NEVADA PLACE NAMES

NEVADA
PLACE NAMES

A GEOGRAPHICAL DICTIONARY

Helen S. Carlson

UNIVERSITY OF NEVADA PRESS
RENO & LAS VEGAS

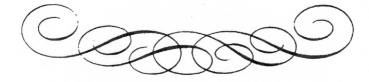

Grateful acknowledgment is hereby made to the
Nevada Silver Centennial Commission
for their early financial support of this book.

University of Nevada Press, Reno, Nevada, 89557 USA
Copyright © 1974 by Helen S. Carlson
Manufactured in the United States of America
All rights reserved
Text design by Dave Comstock
Cover design by Kathleen Szawiola

Library of Congress Cataloging-in-Publication Data
Carlson, Helen S. 1917–1996.
Nevada place names: a geographical dictionary.
Bibliography: p.
1. Names, Geographical—Nevada. 2. Nevada—History. I. Title
F839.C37   917.93   74-13877
ISBN 0-87417-094-X

The paper used in this book meets the requirements of American National Standard
for Information Sciences—Permanence of Paper for Printed Library Materials,
ANSI Z39.48-1984. Binding materials were selected for strength and durability.
This book has been reproduced as a digital reprint.
08   07
6 8 9 7 5

ISBN-13: 978-0-87417-094-8 (pbk. : alk. paper)

To my husband John

CONTENTS

FOREWORD

A SCRAP of ancient Sanskrit verse has been translated, and somewhat modernized by Arthur Ryder, as follows:

> When a book, or a daughter, comes out,
> The author is troubled with doubt,
> A doubt his emotions betray—
> Will she come to good hands?
> Will she please as she stands?
> And what *will* the critics say?

I am sure *Nevada Place Names* will come to many appreciative hands—I trust even the critics may find good words to say—and it suggests a daughter in more ways than in having a debut. Like a charming girl, a good book like this may delight many people for many reasons, and it may take half a lifetime of love and labor. This book has; a bit of background may suggest what it cost in devotion and trained intelligence.

Nevada place names have attracted devotees for a long time. A WPA project produced a small book, and many individuals collected names as a hobby, perhaps most notably David Myrick, who utilized his position as a Southern Pacific executive to record information about naming. But the serious study of Nevada onomastics by a trained specialist began only with Prof. Muriel J. Hughes, who spent the year 1944–45 on the Reno campus. She assembled previous work, set up a permanent file for names, and with her students started investigations in the state archives. The next year we lost her to the University of Vermont, where she has recently been recognized with an honorary doctorate, in addition to her Ph.D. from Columbia. When I returned to the campus in 1945 from a research fellowship, I found I could not pursue the study with the vigor she had, but I kept the project alive in a desultory fashion, starting one graduate student after another on place-naming.

At length I found the right one. Helen Carlson came here in 1952, and by 1955 she had taken a master's degree with a thesis on the Comstock mining names. Thereafter she wrote articles on Nevada naming, and went to the University of New Mexico to study under Prof. T. M. Pearce, author of *New Mex-*

ico Place Names—Nevada was not at that time authorized to offer a doctorate. By 1959 she had earned her Ph.D. degree, and the next year her manuscript was accepted by the University of Nevada Press, presumably to become part of the state centennial celebration.

But a good dissertation is not usually as yet a good book. During the succeeding years, while Mrs. Carlson became Professor Carlson at Western Illinois University and then at Purdue, she rewrote her manuscript repeatedly, adding names that had been missed, taking advantage of more recent research especially on Indian names, tightening her style, utilizing materials available here but not so accessible in New Mexico, and adding the excellent essay she has called "The Name-Givers." During the academic year 1972–73 she spent a sabbatical year here, working with the publisher's editors on the final revision. Now the job is done. The study of Nevada place names is not over, of course; it will never be, but at last we have a good book, from which any future study must start.

I pointed out above that *Nevada Place Names* should appeal to several sorts of users, and this characteristic may warrant explanation. Many books have a single, sharp purpose, and are the better for such specialization. Mrs. Carlson has tried to make her book welcome to several sorts of users, to fill various needs. Partly as explanation of this intent, partly as justification, a glance at potential users may be in order.

Some books on place names are almost exclusively reference works. Such volumes have their use, for reference librarians, for writers or speakers who want to check facts, for anybody who needs to harness the knowledge explosion as a controlled source of intellectual power. For a long time there was no adequate book for Nevada, which remained *terra* almost *incognita* so far as names were concerned. Now, George R. Stewart, who knows American naming if anybody does, has included Nevada among the dozen continental states for which there is an adequate book, and mainly because of Mrs. Carlson's volume. It will serve reference needs; it is objective, as full as could be expected, and it embodies the best onomastic methods, although admittedly it could be perhaps half the size if it were intended only for reference.

The book should provide good browsing. Some books on names do little more; they might be catalogued under "Quaint Doings of Our Ancestors," and the author of *Nevada Place Names* has not hesitated to include both historical and folkloristic bits, partly because they provide good fun, partly because they too are revealing—folklore if it is not very pertinent for historical fact is significant for the nature of human minds. Some tales she has wisely omitted. The reader will not here be assured that the mines at Tonopah were discovered by Jim Butler's mule, which is reputed to have had a short temper and an inept hind leg. According to a widely told tale, the mule aimed a kick at Jim, missed, and knocked a nugget off a nearby ledge. The legend is told of hundreds of mines, but if it ever happened the blunder must have been rare, and there is no reason to connect it with Tonopah. The tale, of course, is a double libel, first on the inaccuracy of mules, which are skillful creatures, and second on the intelligence of prospectors, who may not have been research geologists, but at the worst knew more about the mineral properties of rocks than did their jackasses. But even without the antics of Jim Butler's traveling companion, *Nevada Place Names* should make good reading.

The book provides the basis for serious study. Toponymy is an adjunct of both geography and history. Names are redolent of the times and the minds that gave them birth; consider Lousetown Road, Yellow Jacket Mine, West Gate Station, Stonewall Mountain, Shakespeare Cliff, Telegraph Canyon, Skedaddle Creek, Toquop Wash, Sam's Camp, San Jacinto Ranch, Fiddlers Green, Indian Mike, Burning Moscow, Jackpot. They tell us something of the kinds of men and women these early settlers were, whence they came, how they spoke, how their minds worked, and what they thought. Of course a name like Stonewall Mountain may reveal an awareness of picturesque scenery, the labors of pioneers confronted with an insuperable barrier, or loyal Secessionists commemorating a lost leader, Stonewall Jackson, which is one reason we need a book like *Nevada Place Names* to sift the evidence.

And the book will aid the study of language; we do not know how man invented language, but we know it did much to make him human and that naming is somehow at the root of it. In Nevada we have uncommonly interesting and revealing naming, partly because the history of the state is so varied, partly because it is so recent that we can often discover what happened and why it happened. In Europe we may be able to ferret out the origin of a name, but we can seldom more than guess at purposes behind the giving of a name.

For such reasons I applaud the inclusion of Mrs. Carlson's study of the name-givers. Nevadans have developed engaging onomastic habits. Many names have apparently grown in accordance with practices that seem to be worldwide; a town is called Ruth and a mountain Rose because a proud parent wanted to commemorate his daughter, and Dry Creek was called that because it became dry in summer while another remained wet. But some naming was characteristic of the Great Basin, or people who made their mark on the Old West, not exclusively in Nevada but exclusively in areas not previously well studied.

Consider the veteran prospector as a sower of names. Whether he was a "boomer" or a "loner," he had been in many rushes. He had staked many claims, most of them worthless or nearly so, and every time he planted stakes he gave the place a name. He was likely to have developed his own notion of propriety in nomenclature; he had a store of appropriate names, or he had one name he had been lucky with—Ophir, Jackpot, Lucky Boy, Golconda, or whatever. Or perhaps in the excitement of a strike he could think of only the title he had used last time, Silverado or Gold Hill. Such names usually died where they were given; most claims came to little or nothing. But if this particular Silverado became a working mine, there would be a Silverado Road to it, and a nearby stream might become Silverado Creek, running from the Silverado Mountains. The tents and shacks that sprouted there could be Silverado City, followed by Silverado Township and even Silverado County. This sort of thing happened all over Nevada and the adjacent West. Now we have it described in a volume that happily combines good fun and apt scholarship. *Nevada Place Names* will be a delight to many Nevadans—even to many Californians, for Nevada was once part of California—along with Westerners generally, and to persons throughout the world who welcome a good book on an important subject not previously well treated.

CHARLTON LAIRD

University of Nevada, Reno

PREFACE

PREPARING a book on place names is in many ways as precarious an undertaking as sitting astride a tiger. Where, when, and how does the rider dismount, as the tiger runs into the academic forests of history, geology, geography, language, and folklore? Attempts to control the vagaries of the tiger and the place name are ambitious, but worthwhile when successful.

The origin of place names in Nevada has been traced by means of the settlement pattern of the state. To say that the name-giver placed a name because he felt a need to distinguish one place from another is to state the obvious. Even though the full complexity of his motivations is usually unknown, the mechanisms of origin can be considered in a historical context. Pinpointing names by grid coordinates seemed less useful than relating names to larger, or better-known places, in a land of which roughly 87 percent is public domain and where vanished names are of some historical importance. For the benefit of the general reader, therefore, the locations of the names are given in an onomastic rather than a numerical context.

Because the first permanent citizenry of any size in Nevada was made up of those peoples drawn by the gold and silver rushes, this dictionary contains the names of many mines and most mining districts, active and abandoned. These names have endured in the nomenclature and have not proved trite. A long entry usually means a name long important in the state. The "Ophir" entry is the lengthiest in the dictionary because the discovery of the Ophir Mine is the discovery of the Comstock Lode. In addition, the entries (individual names or group names) include all counties and county seats; all present post offices, and past when known; state and national parks and monuments; and railway stations. The names of all present-day cities, towns, and known settlements have been entered, as well as those of former settlements, mining camps, way stations, and stage and Pony Express stops, when information was available. Major and minor natural features have been treated fully, when pertinent details were forthcoming. Some ranch and brand names have been applied to land features and included in the entries for that reason. In general, names were omitted if only geographical details were available and the places were not considered important enough either historically or geographically to be listed. No names that are meaningful to Nevadans have been intentionally passed over, unless there was nothing to state about them. Neither improbable folklore nor carefree etymology has been intentionally included.

Although a dictionary of everchanging and elusive place names cannot be exhaustive or definitive, it can serve as a basis for the revision it immediately invites. Additional studies are needed from local authorities and specialists who want to ride the tiger.

Among the great number of excellent sources consulted, those that have been especially valuable are anthropological and archaeological publications of the Nevada State Museum and of the Desert Research Institute of the University of Nevada; the historical publications of the University of Nevada Press; the historical-cartographical work of Carl I. Wheat; and the regional studies of Walter Averett, Edna Patterson, Myrtle T. Myles, and Grace Dangberg.

My debt to the many who have assisted over the years in the production of this book is huge. For their interest and willing helpfulness, I extend my thanks to those persons who have been in charge of the various county archives and to former and present staff and members of the Nevada Historical Society (especially the late Clara Beatty), Nevada Bureau of Mines, Nevada State Museum, Nevada State Park System, Nevada State Highway Department, Nevada State Library, the libraries of the University of Nevada and the Mackay School of Mines, and the Washoe County libraries in Reno and Sparks.

I acknowledge a special debt to Professor Russell R. Elliott (history) and Emeritus Professor Vincent P. Gianella (geology) of the University of Nevada for reading the manuscript in its various stages and suggesting much-needed changes that were incorporated. David F. Myrick, an authority on Nevada and California railroads, has my deep appreciation for the generous aid he volunteered concerning a body of significant, but rapidly disappearing, railroad station names. To Thomas Matthews Pearce, Emeritus Professor of English, the University of New Mexico, for his enthusiastic guidance and common interest in onomastics, my thanks are inexpressible. Because he was the prime mover and has been a continuing inspiration and mentor, since my first investigation into place names, my debt to Charlton Laird, Emeritus Professor of English, University of Nevada, is inestimable. Without the patient help and thoughtfulness of Robert Laxalt, Director, and N. M. Cady, Editor, University of Nevada Press, and the unlimited understanding of my husband John, the manuscript would have remained unpublished.

None of these organizations or individuals is responsible for the inevitable mistakes in presentation and interpretation. Errors of commission and omission are solely mine.

H.S.C.

Reno, Nevada
August 1973

INTRODUCTION

THE NAME GIVERS

THE state of Nevada has an area of 110,540 square miles, a mean elevation of 5,500 feet, and lies almost wholly within the Great Basin, the only drainage area within the United States out of which no rivers or watercourses flow to the oceans. This semiarid state, seventh largest in area, has an average annual precipitation of nine inches. Long stretches of desert and uncultivated lands are fluted by broken chains of mountains trending generally north and south and varying from five to twenty miles in width at their bases. The mountain ranges are separated by flat-bottomed alluvial valleys which hold either lakes or barren desert and alkali flats. With the exception of the alkali flats, no portion of Nevada is devoid of vegetation even in the dry seasons. Shad scale, creosote bushes, and sagebrush are typical of the desert shrubs covering the valleys. On the lower mountain slopes grow stunted piñon, juniper, and other hardy trees and shrubs. At the higher elevations, coniferous and alpine vegetation thrives. Ancient, gnarled forests of bristlecone pine (the oldest known living thing) are at elevations of ten thousand feet or higher in eastern Nevada. A major orographic feature, the Sierra Nevada, forms a part of the western boundary of the state, which follows the 120th meridian from the 42nd to the 39th parallel, then crosses diagonally to the intersection of the 35th parallel with the Colorado River.

Two ancient bodies of water once covered parts of the state: the western portion of old Lake Bonneville on the northeastern border, and nearly all of the old Lake Lahontan area in northwestern Nevada. The latter extended east of Winnemucca about twenty miles, north to just inside Oregon (at McDermitt), west into California's Honey Lake Valley, and south to the vicinity of Hawthorne. Lake Bonneville has shrunk to the present Great Salt Lake in the state of Utah. Evaporation of Lake Lahontan has reduced its level to several residual and increasingly alkaline lakes, or "evaporation pans," in Nevada, notably Pyramid, Winnemucca, Carson, and Walker lakes and the Carson and Humboldt sinks. The rivers and principal streams of the state are the Muddy and the Virgin rivers in the south, the Owyhee in the northeast, the Humboldt in the north, and the Truckee, Carson, and Walker in the west.

Although the prehistory of Nevada is imperfectly known, most geologists, anthropologists, and archaeologists believe the first human beings lived there from 11,000 to 13,000 years ago among such animals as Pleistocene elephants, horses, and camels. Recent excavations point to the archaeological site at Tule Springs, fifteen miles northwest of Las Vegas, as man's first known home within the present state area, perhaps 12,400 years ago. Later prehistoric peoples were developing more complex societies along the shore of ancient Lake Lahontan (Lovelock) and in the Pyramid Lake area (when Northern Paiutes penetrated the regions), and along the lower Muddy River (when the Southern Paiutes intruded). Early rock art, widespread over the state and along migratory game trails, dates from 3000 to 5000 B.C. to the time of the arrival of the Numic-speaking (Shoshone) people, ca. A.D. 1300.

The origin of place names in Nevada follows the settlement pattern of the state. The name-givers can thus be grouped as follows: American Indians; fur trappers and explorers; early emigrant parties and religious groups; prospectors and investors in mining and related enterprises; ranchers and town-builders; trading, stage, and pony line station operators and railroad builders; and government officials and agencies.

AMERICAN INDIANS

When the first trappers appeared in the 1820s, Indians occupying the area now known as Nevada were Numic-speaking (Plateau Shoshonean) people and the Washo, a small tribe of the Hokan linguistic stock. Alfred L. Kroeber (1907) divided Plateau Shoshonean (his term) linguistic groups into Mono-Paviotso, Shoshoni-Comanche, and Ute-Chemehuevi. John Wesley Powell's earlier (1874) term "Numic" (for Plateau Shoshonean) recently has been readopted and division names more consistent with his terminology suggested: Western Numic, Central Numic, and Southern Numic. Major subclassifications of Western Numic were Paviotso, Mono, Owens Valley Paiute, Northern Paiute, and Bannock; of Central Numic, Panamint and Shoshoni (including Western Shoshoni and Gosiute); and of Southern Numic, Kawaiisu and Ute (including Chemehuevi and Southern Paiute dialects). Even though twenty-seven tribal groups are known to have been in the state, Indian place names derive from three major Numic-speaking groups: Shoshoni (usually spelled Shoshone), Northern Paiute, and Southern Paiute. Two non-Numic tribes, the Washo and the Mohave, are also represented in the nomenclature (Fowler, pp. 5–7; RRE, Hist., p. 25).

The peaceable and inoffensive Washo tribe was eventually restricted by the Mono-Paviotso and the hostile Northern Paiutes to an area along the base of the Sierra Nevada which extended from south of Honey Lake to Sonora Pass. The tribal name Washo, from *washiu* or *wasiu* meaning 'person' in their own language, was given to a few places in the western part of the state:

Washoe County, Washoe Hill, Washoe Lake, Little Washoe Lake, and Washoe Valley. In addition to the tribal name, Tahoe, 'lake water' or 'sheet of water,' and probably Wabuska, 'white grass' or 'vegetation,' are Washo names. Both features were important to the survival of a society of hunters, fishermen, and gatherers. Desert grasses were stored or ground into flour for baking or making soup (RRE, Hist., p. 28). Two Mohave names of secondary application appear in southern Nevada. The tribal name is used for the lake created north of Davis Dam on the Colorado, and is the old name for a valley extending from Davis Dam to Needles, California. Ireteba Peaks, a part of the Opal Mountains south of Eldorado Canyon in Clark County, commemorates Ireteba, a Mohave Indian guide with the Joseph C. Ives expedition of 1857 and 1858.

Aside from the area occupied by the Washo on the western boundary of the state and the Mohave along the northern bank of the Colorado River, the entire state was roamed by Numic-speaking peoples. Western Numic place names in Nevada are largely Northern Paiute, but also reflect the presence of the Bannocks and the Mono. The Toquimas, a Mono band living in the lower Reese River Valley, took their name from the Toquima Range in north central Nevada, extending from Nye County northward into the southeastern corner of Lander County. The translation 'black backs' may be erroneous, or possibly describes the mountains. According to Powell, these small tribes were called "land-nameds" in the Indian idiom (Fowler, p. 107). The Bannock, from *panaíti,* their own name, although inhabiting the land north of and adjoining the Northern Paiutes, were a horse-using group that roved widely in the state. The tribal name Bannock seems to have vanished from present-day Nevada names, but exists in the historic nomenclature for a town and post office at the mouth of Philadelphia Canyon on the south edge of Battle Mountain in Lander County. Tippipah, 'rock-water,' is a Bannock name indicating a spring flowing from rocks. The spring was an Indian campsite in Nye County.

The largest group of the Western Numa in Nevada were the Northern Paiutes who occupied an area from west of Winnemucca in the north to just west of Tonopah in the south. In addition to the tribal name (Pahute, Piute, Paiute), which is commemorative of either or both the Northern Paiutes and the Southern Paiutes, depending upon the region of application, the names of individual chiefs are in the nomenclature. The station name honorific of Chief Numana is one of a group of vanishing railway names. Nache Peak and Natchez Pass, although graphic variants, commemorate Chief Na(t)ches. Natches, the name for an early gold camp, appears only in the historic nomenclature. The most enduring of the chieftain names are Winnemucca, honoring Poito (Old Winnemucca), and Truckee, named for an earlier Northern Paiute chief, who served as a guide for John Charles Frémont. The Kamma ('jackrabbit') Mountains and Tohakum ('hare or white rabbit') Peak are named for small game important to the Indian for both food and clothing. The mountain hare, much larger than the valley hare, is gray in the summer and snow white in the winter. The name of the Sahwave ('sage or sagebrush') Range reflects the importance of this vegetation to the Great Basin ecology. The edible roots of the white sage were used extensively, and the inner bark of sagebrush was made into a substance that could be used for apparel and twine (RRE, Hist., pp. 27–29). Two settlement names, Beowawe, 'gate,' and Tonopah, 'greasewood spring,' probably are Northern Paiute, but could be Western Shoshone.

A larger body of place names derives from Southern Paiute bands of Southern Numic-speaking peoples. Based upon his extensive research in the American West, between 1867 and 1881, John Wesley Powell concluded that an Indian's name was a title deed to his home. "An Indian will never ask to what nation or tribe or body of people another Indian belongs but to 'what land do you belong and how are you land named?'" (Fowler, p. 38). Southern Paiute tribes of the land-nameds category include the Moapariats (Moapats) of Moapa Valley, the Pahranaguts of Pahranagut(gat) Valley and the Paroompats of Pa-room Spring. The Numic (Shoshonean) generic *pah, pai, pa, ba,* meaning 'water,' probably the most significant single feature of the Indian place names of Nevada, is contained in the names of these bands that had established their rights to well-watered districts. Among the several Southern Paiute names containing this generic are Ivanpah, 'good, clear water,' Timpahute, 'rock water people,' Pahrump, 'water rock,' Tupapa, 'emerging water,' and Pahroc, 'water underground(?).' One of the most important foods gathered by the Indians was the pine nut of the piñon pine, for which Tiva Canyon is named. Toquop Wash was named for the 'black tobacco' weed sought by the Indian.

The Central Numa (Western Shoshone and Gosiute) lived in the eastern half of Nevada, with Southern Paiutes to the south and Northern Paiutes to the west. Powell and G. W. Ingalls reported in 1873 that 204 Gosiutes and 1,945 Western Shoshones were living in eastern Nevada (Fowler, p. 105). In this part of the state, Indian reservations, mountain ranges, peaks, creeks, passes, mining districts, railway stations and post offices have been named for both tribes. White Horse, a Gosiute war chief, is commemorated by a mountain in the Goshute Range. Toano(a), 'pipe-camping-place,' for some association with a tobacco pipe; and Napias, 'money, paper,' complete the known Gosiute place names in Nevada (GRS, Amer., p. 485). The largest group of indigenous Indian place names in the state derive from Western Shoshone.

The known place names given by and for the Western Shoshone are similar in many respects to those of other Indian groups in Nevada. The honored chiefs Timoak and Chokup have been commemorated by the Te-moak Indian Reservation and Chokup Pass (renamed Railroad Pass). The Toiyabe Range, from Shoshone *toyap,* 'mountain,' was part of the region of the land-named Kaidatoiabe. The Shoshone generic also occurs in the name of the Desatoya Mountains. Illapah, from *illa,* 'rock,' and *pah,* 'water,' corresponds to Western Numic (Bannock) Tippipah, and Southern Numic (Southern Paiute) Pahrump, all apparently indicating a spring flowing from rocks.

Jarbidge, a place name of somewhat different character, still endures in the present-day nomenclature. The name of the canyon so denoted has been adopted for a river, mountain range, mountain peak, mining district, post office, and town in the area. *Jahabich* (or *Tswhawbitts*) was a mythical devil giant that roamed the canyon and feasted on Indians. Hunting parties are known to have camped in nearby caves as early as ten thousand years ago. Western Numic speakers came into the region at some time after 1150 A.D. Presumably many Indian names, expressing fear or reverence, have vanished from the name-body, or are unknown. Elder George W. Bean, a Las Vegas missionary of the Church of Jesus Christ of Latter-Day Saints, wrote of the southern Nevada Indians on December 11, 1855, "there is hardly a mountain or canyon that is not reverenced upon some account or other." The name Tybo, 'white man,' relates to the time of contact with the white man in this region of Nye County.

The number of known Shoshone place names has been augmented through the efforts of field workers who have submitted them to the United States Board on Geographic Names. Unofficial designations for some features in the Western Shoshone Indian Reservation include Dirdui Panguipa Honops, 'little fishes creek'; Disiguoy Honops, 'grassy hill creek'; Nayantovoy, 'standing Indian creek'; Narino Honguy, 'back of a saddle hill'; and Nagomina, 'break-neck creek.'

The only indigenous Indian names that can be dated with any certainty are of secondary application and are honorific of chiefs and tribes. It is probable that all of these were applied in the second half of the nineteenth century. Most settlement names were placed secondarily, ostensibly because of some incident, by prospectors, railroad builders, and early settlers, also during the second half of the nineteenth century. The oldest names of the group are those of the mountain ranges, peaks, and canyons, and the often vanished river, creek, and spring names. Further investigation into the known tribal names listed by Indian agents and into the areas which these tribes inhabited may lead to the discovery of early, unrecorded Indian place names of Nevada, antedating by many years those names placed by the first white trappers and explorers in the Great Basin.

FUR TRAPPERS AND EXPLORERS

The first non-Indians known to have entered Nevada were Francisco Garcés, who "passed the Needles and penetrated a short distance across the present boundary of the state of Nevada" in 1776; Peter Skene Ogden, who made a slight entrance into the northeast tip in 1826; and Jedediah Strong Smith, who crossed the southern tip of the state in 1826 (GGC, p. 36; RRE, Hist., p. 36). These early explorations contributed little to Nevada toponymy beyond names for the Colorado, the Bruneau, the Owyhee, the Virgin, and the Amargosa rivers, which Nevada shares with adjoining states, and a campsite, Las Vegas, on the Old Spanish Trail. Other Spanish and French place names within the confines of the present state area seemingly were placed subsequent to the Smith explorations of 1826. Smith first entered Nevada near the present-day town of Mesquite and followed the Meadow Valley Wash and the Virgin River, which he originally named for John Quincy Adams. The name Adams River has been lost, but the name Muddy, recorded by Smith's clerk, is the present designation for that river. A salt deposit described by Smith is the earliest mentioned mineral deposit in Nevada.

In 1828 Peter Skene Ogden led trappers of the Hudson's Bay Company into northern Nevada slightly east of present-day Denio. On November 9, greatly surprised at coming upon a river (the Humboldt) abounding in beaver, and thinking it was a branch of the Sandwich Island River (the Owyhee), he named it Unknown River (GGC, p. 116; EMM, Nev., pp. 67–68). In the summer of 1829, he suggested that the name be changed to Paul's, in honor of Joseph Paul, one of his party of trappers who had died and was buried on the riverbank. Before 1845, the river probably was best known as Mary's. Mary is said to have been a Shoshone woman, the wife of either Peter Skene Ogden or one of his trappers (HHB, Nev., p. 36; HMC, p. 84; FNF, p. 56; MA, p. 22).

In his notes, Ogden mentioned that Unknown River was known to trappers as Swampy River. Unknown free-trappers, who also called the river Ogden's, are thought to have named Salmon Falls Creek, a tributary to the Snake River in Elko County, and Delano in northeastern Elko. Lamoille Creek (Elko) was named for a French Canadian trapper who had a cabin there in the 1850s. McCoy Creek, in northern Lander County, commemorates Thomas McCoy, also a trapper.

All of Ogden's names for the Humboldt River have fallen out of use excepting Mary's, which now denotes a tributary in Elko County. Although he was unsuccessful in affixing a permanent name to the Humboldt, he was unquestionably the first white man to explore it from near its sources to its sink in the Nevada desert (JGS, I, pp. 39–44).

The propensity of Smith and Ogden to give commemorative names to land features apparently was not shared, at least not in Nevada, by the hunter, trapper, and Indian fighter Joseph Reddeford Walker. The expedition under him, sent out by Captain Benjamin Louis Eulalie de Bonneville, entered Nevada in August, 1833. Following approximately the present route of the Southern Pacific Railroad, the party soon came upon the Humboldt River and named it Barren, a name which they thought highly appropriate to the country and to the natives belonging to it. Early in September some of Walker's men killed two or three Indians near the sink of the Humboldt. A day or so later almost a hundred more Indians came boldly near the camp; thirty of Walker's men closed in and shot thirty-nine of them, and the other Indians fled into the high grass. In consequence of this fight, Walker named some nearby shallow ponds Battle Lakes.

Only one name other than Barren and Battle Lakes is known to have been given by Walker to a geographic feature of Nevada, and that was while he was a guide for Frémont in 1845. Kern records that six miles distant from the Humboldt, Walker named a creek Walnut (Trout) "from one of his trappers having brought into his camp a twig of that tree found near its head; a tree scarcely known so far west as this" (JGS, I, pp. 45–58, 95). In contrast to Jed Smith and Peter Ogden, for whom, apparently, no Nevada places are named, Joseph Walker is commemorated by the names of several important features.

The fame of the fur trade, the romance of exploration, and the meager, often inaccurate, reports of the land beyond the Rocky Mountains aroused the country's interest in the Far West. In 1843, Captain John Charles Frémont was ordered to survey the wilderness west of Frémont's Peak. From his camp on the Oregon border, Frémont entered Nevada on December 26, 1843, and traveled nearly straight south to the southeast end of Pyramid Lake. From here he followed the Truckee River to the Big Bend (Wadsworth), then went along the Carson River to Antelope Valley, and finally on to the East Walker River, which he followed into California. In the spring of 1844, he followed the Old Spanish Trail eastward from California, reaching the Amargosa River on April 28 and the springs at Las Vegas the next day. From there he journeyed to the Muddy and Virgin rivers, and on into Utah (GGC, pp. 208–216). In the late fall of 1845 he crossed Nevada again, going south from Pilot Peak to the Toano Range near Wendover, then west into Ruby Valley, and southwest to Walker Lake. Some of his party, under Kern and guided by Walker, went west through Secret Canyon and on to the Humboldt near present Halleck (VPG).

Frémont's vivid reports of his explorations explain the descriptive names he gave. His name for the plateau of 210,000 square miles between the Sierra Nevada and the Wasatch Mountains, covering western Utah, most of Nevada, and eastern California, was Great Basin (JCF, Report, p. 276; Frémont Map). During his explorations in Nevada in 1843, he camped at a hot spring and named it Boiling Spring. He discovered a lake, "a sheet of green" that "broke upon our eyes like the ocean," on January 10, 1844. A remarkable rock in the lake which, "from the point we viewed it [on January 13, 1844], presented a pretty exact outline of the great Pyramid of Cheops . . . suggested a name for the lake; and I called it Pyramid Lake" (JCF, Report, p. 217). On January 15 he wrote that "an Indian brought in a large fish to trade, which we had the inexpressable satisfaction to find was a salmon trout," and on January 16, "this morning we continued our journey along this beautiful stream, which we naturally called the Salmon Trout River" (JCF, Report, pp. 218–219). Frémont ascended Red Lake Peak on February 14, 1844, with Charles Preuss, his topographer, from which they had a "beautiful view of a mountain lake . . . about fifteen miles in length, and . . . entirely surrounded by mountains" (JCF, Report, p. 234). Mountain Lake is the name for Lake Tahoe on his 1845 map. In April of 1844, Captain Frémont reached the Amargosa and noted, "It is called by the Spaniards *Amargosa*—the bitter water of the desert" (JCF, Report, p. 264). Later he camped near some springs where Las Vegas is now situated. "After a day's journey of 18 miles, in a northeasterly direction, we encamped in the midst of another very large basin, at a camping ground called *las vegas*—a term which the Spanish use to signify fertile or marshy plains in contradiction to *llanos,* which they apply to dry and sterile plains" (JCF, Report, p. 266). In October, 1845, he saw a peak-shaped mountain, forty or fifty miles distant and "to the friendly mountain," as well as to the creek flowing down its eastern slope, gave the name Pilot Peak (JCF, Report, pp. 264, 266). With the exceptions of Salmon Trout River (Truckee), Mountain Lake (Tahoe), and Boiling Spring (Gerlach Hot Springs), Frémont's descriptive names have endured in Nevada.

Captain Frémont's reports also provide his motivation for bestowing names to commemorate members of his expeditions. He had named the Carson River for his "true and reliable friend, Kit Carson," and the Walker River, Walker Lake, and Walker Pass for Joseph Walker, a man "celebrated as one of the best and bravest leaders who have ever been in the country" (JCF, Report, pp. 110, 155). In 1844 Frémont crossed the Sierra Nevada about twenty to twenty-five miles northwest of Tehachapi Pass and about due east of Bakersfield. He thought he was using Walker's Pass and so named it. "This pass," he wrote, "reported to be good, was discovered by Mr. Joseph Walker, of whom I have already spoken, and whose name it might therefore appropriately bear" (JCF, Report, p. 248). Under date of November 24, 1845, he explained that "the place appointed for meeting the main party was on the eastward shore of Walker Lake near the point where the river which I had given the same name enters it" (JGS, I, p. 39).

The many named northern river, explored by Ogden and Walker and followed by others who trapped or took the route to California, has been known as the Humboldt since Frémont named it in 1845, for Baron Friedrich Heinrich Alexander von Humboldt (1769–1859), German naturalist, traveler, and statesman. Remaining northern Nevada names given by Frémont in honor of his men and chosen to record their "rivalry . . . in finding good camps [and] their judgment of the country," are the following: Whitton Springs, named for the man who discovered it and known to emigrants as Mound Spring, presently designated Chase Spring; Crane Spring, named for one of his Delaware Indians; and Connor Spring and Basil Creek, named for two other members of the expedition.

Ten years after Frémont's third expedition, Lieutenant E. G. Beckwith also named places in northern Nevada during his explorations of the forty-first parallel, for a Pacific railroad route. Following Beckwith, Arnold Hague and S. F. Emmons explored the fortieth parallel. These explorations account for the names of a few land features in Pershing, Lander, and Churchill counties. During his exploration of the Colorado River in 1857–58, Lieutenant Joseph C. Ives left some names in Clark County.

Beckwith's Fish Creek and Antelope Butte and Ives's Opal Mountains, the latter named for some "opalescent chalcedony" found there by Dr. Newberry (WA), Black Canyon, and Cottonwood Island (now under Lake Mead) are the descriptive names of the group. A pass, named Madelin, was recorded by Beckwith in memory of an emigrant child who had been killed by Indians nearby (Gudde). Beckwith named Franklin Lake in honor of President Franklin Pierce. Hague commemorated the famous English astronomer, Sir George Biddell Airy, by naming Mount Airy for him, and he designated a range in Lander, Pershing, and Churchill counties the Augusta Mountains (VPG). The name of the Kamma Mountains, Northern Paiute 'jackrabbit,' was recorded by Hague. Members of the Ives expedition were rewarded by Lieutenant Ives when he named Ireteba Peaks for his Mohave guide of that name and probably the Newberry Mountains for Dr. Newberry.

In 1859, Captain James Hervey Simpson of the topographical engineers led an expedition of sixty-four men, sent by the government to locate a wagon road from Camp Floyd (forty miles south of Salt Lake City and near Lake Utah) to Genoa, a settlement of Latter-Day Saints in western Nevada. The route he explored became that of the Pony Express, the Overland Telegraph, and the Overland Mail, and later was known for the most part as the Lincoln Highway (U.S. 50) through central Nevada. Between May 2, 1859, when he left Camp Floyd, and August 5, 1859, when he returned, Simpson placed and recorded more Nevada names than any of his trapping and exploring predecessors. In addition to naming places to honor and reward the men of his expedition and to giving apt descriptive names, he showed a real respect for native nomenclature, taking care and time to learn, whenever possible, the Indian place names and to record them in phonetic spelling.

He gave simple and direct reasons for applying such names as Edwards, Huntington, Lowry, Murry, Pete's, Buell, Cooper's, and Reese. He allowed his party to name a lake, park, and pass for him, but demurred at their so naming the nearby creek, explaining "as it has been my rule to preserve the Indian names, whenever I can ascertain them, and Ton-a-ho-nupe is the name of the creek, I shall continue so to call it" (JHS, p. 77). Also honorific are the names of the Goshute Range and Chokup Pass.

Simpson's descriptive names for land features in central Nevada are East Gate, Middle Gate, and West Gate, Alkaline Valley, Dry Flat Valley, Gate of Hercules, Red Canyon, and Black Mountain. Those names descriptive of the water are of like practicality: Cold Springs and Deep Creek. Additional descriptive Indian names recorded by Simpson (*Totsaarh, Ungopah, Sedaye, Kobah, Pangqueowhoppe, Wonstindamme,* and *Tahou*) bring to a close the account of the names known to have been placed by those who trapped the streams or, in some official capacity, explored Nevada and blazed trails followed by the emigrants.

EARLY EMIGRANT PARTIES AND RELIGIOUS GROUPS
Few emigrants crossed Nevada before the discovery of gold by John Marshall, on January 24, 1848, in a tailrace at Sutter's Mill in California. Most had traveled the Oregon Trail to Fort Hall and down the Snake and

Columbia rivers. A small number seeking a more direct route to California followed the trails opened by Peter Skene Ogden in 1828 and by Joseph Walker in 1833 and 1834.

Thirty-two members of the party of John Bidwell and John B. Bartleson crossed Nevada in 1841. They entered the state near the mountain later to be named Pilot Peak by Frémont, crossed the Ruby Mountains, and followed the Humboldt River. After passing through the long valley of the Humboldt, they camped at the Humboldt Sink, crossed the Carson River, and following the Walker River, made camp in Antelope Valley (probably named by the party for the pronghorn antelope ranging there). They followed the Walker to the eastern base of the Sierra Nevada and took Sonora Pass over the mountains (VPG).

The Bidwell party had generally followed the trail opened by Joseph Walker in 1833. In 1843, Walker guided the J. B. Chiles party of fifty over the northern route that he had used in 1834. In Nevada this route went through Thousand Springs Valley in northeastern Elko County to the headwaters of the Humboldt River. He guided this, the first group to cross the Great Basin with wagons (which they abandoned near Owen's Lake), south along the eastern base of the Sierra Nevada into Walker's Pass and thus to California.

The Stevens-Murphy party of about a hundred men, women, and children, led by Elisha Stevens, followed Walker's route from Fort Hall to the Humboldt in 1844. From the Humboldt Sink, they crossed the desert to the Truckee River, which they followed to Truckee Pass to cross the Sierra Nevada. A Northern Paiute called Captain Truckee befriended the party and offered to guide them. He became a great favorite with the group, and when they reached the lower crossing of the Truckee, they named the river for him (MA, pp. 24–25). The Stevens-Murphy party is the first known to have taken the Truckee River route to California and to have taken wagons across the Sierra Nevada (VPG).

Other parties known to have followed Walker's route from Fort Hall to the Humboldt in 1845 were a party of twelve men traveling by saddle and pack animals; a party of fifteen led by William Sublette; and the Grigsby-Ide party with about fifty men and as many women and children, who arrived at Sutter's Fort on Christmas Day of that year.

A third northern route was that opened by Frémont in 1845 from the Jordan River, south of Great Salt Lake, across the desert to Pilot Peak. After the Bidwell-Bartleson party in 1841, the first emigrants known to have followed this route were the Edwin Bryant party in 1846, led by Lansford W. Hastings, for whom this southern portion was named the Hastings Cutoff. The Hastings-led group went through Silver Zone Pass in the Toano Range, crossed the Pequops southwest of Shafter, went south in Ruby Valley and through Harrison Pass, then north to the Humboldt River a few miles southwest of the site of Elko (VPG). Since the Bryant party was equipped with saddle horses and pack animals, they crossed the desert in safety; however, the hardships suffered during the trip caused Bryant to attempt to dissuade emigrants with wagons from taking the same route. This route, highly advertised as a time-saver, was the one taken by the Donner party.

The Applegate Trail in northwestern Nevada was opened in 1846 and named for Jesse Applegate, who led a small party of men over it. They went from the Rogue River in Oregon, past Lower Klamath Lake, south of Goose Lake, and into Nevada, where they crossed the Black Rock Desert to connect with the Humboldt route near the present site of Mill City. The Lassen Cutoff (1848), named for Peter Lassen, was also in the northwestern part of Nevada. From Mill City it followed the Applegate through High Rock Canyon to the south end of Goose Lake. From there to the Sacramento Valley, it was known as Lassen's (VPG; JGS, I, pp. 101–110). In 1851 William Nobles established the Nobles Road which left the Lassen route at Black Rock and went directly west into the Honey Lake region in California (RRE, Hist., p. 48). Bancroft estimated that three hundred emigrants bound for California crossed Nevada in 1846.

During the following year, it has been estimated, perhaps two hundred people arrived at Sutter's Fort via the Humboldt River route. While Brigham Young and the Latter-Day Saints were on the trek to Great Salt Lake, which they reached in 1847, some members of his train were taken into the United States Army and marched to San Diego to fight in the Mexican War (which was over when they arrived). This Morman Battalion was honorably discharged. To rejoin their people, some members went to Great Salt Lake via the Humboldt route in 1847 (after assisting General Stephen Watts Kearny in burying the dead from the unfortunate Donner party). Others apparently crossed southern Nevada. A stone found north of Las Vegas was carved "F. D. Byer, 1847." It is believed that Mr. Byer was a member of the Mormon Battalion who perhaps became a prospector on the return.

The wave of emigration across Nevada grew a hundred-fold after the discovery of gold in California. The Rich-Bigler party, including missionaries from Salt Lake City, set out for San Francisco in 1849 via the Spanish Trail. A group led by C. C. Rich left the main party at Parowan to search for a more direct route. After traveling parallel to the Spanish Trail for about ten miles, they turned northwest and entered the Meadow Valley Wash, which they named Providence. When they reached Coyote Springs and the party split again, they named the springs Division. Discovering the untried route perilous and determining to go back to the Spanish Trail, Rich led his group through Arrow Canyon, naming it Double Canyon, and eventually rejoined the main party at California Crossing on the Muddy River (WA). Another group going from Utah Lake to Los Angeles broke away from their experienced leader, Jefferson Hunt, and formed the Manly-Bennet party, or Death Valley Forty-Niners. The party crossed southern Nevada, following a route north of the Charleston Mountains, across the Amargosa Desert, and into Death Valley.

It was during 1850 that the Mormons of Great Salt Lake established a trading station in Carson Valley for the benefit of the emigrants who, upon reaching the eastern base of the Sierra Nevada, were usually destitute. They had often lost their cattle from the lack of good grass and wholesome water and had been forced to discard most of their goods in the crossing of Nevada.

In 1854 Frémont led a private expedition across the thirty-eighth parallel in Nevada, following a route a little to the north of the Jayhawkers' trail across southern Nevada. At the same time, Mormon missionaries were settling in the Virgin and Santa Clara river valleys to administer to the Indians.

Emigrants following the Humboldt (the principal route of the migration to California) or other routes, did not find beaten paths except when canyons and passes made it imperative that all groups converge to a single road. Otherwise they scattered out over level country to secure good forage for their stock and to find good springs and watercourses in the semiarid land. Valley of Fountains was T. H. Jefferson's name for Ruby Valley in 1849. The names they left in the 1840s and early 1850s are an index to both the difficulties experienced and the pleasures anticipated in the western push of the pioneers.

Of crucial importance to all of the pioneers was a knowledge of the locations of mountain passes, river crossings, acceptable campsites, and dreaded alkali deserts. New Pass, named by a pioneer who felt that he had discovered a new pass through the mountains, was on one of the principal routes through central Nevada. Emigrant Pass, a narrow divide on the Humboldt route, was east of Emigrant Spring (presently on Interstate 80, west of Carlin), a campsite where respite from the alkali dust and heat could be gained. A hot spring in the Forty Mile Desert was called Spring of False Hope because oxen suffered from drinking its water and there was no forage. California Crossing named the place where the California Trail crossed the Muddy River. Lower Emigrant Crossing (Wadsworth) was at the Big Bend of the Truckee River. French Ford or French Bridge (Winnemucca) was a noted crossing place on the Humboldt River, as was Gravelly Ford near present-day Beowawe.

Emigrant Valley was one of those traversed by the Death Valley Forty-Niners. Big Meadows was a natural meadow and tule swamp where emigrants rested as they prepared to cross the most dreadful portion of the trial to California, the Forty Mile Desert. Pioneers on the Fort Hall–Humboldt River Trail camped at springs scattered over a meadow; they referred to the springs as wells, and the campsite became known as Humboldt Wells, and later as Wells, which name it still bears.

Antelope Springs on the Applegate Cutoff to Oregon was named by the Applegate party, as was Rabbit Hole Springs, the last place where emigrants could get water before crossing the Black Rock Desert (VPG). Because the pioneers who camped on the Carson River were sometimes undecided whether to continue westward or to follow the river south, they called the campsite Ponderers' Rest. Deserts were often named for the number of miles that had to be endured in crossing them. The Twelve-Mile Desert was east of Ponderers' Rest, the Twenty-Six-Mile Desert was west of Ragtown, and the Forty Mile Desert was between the Humboldt and Carson sinks.

Also important to those of the great migration to California were the landmarks, usually named descriptively. A conspicuous black rock rising above white alkali flats was named Black Rock, and the desert around it, the Black Rock Desert. Later emigrants over the Applegate Trail would know that Peter Lassen had been killed by hostile Indians in the Black Rock Range. The Lassen Cutoff passed through High Rock Canyon, named for its narrow, high rock walls. A ragged, broken mountain with a protusion of granite was named Granite Point by some pioneer on the Humboldt route. Iron Point denoted an emigrant pass—a low ridge with barren sides and summit of reddish rock which indicated the presence of iron.

Other significant names on the trail might denote a station, such as Ragtown, where exhausted and thirsty emigrants rested after crossing the Forty Mile Desert. Two visitors of 1855 found that it consisted of "three huts, formed of poles covered with rotten canvas full of holes" (JGS, I, p. 123). At Ragtown the emigrants are said to have washed their ragged garments in the Carson River and to have spread them on the bushes to dry. Such significant names included those of creeks named for animals encountered in the area, such as Goose Creek and Rattlesnake Creek, and those of valleys named for the glittering crystals of quartz and red garnets found there, such as Diamond and Ruby valleys.

Only rarely would the emigrants attempt to perpetuate their own names or the names of others in the toponymy of Nevada. One pioneer stayed by a small stream on the Humboldt route for a time, recruiting his stock. He named the stream Maggie Creek for his daughter.

Of importance, at least to individual groups, must have been Forty-Nine Lake, named for an 1849 crossing, and Continental Lake, also named for the journey. Incident names were given because some misfortune occurred at a place. Misery Lake is said to have been named by the Death Valley Forty-Niners who camped there and, after untold hardship, later reached and named Death Valley itself. Battle Mountain was named for an incident on the trail involving the Shoshones, and some small lakes or dry sinks were named Massacre because forty men of an emigrant party were killed by Indians in a battle there and interred in a common grave. Susan O'Brien, whose father, mother, and brother had been killed by Indians, escaped from the latter's captivity and jumped from the top of a high bluff overlooking the Carson River. The place of the suicide was named Susan's Bluff (MTM). Thus the place names reflect the immense difficulties of crossing Nevada, the great barrier to the California goldfields, and also the rare pleasure felt by those who had surmounted the obstacles. William Lewis Manly, one of a party decimated while following what is now called the Jayhawker Trail, recounts that the survivors of the party took off their hats prior to leaving Death Valley, "and then overlooking the scene of so much trial, suffering, and death, spoke the thought uppermost, saying: 'Goodbye, Death Valley' " (JGS, I, pp. 584–85). Another group, upon having crossed the Black Rock Desert, suddenly entered a pleasant valley on the Nevada-California line and named it Surprise (Gudde).

The site of the roofless, floorless trading post established and operated by Hampden S. Beatie during the summer of 1850 at the eastern base of the Sierra Nevada was taken up by Colonel John Reese in 1851. He built a log house nearby, and the place was known as Mormon Station, the first permanent settlement in Nevada. Elder Orson Hyde renamed the little Mormon settlement Genoa in 1856. Elder Hyde also laid out and named Franktown, where he ran a sawmill until 1856. Hiram and Israel Mott founded Mottsville. In addition to building Mormon Station and running a ranch there, Colonel John Reese later acted as a guide for James H. Simpson, who named the Reese River for him. While these tiny settlements were being established in western Nevada, much larger groups of Mormon people were exploring and settling in southern and eastern parts of the state.

The Mormon missionaries and colonizers of southern Nevada built adobe houses and an adobe fort to protect themselves from the Indians. Utilizing the great springs for purposes of irrigation, they raised fields of grain, planted peach and apple orchards, and established towns and flourishing business enterprises. Among the names given to commemorate members of the group are Bringhurst, named for William Bringhurst, the leader of Las Vegas Mission until 1860; Bunkerville, named for Edward Bunker, a member of the Mormon Battalion, who did much toward laying the foundation of the town; Simonsville, named for Orrawell Simons, who built a mill at the site formerly known as Mill Point (WA); Callville, a settlement founded by Bishop Anson W. Call to serve as a landing at the big bend of the Colorado River; and Bonelli Peak, named for Daniel Bonelli. Two townsites now under the waters of Lake Mead, Saint Joseph and Saint Thomas, were named in honor of Joseph W. Young, the son of Brigham Young, who helped to colonize Muddy Valley, and Thomas S. Smith, who led a Mormon migration to Moapa Valley.

Rioville, Westpoint, and Overton also denoted early Mormon settlements. Mission Canyon, Mount Moriah, Piute Springs, Badger Bench, Pipe Springs, Big Salt Cliff (also called St. Thomas, or Salvation Salt Deposit), Pockets, an old watering place in a narrow wash (WA), and perhaps Meadow Valley were some of the names the Mormons gave to land features. Several names given by J. H. Martineau, historian for the Desert Mission of 1858, have been lost: Desert Swamp Springs (Butterfield Spring), Three Butte Valley (Cave Valley), Badger Valley (Clover Creek Valley), Willow Springs (Indian Springs), and Cricket Spring. The Mormons also discovered and developed mines. One of the oldest mine names of the state is Potosi, which designated a lead mine worked at least as early as the eighteenth century. The mine was pointed out to the Mormons by an Indian in 1856, and Nathaniel V.

Jones, whom Brigham Young assigned to develop it, named it for the Potosi District in Wisconsin, where he was born (WA).

Daniel Bonelli's various pursuits and accomplishments made him one of the most famous of the pioneers of southern Nevada. He brought vines from Europe and planted the first vineyard in Nevada at Las Vegas. Bonelli's Ferry, at the junction of the Virgin River with the Colorado, served travelers on the main road from Utah to Arizona in the early days. An avid prospector, Bonelli was the discoverer and owner of three mines which he named the Cleopatra, the Czarina, and the Virgin Queen (WA). The naming habits and histories of individual prospectors are seldom as detailed or as readily available as they are in the case of Daniel Bonelli.

PROSPECTORS AND INVESTORS IN MINING
AND RELATED ENTERPRISES

The mining era brought about an international movement of men, methods, and ideas to California. Among the ideas the men carried along with them were the mining codes which were a product of the common experience of miners in several parts of the world in dealing with the problems of their trade (BH, pp. 127–67; EL, pp. 43–91). A less formal part of their practical education was the acquisition of a stock of well-used mine names of a durable, sometimes distinctive quality. Rapid disposition or transfer of claims, economic depressions, and rumors of new strikes kept most of the prospectors on the move and resulted in a corresponding fluidity in the mine names.

Two California-bound prospectors, William Prouse and John Orr, discovered gold in Gold Canyon, Nevada, in 1849, while they were waiting for the mountain passes to clear of snow. In June of 1859 miners struck the Ophir outcroppings—one of the world's greatest silver lodes. In the rush that followed, most of those who came to Washoe (as the region was then known) were part of the exodus from California and had "been engaged more or less in placer mining" (SM, 1866). In a series of articles regarding early locators and miners, Dr. Henry De Groot told how California miners, a year prior to the Comstock discovery, had gone to British Columbia only to meet disappointment and to return to California; "once on the wing, however, the most of these men remained uneasy and ready for a new flight should anything occur to set them in motion" (CP, 8/19/76, p. 28). J. Ross Browne took "A Peep at Washoe" in 1860 and described the feverish activity there:

The whole country was staked off to the distance of twenty or thirty miles. Every hillside was grubbed open, and even the desert was pegged, like the sole of a boot, with stakes designating claims. Those who could not spare time to go out "prospecting" hired others, or furnished provisions and pack-mules, and went shares (JRB, p. 82).

Sixteen thousand claims were located on the Comstock alone (JHS, p. 20; EL, p. 415), but the prospectors seldom derived much benefit from their discoveries. Closed mines, unemployment, or other reversals set them in motion again, and during 1864 and 1865, ten thousand people left the Comstock (EL, pp. 227–29; GHS, p. 60). New rushes in Nevada continued to occur even into the twentieth century, and prospecting is still carried on at the present time. A latent hope that almost reaches a firm conviction in the Nevada prospector is that he is likely almost any day to strike a lead that will be greater than the Comstock.

The following accounts of a few discoveries show the naming practices of the first prospectors. Ante-Comstockers saw a towering peak catch the first light of the morning sun and named it Sun Peak. When the area began to look promising and still others arrived, they called their settlement Pleasant Hill Camp. Ophir was selected for the claim name when they uncovered the top of a bonanza and washed gold from it. Bishop, Camp, and Rogers made a location on the Comstock and named it the Yellow Jacket, "because of the fact of the locators' finding a nest of yellow-jackets in the surface rock while they were digging about for the purpose of prospecting the vein" (DDQ, p. 36). Jim Butler discovered Tonopah; when his wife Belle staked a claim, she named it Mizpah for an inscription in her wedding ring. A. J. Leathers, having been led to rich ore by Napias Jim, an Indian, staked his claim and named it the Hidden Treasure. Frank (Shorty) Harris and E. Cross discovered rich ore in the range of hills northwest of Beatty; the ore was genuine green bullfrog rock with free gold scattered through it, so the claim name was the Bullfrog. John C. Humphrey and his partners discovered gold in a ledge of silicified lime outcroppings in April, 1905, and their location notice read the April Fool. Isaac Newton Garrison picked up a rock to throw at a jackrabbit. The rock he was holding turned out to be a rich piece of silver ore; the discovery was the Jackrabbit Mine.

If the itinerant prospectors may be said to have filtered into a mining area, the owners and investors helped to make up the so-called rush. B. August Harrison (the locator of the Sierra Nevada Mine on the Comstock) showed some ore to Judge James Walsh of Grass Valley, California. Judge Walsh had Melville Atwood, an assayer of Grass Valley, make the test. Although the high value of the ore was not known until late at night, by the early hours of the morning Judge Walsh had started for the Eastern Slope on horseback. The test could not be kept secret, and by nine o'clock that morning half of the town of Grass Valley knew of the great strike. The Washoe rush had started. "In a few days hundreds of miners had left their diggings in California and were flocking over the mountains on horseback, on foot, with teams, and in any way that offered" (MA, p. 61). The names of Walsh, Atwood, and Harrison appear on the first location notice entered in *Gold Hill Book A* which, in 1859, was kept on a shelf back of a saloon bar. Harrison became associated with Solomon Geller, another responsible citizen, and they formed the Geller Ledge and Harrison Company. A prominent Eagle Valley resident, Abraham V. Z. Curry, and his partner Alvah Gould, became owners of a mine and named it the Gould and Curry. Richard D. Sides, who had previously owned a sawmill and was a rancher in Eagle Valley, took up some ground and named it Sides. Such people account for place names like Belcher, Burke and Hamilton, Hale and Norcross, Raymond & Ely, Pioche, Getchell, Kimberly, and Delamar. Feminine names for mines were also probably placed by the owners and investors.

The naming habits of the itinerant prospector and of the mine owners or investors create a sharp distinction in the name body: the traditional terminology of the former as opposed to names placed to commemorate the latter. The traditional names fall into three broad classifications: names that were thought to be auspicious, that had a learned or classical flavor, or that were of a homey nature.

Auspicious designations signify real or anticipated characteristics such as personal fortitude, the type of mineral deposit, good fortune, or opulence. Names reflecting personal fortitude in the miners include Confidence, Honest Miner, Perserverance, Independent, Defiance, Pickaway, and Neversink.

Names relating to the minerals are, of course, as various as the ore deposits. In addition to the numerous mine names relating to gold, silver, and copper are the following: American Borax, Bullion, Chloride, Coaldale, Cyanide Wash, Eagle Salt Marsh, Galena, Radio Crystal, Sulphur, and Sodaville. Also relating to ore deposits are the "blue" names indicating turquoise: The Blue Gem Lease, the Blue Jay, and the Blue Eagle claims.

Denoting opulence were such popular mine names as Empire, Ophir, and Potosi. Empire was chosen because it had been used for mines in at least eight California counties plus Idaho and New Mexico. The Ophir mines of King Solomon provided a name for mines, mining districts, mining camps, and mountains, and Potosi became popular after the fabulous output of the Bolivian mines became known to the world.

Other mine names denoting good fortune and opulence were Lucky Hobo, Home Ticket, Ready Pay, Hidden Treasure, Paymaster, Eldorado, Wonder, Good Hope, and Jubilee. Emphasizing great size or first position are such names as Mammoth, Keystone, Prince Royal, and Jumbo. The gambling instinct is represented by Big Casino, Four Aces, Jackpot, Seven Up, and Solo Joker.

A second group of mining names has a learned or classical flavor: Caledonia, Aurora Borealis, Bacchus, Sphinx, Macbeth, Faust, Lord Byron, and Socrates. James M. Corey is said to have named Aurora for the goddess of dawn, and to have selected Esmeralda, the gipsy dancer in Victor Hugo's *Notre-Dame de Paris,* because the mining district he was naming was to be a "wild dance of death or disappointment to thousands" (RC, p. 38).

Homey names constitute the largest group in the traditional category. Among these names are the ones given to commemorate famous persons like Columbus, Jefferson, Kit Carson, and Montezuma. Locomotive and Railroad recall the railroad era. Many transfer names probably commemorate the place of birth of a prospector: Quaker City, Montana, Philadelphia, Klondike, and

Northumberland, among others. National was named for the discoverer's National automobile, and the discovery of the Pony Ledge was made in a canyon on the route of the Pony Express.

Among traditional incident names of the homey category are Bean Pot, Accident, Sandstorm, and the previously mentioned Jackrabbit and Yellow Jacket. The Monkey Wrench Mine got its name because members of the Riggs family, using a monkey wrench found in a small ravine, broke a small piece off a ledge with it and were rewarded with a strike which they named for the incident (CGL, pp. 78–84). The famous Hogpen Shoot in the Lucky Bar Mine at Delamar received its name when hogs in a pen built on the side of a hill rooted the dirt off some gold outcroppings (WA).

Named for the incident of the mine's having been discovered at a certain time are April Fool, Christmas, Sunrise, and January. Names exhibiting homey folk humor are the traditional Pick Handle, Thirsty, Whisky, and Lousetown. Apparently the prospectors found the frequent *pah* element in the Indian names amusing. They coined the hybrid Windypah, from *windy* and Southern Paiute *pah,* 'water.' The original discoveries at Goldfield were designated Grandpa(h) in jest at Tonopah (SPD, p. 861).

Whereas the individual prospectors drew on a name-hoard of well used mine names, the investors in mines and mills usually affixed their own names (Caselton, Blair, Hamilton, Weed Heights) to their mines. After forming partnerships, they sometimes added the partner's name (Best & Belcher, Raymond & Ely), or after consolidating, often adopted the name of the district or lode (Consolidated Virginia, Comstock Merger Mines, Inc.).

The names of important individual mines have endured to a surprising degree in Nevada, the most important claim in an area frequently giving its name to the entire district.

The "district" was declared by naming and defining boundaries. It was intended to cover the discovery and was therefore large or small according to the extent and richness of the deposit. The "mining district" was sometimes coextensive with a county or township. It was sometimes very large, as the Reese River District in Nevada, which was about twenty-five miles from north to south (JGS, I, pp. 169–170).

The name of the mining district usually was adopted for the camp which sprang up to serve it and frequently for the mountain from which the ore was taken, for a nearby creek, the post office, and the stage or railroad station. The discovery of a new lead or richer ore body in the same area would often give a new name to the district and the camp, but the older name would not be lost.

RANCHERS AND TOWN–BUILDERS

At first attracted to the state because of mineral discoveries, many members of the westward migration who settled in Nevada came to realize the potential value of valleys and meadowland for stock-growing and farming. Irrigation made it possible to produce vegetables in some southern areas, and melons, tomatoes, and potatoes in the western valleys. The principal crops, however, were wild hay, alfalfa, and grain for cattle. (At present, fourteen of the sixteen counties of Nevada derive the major portion of their income from farming and livestock.) The individual ranches were from six thousand to over a hundred thousand acres in size, although most of the grazing area was public domain. Some of the largest ranches, as well as smaller ones, were settled in the 1860s, and the names of the owners became designations for mountains, valleys, caves, springs, post offices, and towns.

Orographic features ordinarily bear the surname of a pioneer settler. Some of the peaks so named are Adams, Doherty, Garrett, Heusser, Springer, and Wilson. The Nightingale Mountains, a name devised by folk etymology, has been corrupted from Nightengill, in honor of Alanson W. Nightengill, a captain in the Truckee Rangers of the Washoe Regiment which engaged in the Pyramid Lake Indian War of 1860, to Nightengale, to the present Nightingale. Daggett's Pass, Hickerson Summit, Lehman Cave, and Arnold, Latham, and Lewis bottoms also bear the surnames of early settlers. Canyon and valley names follow the same pattern, as shown in such canyon names as Cahill, Hays, Kershad, and Kyle, and in the valleys named Jakes, Lemmon, and Smith. The given names of Billy Joe Smith, however, appear in Billy Joe Basin.

Those who lived on or near hydrographic features are commemorated by creek names: Chiatovich, Griswold, Hulse, Peterson, and Winter; by the designations for springs and wells, as in Becky, Hinds, and Walley; and by Angel Lake. The hydrographic features, in a few instances, bear the full name of the honored early settler: Tom Cain Creek, Decker Bob Creek (commemorating a Shoshone of that name), and Warren Able Springs.

Also bearing the surname of the settler were those post offices operated at ranches strategically located to serve mining districts and other settled areas. With the rancher or his wife serving as postmaster, the family name commonly was adopted for the post office. Such names include Barrett, Currie, Fletcher, Sutcliffe, Tippett, and Yoacham.

In like manner, the name of a ranch owner, of the first settler, of a prominent businessman, or of an individual promoter or surveyor often became that of a Nevada townsite. Frequently the surname alone became the settlement name: Beatty, Carlin, Doutre, Fallon, Stewart, Wilkins, Lovelock, Olinghouse, and Parker. At other times, the surname was combined with -ville, -town, or -ton to form such names as Downeyville, Gardnerville, Reipetown, and Dayton.

As often as not, however, the pioneer settlers gave names that described the areas in which they lived, or the occupations that engaged them, that were related to some memorable incident, or that exemplified frontier humor. Occasionally, they named to commemorate a famous personage, a war, their homeland, or created an appropriate coinage.

Descriptive of the area were Alamo, associated with cottonwood trees, and Grass and Clover valleys, with the abundant grass and clover growing in them. The haze usually present in one large valley induced the settlers to name it Big Smoky. Artesia was descriptively named for artesian wells nearby. Taking their names because of their locations are Centerville for its central position, and North Fork for its being on the North Fork of the Humboldt River. Deerlodge, Duckwater, and Sage Hen were named for indigenous game.

Other descriptive names recall the diverse occupations of the early ranchers and town-builders. A mountain range was named Seven Troughs from a series of seven watering troughs which stockmen had placed in a canyon. Mill Point and Sawmill Canyon were the sites of mills operated by early settlers. A canyon where beef was killed for the town butcher shops was named Slaughterhouse. Bootleg Canyon was named for a still provided for the convenience of construction workers at Hoover Dam. The YP and Diamond A deserts (flats used as rangeland) are named for cattle brands. "Dave," a sorrel stallion, is commemorated by a creek so named (EP).

Some names recall a particular incident. When the rising waters of Lake Mead trapped a bighorn sheep on one of the Overton Islands, the incident produced the name Bighorn Island (WA). When settlers learned that local Indians believed a concavity in the earth containing hot springs was the abode of a devil, they named the place Devil's Punch Bowl, currently euphemized to Diana's Punch Bowl. A settler roped a bear on a northern Nevada mountain named Bear. Sheepshead Ranch in the Smoke Creek Desert was named for nearby Sheepshead Springs, which got its name from the head of a mountain sheep nailed to a tree at the site.

That certain events or circumstances were thought humorous is revealed in some of the place names attributed to the settlers. A poor locality near Pioche was called Fiddler's Gulch, and a small settlement near Dayton, the home of some shiftless and happy-go-lucky families who spent their time dancing and playing, became known as Fiddler's Green. Also near Dayton was the ranch of a known atheist; the ranch and the surrounding area were dubbed New Jerusalem. A group of men digging an irrigation ditch in the southern part of the state had nothing to drink but the purgative waters of the Rogers and Blue Point springs. As a result, several workers lost weight, and the stream below the springs was named Slim Creek (WA).

Some famous personages commemorated by settlers in the names they placed are Admiral George Dewey, whose name was given to the post office Dewey, in the valley of the Virginia Range; Chester A. Arthur, commemorated by Arthur, a post office established in 1881; and General Thomas Jonathan Jackson, in the name of the Stonewall Mountains.

Buena Vista Valley was settled by men from the South who had fought against Santa Ana at Buena Vista on February 23, 1847, and who named the valley to commemorate the battle. Several features were named Dixie by Southern sympathizers in the early 1860s. A place so denoted in Pershing County was renamed Unionville because of the loyalty of the settlers during the Civil War.

Named to commemorate their native homelands were Minden, so called by the sons of Henry Fred Dangberg, Sr., for the place of their father's birth in Germany, and Engadine, an early post office in Round Valley, named by Joseph D. Delmue and his brothers for the place of their birth in Switzerland (WA).

Lastly, representative names coined by the town-builders are Nyala (a settlement in northern Nye County), from the county name plus a diminutive, and Adaven (Nevada spelled backwards), selected for a post office in Elko County, a town in Nye County, and as an early name for Las Vegas.

As name-givers the ranchers and town-builders are the second most influential group, having placed around half as many names as the prospectors and investors. The number would be increased to a degree were it not that, for the purposes of this inquiry into the habits of the name-givers, those ranch owners who also operated stage and pony line stations have been considered with those who named the railroad stations in the state.

TRADING, STAGE, AND PONY LINE STATION OPERATORS AND RAILROAD BUILDERS

The opening of the West led to the building of numerous way stations along the main routes of travel. The trails explored by Smith, Ogden, Walker, Frémont, and Simpson became liberally dotted by the names of independent trading posts and stage and pony line stations, and with the building of the railroads, the names of agency and nonagency stations and of sidings began to appear in hitherto remote areas.

Most of the early trading and mail stations have crumbled to dust, and many of their names have vanished. Also largely gone are the names along the routes of the twenty-seven shortline railroads built mainly to transport ore from the mines and in most instances abandoned when the ore bodies gave out. The loss of most of the early station names on the emigrant trails and on small stage and freight routes is attributable to the station proprietor's habit of affixing his own name, usually possessive, to the place—a subsequent change of owner meant a change of name. Improvements in transportation and communication often meant the discontinuance of the station and subsequent loss of the name.

For example, Jamison's Station on the Truckee River, named after its owner, became Stone and Gates' Crossing when John F. Stone and Charles C. Gates bought it, but the locality is now known as Glendale. Other trading posts of the 1850s were Fuller's Crossing on the Truckee River, named for C. W. Fuller, which later became Lake's Crossing in honor of Myron C. Lake, and eventually Reno; and Hall's Station, so called when owned by Spafford Hall, which became McMarlin's Station when purchased by James McMarlin, and is presently Dayton. Names showing the nationality of the owner were Dutch Nick's Station on the Carson River (now New Empire), and French Ford or French Bridge, built by Frank Band on the Humboldt River and now known as Winnemucca.

A few station names of the 1850s did not commemorate the owner, but were adopted from nearby land features or recalled incidents. Clear Creek Station was on Clear Creek; Eagle Station has become Carson City; and Asa L. Kenyon's trading post at the edge of the Forty Mile Desert—"three huts, formed of poles covered with rotten canvas full of holes"—was called Ragtown Station.

Important mineral discoveries in other parts of the state increased the need for stations to serve the new mining camps. Names placed to commemorate station owners still predominated, but descriptive names increased in number, particularly those describing location and distance. Cradlebaugh's Bridge and Sweetwater Station were built on the road to Bodie and Aurora. River Bed Station, on the old river bed of the Carson River, was on the road from Virginia City to Reese River. Coates's Wells was a station and watering place on the way to Austin, and Manseau's Half-Way House, also on the road to Reese River, was half way between Virginia City and Carson. Travelers in northern Elko County made a regular meal stop at Dinner Station, and a station near East Gate, cut from soft white rock, was named White Rock Station.

In addition to the independent and small stage-line way stations there were stopping places on the Pony Express and Overland Mail routes, both of which followed the wagon road explored by Captain James H. Simpson through central Nevada. Occasionally these posts were named for the mail agents who operated them; more often they were given older place names taken from the surrounding areas.

There had been regular mail service across Nevada since 1851, by pack mule, covered wagon, and stage. Major George Chorpenning, pioneer stage operator through Nevada, had a route from Sacramento to Salt Lake City from 1851 to 1859. Senator Gwinn of California, said to have conceived the idea of the first horse-relay mail service, prevailed upon William H. Russell, Alexander Majors, and William Waddell, who had been transporting freight from Kansas to California since 1854, to organize the Pony Express. They bought up two lines running out of Salt Lake City: the Hockaday line to the east and the Chorpenning line to the west. Upon winning the mail contract in January, 1860, they set up stations, hired two hundred additional station keepers, and from eighty to ninety express riders, to be distributed along the central route from St. Joseph, Missouri, to Sacramento, California. Service began simultaneously at both ends of the route on April 3, 1860, and ended eighteen months later when the transcontinental telegraph wire went into operation on October 25, 1861. In Nevada, the pony riders covering the Simpson route traveled a dangerous 407-mile stretch with twenty-nine stations, beginning with Deep Creek at the eastern end and ending with Friday's, west of Genoa.

Egan Canyon Station is one of the two names on the route known to stem directly from men in the employ of George Chorpenning. It was named after Major Howard E. Egan (a rider for Chorpenning's pioneer mail service), who was the first to prove the Egan Cutoff, a route across central Nevada which was more practicable than the Humboldt route. Roberts Creek Station was named for Bolivar Roberts, a division superintendent of the Pony Express.

Of the seven stations named to commemorate station keepers, three are honorific of men whose full names are unknown: Jacob's Wells (between Ruby Springs and Diamond Springs), Grubbs Wells, and Friday's Station. Jacob's Station (between Simpson's Park and Dry Wells stations) was named for George Washington Jacobs, mail agent; Buckland Station was named for Agent Samuel S. Buckland; and a station on the Carson River originally called Miller's was renamed Reed for Agent G. W. Reed.

The remaining commemorative station names along the line of the Pony Express honor Kit Carson (Carson Sink), James H. Simpson (Simpson's Park), Edward Jagiello of the Simpson expedition (Edward's Creek), Lieutenant J. L. Kirby Smith, assistant to Simpson (Smith Creek), John Day, the surveyor (Dayton), Major A. J. Schell, United States commander in charge of a detachment of troops for the protection of the mail (Schell Creek), and General Sylvester Churchill (Fort Churchill).

Thirteen of the Pony Express way stations set up by Russell, Major, and Waddell took their names from nearby land features, descriptively named prior to 1860: Antelope Springs, Butte, Deep Creek, Desert, Diamond Springs, Dry Creek, Dry Wells, Mountain Springs, Ruby, Sand Hill, Sand Springs, Sulphur Springs, and Westgate. Genoa had been so named by Mormon Elder Orson Hyde because a cove in the mountains there reminded him of the harbor of Genoa, Italy. Although most of the Pony Express stations have vanished or stand in ruins, most of their names have remained.

The stages of the Overland Mail followed essentially the same route across Nevada as had the riders of the Pony Express. The stage drivers and Wells Fargo guards risked their lives on each trip, and the station agents experienced the isolation and usual dangers from marauding Indians. On March 22, 1863, some Indians under War Chief White Horse killed the keeper of Eight-Mile Station, starting the Goshute War (also called the Overland War of 1863), which cost the Overland Stage Company in Utah and Nevada one hundred and fifty horses, seven stations, and sixteen men (SPD, pp. 155, 183).

Of the thirty-three stations on the line, as compiled in Root and Connelley's *The Overland Stage to California,* seventeen retained the same names that they had earlier had as Pony Express stations: the surviving descriptive names were Antelope Springs, Spring Valley, Butte, Mountain Spring, Diamond Springs, Sulphur Springs, Dry Creek, and Cold Spring; the commemorative names were Schell Creek, Jacob's Wells, Robert's Creek, Simpson's Park, Edward's Creek, Dayton, Carson, Genoa, and Friday's.

The remaining sixteen names were either changed or new, and were both descriptive and commemorative. For example, Prairie Gate, instead of Deep Creek, was the first station on the eastern end of the line in Nevada. Gold Canyon replaced the Egan Canyon Station; Ruby Valley denoted Ruby Station; Overland Ranch in Ruby Valley supplied grain for the horses of the stage line

and furnished a name for Overland Lake in the Rubies (EP); Cape Horn was
established midway between Dry Creek and Simpson's Park; and old Jacobsville Station, northwest of Austin, was known as Reese River. Dry Wells was
replaced by Mount Airy, Westgate by Middle Gate, Carson Sink by Stillwater,
and Reed by Desert Wells, later changed to Nelson's.

Lost names of the Overland Mail stations were few. The fact that the
bulk of the names on the central mail routes through the state were taken from
the land, or commemorated the men who were intimately connected with the
exploration and history of Nevada, assures some permanency.

The transporting of mail and passengers, at first by pack mule, covered
wagon, pony line, and stage line, ultimately became the province of the railroads. Four trunk lines crossed or entered the state, a minimum of twenty-
seven short lines were built mainly to transport ore, and many names were
added to the nomenclature of Nevada. Except for the Nevada Northern Railroad, the short lines and narrow-gage roads either are defunct or have been
taken up as spurs, branch lines, or parts of the main lines by the three first-
class railroads that now cross the state.

The name of a railroad usually indicated where it started, where it was
going, or where it would like to go. The name of the first transcontinental, the
Central Pacific (Southern Pacific) came from the "Central" Overland Stage
route. Most nineteenth-century short lines in Nevada were named as appropriately: Virginia and Truckee, Eureka Mill, Lake Tahoe Narrow Gauge,
Sutro Tunnel, and Oregon Short Line. Named with more optimism was the
Carson and Colorado (Southern Pacific), planned to connect Carson City,
Nevada, with the Lower Colorado River, but actually taking a southwesterly
route to California from Sodaville, Nevada (DM, GHK, Bonanza, pp. 72–73).
In 1900 the Southern Pacific bought the Carson and Colorado and changed its
name to Nevada and California. Lines named for twentieth-century boom
towns were Tonopah Railroad, Tonopah and Goldfield, Las Vegas and Tonopah, and Tonopah and Tidewater (the first railroad to attempt to enter Nevada
mineral discoveries from the south).

The station names adopted by the builders of the Nevada Northern
are representative of those names chosen by other railroad builders. Steptoe
was named to commemorate Colonel E. J. Steptoe, a famous fighter of the
Old West who was sent into eastern Nevada to quell reported Indian uprisings
in the 1860s, and Shafter was named to commemorate General W. R. Shafter,
a commander in the United States Army in Cuba during the Spanish-American
War. Other station names honorific of the military are Reno, Wadsworth, and
Halleck.

Cherry Creek, named for chokeberries in the canyon and adopted for a
station name, is typical of the names selected by early emigrants, traders, and
explorers. Among such names are Amargosa, Cedar, Cold Springs, Iron Point,
Pyramid, and Las Vegas. Currie and McGill were named for early ranchers
Joseph H. Currie and William N. McGill. Some other station names which

honor ranchers and early settlers are Carlin, Deeth, Gerlach, Lovelock, and Sutcliffe.

Station names on the Nevada Northern that commemorate the mining investors are Kimberly, named for Peter L. Kimberly; Ely, named for Smith Ely; and Ruth, named for the daughter of D. C. McDonald, an owner of claims in the area. Similar names on other lines and stemming from the mining industry are Austin, Lewis, Sloan, Sutro, and Virginia City, among others.

The name Cobre is representative of those names chosen by the rail-road builders which were not already in use in an area, but appropriate to it. At a meeting of the railroad people to select a name for the rail junction, O. H. Hershey, who had just returned from Mexico and was still speaking some Spanish words, suggested the Spanish word for copper to denote the northern terminal of a railroad built to serve the copper fields to the south (DM). Among this group chosen by the railroad builders and particularly appropriate to the area are Mina, Caliente, and Marmol, named for nearby rich ore, hot springs, and marble deposits. Appropriate to the terrain are such names as Mirage, Sage, Clifton, Borax, and Summit.

A small group of names have to do with the business of railroading. Adverse was named for a point where the track runs counter to the grade, and Hiline denotes a junction on the Nevada Northern where the high line to a smelter takes off from the main line (DM). Woodyard and Cottonwood, built to reach wood supply stations, are reminiscent of the old woodburning loco-motives. Tie House, Junction, and Scales relate to the industry. Also to be included in this group is Washout, the name of a station on the Carson and Colorado that washed out each year when the snows melted. Some names of the group are identifiable by a generic, peculiar to the industry: Amargosa Siding, Gravel Pit Siding, Smiley's Spur, and Cedar Switch.

Only a few names are known to commemorate the builders and officials of the railroads—for example, Bridges, Ledlie, Yerington, and Garnet. It is probable, however, that many station names, apparently surnames and of unknown origin, fall into the same category. Other railroad names of undeter-mined origin are Ocala, Rasid, Coin, and Tulasco. Some are blend words, such as Weso, combining the names of the Western Pacific and the Southern Pacific; Idavada, a Western Pacific Station on the Idaho and Nevada line; and Melandco for the Metropolis Land Company. Although no pattern is readily discernible in the railroad names, a number apparently useful for their brevity and distinctiveness end in the letter *o*. Among the short names in this series are Argo, Bango, Elko, Jungo, Pardo, and Sano.

GOVERNMENT OFFICIALS AND AGENCIES

Before the creation of the Territory of Nevada by Congressional Act of March 2, 1861, the present state area had been a Spanish possession until 1822, and from then until the concluding of the treaty of Guadalupe Hidalgo on February 2, 1848, it was part of Mexican Territory. From 1849 to 1850 the area had been included in the Mormon "State of Deseret," established with boundary changes, as the Territory of Utah by Congress on September 9, 1850 (AJM, pp. 14, 21). The bill for the organization of Sierra Nevada Territory was presented to the Committee on Territories early in 1858 by Delegate James M. Crane, but the committee shortened the name to Nevada (OPN, p. 2; JHS, p. 91; GRS, p. 304). The name Sierra Nevada as submitted by Delegate Crane is Spanish for "snow-covered jagged mountain range," and is the name of the mountains which formed the western boundary of the territory. The range had been named on April 3, 1776, by Padre Pedro Font, as he viewed it from the California side (Gudde). The region east of the Sierra Nevada had been known generally as the Eastern Slope, or Washoe, since it was the habitat of the Washo Indians. Other official names of the territory were those of the counties and of the camps and forts established by the military for the protection of emigrant parties, traders, prospectors, and settlers.

The first forts and camps were established subsequent to the killing of five men on May 7, 1860, by Indians at Williams Station on the emigrant trail. Four detachments, consisting of 105 volunteers, made a revenge march on May 12. Many of the men, not believing the Indians would fight, started out with the watchword "An Indian for breakfast and a pony to ride" (SPD, p. 51). Seventy-six of them were killed in a battle three miles from Pyramid Lake. Aided by United States soldiers, they defeated the Indians in a second battle near Pyramid Lake on June 2, 1860. As a result of the two battles, several temporary camps and two permanent forts were established. Other territorial forts were built, too, because of later Indian uprisings.

In his account entitled "Early Nevada Forts, Posts and Camps," Colonel George Ruhlen explains that "forts of the permanent type were named by the Secretary of War upon the recommendation of the military commander in whose department they were located," and that camps or bivouacs, to be temporarily occupied from a few days to several months, were "given names or numbers by the officers responsible for their establishment, or by higher commanders" for purposes of identification. Commemorative names for early territorial forts and camps honored United States Army officers, Nevada volunteers in the Indian wars, a prospector on the Comstock, and a territorial governor.

Fort Haven, an earthwork thrown up by soldiers on June 6, 1860, about one mile from Pyramid Lake on the Truckee River, was named for Major General J. P. Haven of the California Militia, who had participated in the battle of June 2, 1860, as a volunteer in the Washoe Regiment. Fort Churchill was established by Captain Joseph Stewart, in command of "The Carson River Expedition." The site was selected on July 20, 1860, and, at the request of Captain Stewart, named for General Sylvester Churchill, Inspector General.

Two temporary camps were named for Nevada volunteers in the Pyramid Lake Indian battles of 1860. Camp Ormsby, on the Truckee River ten miles from Pyramid Lake, was established by Captain Stewart on June 2,

1860, and named for Major William M. Ormsby, a prominent pioneer and one of the founders of Carson City. Major Ormsby had been killed leading the "Carson City Rangers" in the battle of May 12, 1860 (SPD, pp. 51, 52, 58; MA, pp. 527–28; Ruhlen). A temporary earthwork, constructed by the Washoe Regiment of Nevada volunteers prior to the battle of June 2, was situated about midway between Pyramid Lake and Wadsworth on the Truckee River. The fort was named for Captain Edward Faris Storey, who lost his life on that day (MA, p. 569; DDQ, p. 80; Ruhlen).

After the initial victory of the Paiutes, the women and children who remained at Virginia City "were corralled for safety in a large stone hotel that was being built by Peter O'Riley" (DDQ, p. 79). The name Fort Riley commemorates this man who, with Patrick McLaughlin, is credited with having discovered the Ophir bonanza and the Comstock Lode in June, 1859.

Camp Nye, established five miles north of Carson City in June, 1862, served as a base and depot for Nevada and California volunteers serving in Nevada during the Civil War. The camp was named for James Warren Nye of New York, who was commissioned Governor of Nevada Territory on March 22, 1861 (Ruhlen; AJM, p. 21).

Other territorial military establishments took their names from the surrounding area. Military forts had been constructed at Salt Lake City and Carson Valley, leaving the route of the Overland Mail unprotected for six hundred miles. Fertile Ruby Valley, located about midway between the two posts, was selected as the site for a new camp, established on June 10, 1860. The fort, which adopted the name of the valley, was redesignated Camp Ruby on January 1, 1867. Camp Smoke Creek, named for the creek where it was located, was established on December 15, 1862, near a stage station, five miles east of the California-Nevada line. The troops were stationed there as a protection against hostile Indians in the Honey Lake region.

Of the commemorative names of the early territorial camps and forts, four ultimately became the designations for counties. Smoke Creek and Ruby still denote land features, as they did prior to the establishment of the camps. Also, the local name for the territory was preserved with the creation of Washoe County by act of the first territorial legislature on November 25, 1861.

Also created by the act of November 25, 1861, and named commemoratively, were Lyon and Douglas counties. The names honor Stephen A. Douglas, an American political leader and chairman of the Committee on Territories, who died in 1861, and Captain Robert Lyon of the Pioneer army who came to Nevada in June, 1850, by wagon train and was a hero of the Indian wars (SPD, pp. 22, 37; M&S, p. 144; MTM).

Subsequent to the achievement of statehood in 1864, the Nevada legislature created and named additional counties, usually because of significant mineral discoveries. The new counties were named for nationally known persons, for mining districts, and for the character of the land.

Lincoln County, created February 25, 1866, commemorated the martyred president, and Pershing County, created March 18, 1919, honored General John Joseph Pershing. Clark County was named in honor of William A. Clark, United States Senator from Montana, who built the San Pedro, Los Angeles, and Salt Lake Railroad, later purchased by the Union Pacific (M&S, p. 162; OPN, p. 4). White Pine County was named after the White Pine Mining District, so called because of the heavy stand of trees in the range which were thought to be white pine (RRE; M&S, p. 158). A county created from the northern portion of Esmeralda County in 1911 was named Mineral because it is a highly mineralized area (SPD, p. 957). Forts, bases, and depots established since 1864 in the state of Nevada have usually been named for officers; a few have been named for land features.

Significant dams in Nevada, like the military installations, have been named for government officials. Davis Dam on the Colorado River was named in honor of Arthur Powell Davis, Director of Reclamation from 1914 to 1923. Lahontan Dam, completed in 1915, formed Lahontan Reservoir to store the waters of the Truckee and Carson rivers. The name, stemming from that of ancient Lake Lahontan, honors Baron de Lahontan, French officer and traveler. Hoover Dam, originally called Boulder Dam, was officially renamed in 1947 to commemorate Herbert Hoover, the thirty-first president of the United States. Lake Mead, created by Hoover Dam, commemorates Elwood Mead, Commissioner of the Bureau of Reclamation, who recommended the awarding of the bid for the construction of Boulder Dam in 1931 (JGS, I, p. 558).

State officials are responsible for the designations of the Nevada State Parks, created by statutes of 1925 and 1935, and for the place names therein, such as Elephant Rock and Beehive Rock, as well as the studiedly arresting toponyms, Enchanted Formations, Rainbow Vista, Atlatl Rock, Flaming Fire, and Fire Alcove. Such sophisticated periphrastics as Valley of Fire State Park and Court of Antiquity belong to the same group. Local history is preserved in such names as Mouses Tank Picnic Area in the Valley of Fire State Park. "Mouse," a shy and elusive Southern Paiute, hid from white settlers in the 1890s near a natural sandstone tank, hollowed out by the force of water.

United States postal authorities, as official arbiters, apparently allowed local usage to govern their name decisions. A choice was dictated only when it became necessary in order to avoid a duplication of names, to settle a controversy over them, or to provide a name when no prior name existed. Since the advent of the Zone Improvement Program, post office names have been superseded by five-digit numbers. Selected examples of past name choices made by these officials, therefore, are sufficient to the purpose of this inquiry.

Settlers in a gold mining camp in Elko County asked for the name Gold Circle. The postal authorities refused to approve the name because too many post offices in Nevada at that time were using *gold* in their names and suggested Midas, which denoted the post office from 1907 to 1942 (NM, p. 126; F&T). A controversy over the name to be given to a settlement in Mound Valley, Elko County, led postal authorities to select the name Jiggs from a list submitted by local ranchers for the post office established December 18, 1918 (RC, p. 57; F&T). Prior names for the settlement and post office had been Dry Creek (1874–1879), Mound Valley (1879–1881), Skelton (1884–1911), and Hy(i)lton (1911–1913). The post office commemorates the comic-strip character Jiggs, his altercations with his wife Maggie symbolizing the name controversy among the ranchers (Nev. Guide, p. 162; OPN, p. 25). Gravelly Ford, a post office established in 1869, was reestablished as Beowawe in 1870 when a railroad station was built a little distance from the old emigrant crossing.

The importance of the United States Board on Geographic Names as name-giver or official arbiter tends to increase in Nevada. Names formally submitted to the Geographic Board by its field workers and by various other agencies apparently are approved when local usage and etymology sanction the approval. Correctness, uniformity, and local history are also among matters of its concern. An examination of the *Decisions* affords ample evidence of the willingness with which the board both reverses and alters decisions with celerity, when the action is warranted.

New names proposed by or submitted to the board for unnamed features, sometimes for publication purposes, may be descriptive and are often in keeping with other names in the area. The Halfpint Range, "so named in 1962 because of its relatively low and broken relief in contrast to many nearby ranges," is in the same general area as the Pintwater Range. Other names given because they are in keeping with the vernacular of the geographical names in a region include Cockeyed Ridge, a ridge with an asymmetrical profile; Busted Butte, a hill with the ledges on its side offset by a fault, giving it a broken appearance; Big Burn Valley, a valley conspicuously marked by a large burned area; and Grimy Gulch, where finely weathered rock makes one feel grimy on a windy day.

Commemorative names may honor persons of local importance, such as Streuben Knob, named for a mine operator; Winter Creek, named for a longtime resident of the area; and Steele Lake, named for a settler of the 1860s. Historical personages of greater than regional importance are also honored. King Peak in the Ruby Mountains is "named for Clarence King (1842–1901), leader of the Fortieth Parallel Survey and first Director of the United States Geological Survey" (USGB 7002). Mount Fitzgerald, also in the Rubies, commemorates President John Fitzgerald Kennedy (USGB 6601).

Recent incident names are also appropriate: Dead Horse Flat was named for the saddled skeleton of a horse found on the flat; Parachute Canyon for a parachute found in the canyon; and Basket Valley for Indian baskets discovered in a cave in the valley.

Innovative naming occurs in the designations of minor features. Ridges and buttes are carefully described and precisely named. Crested Wheat Ridge is "named for the wheatgrass that grows on the ridge"; Andesite Ridge is "named for the andesite lava found on the western part of the ridge"; and

Shingle Buttes "are capped by layers of welded tuff that appear as shingles" (USGB 6903). Color adjectives new to the Nevada name body are usefully employed. Pink Holes Hill was named for its color and its numerous wind-eroded holes. Amethyst Peak was named for its cap rock, which has an amethyst color in the sunshine. Orange Lichen Creek takes its name from the "orange lichens which cover the exposed welded tuff" (USGB 6103; 6903).

It is probable that the macabre name belt of southwestern Nye County originated with the Geographic Board. Specter Range, Skeleton Hills, and Skull Mountains were officially so named in the *Fifth Report of the United States Geographic Board, 1899–1920*. The names properly complement that of Death Valley to the west. Goblin Knobs, a group of hills also in Nye County, were so named in 1971 because "local tuff weathers into hoodoos and weird knobs."

The name for Spirit Mountain, near the southern tip of Nevada, was chosen by the Geographic Board over Deadman, Dead, Newberry, and North. Precedent for such names in the southern Nevada desert areas was established by the Indians: Nüvant, the Southern Paiute name for Charleston Peak in Clark County, "was the most famous place in the mythology of both the Chemehuevi and the western bands of the Southern Paiute" (Kroeber, Handbook, p. 596). Fallout Hills, denoting an orographic feature in Lincoln County, was a name submitted by the Geologic Division of the Geological Survey to the Geographic Board and accepted because "during 1957–1958 this area was contaminated by radio-active fallout related to A-bomb tests in the Nevada Test Site, a few miles west" (Kilmartin). The historicity of Spirit Mountain and Fallout Hills may well certify to the eloquence of name-givers in describing and recording the pursuits of man.

METHOD OF
PRESENTATION OF THE NAMES

All entries are arranged alphabetically as determined by the initial letter of the specific part: Lake Tahoe, see under Tahoe; Mount Davidson, see under Davidson. When the generic (class) becomes a part of the specific as in the town name Mount Montgomery, the entry is under Mount. County names, enclosed in parentheses, follow the entry if all names in the group are in the same county. For practical purposes and close documentation, a key to the Bibliography, Maps, and Railroads has been utilized throughout.

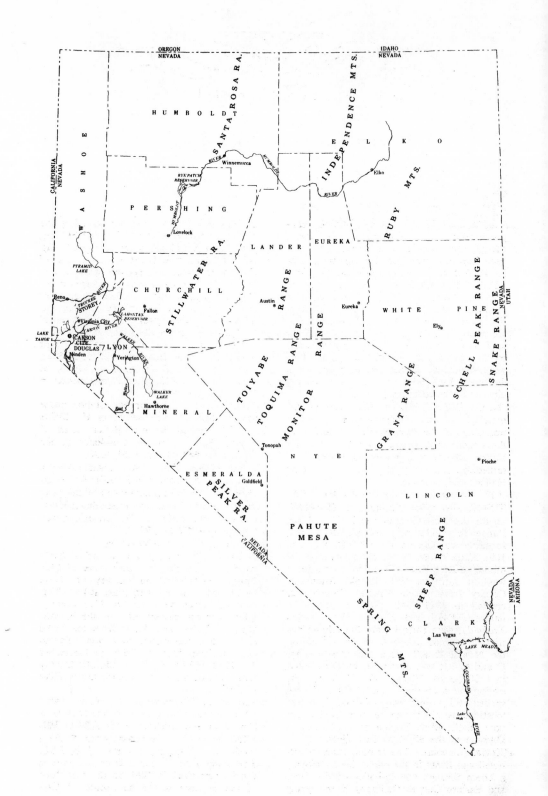

THE PLACE NAMES

ABBOTTS. ABBOTTS FORK, a canyon heading on the west slope of the Bristol Range, about one mile northwest of Stampede Gap in Lincoln County, commemorates J. W. Abbott, an early settler in the area. **ABBOTTSVILLE** (Clark) was the name for land on which the AT and SF RR built the terminal of the former Barnwell and Searchlight branch line in 1907. Local objection to the establishment of the terminal on this land about a mile west of Searchlight, owned by the Searchlight Terminal Townsite Company, caused the citizens to apply the name derisively for F. J. Abbott, the managing director of the company (WA; DM).

ACKLER CREEK (Elko). The name of this mountain stream, which rises on the northwest slope of the East Humboldt Range and flows generally northwestward into Starr Valley, commemorates George Ackler, who settled on the creek after serving at Fort Halleck (EP, p. 7; NK 11–12).

ACME (Mineral). **ACME MINING DIS-TRICT,** also called *Fitting* and *Kincaid,* is on the southeast slope and end of the Gillis Range, four miles north of **ACME TANK,** formerly a siding on the SP RR (VPG, p. 109). *Kincaid* may be the oldest name of the mining district, since a location of this name was on Martinez Hill in old Esmeralda County from which Mineral County was created in 1911 (SM, 1867, p. 36). Both names, **ACME** and *Kincaid* (also spelled *Kinkaid*), were shifted from the mining district to become designations for sidings on the N and C RR when the narrow-gauge C and C RR was purchased by the SP RR in 1900 (GHK, V&T, p. 19; NJ 11–4). The station name on the C and C RR had been spelled still a third way *Kinkead.* The two locations between Thorne and Luning are now on the Mina Branch of the Salt Lake Division of the SP RR (Haw. Quad.; T75).

ACOMA (Lincoln). The mining camp so denoted was lively in the early 1900s, enjoying a boom through the activities of the Utah and Eastern Copper Company in the spring of 1904 (DM). The camp was served by the old Clark Road, or the SPLA and SL RR, built in 1905 and purchased by the UP RR. **ACOMA** station is twenty-six miles east of Caliente in the eastern portion of the county (NJ 11–9). The name was transferred probably from some older settlement, such as that in Valencia County, New Mexico, and means *ako,* "white rock" and *ma,* "people" or "people of the white rock," in the Keres Indian language (Pearce, p. 2). **ACOMA** post office, with one interruption (1908–1909), served the area from April 29, 1905, to November 15, 1913, when it was moved to Caliente (FTM, p. 1).

ACTON (Clark). This popular station name was applied by the builders of the SPLA and SL RR to the first station north of Moapa. The station was abandoned by the UP RR in 1949 (OG, p. 1257; WA).

ADAMS PEAK (Humboldt). Charles Adams, who founded a colony in Paradise Valley on May 10, 1865, is commemorated by this peak in the Osgood Mountains in southeast Humboldt County (SPD, p. 171). *Adam* is a variant spelling (GHM, HU 1).

ADAMS RIVER. See **VIRGIN.**

ADAVEN. The name, *Nevada* spelled backwards, was applied to a post office of Elko County, established on January 11, 1916, by an order rescinded in June, 1916 (FTM, p. 1). A small settlement of Nye County, lying near the eastern edge of the Nevada National Forest and dating from the 1870s (RC, p. 36), was served by a post office so denoted from May 1, 1939, to November 30, 1953 (FTM, p. 1). A Lincoln County settlement of this name is northwest of Hiko (WA).

ADELAIDE (Humboldt). A mining camp which flourished at the turn of the century as a result of the purchase of the **ADELAIDE MINE** in 1897 by the Glasgow and Western Exploration Company (Census, 1900; DM). The camp took its name from the mining district organized in 1866 on the east slope of the Sonoma Range and south of Golconda. The district was named for an early woman settler, but is now better known as *Gold Run* (VPG, p. 72).

ADOBE. Features are so named for the alluvial or playa clay in a region. **ADOBE FLAT** (Pershing) forms a portion of Granite Springs Valley, lying west of the Trinity Range. A settlement of the 1860s in that portion of Humboldt County from which Pershing County was created in 1919; named for adobe buildings, which comprised most of the settlement (HHB, Nev., p. 264; DB, p. 1). Humboldt House post office served the area (TF, p. 15). An Elko County name group may stem from **ADOBE** (Doby) **SUMMIT,** a pass in the **ADOBE RANGE** about seven miles northwest of Elko and two miles south of **ADOBE RANCH.** The summit was named by early freighters or by stagecoach drivers for rain-slick, heavy clay. **ADOBE CREEK** and **EAST ADOBE CREEK** complete the name group. Field reports of the United States Geological Survey indicate that local opinion is divided as to the spelling of the summit name, but that most people in the area pronounce it "Doby" even while spelling it "Adobe" (DL 61).

ADOTH (Washoe). The name was applied by railroad officials to a former station of the SP RR, opened February 10, 1904, at Ninth Crossing on the Truckee River, by report of the *Reno Evening Gazette*. The station served the newly organized Ninth Crossing Gold Mining Company (DM).

ADVANCE GULCH (Lincoln). The wash, southwest of Pioche, runs eastward from the **ADVANCE MINE,** for which it was named (WA).

ADVERSE (White Pine). The name of this railroad siding, northeast of Lavon, is descriptive of the "adverse grade" track there, so called because the track runs counter to the grade (SG Map 9; DM).

AFTON (Elko). A short-lived settlement, north of Metropolis, a post office (September 26, 1914–January 15, 1918); believed to have been so named by settlers for their earlier home at Afton, Wyoming (FTM, p. 1; EP, p. 7).

AGORT PASS (Elko). A pass, nine miles southeast of Contact and between Blanchard Mountain, on the north, and Knoll Mountain, on the south; "named for Chris Agort, early immigrant, who discovered and worked the first copper deposits in this area" (USGB 6902).

AGUA CHIQUITA SPRING (Clark). The spring is in Catclaw Wash and west of Gold Butte (WA; GHM, CL 2). The Spanish generic *agua,* "water" was often applied to springs; the Spanish diminutive *chiquita* is derived from *chico,* "little."

AIKEN. AIKEN CREEK (Nye), named for an early settler, empties into the Reese River at a point west of Toiyabe Peak near the Lander County line. **AIKEN CANYON** (Eureka), south of Mineral Hill and east of State Route 20, takes its name from nearby **AIKEN SPRING** (NK 11–11; Dir. 1971).

AIRY (Lander). A peak in the Shoshone Mountains west of Reese River, named for Sir George Biddell Airy (1801–1892), English scientist, by Arnold Hague of the Fortieth Parallel Survey. The name was adopted for **AIRY MESA** in the range and for a station on an old overland mail route (JGS, I, p. 136; VPG; OPN, p. 39). See **MOUNT AIR(E)Y STATION.**

ALABAMA. A mine east of Awakening in the Slumbering Hills in Humboldt County; a mining district, discovered in 1871 about forty miles north of Wells and named by a Mr. Knoll, one of the discoverers, for his native state. Wells post office served the district (GHM, HU 1; EP, p. 7; TF, p. 15).

ALAMEDA CANYON (Churchill). The name, Spanish "poplar (or cottonwood) grove," for a canyon on the east slope of the Stillwater Range, extending to Dixie Valley, about thirty-four miles northeast of Fallon (USGB 5904). See **COTTONWOOD.**

ALAMO (Lincoln). This principal town of Pahranagat Valley was laid out about 1900 by Fred Allen, Mike Botts, Bert Riggs, and Thomas F. Stewart and settled largely by people from Fredonia, Arizona (WA). The locality, which for a time became a mecca for horse thieves and rustlers (Nev. Guide, p. 178), is on U.S. 93 about 110 miles north of Las Vegas. It has a post office, established May 12, 1905 (FTM, p. 1), and a yearly rodeo. Although the name is perhaps commemorative of the famous battle (OPN, p. 42; RC, p. 36), a more plausible conjecture is that the Spanish term *alamo,* "poplar," is descriptive and denotes the presence of the poplar, or cottonwood, tree in the area. The **ALAMO MINE** (Clark), a copper mine high on the west face of Frenchman Mountain, was located by John F. Miller and first named the *Johnny Stump* (WA). A mining district in Churchill County, organized prior to 1866, was named **ALAMO** (SM, 1867, p. 28). The name also denoted a Hereford stock farm south of Reno (Washoe), owned by former governor John Sparks, as well as a mining camp, described April 14, 1906 (*Reno Evening Gazette*), as newly located near Cooney Springs in Storey County (DM). See **SAN JACINTO.** Numerous features of Nevada named *Cottonwood* attest to the preference of the early name-givers for the English word. See **COTTONWOOD.**

ALANS (Churchill). An early way station, south of Carson Lake and east of Fort Churchill on the road to Dayton; named for its owner (HHB, Nev., pp. 261–62; NHS,

1913, p. 178; 1881 Map). The station was served by Dayton post office (TF, p. 15).

ALAZON (Elko). The first station west of Wells on the SP RR. The station is a non-agency with telegraph and marks the east end of the WP RR and SP RR paired track operation to Weso (T75 Map).

ALCATRAZ ISLAND (Esmeralda). Both Alcatraz (Spanish "pelican") Island and Goat Island are in the southern half of the large salt marsh which lies west and north of Silver Peak (Lida Quad.). A new application of the already established names for islands in San Francisco Bay probably was made for honorific purposes by an early settler in the county.

ALDER. Features named for alder shrubs growing in the region include **ALDER CREEK** and **ALDER CREEK RANCH** at the west side of the Pine Forest Mountains and southwest of Denio in Humboldt County (NK 11–7; Dir. 1971). **ALDER,** a mining district of Elko County, also named *Tennessee Gulch,* eight miles north of Gold Creek and northwest of Charleston, takes its name from a Montana district so named. **ALDER MOUNTAIN** is a peak northeast of Horse Heaven Flat (VPG, p. 36; EP, p. 8; OPN, p. 21; GHM, EL 3).

ALDRICH (Pershing). A mining district, better known as *Iron Hat,* on the east slope of the Sonoma Range and twenty miles southwest of Valmy (VPG, p. 152).

ALEXANDER (Elko). A post office south of Tuscarora from May 25, 1895, until July 31, 1901 (FTM, p. 1). The name commemorates C. D. Alexander, an early postmaster (OR, 1899).

ALHAMBRA HILL (White Pine). The peak is at the southeast end of the Diamond Range. It probably takes its name from the famous palace near Granada in Spain made popular by Washington Irving's book *The Alhambra* (OPN, p. 72).

ALICE GENDRON CREEK (Nye). The creek south of Toiyabe Peak in the Toiyabe Range (SG Map 6) was named in honor of a pioneer woman.

ALIDA (Esmeralda). A valley and a spring in the extreme eastern part of the valley, between Mount Magruder and Montezuma, were named during the Wheeler Survey of 1871–72 for Alida, the wife of David Buel of Austin, who was with the surveying group (Wheeler 1871 Map; MM; Wheeler, 1872, p. 47). **ALIDA VALLEY** was the name adopted for a settlement, also known as *Lida Valley* (Census, 1900), and for a mining district thirty miles southwest of Goldfield (HHB, Nev., p. 260). Variant names for the mining district are *Tule Canyon* and *Lida,* the latter having greatest currency (VPG, p. 56). See **LIDA.**

ALKALI. The geographical name has been widely used in western Nevada for various soluble mineral salts found in natural water and arid soils, with the generics *creek, lake, valley,* and especially *flat.* **ALKALI FLAT** designates areas in Churchill, Humboldt, Lyon, Mineral, Nye, Pershing, and Washoe counties, as well as in Elko County, where one flat is east of Franklin Lake and another is southwest of Pilot Peak (Car. Sink 1908; Well. Sheet; Haw., Tono., Wab. Quad.; NK 11–12; NK 11–10). A tendency to vary the specific appears on later maps and in later listings. *Turupah* denotes an alkali flat north of Eightmile Flat and *Bass* one southeast of Carson Lake (Dir. 1971; Car. Lake 1951). The name appears with more than one generic in **ALKALI FLAT RESERVOIR** (Humboldt) and **ALKALI LAKE WILDLIFE MANAGEMENT AREA** (Lyon). **ALKALI VALLEY** (Mineral) extends from a point southwest of Powell Mountain into Mono County, California (USGB 6002). Captain James H. Simpson chose *Alkaline* as the name for a valley on his route in 1859. "Twenty miles from camp [Middle Gate (Churchill)] we attain the summit of the range dividing Dry from a valley I call Alkaline Valley, on account of its whitish alkaline appearance from saline efflorescence" (JHS, p. 84). His map name is **ALKALI VALLEY** (Wheat IV, 137).

ALLEGHENY (Elko). The name derives from the Delaware Indian name for the Allegheny River (HK, p. 39). In Nevada, Allegheny is the designation for a creek in northern Elko County and a peak southeast of Mountain City (Dir. 1971; SG Map 11). **ALLEGHENY MINING DISTRICT,** also called *Ferguson Spring,* is on the west side of the Goshute Range at Don-Don Pass, thirty miles south-southwest of Wendover. The district was named for George Washington Mardis, an early Indian scout and prospector called "Old Allegheny." Mardis was given the nickname because he was fond of talking about the Allegheny Mountains of his native Pennsylvania (VPG, p. 41; OPN, p. 21; EP, p. 8).

ALLISON (Eureka). A creek north of Bald Mountain in the Monitor Range; named for **ALLISON,** an early settlement in the southwestern part of the county, served by Eureka post office (GHM, EU 1; TF, p. 15).

ALLRED (Nye). An early post office, established April 17, 1911, and discontinued October 31, 1912 (FTM, p. 1).

ALPHA. One of the most populous of the sixteen way stations in Eureka County on the E and P RR; named late in 1874 when the railroad reached the site (1881 Map; TF, p. 15). Although the settlement, thirty-five miles northwest of Eureka, once had stores, saloons, and a fair-sized hotel, by 1880 the population had been reduced to fifty people.

At present, practically nothing remains at the site (MA, p. 285; DM; Census, 1880; NM). **ALPHA** post office first existed from 1877 until 1886. It was reestablished in 1919 and remained in operation until 1924 (FTM, p. 1). **ALPHA BUTTE** (Humboldt). A hill, southwest of Winnemucca and just north of the Pershing-Humboldt county line; named for its position in relation to other peaks (OPN, p. 35). **ALPHA** (Storey). A claim staked in 1859 between the Exchequer and the Consolidated Imperial mines on the Comstock Lode. The name origin is unrevealed; however, transient miners who were a part of the California exodus could have applied it to the Comstock mine. Bancroft's map of the Northern Mines of California shows the Alpha existing as early as 1849–50 (HHB, Cal., p. 368). Gudde places the date at 1852 or 1853. "Alpha (Nevada). Two early mining camps on the South Fork of Yuba River were called Hell-Out-for-Noon and Delirium Tremens ('The Knave,' Sept. 15, 1946). In 1852 or 1853, when the country began to become respectable, these names were changed to Alpha and Omega, the first and last letter of the Greek Alphabet" (Gudde, p. 8). The Alpha is carried as a patented claim on the Storey County tax roll (AR, No. 63). **ALPHA** (Pershing). See **ECHO.**

ALPINE. A mining district of Churchill County, also called *Clan Alpine,* organized in 1864 on the eastern slope of the Clan Alpine Range, fourteen miles north of Eastgate. The village of **ALPINE,** seventy-five miles east of Fallon, had a little over one-hundred people in 1899, and a post office of this name served the settlement from August 6, 1894, to November 14, 1914 (VPG, p. 11; NHS, 1913, p. 183; Census, 1900; OR, 1899; FTM, p. 1). Both the village and the mining district were named for the nearby Clan Alpine Range. **ALPINE** (Esmeralda). A mining district (gold) near Lone Mountain, west of Tonopah (VPG, p. 50).

ALUM. Creeks named for the presence of alum in solution in the water are south of Lucky Boy in Mineral County, northeast of Hunter Lake in Washoe County, and southwest of Tule Summit in Esmeralda County (GHM, MI 1; WA 1; ES 2). The last, an intermittent stream flowing from Poison Spring to Cottonwood Creek, furnished a name for **ALUM CREEK,** an early settlement served by Aurora post office (HHB, Nev., p. 260; TF, p. 15; 1881 Map; USGB 6002). **ALUM MINING DISTRICT,** ten miles south of Blair Junction in Esmeralda County, took its name from a nearby alum deposit and mine (VPG, p. 50).

ALUNITE (Clark). A town on U.S. 95, twenty-two miles southeast of Las Vegas and two miles west of Boulder City, named for the **ALUNITE MINING DISTRICT.** The district took its name from the **ALUNITE MINE,** opened in 1908 by Professor Robert T. Hill, a mining geologist, and was descriptively named for the alunite mineralization. Other principal mines of the district, also denoted *Vincent,* were the Quo Vadis, Lucky Dutchman, Bean Pot, and Spearhead (WA; VPG, p. 22; Dir. 1971; OPN, p. 13).

AMADOR (Lander). A former town of the Reese River area, reported in the *Gold Hill News* of December 19, 1863, to have been laid out by Messrs. B. T. Hunt, Bowe, Chase, Matheny, Meek, and Kinsey. The once-thriving mining camp, seven miles north of Austin, was a candidate for the Lander County seat in 1863, with seven-hundred qualified voters among its fifteen-hundred inhabitants. Austin won the decision and Amador was deserted by 1869. A territorial post office established April 6, 1864, continued operations for two years (DM; NM; NHS, Nev., p. 260; 1881 Map; FTM, p. 1). The name has been retained for the mining district, six miles north of Austin on the west slope of the Toiyabe Range. The district is known also by the names *Reese River, Austin,* and *Yankee Blade* (VPG, p. 88). Although the literal meaning of the word is "lover" in Spanish, it is here a surname, if, as is likely, the name was transferred from Amador County, California (created May 11, 1854), and named for Don Pedro Amador or his son José Maria (NS, p. 310; Gudde, p. 9).

AMARGOSA (Nye). Ten miles north of Beatty at Springdale, the **AMARGOSA RIVER** rises from springs and flows southeast to the California line, where it turns northwest and becomes lost in Death Valley. The water of the Amargosa often contains salt, soda, sulfates, and other minerals which give it a nearly red color and make it poisonous to animals. The stream sinks into an underground channel in the desert (OPN, p. 52; NHS, 1922, p. 163; JGS, I, p. 261). In April of 1844, Captain Frémont noted, "It is called by the Spaniards *Amargosa*—the bitter water of the desert" (JCF, Report, p. 264). Letters and journals of the forty-niners show the use of names other than *Amargosa* for this river. In his recollections of his journey from Salt Lake City to Los Angeles in 1849, Leonard Babcock writes of *Alkali Creek;* Thomas Kealy and Joseph P. Hamelin, Jr. refer to the river as *The Bitter Water* and *Bitter Water Creek* (LRH, XV, pp. 67, 92, 106). Henry W. Bigler and Charles C. Rich call it *Saleratus Creek,* as does Addison Pratt, spelling the name Salaratus however. Concurrent usage is shown in a Morman Way-Bill of 1851: "Amagoshe or Saleratus creek; let no animals drink the saleratus water" (LRH, II, pp. 94, 167, 190;

XV, p. 322). The 1855 railroad survey map by Parke shows **AMARGOSA,** while an 1856 map by S. Augustus Mitchell has the variant spelling *Anorgosa* (Wheat IV, 49, 83). The Wheeler Map of 1871 delineates the Amargoza Desert and Mountains and the Swampy Bed of the Amargoza. The **AMARGOSA DESERT,** containing no permanent lakes, no living streams, and almost destitute of vegetation except for grass growing near a few springs, extends from the Funeral Mountains to Bullfrog, Nevada, and is covered with volcanic ashes, scoria, alkali flats, and sand (JGS, I, p. 261). An order issued to establish a post office named *Amagosa* on December 14, 1901, was rescinded in November of 1902. On December 3, 1904, **AMARGOSA** post office was created and remained operative until March 21, 1905. **AMARGOSA STATION** was the name adopted by officials of the defunct LV and T RR in 1906 for a rail point, also called *Johnnie Siding,* which served as a shipping point for the Johnnie district. When the builders reached this site and sank a well, they thought the brackish water encountered had a relation to the bitterish river so named (CHL, p. 185). In March of 1906, H. H. Clark laid out a townsite and named it **AMARGOSA.** Six months later Clark founded Bullfrog, Nevada, nearer the Original Bullfrog Mine, and the entire population of Amargosa moved to the new site in one day's time (FTM, p. 1; WA; DM; Furn. Cr. Quad.).

AMAZON (Elko). A mining district located in 1877, twenty-five miles northwest of Tuscarora (OPN, p. 21). The name ultimately commemorates the Amazon River of South America, said to have been so called because Orellana and early Spanish explorers thought they saw female warriors on its banks.

AMBER (Clark). The name for a siding near Logandale on the Moapa Valley branch of the UP RR (OC, p. 1261; Dir. 1971); formerly a local name for a mountain northeast of Charleston Peak and approximately thirty miles northwest of Las Vegas (WA). Although the circumstances of the naming are unknown, it is likely that an early settler, or a prospector, was so honored. See **ANGELS PEAK.**

AMERICAN (Pershing). The name for a canyon southwest of Gold Mountain and for a mining district, organized prior to 1866 and also called *Spring Valley* and *Fitting,* in the Humboldt Range, fourteen miles by road west of Oreana (VPG, p. 163; SM, 1867, p. 52; Love. Quad.; NK 11–10). **AMERICAN CANYON MINING DISTRICT,** also called *Rochester* (q.v.) is nine miles west of Oreana in the West Humboldt Range (NK 11–10). The discoverers of placer gold in 1871 must have named the canyon before L. F. Dunn

leased claims to Chinese miners, who from 1881 to 1896 are said to have produced an estimated $10,000,000 from gold deposits there. Of the many lodging houses, stores, and a joss temple, only rock ruins remain (NM; VPG, p. 157; M&M, p. 167).

AMERICAN CITY (Storey). The town was laid out on American Flat (q.v.) in January, 1864, by a Gold Hill company with large capital. The Territory of Nevada refused the company's offer of $50,000 for removal of the state capital from Carson City to American City, which flourished during the days of the big bonanzas (NHS, 1913, p. 197; 1922, p. 31). A post office of this name was in operation from March 6, 1866, until February 3, 1868 (FTM, p. 1).

AMERICAN FLAT (Storey). This claim was located as the *American* and was first worked in June, 1859. Later the company joined with the Baltimore Consolidated to sink a shaft near the dividing line of the two claims (Dir., 1865, p. xxxii). **AMERICAN FLAT,** for which the mine was named, is south of Gold Hill. According to Emanuel Penrod, the early partner of Henry Comstock, for whom the great Comstock Lode was named, the flat was mined by Americans in the early days, rather than by Mexicans or Chinese and, therefore, was named *American* Flat (NHS, 1913, p. 201). In support of Penrod's explanation, it may be noted that William Wright gives a similar reason for the naming of the famous Mexican Mine on the Comstock. The mine was operated by Mexican methods (DDQ, p. 43). The American Flat name complex is historically important in Nevada. **AMERICAN FLAT RAVINE** was the name given to a little canyon opening out of American Flat. Hosea and Allan Grosch, two brothers who were among the earliest prospectors in the area, lived in a stone cabin there in 1857. **AMERICAN FLAT WASH** was a stream in the ravine. During the summer of 1858, Henry Comstock prospected there, aided by the Paiute Indians (NHS, 1913, p. 201). See **GRIZZLY HILL.**

AMETHYST PEAK (Nye). "One of the Twin Peaks, in the Hot Creek Range 2 mi. SW of Tybo; named for its cap rock that appears amethyst in color under the sun" (USGB 6903).

AMOS (Humboldt). A mail stop at the junction of State Route 8A with a dirt road. Although Amos was largely settled about 1910, it had a post office by January 30, 1889, which served the area until 1926 (Nev. Guide, p. 214; OPN, p. 35; FTM, p. 1). Thirteen miles from Amos and thirty miles northwest of Winnemucca in the Slumbering Hills is the **AMOS MINING DISTRICT** (VPG, p. 70). This district is generally known as *Awakening.* Folk humor is obviously at play when prospectors in the Slumbering Hills call their strike the Awakening. See **ANDORNO.**

ANAHO ISLAND (Washoe). The largest island (247.73 acres) in Pyramid Lake and at its south end; noted as the world's largest rookery for the white pelican. By Presidential Proclamation of September 13, 1913, **ANAHO ISLAND BIRD REFUGE** was established. By Executive Order No. 2416 of July 25, 1940, the island was made a national wildlife refuge (OPN, p. 66; HPS, 1/24/54). The name is commemorative of Anaho Bay, the chief harbor of Nuku Hiva Island in the Marquesas of the South Pacific. Anaho Island appears on an 1893 map of Glendale, Nevada, and vicinity.

ANCHORITE (Mineral). The official designation for a summit and a group of hills at the western extremity of the Excelsior Mountains in the Toiyabe National Forest (Dir. 1971; Haw. Quad.; NJ 11–4).

ANDERSON. A gypsum deposit west of Overton in Clark County was discovered in **ANDERSON WASH** (which drains north along the east side of Weiser Ridge and joins the Muddy River at the Narrows) by W. C. ("Dad") Anderson. Both **ANDERSON GYP,** the name of the deposit, and Anderson Wash honor the discoverer. **ANDERSON RIDGE** (Clark) denotes a ridge lying south of Gold Butte (WA). Other features in Nevada bearing this surname include a canal in Eureka County; canyons in Lincoln and Humboldt counties; a creek and a spring in Elko County. **ANDERSON** (Elko) denoted a post office near Tuscarora in operation from April, 1900, until September, 1905 (FTM, p. 1). **ANDERSON ACRES** (Washoe) is the name for an unincorporated town on U.S. 395, about nine miles north of Reno, between Black Springs and the state line (Dir. 1971).

ANDERSONS (Washoe). A large ranch and station along an old stage line was owned by William Anderson and situated three miles south of Reno near Moana Springs. After being purchased by John Sparks, former governor of Nevada, the site became known as the Sparks Ranch (MA, p. 565; SPD, p. 1029; HHB, Nev., p. 256). **ANDERSONS** was also the name of a station on the V and T RR between Huffakers and Reno.

ANDESITE RIDGE (Nye). A ridge seven miles northeast of Moores Station; "named for the andesite lava found on the western part of the ridge" (USGB 6903).

ANDORNO (Humboldt). A name of undetermined origin for a stream heading in the Humboldt National Forest on the western slope of the Santa Rosa Range and flowing to a reservoir just south of **ANDORNO RANCH,** about thirty-five miles north of Winnemucca (USGB 6102). An old stage stop so denoted was called also *Awakening Peak* and *Paradise Valley.* Variant spellings are *Andornia* and *Andorinia* (USGB 6102; SG Map 12).

ANGEL. In Elko County, a trout-filled snow lake in the East Humboldt Range, twelve miles south of Wells; named for Warren M. Angel who had a ranch below in Clover Valley in the 1870s (JM; EP, p. 8; NK 11–9). **ANGEL ISLAND** (Esmeralda). An isolated hill in Clayton Valley, about three miles east of the hills named Alcatraz Island and Goat Island and eighteen miles west-northwest of Goldfield. The name *Angel Island* continues the analogy to the islands of San Francisco Bay. The three Esmerala County hills, or islands, are along the playa of Clayton Valley (DL 60). See **ALCATRAZ ISLAND. ANGEL(S) PEAK** (Clark), northeast of Charleston Peak in the Spring Mountains, perhaps was known in the early days as *Amber Mountain* (WA; Dir. 1971).

ANNA. This feminine given name designates a mountain in Nye County, about fifteen miles south of Fairview Peak (USGB 5904; OPN, p. 52), with a variant *Annie* (1881 Map; GHM, NY 2); and in combined form **ANNAVILLE,** an early post office in Elko County, in operation from October 10, 1872, until October 21, 1874 (FTM, p. 1). The diminutive suffix appears in **ANNIE CREEK,** a tributary of the Bruneau River, southwest of Charleston in northern Elko County (SG Map 11); "named for Annie Bieroth who lived in the area" (EP, p. 10).

ANTELOPE. The prevalence of the pronghorn antelope in the early days of discovery and settlement in Nevada is evidenced by the widespread use of the name with the generics: *butte, canyon, creek, meadow, mountain, peak, range, spring, valley,* and *wash.* The name was also adopted for settlements, mines, and mining districts. **ANTELOPE SPRING** (Pershing). These springs were discovered and presumably named by the Applegate party in 1846 as they were laying out the Southern Oregon Road (Applegate Trail). It was a noted stopping place for emigrants on the Applegate Trail to southern Oregon and the Lassen Cutoff to California. **ANTELOPE VALLEY,** extending from Douglas County, Nevada, into Mono County, California, provided a campsite for the Bidwell-Bartleson party in 1841 and possibly for Joseph Walker in 1833 (VPG). "It was named from a large herd of antelope, perhaps thirty to fifty, which roamed through the valley in the early days" (NHS, 1913, p. 190). **ANTELOPE CREEK** denotes streams in Elko, Humboldt, Lander, and Nye counties. According to J. H. Simpson in the report of his explorations in 1859, the creek in Nye County was called *wonst-in-dam-me* by Digger Indians (JHS, p. 74). **ANTELOPE**

VALLEY (White Pine), between the ANTE-
LOPE RANGE and the Goshute Mountains,
appears on the Simpson map of 1859. The
valley was part of the homeland of the
Gosiute who held antelope drives there.

ANTELOPE SPRINGS, said to have been
named *Kwadumba,* "antelope water" by the
Shoshone (M&M, p. 204), in the southwestern
part of the valley, was the site of an Overland
Stage station on the old route between Ham-
ilton and Elko and a "pony" stop twenty-five
miles southeast of Schell Creek Station (Nev.
Guide, p. 254; Nevada I, 1961, pp. 8–9; DM;
1867 Map). Other springs so named are in
Elko, Eureka, Lander, Nye, and Pershing
counties. A new mining camp in February, 1912, was named for the ANTELOPE
SPRINGS MINING DISTRICT of Nye
County, at the south end of the Cactus
Range, thirty miles east-southeast of Goldfield. Another district so denoted, also called
Relief, lies between Antelope Springs and
Buffalo Peak in the West Humboldt Range,
twenty-two miles by road east of Lovelock,
in Pershing County (VPG, pp. 121, 157).

ANTELOPE BUTTE denotes mountain peaks
in west-central Lander County and south of
Snow Water Lake in Elko County. The name
appears on Beckwith's 1855 map (Dir. 1971;
1881 Map; Wheat IV, 74). An old road ran
westward from Caliente (Lincoln) through
ANTELOPE CANYON to Hiko, Alamo,
Delamar, and other early camps. *Dead Man's*
is said to have been an earlier, local name
for this canyon which is now the site of a
railroad quarry for track ballast (Dir. 1971;
WA). ANTELOPE STATION (Humboldt)
is on the WP RR main line, forty-four miles
southwest of Winnemucca (T154). ANTE-
LOPE RUN, a settlement of old Roop
County, was ten miles northwest of Poeville
(TF, p. 15; 1881 Map). The frequency of
the name in certain areas would indicate a
shift from one generic to another. In southwestern Eureka County, at the northern end
of the Monitor Range in the Toiyabe National Forest, ANTELOPE PEAK rises to
a height of 10,220 feet. The ANTELOPE
RANGE lies west of ANTELOPE VALLEY.
Features in the valley so named are ANTE-
LOPE WASH, ANTELOPE MEADOW, and
ANTELOPE SPRING. A mining district in
the southwestern corner of Eureka County
also bears the name, as did ANTELOPE, a
Eureka County post office established on
February 8, 1904, to serve the district, transferred into Nye County in April of 1905,
and discontinued July 31, 1908 (NJ 11–2;
VPG, p. 63; FTM, p. 1). The name complex
probably stems from the imposing landmark,
Antelope Peak, in Eureka County.

ANTHONY (Elko). The name denotes a non-
agency siding on the Salt Lake Division of

the SP RR main line between Holborn and
Moor (T75).

ANTIMONY (Humboldt). A mining district
so named was organized in the southern
portion of Humboldt County. William Clark,
J. W. Graves, and others discovered thirteen
distinct antimony-bearing veins in the district
in 1875. In order to transport the ores from
the mines, a wagon road was constructed in
the summer of 1875 to intersect the Winnemucca and Austin road at a point ten miles
from Shoshone Springs (SM, 1875, pp.
59–61).

ANTLER PEAK (Lander). A peak in the
Battle Mountain Range, northwest of Telluride (Son. R. Quad.); the circumstances of
the naming are unknown.

ANTONIO WELLS (Mineral). A Nevada
landmark and the site of the former AN-
TONIO STATION, in the eastern part of the
county and southwest of Goldyke. *Antones
Well* is a variant (SG Map 5; Tono. Quad.;
Dir. 1971).

APACHE (Lyon). The name, honorific of a
tribe of nomadic Athapascan Indians of
northern Mexico and the southwestern United
States, was applied to a town below Ramsey
Station on the former C and C RR, according to the *Lyon County Times* of August 4,
1906 (DM).

APEX. One of the original stations on the
SPLA and SL RR in Clark County near
APEX SUMMIT, eighteen miles north of
Las Vegas (WA). The station name was
retained by the UP RR which purchased the
line. A mining district of this name is twenty
miles northeast of Las Vegas on U.S. 91 in
Clark County (VPG, p. 22). APEX URA-
NIUM (Lander). This company has thirty-
nine claims six miles south of Austin, in the
Toiyabe Range, east of Reese River Valley.
The company took over the property under
agreement with Joe Rundberg, who with his
son, found the first uranium ore in this district in 1953 (FG, Uran.).

APRIL FOOL (Lincoln). The calendar name
was chosen by Frank Wilson and D. A.
Reeves for a mine they located in the
Ferguson district on April 1. The April
Fool was the largest producer in the camp
between 1892 and 1902 (JWH; WA). See
DELAMAR.

AQUEDUCT (Nye). AQUEDUCT MESA, on
the northeastern side of Ranier Mesa, sixty-
eight miles southeast of Goldfield (USGB
6801), takes its name from THE AQUE-
DUCT, a canyon extending from the mesa
to Yucca Flat (USGB 6002).

ARABIA (Pershing). The mines of the ARA-
BIA DISTRICT were discovered by George
Lovelock in 1868, according to the February
1, 1907, issue of the *Lovelock Tribune* (DM).
Attracted by the rich ore of the Montezuma
mine, early settlers created a small mining

camp seven miles north of Oreana. Extensive mine workings and some rock ruins remain (NM). All of the eleven original mines of the Arabia Mining District, except two, were owned by one company. Now better known as *Trinity*, the district is five miles west of Oreana on the east flank of the Trinity Range (SM, 1875, p. 67; VPG, p. 165).

ARC DOME (Nye). By decision of the United States Board on Geographic Names, the mountain, altitude 11,775 feet, was named *Arc Dome*, "not Bald" (USGB–2, p. 27). The name is descriptive of its shape. Variant names for this mountain in the Toiyabe Range are *Toiyabe Dome* and *Toyabe Dome* (Tono. Quad.; NJ 11–5; USGB 7002). See **TOIYABE.**

ARDEN (Clark). A station on the UP RR, as it had been on the earlier SPLA and SL RR, ten miles southwest of Las Vegas; formerly the site of the Arden Plaster Company mill, which was in operation from 1909 until 1919. The station served the **ARDEN MINING DISTRICT,** five miles west of it in the Spring Mountains. **ARDEN** post office, established July 24, 1907, in Lincoln County, was within the boundaries of Clark when that county was created on March 5, 1909 (VPG, p. 22; OPN, p. 13; WA; FTM, p. 1). Since both the station name and the post office name antedate the discovery of the gypsum and silica sand deposits of the Arden district in 1909, apparently milling and mining officials adopted the station name.

ARDIVEY, MOUNT (Nye). A name of undetermined origin for the principal peak in the southern portion of the Shoshone Mountains between Grantsville and the Cloverdale Ranch (NJ 11–5).

ARGENTA (Lander). A non-agency siding on the SP RR between Mosel and Rosny. Although Argenta had the distinction of being the first CP RR station in Lander County, it had the misfortune of being located too far from the natural roadway to Austin and to the ores of the Battle Mountain Range for convenience and profit. In 1870, the citizens migrated en masse, moving business establishments, merchandise, and dwellings to Battle Mountain Station, a point of departure for Austin (BLK, pp. 42, 88–89). A guide book of 1873 contains the following description: "This was formerly a regular eating station and the distributing point for Austin and the Reese River country, now only a signal station, with few buildings" (GAC, p. 144). **ARGENTA** post office, established on December 4, 1868, was removed to Battle Mountain on February 24, 1874 (FTM, p. 1). Argenta siding is now a rail point for barium from the Shoshone Mountains and for hay from the Humboldt River ranches (Nev. Guide, p. 127). The traditional name for the native ore is said to have been

applied to the siding by Judge E. B. Crocker, brother of Charles Crocker, who was in charge of the construction of the CP RR (DM). Judge Crocker might have been the one who suggested the descriptive name for the present site of Reno; the *Eastern Slope* of April 11, 1868, published at Washoe City, reported that Argenta was the new name for Lakes Crossing. See **RENO. ARGENTA MINING DISTRICT,** presumably named for the settlement, is twelve miles east of Battle Mountain and four miles southeast of the siding (VPG, p. 81). Other shift names nearby are **ARGENTA BUTTE** and **ARGENTA RIM** denoting a peak and a mountain in the northern extremity of the Shoshone Range (Dir. 1971; NK 11–11).

ARGENTINE. Two early mining districts were named for the silver ore. The Carson City district was located in 1859 in the mountains east of Washoe Valley, west of Virginia City, and just north of Eagle Valley. A second district was located in Washoe County (SM, 1867, pp. 18, 21–25; NHS, 1913, p. 187).

ARGENTITE (Esmeralda). A mining district discovered in 1920, twenty-four miles west of Silver Peak; named for native silver sulfide (OPN, p. 30; VPG, p. 50). **ARGENTITE CANYON** in the Silver Peak Range is named for the mining district (Dir. 1971).

ARGO (Lyon). The first non-agency siding west of Darwin on the main line of the SP RR; perhaps named for Argo in Cook County, Illinois, or in Scott County, Iowa, but stemming from Greek legend, the ship on which Jason sailed to find the Golden Fleece (T75).

ARIZONA. The name for a peak between Pioche and Mendha, north of Highland Peak in the Highland Range, in Lincoln County (GHM, LN 1), and for a famous mine in the Echo district of the West Range in old Humboldt (presently Pershing) County (SM, 1866, pp. 49–50). **ARIZONA MINE** (Elko) is southeast of Granite Peak in the Granite Range (GHM, EL 4). Honorific of the State of Arizona, the name "is derived from Papago Indian words, *ali* ('small') and *shonak* ('place of the spring'), or 'place of the small spring'" (Barnes, p. xv).

ARLEMONT (Esmeralda). A town thirty miles west of Silver Peak and ten miles north of Dyer (OPN, p. 30), served by a post office from July 13, 1916, until September 30, 1932 (FTM, p. 1). *Arles,* often construed as singular, came into Middle English via Old French, deriving from Latin *arrhula,* "earnest money." Joined with French *mont,* "hill," the composite results in an auspicious place name, popular in mining country.

ARNOLD. A settlement northeast of Shafter in Elko County (SG Map 2). **ARNOLD BOTTOM** (Clark). A part of the east side of the Virgin River Valley, immediately below Riverside; named for Richard Arnold, who owned a farm there (WA).

ARROW CANYON (Clark). A canyon about nine miles northwest of Moapa in the ARROW CANYON RANGE. The mountain range trends generally north-south; its south end is approximately twenty-three miles northeast of Las Vegas (USGB 6001; 6002). Henry W. Bigler described the canyon November 17, 1849. "The Bed of the River [Pahranagat Wash] past through a mountain for about 3 miles, a solled mass of Rocks perpendicular to the highth of from 500 to 1000 feet high on either side of the Creek, the passage is about 10 yards wide, the bed of the creek was dry, thare was several holes of water found standing. about half way through we found whare the indians had shot over head about 80 feet into a crivis as if they wished to pry off a large shelv in Rock. probable thare was more than 200 arrows sticking thare" (LRH, II, p. 162). According to a local legend, at one time when the Moapa Valley Paiutes and the Pahranagat Valley Paiutes were at war, two of their war parties met suddenly in the canyon. Rather than engage in what would surely prove to be a mutually disastrous combat within the narrow rock confines, the two parties called a truce and fired all their arrows high into the canyon walls. Their ceremony of the arrows is said to have become a yearly event (WA).

ARROWHEAD. Two early settlements of this name were in Lyon County, four miles southwest of Rockland, and in Nye County, twelve miles southeast of Warm Springs on U.S. 6. The latter, a small camp consisting of a post office (in operation from 1919 to 1924), a boarding house, a store, and a blacksmith shop, was abandoned in the 1930s. Only cement foundations and rubble have survived (FTM, p. 1; NM). The Nye County camp took its name from the ARROWHEAD MINING DISTRICT which is sixty-five miles east of Tonopah, in the north end of the Reveille Range (VPG, p. 121). ARROWHEAD (Clark) denotes a siding at the Glendale bulk oil plant, on the UP RR branch line from Moapa to Overton, about forty-five miles north of Las Vegas (WA). ARROWHEAD TRAIL, presently U.S. 91, is in the southern tip of the state. In Nevada, the old trail ran from Overton through the Valley of Fire, following east of the Dry Lake Range to Las Vegas, then southerly to Eldorado Pass, Searchlight, and on into California (WA). These features were either named for a configuration or for the finding of arrowheads in the region.

ARROWLIME (Clark). A UP RR siding, twenty-two miles north of Las Vegas, near the quarry and plant of the U.S. Lime Products Company at the southern extremity of the Arrow Canyon Range. The toponymic compound derives from the names of the range and the company. A variant map spelling is Arrolime (WA; NJ 11–12).

ARTESIA (Lyon). A settlement, lake, and post office (1914–1926) of northern Smith Valley; named for artesian wells in the surrounding area (FTM, p. 1; VPG).

ARTESIAN WELL (Lander). A station on the NC RR, fifteen miles from Battle Mountain and between Galena and Mound Springs; named for a well in the vicinity. On February 6, 1889, an act was passed relative to "encouraging the sinking of artesian wells and the assistance of other means of irrigation for the arid lands situated within the state of Nevada" (JGS, I, p. 369). Under this act a number of artesian wells were sunk in different parts of the state.

ARTHUR (Elko). The town, settled in 1874, is twenty-three miles southeast of Halleck in Ruby Valley between the East Humboldt and the Ruby ranges. Except for about a two-year interval, ARTHUR was a post office from April of 1881 until June of 1951, and served ranchers in the north end of Ruby Valley. The name commemorates Chester A. Arthur, who became the twenty-first president of the United States in 1881 (Nev. Guide, pp. 120, 165; 1881 Map; OPN, p. 21; FTM, p. 1; ECN Map).

ASH (Carson City). A canyon west of Carson City, the site of the ASH SAWMILL on Mill Creek, near Gregorys Mill in 1859 (NHS, 1926, p. 390; Bancroft Map; DM); named for Alexander Ash(e), builder and owner of the mill (also called Ashes Mill), who moved to Chico, California, in 1890 (Reno Evening Gazette).

ASHBY (Mineral). A mining district in the early days, twenty miles northwest of Mina; named for George A. Ashby, one of the owners (OPN, p. 48).

ASH CREEK. A creek and a flat in Lincoln County, east of Elgin, and a spring in the Red Rock area of Clark County, were so named for the desert ash which grows in profusion in some areas of southern Nevada (VPG; WA).

ASHDOWN (Humboldt). A mining district located in 1863 in northwestern Humboldt County at the Oregon line and named for the chief mine in the district (OPN, p. 35). A post office named for the district was in operation from 1904 until 1909, reestablished in 1920, but removed to Denio on December 31, 1921 (FTM, p. 1).

ASH MEADOWS (Nye). Meadows and springs on the southeast edge of the Amargosa Desert, in southern Nye County along the California state line, were so named for the leather-leaved ash trees which grow in abundance there. Variant names are Ash

Meadow Valley and *Meadow Valley* (1881 Map; WA; VPG; Furn. Cr. Quad.). Devils Hole in Ash Meadows is probably one of the springs visited by William L. Manly in 1849 when he conducted his party through that section of Nevada. Later a tent station, with sleeping tents and a saloon, was established by Dad Fairbanks (a freighter between Las Vegas and Beatty) at springs which eventually became a source of water for Greenwater, California (DM). See **DEVILS HOLE.** A spring near Devils Hole is named **ASH TREE SPRING** (VPG).

ASH SPRINGS (Lincoln). A community on U.S. 93, north of Alamo, named for a group of large springs nearby; and springs about five miles south of Bunker Peak, in the Clover Mountains southeast of Caliente; named for the desert ash trees growing there (Dir. 1971; NJ 11–9; WA).

ASHTON (Nye). Formerly a station in the Amargosa Desert, northwest of Leeland on the T and T RR; probably named by railroad builders for nearby small ash trees which differ markedly from associated desert vegetation (VPG; Furn. Cr. Quad.).

ASPEN (Churchill). A mining district in the extreme southeast portion of Churchill County, eight miles east of Broken Hills, discovered in March, 1909 (VPG; DM); named for the white-limbed quaking aspen *(Populus tremuloides)* in the region.

ASTOR (Washoe). A settlement and a mountain pass northwest of Zenobia, near Pyramid Lake (Gen. Land Off. Map). The name, if applied by early trappers, may commemorate the fur merchant, John Jacob Astor.

ATCHISON (Storey). One of the early claims on the Comstock Lode. In October, 1886, Emanuel Penrod wrote: "Threats were made to cut down claims to two hundred feet, so we each six of our company selected his man, and deeded off fifty feet each, making 300 feet in all. This 300 feet came off the north end of the Ophir. This was afterwards called the Atchison" (MA, p. 56). The claim was named for T. J. Atchison who recorded it on September 1, 1859 (GH–A). **ATCHISON QUARTZ MILL** was built in 1863 at Washoe City and was second in size only to the Ophir Mill.

ATHENS (Nye). A mining district thirty miles northeast of Mina in the northeastern portion of the Cedar Mountains (VPG, p. 121); ultimately commemorative of the Greek city.

ATLANTA (Lincoln). A mining district discovered in October, 1907, by Mrs. Belle Fisher (a camp cook for assessors in an area at the north end of the Wilson Creek Range) about forty miles northeast of Pioche. After finding free gold, Mrs. Fisher staked four claims and started the Atlanta boom. Principal producers in the district were the Atlanta, Bradshaw, Silver Park, and Solo

Joker (WA; VPG, p. 92). A post office, named for the district, served the small camp from September 4, 1909 until May 31, 1920 (FTM, p. 2). Alternate names for the mining district are *Silver Peak* and *Silver Springs.*

ATLATL ROCK (Clark). A sandstone feature with numerous petroglyphs in the Valley of Fire State Park; named for a primitive throwing stick used by Indians for hurling spears and darts or javelins (WA; JGS, I, p. 2).

ATWOOD (Nye). A town that grew up as a result of rich ore discoveries in 1901 in the Paradise Range, thirty-two miles northeast of Luning. **ATWOOD** post office dated from February, 1906, to January, 1908. The settlement, of which little remains, was named for **ATWOOD MINING DISTRICT** whose most widely accepted designation is *Fairplay* (NM; VPG, p. 127; FTM, p. 2). The district was named for its discoverer.

AUBURN (Washoe). A post office and village, laid out in 1865 and subsequently absorbed by Reno. The settlement grew up because of the presence of the Old English Mill which had been built by Horace Countryman and his brother (NHS, 1924, p. 96, n. 1). For reasons unknown, Colonel O'Connor, who was associated with the mill, changed its name to Auburn. The mill, situated two miles northwest of Sparks, operated perhaps as late as the early 1890s. After absorption of the village by Reno, the name *Auburn* was lost. All that remains of the mill is the five-mile "English Mill Ditch" (JGS, I, p. 254; NHS, 1911, p. 92; 1926, pp. 336, 343; HPS, 1/29/56).

AUGUSTA MOUNTAINS (Lander, Pershing, Churchill). The north-south trending mountain range, named by Arnold Hague, one of the surveyors of the Fortieth Parallel, lies between the Fish Creek Mountains and the Clan Alpine Mountains (USGB 5904; Gen. Land Off. Map). **AUGUSTA** was also the name of an early mining district in Churchill County (SM, 1867, pp 28–29).

AULD LANG SYNE (Pershing). This peak, in the northern part of the East Range northeast of Mill City, was prominent as a producer of gold and silver (Gen. Land Off. Map; OPN, p. 60). The place name ultimately commemorates *Auld Lang Syne* (c. 1789), written by the Scottish poet, Robert Burns.

AURA (Elko). The mining district was discovered by Jesse Cope and party in 1869 on the eastern slope of the Bull Run, or Centennial, Range, ninety-five miles north-northwest of Elko (VPG, p. 36; OPN, p. 21). Renewed activity in the district resulted in the settlement of **AURA,** a new town thirty miles northeast of Tuscarora, according to a report in the *Nevada State Journal* of May 24, 1907 (DM). A post office so named was established July 5, 1906, and remained in operation until September 30, 1921, when it was moved to Mountain City (FTM, p. 2). The name derives from *aurum*, being descriptive of gold deposits there. Alternate names for the mining district are *Bull Run* and *Columbia*.

AURORA. A boom camp which mushroomed in the early 1860s as a result of the discovery of a rich quartz vein on the steep slope of Mount Corey by E. R. Hicks, in company with J. M. Corey and James M. Braley. Only four miles from the California line, for a time Aurora was the county seat of both Mono County, California, and Esmeralda County, Nevada Territory. The Ives and Kidder survey placed Aurora in Nevada Territory. The first rush was made up of men from Monoville, California, where the assay had been made in August of 1860. Esmeralda Mining District was formed and named for the region which was then known as Esmeralda. J. M. Corey, for whom Mount Corey is named, is credited with having named the region *Esmeralda* but, in the late 1860s, he is reported to have changed the name of the new settlement to Aurora for the goddess of dawn of classical mythology. Among the five-thousand settlers in Aurora, Mark Twain dwelt and prospected for a time. Seventeen stamping mills were required to handle the ore output (M&S, pp. 139–40; RC, pp. 37–38; OPN, p. 48; HHB, Nev., pp. 259–60). The mining district suffered a general collapse in 1864; however, there was renewed activity from 1884 to 1886 and again from 1906 to 1918. Except for a period from May, 1897, until January, 1906, **AURORA** post office operated from 1866 until 1919 (DM; FTM, p. 2). Variant names for the district are *Esmeralda* and *Cambridge* (SM, 1867, pp. 30–37; VPG, p. 109). The name of the arc-shaped valley, about three miles southwest of Powell Mountain, has been changed officially from *Aurora* to *Alkali* (USGB 6002). **AURORA MINING DISTRICT** (Elko) was discovered in December, 1875, and named for the earlier camp in the Esmeralda region (HHB, Nev., p. 277; SM, 1875, p. 26). See **ESMERALDA**.

AURUM (White Pine). A silver mining camp and stop on a stage mail route, northwest of Ruby Hill near Birch Creek and thirty miles northeast of Ely. The settlement reached its height in 1872, at which time the **AURUM MILL,** situated near the mouth of Silver Canyon on the east slope of the Schell Creek Range, milled the ores from Ruby Hill (ECN Map). Dr. Brooks, for many years the only physician in the district, built the stamp mill with the aid of Boston capital (NHS, 1924, p. 295). **AURUM** post office was active from April 4, 1881, until May 31, 1938. The name (Latin "gold") was also spelled Auram (OR, 1883; FTM, p. 2). **AURUM MINING DISTRICT,** which saw a flurry of activity again in 1905 and 1906 (DM), is in the northern part of the Schell Creek Range, eighteen miles southeast of Cherry Creek. The district is designated variously as *Muncy Creek, Queen Springs, Ruby Hill, Schellbourne, Schell Creek, Siegal, Silver Canyon,* and *Silver Mountain* (VPG, p. 176; NHS, 1924, pp. 304, 323, 432).

AUSTIN (Lander). Austin, a famous silver camp of 1862, is on U.S. 50, almost in the middle of the state. The *Mining and Scientific Press* of March 24, 1883, states that David Buel laid out the townsite and "named it for his partner, Alvah C. Austin"; whereas the *De Lamar Lode* of April 30, 1903, reports that John Austin is the pioneer so honored (MM; DM). The name is said also to commemorate Leander Kelse Austin, an uncle of George Austin, the developer of the Jumbo Mine in Humboldt County (OPN, p. 36). Another version of the name story relates that the town was named by David Buel, for his native city, Austin, Texas (MM; Nev., I, 1963, p. 25). The site originally had been named *Pony,* since it was in a steep Toiyabe canyon so denoted. Riders of the Pony Express had designated the canyon thus, because they often shortened their route by taking it instead of the usual pass (HHB, Nev., p. 264). In May, 1862, William M. Talcott, a station agent for the Overland Stage in Jacobsville (eight miles southwest of what was to become Austin), stumbled over some rich silver float in Pony Canyon, and named the discovery the *Pony Ledge* (MA, p. 461; Nev. Guide, p. 258). The resulting Reese River excitement brought an estimated 10,000 people to the area in 1863, and Austin was created, with city lots selling for about $8,000 in gold. In March, 1863, John Frost built the first dwelling in Austin, a cabin of logs. He and his partners were instrumental in forming the Manhattan Company, named by New York capitalists who bought it (MM). A territorial post office was established on November 20, 1863 (FTM, p. 2). The first settlement was around the camp and mine of two men named Marshall and Cole and was called *Clifton*. Later a site farther up the canyon was selected, and on February 17, 1864, Clifton, Austin, and Upper Austin were incorporated as the City of Austin (MA, p. 467). Austin was made the seat of Lander County (created December 19, 1862) comprising what are now Lander, Eureka, White Pine, and Elko counties, or roughly one-third of the state. The decline of Austin had begun by the time of the completion in 1880 of the NC RR, of which it was the southern terminus. **AUSTIN JUNCTION** designated the point of connection of the NC RR and the AC RR, which for a short time was operated by mule-power (MA, p. 284; Nev. Guide, p. 260; GHK, Bonanza, p. 126).

In addition to having been the center of one of the greatest mining areas in the state, an agency for Wells Fargo, a relay point on the transcontinental telegraph, and the home of Emma Nevada, internationally known opera star of the nineteenth century, Austin also has the distinction of being the home of the only newspaper in Nevada published con-tinuously since May 16, 1863. The *Reese River Reveille* bids fair claim to equal the fame of the *Territorial Enterprise* of Virginia City and probably has been as often quoted. The Lander County seat serves as a point of distribution and an educational center for isolated ranching and mining communities. Uranium ore was discovered in the Reese River Mining District in 1953. See **APEX.**

AVALON (Mineral). An early town laid out on the west side of Walker Lake directly opposite Gillis, in December, 1906, was about twelve miles south of Schurz by a fair wagon road. The old Penrod Mine is at the site (DM).

AVENEL (Elko). A non-agency siding on the SP RR main line just west of Elko. The name may be a transfer from Avenel, New Jersey (OG, pp. 312, 1267), or a corruption of Avenal, California, from the Spanish word for "oat field" (PTH, p. 18).

AVERETT SPRING (Lincoln). The spring, about twelve miles northwest of Carp, was named for C. L. Averett who developed and patented it for stock-watering purposes (WA).

AWAKENING. See **AMOS.**

AXHANDLE SPRINGS (White Pine). The springs were at the southeast corner of a farm owned by William McGill, present site of the town of McGill. The name derives from an incident which occurred there. J. R. Withington and John Cowger had a fight over water rights, during which Mr. Cow-ger effectively wielded an axhandle (NHS, 1924, pp. 394–95).

AZTEC (Clark). This name for a wash drain-ing east from Knob Hill, south of Eldorado Canyon, and for a tank near the Contact Mine on the eastern slope of Potosi Moun-tain in the Spring Mountains, is commemora-tive of a Nahuatl people that founded the Mexican empire conquered by Cortez in 1519 (WA; Dir. 1971).

AZURE RIDGE (Clark). A ridge about six miles east of Gold Butte and a mine of the Gold Butte district named for the ridge. **AZURE RIDGE DRAW** is a wash which runs east from Azure Ridge to Grand Wash Bay (WA; Dir. 1971).

AZURITE (Churchill). A post office in north-central Churchill County from April 9, 1901, until December 14, 1901 (FTM, p. 2).

B

BABBITT (Mineral). This settlement, essentially one community with Hawthorne, is operated by the Navy (DRL, p. 14). Cap-tain H. S. Babbitt, in 1935, was Inspector of Ordnance in Charge of the Naval Ammuni-tion Depot at Hawthorne (JGS, II, p. 445).

BACON. The **BACON CLAIM** on the Com-stock Lode (Storey) was named for Hiram Bacon, the original locator, in 1859 (HHB, Nev., p. 106). Bacon owned other valuable ground in the area and became wealthy through the sale of these properties. Accord-ing to report, he was unfortunate in marry-ing a woman who systematically plundered him. A few years later he died in an alms-house at Placerville (HDG, CP, 10/14/76). Although the Bacon Claim was taken up by the Consolidated Imperial, the name has been retained (AR, No. 58). The surname occurs in **BACON CANYON** (Pershing) and **BACON SPRINGS** (Nye). **BACON RIND** is the name for a flat north of Sparks in Washoe County (Dir. 1971).

BADE (Lander). A creek southeast of Aus-tin; **BADE FLAT,** a state recreational ground and game refuge, also southeast of Austin (Dir. 1971; Park Map).

BADGER. Several features of Nevada have been named for the western badger, or its burrows, found in all heavy sage-covered areas of the state. **BADGER FLAT** (Church-ill) denotes a valley between the Clan Alpine and Louderback mountains about thirty-eight miles east of Fallon (USGB 5904). **BADGER GULCH** is a canyon in Nye County, and **BADGER** (Carson City) and **BADGER HOLE** (White Pine) are designations for springs (Dir. 1971). A mining district dis-covered ten miles northeast of Virginia City, by report of the *Reno Evening Gazette* on June 2, 1906, was named **BADGER** (DM). East of Tennessee Mountain in northern Elko County, **BADGER CREEK** empties into the Bruneau River. **BADGER** (Hum-boldt, Washoe) denotes a creek flowing through **BADGER MEADOWS** in north-west Humboldt County and northeast Washoe County and a mountain which trends north-west-southeast across the county line (NK 11–7; SG Map 11; JML, p. 14). A sand flat of Clark County, east of Overton in the Virgin River Valley and at the foot of Hunts-man Hill, was named **BADGER BENCH** for the numerous badgers to be found in the area (WA).

BAILEY (Lander). Formerly a station, nine-teen miles from Battle Mountain, on the now defunct NC RR, and a post office, established

January 5, 1880, and discontinued by order of November 12, 1887. Both names commemorate E. L. Bailey, who was postmaster from 1880 to 1885 (FTM, p. 2; 1881 Map; OR).

BAKER (White Pine). The post office, near the ranch of George W. Baker, one of the earliest settlers in Snake Valley, was established on February 18, 1895, discontinued on September 14, 1901, but reestablished November 1, 1909 (NHS, 1924, p. 363; FTM, p. 2). The town, BAKER LAKE, and BAKER CREEK, on the eastern slope of Mount Wheeler in the Snake Range, were named for the early rancher. The BAKER CREEK CAVES have walls with pictographs and may contain cultural deposits of historical value (JML, p. 14; M&M, p. 205; NJ 11–6; Garr. Quad.).

BAKER, FORT (Clark). The name was applied by Colonel James H. Carleton in orders issued by him on December 19, 1861, to the effect that the old fort, built by Mormon settlers in 1855, would be garrisoned by California Volunteers for the purpose of guarding the road from Salt Lake City to San Bernardino. Colonel Edward Dickinson Baker (1811–1861) is commemorated. The location of the original fort at Las Vegas is marked by a monument and tablet, a restored building which serves as a museum, and fig trees planted by the original Mormon settlers before their recall to Salt Lake City in 1857 and 1858 (Ruhlen).

BAKING POWDER FLAT (White Pine). A flat at the north end of Spring Valley, in an area of low sand dunes and dry lakes; named for the quartz and feldspar of the sand and for alkali efflorescences, which combine to give the flat a white, finely powdered appearance (NJ 11–6).

BALD MOUNTAIN. The name, descriptive of mountains which appear to be relatively devoid of vegetation at their higher elevations, designates a peak in Nye County, in the Toquima Range and north of Manhattan; a mountain in Mineral County, west of Walker Lake, in the Wassuk Range near the Lyon County line; a peak in the Timpahute Range and south of the Tempiute Mine, in Lincoln County; a peak in White Pine County, at the south end of the Ruby Range, for which a mining district, located south of the peak, was named (OPN, pp. 48, 52, 72; WA); and a mountain in northern Washoe County, with BALD MOUNTAIN CANYON heading at its south end, northeast of Long Valley, and BALD MOUNTAIN LAKE, north of the mountain in the Sheldon National Antelope Refuge (NK 11–7). BALD MOUNTAIN (Washoe) was the name selected for a post office, established by an order of June 8, 1908, but rescinded before operations commenced (FTM, p. 2).

BALTIC SWITCH. See SCALES.

BAMBERGER ROAD (Lincoln). The main road between the Meadow Valley Wash and the bonanza gold camp, Delamar, in the early twentieth century was named for Simon Bamberger. In 1902, Bamberger formed the Bamberger-Delamar syndicate which purchased most of the producing properties of the Delamar Mining District (WA).

BANGO (Churchill). The first station south of Hazen on the Mina Branch of the SP RR. Although the reasons for the naming are unknown, it seems likely that officials of the SP RR named this non-agency siding, since the name is not shown on the list of stations of the C and C RR (MA, p. 287), which later became the Mina Branch. The toponym probably was transferred from an older place. The United States Board on Geographic Names established *Baugo* (not *Bango*) as the name of a township in Elkhart County, Indiana (USGB 1–2–5).

BANNOCK (Lander). A locality, former townsite, and post office (November 5, 1909–July 15, 1910), on the south edge of Battle Mountain and at the mouth of Philadelphia Canyon; named for the Bannock Indians, from *Panaiti*, their own name (USBG 6003; FTM, p. 2; FWH, p. 129). The Bannocks were a subdivision of the Western Numa (Fowler, p. 6).

BAR (Eureka). A post office near Eureka in operation from November 16, 1896, until October 31, 1898 (FTM, p. 2).

BARBEE (Pershing). This early mining district was located three miles from Humboldt House, an early station of northern Pershing County. The district was named for Judge Barbee, a pioneer (DM).

BARBER. A stream in the Carson Range, north of Jobs Canyon and west of Sheridan, in both Douglas County, Nevada, and Alpine County, California (SG Map 3). BARBERSVILLE (Pershing) was an early camp serving placer miners in BARBER CANYON near Dun Glen. The name commemorates Charley Barber, who developed ledges in the area (1881 Map; DB, p. 6; DM).

BARCELONA (Nye). An early silver camp (Census, 1880) on the southeast flank of the Toquima Range; named for the BARCELONA MINE in the Spanish Belt Mining District, which was discovered in the summer of 1871 by a Castillian grandee, Emanuel San Pedro, who led a party of Mexicans on a prospecting expedition from California into Nevada (SM, 1875, p. 104; VPG, p. 122; 1881 Map; SFH, p. 2). See SAN PEDRO and SPANISH. San Pedro named the mine for the city in Spain, founded by Hamilcar Barca of Carthage in the third century B.C.

BARCLAY (Lincoln). A station in Clover Valley on the UP RR, southwest of Acoma and nineteen miles northeast of Caliente (Freese, Map 2; WA). Although the town was settled largely in 1905 with the completion of the SPLA and SL RR, a post office had been in existence since April 24, 1899, and probably took its name from its first postmaster. Postal operations, which were suspended on April 29, 1905, were resumed on December 16, 1907, and continued until January 14, 1910 (FTM, p. 2).

BARD (Clark). Formerly a non-agency station on the UP RR, between Arden and Sloan, about thirteen miles southwest of Las Vegas; named for the **BARD MINING DISTRICT**, which commemorates either D. C. Bard, a noted mining engineer and geologist who was prospecting in the area, according to the *Lincoln County Record* of March 24, 1905 (WA; VPG, p. 22; DM), or Senator Thomas Bard, of California, who owned nearby mining claims (WA).

BAREFOOT BOY (Clark). An old mine of this name was near the Keystone Mine in the Goodsprings Mining District, eight miles northwest of Jean. The mill built to handle the ore was called the **BAREFOOT** (WA; VPG, p. 26).

BARE MOUNTAIN (Nye). A peak and a short mountain range in southwestern Nye County; a mining district on Bare Mountain just east of Beatty. The name of the peak, descriptive of its bare, naked appearance, was applied to the range and to the mining district, also known as *Flourine, Telluride,* and *Beatty* (VPG, p. 127; OPN, p. 52; Furn. Cr. Quad.).

BARNES (White Pine). An early post office near Preston, established July 28, 1902, and discontinued February 28, 1907 (FTM, p. 2).

BARNEY MEADOWS (Nye). A creek in northwestern Nye County, emptying into Peavine Creek. **BARNEY MEADOWS PASTURE** lies west of the creek. The person so honored remains unidentified (Dir. 1971; SG Map 5).

BARREL SPRING(S). Springs in Elko, Esmeralda, Lander, Mineral, Nye, Pershing, Washoe, and White Pine counties; named "by association with a barrel . . . because barrels were often set into springs to provide a collection basin" (GRS, Amer., p. 36). **BARREL SPRINGS**, a town in northwest Pershing County, takes its name from nearby springs so denoted (Dir. 1971).

BARREN (Nye). The name for a butte, five miles southwest of Yucca Pass and immediately west of **BARREN WASH,** an intermittent watercourse, extending from Mid Valley to Frenchman Flat, approximately five miles south-southeast of Yucca Pass. By decision of the United States Board on Geographic Names (USGB 6201), the name for the butte and the wash is not *Four Corners.*

BARRETT. A canyon north of Meadow Creek in the Shoshone Mountains and an early post office, in Nye County; named for J. T. Barrett, early settler and first postmaster. **BARRETT** post office operated from May 24, 1882, until January 23, 1885 (OR; FTM, p. 2; GHM, NY 2). **BARRETT SPRINGS** (Humboldt). At the springs so named the townsite of **BARRETT SPRINGS** was laid out eight miles northwest of Winnemucca on July 4, 1907, as a result of ore discoveries and the attending rush to the site (DM, *Reno Evening Gazette,* 7/6/07; GHM, HU 1).

BARTH (Eureka). The name of a rail point between Cluro and Palisade, where the SP RR and WP RR connect (T54).

BARTLETT (Humboldt). A mountain named **BARTLETT BUTTE** in the north end of the Black Rock Range and a creek on the eastern flank of the northern Black Rock Range. **BARTLETT CREEK,** a town settled in the early 1880s, was served by Winnemucca post office (1881 Map; Census, 1900; HHB, Nev., p. 264; VPG; Dir. 1971).

BASALT. The small settlement **BASALT** on U.S. 6 in the southwestern part of Mineral County was formerly a station on the early C and C RR. It now serves as a minor supply center for prospectors. A post office so denoted was established by order of March 20, 1906, rescinded on August 9, 1906 (Nev. Guide, p. 245; Haw. Quad.; FTM, p. 2; Dir. 1971). The name derives from the rock in the area. **BASALTIC CAÑON** appears on R. M. Evans's 1860 map of the Washoe Mining Region (Wheat V (I), 16). **BASALT** is the name for a hill west of Silver City in Lyon County (NJ 11-1; Dir. 1971). In Nye County, **BASALT RIDGE** is a ridge on the north side of Pahute Mesa, immediately south of Silent Butte and fifty miles southeast of Goldfield (USGB 6302), and **BASALT BUTTE** denotes a butte six miles southeast of Moores Station; "named for its cap rock of black basalt" (USGB 6903). **BASALT PEAK** was an earlier name for Big Kasock Mountain, a peak in Mineral County (1881 Map).

BASIL CREEK (Lander). On November 14, 1845, John Charles Frémont named a small stream at the north end of Big Smoky Valley for one of his men. The possessive form **BASILS CREEK** appears on John R. Bartlett's 1854 map of the exploration and survey by the United States and Mexican Boundary Commission and on the 1855 Colton map of the Territories of New Mexico and Utah, but has since been lost (Wheat III, 240; IV, 1; JGS, I, p. 94).

BASIN SPRING. The name for a spring in Eureka County and for a spring west of Mormon Well, situated in the basin east of the Sheep Range in Clark County (Dir. 1971; WA).

BASKET VALLEY (Nye). A canyon extending along the northeast edge of Pahute Mesa, to Kawich Valley, about twelve miles south-southeast of Quartzite Mountain; named for Indian baskets found in a cave in the canyon (USGB 6302).

BASSETT (White Pine). Frank and Manton Bassett were early settlers in the county. A small settlement so named on **BASSETT CREEK,** and **BASSETT LAKE,** northwest of McGill in Steptoe Valley, commemorate one or both of the ranchers (NJ 11–3; NHS, 1924, pp. 303, 307; Dir. 1971).

BATTLE CREEK. BATTLE CREEK MINE (Elko) takes its name from a creek rising northeast of Overland Lake in the Ruby Mountains. The creek was so named after two ranchers, A. W. Gedney and William Myers, fought with shovels over division of the creek water for irrigation purposes (EP, p. 11). **BATTLE CREEK RANCH** (Humboldt) is named for a creek on the northeastern slope of the Black Rock Range. **BATTLE CREEK** (Lander) is a creek northeast of Stony Point in Shoshone Mesa (NK 11–12; NK 11–7; GHM, LA 2).

BATTLE LAKES (Pershing). A name given by Joseph Reddiford Walker, explorer of the Great Basin in 1833–1834, to some shallow ponds at the mouth of the Humboldt River, because of encounters with the Indians there. Zenas Leonard, a member of the Walker party, recorded in his Journal "we at length arrived in the neighborhood of the lakes at the mouth of Barren [Humboldt] River, and which we had named Battle Lakes" (JGS, I, p. 57; NHS, 1920, p. 231). Peter Skene Ogden had also encountered armed Indians near the Humboldt Sink, on May 30, 1829, but succeeded in appeasing them with tobacco (GGC, p. 123).

BATTLE MOUNTAIN (Humboldt, Lander). A Shoshone raid either on an emigrant party, or on the John Kirk road-building party, in 1857, and the resulting skirmish gave rise to the name of the range where the event occurred. A mining district was organized in 1866 in the northwestern corner of Lander County to include within its boundaries the whole **BATTLE MOUNTAIN RANGE,** for which it was named (SM, 1875, pp. 77–99; MA, p. 473; GHK, Bonanza, p. 104). A small settlement which grew up here, near Copper Basin Spring, was also known as **BATTLE MOUNTAIN.** With the arrival of the CP RR, this settlement, complete with name, moved to the present location of the town (BLK, pp. 105–106; Wheeler 1871 Map). Robert Macbeth, or McBeth, one of the owners of the Buena Vista Mine in the **BATTLE MOUNTAIN MINING DISTRICT,** applied the name to the new town, but it is not known whether Macbeth named the original Copper Basin Spring

settlement which moved, or whether the name was newly applied to the station on the railroad (HHB, Nev., pp. 268–269, n. 12; SM, 1875, pp. 77–79). **BATTLE MOUNTAIN** post office, established June 2, 1870, was discontinued, with Argenta serving its patrons, from October 30, 1872, until February 24, 1874, when it was reestablished (FTM, p. 2).

BATTLE MOUNTAIN was the northern terminal of the NC RR, a narrow-gauge line running ninety-three miles to Austin. The shops were at Battle Mountain. According to Myron Angel, "The only visible improvement resulting from the construction of the Nevada Central Railroad has been the building of round houses" (p. 471). The charter of the NC RR expired in 1938, and its business was taken over by motor trucks (Nev. Guide, p. 128). The twelve-mile Battle Mountain and Lewis Railroad was completed July 30, 1881, and extended from Galena on the NC RR to the mining town of Lewis. The property of this road was sold at auction in March, 1882 (BLK, p. 75; MA, p. 284; HHB, Nev., p. 239; GHK, Bonanza, pp. 127–128). The Northwestern Stage Company also ran stages daily from Battle Mountain to Galena, Austin, and to the Battle Mountain Mining District, the principal producers of which were the Miner's Hope and the Caledonia of the Little Giant Lode; the Humbug, Mammoth, and Restoration of the Trinity Lode; the Buena Vista, White and Shiloh, and the Copper Cañon mines (GAC, p. 146; SM, 1875, pp. 77–82; Wheeler, 1872, p. 40). The town is presently a supply center and shipping point of the SP RR and the WP RR. **NORTH BATTLE MOUNTAIN** is also a station on the main line of the WP RR.

BAUER (Lincoln). The magnesite deposit, located near Horse Springs and about nine miles north of Gold Butte, was named for Albert and Harvey Bauer, who discovered it about 1925 (WA).

BAUVARD (Elko). The site of an engine terminal of the SP RR, established in February, 1904, with the completion of the Lucin Cut-off across Great Salt Lake and the discontinuance of the old terminal at Terrace, Utah (DM). A post office, named for the terminal, existed from June 4, 1904, until February 27, 1912. Both the engine terminal and the post office were moved to Montello (FTM, p. 2; DM). A variant is *Banvard* (EP p. 11).

BAXTER SPRING (Nye). The early name for the settlement east of San Antonio and at the southern end of the Toquima Range was **BAXTERS** (Wheeler 1871 Map). It was renamed **BAXTER SPRINGS** and had a Belmont mailing address in the early 1880s. The town flourished briefly in 1906 when gold was discovered west of the spring which retains the name of the unidentified early settler (TF, p. 15; M&M, p. 141; Dir. 1971; NJ 11–5).

BAYARD (Elko). A former post office of central Elko County, in operation from August 28, 1886, until February 2, 1889, when Halleck became the mailing address for its patrons (FTM, p. 2).

BEACON ROCK (Clark). The island so named is in Lake Mead, at the mouth of Boulder Canyon. Variants are *Callville Island,* honorific of Anson Call, and *Bighorn Island,* so denoted because a mountain sheep was once trapped there by the rising waters of Lake Mead (WA; GHM, CL 2).

BEAN POT (Clark). This gold mine, also known as the *Blue Quartz,* presumably was named by Nels Jorgenson, who is believed to have discovered it about 1932 in the Alunite Mining District, at the south end of Bishop Mountain (WA).

BEAR (Elko). Features of northern Elko County named for wild bears that once lived there include **BEAR CREEK** near the Idaho boundary and **BEAR SPRING** west of Contact. **BEAR MOUNTAIN,** a peak northwest of Contact, "was so named because Bill O'Neil roped a bear on it in the 1890's" (EP, p. 11). **BEAR PAW MOUNTAIN** is at the northern end of the Jarbidge Mountains (JML, p. 14; NK 11–9; GHM, EL 3).

BEATTY (Nye). The name of the town commemorates M. M. Beatty, locally known as "Old Man" or "Jim" Beatty, who owned a ranch there. The town was laid out in 1904 or 1905, during the time of the Rhyolite boom (MM). The *Rhyolite Daily Bulletin* of December 15, 1908, reported that M. M. Beatty, the founder of the town, had died at the age of seventy-three, following a fall from a wagon (DM). The post office at Beatty was established on January 19, 1905 (FTM, p. 2). In the first decade of the twentieth century, Beatty was important as a freighting point for nearby boom areas.

> The rapid growth of the new communities and their increased demands for supplies of all kinds, and the obvious desire of mine operators to get their ore to the smelters, forced a breakdown in the freighting system. Freight tie-ups all along the different freighting routes were the inevitable result of the increasing demands of these districts. These continuous freight tie-ups and the rapid accumulation of vast dumps of low grade ores, convinced the mine owners and business men that railroads were the only answer to efficient and more rapid development of the mining areas. (RRE, p. 3)

For a time Beatty was served by three railroads. The LV and T RR reached Beatty on October 22, 1906, the BG RR in April of 1907, and the T and T RR on October 27, 1907 (RRE, pp. 8–9). The town is on the Amargosa River in southwestern Nye County, on U.S. 95 at a junction with State Route 58.

BEAVER. A creek, southwest of Charleston in Elko County; **BEAVER SPRING** is on its east fork and **BEAVER CREEK RANCH** on its west fork. A peak and a mining district so named are south of Tuscarora and west of the Independence Mountains. **BEAVER** post office was in operation from January 10, 1896 to April 15, 1908, when Deeth became the mailing address for its patrons (OPN, p. 21; FTM, p. 2; Dir. 1971). **BEAVER DAM STATE PARK** (Lincoln) is east of Caliente near the Utah line, approached by a branch road from U.S. 93 (Park Map). **BEAVER DAM WASH** heads in the Dixie National Forest in Utah, trends generally westward into Nevada, then south-southeastward, crossing back into Utah, then into Arizona to the Virgin River, approximately one mile northeast of Littlefield (DL 60). *Beaver* is usually an animal name classified under incident, but *Beaver Dam* may be descriptive of the soil, the productive beaverdam land sought by pioneers (LAM, p. 43). The presence of the name *Beaver,* alone or in various combinations, in over sixty separate listings of the railway guide (OG, p. 1272) is an indication of its popularity in the United States and Canada.

BECHTEL (Clark). The name, honorific of the president of Bechtel Construction Company, one of the six companies engaged in the building of Hoover Dam, was given to a siding on the former Bureau of Reclamation railroad at the site of a steel fabrication plant producing pipe for the dam (WA).

BECKER CREEK (Nye). A tributary of the Reese River, east of Ione; named for an early settler who had a ranch on the creek (Dir. 1971; MM).

BECKY (White Pine). **BECKY SPRINGS** denotes a locality at a point of juncture of U.S. 50 and 93; named for nearby springs. **BECKY PEAK** is at the north end of the Schell Creek Range (Dir. 1971; NK 11–12).

BEEHIVE ROCK (Clark). An eroded sandstone formation in the Valley of Fire State Park, about ten miles northwest of Overton; named for its resemblance to a beehive (WA).

BEER BOTTLE PASS (Clark). A name of undetermined origin for a pass through the Lucy Grey Mountains, just east of Jean, in southwestern Clark County (Dir. 1971; WA).

BELCHER. A canyon and a basin in northern Nye County, south of Twin River (NJ 11–5); a mill in Storey County between Gold Hill and Virginia City on the former V and T RR; an important mine on the Comstock Lode. The mine was named for E. Belcher, one of the men who staked the claim in

1859 (GH–A; JJP, p. 113; MA, p. 58; TW, p. 45). Henry Comstock, whose name also appears on the location notice of June 27, 1859, refers to Ed. Belcher. The Belcher included 1,040 feet along the Comstock Lode, between the Overman and the Crown Point mines (IH; FCL, p. 228). Proof of labor on the mine is filed by the Sutro Tunnel Coalition, Inc. (AAL).

BELLANDER (White Pine). The locality so named and **BELLANDER RANCH**, northwest of Baker in Snake Valley, commemorate the Bellander family, early settlers in the area (NJ 11–3; RRE).

BELLEHELEN (Nye). The early twentieth-century mining camp so named was about fifty miles east of Tonopah in the north end of the Kawich Range. The order to establish a post office, dated April 27, 1907, was rescinded January 19, 1908. Operations were resumed from October 15, 1909, until November 15, 1911. **BELLEHELEN** post office and **BELLEHELEN RANCH** were named for the mining district (NJ 11–5; Dir. 1971; FTM, p. 2; VPG, p. 122).

BELLEVILLE (Mineral). Founded in 1873, Belleville became an important mill town on the C and C RR when nearby Candelaria was booming. A post office so named was established December 30, 1874, discontinued December 22, 1894, and reestablished in August of 1915 to operate until April 30, 1918. The euphemistic name *Belleville* (French "beautiful city") derives from the Northern Belle Mining and Milling Company, which operated two twenty-stamp mills to handle the ore from its mines at Candelaria. Only massive mill walls remain to mark the site of this once prosperous town of southern Mineral County (DM; HHB, Nev., p. 259; HPS, 1/24/54).

BELLEVUE (Eureka). The peak, southwest of Eureka and northwest of the northern extremity of Little Smoky Valley, was named for its scenic beauty (OPN, p. 33; Dir. 1971).

BELL FLAT (Churchill). A flat lying at the north side of a valley about five and one-half miles south of Fairview Peak; perhaps named for Thomas Bell, one of the owners of the Union Mill and Mining Company (USGB 5904; SPD, p. 413).

BELL MOUNTAIN (Churchill). Charles Bell, an early prospector, is commemorated by this mining district, forty-three miles southeast of Fallon (OPN, p. 9).

BELMONT (Nye). This noted mining district was organized as a result of a rich strike made in February of 1865, fifty miles north-northeast of Tonopah and fifteen miles northeast of Manhattan on the southeast flank of the Toquima Range. The rush to the newly created camp was of such proportions that the 1867 legislature made Belmont the seat of Nye County (1867 Map). The courthouse

was built in 1874. During this time Belmont was the most flourishing town of eastern Nevada and an active trading center for miners and cattle ranchers (SM, 1875, p. 102; VPG, p. 122; M&S, p. 153). **BELMONT** post office was first established on April 10, 1867, and discontinued on May 31, 1911, until its reestablishment on September 27, 1915. The post office was discontinued a second time on August 31, 1922, and Manhattan became the mail address of the patrons of the old Belmont office (FTM, p. 3). The county seat was moved to Tonopah in 1904. Belmont, from the French *Beaumont*, "beautiful mountain," was named for its location at the base of the Toquima Range.

BELMONT–CLOVERDALE ROAD. See **CLOVERDALE.**

BELTED (Nye). **BELTED PEAK** is the most northerly summit of the **BELTED RANGE**, east of Kawich Valley and north of Gold Meadows; named for outcroppings of rock that resemble a belt (USGB 6302; Kaw. Quad.; Dir. 1971).

BEND (Elko). A creek south of Tennessee Mountain in northern Elko County (SG Map 11); a name traditionally given to a stream that curves.

BENIN (Humboldt). A non-agency siding on the Salt Lake Division of the SP RR between Winnemucca and Rose Creek (T75). The French word meaning "propitious" is probably not descriptive, but commemorative of one of the various features in Africa so named.

BENNETT (Lincoln). A pass between Chief Mountain and the Highland Range, immediately west of **BENNETT SPRING** on the north end of Chief Mountain. It is locally known as **BENNETT SPRING MOUNTAIN** and lies west of Panaca, at the south end of the Highland Range. The group toponym derives from the spring which was on the old road between Pioche and Hiko. William H. Dame headed a party of Latter-Day Saints who fled to Lincoln County, Nevada, from Salt Lake City in the spring of 1858, seeking refuge from Colonel Albert S. Johnston's contingent of United States troops. Mr. Dame named the spring for Asabel C. Bennett, the party's guide (WA: JGS, I, p. 125). **BENNETTS SPRING** appears on J. H. Martineau's 1858 chart of the Desert Mission explorations (Wheat IV, 129).

BEOWAWE (Eureka). Most accounts credit the Paiute Indians with having named Beowawe because of a conformation of hills which causes the station to appear to be standing in an open gateway, the term itself said to mean "gate" in Northern Paiute. An early guide book describes the first station west of Cluro: "At this point, nature has so fortified the entrance of the valley, that a handful of determined rangers could hold the entrance against any force the savages could bring against them" (GAC, pp. 142–143). A later writer on the railroads was unconvinced by this interpretation. In *Main Line* (1948), Ernest La Marr King related a legend concerning the naming and involving J. A. Fillmore, one of the early managers of the CP RR.

Fillmore . . . was a huge man weighing some three hundred pounds, with a body width which was amazing. One of Fillmore's first chores was examination of a region with an eye to determining where townsites should be established. Locations had to be designated and names provided for the proposed new towns. Fillmore and his party were on a rear work train and stopped in an area with only sagebrush. Fillmore wandering about came upon some members of the Paiute tribe. They appeared to be frightened because of his size and ran away shouting "Beo-wa-we! Beo-wa-we!" The name was adopted and only later was it discovered that in Paiute Beo-wa-we means "great posterior." (ELK, pp. 185–187)

Students of Nevada railroad lore substantially support the legend repeated by Mr. King, insofar as it relates to the derriere; however, their translation of *Beowawe* as "big-ass Indian woman" rules out Mr. Fillmore, the progenitor of the tale (KWC). Beowawe is also said to be a Shoshone word, meaning "big wagon." According to Frederick W. Hodge, Beowa*wa* (1881 Map) seems to be the name of a man (FWH, I, p. 142). Lack of conclusive evidence precludes a positive statement of the origin and meaning of this Nevada place name.

The settlement, six miles off Interstate 80 on State Route 21 at the Humboldt River, was for a long time a Northern Paiute campsite, as was the active geyser area, seven miles south of Beowawe. An emigrant campsite to the east, known as Gravelly Ford, was described in an early guide book. "The river here spreads over a wide, gravelly bed, and is always shallow so that it is easily crossed" (FES, pp. 183–184). After 1868 and the establishment of the railway station, Beowawe became a supply point for mining districts in the Cortez Range (MA, p. 438). **BEOWAWE** post office was established on April 15, 1870 (FTM, p. 3).

BERLIN (Nye). A peak and a mining district on the southwest slope of the Shoshone Range in northwestern Nye County. **OLD BERLIN** mining camp in West Union Canyon, four miles south of Ione, had an estimated 1,400 inhabitants at one time. A post office of the same name served the camp from July 10, 1900, until December 18, 1918, at which time it was moved to Ione (FTM, p. 3). Ichthyosaur fossil beds were found in 1928 about a mile and a half from the site of the old camp. German prospectors in the area may have named the camp in commemoration of the old world city (KU; OPN, p. 53).

BERMOND (Churchill). A name of undetermined origin for a post office, thirty miles southeast of Fallon in Churchill County and in operation from November 20, 1920, until May 31, 1926 (FTM, p. 3).

BERNICE (Churchill). An antimony and silver mining camp on the north end of the Clan Alpine Range, forty-one miles northeast from Frenchman, U.S. 50; a mining district, sixty miles northeast of Fallon, on the east side of Dixie Valley; a post office at the mining camp from July 5, 1883, until June 6, 1894 (NHS, 1913, p. 178; OPN, p. 9; NM; FTM, p. 3).

BERRY (White Pine). A creek in the Schell Creek Range, east of Adverse and tributary to Duck Creek; named for John Berry, who operated a sawmill at the site in the early 1870s (Dir. 1971; NHS, 1924, p. 300).

BEST AND BELCHER (Storey). This Comstock claim consisted of 537 feet between the Gould and Curry and the Consolidated Virginia (IH; FCL, p. 228). E. Belcher (q.v.) and a man named Best, for whom the claim was named, disposed of their interests which they had purchased from Henry Comstock, at an early date; according to Smith, they were the original locators in 1859 (HDG, CP, 12/23/76; GHS, p. 11). Best might have been the man mentioned by Wells Drury. "It used to be the custom to have riding tournaments up in Honey Lake Valley, but John Best won so many prizes that the others got tired" (WD, p. 11). S. M. Best was listed as "a witness not allowed" in a case of petit larceny, Territory of Utah versus Charlie Kensler, accused of stealing about twelve dollars in gold dust from the Stebbins bar, and tried before Judge Orson Hyde on February 1, 1856 (WSJ-2). The Best and Belcher is a patented claim (AR).

BETTY O'NEAL (Lander). A mining camp and district situated twelve miles southeast of Battle Mountain on the west slope of the Shoshone Range were named for the **BETTY O'NEAL** (O'Neil) **MINE** which was located in 1880. The district enjoyed a bonanza in the 1920s when Noble Getchell reopened the old mine (BLK, p. 75; OPN, p. 40; NM; Dir. 1971; Gen. Land Off. Map). The post office, bearing the variant name Betty *Oneal*, operated from June 22, 1925, until April 26, 1932 (FTM, p. 3).

BEULAH (Washoe). A post office in northwestern Washoe County, near Vya, from December 30, 1913, until May 31, 1920 (FTM, p. 3).

BEWS (Elko). An early stage station at the **BEWS RANCH**; a station on the NN RR in

1907; "named for a Mr. Bews, a native of England who ran the stage stop and ranch" (EP, p. 12). This name was once selected for a proposed junction point of the NN RR and WP RR, near Shafter (DM).

BIG BEND. The BIG BEND of the Carson River begins at Fort Churchill (Lyon) and extends down the river for about eight miles, where it bends and flows back the same distance. It is the largest river bend in the area and is sometimes called *Horseshoe Bend*. The BIG BEND of the Truckee River is near Wadsworth (Washoe), where the Truckee turns and flows northward to Pyramid Lake (NHS, 1913, p. 208; DM). BIG BEND (Humboldt River) appears on W. Wadsworth's map of the Overland Route, published in 1858 (Wheat IV, 106).

BIG BURN VALLEY (Nye). A basin-like valley, conspicuously marked by a large burnt area, immediately south of Pahute Mesa and east of the northern half of Split Ridge (USGB 6302; DL).

BIG CANYON (Washoe). The locality, west of Pyramid Lake and between Zenobia and Sutcliffe, takes its name from the canyon in which it is situated (NHS, 1911, p. 91; SPD, p. 1029).

BIG COTTONWOOD. See COTTONWOOD.

BIG CREEK. In Lander County, BIG CREEK, a station on the NC RR about three miles north of Clifton, took its name from an important town of the 1860s on BIG CREEK, a stream on the western slope of the Toiyabe Range about twelve miles south of Austin. Only stone ruins remain of the once flourishing settlement, where miners paid two dollars each to hear the famed American humorist, Artemus Ward, lecture in the Young America saloon, in 1864 (NM; HNS, p. 129; NJ 11-2). BIG CREEK RANCH (Humboldt), northwest of Quinn River Crossing, takes its name from a creek rising on the east side of the Pine Forest Range (NK 11-7). A Nye County ranch, south of Nyala, and a canyon in the Quinn Canyon Range are so denoted (NJ 11-6). See LITTLE.

BIG DEVIL. See DEVIL PEAK.

BIG DUNE (Nye). A sand dune, altitude 2,-175 feet, south of Roses Well in the Amargosa Desert near the California border; a mining district, named for the dune and lying to the west of it, twenty miles south of Beatty (OPN, p. 53; VPG, p. 131; Dir. 1971).

BIGHORN ISLAND. See BEACON ROCK.

BIG INDIAN MOUNTAIN (Mineral). The name designates a mountain, north of Corey Peak and west of Hawthorne in western Mineral County (Kaw. Quad.).

BIG KASOCK (Mineral). A name of undetermined meaning for a peak in northern Mineral County near the Churchill County line (OPN, p. 49; NJ 11-1).

BIGLER. See TAHOE.

BIG MEADOWS. A name descriptive of the meadows in the neighborhood of Williams Station in Lyon County (NHS, 1913, p. 208). BIG MEADOWS (Pershing). "At the time of the great western migration the Humboldt completely disappeared as a river about two miles northeast of the present town [Lovelock]. What was left of the water spread out thinly over a fairly good-sized area, forming a natural meadow and a tule swamp; this was the Big Meadows of travelers on the Humboldt Road" (Nev. Guide, p. 135). Emigrants rested here and prepared for the forty-eight-hour trip across the Forty Mile Desert, at the sink of the Humboldt, the most dreadful portion of the trail to California (AEH).

BIG MUDDY (Clark). A mining district named for the Muddy River and situated near Overton, in northeastern Clark County (OPN, p. 14). See MUDDY.

BIG SALT CLIFF (Clark). A cliff of salt that was west of the Virgin River and approximately three miles south of Saint Thomas, and is now under the waters of Lake Mead. This orographic feature, named by the early Mormons of Clark County, was also known as *St. Thomas Salt Deposit, Salvation Salt Deposit, Salt Point,* and *Salt Mountain*. The last name appears on George M. Wheeler's 1871 map. The cliff, 100 to 150 feet high and about one-half mile long, is fabled to have been three miles long, all salt, and as clear as glass (WA). It was the site of the salt cave or Indian mine reported by Jedediah Smith in 1826, the first mineral deposit to be reported from the Great Basin (VPG). See SAINT THOMAS and SALT.

BIG SMOKY VALLEY. The name is descriptive of the haze over the valley, which extends generally southwestward from the southwest end of the Simpson Park Mountains to the northeast end of the Silver Peak Range, in Lander, Nye, and Esmeralda counties. Alternate names for the feature are *Great Smoky Valley* and *Smoky Valley,* the latter occurring more frequently (USGB 6201; OPN, p. 53; 1867 Map). See LITTLE SMOKY VALLEY.

BIG SODA LAKE (Churchill). The lake was discovered by Asa L. Kenyon in 1855 and so named because of the soda made from the water. It consists of about seventy-five acres of land below the general level, approximately four miles northeast of Leeteville. Variants are *Nevada Soda Lake* (NHS, 1913, p. 176) and *Soda Lake* (Car. Sink 1908; 1881 Map).

BIG SPRING(S). The name has been applied to springs in Elko, Esmeralda, Humboldt, Lander, Nye, and White Pine counties; creeks in Elko and White Pine counties; and washes in Nye and White Pine counties. **BIG SPRING BUTTE** and **BIG SPRING TABLE,** a mountain and a flat, and **BIG SPRING RESERVOIR** are in northwestern Humboldt County, near the Oregon boundary (NJ 11–6; NK 11–7; Dir. 1971).

BIG WARM SPRINGS (Nye). The springs so designated are east of the south end of the South Egan Range, in White River Valley at **WARM SPRINGS RANCH** (Cad. Map; NJ 11–6).

BILLY GOAT PEAK (Clark). A name of undetermined origin for a peak about one mile west of the Nevada-Arizona boundary and approximately one and a half miles south of Whitney Pass (USGB 6002).

BIRCH (Eureka). A settlement, twenty-six miles northeast of Eureka on the west side of the Diamond Mountains, and its post office were named to commemorate James E. Birch, a pioneer stage driver. The post office, established August 28, 1901, was discontinued July 31, 1926, at which time Eureka became the mail address of its patrons (OPN, p. 33; FTM, p. 3).

BIRCH CREEK (Lander). A creek fourteen miles southeast of Austin, heading on the east slope of the Toiyabe Range, northeast of Toiyabe Peak, and flowing through **BIRCH CREEK RANCH** into Big Smoky Valley; named for white birch along the stream banks (VPG; NJ 11–2).

BIRD CREEK (White Pine). B. B. Bird, one of the earliest settlers of White Pine County, is commemorated by the name of this creek, east of Duck Creek Dam in the Schell Creek Range (NHS, 1924, p. 300; NJ 11–3).

BIRD SPRING (Clark). A spring, six miles northeast of Goodsprings and southwest of Las Vegas, and a summit, both in the **BIRD SPRING RANGE** which extends from Goodsprings to Blue Diamond (WA; DM; Blue D. Quad.; 1956 Map; NI 11–3).

BISBYS (Churchill). A station on the road from Virginia City to the Reese River mines via the Twenty-six-Mile Desert, eleven miles east of Old River Station on the Overland Stage route (NHS, 1913, p. 178; JGS, I, p. 136); named for the owner of the way station.

BISHOP MOUNTAIN (Clark). The name of this mountain, which lies between Railroad Pass and Eldorado Pass in southeastern Clark County, is honorific of the Bishop family who owned a ranch in Las Vegas Wash and some mining properties near the Bean Pot Mine (WA).

BISHOPS (Elko). **BISHOPS CREEK,** northwest of Wells, was followed by most of the early emigrants coming in from Fort Hall, Idaho. Shift names in the area are **BISHOP CREEK RESERVOIR** and **BISHOP FLAT. BISHOPS** was a station on the first trans-

continental railroad, eight miles northeast of Deeth (VPG; FES, p. 176; 1867 Map; 1881 Map; Dir. 1971). The identity of the pioneer so honored is unknown.

BISMARK (Carson City). The name, perhaps given by German settlers, denotes a peak southeast of Carson City and west of Eldorado Canyon, in the Pine Nut Range (OPN, p. 19; NJ 11–1; Dir. 1971). An earlier spelling of the name was *Bismarck* (Car. City Quad.).

BITTER (Clark). The Clark County name complex is descriptive of the bitter waters, usually springs, that will support some forms of life, but that are not palatable enough for consumption by human beings. The Amargosa River was known as *The Bitter Water* and *Bitter Water Creek* by some of the forty-niners. See **AMARGOSA. BITTER SPRING** is a spring on the eastern slope of the Muddy Mountains. **BITTER RIDGE** is the sharp ridge dividing White Basin from **BITTER SPRING VALLEY** (WA; NJ 11–12). Another ridge so named runs northeast of Red Bluff Springs, east of Overton Beach. Alkali springs of this designation have furnished names for **BITTER WASH** (Echo Canyon) and **BITTER SPRINGS WASH** in which they are found. Valley of Fire Wash and Mud Wash also have alternate names with the descriptive specific *Bitter* (WA; NJ 11–12; LRH, XV, pp. 67, 92, 106).

BLACK. The color adjective occurs frequently in Nevada, with a variety of generic terms, for orographic features that are distinguished by their dark composition of rock or black tuff tops. **BLACK BUTTE** denotes peaks in Nye and Clark counties and a mountain in White Pine County, from which the **BLACK BUTTE MINE** takes its name (Dir. 1971; WA). **BLACK CLIFF** and **BLACK CONE** are names for peaks in Nye County. **BLACK HILL** is the name for a peak in Lincoln County and a hill in Clark County. **BLACK KNOB SPRING** (Pershing) is named for **BLACK KNOB,** a mountain south of Rochester in the West Humboldt Range (Dir. 1971; NK 11–10). **BLACK POINT** designates a mountain in Eureka County and two peaks, as well as a mountain, for which **BLACK POINT WELL** is named, in White Pine County (NJ 11–3). **BLACK RIDGE** is the name for a ridge about fifteen miles northwest of Mercury, in Nye County, and for a mountain range in Humboldt County (USGB 6201; Dir. 1971). **BLACK MOUNTAIN,** the name most frequently used, denotes peaks and mountains in Clark, Elko, Esmeralda, Mineral, Nye, and Washoe counties and a mountain range in Clark County (Dir. 1971). Two mining districts called **BLACK MOUNTAIN** were named for the place where the ore discovery was made. One, also known as

Silver Star, is in the Excelsior Mountains, southwest of Mina in Mineral County, and the other is south of the Alunite district in Clark County (VPG, p. 118; 1881 Map). The account of Captain J. H. Simpson, dated June 4, 1859, probably best describes the name process involved. "Mountains in the distance [Churchill County] perfectly devoid of timber, and of a thirsty, ashy hue, except the last range we crossed, which is of a dark-brown appearance, approaching black, and therefore called Black Mountain" (JHS, p. 14).

BLACKBIRD (Lander). **BLACKBIRD CREEK** flows from the east slope of the Toiyabe Range to **BLACKBIRD RANCH** and into Big Smoky Valley (NJ 11–2; SG Map 6; Dir. 1971).

BLACKBURN (Eureka). The former station on the E and P RR was situated at the point where the tracks crossed the Austin road. The mailing address was Mineral Hill (1881 Map; TF, p. 15).

BLACK, CAMP. Of the several camps of this name established during 1865 and all of a temporary nature, one, an outpost of Fort McDermitt, was at Massacre Lake in Washoe County and another was in Paradise Valley in Humboldt County. The latter was garrisoned in July and August, 1865, by California Volunteers under the command of Captain Albert Hahn. The name of this camp was honorific of Colonel Henry Moore Black, a native of Pennsylvania (Ruhlen).

BLACK CANYON. The canyon in Clark County so named is that part of the Colorado River Canyon in which Hoover Dam was built. The name appears on the Joseph C. Ives 1858 map of the Rio Colorado of the West (WA; Wheat IV, 98). Other canyons of this name are in Esmeralda, Lincoln, Pershing, and Washoe counties (Dir. 1971).

BLACK DIABLO (Pershing). The **BLACK DIABLO** (Spanish "devil") is a manganese mine at the southern end of the Sonoma Range, twenty miles south of Golconda (Hwy. Map). The color adjective is descriptive of the black manganese ore.

BLACK FOREST (Elko). The settlement grew up in 1872 between Wells and Currie, on the east slope of Spruce Mountain, and adopted a name descriptive of the dark appearance of the trees in the vicinity. A mine and a post office (1926–1943) were named for the settlement (OPN, p. 21; FTM, p. 3; Dir. 1971).

BLACK GLASS CANYON (Nye). A name of unknown meaning for a canyon running from Pinnacles Ridge in Yucca Mountain to Yucca Wash near its mouth on Fortymile Canyon (DL 58).

BLACK HORSE (White Pine). A mining district organized in the first decade of the twentieth century on the east flank of the

Snake Range, forty-nine miles east-southeast of Ely. A post office of the same name served the mining camp from September 17, 1906, until March 24, 1914, when Osceola became the mail address of its patrons (VPG, p. 177; FTM, p. 3).

BLACK ISLAND (Clark). The island so named is southeast of Las Vegas Beach in Las Vegas Bay (NJ 11–12; Dir. 1971).

BLACK JACK (Clark). A mine at the southern extremity of Tramp Ridge, near Gold Butte, at the south end of the Virgin Mountains (WA; Dir. 1971).

BLACK ROCK. A conspicuous black hill of Humboldt County rising above white alkali flats was first described by Frémont on January 2, 1844, as a black "rocky cape, a jagged, broken point, bare and torn." It became a noted landmark, serving emigrants to Oregon using the Applegate Trail, in 1846, and emigrants to California, in 1849 and later years. The name appears on Bruff's 1849 map (Wheat IV, 95). The rock provided a name for the **BLACK ROCK DESERT**, which extends north from northwest Pershing County and the Granite Creek Desert into Humboldt County, an area once occupied by the waters of ancient Lake Lahontan. John A. Dreibelbis gives the name of the desert on his 1854 map of a route for a Pacific Railroad (Wheat III, 167). Also named for the rocky headland were the **BLACK ROCK RANGE**, mountains west of the Black Rock Desert, and the **BLACK ROCK MINING DISTRICT**, organized in 1864 in Humboldt County (NHS, 1911, p. 117; SM, 1867, p. 55; USGB–5). The mountain range is delineated on Beckwith's map of 1855 (Wheat IV, 74). The Black Rock Range had been the scene of mining rushes as early as the 1850s, and it was here that Peter Lassen was killed while on a prospecting trip (VPG). **BLACK ROCK SPRINGS**, a watering spot on the Applegate Trail, was known as **BLACK ROCK SPA** and is so named on a map illustrating Horn's *Overland Guide to California and Oregon,* published in 1852 (Wheat III, 129). Canyons named **BLACK ROCK** are in Lander, Nye, and Pershing counties (Dir. 1971). **BLACK ROCK SPRING** (Churchill) was the name of a settlement, north of White Cloud City and east of Humboldt Lake. Salinas was its mail address (1881 Map, TF, p. 15).

BLACK SPRINGS (Washoe). The name for a town on U.S. 395, east of Anderson Acres, and a post office established October 16, 1947 (FTM, p. 3; NJ 11–1; Dir. 1971).

BLACKTOP BUTTES (Nye). The three hills on two ridges which are at the southwest end of Split Ridge and about four miles north of Buckboard Mesa are so named because they are composed of yellow and grey tuff capped by a layer of black tuff (USGB 6302).

BLACK WARRIOR (Washoe). The peak so named is west of the Churchill County boundary in the Truckee Range. As seen from the west side of Pyramid Lake, the outline of the mountain provides an outstanding silhouette of a recumbent figure (OPN, p. 66; AEH). **BLACK WARRIOR SPRING** takes its name from the mountain (Dir. 1971).

BLAINE (Elko). The post office, situated on the Brennan Ranch, was in operation from May 26, 1884, until December 31, 1914, when it was moved to Lamoille. The name commemorates James Gillespie Blaine (1830–1893), the Republican presidential candidate in 1884 (FTM, p. 3; EP, p. 12).

BLAIR (Esmeralda). The townsite of Blair was laid out in 1906, subsequent to the purchase of the old Silver Peak mines by the Pittsburg Silver Peak Gold Mining Company and the resultant acquisition of all the land around Silver Peak by numerous speculators. Various names, including North Silver Peak and Silver City, were suggested at a conference held by Martin L. Effinger, a Salt Lake City promoter, James Freeborn, the general manager of the mining company, and Orlando McCraney, the mining engineer. The name offered by McCraney, and finally agreed upon, was Blair, honoring John I. Blair, a capitalist who had furnished money for the development of the mine in the 1860s (DM). **BLAIR JUNCTION**, at the junction of the T and G RR with a spur running south to Blair, took its name from the mining town. **BLAIR** post office was established November 8, 1906, and operated until December 8, 1916, the year when the dismantling of the mill of the Pittsburg Silver Peak Gold Mining Company was begun. **BLAIR JUNCTION** post office, except for a two-month interruption of service, operated from November 18, 1920, until September 29, 1923 (FTM, p. 3).

BLANCO (Lander). The Spanish heraldic term *blanco*, "argent," designated a post office in northwestern Lander County from July 12, 1887, until October 11, 1888, when the name was changed to Galena (FTM, p. 3). See **GALENA**.

BLEY (Mineral). A short-lived post office of southwestern Mineral County, established July 9, 1914, and discontinued July 31, 1915, at which time Mount Montgomery became the mail address of its patrons (FTM, p. 3).

BLIND MOUNTAIN (Lincoln). A name of obscure origin for a mountain at the south end of the Bristol Range and for a group of springs on the mountain. **BLIND MOUN-TAIN MINING DISTRICT**, later renamed *Bristol*, was organized in April, 1871, and was located northwest of Pioche and north of the Highland Mining District (WA; Wheeler 1871 Map). See **BRISTOL**.

BLISS. A settlement, a creek, and the meadows in Carson City, near Secret Harbor on Lake Tahoe; named for Duane L. Bliss. In 1873, the firm of H. M. Yerington and Duane L. Bliss began a lumber business at Glenbrook (HHB, Nev., p. 254). **BLISS** (Humboldt), a station on the main line of the WP RR, is six miles west of Golconda. **BLISS PEAK** (Douglas). See **DUANE BLISS PEAK**.

BLITZEN, MOUNT (Elko). A mountain located fifty miles northwest of Elko. Tuscarora Mining District was organized on its east flank. The German name was given because an electrical storm occurred at the time of the naming (Gen. Land Off. Map; VPG, p. 48).

BLOODY RUN (Humboldt). A mountain range named **BLOODY RUN HILLS** extends northward from the northeast end of the Krum Hills, west of the south end of the Santa Rosa Range and east of Silver State Valley. **BLOODY RUN PEAK** is at the south end of the range. The circumstances of the naming are unknown (NK 11–8; Dir. 1971).

BLUE. Features named for the bluish cast of rock or water include **BLUE MOUNTAIN**, a mountain north of State Route 49 and west of Winnemucca in southern Humboldt County, and a mountain southeast of Caliente and west of Beaver Dam State Park in western White Pine County; **BLUE LAKE**, a deep glacial lake near the summit region of the Pine Forest Range, about three miles north of Duffer Peak in northern Humboldt County, and a lake southwest of Baker in White Pine County; **BLUE SPRINGS**, springs near Ward in the Egan Range in White Pine County. An early settlement in Nye County was named **BLUE SPRINGS**, and Belmont was the mail address for its inhabitants (NK 11–10; Dir. 1971; TF, p. 15; VPG).

BLUEBELL (Lincoln). A lead-silver mine owned and probably named by James Kelley in 1917; located about thirty miles north of Indian Springs, ten miles south of Groom, and within the boundaries of the Las Vegas Bombing and Gunnery Range (WA).

BLUE BOY. See **BLUE EAGLE**.

BLUE DIAMOND (Clark). A post office, twenty-eight miles south of Las Vegas; named for the Blue Diamond Corporation, which operates a board-plaster mill there. The company was founded by J. W. Jamison at Tehachapi, California, in 1900 and given the brand name for a high-quality lime product. Jamison, along with his partners William Hay and W. G. Bradley, purchased the Nevada gypsum mine in 1923. The mill, built in 1941, and the hill on which it was located, both took the name of the mine, and the old settlement of Cottonwood (named for Cottonwood Springs there) also became known as **BLUE DIAMOND,** with the establishment of a post office so denoted in 1942. The post office name, first recorded as *Blue Diamondville* on July 1, was officially changed to *Blue Diamond* on December 1, 1942 (RC, p. 41; WA; FTM, p. 3).

BLUE EAGLE. A turquoise mine, southeast of Battle Mountain in Lander County, located by Harold Johnson, William Van Alder, and Ted Johnson. The trio also located the following glory holes: Blue Matrix, Big Blue, Blue Boy, Turquoise Boy, and Color Back. The locations are called the **BLUE EAGLE** claims. At one time Ted Johnson climbed out of a pit at one of the Blue Eagle claims and sat on a rattlesnake. Johnson got away, and one of the partners killed the snake. "When Johnson got back his breath the other boys insisted on renaming the claim 'The Rattlesnake' and it is on file as such in the recorder's books at Austin" (HPS, 1/24/54). **BLUE EAGLE SPRINGS,** north of Butterfield Springs, furnished a name for **BLUE EAGLE,** a ranching district west of the Grant Range in eastern Nye County (ECN Map; MM). Duckwater was the early mail address for the inhabitants of **BLUE EAGLE** (TF, p. 15).

BLUE GEM LEASE MINE (Lander). A large vein of turquoise discovered on the claims of the Copper Canyon Mining Company, south of Battle Mountain (HPS, 1/24/54).

BLUE JACKET (Elko). A creek and a peak southeast of White Rock in the Bull Run Mountains; named for the **BLUE JACKET MINE.** Columbia was the mail address for the mining camp (TF, p. 15; Dir. 1971).

BLUE JAY (Esmeralda). This turquoise mine is still extensively operated and is located on the southern slope of Lone Mountain, just south of Millers and about sixteen miles southwest of Tonopah. The mine is also called the *Lone Mountain,* and "among the traders and the Indians, no mine is better known than the Lone Mountain" (HPS, 1/24/54).

BLUE LIGHT (Mineral). The designation for a famous old copper mine of the Garfield Mining District, in the Garfield Hills and west of Mina; the site of renewed mining activity in 1906 (DM; VPG).

BLUE MATRIX. See **BLUE EAGLE.**

BLUE POINT. A name for the eastern tip of the Muddy Mountains, on the south side to the Valley of Fire, and for a spring on **BLUE POINT MOUNTAIN** in Clark County (WA; Dir. 1971). **BLUE POINT SPRING** (Elko) denotes a spring and an early settlement, north of Elaine, named for the spring. Wells was the mail address for

the settlement (Dir. 1971; 1881 Map; TF, p. 15).

BLUE QUARTZ. See **BEAN POT.**

BLUE WING (Pershing). The **BLUE WING MOUNTAINS,** a short range northwest of Granite Springs Valley between the Seven Troughs and the Nightingale ranges, were so named for the presence of blue rock formations. **BLUE WING SPRING** takes its name from the range (OPN, p. 60; Love. Quad.; Dir. 1971).

BOB CREEK (Eureka). A creek in the northern portion of the county north of Beowawe, flowing from the west slope of the Tuscarora Mountains across **BOBS FLAT** (NK 11–11). The name may have resulted from an incident with wildcats in the area.

BOBTOWN (Lander). Formerly a station on the NC RR, milepost 49, southeast of Battle Mountain (DM).

BODIE (Mineral). A creek west of Aurora and a mining district, twelve miles south of Aurora, both formerly in old Esmeralda County (NJ 11–4; SM, 1867). W. S. Bodey was the first to discover gold in the **BODIE MINING DISTRICT,** and the site of the mining camp which grew up there is now w.thin the California boundary in Mono County (California Registered Historical Landmark No. 341). The given name of the discoverer has been recorded as *Waterman* (Gudde, p. 32) and *William* (EWB, p. 77). A variant spelling of the surname *Body* appears in Davis (SPD, p. 235), Gudde (p. 32) and Stewart (GRS, Amer., p. 51). The camp and creek were named for Bodey, though the spelling is thought to have been changed either to preserve the correct pronunciation (Gudde, p. 32) or because of a sign painter's mistake (EWB, p. 77). Bodey located the first quartz claim in the district in the fall of 1859. In the early spring of 1860, he was caught in a blizzard in Cottonwood Canyon, lost his way, and died in the snow (SPD, p. 235).

BOILING SPRING(S). Hot springs three miles north of Gerlach in Washoe County; named by John C. Frémont who camped at the site in 1843 (SHM 152; 1867 Map); and springs in White Pine County on the old road to Hot Creek (Cad. Map). The name also appears on Colton's 1855 map of New Mexico and Utah Territories (Wheat IV, 1). **BOILING SPRING** (Nye) was an early settlement with a Belmont mailing address (TF, p. 15).

BOLIVIA. The mining district, in both Churchill and Pershing counties and better known as *Table Mountain,* is sixty miles southeast of Lovelock, at the northern end of Dixie Valley, and about fifty-five miles north of U.S. 50 (VPG, p. 19). **BOLIVIA MINE** (Humboldt) was served by Winnemucca post office (TF, p. 15).

BONANZA. Mexican silver-miners on the Comstock (Storey) held faith in their aphorism, "So many days as you are in borrasca, so many days shall you be in bonanza," to the extent that they would contract their services, with the simple understanding that they be allowed to work as much time in a rich body of ore as they had spent in barren rock trying to find it. For a mining company to be "in borrasca" was to be out of luck; to be "in bonanza" was to be in good luck. Although many bonanzas were discovered on the Comstock, as well as throughout Nevada, the rich ore body located in the California and the Consolidated Virginia mines, which produced about $105,000,000, became known as the **BIG BONANZA**. It was determined by Dan De Quille (William Wright), the first historian of the great silver lode, that "not alone to the deposit of ore in one or two mines, but to the whole Comstock lode should be given the name of the 'Big Bonanza' " (FCL, p. 224; DDQ, p. 384). Otherwise used sparingly in Nevada as a place name, **BONANZA** designates, in Clark County, a hill, a former mining camp, and a wash draining west from Table Mountain past the hill and camp. The name has been retained for the wash; whereas the hill and the old camp have become better known as *Root* (WA). See **ROOT**. **BONANZA** (Nye) formerly denoted a townsite south of Ladd Mountain. The town was deserted in 1905 when its inhabitants joined the rush to Rhyolite (DM).

BONELLI (Clark). Presently the name for a peak at the southern extremity of the Virgin Mountains and south of Gold Butte and for a mine of the Gold Butte district; formerly an alternate name for the *Virgin Queen*, a salt mine (now under the waters of Lake Mead) about five miles above **BONELLIS FERRY**, which operated at the junction of the Virgin River with the Colorado and served travelers on the main road from Utah to Arizona in the early days. The name commemorates Daniel Bonelli, one of the most famous of the pioneers of southern Nevada. In addition to being a discoverer and developer of mines and the owner of a ferry, he owned a large hay and vegetable ranch near the junction of the Virgin with the Colorado. Having been on a mission to Spain and France for the Church of Jesus Christ of Latter-Day Saints, Bonelli brought vines from Europe and planted the first vineyard of Nevada at Las Vegas (OPN, p. 14; WA; SPD, p. 221; JGS, I, pp. 621–25; NJ 11–12).

BONITA. The Spanish diminutive meaning "pretty" is a place name for a canyon in the Eugene Mountains, northwest of the Nevada Massachusetts Tungsten Mine, in Pershing County (Love. Quad.); for a mining district, also known as *Snake* and located south of Baker on the east slope of the Snake Range, in White Pine County (VPG, p. 184); and for a former post office of Nye County, established August 2, 1907, and rescinded by order of March 19, 1908 (FTM, p. 3).

BONITA SPRINGS (Humboldt). The mining camp which grew up as a result of the discovery of Red Butte Mining District, forty miles from Humboldt House in the Antelope Range, was named Bonita Springs by W. M. Anderson. He was from Salt Lake City and the discoverer of the rich copper there, by report of the *Reno Evening Gazette* on September 24, 1907 (DM).

BONNIE BRIAR (Humboldt). This post office operated in Humboldt County from June 15, 1908, until August 31, 1911, when Mill City became the mailing address for its patrons (FTM, p. 3).

BONNIE CLAIRE. The name, as well as *Old Gold Mountain* and *Oriental Wash*, is an alternate for the *Tokop Mining District* (Esmeralda), located fifteen miles west of **BONNIE CLAIRE (CLARE)**, a former station on the BG RR. The name commemorates the daughter of an early settler from eastern Europe. A prior name for the station was *Montana*. **BONNIE CLARE**, a Nye County post office originally named *Thorp*, was established July 13, 1909, and discontinued on December 31, 1931 (VPG, p. 61; Lida Quad.; FTM, p. 3).

BOONE. A creek northwest of Mount Callahan at the northern end of the Toiyabe Range in Lander County and **BOONE CREEK RANCH**. The ranch was known as **BOONS** in the early 1880s. Battle Mountain was the mail address (NJ 11–2; Dir. 1971; TF, p. 15). **BOONE** (Elko) denotes a canyon and a spring southeast of Currie. Also in the area are **BOONE SPRING HILLS** and **BOONE SPRINGS**, a locality north of Becky Springs (NK 11–12; Dir. 1971; 1956 Map).

BOOTLEG (Clark). A canyon west of Boulder City, the site of several small tunnels where a still was operated during the construction of Hoover Dam; a spring west of Mormon Well; a spring north of Mountain Springs (WA; Dir. 1971).

BORAX (Clark). A station on the UP RR, south of Jean and near the western border of the county; settled in 1905 upon completion of the SPLA and SL RR and named for borax deposits there. **BORAX WASH** drains into West End Wash (OPN, p. 14; WA; Freese, Map 1; NI 11–3).

BOSS MINE (Clark). The discovery in 1915 of platinum in this mine of the Goodsprings district led to the creation of *Platina*, a short-lived mining camp in Mesquite Valley (WA). See **PLATINA**.

BOULDER. A valley, a flat, and a creek in

Eureka County, west of the Tuscarora Mountains, north of the Humboldt River, and east of the Sheep Creek Range (OPN, p. 33; NK 11–11; NK 11–12); a creek and a lake in the East Humboldt Range in central Elko County; a small lake, the southernmost of a group of lakes in northern Washoe County (NK 11–7). **BOULDER CUESTA** (Nye) is a crescent-shaped cuesta on Pahute Mesa, approximately two miles east of the peak of Black Mountain and twenty-seven miles north-northeast of Beatty (USGB 6302). **BOULDER CANYON** (Clark) is north of Black Canyon (q.v.) on the Colorado River, the site of Hoover Dam.

Whereas the preceding geographical features were named for the presence of boulders in the various regions, the Boulder Canyon Project, enacted into law on December 21, 1928, was so called because Boulder Canyon was thought to be the best location for the dam at that time. Later Black Canyon was selected. Water was turned in behind the dam, which was first put into use in 1936, on February 1, 1935 (JGS, I, p. 570). With a maximum height of 726 feet, the dam is the highest in the United States. Originally and from 1933–1947, the name was *Boulder Dam;* during 1932–1933, it was called *Hoover Dam* and officially renamed so in 1947. Although locally these names for the dam often are used interchangeably, a *Boulder* name complex has appeared in southern Clark County. **BOULDER BASIN,** also known by the toponyms, *Callville Basin, Lower Basin, Lower Division,* and *Lower Lake,* is that portion of Lake Mead lying between Hoover Dam and Boulder Canyon. **BOULDER BEACH** is several miles upstream from Hoover Dam (WA). The **BOULDER ISLANDS** are in Lake Mead, near Boulder Beach, and **BOULDER PEAK** rises north of Boulder Canyon (Freese, Map 1; SG Map 47; WA). **BOULDER DAM RECREATION AREA** and **BOULDER CANYON WILD-LIFE REFUGE,** as well as **BOULDER CITY,** derive their names from the canyon. The city, designed as a model town by S. R. de Boer, served as the dam's construction camp, later becoming its administrative center under the jurisdiction of the Department of the Interior, Bureau of Reclamation. The bureau chose the name Boulder City over the alternate proposals: Hoover City, Adaven, Hidam, and Wilbur. A post office, established April 15, 1931, and a mining district, twenty-three miles southeast of Las Vegas, were named for Boulder City, as was **BOULDER JUNCTION,** the point between Bracken and Pierce about eight miles southwest of Las Vegas, where the Boulder City branch leaves the main line of the UP RR (RC, p. 42; WA; VPG, p. 23; FTM, p. 3; OPN, p. 14; NI 11–3; NJ 11–12).

BOUNDARY. The name was given to the highest peak in Nevada (altitude 13,143) because of its position at the western point of Esmeralda County near the California line, in Inyo National Forest; to a hill in Clark County, situated where the Nevada-Arizona boundary meets the Colorado River between Grand Wash and Iceberg Canyon; to a point, the southwest tip of Boundary Hill; and to a butte, named for its position on the Thirty-seventh parallel, about one mile north of Beatty Wash and three miles west-northwest of Dome Mountain, in Nye County (OPN, p. 30; WA; DL 58; Dir. 1971).

BOVARD (Mineral). A mining district about twenty-two miles northeast of Hawthorne on the east slope of the Gabbs Valley Range, organized in May, 1908, consequent to mineral discoveries made the previous month (VPG, p. 110; DM).

BOWERS. Lemuel Sanford ("Sandy") Bowers was the owner of ten feet of a claim of fifty feet on the Comstock Lode (Storey), staked by him and three others in 1859. His wife had already acquired the ten feet adjoining Sandy's claim from James Rogers, one of the partners. This claim, consisting of twenty feet, was known as the *Sandy Bowers Claim* (HHB, Nev., pp. 109–10; MA, p. 39). The Bowers Claim is still known by that name although it was later included in the Consolidated Imperial and, presently, is controlled by the Sutro Tunnel Coalition, Inc. (AAL). Both Sandy, who came overland from Missouri, and Mrs. Bowers, who came to the Utah Territory with the Mormons, were of Scotch descent. He was "a rough, honest fellow and well liked by his companions, though not so canny and circumspect in his worldly affairs as his countrymen are commonly reputed to be" (HDG, CP, 11/25/76; MA, p. 39; VF; SP). One of the first of the Comstock millionaires, Sandy built the **BOWERS MANSION** in 1864 near Washoe Lake in Washoe County on U.S. 395. The two-story sandstone structure has been restored, and the grounds have become a picnicking resort.

BOWLERVILLE (Nye). A mining camp of the early twentieth century, a few miles south of the Johnnie Mine; named to commemorate Fred Bowler, who owned a mine there (WA).

BOWL OF FIRE (Clark). A basin in upper Callville Wash (WA); named for its red sandstone. See **VALLEY OF FIRE.**

BOWMANS (Nye). The name was adopted in June of 1908 for a new camp, on the west side of upper Smoky Valley, near the site of the old stage station called Minniums (MM; DM).

BOX. The name, descriptive of a box-shaped feature, or one with a "blind" end, denotes a canyon in the Anchorite Hills, west of Whisky Flat in Mineral County; a canyon southeast of Antelope Siding in Pershing County; a canyon south of Copper Canyon Mine in Lander County; and a wash near Overton that drains into the Muddy River Valley in Clark County (Dir. 1971; NK 11–10; WA). **BOX SPRINGS** (Eureka), a locality of the 1880s north of Blackburn, was served by Mineral Hill post office (TF, p. 15; 1881 Map).

BOYD. William H. Boyd is commemorated by **BOYD TOLL ROAD** and **BOYD BRIDGE** built by him in Carson Valley (Douglas) in 1861. The road, which joined the Cradlebaugh Toll Road (q.v.), was called *Telegraph* in 1863 for the telegraph line alongside it (HSM 124). The surname also designates a creek in the Independence Mountains, south of Jack Creek, and a spring near **BOYD RESERVOIR,** northwest of Lamoille in Elko County; named for Q. Boyd who built **BOYDS DAM** in 1909 (EP, p. 13), **BOYD CANYON** (Nye) is southwest of Round Mountain on the east slope of the Toiyabe Range. **BOYD BASIN** (Humboldt), about one hundred miles northwest of Winnemucca in the Pine Forest Range, was the site of rich ore discoveries made in 1907. **BOYD** (Lincoln) was a railroad station north of Elgin on the former SPLA and SL RR (NK 11–12; DM; Dir. 1971).

BOYER (Churchill). A mining district and a former post office (April 27, 1896–January 31, 1914) in Dixie Valley, about sixty miles southeast of Lovelock. The district is known also as *Table Mountain*. The name commemorates Alva Boyer, the discoverer of copper ore on Table Mountain and the postmaster of the settlement (FTM, p. 3; OPN, p. 9; VPG, p. 19).

BOZ MINE (Esmeralda). A mine of old Esmeralda County, located on Middle Hill (SM, 1867, pp. 33–34); named to commemorate Charles Dickens, the English novelist who wrote under the pen name *Boz* in the early 1830s.

BRACKEN (Clark). The name of the station five miles south of Las Vegas, on the UP RR, appears to be commemorative of either Walter R. Bracken, a native of Steubenville, Ohio (who was one of the first men to settle in Las Vegas and was identified with the SPLA and SL RR), or for Dr. J. K. Bracken, who was agent for that railroad during its construction (SPD, pp. 799, 1090; DM; NJ 11–12).

BRACKET PEAK (Nye). A peak fifteen miles southeast of Tybo and northeast of Tonopah; perhaps named for the same reason as Bracket Mountain, Clackamas County, Oregon, because "it resembled a printer's bracket, or brace, placed horizontally with the point up" (OPN, p. 53; LAM, p. 66).

BRADLEYS. A settlement of the 1880s in Mound Valley, served by Dry Creek post office; **BRADLEY CREEK** rising on the west flank of the Ruby Mountains, both in Elko County; named to commemorate L. R. Bradley who took up a ranch in the valley in 1865 and served as governor of Nevada from 1871 to 1878 (TF, p. 15; 1881 Map; EP, p. 13). The possessive name also denoted a former way station on the E and P RR in Eureka County (MA, p. 285).

BRADSHAW (Humboldt). The Winnemucca *Silver State* of February 21, 1881, reported the organization of the **BRADSHAW MINING DISTRICT** at Pollock Springs, the ledges having been discovered during the closing months of 1880 (DM).

BRALEY. See **BRAWLEY PEAKS.**

BRATTAIN (Elko). A name of undetermined origin for a post office established July 16, 1904, and discontinued on March 14, 1906, when Edgemont became the mailing address for its patrons (FTM, p. 3).

BRAWLEY PEAKS (Mineral). A commemorative name for a mountain, earlier called *Mount Braley,* south of Aurora on the California boundary; named for James M. Braley (Brawley) and situated near the mine he discovered in 1860 (SPD, p. 855; Gudde, p. 36; Haw. Quad.).

BREAKNECK CREEK (Elko). A stream flowing from the north slope of Pennsylvania Hill to Silver Creek in the Humboldt National Forest. *Nagomina,* meaning "breakneck," is reported to be the Shoshone Indian name for this stream (USGB 6103).

BREEN (Nye). **BREEN CREEK** on the west side of the Kawich Range and **BREEN RANCH** were named for an early rancher and cattleman of the area (JML, p. 14; Dir. 1971; MM).

BRIDGE. A canyon running southeast through the Dead Mountains below Davis Dam, and a spring north of Eldorado Canyon, named for a natural bridge nearby, both features in Clark County; formerly the name of a station on the transcontinental railroad between Lovelock and Oreana in Pershing County, the station marking the point where the railroad crossed the Humboldt River (WA; 1881 Map; GAC, p. 153).

BRIDGE HOUSE (Douglas). Another name, presumably, for *Cradlebaugh Bridge* (q.v.), a station on the road from Carson City to Bodie (NHS, 1913, pp. 193, 197; HHB, Nev., pp. 254–55).

BRIDGES (Lander). The former station on the NC RR between Hot Springs and Reese River Canyon stations and forty-three miles from Battle Mountain was named for Lyman Bridges of Chicago, who was chief engineer of the NC RR company, formed September 2, 1879 (MA, pp. 283–84). Bailey post office was the mail address for the station (TF, p. 15).

BRIER SPRING (Nye). A name authorized, instead of *Wild Rose*, for a spring in Death Valley National Monument, in the eastern foothills of the Grapevine Mountains, approximately one and a half miles east of Wahguyhe Peak (USGR–5; USGB 5904). **BRIAR SPRING**, a settlement of the 1880s, west of Grant in northeastern Nye County was served by Morey post office (1881 Map; TF, p. 15).

BRINE SPRING (Clark). This spring of the Colorado River was south of Salt Well and near the site of Bonellis Ferry. Stones Ferry, purchased and then moved by Daniel Bonelli in 1869, was about two miles downstream from Brine Spring. Before the spring was covered by Lake Mead, its clear brine sometimes could be seen boiling up through the muddy water of the Colorado (WA).

BRINGHURST. The post office, established August 1, 1855, at Las Vegas Mission, New Mexico Territory (presently Clark County), was named for William Bringhurst by the postal officials "because there was already one named Vegas in New Mexico," according to a letter written by Bringhurst from Big Cottonwood, under date of March 26, 1856 (NHS, 1926, p. 207). At a general conference held by the Latter-Day Saints at Salt Lake City in April of 1855, it was decided that a mission should be established at Las Vegas, a popular camping site in the desert on the Old Spanish Trail. William Bringhurst, nominated by Brigham Young, was made president of the mission and remained in that office until 1858, when he was succeeded by Benjamin R. Hulse. Bringhurst post office was discontinued September 22, 1860 (NHS, 1926, pp. 119, 122, 279; FTM, p. 3). See **LAS VEGAS.**

BRISTOL. A non-agency station on the SP RR, Wadsworth Subdivision, west of Pyramid Lake between Big Canyon and Sutcliffe, in Washoe County (T75). **BRISTOL MINING DISTRICT** (Lincoln), whose earlier name was *Blind Mountain* (Wheeler, 1872, p. 43; Map 1871), was organized by Hardy, Hyatt, and Hall in 1871, sixteen to twenty miles northwest of Pioche and north and west from the Highland Mining District, on the western slope of the **BRISTOL RANGE**. The district is now better known as the *Jackrabbit*, taking its name from the famous mine. The mining camp **BRISTOL CITY** was so named in 1878 (earlier having been called *National City* for the National Mine) with the establishment of **BRISTOL** post office on October 15, 1878 (VPG, p. 96; WA; NM). Although operations were suspended from April 2, 1887, until May 1, 1891, and from March 27, 1893, until April 18, 1907, Bristol remained the name of the post office until April 15, 1908.

Upon its reestablishment on August 30, 1922, the name *Tempest,* for the Tempest Mine, became the official designation for the post office until January 22, 1929, when the name was changed to **BRISTOL SILVER.** The latter name derived from the **BRISTOL SILVER MINES COMPANY,** which took over the properties in the Bristol Mining District in 1925. With only one interruption of service (1932–1936), Bristol Silver post office continued until February 15, 1950, when Pioche became the mailing address for its patrons (FTM, pp. 3–4; WA, SPD, p. 943). In 1880, about five miles west of the Bristol mines, a well was drilled and a mill was built. **BRISTOL WELL(S)** was the name chosen for the town which grew up there (NM; WA). **BRISTOL PASS,** between the Bristol Range and the Ely Range, trends generally westward from Duck Valley to **BRISTOL VALLEY** (WA; Freese, Map 2; 1881 Map).

BRISTOL SILVER. See **BRISTOL.**

BROAD CANYON. Two canyons are so named, one on the eastern slope of the Toiyabe Range, northwest of Clear Creek in Lander County; another in the Bristol Range, running southeasterly from Roe Peak in Lincoln County (WA; Dir. 1971). The specific is "uncommon as a descriptive term, though more used in the East than in the West, probably an indication that it was more used in colonial times than later" (GRS, Amer., p. 60).

BROADWAY (White Pine). A post office in the eastern portion of the county, established July 19, 1893, and discontinued September 7, 1894 (FTM, p. 4).

BROKEN HILLS. The mining district is about twenty miles south of U.S. 50, between the Fairview and Ellsworth ranges, extending from southeastern Churchill County into Mineral and Nye counties. James M. Stratford and Joseph Arthur discovered the district on April 13, 1913. After working the properties until 1920, they sold out to the Broken Hills Silver Corporation. The district was named for the character of the surrounding terrain. When the district was producing, **BROKEN HILLS,** the small mining camp in northeastern Mineral County, served it, and a post office of the same name operated, except for a five-year interruption, from December 1, 1920, until February 28, 1935 (OPN, pp. 9, 49; KU; FTM, p. 4).

BROMIDE FLATS (White Pine). An early mining camp on the west side of the Pine Ridge Range, below the crest (SM, 1875, pp. 164–65).

BRONCO. An early settlement, thirteen miles southwest of Reno in Washoe County; a short-lived post office (October 18, 1872–November 11, 1872) whose operations were transferred to Nevada County, California,

and later to Reno. A variant spelling was
BRONCA (FTM, p. 4; TF, p. 15). The name
is retained in **BRONCO CREEK** (NJ 11–1).
BRONCO MINE is in southern Lander
County (Dir. 1971). The places were named
for the wild or semi-wild horse or pony of
the West.

BRONTE (Washoe). A section house on the
WP RR, in the Smoke Creek Desert, southwest of Gerlach (NK 11–10).

BROOKLYN (Washoe). A small town laid
out and named in 1875 by a New York
company which expected to develop some
claims on the south side of Peavine Mountain, midway between Reno and Verdi. The
United Brooklyn Mining Company made
great expenditure, but little profit on the
mine (NHS, 1911, p. 92).

BROWN. The surname denotes a settlement,
started in 1905, near the Utah line and a
railroad siding at Clover Creek, thirty miles
northeast of Caliente in Lincoln County
(OPN, p. 42; WA); a creek and former settlement, served by Dry Creek post office, in
Huntington Valley of southern Elko County
(1881 Map; TF, p. 15) and named for Augus-
tine W. Browne, an early ranch owner
(EP, p. 13); a post office in Churchill County
in operation from July 14, 1881, until November 28, 1881; and a post office of early
Humboldt County from April 14, 1884, until
February 3, 1887, when Lovelock became
the mailing address for its patrons (FTM,
p. 4). **BROWN** also designates a creek, a
ranch, and a spring southwest of Jiggs in
Elko County. **BROWN MEADOWS** is a flat
north of Wellington in Douglas County (Dir.
1971).

BROWNS. An early stage station, later on
the line of the V and T RR, was built and
owned by Felix Brown. It was seven miles
southeast of Reno in Washoe County and
was the terminus of the Eldorado Flume,
owned by the V and T RR (SPD, p. 1029;
NHS, 1911, p. 86; GHK, V&T, p. 29;
FES, p. 207). **BROWNS CREEK** is north of
Washoe City in Washoe County (NJ 11–1).
BROWNS STATION in Churchill County
was a famous point on the Overland Stage
route and later on the SP RR, sixteen miles
southwest of Lovelock (1881 Map; T1TR).
The station was named for the proprietor
(NHS, 1913, p. 179; FES, p. 198; GAC, p.
154). **BROWNS,** a mining district on the
Pershing County border, on the western
slope of the Trinity Range two miles south
of Toy, was named for Browns Station. The
district is better known now as *Toy* (VPG,
p. 20). The earliest station of this name in
Nevada was **BROWNS STATION,** on the
Carson River about three miles above old
Fort Churchill in Lyon County. The small
stage station was started in 1853 or 1854,
and named for its owner, George Brown

(NHS, 1913, p. 211; HHB, Nev., pp. 73–74;
MA, p. 36). **BROWNS** (Humboldt) was the
name of a post office ordered established
December 6, 1895; however, the order was
rescinded on January 14, 1896, before operations commenced (FTM, p. 4; HHB, Nev.,
p. 264).

BRUCITE (Nye). A settlement on the western slope of the Paradise Range in the
northwestern portion of the county; named
from the deposits of brucite in the vicinity
(Guide Map; VPG).

BRUNEAU (Elko). The river runs north from
the divide between the Humboldt and Snake
River basins and empties into the Snake
River in Idaho. According to Fritz L.
Kramer, the name probably was given in
1811 by the detachment of Astorians under
Ramsey Crook and first appears in 1831 in
the *Journals* of John Work. It commemorates
either Baptiste Pruneau (Bruneau), a hunter,
or Pierre Bruneau, a trapper, or else describes
the color of the water at certain seasons
(FLK, pp. 53–54). A mining district, named
for the river, was two miles from Island
Mountain (SM, 1875). The name *Bruno City*
was perhaps a misspelling of Bruneau (Census, 1860, 1870; HHB, Nev., p. 277).

BRUNER (Nye). A mining district in the
north end of the Paradise Range, fifty miles
northeast of Luning; a post office so named
was twice established to serve the mining
district, from October 17, 1910, until January 31, 1912, and from December 28, 1915,
until its final discontinuance on June 15,
1920 (VPG, p. 124; FTM, p. 4).

BRUNO CITY. See **BRUNEAU.**

BRUNSON (Washoe). A mining camp (by
report of the Winnemucca *Silver State*, dated
February 23, 1881) seventy-five miles north
of Wadsworth and fourteen miles west of the
Washoe-Humboldt boundary in the Miller
Mining District, named for its discoverer,
H. B. Miller (DM).

BRUNSWICK (Carson City). A canyon, south
of the Carson River in the Pine Nut Mountains, and a former station on the V and T
RR, one mile from Empire toward Virginia
City; named for the early **BRUNSWICK
MILL,** built in 1866 on the Carson River
near Empire (NHS, 1913, p. 204; MA, p.
541; GHK, V&T, p. 31; NJ 11–1).

BRUSH CREEK (Elko). A creek east of
Sprucemont in the southeastern part of the
county; a creek tributary to Spring Creek
southeast of Wilkins. The latter "was so
named because the original stock corrals
on this spot were made of brush" (EP, p.
14; GHM, EL 5, 4).

BRUSHY CANYON (Nye). The canyon
heads on Timber Mountain and extends to
Fortymile Canyon, about eleven miles southwest of Ranier Mesa and twenty-six miles

east-northeast of Beatty. It is named for the thick brush in the canyon (DL 61).

BUCASTA (Elko). A post office of north-central Elko County (November 17, 1896–June 29, 1898); apparently a mistake name for *Bueasta*, a blend of the surnames of three men in the area, Frank Buschaizzo, Lou Eastman, and Joe Taylor (FTM, p. 4; EP, pp. 14–15).

BUCK. Features named for the male deer include **BUCK PASTURE** (Washoe), an area good for deer hunting, south of the Sheldon National Antelope Refuge, east of the north end of Long Valley and just south of Bald Mountain; **BUCK PEAK** (Lander), a peak in the Shoshone Mountains, south of Battle Mountain and north of Goat Peak; **BUCK SPRING** (Clark), a spring northwest of Charleston Peak, in the Spring Mountains; and **BUCK CREEK** (Elko), a stream rising northwest of Granite Mountain in the Humboldt National Forest, and a tributary to Savonia Creek, west of the Jarbidge River (NK 11–7; Guide Map; WA; NK 11–9).

BUCKEYE (Douglas). **BUCKEYE CREEK** rises in the Pine Nut Mountains and flows westward into the Carson River through the **BUCKEYE MINING DISTRICT**. The name is derived from the buck brush in the area (NJ 11–1; NHS, 1913, p. 190). **BUCKEYE MINE**. See **EXCHEQUER** and **RUBY HILL**.

BUCKHORN (Eureka). The mining district was organized thirty-five miles south-south-west of Palisade and thirty miles south of Beowawe on the southeast slope of the Cortez Range upon the discovery of rich ore there in 1908 by Joseph Lynn. George Wingfield, who acquired the chief producing mines in the area, erected a 300-ton cyanide mill at Buckhorn. The mill was dismantled in 1916. **BUCKHORN** post office, established February 18, 1910, was discontinued on May 15, 1916, when Palisade became the mail address for its patrons (VPG, p. 63; NM; FTM, p. 4).

BUCKLANDS (Churchill). The Pony Express station between Fort Churchill and Desert stations was named for Samuel S. Buckland, the owner of the station and a toll bridge on the Carson River. Buckland, a native of Licking County, Ohio, went to California via the Panama Canal in 1850 and moved to Carson Valley, Utah Territory, in the fall of 1857. It was at Bucklands station that volunteers from Virginia City, Carson City, Dayton, and Genoa organized into four squads prior to their disastrous battle with the Indians near Wadsworth on May 12, 1860 (Nev. I, 1961, p. 8; REL, pp. 21–23; 1867 Map; NHS, 1917, p. 171; 1922, p. 45).

BUCKLEY (Esmeralda). In 1907, the main town on Walker Lake for boats to Dutch Creek; named for the owner of several claims

in the area. The post office of the same name was established on October 22, 1907, by an order rescinded March 19, 1908 (DM; FTM, p. 4).

BUCKSKIN. Formerly a post office (June 19, 1906–July 21, 1914) and thriving mining camp of Douglas County, twenty miles from Genoa, twelve miles from Wabuska (its shipping point), and eighteen miles east of Carson City, in the **BUCKSKIN RANGE**, west of the Singatse Range. According to the *Goldfield News* of July 28, 1906, a prospector named W. D. Kennedy located quartz claims in the spring of 1906 and named the new camp for his buckskin mare. Prior to the naming of the camp, Kennedy, at one time, was lost in Death Valley; his buckskin horse carried him 150 miles to water. Kennedy rode this same horse to the site which later became the mining camp and named the location Buckskin because of his great attachment to the horse. (DM; NHS, 1913, pp. 197–98; NJ 11–1). **BUCKSKIN MINING DISTRICT** in Douglas County adjoins the Yerington district (Lyon County) and the Mount Siegel district (VPG, p. 33). Orographic features named for color bands showing stratification, or for grayish-yellow "buckskin" boulders include **BUCKSKIN MOUNTAIN**, a mountain southeast of Carlin in Elko County, and a mountain in the northern part of the Santa Rosa Range in Humboldt County; **BUCKSKIN RANGE**, a range west of the Singatse Range and east of Mount Como in Douglas County, and an old local name for the northern part of the Spring Mountains in Clark County (Dir. 1971; Carlin Quad.; NK 11–8; NJ 11–1; OPN, p. 36; Wheeler, 1872, p. 66; WA). See **GOLD PIT**.

BUEL (Elko). Formerly a post office (December 18, 1871–January 7, 1878) and a mining camp; named for **BUEL(L) MINING DISTRICT**, also called *Lucin*, in the Pilot Range about six miles southeast of Tecoma station. The name is honorific of David E. Buel, one of the locators of the district, by report of the *Elko Free Press* of March 10, 1888. When the district was revived in 1907 by The Buel Copper Mining Company, the latter built a four-mile tramway connecting the mine with a spur line, constructed by the SP RR from Tecoma to Tuttle (FTM, p. 4; VPG, p. 43; EP, p. 15; HHB, Nev., p. 277; 1881 Map; DM). See **AUSTIN**. **BUELL VALLEY**, a name given by James H. Simpson for Major Don Carlos Buell in 1859, seemingly has disappeared from the nomenclature (JHS, p. 114; 1867 Map).

BUENA VISTA. The name meaning "beautiful view" is one of the most popular toponyms of Spanish origin in the United States. **BUENA VISTA VALLEY**, between the Humboldt Range and the East Range, in Pershing County, was settled by men from the South who had fought against Santa Ana at Buena Vista (Mexico) on February 23, 1847. They named the valley to commemorate the victory (Son. R. Quad.; OPN, p. 60; NK 11–10). Features named for the valley are **BUENA VISTA CREEK,** rising near Unionville on the east slope of the Humboldt Range and flowing into Buena Vista Valley; **BUENA VISTA MINING DISTRICT,** also known as *Unionville,* organized in 1865, twenty-five miles by road south of Mill City on the eastern slope of the Humboldt Range (1867 Map); and the **BUENA VISTA HILLS,** lying southwest of the southern extremity of the valley in Pershing and Churchill counties (Dir. 1971; NJ 11–1; NK 11–10). **BUENA VISTA** (Clark) denotes a recreational area in the Valley of Fire State Park. A post office so named was established in Esmeralda County on December 14, 1905, but renamed *Sunland* on April 24, 1911 (USGB 6002; VPG, p. 166; SM, 1867, 1875; WA; FTM, p. 4).

BUFFALO. The name appears with moderate frequency in Nevada, especially in the western and central counties, with the generic terms: *canyon, creek, hills, meadows, mountain, peak, slough, spring, summit,* and *valley.* It was also adopted for early stations and settlements, a post office, and a mining district. Natural features were so named for buffalo grass in an area, or for buffalo bushes growing on stream banks. **BUFFALO MEADOWS** (Washoe) is a flat west of the Smoke Creek Desert and north of Twin Mountain. The settlement **BUFFALO MEADOWS** which began in 1865 as a center for a stock-raising district became a station on the WP RR and a post office from March 28, 1879, until November 15, 1913, when Sheepshead became the mail address for its patrons. Buffalo Meadows post office also served the early settlers at nearby **BUFFALO SPRING. BUFFALO SALT WORKS,** near Sheepshead in the late nineteenth century, was named for the meadows, as were **BUFFALO CREEK, BUFFALO SLOUGH,** and **BUFFALO HILLS** (SPD, p. 1029; HHB, Nev., p. 262; DM; FTM, p. 4; NK 11–10; 1881 Map; TF, p. 15; Dir. 1971). **BUFFALO CREEK** (Humboldt) flows from the west slope of the Santa Rosa Range into Quinn River Valley, south of Pine Creek. Former **BUFFALO SPRING STATION** on the creek and near the mouth of **BUFFALO CANYON** was served by Paradise Valley post office. Other canyons of this designation are in Churchill, Douglas, Nye, and Pershing counties (JML, p. 14; HHB, Nev., p. 264; NK 11–8; Dir. 1971; 1881 Map; TF, p. 15). **BUFFALO** (Pershing) denotes a peak south of Rochester in the Humboldt Range; a valley east of the Tobin Range along the Pershing-Lander county line; and a spring.

BUFFALO SPRING, an early settlement, was served by Galena post office. **BUFFALO VALLEY MINING DISTRICT,** also called *Mill Canyon,* is seventeen miles south of Valmy on the west slope of the Battle Mountain Range (NK 11–10; NK 11–11; OPN, pp. 40, 60; VPG, p. 84; 1881 Map; TF, p. 15). **BUFFALO MOUNTAIN** and **SUMMIT** are southeast of Eastgate in Churchill County (Dir. 1971).

BUFFINGTON POCKETS (Clark). The name for water pockets and a dam, southwest of the Valley of Fire in the Muddy Mountains. Numerous petroglyphs are to be found in the canyon above the dam (WA).

BULL. A spring and a creek on the west slope of the Hays Canyon Range; a creek at the north end of the Lake Range, west of Mud Flat; and **BULL RANCH CREEK** east of Vya, near the Humboldt County line, all in Washoe County. The name also denotes a spring and a creek, the latter furnishing a name for **BULL CREEK RANCH** and **BULL CREEK RESERVOIR,** west of the White Pine Range in Railroad Valley, White Pine County. **BULL CANYON** (Lyon) heads on the east slope of the Pine Nut Mountains. The features probably were named for the domestic bull (NK 11–7; NK 11–10; NJ 11–3; NJ 11–1; Dir. 1971).

BULLER MOUNTAIN (Mineral). The name of the mountain, north of Powell Mountain in the Wassuk Range and south of Lucky Boy, may commemorate Sir Redvers Henry Buller, British general and at one time commander in chief in the Boer War (NJ 11–4).

BULLFROG (Nye). This southern Nevada place name stems from the **ORIGINAL BULLFROG MINE,** discovered by Frank ("Shorty") Harris and Eddie Cross on August 9, 1904, in a range of hills about five miles northwest of Beatty. Two "etymological just-so stories" are current concerning the mine name. *Bullfrog* was the name chosen either because Eddie Cross was fond of singing "Oh, the bulldog on the bank and the bullfrog in the pool . . ." or because the ore sample of rich gold was found in green-stained rock and was frog-shaped (OPN, p. 53; DM; WA; NM). The latter theory, except for the shape of the rock, is supported by Charles Labbe. "The ore broken from a surface boulder was the type that gave the name Bullfrog; a green stained quartz with plenty of free gold in the chrysocolla, later sought by every one for Jewelry rock" (CHL, p. 175).

It is probable that *Original* was added to the name of the mine to distinguish it from the mining camp which, by the winter of 1904, had about a thousand people living in tents, dugouts, and rude stone cabins. Freight tie-ups and congested traffic made a demand for rail connections. The BG RR was incorporated in Nevada on August 30, 1905, and building from Goldfield, reached Rhyolite, the most important town of the Bullfrog district on May 22, 1907 (RRE, pp. 16–17; OPN, p. 53). In addition to being adopted for the mining camp, the name spread from the Original Bullfrog Mine to **BULLFROG MOUNTAIN,** on which the mine was located, to the **BULLFROG HILLS,** running northeasterly from the mountain, and to **BULLFROG** post office which served the area from March 21, 1905, until May 15, 1909. **BULLFROG MINING DISTRICT** is also known as *Beatty, Pioneer,* and *Rhyolite.* Only rock ruins remain of the old bonanza camp (Bull. Quad.; FTM, p. 4; NM; VPG, p. 124).

BULLION. Two settlements in early Nevada were so named. The Lander County settlement was the camp for the **BULLION MINING DISTRICT,** twenty-five miles southwest of Beowawe on the east slope of the Shoshone Range. **BULLION MOUNTAIN,** named for the district, is south of Granite Mountain in the Shoshone Range (Census, 1900; VPG, p. 84; Dir. 1971; NK 11–11). **BULLION CITY** (Elko) was an important mining camp southeast of Carlin, serving the **BULLION MINING DISTRICT,** located in 1869 and active until the 1880s (1881 Map). The district, now better known as *Railroad,* is twenty-seven miles south-southwest of Elko and twelve miles southeast of Palisade (ECN Map; NM; VPG, p. 45; 1881 Map; HHB, Nev., p. 277). The post office, named simply **BULLION,** served miners and ranchers of the area from August 8, 1871, until January 31, 1934 (FTM, p. 4). **BULLION MINING COMPANY** (Storey) was the name of a claim staked in 1859 between the Potosi and the Exchequer on the Comstock Lode. The Bullion absorbed the Casser, the Wellington, and the Eastern Slope. Even though the area of the claim was augmented by the consolidation, the popular mine name proved inappropriate for the ground. The Bullion is a patented claim on the Comstock (IH; Dir., 1875; AR; CHS, Mine, p. 177; OL, Silver, p. 68; MA, p. 184; OPJ, p. 75; RWR, p. 499). **BULLION HILL** is an alternate name for the Cortez Mining District, thirty-six miles south of Beowawe in Lander County, and the name of an early mine of White Pine County (VPG, p. 84; RWR, p. 165). **BULLION SPRING** is a spring fifteen miles west of Searchlight in Clark County (WA). **BULLION RAVINE** denotes a canyon in Storey County (Dir. 1971).

BULLIONVILLE (Lincoln). John H. Ely and William H. Raymond established a five-stamp mill at the head of Meadow Valley on a hillside later known as **BULLION-**

VILLE. Several large stamp mills were built at this site, ten miles southeast of Pioche, because it was the nearest point with a sufficient supply of water to the important mines of the Ely Mining District. General A. L. Page, aided by the Raymond and Ely Mining Company, built the narrow-gauge P and B RR, completed in 1874, at a cost of $400,-000 to transport ore from the mines at Pioche to the mills of Bullionville. The first iron foundry of eastern Nevada was erected here for the railroad company in 1873. When an abundance of water was found in the Pioche mines in 1876, Bullionville was no longer necessary for milling purposes, and railroad operations were discontinued. **BULLIONVILLE** post office was established April 27, 1874, discontinued in 1886, re-established in 1892, and discontinued a second time July 27, 1898. Although the town had declined, in 1880, new smelting and concentrating works were erected to work with the tailings deposited by the mills. The smelter burned down in June of 1893 (SPD, p. 931; MA, pp. 484, 488–489; HHB, Nev., pp. 273, 287; FTM, p. 4; Census, 1870, 1880; Wheeler 1871 Map; WTL, p. 16; WA). The name Bullionville reflects the fact that the main purpose of the town was to refine ore into bullion.

BULL RUN (Elko). The **BULL RUN MINING DISTRICT** was discovered by Jesse Cope in 1869, about eighty-nine miles north from Carlin, on the east slope of the **BULL RUN MOUNTAINS,** or *Centennial Range,* a north-south trending range that forms the eastern limit of the valley of the Owyhee. **BULL RUN CREEK** runs through a canyon of the same name, north of Deep Creek, and empties into **BULL RUN RESERVOIR,** which lies west and south of **BULL RUN BASIN.** A peak so named is in the range near Deep Creek in the Humboldt National Forest. The complex probably derives ultimately from the Civil War battles of 1861 and 1862, but the order of naming remains undetermined (Wheeler, 1872, p. 34; SM, 1875; VPG, p. 36; OPN, p. 22; JML, p. 15; Bull. R. Quad.).

BUNKER HILL. BUNKER HILL PEAK is in the Toiyabe Range (in Lander County), south of Austin and west of State Route 8A, which divides Kingston Canyon at its head from Big Creek Canyon. It is probably the peak, as seen from the northeast, that, in 1845, guided Captain Frémont, thought to be the first white man to have entered Big Smoky Valley (OPN, p. 40; MM; NJ 11–2). **BUNKER HILL MINING DISTRICT,** named for the peak, was south of the Santa Fe district (1867 Map) and served by Battle Mountain post office (TF, p. 16). **BUNKER HILL** (Elko) is a peak northeast of Lee

Canyon in the Piñon Range (Carlin Quad.). The peaks were named for the hill near Boston famous in the American Revolution. **BUNKER HILLS** (Lincoln) designates a range in the southeastern part of the county (Dir. 1971). **BUNKER PEAK** and **BUNKER PASS** are about five miles east of Elly Mountain in the Clover Mountains, Lincoln County (WA; Dir. 1971).

BUNKERVILLE (Clark). The old Mormon town so named, east of the Virgin River and a few miles below Mesquite, commemorates Edward Bunker of St. George, Utah, who came to Nevada in 1877 to serve as a missionary to the Indians. The town, formerly called *Mesquite* (not to be confused with present town of Mesquite, six miles northeast of Bunkerville), had been founded earlier in the 1870s by Thomas Dudley Leavitt, Sr. and a few others from Utah; however, with the establishment of the post office on October 27, 1879, the name was changed to **BUNKERVILLE**, honoring Mr. Bunker, a veteran of the Mormon Battalion of the Mexican War (NHS, 1924, p. 247; FTM, p. 4; MA, p. 489; OPN, p. 14; AJ, ix, p. 16; 1881 Map; WA). Named for the town are **BUNKERVILLE MINING DISTRICT**, lying fifteen miles to the south; **BUNKERVILLE MOUNTAIN**, north of Saint Thomas Gap, in the northern end of the Virgin Mountains; and **BUNKERVILLE RIDGE**, three miles north of Virgin Peak Ridge in the Virgin Mountains, and seven and one-half miles south of Bunkerville (VPG, p. 23; WA; USGB 6203).

BURCHAMS (Lander). The possessive name applies to a creek rising on the western slope of the Shoshone Mountains and flowing into Smith Creek Valley, and a spring north of Round Hill; named for an early rancher (NJ 11–2; MM).

BURNED CORRAL CAÑON (Nye). A canyon east of Railroad Valley and on the west slope of the Quinn Canyon Range; named for a wild horse corral which burned in the canyon (JML, p. 15).

BURNER (Elko). A mining district in the **BURNER HILLS** in the northwestern portion of the county, near the Humboldt County line, ten miles west of Good Hope; named for J. F. Burner, an early prospector (OPN, p. 22; VPG, p. 37). **BURNER BASIN**, a valley northeast of Elko Summit in the Elko Mountains, and **BURNER BASIN SPRING**; named for Elijah Burner who used the valley for rangeland (EP, p. 15; GHM, EL 2, 1).

BURNING MOSCOW (Storey). Since this company located on ground first claimed by the Ophir on the Comstock, several litigations contesting title followed. It was purchased by the Ophir in 1865 (GHS, p. 65; EL, pp. 173–77; HHB, Nev., p. 125). According to Davis, when the miners came in the spring of 1859, Henry Comstock was "on deck" deeding ground, and he sold the Burning Moscow, "which seems to have been the second location on the Comstock, the Ophir being the first" (SPD, p. 387). However, a location notice for the *Burning Mosca Ledge Lucky Co.* was dated April 19, 1860, at Virginia City, Utah Territory, and signed by William Bickerstaff and eleven others (VMR–E, p. 101). *Mosca*, Spanish "fly," seems to be of Mexican mining tradition, thus Burning Mosca a distorted version of *firefly*. Folk etymology would account for the change from *Mosca* to *Moscow*. (JRB, Res., p. 91; CMA, pp. 184, 318, 359; RWR, pp. 225, 569). See **YELLOW JACKET** and **MOSQUITO**.

BURNT. A name bestowed because a structure or vegetation in an area has been destroyed by fire, frequently coupled with *cabin* or *mill*, but also appearing with the generics *canyon, creek, peak, spring*, and *summit*. **BURNT CABIN** (Douglas) was four miles from Double Springs on the road from Carson City to Aurora (NHS, 1913, p. 197). **BURNT CABIN** (White Pine) denotes a spring northwest of Smith Valley. **BURNT CABIN FLAT** is south of Horse Canyon on the east slope of the Monitor Range, and **BURNT CABIN SUMMIT** is northeast of Ione in the Paradise Range, both in Nye County. **BURNT MILL CANYON** (White Pine) is a canyon north of Lehman Creek in the Snake Range. **BURNT CREEK** (Elko) is the name for a creek east of Metropolis and for a spring southwest of Jackpot, north of Cottonwood Flat. In Lincoln County, **BURNT CANYON** is south of Jackrabbit in the Bristol Range; **BURNT CANYON CREEK** is north of Ursine in the White Rock Mountains; **BURNT PEAK** is about three miles southwest of Silver King Mountain in the southern part of the Schell Creek Range; and the **BURNT SPRINGS RANGE** is a range of hills along the east side of Dry Lake Valley, about seventeen miles west-southwest of Panaca, named for nearby **BURNT SPRINGS**. **BURNT PEAK** (Nye) is a crescent-shaped mountain just northwest of Quartzite Ridge and about five miles southeast of the south end of the Belted Range (Dir. 1971; WA; NK 11–9; DL 60; USGB 6302).

BURRO (Lander). A name chosen for a real estate mining promotion about fifteen miles northeast of Austin. An order establishing **BURRO** post office on July 19, 1906, was rescinded March 16, 1907 (DM; FTM, p. 4).

BURRO SPRING (Clark). The spring, on the northeast slope of Crescent Peak, and **BURRO SPRING WASH**, draining east to

Lake Mead from Jumbo Basin, south and east of Gold Butte, may have been named for an incident with the desert burro (WA).

BURROWS (Lincoln). The name for a canyon west of Highland Peak in the Highland Range and for outcroppings of dolomite found there, called the **BURROWS DOLOMITE FORMATION** (WA).

BUSH. A name of unknown origin for a mountain in the Bullfrog Hills, north of Rhyolite in Nye County, with the variant spelling *Busch;* a creek heading in the Roberts Mountains of Eureka County and flowing into Pete Hanson Creek in Denay Valley (Bullfrog Quad.; Robt. Mts. Quad.).

BUSTED BUTTE (Nye). A hill between Fortymile Canyon to the east, and the south end of Yucca Mountain to the west; "so named because the ledges on its side are offset by a fault and do not join, giving the hill a broken or 'busted' appearance" (USGB 6302).

BUTLER. A basin and a creek north of Dianas Punch Bowl, in the Monitor Range of northern Nye County; a peak west of Walker Lake on the Mineral-Lyon county line; and a peak in Storey County (OPN, p. 49; Dir. 1971). **BUTLER** post office (Nye) operated from April 10, 1901, until March 3, 1905, when the name was changed to *Tonopah* (FTM, p. 4). Until March of 1904, the masthead of the *Tonopah Bonanza* read "Tonopah (Butler P.O.), Nevada" (DM). The post office name commemorates James L. Butler (1855–1923), the discoverer of Tonopah. See **TONOPAH.**

BUTTE. *Butt* meaning "hillock" or "mount" is generally used in the French form *butte* in the United States. Frémont explains *butte* as a word "applied to the detached hills and ridges which rise abruptly, and reach too high to be called hills or ridges, and not high enough to be called mountains. *Knob,* as applied in the western States, is their most descriptive term in English. *Cerro* is the Spanish term; but no translation, or periphrasis, would preserve the identity of these picturesque landmarks, familiar to the traveler, and often seen at a great distance" (JCF, Report, p. 161). Gudde explains that the word was introduced in the Northwest by French-Canadians of the Hudson's Bay Company, but first used as a generic term by members of the Lewis and Clark expedition (Gudde, p. 42). **BUTTE VALLEY,** extending from west-central White Pine County north into Elko County, and the **BUTTE MOUNTAINS,** west of the valley, are described by Simpson. "It [the valley] is about eight miles wide and takes its name from the buttes or table-hills in it." Concerning the range, he wrote: "The range of mountains limiting it on its west side are

low, and, though covered with cedar, present but little indications of water" (JHS, p. 60; NJ 11–3). **BUTTE GULCH** (White Pine) is a gulch of about a mile's length, extending northeastward to Butte Valley from the lower slopes of Robbers Roost Ridge (USGB 5902). **BUTTE STATION** (White Pine) was between Mountain Springs and Egan Canyon on the line of the Pony Express. In the 1880s Cold Creek was the mail address for the station (Nev. I, 1961, p. 9; Cad. Map; ECN Map; TF, p. 16).

BUTTERFIELD. A Lincoln County spring of this name, southwest of Emigrant Springs and north of the Bristol Mining District, was called *Desert Swamp Springs* by the J. H. Martineau party of Mormons in 1858 (Wheat IV, 132). The mailing address for the locality in the early 1880s was Bristol (1881 Map; TF, p. 15). **BUTTERFIELD** (Nye) denotes a spring, south of Blue Eagle Spring, and a salt marsh south of Mud Flat and west of the Grant Mining District in the Grant Range. The early **BUTTERFIELD RANCH** was served by Tybo post office (1881 Map; Dir. 1971; TF, p. 16).

BUTTERS MILL (Storey). Only rubble remains today of this large cyanide plant, capable of working 350 tons of ore a day. It was built at the base of Sugar Loaf Mountain in the early twentieth century by Charles Butters and his associates, who constructed the plant for the working of tailings in Six-Mile Canyon (SPD, pp. 325, 341).

BUTTONHOOK WASH (Nye). The name for a watercourse, extending from the southwest side of Timber Mountain to Beatty Wash, about thirteen miles east-northeast of Beatty (DL 61).

BUTTON(S) (Humboldt). **BUTTONS** post office was in operation from May 27, 1889, until October 8, 1891, when Paradise Valley became the mail address for its patrons (FTM, p. 4). **BUTTON POINT** is a rest area on Interstate 80, east of Winnemucca. The name is honorific of Frank Button who, with his uncle I. V. Button, drove cattle into the area and began ranching operations in 1873. "Using their famous Double Square brand, they raised thousands of fine horses on the 4,000 square miles of ranchland" (SHM 164).

BYRON. The popular station name was applied to a siding in Clark County, southwest of Moapa and forty-four miles north of Las Vegas on the UP RR, which was abandoned in 1949 (NJ 11–12; WA; OPN, p. 14). **BYRON** was also the name of one of three mining companies reported by Mark Twain in a letter dated February 3, 1863, to have ledges located in the Brown and Murphy Mining District of Lyon County (HNS, pp. 57–58).

CABIN. Features named for cabins that have once stood or are standing nearby include **CABIN CANYON** (Clark), a canyon in the Virgin Mountains, and **CABIN CANYON SPUR,** a ridge named for the canyon and breached by Cabin and Nickel Creek canyons, parallel to and between Virgin Peak Ridge to the south, and Bunkerville Ridge to the north (DL 47); **CABIN CREEK** (Humboldt), a tributary of Martin Creek, southeast of Buckskin Mountain; and **CABIN SPRINGS** (Clark), a spring about four miles south of Sheep Spring on Sheep Mountain, and springs east of Charleston Peak in the Spring Mountains (WA; Dir. 1971).

CACHE CAVE DRAW (Nye). A watercourse extending from the west side of the Belted Range to the south end of Kawich Valley just north of Ocher Ridge and about nine miles southwest of Wheelbarrow Peak; named for "a number of caves along the draw containing Indian caches" (USGB 6302; DL 58).

CACTUS (Nye). A mountain range southeast of Tonopah; **CACTUS PEAK,** at the north end of the range was an active mining area in 1914; **CACTUS FLAT** lies east of the Cactus Range (NJ 11–8; DM). **CACTUS SPRING** is on the eastern slope of the Cactus Range, west of Cactus Flat (JML, p. 15). **CACTUS SPRINGS MINING DISTRICT,** at the northwest end of the Cactus Range, is twenty-four miles east of Goldfield (VPG, p. 125). Various species of cactus grow over a wide area in southern Nevada; the beavertail, the calico cactus, and the barrel cactus are the most common in the Tonopah area.

CAHILL CANYON (Lander). A canyon in the Toiyabe Range southeast of Austin; named for an old Austin family who ranched in the canyon (Dir. 1971; MM).

CAIN. A mountain, formerly named *Lone Peak,* in the Augusta Mountains about fifty-three miles southwest of the town of Battle Mountain and sixty-six miles south-southeast of Winnemucca, in Pershing County; a creek, the name of which was earlier spelled *Cane,* flowing from the north end of Antelope Valley to Reese River, about twenty miles east-northeast of Cain Mountain and thirty-nine miles south-southwest of Battle Mountain, in Lander County; named to commemorate Hiram Cain, an early settler in the area. The correct spelling of the name was verified by official land patents, obtained by Hiram Cain in 1881 (NK 11 11; USGB 6301; DL 51).

CALEDONIA (Storey). On March 16, 1861, the **CALEDONIA MINE** was formed by a consolidation of seven claims and controlled 2,188 feet southeast of the Overman on the Comstock (GH–D, p. 382; IH; FCL, p. 228). The Consolidated Chollar, Gould and Savage Mining Company presently files proof of labor in the Caledonia (AAL). The Caledonia Silver Mining Company was originally entered into the records as the *Clyde Lode and Caledonia Company.* Although Caledonia perpetuates the ancient Roman name for Scotland, its origin in this instance is undetermined. The preference of some miners for names with a learned or classical flavor establishes a tradition in mine-naming. At least three mines named *Caledonia* are known to have existed in California: one in Plumas County, one at Michigan Bluff in Placer County, and another spelled *Calidonia* in El Dorado County (RWR, p. 78; CMA, pp. 182, 318). Also, there was a Caledonia gold mine in Colorado's Wide Awake District (OJH, pp. 225–26). An instance of direct transfer is probably shown in South Dakota; in 1877, the Caledonia mine in the Black Hills District copied the underground methods of the Comstock including square-set timbering (TAR, pp. 212, 216).

CALICO. A term of description for land features distinguished by varicolored rock in desert country. The **CALICO MOUNTAINS,** about thirty miles north of Gerlach in northern Washoe County, were known earlier as the *Harlequin Hills,* a name derived from the costume of many colors worn by the traditional comic pantomimist. The **CALICO HILLS** (Nye), west of Fortymile Canyon and south of Shoshone Mountain, were the site of mining excitement in the early twentieth century. Canon Station, thirty-five miles southeast of Rhyolite on the LV and T RR, was established in October of 1908 to serve the mines of the Quartz Gold Mining Company, located seventeen miles to the north in the Calico Hills. **CALICO** (Clark) denotes a spring, west of Las Vegas and north of Red Rock Wash; a wash lying north of Echo Canyon and draining into the Overton Arm of Lake Mead; the bay at the mouth of Calico Wash, formerly the site of **CALICO SALT MINE,** now covered by Lake Mead (VPG; Furn. Cr. Quad.; DM; WA).

CALIENTE (Lincoln). A town in Meadow Valley Wash at Clover Creek, on U.S. 93 and on a branch line of the UP RR running north to Pioche, thirty-two miles distant. The area surrounding present Caliente was first known as *Dutch Flat* and first settled in the early 1870s with the establishment of the Jackman Ranch. When William Culverwell began the purchase of the ranch in 1874, the site became known as the *Culverwell Ranch* (DM; WA). According to Scrugham, Charles Culverwell had settled on the land in 1875, with squatters' rights; he acquired legal title in 1882 under homestead provisions

(JGS, I, p. 609). After a railroad fight and much litigation between Senator William A. Clark and the Oregon Short Line, the Clark Road (later the UP RR) was extended to Culverwell Ranch, but the station was called *Clover*, or *Cloverdale Station*, for the creek. When first laid out in 1901, the town was called *Calientes* (Spanish *caliente*, "hot") for hot springs in the area. When the post office was established on August 3, 1901, postal officials dropped the *s* from the name (FTM, p. 4; SPD, p. 947). **CALIENTE MINING DISTRICT**, also called *Chief*, is eight miles north-northwest of the town for which it was named (VPG, p. 92).

CALIFORNIA. Two creeks of this name are in northern Elko County, one near **CALIFORNIA HILL** and a tributary to the Owyhee River between Mountain City and Rio Tinto, the other north of **CALIFORNIA MOUNTAIN** on the east slope of the Independence Mountains (SG Map 11; NK 11-9). A few features in Clark County are so named because of their relation to the **CALIFORNIA TRAIL**, that part of the Spanish Trail between southern Utah and San Bernardino, California. **CALIFORNIA CROSSING** denoted the place where the trail crossed the Muddy River, about due south of the present site of Moapa. The trail moved southerly over a low mesa, before traversing the Muddy, and continued west along the river to **CALIFORNIA WASH**, which drains the west side of the Muddy Mountains and the east side of the Arrow Canyon Range (WA). **CALIFORNIA** (Storey). A notice of location of the original California Mine on the Comstock Lode, claiming 450 feet, was dated June 22, 1859 (MA, p. 58). Another notice dated July 2, 1859, states "this company is known as the California Mining Company" (GH-A, p. 22). Angel quotes the Placerville *Semi-Weekly Observer*, July 6, 1859, as follows: "The California Company, a party of miners who recently left Placerville, have a claim which averages $250 per day to the hand with a rocker" (MA, p. 60). The present California company was formed in 1874 and included 600 feet along the Comstock Lode. "In 1874 directors of Consolidated Virginia Mining Company gradually gained control of the Kinney, Central No. 2, California, and Central No. 1 Mining Company, organized a new corporation and called it the California Mining Company" (JLK, p. 246).

Miners in the Mother Lode area must have been honoring their state when they applied the name of California mines which were south of Deer Creek in Nevada County, at Milton in Calaveras County, and in El Dorado and Amador counties (CMA, pp. 179, 318). The California mine on the Comstock, named by California miners from

Placerville, as well as two other Nevada mines by that name in Elko County and in White Pine County (RWR, pp. 135, 186), was given the name because of association. The richness of the California mine on the Comstock, which was valued at $12,000 per inch in 1875 (JLK, p. 74), lent new connotation to this name until it was thought to be auspicious. Mines of this name were also located in Central City and in Pinos Altos, New Mexico, and in Gilpin County, Colorado (RWR, pp. 354, 398-99). The assumption that the name *California* had become synonymous with rich ore is perhaps verified by a placer miner's statement as he worked in the California Gulch in Colorado: "Abe Lee . . . looked up from a pan of gravel and shouted, 'Boys, by the Almighty, I've got Californy in the bottom of this-here pan!' " (GTC, p. 29; GCQ, p. 149). The California mine on the Comstock is presently assessed in Storey County (AR, No. 133).

The word *California* first appeared in a Spanish novel, *Las Sergas de Esplandian*, by Garcia Ordonez de Montalvo, printed in Seville, Spain in 1510 (PTH, p. 44; Gudde, p. 46).

CALLAGHAN (Lander). A peak in the Toiyabe Range northeast of Austin and west of Grass Valley; a creek rising southeast of Mount Callaghan and flowing into Grass Valley; named for an early settler (NJ 11-2).

CALLVILLE (Clark). An early Mormon settlement between Boulder Canyon and Black Canyon on the Colorado River, now under the water of Lake Mead; named for Bishop Anson W. Call, who built a stone warehouse there in 1865. The post office, along with Overton and Saint Joseph, was established as if in Pah Ute County, Arizona, "although the sites had been transferred to Nevada by Act of Congress in 1866 and attached to Lincoln County" (FTM, p. 33). Callville was abandoned in 1869 and its post office, dating from January 25, 1867, was discontinued on June 15, 1869 (FTM, p. 4). **CALLVILLE WASH** drains southwestward from the Muddy Mountains into **CALLVILLE BAY**, Lake Mead, the site of Bishop Call's stone warehouse which was also known in the early days as *Calls Landing* (JGS, I, p. 592; 1881 Map; SPD, p. 219; WA; NJ 11-12). See **BOULDER BASIN**.

CALMVILLE (Esmeralda). A post office, established November 24, 1893, and discontinued October 9, 1895, when Columbus became the mail address of its patrons (FTM, p. 5).

CALVADA (Washoe). Formerly a station on the SP RR at the California-Nevada state line; a coined name commemorating both states (DM).

CAMBRIDGE. An early mining camp and post office of this name were in old Esmeralda County (HHB, Nev., p. 260; 1881 Map; Census, 1900). The post office operated from September 12, 1879, until May 4, 1881 (FTM, p. 5). The **CAMBRIDGE MINING DISTRICT** (Mineral), better known as *Aurora*, is near the California-Nevada state boundary on the eastern slope of the Sierra Nevada, thirty miles southwest of Hawthorne and five miles south of Fletcher (VPG, p. 109).

CAMELBACK PEAK (Churchill). A peak in the Louderback Mountains approximately two miles northwest of Wonder; named for its humped shape (USGB 5904).

CAMP. Military reservations are listed under the specific term of the name. For Camp Halleck, see **HALLECK, CAMP (FORT)**.

CAMPBELL. In Lander County, a settlement on U.S. 50 east of the Desatoya Range near the Churchill County line (Guide Map), and a mining district, also known as *Bullion, Lander,* and *Tenabo;* named for John Campbell, one of the owners of the Osceola Mine (VPG, p. 84; DM), and located twenty-five miles southwest of Beowawe on the east slope of the Shoshone Mountains. Beowawe was the mail address for the early camp (TF, p. 16). **CAMPBELL CREEK** and **CAMPBELL CREEK RANCH** are in the southwestern part of the county (GHM, LA 1). **CAMPBELL** (Lyon) was a station on the NCB RR, a short line carrier connecting with the C and C RR at Wabuska, and running to the Nevada Douglas Copper Mines near Ludwig. Abandonment of the railroad was authorized on January 2, 1947 (NCB Map). **CAMPBELL DITCH** is the designation for a canal southeast of Wabuska. **CAMPBELL VALLEY** denotes a portion of the Walker River Valley, northwest of Weber Reservoir (GHM, LY 1). Two springs southeast of Long Valley, in central White Pine County, are named **CAMPBELL SPRING NO. 1** and **CAMPBELL SPRING NO. 2** (GHM, WP 3).

CAMP STATION (Eureka). A stop on the Overland Stage route, situated thirteen miles southwest of Roberts Creek Station in Root and Connelley's compilation. The Pony Express station at this location was called *Grubbs Well* (JGS, I, p. 136; Nev. I, 1961, 9).

CAMP VALLEY (Lincoln). A name applied to a portion of Ursine Valley in the upper end of the Meadow Valley Wash (WA).

CANA (Lincoln). Formerly a railroad siding between Etna and Stine on the UP RR (WA); probably named to commemorate the village northeast of Nazareth in Galilee, where Christ performed his first miracle.

CANDELARIA (Mineral). The bonanza town of **CANDELARIA** was built up between the Northern Belle and the Vanderbilt mines in 1875. In September of that year only one building was there, but within a month it was a town with many dwelling houses, two hotels, a restaurant, a livery stable, four stores, and eleven saloons (SM, 1875, pp. 33–34). In 1880, according to a contemporary report, while the **CANDELARIA MINING DISTRICT** was booming, water had to be hauled from Columbus and Belleville. Poor water was six cents a gallon; poorer water, impregnated with alkali, was five cents a gallon. With wood at $20 a cord, it took a capitalist to keep a fire going. The district was first known locally as *Pickhandle Gulch,* but because citizens objected and preferred *Metallic City,* another thriving town grew up less than a mile from Candelaria and took the name Metallic City (M&SP, 5/15/80; 10/9/80; 10/30/80). The narrow-gauge C and C RR reached Candelaria in 1882, to handle the ore from the district which produced $50,000,000 in the early days. The branch was abandoned in 1932 (B&C, US West, pp. 169, 172, 174). Although some claims are still worked in a desultory way there, only extensive rock ruins and a cemetery remain of the famous boom town (HPS, 1/24/54; NM).

Variants of the post office name were Candalaria, at the time of establishment on August 18, 1876, Candalara, according to the Official Register of 1879, and Candelaria, as of November 23, 1882, in Esmeralda County. The post office, found to be in Mineral County upon its creation in 1911, continued operations until January 31, 1939 (FTM, p. 5).

The name of the town, post office, and mining district, as well as that of the **CANDELARIA HILLS** (in which the district is situated near the boundary line between Esmeralda and Mineral counties, fifty-three miles northwest of Tonopah and six miles northwest of Columbus Marsh) derives from **CANDELARIA CLAIM**, located on May 22, 1865, and named by its unidentified Spanish discoverers (VPG, p. 111; MA, p. 419; HHB, Nev., p. 259; SPD, p. 56). *Mount Candelaria* was an earlier name for the hills where the claim was located (1881 Map). The Spanish word for "Candlemas Day," also a family surname, may be commemorative or a transfer from the Candelaria Mine, San Dimas, Mexico (M&SP, 2/28/80).

CANE. The specific, frequently applied to a spring, creek, or wash because of cane plants found nearby, has a curiously unstable orthography. **CANE (KANE) SPRINGS** (Humboldt) denotes springs and a locality south of Orovada and north of the Bloody Hills. A mine and a mill so named lie south of the springs (GHM, HU 4). The early settlement was served by Paradise Valley post office (TF, p. 16; 1881 Map) until *Amos* post office was established at the site in 1889 (HHB, Nev., p. 264; JML, p. 15;

FTM, p. 1). **CANE CREEK,** north of Buffalo Spring Station, was an early name for Pine Creek (1881 Map). The name of the triangulation station west of Cane Springs is spelled *Cain* (GHM, HU 4). In Lincoln County, **KANE (CANE) SPRINGS VALLEY** and **WASH,** which run from a point near Elgin to Coyote Springs Valley, are named for nearby **CANE SPRING.** A prominent elevation in the area is named **KANE** (Dir. 1971; GHM, LN 2; WA). **CANE (KAIN) SPRING,** a spring fifteen miles north of Amargosa on Skull Mountain, furnished a name for **CANE SPRING WASH,** southeast of Jackass Flats, in Nye County (Furn. Cr. Quad.; GHM, NY 8). **CANE** is also the name of a creek, tributary to the Reese River, north of Bridges in Lander County, and of a spring and an old "pony" station a few miles above Moapa in Clark County (GHM, CL 2; WA; Son. R. Quad.; GHM, LA 2). **CANE SPRING WELLS** is mentioned in J. H. Martineau's account of the explorations of the Desert Mission in 1858 (Wheat IV, 128).

CAÑON. A station on the LV and T RR between Amargosa and Rosewell, or Roses Well (Furn. Cr. Quad.). The railroad company was incorporated by William A. Clark, the Montana copper king, on September 22, 1905, and construction started in 1906. Between Goldfield and Beatty, the LV and T RR ran parallel with the BG RR until the two lines were consolidated on July 1, 1914. The route of the LV and T RR has been usurped by a modern highway through this desert region of Nye County, and the name of Cañon Station has disappeared from modern maps (RRE, p. 6; JGS, I, pp. 419, 423–24, 527). **CAÑON** (Lander) was an alternate name for *Reese River Canyon,* a station on the NC RR, fifty-three miles southeast of Battle Mountain (DM).

CAÑON CITY (Lander). A short-lived boom town of the 1860s, established at Big Creek on the western slope of the Toiyabe Range, seven miles south of Austin. Although rich silver-bearing ore was found here, the ledges proved to be small and the strike less valuable than anticipated. **CAÑON CITY** post office was established August 19, 1863, and discontinued October 14, 1867 (FTM, p. 5). In January of 1864, Artemus Ward spoke at this mining camp in a saloon constructed of mud and willows (FTM, p. 5; MM; HNS, p. 129).

CANYON. A term employed to show that land features so denoted are either in or near a canyon, actually resulting in a double generic. **CANYON CREEK** denotes a stream in Elko County, rising in the Humboldt National Forest east of Pole Creek Ranger Station, and joining Pole Creek at a confluence north of Choke A Man Draw (NK 11–9); and a creek in Humboldt County rising on the west slope of the Santa Rosa Range, southwest of Buckskin Mountain, and flowing to the Quinn River. The alternate spelling *Cañon* appears on earlier maps. Early *Cañon Station* (Humboldt), named for the creek on which it was situated, was served by Fort McDermitt post office (1881 Map; TF, p. 16; NK 11–8). **CANYON PEAK** (Lincoln) is a peak in the Needle Mountains, east of Ursine on the Utah boundary (GHM, LN 1). In Clark County, **CANYON POINT** denotes a ridge at the mouth of Boulder Canyon, and **CANYON SPRING,** a spring about six miles to the west of Mormon Well, between the Las Vegas and the Sheep ranges (NJ 11–12; WA).

CANYON STATION (White Pine). This station on the Overland Stage road, east of Deep Creek and near the Utah boundary, was attacked by Gosiute Indians who murdered the station keeper and burned the station on March 24, 1863 (SPD, p. 158; 1867 Map).

CAPITOL (Clark). A mining camp, established prior to 1904 about six miles southeast of Nelson in **CAPITOL WASH;** named for the old **CAPITOL HILL** mine (WA; Dir. 1971).

CARBONATE WASH (Nye). A watercourse heading about two miles west-northwest of Oak Spring Butte and trending generally northeastward to an unnamed watercourse in the western portion of Emigrant Valley, about six miles east of the Belted Range; named for "prominent ledges of carbonate rocks which are found on the slopes of the wash" (DL 53).

CARIBOU HILL (Eureka). The name of an isolated hill of massive quartz or quartzite, on which was located the Eureka Consolidated Mine (MA, p. 434). In 1875, the RH RR, five miles in length, was built for the purpose of carrying ore from the Eureka Consolidated Mine to the furnaces at Eureka because "on the road from Eureka to Ruby Hill the mud averages three feet in depth and teamsters find it almost impossible to get their ore wagons from the mines to the furnaces" (M&SP, 11/21/74; GHK, Bonanza, p. 87; MA, p. 286). The name of the hill was originally spelled Cariboo and may have been bestowed by prospectors who knew of the Cariboo Mines of British Columbia which were opened in 1858 (Gudde, p. 51; MA, p. 434). The name of the animal has its origin in eastern Algonquian dialects and signified *pawer* or *scratcher,* "the animal being so called from its habit of shoveling the snow with its forelegs to find the food covered by snow" (FWH, I, p. 206).

CARICO (Lander). **CARICO LAKE VALLEY,** lying between the Shoshone and Toiyabe ranges, southwest of Crescent Valley;

CARICO LAKE RANCH at the northern end of the valley; and **CARICO PEAK** in the Red Mountains west of the valley; named for **CARICO DRY LAKE** (GHM, LA 1 and 2).

CARLIN (Elko). A town on Interstate 80, a connecting point of the SP RR and the WP RR, twenty-four miles southwest of Elko. **CARLIN CANYON** had been an impassable gorge before the CP RR in 1867; therefore, emigrants camped near the site of the present town of Carlin before making a detour northwest through Emigrant Pass in the Mary Creek Mountains (Nev. Guide, p. 125; RC, p. 43). According to an early guide, in the vicinity of Carlin four little creeks came in from the north. In the order crossed, they were called Susie, Maggie, Mary, and Amelia. "Tradition says in regard to these names, that an emigrant was crossing the plains with his family at an early day, and that in this family were four daughters in the order given, and that as the party came to these streams, they gave the name of each one of the daughters to them" (FES, p. 180). The town, settled in the 1860s by J. A. Palmer, S. Pierce, C. Boyen, and James Clark (MA, p. 396), grew rapidly when it became a terminus of the Humboldt Division of the CP RR on December 20, 1868 (GAC, p. 137). Railroad officials named the station for William Passmore Carlin, an officer in the Union Army (SHM 112). A line of six-horse stages ran from Carlin to the Railroad Mining District, Mineral Hill, and Eureka. **CARLIN** post office was established December 4, 1868 (FTM, p. 5). **CARLIN RESERVATION** was situated on Maggie Creek about a mile and a half north of Carlin. By Executive Order dated November 9, 1874, and amended April 7, 1875, 960 acres were reserved. No military post was ever built there, and the land was relinquished to the Department of the Interior on March 20, 1886 (Ruhlen).

CARMAN HEIGHTS (Douglas). Formerly a settlement about eighteen miles southeast of Gardnerville; named for E. W. Carman, an executive of the Longfellow Gold Mining Company located there (DM).

CARP. A post office, a station on the main line of the UP RR, and a locality, first settled in 1907, thirty-eight miles south of Caliente in Lincoln County. The town at first was named *Cliffdale,* descriptive of the cliffs surrounding it (OPN, p. 42). The station was named Carp by railroad officials, in commemoration of an employee, and the operator also served as postmaster since the post office was in the station. At the suggestion of an operator named Tom Casey, postal officials also adopted the name *Carp,* effective December 1, 1925 (WA; FTM, p. 5). An earlier post office of the same name,

in Eureka County, was established April 6, 1888, and discontinued January 3, 1889 (FTM, p. 5).

CARPSDALE (Lincoln). The order, dated June 29, 1918, establishing **CARPSDALE** post office, was rescinded before operations commenced (FTM, p. 5).

CARRARA (Nye). **CARRARA** townsite, on U.S. 95, was laid out May 8, 1913, and named for **CARRARA MINING DISTRICT,** ten miles south of Beatty on the west flank of Bare Mountain. Marble deposits were worked here as early as 1904 by the American Carrara Marble Company, whose plant was dismantled in 1936. A post office served the area from May 24, 1913, until September 15, 1924, when Beatty became the mail address for its patrons. The district was named after the white marble region found near Carrara, a city in northwestern Italy (Gen. Land Off. Map; NM; FTM, p. 5).

CARROLL. A summit in the Desatoya Range, on the boundary line between Lander and Churchill counties; an early mining district and a post office (December 11, 1911–November 30, 1914) named for the summit (JML, p. 15; OPN, p. 9; FTM, p. 5).

CARSON. The western Nevada place name complex honors J. C. Frémont's "true and reliable friend, Kit Carson" (JCF, Report, p. 119). The following excerpt is from a letter written by Frémont at Prescott, Arizona, on March 8, 1881, and quoted by Myron Angel. "Carson River, as well as the others in that region, Humboldt, Walker, and Owens, with the Pyramid and other lakes, were named by me in the winter journey of 1843–44" (MA, p. 26). Christopher Carson (1809–1868), the celebrated guide, had entered western Nevada with Frémont in the winter of 1843–44. The **CARSON RIVER** has its source in the Sierra Nevada, runs generally northeasterly through the northwest section of Douglas County, through Carson Valley, and empties into Lahontan Reservoir. About two miles southeast of the valley, the east and west forks unite to form the main river. **CARSON LAKE,** south of Fallon in the southwest quarter of Churchill County, has an irregular shape and alkaline waters. A name variant is **CARSON LAKE PASTURE** (Dir. 1971; GHM, CH 1). The name *Carson* for the river and the lake appears on the Frémont (Preuss) Map of 1848 (Wheat III, pp. 56–57).

CARSON VALLEY is east of Lake Tahoe, enclosed between the Sierra Nevada and the Pine Nut Mountains. It is one of the principal valleys of Douglas County and furnished a name for the first United States post office within the present boundaries of Nevada. First established in Carson County, Utah Territory, on December 10, 1852, **CARSON VALLEY** post office was within the boundaries of Nevada Territory, created March 2, 1861, and remained a territorial post office until August 20, 1863(?), when the name was changed to *Genoa* (FTM, pp. vi, 5). The "New National Map" by S. Augustus Mitchell, published in 1856, includes the name of the valley (Wheat, IV, 49). **CARSON VALLEY BOTTOMS,** the former name of the Big Bend of the Carson, begins one mile above Dayton in Lyon County and extends twelve miles down the river (NHS, 1913, p. 208). A variant name for the bottom land is **CARSON PLAINS** (Dir. 1971; GHM, LY 1).

The large **CARSON SINK** is in the north-central part of Churchill County, north of Fallon. The sink is so designated on John R. Bartlett's general map of the exploration and survey made by the United States and Mexican Boundary Commission (1850–1853), published in 1854 (Wheat, III, 240). **CARSON SINK STATION,** on the line of the Pony Express, was west of Sand Hill and southeast of Desert Station and named for its location in the sink (Nev. I, 1961, 8). **CARSON SINK RANGE** (Churchill), a principal range of the county, runs north through the central portion. The range is also called *Dun Glen*. Both are local names for part of the Stillwater Range. (NHS, 1913, p. 181; OPN, p. 9). **CARSON SLOUGH** connects the Humboldt and Carson sinks. A toll bridge spanned the slough in 1862. See **REDMAN STATION.** Additional names in the area include **CARSON INDIAN COLONY,** south of Carson City; **CARSON DIVERSION DAM,** northeast of Lahontan Reservoir; and the **CARSON RANGE,** a mountain range extending southerly from north of Lake Tahoe, in Washoe County, into Douglas and Carson City counties (Dir. 1971; GHM, WA 1).

CARSON CITY (Carson City). The capital of Nevada is at the junction of U.S. 395 and U.S. 50, on the route of the Pony Express and the Overland Stage Company. Carson City was also the county seat of Ormsby County (q.v.) until *Statutes of Nevada 1969,* Chapter 213 (SB 75), consolidated Ormsby County and Carson City into one municipal government. The town was served by the now defunct V and T RR (GHK, V&T, p. 31). The first building erected at the site of what was later to become Carson City was called *Eagle Station.*

Early in November of that year [1851] a party, consisting of Joe and Frank Barnard, George Follensbee, A. J. Rollins, Frank Hall, and W. L. Hall, came from Bents Bar [Brent's Bar (Nev. Guide, p. 199)], Placer County, California, for the purpose of mining in western Utah, but finding the pay was not sufficient to warrant them in doing so, they took up, in December, the celebrated Eagle Ranch, where now stands

the State Capitol. . . . An eagle soaring over the heads of the builders was shot and killed by Frank Hall, and the skin stripped from the bird was stuffed and nailed upon the station. This incident furnished a name for the station that was transferred to the ranch, and eventually to the valley that surrounded it. (MA, p. 31)

Many of the early settlers of Eagle Valley were Mormons who, upon leaving in 1857, sold their holdings to John Mankin. Finding Genoa lots expensive, the colorful Abraham V. Z. Curry, with F. M. Proctor, B. F. Green, and J. J. Musser, bought the Eagle Ranch from John Mankin to lay out a townsite (MA, p. 550; Nev. Guide, p. 199). According to Dan De Quille, the town was not regularly laid out until 1858, when Major William M. Ormsby purchased the land and named the place Carson City (DDQ, pp. 6–7). The post office was established on November 18, 1858 (FTM, p. 5). On June 12, 1859, Captain James H. Simpson described the settlement as having about a dozen small frame houses and two stores, Major Ormsby being the proprietor of one (JHS, p. 91). Some Carson City buildings were constructed from stone from the Carson City sandstone quarry, at the prison east of the city, which the state purchased from Curry in 1864 (NHS, 1913, p. 193). See **GOULD AND CURRY.** The name of Eagle Ranch was changed to Kings Ranch (DDQ, pp. 6–7; NHS, 1913, p. 193), but *Eagle* is still used for the valley in which Carson City is situated. The Official Map Washoe Mining Region by R. M. Evans, published in 1860, includes the names *Carson* for the town and *Eagle* for the valley (Wheat V, Pt. I, 16). **CARSON RAPIDS CITY** was near the mouth of Six-Mile Canyon (Lyon) in 1860. "The name was probably derived from the fact that in the Carson River at that place there were some ripples that seemed like rapids to the people who had just passed over the long stretches of desert in crossing Nevada" (NHS, 1913, p. 207). This name also appears on the R. M. Evans map of 1860.

CARTER(S) (Douglas). A station in the 1870s halfway between Twelve Mile House and Double Springs, and **CARTER CANYON,** north of Double Springs; named for Charles Carter, the owner of the station (NHS, 1913, p. 193; SG Map 4B; 1881 Map). Walker River was the mail address for the station (TF, p. 16).

CARVILLE CREEK (Elko). The name of this creek, southeast of Jiggs in the Ruby Mountains, is commemorative of the Edward Carville family, pioneer residents of northeastern Nevada. A son, Edward P. Carville, was governor of Nevada from 1939 to 1945 (JGS, II, p. 496; GHM, EL 1; M&S, p. 307).

CASELTON (Lincoln). A town established by Combined Metals Reduction Company in the 1920s at the south slope of Ely Mountain; named for J. A. Caselton, an official of National Lead Company. The town and its flotation mill, built by Combined Metals in 1941, are connected with Pioche by a branch of the UP RR, called the Prince Consolidated Railroad for the Prince Mine (GHM, LN 1; Freese, Map 2; WA).

CASKET (Churchill). A short-lived post office of eastern Churchill County (June 7, 1882–January 8, 1883); perhaps named by Merrill W. Hoy, the postmaster, by report of the *Battle Mountain Messenger,* July 22, 1882 (FTM, p. 5; DM).

CASTLE. Orographic features thought to resemble castles are often so named. **CASTLE MOUNTAIN** (Eureka) is a peak in the Fish Creek Range. **CASTLE PEAK MINING DISTRICT** (Storey), also called *Red Mountain,* is ten miles north of Virginia City on **CASTLE PEAK** near the Washoe County boundary. **CASTLE ROCK** denotes a peak southwest of Zephyr Cove in Douglas County; a mining district of Esmeralda County, eight miles north of Blair Junction and about thirty-five miles west of Tonopah; and an Overland Mail station of the early 1860s in Lander County, eleven miles northeast of Edwards Creek Station, as given in Poor and Connelley's compilation (VPG, pp. 50, 168; JGS, I, p. 136; Dir. 1971; GHM, EU 1; GHM, DO). **CASTLE LAKE** (Elko), a small lake in the Ruby Mountains, is named for Saxon Castle, an employee of the U.S. Forest Service (EP, p. 18).

CAT CREEK (Mineral). **CAT CREEK,** rising in the Wassuk Range on the southeast slope of Mount Grant southwest of Walker Lake, flows through Wild Cat Canyon. By report of the *Walker Lake Bulletin,* April 11, 1883, **CAT CREEK MILL** was located northwest of Hawthorne on the creek for which it was named. The features were named for the bobcat, which inhabits the intermediate mountain ranges and ledgy country of Nevada (Haw. Quad.).

CATHEDRAL. The name is often applied to orographic features with imposing rock formations reminiscent of a cathedral, and to places near those features. **CATHEDRAL GORGE STATE PARK** (Lincoln). A few miles west of Panaca, 1,578 acres were set aside as a park in 1935. "Striking features of this park are displayed in the peculiar rock weathering. Erosion through the ages has moulded diversified patterns of intrinsic design, fluted the rocks in varied fashions, formed lofty, and in some instances, isolated sentinels resembling cathedral spires" (NP, p. 59; Park and Guide maps). **CATHEDRAL COVE** (Clark) is a cove on Lake Mead at the eastern extremity of **CATHEDRAL PEAKS** for which it was named. **CATHEDRAL ROCK** denotes a peak on the south edge of upper Kyle Canyon and southeast of Charleston Peak in the Spring Mountains (WA). **CATHEDRAL CANYON** (White Pine) is a picturesque gorge on the west slope of the White Pine Range and north of Green Springs (VPG).

CATON (Lander). Formerly a station on the NC RR twenty-three miles north of Austin Junction; named for the Caton family who had a ranch there (MM).

CAVE. CAVE VALLEY, east of the South Egan Range in Lincoln County, was named by the George M. Wheeler Survey made between 1869 and 1873. It had been called *Three Butte Valley* by J. H. Martineau in 1858. During the same year, George Washington Bean led an exploring party and included a description of the valley caves in his report to Brigham Young. "The main cave is half a mile in length and varying in breadth from five to sixty feet. The smaller caves or branches are from ten feet to one hundred yards in length and from ten to twenty five feet wide, they are from seven to twenty five feet high" (Wheat IV, pp. 122–125, 132). The caves and **CAVE VALLEY RANCH** are at the north end of the valley, west of the Schell Creek Range. **CAVE VALLEY** post office was in operation from June 24, 1926, until January 31, 1933 (GHM, LN 1; FTM, p. 5; NJ 11–6). **CAVE VALLEY MINING DISTRICT,** also known as *Patterson* and *Geyser,* is fifty miles south-southeast of Ely (VPG, p. 97). **CAVE CITY** is said to have been the first town in the White Pine Mining District and to have been so named because of the numerous hillside dugouts which served as shelters for the miners. Hamilton later grew up at the site of the old camp (NM, p. 101). Other features of White Pine County named for natural caves are **CAVE MOUNTAIN** and **CAVE CREEK** southeast of Ely in the Schell Creek Range. A spring and a reservoir in the area are named for the creek (GHM, WP 1). **CAVE CREEK** (Elko) designated a post office, established November 5, 1887, and discontinued April 30, 1929, when Ruby Valley became the mail address of its patrons (FTM, p. 5). The post office was at the **CAVE CREEK RANCH,** owned by Thomas Short and situated at the south end of Ruby Valley. The name derives from a great underground lake, from which a river of ice-cold water cuts its way. The cave was explored in the early days by A. G. Dawley and Thomas Short, who built a boat within the narrow opening of the cave. "They passed from one huge cavern to another perhaps a quarter of a mile beyond the opening when at last they were confronted by a large formation resembling a pipe organ arrangement. This they termed the 'Great Organ' " (SPD, p. 822; GHM, EL 1). **CAVE CANYON** is the name of a canyon southwest of Palisade in the Cortez Mountains in Eureka County, and a canyon east of Getchell Mine in the Osgood Mountains in Humboldt County (GHM, EU 2; HU 1). **CAVE SPRING** (Esmeralda) is a spring in the Silver Peak Range, while **CAVE SPRINGS** (Lincoln) denotes a locality where, in 1904, the Utah Construction Company maintained a hospital for the benefit of the men building the railroad in Meadow Valley Wash (JML, p. 15; DM). **CAVE ROCK** (Douglas), through which U.S. 50 passes, is on the shore of Lake Tahoe south of Glenbrook, and was named for the natural cave in it. Population figures for this settlement were recorded as early as 1870 (Census, 1870; AEH; GHM, DO 1).

CEDAR. In Eureka County, **CEDAR CREEK** rises on the east slope of the Monitor Range south of Summit Mountain, and flows into Antelope Valley (NJ 11–2). **CEDAR HILL**, the site of early mineral discoveries, is a small hill near Virginia City in Storey County, north of **CEDAR HILL RAVINE.** Both the hill and the ravine were named for the large growth of western juniper (*Juniperus utahensis* and *Juniperus menosperma*) found there and used for fuel or for timbering in the mines (NHS, 1913, pp. 190–91). **CEDAR HILL MILL** was at the foot of Cedar Hill Ravine. The **CEDAR MOUNTAINS** extend from the northern part of Esmeralda County, along the Nye County line into Mineral County. The mountain range was named for the native growth of trees. **CEDAR MOUNTAIN MINING DISTRICT**, in the northern part of the range, twenty-two miles northeast of Mina near the Nye County boundary, in Mineral County, was named for the range (VPG, p. 112; NJ 11–5). **CEDAR BASIN** (Clark) is a valley south of Gold Butte in which a mining district of the same name was located in 1904 (WA; DM). Other mining districts named Cedar were organized fifteen miles south of Cliff Springs in Lincoln County (DM) and twenty miles west of Mill City in the Trinity Range of Pershing County. The latter district is also called *Antelope* and *Majuba Hill* (VPG, p. 149).

CEDAR, a name often applied by railroad builders, denoted stations on two Nevada narrow-gauge lines and on the SP RR. A side-track station of this name on the SP RR was six miles east of Wells at **CEDAR PASS** (T1SL). "In general this pass resembles a rather rough, broken plateau, bent upward in the middle, forming a natural road bed from the desert to Humboldt Valley. It was once covered with scrub cedar, which has been cut off for wood" (GAC,

p. 128). The station served a camp of wood choppers in the mountains to the west of it (FES, p. 174; SG Map 2). On the E and P RR, **CEDAR** was a way station between Oak and Summit (MA, p. 286; HHB, Nev., p. 285). **CEDAR SWITCH,** or **CEDAR,** was a point between Summit and Francis on the NCO RR which began regular train service on October 2, 1882, from Reno to Antelope, California. The railroad was completed to Lakeview, Oregon, on January 10, 1912. The WP RR purchased the main line out of Reno to Herlong, California, on March 24, 1917; standard gauge operations began on February 4, 1918, the last narrow-gauge train on the line, nicknamed the "Narrow, Crooked, and Ornery," or the "Northern California Outrage," having left Reno on January 30, 1918 (N-C-O Map; DM, pp. 6–14; B&H, p. 506).

CEDAR WASH, one of a group of Lincoln County features named for heavy stands of juniper by early settlers prior to 1870, appears to be the last of these places still to bear the name. The wash drains into Delamar Valley south of Delamar. The **CEDAR MINING DISTRICT,** delineated on George M. Wheeler's 1871 map, seems to be in the area of the present Delamar Mining District. In his 1872 Report, Wheeler explains that "this district was discovered in 1871, and lies on the western side of Bennett Spring [Chief] Mountains and nearly due east from Pahranagat Lake" (p. 43). From this Walter Averett has deduced that the district, if not at the present Delamar, may have been near the Chief Mining District south of Pioche. The proximity of the big wash to the old mining district probably accounts for its name. North and east of Pioche, the name *Cedar* denoted a valley and a mountain range. **CEDAR VALLEY** has vanished as a name for upper Ursine Valley, and the mountains are now called the Wilson Creek Range (WA). **CEDARHURST,** a post office in Ursine Valley, operated from August 11, 1922, until October 31, 1928 (FTM, p. 5).

CENTENNIAL. See **BULL RUN** and **EDGEMONT.**

CENTERVILLE. A settlement in Douglas County two miles south of Waterloo on the road to Woodfords; named for its position in the middle of the valley (OPN, p. 19; NHS, 1913, p. 187). **CENTERVILLE** (Churchill). A small town two miles west of Leeteville; named because of its being at the fork of two roads and serving as a central meeting place (NHS, 1913, p. 173).

CENTRAL. A lake, usually dry, between Boulder Lake and Forty-Nine Lake in Long Valley, northern Washoe County; named for its position (Gen. Land Off. Map; OPN, p. 66). Two mining districts in the Eugene

Mountains are named **CENTRAL**. In Humboldt County, the district, also known as *New Central,* is in the northern part of the Eugene Mountains eight miles southwest of Pronto (VPG, p. 70). Principal producers in the early days were the Teamster, Golden Age, Railroad, Locomotive, Hammond, and Monarch mines (SM, 1875, p. 62). In Pershing County, the district so named and also known as *Mill City* is on the southeast slope of the Eugene Mountains, seven miles northwest of Mill City (VPG, p. 154). **CENTRAL** post office, Nye County, was established by an order of March 22, 1906, rescinded September 19, 1906 (FTM, p. 5). **CENTRAL HILL** (Storey), a ridge between Cedar Hill and Mount Davidson, was the site of the Central Mining Company's mill, incorporated in 1860 (NHS, 1913, p. 191).

Two claims designated as **CENTRAL NO. 1** and **CENTRAL NO. 2** were staked here in 1859. The former, located by John Bishop, included 150 feet along the Comstock Lode. The Ophir and the California mines were at this time considered to be the most important claims along the lode, and the Central ground was so denominated because of its position between the two (DDQ, p. 27; HDG, CP, 12/23/76). It may be assumed that Central No. 2 derives from Central No. 1. Both claims are patented (AR, No. 50, No. 71). There is the possibility of transfer of the name from California, where mines named *Central* were located in Amador, Shasta, and El Dorado counties (RWR, pp. 50, 565–66), or from Lake Superior copper mines where a rich vein, designated the *Central,* was discovered in 1854 (TAR, p. 235).

CENTRASVILLE (Nye). An old mining camp, established in December of 1884 between Ione and Grantsville; named for John Centras who came to the area from Virginia City (DM).

CHAFEY (Pershing). A temporary name for Dun Glen, a settlement and post office at the eastern side of Buena Vista Valley in old Humboldt County, presently within the boundaries of Pershing County. **CHAFEY** post office, established August 4, 1908, existed until March 4, 1911, when the older name *Dun Glen* was adopted again. The name commemorates E. S. Chafey, owner of the **CHAFEY MINE**. *Chaffey* was an alternate spelling (Gen. Land Off. Map; 1910 Map; FTM, p. 5; DM).

CHALK MOUNTAIN (Churchill). By decision of the United States Board on Geographic Names, **CHALK MOUNTAIN**, not *Grey Hills,* denotes the mountain about four miles northwest of West Gate; apparently named for the light gray coloration of its carbonate rocks (USGB 5904; NJ 11–1).

CHALLENGE (Storey). A traditional name for a Comstock claim, consisting of ninety feet, located in 1859 (JAC, p. 1; IH). Later the mine became a part of the Challenge-Confidence consolidation. At the present time the Challenge is a patented claim. Origin of the name is undetermined.

CHALLENGE–CONFIDENCE (Storey). A consolidation of the Burke and Hamilton claim, Challenge claim, and some footage from the Imperial South, totaling 237.5 feet, between the Yellow Jacket and the Imperial mines on the Comstock (IH).

CHAMPION SPARK PLUG MINE (Pershing). A mine in the West Humboldt Range, near Oreana; named for dumortierite formerly produced there. Dumortierite, an aluminum borosilicate, was, at the time the mine was active, the finest known material for spark plugs (HPS, 1/29/56; VPG).

CHARCOAL CANYON (Nye). The canyon three miles southwest of Morey Peak was "named for the charcoal kilns at its mouth" (USGB 6903).

CHARLES SHELDON WILDLIFE REFUGE. In northeastern Washoe County and northwestern Humboldt County, on the Oregon state boundary; perhaps named for Charles Monroe Sheldon (1857–1946), American clergyman and author (Park and Guide maps; NK 11–7). Large protected herds of the pronghorn antelope are on the tablelands of the **CHARLES SHELDON ANTELOPE RANGE** (Nev. Guide, p. 17).

CHARLESTON. A town, formerly a post office (January 31, 1895–July 31, 1951), and a mining district, fifty miles north-northwest of Deeth in Elko County; named for Tom Charles, a miner who lived there in 1895 (OR, 1899; FTM, p. 5; OPN, p. 22; NK 11–9). **CHARLESTON**, formerly a station on the LV and T RR, was in Nye County near the Clark County line (Vegas Quad.). **CHARLESTON MOUNTAIN(S)** is a local name for the central portion of the Spring Mountains, the largest and highest mountain mass in southern Nevada (WA; VPG). **CHARLESTON PEAK** (Clark), altitude 11,912 feet, lying at the head of Kyle Canyon, is the tallest peak in the Spring Mountains, has public camps, picnic grounds, and is a winter-sports area. The peak, called *Nüvant* by the Southern Paiutes, was "the most famous place in the mythology of both the Chemehuevi and the western bands of the Southern Paiute" (Kroeber, Handbook, p. 596). Chosen in 1869 by a topographic mapping group of United States Army Engineers, the toponym is commemorative of Charleston, South Carolina (WA). **CHARLESTON MINING DISTRICT** is thirty miles west of Las Vegas, in the Spring Mountains (VPG, p. 23). **CHARLESTON FOREST PRESERVE.** See **DIXIE.**

CHASE (Elko). A spring on the east side of Spruce Mountain Ridge in southern Elko County; a creek heading in the East Humboldt Range below Steele (Gibbs) Lake and flowing generally northeast into Clover Valley (NK 11–12; SG Map 10; GHM, EL 5). The spring was first named *Whitton(s)* by John C. Frémont in November, 1845, for one of his men who discovered it. The name appears on the Frémont (Preuss) 1848 map and on the S. Augustus Mitchell 1856 map, but has since been lost (Wheat III, 57; IV, 49). Emigrants passing that way in 1846, including the Donner Party and later parties, called the campsite *Mound Springs* (VPG).

CHEROKEE (Lincoln). An old copper-silver mine and district one-fourth mile southeast of Carp in the Mormon Mountains; named for Scott Allen, a Cherokee Indian, who relocated the mine in 1900. "The tribal name is a corruption of Tsálagi or Tsáragi, the name by which they commonly called themselves, and which may be derived from the Choctaw *chiluk-ki*, 'cave people,' in allusion to the numerous caves in their mountain country" (FWH, I, pp. 245–46). The earlier name for the district is said to have been *Long Valley*, named for that part of the Meadow Valley Wash between Leith and Carp, earlier called Long Valley. The name was changed to *Kiernan* in 1908, for John Kiernan who had purchased the ground. The district presently is known as *Viola*, having been named for a daughter of Kiernan (WA; VPG, p. 101).

CHERRY CREEK. The name designates a creek in Elko County northwest of Elk Mountain near the Idaho boundary (NK 11–9); a creek in Garden Valley, west of the Golden Gate Range in Lincoln County (Freese, Map 2); and a stream in northern White Pine County which furnished a name for **CHERRY CREEK,** a settlement and a post office (established June 11, 1873) at the mouth of **CHERRY CREEK CANYON.** The canyon heads in the **CHERRY CREEK RANGE** just north of the Egan Range and about sixty-eight miles southeast of Elko, bounded by Steptoe Valley on the east and by Butte Valley on the west, in Elko and White Pine counties (DL 60). A variant spelling of the post office name was *Cherry-creek* (OR, 1899). **CHERRY CREEK STATION** is west of Cherry Creek on the NN RR, ninety-one miles southwest of Cobre (NK 11–12; NJ 11–3). **CHERRY CREEK MINING DISTRICT** (White Pine) was discovered in 1872, fifty miles north of Ely (SPD, p. 1045; 1881 Map; VPG, p. 177). Some of the principal mines were the Teacup, Exchequer, Pacific, Gray Eagle, Chance, Flagstaff, and Victorine (SM, 1875, pp. 165–66); however, the Star Mine was the leading producer in halcyon days. When the mines

suspended operations, some of the population remained to raise grain and hay and to graze cattle and sheep (JGS, I, p. 320). The creek was named for chokecherries in the canyon through which it flows. The name-spread occurred between 1872 and 1883, when Cherry Creek was one of the chief mining camps of White Pine County. **CHERRY CREEK** in Churchill County runs through **CHERRY VALLEY** on the north side of the Clan Alpine Mountains and empties into Dry Lake. The creek was named for the valley which took its name from wild cherry trees there (NHS, 1913, p. 176; NM).

CHERRY SPRING. A spring approximately four miles south of Sheep Spring in the Sheep Range of central Clark County; an early settlement in Butte Valley (White Pine), north of Cherry Creek which served as a mailing address for its inhabitants (WA; TF, p. 16; 1881 Map).

CHERT RIDGE (Lincoln). A ridge extending northward from the Buried Hills and bordered on the north and west by Emigrant Valley, on the east by the Fallout Hills (USGB 6001); named for the dull-colored, flintlike rock of the ridge.

CHIATOVICH CREEK (Esmeralda). A creek rising in the White Mountains and flowing into Fish Lake Valley north of Dyer; named for the John Chiatovich family. John Chiatovich, born in southeastern Europe, was a pioneer of Virginia City, Nevada. He moved to Fish Lake Valley, hauled some of the first logs from the White Mountains, and operated the mill of the famous Mary Mine for seven years. He took ranch property for his pay (NJ 11–7; JML, p. 15; JGS, III, p. 211). Transformation of *Chiatovich* to *Chlatevigh* (SG Map 15) probably was caused by confusion of sounds.

CHICKEN CREEK (Elko). A creek north of Jack Peak in the Independence Mountains; named for the numerous sage grouse there (GHM, EL 2). **CHICKEN CREEK SUMMIT** is on State Route 11 between Jack Creek and Deep Creek (GHM, EL 1).

CHICKEN SOUP SPRING. See **ELKO.**

CHIEF (Lincoln). The **CHIEF RANGE,** also called *Chief Mountain* and earlier *Bennett Spring Mountain* (WA), is approximately two miles south of the Highland Range and three miles north-northwest of Caliente (DL 60). **CHIEF MINING DISTRICT,** also called *Caliente,* was located in 1870 eight miles north-northwest of Caliente in the range; it had a revival in the 1930s because of the activities of the Caliente Cobalt Mining Company and for a time was known as the *Cobalt* district (Wheeler 1871 Map; VPG, p. 92; WA; SPD, p. 930). Among the principal producers of the district were the Lucky Hobo, Lucky Chief, and Gold Chief. Scottish prospectors named both the Highland

and Chief ranges. See **HIGHLAND CHIEF** and **CEDAR.**

CHILDS STATION (Lyon). An early stage and trading station between Dayton and Silver City; named for the owner, John S. Child (NHS, 1913, p. 211). In 1858, Governor Cumming, who succeeded Brigham Young as governor of Utah Territory, appointed John S. Child probate judge of Carson County (JGS, I, p. 127).

CHIMNEY CREEK. Creeks named for nearby-chimneylike rock formations include a stream rising on the west slope of the Santa Rosa Range and flowing to Tony Creek, north of the Bloody Run Hills in Humboldt County; a creek rising on Elk Mountain, north of Red Point, tributary to Wilson Creek, in northern Elko County near the Idaho line (NK 11–8; SG Map 11). **CHIMNEY CREEK** (Elko), a branch of the South Fork Owyhee River, empties into **CHIMNEY CREEK RESERVOIR,** northeast of Silver Lake. The creek was so named for the chimney of a coke oven that was nearby (NK 11–8; EP, p. 20).

CHINATOWN. See **DAYTON.**

CHINO CREEK (Elko). An intermittent stream rising on the west slope of the Tuscarora Mountains and flowing to Chimney Creek Reservoir (NK 11–8); "named by the Spanish and Mexican buckaroos of the Spanish Ranch for the Chinese who used to cut sagebrush in the area to be used as fuel for the mines" (EP, p. 20).

CHIQUITA HILLS (Clark). A Spanish place name meaning "little" for a group of hills about twenty-five miles south of Searchlight, the site of the **CHIQUITA MINE,** located about 1900 (WA; GHM, CL 3).

CHLATEVIGH. See **CHIATOVICH CREEK.**

CHLORIDE. An early mining camp below the crest of the ridge on the west side of the White Pine Range in White Pine County (SM, 1875, pp. 164–65); a mining district located in 1867, and its camp on the east flank of the Monitor Range in Nye County, later renamed *Danville* (DM; NM). The following account explains the meaning of "chloride camp" to a mining man of the nineteenth century.

> There is a silver ore, usually of a very high grade, in which the silver occurs in the form of a chloride. In the economy of nature rich ore is usually scarce and the chloride veins are often small. Frequently miners through discovery or lease of these small veins arrange to work them carefully and on a small scale without wasting the ore. Thus they made money, whereas by the usual slovenly day's pay methods, the work would not pay expenses. Such miners are called "chloriders" and the work is called "chloriding." A camp where such work is the characteristic one is called a "chloride camp." Gradually, all work for

ore on a small scale, even when the metal is gold, lead or copper, has been termed "chloriding." The term is less used now than in former years. (NHS, 1913, p. 100, n. 8)

CHLORINE (Nye). A town, established in July of 1906 in the northwestern portion of the county, ten miles from Ione; a former station on the LV and T RR, between Roses Well and Gold Center, in the Amargosa Desert (DM; Furn. Cr. Quad.).

CHOATE (Humboldt). The mine was located and the town laid out on Kings River in northern Humboldt County, by report of the *Reno Evening Gazette,* April 6, 1907 (DM).

CHOCOLATE. Features named for the predominantly chocolate coloration of their rock include **CHOCOLATE BUTTE** (Pershing), a butte at the northeast end of the Buena Vista Hills in Antelope Valley (USGB 6002); and **CHOCOLATE MOUNTAIN** (Nye), a peak in the north portion of Yucca Mountain (USGB 6303).

CHOKECHERRY CREEK (White Pine). A stream rising on the east slope of the south end of the Snake Range and flowing generally southeastward into Snake Valley; named for chokecherries growing in the area (NJ 11–6).

CHOKUP PASS (Elko). The pass, now known as *Railroad,* is at the head of Diamond Valley (NK 11–12). Frémont entered the pass on November 11, 1845. The displaced name commemorates a Shoshone Indian chief, known to Captain Simpson in 1859. "Among the Sho-sho-nees who have visited our camp is Cho-kup, the chief of the Humboldt River band of the Sho-sho-nees" (JHS, p. 667; JGS, I, p. 94). In a report dated September, 1856, to Brigham Young, United States Indian Agent Garland Hunt mentions a band of Indians on the Humboldt under Chief *Sho-cup-ut-see* (SPD, p. 33). Colonel Warren Wasson reported the death of *Sho-kup* in a letter to Governor James W. Nye, Nevada Territory, dated June 28, 1862 (SPD, p. 154; MA, p. 178).

CHOLLAR (Storey). The mine name commemorates William ("Billy") Chollar, who located it in Virginia City as a surface or placer claim in 1859. The claim consisted of 700 feet between the Hale and Norcross and the Bullion (IH; JAC, p. 1). Henry Comstock contended that he "staked out" the Chollar and presented it to Billy Chollar, described by De Groot as a clear-headed business man, who, being of a convivial disposition, sometimes spent his money lavishly. After exploring his ground unsuccessfully by means of a tunnel, he sold out and returned to his home at Grass Valley, California, where he engaged in mining until 1867, or 1868. At that time he went to

Connecticut where he reportedly died (GDL, Saga, p. 35; HDG, CP, 12/30/76). The Comstock Chollar is a patented claim (AR, No. 61).

CHOLLAR–POTOSI (Storey). Billy Chollar sued the adjoining Potosi Company in December, 1861, claiming trespass; the $1,300,-000 suit lasted until 1865 when the two companies were consolidated as the Chollar-Potosi Mining Company. The consolidation lasted until 1878 when it again became two companies (IH; EL, pp. 151–163; OL, Silver, p. 35; MA, p. 613).

CHOLONA (Pershing). A name of uncertain meaning for a station on the WP RR main line, ten miles northeast of Trego at the southeast edge of the Black Rock Desert (T54; Dir. 1971).

CHUKAR CANYON (Nye). This canyon, named for the red-legged partridge commonly called the chukar, extends from the southeast side of Timber Mountain to Fortymile Canyon, about nineteen miles east-northeast of Beatty (DL 61). "The first known introduction of chukars into Nevada appears to have been made in 1935" (GCC, p. 13).

CHURCHILL. A county in west-central Nevada, created by territorial act of November 25, 1861, which organized the first nine counties of Nevada Territory. County seats have been as follows: Bucklands, by act of November 25, 1861; La Plata by act of February 19, 1864; Stillwater, by act of the state legislature in 1868; and Fallon, by an act approved March 5, 1903 (SPD, pp. 786–794; M&S, pp. 149–50; OPN, p. 3). The first mineral discoveries in Churchill County were made in the Silver Hill District in 1860. By 1865, Mountain Wells, Clan Alpine, and Desert districts were producing (SM, 1865, pp. 28–29). Presently, in addition to its importance in agriculture, the county is also a center of honey production in Nevada (M&S, p. 197).

Churchill County was named for **FORT CHURCHILL** in Lyon County. The killing, by already restive Indians, of several white men who, according to report, mistreated some Indian squaws at Williams Station on the Overland Trail, precipitated the Pyramid Lake Indian War of 1860 and the building of Fort Churchill. "The Carson River Expedition," dispatched to Nevada under the command of Captain Joseph Stewart, arrived at the site for the new fort on the Big Bend of the Carson River on July 20, 1860, following their fight with the Paiutes near Pyramid Lake on June 2. Shortly thereafter, at the suggestion of Captain Stewart, the fort was named in honor of General Sylvester Churchill. Sylvester Churchill, a native of Vermont, first became a commissioned officer on March 12, 1812, Inspector General on June 25, 1841, and Brigadier General on February 23, 1847, for gallant and meritorious conduct at the Battle of Buena Vista, Mexico (Ruhlen).

With the establishment of Fort Churchill and the concentration of the Paiutes on reservations, Indian warfare in Nevada returned to simply a matter of occasional murder, robbery, or minor crimes. The fort served as headquarters and main supply depot for the Nevada Military District throughout the Civil War; as a station on the Pony Express, between Bucklands and Reeds stations; and as the eastern terminal of Fred A. McBee's Placerville, Humboldt, and Salt Lake Telegraph Company's line. Nevada's first and most important military reservation (ordered abandoned by a directive dated May 19, 1868) was vacated a short time after the building of the transcontinental railroad. The fort was sold at auction for $750 in 1870, and the reservation was relinquished to the General Land Office on June 15, 1871. Until 1935, when Fort Churchill was designated a state park and historic landmark and when some restoration work was started by the Civilian Conservation Corps, there was nothing left at the site except a ranch bearing the same name (Ruhlen; HPS, 1/24/54; MA, p. 360; Nev. Guide, p. 268; NHS, 1913, pp. 218–19; JGS, I, p. 142; Dir. 1971; NJ 11–1).

FORT CHURCHILL post office was established on October 9, 1860, and discontinued for the first time on December 19, 1861, operating again from November 22, 1878, until February 14, 1882, and from April 10, 1905, until September 9, 1924 (FTM, p. 10). **CHURCHILL** (Lyon), a station, milepost 26, on the Mina Subdivision of the SP RR between Weeks and Wabuska, was earlier called *Fort Churchill Station* (DM, T75; NJ 11–1). **CHURCHILL VALLEY,** on the lower Carson River in which Lahontan Reservoir is situated, is east of the station. **CHURCHILL CANYON** is northwest of Wabuska and extends into Douglas County. **CHURCHILL BUTTE** is the name of a peak, north and a little west of Fort Churchill (Wab. Sheet; Car. Sink 1908; Nev. Terr. Map).

CIRAC VALLEY. The valley extends from the Royston Hills in Nye County to Cedar Mountain in Esmeralda County and is thirty miles northwest of Tonopah. The name commemorates "Lewis Cirac, a pioneer settler and prospector in the area" (USGB 7101). **CIPAC MINE** appears on a 1907 map (Tono. Quad.).

CIVET CAT (Nye). A canyon extending from Pahute Mesa to Stonewall Flat, about five miles northeast of Stonewall Mountain and twenty miles east-southeast of Goldfield; a cave in the upper reach of Civet Cat Canyon, approximately one mile east-northeast of the site of Gold Crater; named for the small spotted skunk (genus *Spilogale*) found in the western states (USGB 6303).

CLAIM CANYON (Nye). The canyon so named extends from Yucca Mountain, just northwest of Chocolate Mountain, to Yucca Wash, about one mile northeast of The Prow and eleven miles west-southwest of Topopah Spring (USGB 6303).

CLAN ALPINE (Churchill). The **CLAN ALPINE MOUNTAINS** are "separated on the north from the Augusta Mountains by a stream which drains into Dixie Valley and from the New Pass Range by a pass, bounded on the south by the pass at West Gate, and separated on the west from the Louderback Mountains by Badger Flat and Hercules Canyon" (USGB 5904). **CLAN ALPINE MINING DISTRICT**, also known as *Alpine*, was organized in 1864 on the east slope of the Clan Alpine Range fourteen miles north of Eastgate (SM, 1867, pp. 28–29; KU; 1867 Map; VPG, p. 11). Because ore returns diminished, **CLAN ALPINE MILL**, built in 1866, was removed to White Pine County in 1867. **CLAN ALPINE**, a settlement and post office (March 12, 1866–May 21, 1868) in the range, served the mill and the mining district (HHB, Nev., pp. 261–62; OPN, p. 10; NHS, 1913, p. 183; FTM, p. 5). It is probable that the first application of the name in Nevada was coincident with the discovery of the district in 1864 and that the descendants of Alpin King of Scots (fl. 787), whose patronymic MacAlpine is usually termed the Clan Alpine, are commemorated. Sir Walter Scott's historical novel concerning Rob Roy, a descendant of Alpin, may have been influential.

CLARK. **CLARK COUNTY** was created from southern Lincoln County by an act of the state legislature, dated February 5, 1908. Las Vegas was made the seat of the county when it was created. Now an expanding industrial and entertainment center, the site has been desirable since 1830 when it was a campsite on the Old Spanish Trail (OPN, p. 4; M&S, pp. 162–63; Nev. II, 1962, 22–25). The county name honors William A. Clark, United States Senator from Montana, who built the SPLA and SL RR, also known as the Clark Road and the Salt Lake Route and purchased by the UP RR. The first regular passenger trains left Salt Lake City and Los Angeles at the same hour, inaugurating the service of the SPLA and SL RR on June 2, 1905, the day the last spike was driven at Jean, Nevada (M&S, p. 162; JGS, I, p. 419).

CLARK (Storey) denotes a mountain mass, south of the Truckee River and northeast of Long Valley Creek, about fourteen miles east-southeast of Reno (USGB 5904); a post office established November 2, 1906, rescinded in the spring of 1907, again established in 1912, and finally discontinued July 31, 1919 (FTM, p. 6); and a station on the SP RR, twenty-two miles east of Reno, between Thisbe and Patrick (1881 Map). James Clark, a boss over Chinese laborers who were imported for the building of the CP RR, settled at the site around 1862. He was known as Uncle Jim Clark, and the station name commemorates him (NHS, 1911, p. 87; SPD, p. 1029). A timetable of 1892 (T1TR) lists this station as *Clarks* on the Truckee Division.

CLARKDALE (Nye). A gold-silver mining district, also known as *Tolicha* and *Monte Cristo*, located in Pahute Mesa twenty-six miles north of Beatty (VPG, p. 139).

CLARKE (Nye). An early mining district near Ivanpah, situated partly in Nevada and partly in California; named for Clarke Mountain in San Bernardino County, California, the site of the first discoveries in the district (Wheeler, 1872, p. 53). Alternate names for the mountain are *Clarkes Peak* (Wheeler 1871 Map) and *Clark Mountain* (Gudde, p. 62).

CLARKS (Washoe). A post office in operation from April 19, 1890, until March 29, 1894, at which time Reno became the mail address for its patrons (FTM, p. 6).

CLARKS STATION (Storey). See **CLARK.**

CLARKS WELL (Clark). The well is on the southeast slope of Crescent Peak, approximately ten miles west of Searchlight (WA; Dir. 1971).

CLAYTON (Esmeralda). Joshua E. Clayton, an early settler, is commemorated by **CLAYTON VALLEY**, a complete interior basin lying east of the Silver Peak Range (Wheeler, 1872, p. 78; OPN, p. 30; NJ 11–8). **CLAYTON RIDGE** is at the southeast side of Clayton Valley from which it takes its name (DL 60).

CLEAR CREEK. A mountain stream running from the Sierra Nevada to the Carson River, partly on the boundary line between Douglas and Carson City counties (GHM, CC 1). **CLEAR CREEK STATION**, about five miles south of Carson City near the creek for which it was named, was a famous stage station and a headquarters for sheepherders. An anecdote of local interest concerning Clear Creek is of a man seeking political office, who decided his chances for winning were better in Ormsby County (now called Carson City) than in Douglas County. He changed the course of the creek so that it ran south of his property and gave him official residence in Ormsby County (NHS, 1913, p. 187). Clear Creek was one of the four election precincts organized December 24, 1861. Three large sawmills were built on its banks in 1862 (SPD, pp. 975, 980).

CLEAR CREEK MINING DISTRICT, organized in 1859 in the spurs of the Sierra Nevada west of Carson City, was abandoned, then worked again in 1874 (NHS, 1913, p. 187). The name appears on Henry De Groot's Map of the Washoe Mines of 1860 (Wheat IV, 189). **CLEAR CREEK FOREST CAMP GROUND** lies southwest of Carson City (Dir. 1971; NJ 11–1). The name complex derives from the creek, described by James H. Simpson in 1859 as a "beautiful stream" (JHS, p. 92).

Other streams so named include a tributary of Deep Creek in the Independence Mountains of Elko County (JML, p. 15; SG Map 11); a tributary of the Reese River north of Stewart Creek and a creek which empties into **CLEAR LAKE** east of Monitor Peak in the Monitor Range, both in Nye County; and a stream, also known as *Bowman Creek,* which rises on the east slope of the Toiyabe Range in Lander County, and flows southeastward into Big Smoky Valley in Nye County (NJ 11–5; SG Map 6; NJ 11–2). **CLEAR CREEK** (Washoe) is tributary to Squaw Creek in the Granite Range (GHM, WA 2). An early mining district of Pershing County south of the Sonoma district in the East Range was named for **CLEAR CREEK,** a stream south of Raspberry Creek, later called *Dun Glen Creek* (TF, p. 14; 1881 Map; GHM, PE 2).

CLEAVER (Lyon). A former station on the C and C RR, southeast of Wabuska in Railroad Valley; **CLEAVER PEAK,** northwest of the station and at the northeast extremity of the Walker Lake Indian Reservation (1881 Map; Wab. Sheet). The name honors Kimber Cleaver, born near Toronto, Canada, on July 10, 1837. He became a rancher in Lyon County in 1873 (MA, p. 499).

CLEMENS (Churchill). A post office of north-central Churchill County established October 29, 1892, and discontinued June 26, 1895, when Lovelock(s) became the mail address for its patrons (FTM, p. 6).

CLEOPATRA (Clark). Daniel Bonelli, a prominent early settler of southern Nevada, discovered and named the **CLEOPATRA,** a manganese mine. **CLEOPATRA WASH,** in which the mine was located, trends eastward from the Black Mountains and empties into **CLEOPATRA COVE** at a point below Surprise Reef (WA). Both the wash and the cove took their names from the mine which commemorates the Egyptian Queen, Cleopatra VII (or VI), died 30 B.C. See **BONELLI.**

CLEVE CREEK (White Pine). An intermittent stream rising on the eastern slope of the Schell Creek Range and flowing into Spring Valley. **CLEVE CREEK BALDY** is named for the stream, which rises on its eastern slope (JML, p. 15; NJ 11–3).

CLEVELAND (White Pine). A settlement and post office of early White Pine County; named for Abner C. ("Cleve") Cleveland, who was born in Skowhegan, Maine, in 1838 and migrated to California in 1862. He lived in western Nevada during territorial times, but joined the rush to White Pine, taking up a ranch in Spring Valley. He also established the **CLEVELAND GRADE** through Illipah Canyon and to Pioche (NHS, 1911, p. 77; 1924, pp. 274, 367; SPD, p. 183; JGS, II, pp. 103–105). The post office was established as **CLEVELAND** on July 24, 1882, operations being discontinued on February 15, 1905. **CLEVELAND RANCH,** the largest ranch under fence in Nevada in 1910, furnished a name for a post office, established April 19, 1917, and discontinued on November 17, 1924 (FTM, p. 6; DM). See **TAFT.**

CLIFFDALE (Lincoln). A locality, settled about 1907, thirty-eight miles south of Caliente; named for the cliffs sourrounding it. A post office, named for the settlement, served the area from June 7, 1921, until December 1, 1925, when postal officials changed the name to *Carp* (FTM, p. 6; WA). See **CARP.**

CLIFFORD (Nye). A gold-silver mining district and a former mining camp, thirty-five miles east of Tonopah; discovered in 1905 by John Peavine, an Indian from Tonopah, by report of the *Carson City News* of September 25, 1908, and named for two brothers, James and Edward M. Clifford (VPG, p. 125; DM).

CLIFFS, THE (Clark). The cliffs so named are along the south shore of Las Vegas Bay on Lake Mead, nine miles northeast of Henderson. A variant name is *Brush Hole* (USGB 7202).

CLIFSIDE (Elko). A station on the main line of the WP RR about three miles southeast of Silver Zone Pass; named for a nearby cliff (T54). **CLIFSIDE WELL,** southeast of the station for which it is named, has a variant spelling *Cliffside* (GHM, EL 5; Dir. 1971).

CLIFTON. A high hill behind this water-tank siding in Lyon County on the old C and C RR, eighteen miles from Mound House, probably caused railroad officials to choose the name (GHM, LY 1; NHS, 1913, p. 206). **CLIFTON** (Lander) denoted a settlement at the mouth of Pony Canyon, which grew up as a result of the discovery of silver ore in 1862. A post office so denoted operated from March 26, 1863, until February 20, 1864 (NM; FTM, p. 6). See **AUSTIN.**

CLINTON (Lander). The name of undetermined origin denoted a short-lived post office of Lander County, dating from April 23, 1864, to December 23, 1864 (FTM, p. 6).

CLIPPER GAP (Lander). A natural defile in the Toquima Range in southern Lander

County. **CLIPPER GAP CANYON** runs northwest from Clipper Gap to Big Smoky Valley (Robt. Mts. Quad.).

CLOUD (Lincoln). Formerly a siding on the UP RR, thirty-four miles south of Caliente and in the Meadow Valley Wash. Originally named *Saint George,* in 1920 the siding was renamed *Rappelje* in honor of a railroad official. The name *Cloud* was adopted about 1928 and remained the railroad designation until the abandonment of the siding in 1949 (WA; Freese, Map 2).

CLOVER. A place name often chosen by early settlers to describe geographical features, usually creeks or valleys, having an abundant growth of these trifoliate plants. **CLOVER CREEK** (Lincoln), tributary to the Meadow Valley Wash, drains the **CLOVER MOUNTAINS** (also called **CLOVER VALLEY MOUNTAINS**) from a point east of Caliente. This group of mountains is immediately southeast of Caliente, within Lincoln County, Nevada, and Washington County, Utah (DL 60; GHM, LN 2). The valley of Clover Creek, which takes its name from the creek, had been called *Badger Valley* by James H. Martineau, the historian of the "Southern Exploring Company," a Mormon group organized in April, 1858 (Wheat IV, 126–27). It was settled by the Edwards, Atchison, and Syphus families in 1865, until Indian troubles drove them away. In 1869, Lyman L. Woods, sent by Brigham Young to settle in the region around the Muddy River, entered Clover Valley and asked permission to settle there. **CLOVER VALLEY** post office was established in Washington County, Utah Territory, on April 10, 1871, with Lyman Woods serving as postmaster (FTM, p. 35), and was registered as a Nevada post office from September 10, 1873, until November 5, 1887. See **CALIENTE.** The Lincoln County settlement served as a supply source for railroad builders in the county (1881 Map; NJ 11–9; JGS, I, p. 602). **CLOVER CREEK** (Nye) rises on the eastern slope of the Monitor Range and flows generally eastward into Little Fish Lake Valley (NJ 11–5). **CLOVER VALLEY** (Elko) lies south of Wells, bounded by the East Humboldt Range on the west and by Independence Valley and Spruce Mountain Ridge on the east (NK 11–9; NK 11–12). A post office so named served the residents of the valley from October 18, 1872, until September 10, 1873, and again from July 12, 1921, until October 31, 1924, when Wells became the mail address for its patrons (FTM, p. 6). From January 7, 1896, until March 14, 1903, the name of the postal station was shortened to *Clover* (Cad. Map; FTM, p. 6).

CLOVER CITY (Elko). From December 11, 1918, until January 18, 1921, **CLOVER CITY** was the official designation for *Tobar* post office (FTM, p. 6), denoting a Mormon colony on Tobar Flat (EP, p. 20).

CLOVERDALE (Nye). This early settlement in central Nevada was southwest of the Toiyabe Range, about twenty-two miles west of Manhattan. The post office was first established on January 26, 1886, by an order rescinded on July 24, 1886. On September 21, 1888, the post office was reestablished and operated until October 13, 1899, when San Antonio became the mail address for its patrons (FTM, p. 6; 1881 Map). The Belmont-Cloverdale wagon road was a principal highway of the desert in the 1860s (JML, p. 15; SPD, p. 971). **CLOVERDALE CREEK** flows southward from Indian Valley to **CLOVERDALE RANCH. CLOVERDALE SUMMIT** takes its name from the creek (NJ 11–5; GHM, NY 2).

CLURO (Eureka). A station on the main line of the WP RR and on a spur of the SP RR, seven miles east of Beowawe. Near Cluro, the old emigrant road crossed the Humboldt River at Gravelly Ford (T75; T1TR; 1881 Map; GAC, p. 141).

COAL. Places in Nevada named for local coal deposits include **COAL VALLEY,** a valley lying between the Seaman and Golden Gate ranges in Lincoln and Nye counties (GHM, NY 5, LN 4); **COAL SPRING,** a spring west of Lovell Summit in the Spring Mountains in Clark County; **COAL CREEK** (Washoe), a stream southwest of Nixon in the Pah Rah Range; **COAL CANYON** (Pershing), a canyon south of Rochester Canyon in the West Humboldt Range (GHM, CL 1, WA 1, PE 2). Coal deposits northwest of Halleck in Elko County, formerly designated **COAL** or **COAL SHAFT** (TF, p. 16; 1881 Map), have given rise to a name group. **COAL CANYON MINE** is named for **COAL CANYON** which heads south of Tower Mountain in the Independence Mountains. **COAL MINE** is the name of a prominent elevation east of the mine. **COAL MINE CREEK** and **COAL MINE SUMMIT** are south of the canyon (NJ 11–6; VPG; GHM, EL 3).

COALDALE (Esmeralda). The settlement on U.S. 95, north of Emigrant Peak and east of Columbus Salt Marsh, was named in the 1880s when William Groetzinger (Groezinger), a German prospector, while working under a grubstake agreement with William A. Ingalls, discovered deposits of bituminous coal in the area (SPD, p. 885). A post office, in operation from October 6, 1904, until July 28, 1908, and a station on the now defunct T and G RR were named for the settlement (FTM, p. 6; Tono. Quad.).

COATES WELLS (Churchill). A station and watering place, twelve miles east of Fort Churchill and eighteen miles west of Carson Lake, on the old road to Austin. This early station name commemorated the owner (NHS, 1913, p. 179; HHB, Nev., p. 261; TF, p. 15).

COBB CREEK. The commemorative name for a stream rising southeast of Bald Mountain in the Humboldt National Forest, southwest of Mountain City in Elko County, and for an intermittent stream rising at the north end of the White Rock Mountains in northeast Lincoln County, and flowing to Hamblin Valley Wash (Dir. 1971; NJ 11–6). The Elko County creek "was named for Mr. Cobb, an Oregonian, who came to the Mountain City area around 1870" (EP, p. 21).

COBRE (Elko). A town on the Elko Subdivision of the SP RR and the northern terminal of the NN RR. The earlier station name was *Omar,* perhaps commemorating a caliph, or Omar Khayyam, the poet. As a result of the copper discoveries in the Robinson Mining District, the rail junction was named *Cobre* (the Spanish word for "copper") at the suggestion of O. H. Hershey, who had recently returned from Mexico and was present at a meeting held by railroad officials for the purpose of selecting a name (DM). The NN RR, controlled in the beginning by the Nevada Consolidated Copper Company, was incorporated on May 29, 1905. Work began from Cobre on September 9, 1905, and the first shipment of blister copper from the Robinson district was made August 7, 1908. Prospering from its beginning, the NN RR has hauled more mineral wealth than any other short line railroad in Nevada (RRE, pp. 10–12; Gen. Land Off. Map). With one two-year interruption, **COBRE** post office was in operation from March 12, 1906, until May 31, 1956 (FTM, p. 6).

COCKEYED RIDGE (Nye). The ridge so named is about seventy-eight miles northwest of Las Vegas in the Halfpint Range. The name was applied to the ridge in 1963 and is descriptive of its asymmetrical profile (USGB 6301).

COFFIN. An early station so named was eight miles south of Wadsworth on an old toll road, in Lyon County. The station operators, James Coffin and his two brothers, are commemorated (NHS, 1913, p. 212). **COFFIN** (Elko) is the name of a mountain in the Sulphur Springs Range (GHM, EL 1).

COIN (Elko). A town and side track station on the SP RR and the WP RR, between Elko and Halleck (T75; T54). Settlement of the town began with the completion of the transcontinental railroad to this point in 1869, when railroad officials named the station (OPN, p. 22). **COIN** formerly denoted a mining camp active in 1907, twenty miles northwest of Winnemucca, in Humboldt County (DM).

COLADO (Pershing). A station on the SP RR, between Woolsey and Kodak; named by railroad officials (T75; NK 11–10).

COLD. In Churchill County, **COLD SPRINGS** denoted "a small running brook of icy-cold, pure water, which I call Cold Spring, and which, after running a few hundred yards, sinks" (JHS, p. 106); **COLD SPRINGS STATION,** on the old Overland Trail and on the line of the Pony Express, was ten miles southwest of Edwards Creek and fifteen miles east of West Gate at the base of the mountain from which the stream flowed. Simpson called the mountain *Sedaye* (JHS, p. 106; NHS, 1913, p. 173). Also named for nearby cold springs was a station on the former NCO RR, northwest of Lemmon Valley in Washoe County (Reno Sheet). **COLD SPRING** is the term of relative description for a spring east of Alkali Flat and northeast of Hot Spring in the northwest extremity of Nye County (Haw. Quad.). **COLD CREEK** is the name for a stream which rises on the western slope of the Ruby Range and flows into Lamoille Valley, northeast of Lamoille in Elko County; a creek flowing from the eastern slope of the Diamond Range into Gilson Valley in White Pine County; and a settlement on the creek. A post office so named served the settlement from April 7, 1879, until March 28, 1913, when Simonsen became the mail address for its patrons (Freese, Map 3; ECN Map; FTM, p. 6). **COLD CREEK SPRING** (Clark), northeast of Charleston Peak and west of Willow Spring in the Spring Mountains, takes its name from **COLD CREEK,** which flows generally northward from the Spring Mountains toward Indian Springs (Vegas Quad.). In Lincoln County, a spring so denoted is about three miles southwest of Panaca (WA).

COLE. A commemorative name of undetermined origin for a creek east of Sprucemont, and a creek south of Carlin, both in Elko County; a spring and **COLE MOUNTAIN,** a peak northwest of Stonewall Flat, in Nye County; **COLE SPRING WASH** south of Sagehen Wash in the Wilson Creek Range, in Lincoln County (GHM, EL 1, 5; NY 7; LN 1).

COLEMAN. The surname denotes a valley which extends from Washoe County, Nevada, into Lake County, Oregon; a creek flowing through the valley; a ranch on the creek (GHM, WA 3). **COLEMAN CREEK** (Humboldt) rises on the east slope of the Santa Rosa Range and flows into Paradise Valley (NK 11–8). **COLEMAN CANYON,** near Gold Creek in Elko County, takes its name from the **COLEMAN MINE** (EP, p. 21).

COLONY (Lyon). The station on the former NCB RR between Hudson and Ludwig presumably took its name from the **COLONY RANCH,** near Hinds Hot Springs. Many

Californians came to Colony Ranch, later called *Simpson Colony*, and formed a **COLONY DITCH** and townsite. The name derived from the ideal of the promoters to have a model cooperative, or colony (NCB Map; Dir. 1971; NHS, 1913, p. 217).

COLORADO. This Spanish descriptive adjective meaning "red" is a name of limited application in Nevada and stems from the Colorado River. In August, 1540, Captain Fernando Alarcón named the river *El Rio de Buena Guia* ("river of good guidance") in commemoration of the motto on Viceroy Mendota's coat of arms. In 1540 and 1541, Cárdenas and Díaz called the river *Rio del Tizon* ("firebrand river") after seeing Indians carrying firebrands. Other early names for the river were *Rio Grande de Buena Esperanza* ("great river of good hope"), applied by Juan de Oñate in 1604, *Rio de los Martires* ("river of the martyrs"), given by Eusebio Kino, and *Rio Colorado* and *Rio del Norte,* adopted by Juan Mateo Manje in 1699. In 1700 and 1701, Kino applied the names *Rio Colorado, Rio del Norte,* and *Rio Colorado del Norte* ("red river of the north"). The river was called *Buqui Acqumuri* (Pima Indian for "red river") and *Gritetho* (Cocomaricopas for "great" or "grand river") by Fr. Sedelmayr in about 1746. Other Indian names were *Pa-ha-weap* (Southern Paiute for "water deep down in the earth") and the Navajo name *Pocket-to* (Gudde, pp. 67, 68; Barnes, p. 141).

Erwin G. Gudde has determined that "the name Colorado was first applied by the Oñate expedition in October, 1604, to what is now the Little Colorado in Arizona, 'because the water is nearly red' " and that the name was transferred to the larger river by Kino in 1699; whereas Byrd H. Granger attributes the name origin to Garcés' translation of the Yuma Indian name *Javill* or *HahWeal,* meaning "red," as *Rio Colorado* (Barnes, pp. XIII, 141). *Javill* is also said to have been applied because the river ran through an area of red rock.

The hybrid name *Colorado River,* which is thought to have appeared for the first time on Cary's Map of 1806 (Gudde, p. 67) is the English equivalent of *Rio Colorado* shown on the Bernardo Miera y Pacheco map of the Dominguez-Escalante expedition, 1776, extant in six manuscript copies and containing "enough geographical, historical, and anthropological data to make them the rival of Escalante's diary" (GGC, p. 49; VPG). Miera had accompanied Fr. Silvestre Vélex de Escalante and Fr. Atanasio Domínguez in 1776 when they traveled from Santa Fe, New Mexico, to Monterey, California. On this journey and one through Oraibi the previous year, Fr. Escalante referred to the Colorado as the *Rio Grande de los Cosninas,* probably a corruption of *Coconino,* since the Coconinos lived west of Oraibi in the area of the present Coconino County, Coconino Plateau, and Coconino sandstone. A letter written late in 1775 to the governor of New Mexico and diary entries for October 16, and October 20, 1776, by Escalante, indicate that he knew the *Rio Cosnina* to be the *Rio Colorado.* Fr. Escalante's name appears on Miera's map as *Silbestre Veles* (VPG; GGC, pp. 43–47).

In 1826, Jedediah Strong Smith called the river the *Seeds Keeder.* Variants are *Seedekeeden, Seeds Keeden,* and *Seedskeedeer* (GGC, pp. 155, 199; JGS, I, p. 26; NHS, 1920, p. 216). According to Rufus Wood Leigh (p. 137), the Crow Indian name for the Green River in Utah was *"Seeds-ke-dee Agie,* for 'Prairie Hen River'—*Agie* meaning 'river.' " Since the Colorado River receives the Green River in Utah, it seems likely that Smith applied the Crow name for the tributary to the larger river.

American cartographers of the 1840s and 1850s referred to the Red River of the West or Red River of California. Whipple's sketches of 1853 mentioned the Southern Paiute name *Uncah Pah* (*Pah* means "water") and the Yuma name *HahWeal Asientic* (of undetermined meaning).

The application of the color adjective "red" by numerous Spanish name-givers, as well as by Pima and Yuma Indians and American explorers, who viewed the river from various locations, would indicate that the name is descriptive of the water and alludes to the heavy mud load carried by the river (WA).

COLORADO MINING DISTRICT (Clark), also called *Eldorado Canyon,* was named for the river and is twenty-four miles northeast of Searchlight, in the Opal Mountains (Wheeler 1871 Map; VPG, p. 24).

COLORADO PLACER MINE (Pershing) is west of Vernon in the Bluewing Mountains (GHM, PE 1).

COLOR BACK MINE (Lander). See **BLUE EAGLE.**

COLUMBE(R)T CREEK (Elko). The name for a creek northwest of Jarbidge (GHM, EL 3; SG Map 11); "named after Pete Columbert, a horse king in the vicinity from 1868 to 1890" (EP, p. 21).

COLUMBIA. This poetic name for America (especially the United States), deriving from Christopher Columbus, occurs in at least four Nevada counties. In early December of 1902, W. A. Marsh and H. C. Stimler, prospectors from Tonopah, located claims just north of the summit of **COLUMBIA MOUNTAIN,** near Goldfield in Esmeralda County. Their claims were recorded, along with those of Jim Butler and Tom Kendall, and the district was called "Grandpa in jest at Hinnepah . . . and Tonopah, believing they had found the grandpa(h) of all, the old man" (SPD, p. 861). The entire region around Columbia Mountain was known as Grandpa until, by resolution of October 20, 1903, the name of the district was changed to Goldfield (SPD, pp. 866–67; Gen. Land Off. Map). A post office so named operated from November, 1904, until May, 1919. Also in Esmeralda County were **COLUMBIA JUNCTION,** formerly a station on the T and G RR, just north of Goldfield (Lida Quad.), named for the mountain, and **COLUMBIA MINE,** located on Last Chance Hill in the early days (SM, 1866, pp. 34–35). In Clark County, a pass in the Spring Mountains on the road between Jean and Sandy is so denoted, having taken its name from the nearby **COLUMBIA MINE** (Freese, Map 1; WA). **COLUMBIA** (Elko) designates a creek north of Bull Run Mountain and east of Bull Run Creek, northeast of Aura, and a mining district, better known as *Aura,* located in 1869 on the eastern slope of the Bull Run Range (1881 Map). A post office, about ten miles southwest of Mountain City, was named for the Columbia district, which it served from February 24, 1879, until November 27, 1882, and again from January 30, 1883, through September 15, 1902, when Mountain City became the mail address for its patrons (FTM, p. 6). **COLUMBIA** (Humboldt) is an alternate name for the *Varyville* Mining District, at the south end and on the east slope of the Pine Forest Range, twelve miles to the west of Quinn River Crossing (SM, 1867, pp. 34, 35; VPG, p. 77).

COLUMBUS. After the Aurora excitement, **COLUMBUS MINING DISTRICT** was the first persistent mining district to organize in Esmeralda County. Mexican miners who made the locations in December, 1864, were replaced soon after by Germans, Americans, and Slavonians, in ownership of claims and in control of the district. Principal producers among the five-hundred to six-hundred locations made in the twenty-mile-square district were the Mount Diablo, Black, Metallic, Columbia, Northern Belle, Peru, Potosi, Bellmarte, Pappinaux, and Vulture (SM, 1867, pp. 148–151; Wheeler, 1872, p. 48; 1871 Map). The town of **COLUMBUS** (now abandoned), about eight miles southeast of Candelaria, was laid out near the edge of a salt marsh in 1865 (Haw. Quad.) and named for the district. The Candelaria claim was located in 1865, and Columbus prospered because of its close connection with the new town, whose residents had to have water brought from Columbus. Except for a few months in early 1871, a post office of this name operated from April 2, 1866, until March 2, 1899 (FTM, p. 6; SPD, pp. 855–56; 1881 Map; SM, 1867, pp. 37–44).

COLUMBUS SALT MARSH took its name from the town. In 1872, the Pacific Coast Borax Company began extensive operations there, under the leadership of William T. Coleman, Chris Zabriskie, John Ryan, and Francis Marion ("Borax") Smith. The latter, in 1904, incorporated the T and T RR, the first railroad to attempt entrance to Nevada mineral discoveries from the south (NM, p. 113; Nev. Guide, p. 222; RRE, p. 6). **COLUMBUS** (Lander) was the name of an early mining district, located twenty miles north of Austin on the western slope of the Toiyabe Range (SM, 1867, pp. 97–103).

COMB PEAK (Nye). The peak, named for its resemblance to a cock's comb, is at the east end of Yucca Mountain, about two miles south-southeast of Vent Pass and seven miles west-southwest of Topopah Spring (USGB 6303; DL 58).

COMET (Lincoln). The **COMET** and **SILVER COMET** mines, located in 1882 on the west end of the Highland Range, furnished a name for **COMET PEAK,** the site of discovery, about fourteen miles southwest of Pioche. **COMET,** a station on the UP RR, is southeast of the peak (WA; VPG, p. 93; GHM, LN 1).

COMMONWELTH (Washoe). Formerly a station on the V and T RR, between Washoe and Steamboat. Although the name has been spelled Commonwealth, the original station name apparently was without the *a,* as it is given by Gilbert H. Kneiss (V&T Map).

COMO. In northeast Douglas County, **MOUNT COMO,** at the head of Churchill Canyon in the Pine Nut Mountains, was named presumably by Italian settlers for Lake Como, a lake in a mountainous resort area of Lombardy, in northern Italy (NJ 11–1). **COMO,** a mining camp of the 1860s on the high slopes of Mount Como, was about fifteen miles southeast of Dayton by road. A post office, named for the camp, served the area from December 30, 1879, until January 8, 1881, and again from May 29, 1903, until February 28, 1905 (FTM, p. 6). **COMO MINING DISTRICT,** named for Mount Como, is in the north-central portion of the Pine Nut Mountains, ten miles southeast of Dayton (VPG, p. 103).

COMSTOCK (Storey). The **COMSTOCK LODE,** one of the greatest mining camps in the world, was discovered in 1859 on the eastern flank of Mount Davidson in the Washoe (Virginia) Mountains. The gold and silver lode had many bonanzas, but it was fourteen years after the discovery that the "Big Bonanza" was discovered through the efforts of John W. Mackay, James G. Fair, William S. O'Brien, and James C. Flood. Until about 1886, the Comstock yielded approximately half the silver output of the United States. The district was named for the Washo Indians and called *Washoe* before the discovery. This Indian tribe lived along the base of the Sierra Nevada, from below Honey Lake to the west fork of the Walker River (ALK, Handbook, p. 70; DDQ, pp. 34, 361–62). After the discovery, the lode was named for Henry Comstock, a prospector called "Old Pancake" by his associates because he would not take time to make bread (DDQ, p. 10; HHB, Nev., p. 98; GTM, p. 70; HDG, CP, 8/12/76).

According to his own statement, Comstock was Henry Thomas Paige Comstock, son of Noah Comstock of Cleveland, Ohio, and was born in Canada in 1820 (HHB, Nev., p. 98). A genealogy gives his name as Henry Tompkins Paige Comstock and states that he was born in Trenton, Ontario, Canada, in 1820, of a distinguished Connecticut family related to Daniel D. Tompkins, governor of New York in the early nineteenth century and once vice-president of the United States. Henry Comstock came to Nevada from Santa Fe, New Mexico, in 1853. He had been a trapper for the American Fur Company (NHS, 1911, pp. 69–71). Comstock sold the greater portion of his interest to Judge James Walsh, "the California rock sharp." The following partially explains why the Comstock Lode bears his name. "In making out the deed whereby this claim was conveyed to Walsh, it was, for want of a better name described as the "Comstock ground," a style of description which, having been adhered to in all subsequent sales of the property or portions thereof, caused this term to be at length applied to all portions of the lode" (HDG, CP, 6/29/76). For details concerning the discovery of the Comstock Lode, see **OPHIR.**

The town of **COMSTOCK** was a temporary settlement that grew around a mill, now in ruins, built in 1921 in the southeast portion of American Flat. United Comstock Mining Company and Comstock Merger Mines, Inc., which took over the former in 1924, initiated a renaissance of treasure hunting on the Comstock for a time, with the working of low-grade ores (HPS, 1/24/54; FCL, p. 224). A post office named for the town was in operation from January 9, 1923, until February 15, 1927, when Gold Hill became the mail address for its patrons (FTM, p. 6).

CONDOR (Lincoln). A canyon north of Panaca, the narrows of the Meadow Valley Wash (WA); named for the vulture. Bullionville was the mail address for former **CONDOR MILL,** named for the canyon (TF, 16). The canyon is traversed by the Pioche Branch of the UP RR.

CONFIDENCE. As staked in 1859, the claim included 130 feet along the Comstock Lode. It was later consolidated with three other claims to form the Challenge-Confidence (IH). Although the ground was staked in 1859, records under date of March 23, 1860, state "this company shall be known as the Confidence Co." (GH–B, p. 169). The mine is assessed in Storey County (AR, No. 60). Gudde (p. 69) shows the use of this name for a mill and for a settlement in Tuolumne County, California, mentioned in 1880. The date of the naming of the Confidence mine in Tuolumne County for which the settlement was named is not known (CMA, pp. 187, 359; PTH, p. 64). The time of the discoveries of Confidence mines in Kern and Fresno counties, California, is undetermined (JRB, Res., pp. 208–09). If the discoveries were post-Comstock, transfer from the eastern slope to the western slope could have occurred. Direct transfer also could have been the cause for the naming of the Confidence Mine in Lander County, Nevada (RWR, p. 130). Discounting the possibility of simple transfer of names, the prospectors in their rugged, sometimes hostile, surroundings were prone to rely upon word magic. Curle mentions the Confidence mine in the Matabeleland District in Rhodesia (JHC, p. 147).

CONGRESS. A creek in northern Pershing County; named for the old **CONGRESS MINE,** located in the early 1860s in the Buena Vista (Unionville) Mining District on the east flank of the Humboldt Range (SM, 1867, p. 52; GHM, PE 2). Another mine so named is west of Johnnie in southern Nye County (GHM, NY 8).

CONNOR. The name denotes a creek in northwestern White Pine County, east of the Diamond Mountains and near the Eureka County boundary. The variant name is *Conners Creek* (GHM, WP 3). On November 11, 1845, Captain Frémont entered Diamond Valley and named a spring just north of Eureka, in Eureka County, for Connor, one of his men (JGS, I, p. 94). **CONNOR** (Lincoln) is the designation for a canyon extending northeasterly from **CONNOR PEAK,** east of Highland Peak, and for a spring five miles west of Pioche (WA; Dir. 1971). These were named to commemorate Colonel P. E. Connor of Fort Ruby, who was sent to Pahranagat Valley in 1864 with a cavalry unit. According to Charles Gracey, "his men had located many claims both in Pahranagat and in the Pioche country" (NHS, 1909, p. 109).

CONNORS PASS (White Pine). The pass in the Schell Creek Mountains, on U.S. 50 southwest of Ely, may have been named for Colonel P. E. Connor, who established Fort Ruby in Ruby Valley, White Pine County, in September, 1862 (HWY Map; Ruhlen). See **RUBY, FORT.** Another version of the name origin is that the name of the pass is incorrectly spelled, since it is commemorative of a Mrs. Conners (RRE).

CONRAD CREEK (Elko). A stream, rising on the west slope of the Ruby Mountains, north of Lamoille Creek, and flowing into Lamoille Valley (NK 11–12); named to commemorate Jacob Conrad who settled near the creek in 1870 (EP, p. 22).

CONSOLIDATED IMPERIAL (Storey). The present Imperial mine has a total of 451 feet along the Comstock Lode and is between the Alpha and the Challenge-Confidence. The consolidation was effected on April 13, 1876, and twelve claims were absorbed: Triglone and Co., Imperial North, Bacon, Empire North, Eclipse, Trench and Co., Bowers, Piute, Consolidated, Rice and Co., Empire South, and Imperial South (IH; MA, p. 614). The claim name *Imperial* was selected in recognition of that company's ownership of the most footage along the lode. The Consolidated Imperial is included on Storey County tax rolls (AR, No. 193).

CONSOLIDATED VIRGINIA (Storey). The largest ore body on the Comstock Lode was discovered in the Consolidated Virginia mine in 1873. The mine was named for the Virginia Mining District which took its name from Virginia City. Most accounts credit James Finney, or Fenmore, or Fennimore (familiarly known as "Old Virginny," for his native state), with naming the famous mining camp (JJP, p. 237; GTM, p. 70; SPD, p. 228; GHS, p. 5; DDQ, p. 10; MA, p. 51). The present Consolidated Virginia includes 710 feet lying between the Best and Belcher and the California; however, at the time of the discovery of the largest bonanza, which produced about $105,000,000 (FCL, p. 224), all of the claims between the Best and Belcher and the Ophir had combined to sink a shaft under the name of the Consolidated Virginia (IH; GTM, p. 106; OL, Silver, p. 133; MA, p. 612). This mine is assessed in Storey County (AR, No. 155). See **VIRGINIA**.

CONTACT (Elko). A community on the west bank of Salmon Falls Creek, about fifteen miles southwest of Jackpot, and a station on the branch of the UP RR which runs between Wells and Twin Falls, Idaho. Both were named for **CONTACT MINING DISTRICT**, organized about fifty miles north of Wells about 1895. The mining district was named descriptively because it was on the "contact" of limestone and granite. The post office so named was established February 6, 1897 (FCL, p. 40; OPN, p. 22; Nev. Guide, p. 172; DL 47; FTM, p. 6). See **KIT CARSON**.

CONTINENTAL (Humboldt). A lake at the north end of the Pine Forest Range in northwest Humboldt County; presumably named by an emigrant party to commemorate their continental journey (OPN, p. 36).

COON CREEK (Elko). A trout stream southwest of Jarbidge in the Humboldt National Forest; also **LITTLE COON CREEK**. The name, probably derived from some incident with the raccoon, was adopted for **COON CREEK PEAK** and **COON CREEK SUMMIT**, southeast of the creek (GHM, EL 3). A second creek so designated is tributary to Goose Creek north of Sugar Loaf Peak, in the northeastern part of the county (GHM, EL 4).

COOPER. COOPER(S) PEAK (Eureka), southeast of Tonkin in the Roberts Mountains, apparently was named by Captain James H. Simpson in 1859; the name appears on the map of his explorations across the Great Basin of Utah (Wheat IV, 137). **COOPER CANYON** and **WASH**, north of Taylor Canyon in the Schell Creek Range, White Pine County, were named for **COOPER MINING DISTRICT**, northeast of the Taylor district. The mail address for the early mining camp was Ward (1881 Map; TF, p. 16; GHM, WP 2). The personal name also denotes **COOPER INCORPORATED RANCH** north of Millett in Big Smoky Valley, Nye County (GHM, NY 2). **COOPER SPRING** (Clark) is an alkali spring, northwest of Gass Peak in the southwest end of the Las Vegas Range. The name is of unknown origin, but nearby outcroppings of copper suggest that *Cooper* is a mistake name for *Copper*, the spring perhaps having been named for the associated mineral (Vegas Quad.; WA).

COPE (Elko). A mining district, better known now as *Mountain City*, in the northwest part of the Bull Run Range in northern Elko County. The district was discovered in 1869 by Jesse Cope and named for him (VPG, p. 44; OPN, p. 22). After listing the following principal mines of the district: Mountain City, Pride of the West, Argenta, Excelsior, Independent, U.S. Grant, Eldorado, Crescent, Idaho, Nevada, Emmett, and Saint Nicholas, George M. Wheeler (1872, pp. 34–35) observed: "A study of names on the recorder's books of the many mining districts furnishes much of an index to the character of the miners and prospectors, who often place no little stress and pride upon the names selected with so much solicitude." According to S. Frank Hunt, "Cope and Dixon, two miners on their way from Boise, Idaho, to Pioche, Nevada, made the first discovery of silver veins while enroute" (SFH, pp. 7–8).

COPENHAGEN. The name for a creek and a canyon heading on the west slope of the Monitor Range, near Butler Basin in Nye County, and extending to Antelope Valley in Eureka County (GHM, NY 3, EU 1).

Since the circumstances of the naming are unknown, it is only possible to conjecture that the toponym was applied either to commemorate Copenhagen, Denmark, or to describe the dull, light blue color of the mountain stream.

COPPER. The earliest Nevada place name of record, descriptive of this ore, is **COPPER CAÑON (CANYON)** in the Battle Mountain Mining District of Lander County. In his report of 1872, George M. Wheeler (p. 40) described the surface ores of the Virgin and Lake Superior mines of Copper Cañon as "carbonate of copper and red oxide, and the deep-seated copper glance." **COPPER,** a Lander County post office, operated from May 3, 1906, until November 15, 1906, when Battle Mountain became the mail address for its patrons. The postal name derived either from **COPPER BASIN,** southwest of Battle Mountain, where ore was discovered near **COPPER BASIN SPRING,** or from Copper Canyon. Both Copper Basin and Copper Canyon are alternate names for the Battle Mountain district, organized in the 1860s (NK 11–11; VPG, p. 81). The name *Copper* appeared in at least nine Nevada counties subsequent to copper discoveries made early in the twentieth century. **COPPER BASIN** (Elko) is at the head of **COPPER CREEK,** in the **COPPER MOUNTAINS,** the site of the **COPPER MOUNTAIN MINING DISTRICT,** fifty miles north-northwest of Deeth and southwest of Jarbidge, near Coon Creek Peak (NK 11–9; JML, p. 15; VPG, p. 57). An order authorizing the establishment of **COPPER CANYON** (Lander) post office on August 31, 1917, was rescinded. Other canyons so denoted are situated west of Walker Lake in the Wassuk Range, in Mineral County; a few miles above Nelson, in Clark County; and east of Spring Valley in the Schell Creek Range, in White Pine County (Haw. Quad.; WA; Ely Quad. 1916, 1952). **COPPER CREEK** (White Pine) is tributary to Ellison Creek in the Horse Range (GHM, WP 1). **COPPER HILL** (Mineral) was formerly a station on the SP RR, between Modoc Siding and Gillis, east of Walker Lake (Haw. Quad.). **COPPERHILL** (Esmeralda) was the designation for a post office established December 5, 1907, and discontinued by order of January 15, 1914 (FTM, p. 7). The great copper discoveries in White Pine County made at Ely in 1906 resulted in the names of **COPPER FLAT,** a station on the NN RR near Ruth, and of **COPPER CANYON** (M&S, p. 118; Ely Quad. 1916, 1952). **COPPER KETTLE MINING DISTRICT** was the name selected when copper was discovered in Grimes Canyon, northeast of Fallon on the west slope of the Stillwater Range in Churchill County (NJ 11–1). The

Lovelock Tribune of July 26, 1907, reported the change of the canyon name from *Grimes* to *Copper Kettle* (DM; Car. Sink 1908; OPN, p. 10). In Clark County, a copper mining district known as **COPPER KING** is fifteen miles south of Bunkerville, and **COPPER MOUNTAIN** is the name for a small mountain approximately four miles northeast of Searchlight and south of Opal Mountain, the site of copper discoveries in the early 1900s (Nev. Guide, p. 119; NI 11–3; VPG, pp. 23, 57; WA). **COPPER RUN** denoted a copper camp which grew up near a large copper lode about sixteen miles southeast of Yerington in Mineral County, by report of the *Reno Evening Gazette,* November 27, 1906 (WA). **COPPER VALLEY** (Pershing) is the name for a valley, south of Granite Spring Valley, and for a mining district, also called *Ragged Top,* on the west slope of the Trinity Range, ten miles by road west of Toulon (OPN, p. 10; VPG, p. 157; NK 11–10).

COPPEREID (Churchill). A copper camp and post office (April 8, 1907–June 15, 1914), thirty-five miles southeast of Lovelock in the Stillwater Range, east of the Carson Sink. The coined name commemorates John T. Reid, who carried on exploration works in copper mines there (Car. Sink 1908; NHS, 1913, p. 179).

COPPERFIELD. A station so named on the WP RR in Washoe County serves nearby copper mines (OG; NJ 11–1). The name was adopted for a post office in Esmeralda County, established May 7, 1907, by an order rescinded February 13, 1908 (FTM, p. 7). The post office took its name from **COPPERFIELD,** a copper camp which sprang up in April, 1907, in the Fitting (Acme, Kincaid) Mining District, at the site of Acme Station on the old C and C RR (DM). See **ACME.**

CORAL CANYON (Clark). A name descriptive of the coloration of Jurassic sandstone in an area of the Valley of Fire State Park, west of Lake Mead and southwest of Overton (NP; Park Map; WA).

CORAL HILL (Elko). The name (derived from the coloration of hills there) of this post office, established March 25, 1870, discontinued July 19, 1871, and reestablished May 1, 1874, to operate until March 14, 1877, was changed from *South Fork,* a name which referred to that branch of the Humboldt River (FTM, p. 7; 1881 Map).

CORDERO MINE (Humboldt). A mine west of Quinn River and eleven miles by road southwest of McDermitt. The Spanish word meaning "lamb" may be a surname (HWY Map).

COREY (Mineral). A mountain peak in the Wassuk Range about ten miles southwest of Hawthorne, the site of the **MOUNT CORY**

MINE; a creek rising in the Wassuk Range between Corey Peak and Big Indian Mountain, and flowing eastward to a plain where it disappears about three miles southwest of Hawthorne (M&SP, 4/5/84; NJ 11–4). The name is honorific of J. M. Cor(e)y, a prospector who, in company with James M. Braley and E. R. Hicks, discovered the mines at Aurora. Although Major G. W. Ingalls records the names of Washington Cox Corey and M. A. Braly as the discoverers of Aurora (SPD, p. 73), the consensus seems to be that the initials of both Corey and Braley were *J. M.* (MA, p. 415; SPD, pp. 235, 849; OPN, p. 49; Nev. Guide, p. 220; USGB 6002; Haw. Quad.). A 1960 decision of the United States Board on Geographic Names officially designates the mountain *Corey* Peak, not *Cory* Peak; however, the Army Map Service (NJ 11–4) shows the latter name, as does the official highway map of Nevada (1973).

CORMORANT ROCK (Clark). An island of the Overton Arm of Lake Mead, lying below Surprise Reef (WA); named for the voracious sea bird.

CORN CREEK (Clark). Formerly a station on the LV and T RR in Las Vegas Valley, between Tule and Owens; **CORN CREEK DUNES,** sixteen miles northwest of Las Vegas, in Las Vegas Wash; named for nearby **CORN CREEK SPRINGS.** Archaeologists have found evidence that campfires were built at the dunes site between four and five thousand years ago (Wheeler 1871 Map; 1881 Map; NJ 11–12; Vegas Quad.; JWC; M&M, p. 25).

CORNUCOPIA (Elko). A mining district sixty-five miles north-northwest of Elko; named for the richness of the terrain (GHM, EL 2; 1881 Map). The Leopard (discovered by Mark Dufrees in 1872) and the Chloride mines were the first locations made. The camp which grew up because of the discoveries had a mill, stores, restaurants, lodging houses, saloons, and a stage line to the SP RR. The district was served by **CORNU–COPIA** post office from November 3, 1873, until October 16, 1883, when Tuscarora became the mail address for its patrons (SM, 1875, pp. 20–21; EP, p. 23; VPG, p. 38; HHB, Nev., p. 277; FTM, p. 7).

CORRAL. Features named for corrals in the area include canyons in Elko, Lander, and Nye counties; creeks in Elko and Humboldt counties; and springs in Lander, Lyon, and Nye counties (Dir. 1971). **CORRAL CANYON** (Nye) is a canyon ten miles southwest of Morey Peak, "named for the corral at its mouth" (USGB 6903). **CORRAL CREEK** (Elko) denotes a tributary of the South Fork Humboldt River, named for sheep corrals in the area; a creek in the Diamond A Desert, near the Idaho boundary, named for the Bearfoot Corral. The horse corral was so

named in 1884 when Frank Salaras and Juan Feliz drove three bears (that had been near wild horses) into the corral and killed them (EP, p. 23).

CORSERS (Douglas). An early station, also known as *Cossers,* two miles from Van Sickles on the road to Aurora, was named for its owner, W. D. Corser (NHS, 1913, p. 193) or Walter Cosser (NHS, 1924, p. 18). A stream in Carson Valley, four miles west of Minden, is named for the early station owner and designated **CORSSER CREEK,** with a variant *Cosser,* by decision of the United States Board on Geographic Names in 1970 (USGB 7001).

CORTEZ. A town at the mouth of **CORTEZ CANYON** and a mining district on the southwest slope of Mount Tenabo, near the southwest end of the **CORTEZ MOUNTAINS** which extend southwest to northeast across north-central Eureka County from Lander County (1881 Map; NK 11–11). The name honors Hernán Cortés, the Spanish conqueror of Mexico. In 1864, a Dr. Hatch of Austin relocated the **CORTEZ MINE,** an old Indian turquoise mine (SM, 1875, pp. 54–55). Although the ground was not hard to work and plenty of the semiprecious stone was easily accessible, the Indians apparently had abandoned the mine, perhaps at the time of the Spanish conquest of Mexico. George Schmidtlein discovered stone tools lying about the mine in 1912. The production of this mine, which has been developed into the state's largest producer of turquoise, has been estimated at $6,000,000 (HPS, 1/24/54). The mining camp of **CORTEZ,** situated on the Lander-Eureka boundary, about forty miles southeast of Battle Mountain, was included in the Ninth Census (Census, 1870) and was served by a post office of the same name from January 3, 1868, to October 12, 1869, from June 25, 1892, until June 15, 1915, and from January 3, 1923, until February 15, 1943, dates reflecting the periods of greatest activity in the mining district (FTM, p. 7).

CORWIN (Eureka). An early settlement, mentioned by Bancroft (HHB, Nev., p. 285), and a post office, established December 6, 1878, and discontinued October 31, 1879 (FTM, p. 7); probably named for the postmaster.

CORYVILLE (Esmeralda). A mining camp of the 1880s, in a canyon near the mines of Corey Peak, in that portion of old Esmeralda County included in Mineral County when it was created in 1911, and a post office (April 16, 1883–May 16, 1888). The name commemorates J. M. Corey, one of the discoverers of Aurora (FTM, p. 7; HHB, Nev., p. 260; DM). See **COREY.**

COSGRAVE (Pershing). A name of unknown origin for a station on the Winnemucca Subdivision of the SP RR between Mill City and Rose Creek, about thirty miles south-west of Winnemucca (T75; T1TR).

COTTONWOOD. The place name denotes over sixty features, widespread throughout the state, and is descriptive of the cotton-wood tree, so named because its seeds discharge a cottony substance. The cottonwood grows quite generally along the rivers and streams and in the canyons of Nevada, and often attains a height of sixty feet in the Humboldt Range. Under date of January 15, 1844, Captain Frémont noted that "groves of large cottonwood, . . . at the mouth of the river [Truckee], indicated that it was a stream of considerable size." During his 1858 exploration, Lieutenant Ives named **COTTONWOOD ISLAND,** presently under the waters of Lake Mohave, for the cottonwood trees he saw growing there (WA). The name, popular with ranchers and town builders, was also employed by railroad builders. A station at the end of a seven-mile spur, running south out of Hawthorne, Mineral County, and built in 1890, was named **COTTONWOOD** for the fuel this station furnished the wood-burning locomotives of the C and C RR (DM). In northern Nevada, **COTTONWOOD** (Elko) denotes a creek north of Carlin, tributary to Maggie Creek; a tributary of Salmon Falls Creek near the Idaho boundary; a stream north of Jiggs, tributary to Huntington Creek; a tributary of the North Fork Humboldt River in the central portion of the county, and an early post office (December 14, 1869–July 12, 1870). **LITTLE COTTONWOOD CREEK** is on the west slope of the Ruby Mountains (NK 11–11; NK 11–12; NK 11–9; FTM, p. 7). Also in the northern part of the state are the **COTTONWOOD RANGE** (Santa Rosa Mountains), sixty miles north of Winnemucca, and **COTTONWOOD CREEK** rising in the Santa Rosa Range and flowing into Paradise Valley (NK 11–9), both in Humboldt County.

Another concentration of the name appears in Nye County: **COTTONWOOD CREEK,** south of Dianas Punch Bowl in the Monitor Range; **BIG COTTONWOOD CREEK,** east of Sheep Mountain in the Monitor Range; **LITTLE COTTONWOOD CREEK,** north of Big Cottonwood Creek; a creek in the Shoshone Mountains, south of Grantsville; **COTTONWOOD CANYON** and creek, heading on the west slope of the Paradise Range and trending generally northwestward into Gabbs Valley; and **COTTONWOOD WASH,** a watercourse trending from the west slope of the Toiyabe Range to the Reese River, south of Reese River Butte (NJ 11–2; SG Map 5; NJ 11–5).

Significant features of Clark County named for the cottonwood include the following: **COTTONWOOD CANYON** draining east-ward from Jumbo Peak into **COTTON-WOOD WASH; COTTONWOOD COVE (LANDING),** a vacation spot on the Nevada shore of Lake Mohave, named for and lying above the former Cottonwood Island; and **COTTONWOOD PASS,** between Goodsprings and Blue Diamond. The pass, as well as **COTTONWOOD VALLEY** (extending southeastward from Blue Diamond), took its name from the famous **COTTONWOOD SPRINGS,** a campsite on the Spanish Trail, "a beautiful locality on the eastern slope of the Spring Mountain Range," in the words of Wheeler, "where the Indians cultivate a few acres, raising pumpkins, melons, and corn" (Wheeler, 1872, pp. 17, 70). The valley name appears on Lt. Ives' map of the Rio Colorado of the West dated 1858 (Wheat IV, 98). The town which utilizes the water of the springs and was formerly called **COTTONWOOD** has been renamed *Blue Diamond.* Other springs named for the cottonwood are about five miles east of West End on the old Callville Road and in Cottonwood Canyon, east of Jumbo Peak (NI 11–3; NJ 11–12; 1881 Map; WA).

In the eastern portion of the state the name denotes a creek rising on the east slope of the White Pine Range and tributary to Ellison Creek, in White Pine County; a canyon draining the southwest flank of Clover Mountain and emptying into the Meadow Valley Wash between Leith and Kyle; a spring north of Boyd and east of the Meadow Valley Wash; and an early settlement, all in Lincoln County (NJ 11–6; Census, 1900; WA; NHS, 1926, p. 283; JML, p. 15; OPN, p. 14; SG Map 8A). **COTTONWOOD CANYON** (Lander), the most centrally located feature of the name, is north of Austin in the Toiyabe Range.

In western Nevada features so named include creeks in Mineral County, both rising in the Wassuk Range, one emptying into the west side of Walker Lake, north of Rose Creek, the other flowing eastward from Buller Mountain to Whisky Flat (NJ 11–4; SG Map 4); a locality in Pershing County, northeast of Oreana (SG Map 1); an early settlement in Churchill County (Census, 1900) and **COTTONWOOD CANYON** (Churchill), a mining district discovered in 1861, sixty-five miles southeast of Lovelock near the northwest end of Dixie Valley (OPN, p. 10; VPG, p. 19; NHS, 1913, p. 173); a creek and its south fork, northwest of Wichman in the Bald Mountain area of Lyon County; a creek in Washoe County, rising northeast of Spanish Spring Peak in the Pah Rah Range and flowing into Warm Springs Valley (NJ 11–1; SG Map 4). In Esmeralda County, **COTTONWOOD CREEK** is an intermittent stream heading in springs about a mile southeast of Poison Springs and south of Walker

Spring, in Nevada, and flowing southward into California (USGB 6002). **COTTON-WOOD WELL,** a settlement west of Dead Horse Well in old Esmeralda County, was served by Wellington post office (HHB, Nev., p. 260; TF, p. 16; 1881 Map).

COUGAR. The name of the indigenous animal has been applied to a mountain, north of Marys River Peak, and to a creek, southeast of Jarbidge, in the Jarbidge Mountains of northern Elko County; also to a canyon in Lander County, south of Kingston Creek in the Toiyabe Range near the Nye County line (Dir. 1971).

COUNTY LINE POND (White Pine). A small, stock-watering pond on the west shore of Ruby Lake; named for its position near the Elko County boundary (VPG).

COURT OF ANTIQUITY (Washoe). A flat-topped prominence between Interstate 80 and the Truckee River, immediately east of the west foot of the Virginia Range, is a state recreational area. The name is based on a legend that aborigines once met here in council. Petroglyphs are distinguishable on the stone floor and walls (Nev. Guide, p. 141; Park Map).

COW. The name derives from strays, or from herds of cattle, and is represented in seven Nevada counties. Streams denoted **COW CREEK** are southeast of Jackpot and southeast of Owyhee, both in Elko County; tributary to Rabbithole Creek, northwest of Placeritas in Pershing County; west of Daisy Creek in the Fish Creek Mountains of Lander County; and on the east slope of the Calico Mountains in Humboldt County (GHM, EL 3, 4; PE 1; LA 2; HU 3). Canyons so named are southeast of Grantsville in Nye County; southeast of Rochester in Pershing County; and on the east slope of the Simpson Park Range in Lander County (GHM, NY 2; PE 2; LA 1). **COW CANYON CREEK** (Churchill) is north of Mount Grant in the Clan Alpine Range (GHM, CH 2). In Clark County, **COW SPRING** designates a spring in the McCullough Range, a spring northwest of Searchlight, and is an alternate name for *Threemile Spring,* east of Las Vegas. **COW CAMP SPRING** (Clark) is southwest of Mormon Well and west of Sheep Peak in the Sheep Range (WA; Dir. 1971).

COYOTE. Relatively few features in Nevada bear this popular place name, derived from the Aztec word *coyotl* for "prairie wolf." The Great Basin coyote is found in the Sierra Nevada and the desert coyote throughout the state. **COYOTE HOLE(S)** is the designation for coyote-dug wells on Sarcobatus Flat, in Nye County, and in the Duck Valley Indian Reservation, south of Stateline Well, in Elko County (VPG; NK 11–8).

COYOTE SPRING (Lincoln), an old campsite, is west of Hoya in **COYOTE SPRING VALLEY,** which extends south from Maynard Lake toward Muddy River Valley (WA; OPN, p. 43; JML, p. 15; LRH, II, p. 160, n. 28). A spring of Nye County so named is at the south end of the Paradise Range (VPG). **COYOTE PEAK,** a peak in the western portion of the Timpahute Range, and **COYOTE SUMMIT,** south of Tempiute on State Route 25, are in Lincoln County (NJ 11–9). **COYOTE CREEK** is the name of a stream southeast of Charleston, which empties into **COYOTE LAKE,** in Elko County, and for a tributary of Maggie Creek in the northeast corner of Eureka County (NK 11–9; NK 11–11). **COYOTE CANYON** (Churchill) extends from the east slope of the Stillwater Range to the south end of Dixie Valley, thirty-one miles east of Fallon (USGB 5904). **COYOTE CUESTA** (Nye) is a cuesta ridge south of the Gabbard Hills and north of the west end of Gold Flat, about thirty-nine miles east-southeast of Goldfield (USGB 6303).

C P (Nye). The canyon so named extends from the **C P HILLS,** for which it was named, to Yucca Flat, a few miles northwest of Yucca Pass. The term meaning "control point" has reference to a control point, for some purpose, which was on an elevation in these hills (USGB 6201; Kilmartin).

CRADLEBAUGH (Douglas). The name commemorates William Cradlebaugh who built **CRADLEBAUGH BRIDGE** on **CRADLEBAUGH TOLL ROAD** in 1861. The bridge was the first across the Carson River in Carson Valley (Dangberg, CV, p. 105). A post office named **CRADLEBAUGH** operated for two brief periods, from April 10, 1895, until September 26, 1896, and from August 22, 1898, until January 15, 1900 (FTM, p. 7). William was the younger brother of John Cradlebaugh who was commissioned as Associate Justice of the Supreme Court of Utah by President Buchanan on June 4, 1858, and assigned to the district which included Carson County in 1859 (Car. City Quad.; SPD, pp. 260, 276; NHS, 1917, pp. 174–176). See **BRIDGE HOUSE.**

CRANE. A canyon of Nye County, heading on the west flank of the Toiyabe Range and trending northwesterly to Reese River Valley, north of Ophir Wash (Dir. 1971); a small creek in Elko County, tributary to the south fork of the Humboldt River and named by Frémont for one of his Delaware Indians when he camped there on November 8, 1845. At this point, Frémont gave the name *Humboldt* to the range of mountains and the river (FSD, pp. 282–89; JGS, I, p. 90; VPG).

CRESCENT. A valley along the Eureka-

Lander county line between the Cortez and Shoshone ranges, southwest of Beowawe; named descriptively for its shape (OPN, p. 40). **CRESCENT MINING DISTRICT** (Clark) was located six miles east of Nipton, on the west flank of **CRESCENT PEAK,** by an Indian named "Prospector Johnnie," in 1894. "The district takes its name from the crescent formed by the mountains, with the crescent opening toward the west, and Crescent Peak near the center" (WA). Other features in the area, named for the district, are **CRESCENT SPRING,** a spring about three miles west of the peak, and **CRESCENT,** a former mining camp established on the northwest side of the peak, and its post office, which was in operation from August 4, 1905, until July 31, 1918 (WA; FTM, p. 7; VPG, p. 23; Freese Map 1; OPN, p. 14).

CRESSID (Churchill). Formerly a station on the SP RR, five miles northeast of White Plains, near Humboldt Lake. The name derives from the faithless Cressida, or Criseyde, of medieval legend. Perhaps the railroad builders felt that the countryside shared her dominant characteristic (T1TR; NHS, 1913, p. 173).

CRESTED WHEAT RIDGE (Nye). A ridge fifteen miles north of Moores Station; "named for the wheatgrass that grows on the ridge" (USGB 6903).

CRESTLINE (Lincoln). A non-agency siding on the UP RR, thirty-four miles northeast of Caliente near the Utah line; named for the station's position at the summit (NJ 11-9; WA).

CRICKET CREEK (Elko). A stream, south of Melandco, tributary to Bishop(s) Creek west of Bishop Creek Reservoir. Emigrants coming in from Fort Hall, Idaho, and following Bishop Creek may have named the tributary upon encountering the "Mormon cricket" there. This huge crawling (rather than flying) insect lays its eggs in the ground in late summer, and by early spring they begin to hatch. "By mid-summer the insects are moving in close formation over hill, valley, and whatever is in the way. The column rarely swerves; if a stream blocks the line of march the crickets go as far out as possible on rocks and over-hanging grasses and willow branches, then drop into the water and swim" (Nev. Guide, pp. 124-25; Freese, Map 3). The naming process is best explained in the Journal of James H. Martineau, historian of a party of Mormons called "Southern Exploring Company." Under date of May 23, 1858, the account reads "found a good spring . . . which we named Cricket Spring, from the great number of those insects about" (Wheat IV, 135). This

spring name apparently has vanished from Nevada nomenclature.

CRIPPLE CREEK (Churchill). The *Tonopah Miner* of October 6, 1906, reported that a new townsite so named had been laid out about two miles from Eastgate on the west slope of the Desatoya Range (DM). Promoters named the town for Cripple Creek, the great gold-producing district of central Colorado.

CRITTENDEN (Elko). **CRITTENDEN CREEK,** not *Silva* or *Silver* Creek, is the name of an intermittent stream which heads in **CRITTENDEN SPRINGS** and flows through **CRITTENDEN RESERVOIR** to Thousand Spring Creek about fourteen miles north of Montello (USGB 6303; NK 11-9).

CROOKED CANYON (Lander). The canyon, heading on the east slope of the Toiyabe Range and extending into Big Smoky Valley, is named for its natural contours (NJ 11-2).

CROSBY. A post office of old Lincoln County, established near Bunkerville, presently within the boundaries of Clark County, in operation from February 1, 1883, until May 24, 1883, when its name was changed to *Overton* (FTM, p. 7). The toponym commemorates an early settler, either Jesse Crosby who owned a ranch there in 1883 (WA), or Sam Crosby who is said to have put up a store and post office on this mail route from Muddy Valley to St. George, Utah (NHS, 1924, pp. 249-250).

CROW. The name denotes a canyon on the western slope of the Toiyabe Range, south of Austin in Lander County (SG Map 6), and a former corral, named for and constructed by George Crow, at the crossing in the Meadow Valley Wash, a few miles above Elgin in Lincoln County (WA).

CROW SPRINGS (Esmeralda). A name of undetermined origin for springs in the Monte Cristo Range (Tono. Quad.). **CROW SPRINGS MINING DISTRICT,** eleven miles northwest of Millers, was named for the nearby springs (VPG, p. 51).

CROWN PEAK (Churchill). The mountain is about three miles southwest of Wonder and was so named because it is the highest peak in the Louderback Mountains (USGB 5904).

CROWN POINT (Storey). This claim on the Comstock consisted of 540 feet, staked in 1859, between the Belcher and the Kentuck mines (IH). **CROWN POINT RAVINE,** which took its name from a large rock nearby (NHS, 1912, p. 191), is south of Virginia City; however, there is no information to indicate that the mine was named for the ravine. Crown Point was a popular name with California prospectors, mines bearing this name being located in Amador, El Dorado, Nevada, and San Bernardino counties (ESMB, pp. 429-430, 499; CMA,

p. 318). The Crown Point is a patented claim assessed in Storey County (AR, No. 194). **CROWN POINT** was also the name given to the great trestle over which the V and T RR ran at Gold Hill, since replaced by an earth fill (VPG; AEH).

CRYSTAL (Clark). The UP RR non-agency station of this name, abandoned in 1949, was about thirty-five miles northeast of Las Vegas, at the junction of U.S. 93 and the unpaved Valley of Fire Road, and was named for nearby crystal deposits (Freese, Map 1; OPN, p. 14; WA). **CRYSTAL PASS** is about two miles south of Goodsprings in the southwestern portion of the county (WA).

CRYSTAL BAY (Washoe). A bay at the north end of Lake Tahoe; named for its clear water. A resort and a post office, established September 3, 1937, are on the western shore of this bay for which they were named (Tahoe Map).

CRYSTAL PEAK. The former town, three miles north of Verdi in Washoe County, was laid out in 1864, partly in Nevada and partly in California. It was the first Nevada settlement to benefit from the temporary prosperity of railroad construction and was reputed to be the rowdiest town in the western part of the state. The town was named by the Crystal Peak Company for crystallized gold quartz found in a mountain a few miles to the west. The name of **CRYSTAL PEAK** post office, established in Washoe County on July 25, 1864, was changed to *Verdi* on March 30, 1869 (FTM, p. 7). **CRYSTAL PEAK MINING DISTRICT** was organized in the early 1860s and is located ten miles northwest of Reno (JGS, I, p. 254; SPD, pp. 1029–30; SM, 1867, pp. 21–25; VPG, p. 172).

CRYSTAL SPRING(S). Springs named for their clear water are found in two southern Nevada counties. Four springs in Nye County so denoted are situated northeast of Currant, south of Springdale, east of Johnnie, and northwest of Ash Meadows. **CRYSTAL SPRING** (Lincoln), south of Hiko, furnished a name for nearby **CRYSTAL WASH** (GHM, NY 4, 8; LN 4). Hiko was the mail address for the early settlement named for the spring (TF, p. 16; 1881 Map).

CULVERWELL RANCH. See **CALIENTE.**

CUPRITE (Esmeralda). The station on the now defunct BG RR served the nearby gold camps of Lida, Hornsilver, Bonnie Clare, and Tule Canyon in the early twentieth century. **CUPRITE** post office existed from April 30, 1907, until July 31, 1909, when Goldfield became the mail address for its patrons (NM; FTM, p. 7). The **CUPRITE HILLS** are east of Lida and south of the Goldfield Hills (GHM, ES 2). The name derives from the **CUPRITE MINING DIS-**

TRICT, fourteen miles south of Goldfield, which was named for copper deposits (VPG, p. 51). Cuprite is native red copper oxide, containing 88.8 percent copper.

CURRANT. Creeks named for wild currants growing nearby are found in Elko County, where a tributary of Wild Cat Creek, north of the latter's confluence with Marys River, is so denoted, and in northeastern Nye County. Taking their names from the Nye County creek are **CURRANT,** a settlement on U.S. 6, and a post office, established on April 16, 1883, and reestablished on September 19, 1892, and again on August 31, 1926, operations being suspended on December 31, 1943; **CURRANT MINING DISTRICT,** located east of Currant; **CURRANT MOUNTAIN,** south of Duckwater, in the White Pine Mountains; and **CURRANT SUMMIT** on U.S. 6 in the Horse Range, northeast of the settlement (FTM, p. 7; VPG, p. 126; NJ 11–6; NK 11–9).

CURRIE (Elko). A post office, established August 8, 1906, and a station on the NN RR, northeast of Cherry Creek on U.S. 93; named for Joseph H. Currie, a ranch owner on Nelson Creek in 1885 (OPN, p. 23). Lieutenant E. G. Beckwith of the Pacific Railroad Survey camped at the site in 1854. The **CURRIE HILLS** and **CURRIE CANYON,** east of the town, and **CURRIE GARDENS,** a flat southwest of the town, also commemorate the early rancher (NK 11–12; GHM, EL 5).

CURRYS WARM SPRINGS (Carson City). The name of a hotel and swimming baths, built by Abraham V. Z. Curry in the early days on the site of the present state prison at Carson City (NHS, 1913, p. 193). See **GOULD AND CURRY.**

CURTIS (Lander). A former station on the NC RR between Catons and Ravenwood; named for A. A. Curtis, treasurer of the NC RR company, formed on September 2, 1879 (MA, p. 283).

CYANIDE WASH (Lincoln). The wash near Delamar, in the central portion of the county, is named for a cyanide tailings pile located there (WA).

CYRUS NOBLE MINE (Clark). A mine in the Searchlight Mining District on the east side of Piute Valley, about twenty miles southwest of Eldorado Canyon (WA). A prospector named Jim Coleman located the claim, which later is said to have sold for $100,000, and traded the ground for a bottle of whiskey of this brand name (DM).

CZARINA MINE (Clark). The mica mine was discovered by Daniel Bonelli, prominent southern Nevada pioneer, near the Nevada-Arizona boundary, southeast of St. Thomas, and is now under the waters of Lake Mead (WA). Maria, wife of Alexander II of Russia, probably was being commemorated by

Bonelli who also discovered and named the Cleopatra and the Virgin Queen mines.

DAD LEES (Pershing). A desert trading post at the junction of U.S. 50 and Interstate 80 near Oreana (Guide Map); named for Dad Lee who died in 1936 still insisting that he was William F. Cody, the famous Buffalo Bill (Nev. Guide, p. 135).

DAGGETT(S). A pass on the Kingsbury Grade, east of Lake Tahoe in Douglas County, and **DAGGETT TRAIL,** earlier called *Georgetown Trail;* "so named for the reason that near Rubicon Point on the southwest shore of Lake Tahoe, it joined the trail to the Mother Lode town of Georgetown, which was situated approximately 15 miles east of Auburn, California. The name of Daggett was attached to this trail when Dr. C. [Charles] D. Daggett, in 1854, staked out a claim to 640 acres embracing its debouchment. After this considerable acquisition the name Georgetown gave way to that of Daggett Trail and Pass" (Dangberg, CV, p. 43). Two 1860 maps of the Washoe mining region, by Henry De Groot and R. M. Evans, show Daggetts Pass (Wheat IV, 189; V (I), 16). **DAGGET** (Eureka) denotes a spring and a creek, northeast of Antelope Peak in the southern portion of the county (GHM, EU 1; Mark. Sheet).

DANVILLE (Nye). The gold-silver mining district of this name was organized in the 1860s on the east flank of the Monitor Range, south of Clear Creek in northern Nye County. The name, probably chosen to commemorate an older place so denoted, also designates a canyon in the Monitor Range, a former mining camp, and a post office (November 21, 1883–September 8, 1884) established to serve the district (VPG, p. 126; 1881 Map; NM; FTM, p. 7).

DARROUGHS HOT SPRINGS (Nye). Frémont stopped at this hot springs during his third expedition in 1845 and mentions in his *Memoirs* that the waters had been used by the Indians for centuries. The station, originally a rock cabin called *Hot Springs,* in Big Smoky Valley east of Cove Canyon, was later named for the family of James T. Darrough who have owned it since the 1880s (MM; GHM, NY 2).

DARWIN (Churchill). A station between Argo and Hazen on the Sparks Subdivision of the SP RR (T75); perhaps named in commemoration of Charles Robert Darwin, English naturalist. See **PATNA.**

DAVE CREEK (Elko). Northeast of Jarbidge and west of the East Fork Jarbidge River, Dave Creek flows from northern Elko County into Idaho. "Dave," a sorrel stallion owned by Kitty Wilkins who ranged horses in the area, is commemorated by the creek name and nearby **DAVES TABLE** and **DAVES SPRINGS** (GHM, EL 3; EP, p. 24).

DAVEYTOWN (Humboldt). The settlement in the Quinn River Valley, west of the southern end of the Santa Rosa Range and about twenty-four miles north-northwest of Winnemucca (USGB 6003) takes its name from the **DAVEY MINE.**

DAVIDSON, MOUNT (Storey). A peak (altitude 7,870), the highest point in the Virginia (Washoe) Range and the site of Virginia City. Mount Davidson was called *Sun Peak* by the early miners (DDG, p. 105; MA, p. 55; GTM, p. 69; Dir. 1875, p. ix), also *Sunrise Peak* (Dir. 1875, p. ix). Bancroft gives *Mount Pleasant* as being later than Sun Peak (Nev., p. 93). George D. Lyman cites the *San Francisco Alta* of February 14, 1875, which mentions *Sun Mountain* (GDL, Saga, p. 80). Recent maps show *Mt. Davidson* (Car. City Quad.) and *Mt. Davidson (Sun Mountain)* (Curran Map). There is almost general agreement from William Wright on down that the name was changed to Mount Davidson to honor Donald Davidson, State Geologist of California, who climbed the mountain. Exception is taken by Bancroft, who says the mountain is named for Professor George Davidson and is a fitting tribute to his genius (HHB, Nev., p. 93, n. 1).

DAVIS. A creek in eastern Esmeralda County, northwest of Dyer; a creek north of Ophir Creek and south of Washoe City in Washoe County (GHM, ES 1; WA 1). **DAVIS STATION** (Lyon) was on the Overland Trail, thirty miles east of Dayton at the lower end of the Big Bend of the Carson, and was named for C. M. Davis, the proprietor (NHS, 1913, p. 212).

DAVIS DAM (Clark). The earth and rockfill dam, constructed across the Colorado River, is sixty-seven miles south of Hoover Dam. The dam site was selected in 1924; the name for the proposed dam was chosen to commemorate Arthur Powell Davis, Director of the Bureau of Reclamation from 1914 until 1923 (WA). **DAVIS DAM** post office, established May 1, 1947, in Clark County, Nevada, was transferred into Mohave County, Arizona, on December 1, 1950 (FTM, p. 7).

DAYTON (Lyon). The town of Dayton, one of the oldest in the state, is at the end of the Twenty-six-Mile Desert, across the Big Bend of the Carson River. Emigrant parties, undecided whether to follow the river south or to continue westward, called the campsite *Ponderers Rest* (Nev. Guide, p. 269). In 1849, gold was first discovered in Nevada by one of these parties in Gold Creek, which flowed from Gold Canyon to the Carson River, near the present site of Dayton (M&S, p. 58; Car. City Quad.). At some time prior to June, 1853, Spafford Hall of Fort Wayne, Indiana, established a permanent station, erecting a substantial log house near the mouth of Gold Canyon, called *Halls Station,* or *Gold Creek Station* (MA, p. 35; M&S, p. 66). In 1854, Hall sold the station to James McMarlin who had come across the plains with him, and the post became known as *McMarlins Station.* On October 27, 1855, John Reese and others of Mormon Station (Genoa) were given a franchise to build a ditch to take water from the Carson River for use in Gold Canyon for mining and other purposes. Chinese, imported to work on the ditch, made up a majority of the population. At times more than two hundred Chinese were at work at *Gold Canyon Flat Diggings* (DDQ, p. 9; NHS, 1922, pp. 21–22). The site became known as *Chinatown* in 1856. Although non-Chinese residents objected to the name and adopted *Mineral Rapids* and *Nevada City* as more suitable designations, Chinatown is the name appearing on Captain James H. Simpson's 1859 Map of Wagon Routes in Utah Territory and on R. M. Evans' Official Map Washoe Mining Region, published in 1860 (Wheat IV, 140; V (I), 16). According to Myron Angel (p. 75), the place seems to have been known as *Clinton* at one time. The town was officially named **DAYTON** as a result of a meeting held by the citizens on November 3, 1861 (DDG, p. 10). The name honors John Day, a surveyor passing through the settlement, who agreed to plot the town on the condition that the citizens would name it for him. John Day was elected Surveyor General of Nevada in 1868, in 1870, and in 1874 (NHS, 1922, p. 27; HHB, Nev., p. 189, n. 35). Dayton was the county seat of Lyon County until February 10, 1911 (M&S, p. 145). The post office was established in Nevada Territory on January 15, 1862 (FTM, p. 7; C&C, p. 588; Nev. Terr. Map). During bonanza days, a toll road ran from Gold Hill to Dayton, which was also a station on the former C and C RR. Chinatown, Dayton, and Gold Canyon are alternate names for Silver City Mining District, nine miles northeast of Carson City on the southeast slope of the Virginia Range (VPG, p. 105).

DEA (Esmeralda). A name of undetermined meaning for Rhodes post office from October 19, 1907, until May 4, 1908 (FTM, p. 7).

DEAD (Clark). The name for a mountain range, running parallel to the Colorado River from south of Searchlight, Nevada, into California; descriptive of the lifeless area (Wheeler 1871 Map). According to Indian legend, **DEAD PEAK**, also called **DEAD MOUNTAIN**, in the north end of the range, was Hell or *avickvome,* because it was cold and rainy (OPN, p. 15; GHM, CL 3). The name of the mountain appears on Joseph C. Ives' 1858 map of the Rio Colorado of the West (Wheat IV, 98). The northern part of the range is now called the *Newberry Mountains* (q.v.).

DEAD BULL CANYON (Lincoln). A canyon of the Highland Range extending into Anderson Canyon, north of Highland Peak (WA; Dir. 1971); named to mark an incident connected with the killing of a bull, or the encountering of a dead one.

DEAD CAMEL MOUNTAINS (Churchill). A mountain range southwest of Fallon near Lahontan Reservoir, which lies at its western base; so named because one of the camels used for carrying salt to the mines of the Comstock was found dead there (VPG).

DEAD HORSE FLAT (Nye). A flat basin on Pahute Mesa just east of the head of Grass Spring Canyon and about two miles northeast of the mouth of North Silent Canyon; "so named because a saddled skeleton of a horse was found here" (USGB 6302).

DEAD HORSE SPRINGS (Lincoln). A vanished name for springs west of Coyote Springs and south of Maynard Lake. In the narrative of his overland journey in 1849, Jacob Y. Stover explained the name. "We camped for the night at Dead Horse Springs, as we called it. In the morning we killed our first horse to eat here, an old gray one of mine" (LRH, II, p. 279).

DEAD HORSE WELL(S) (Mineral). A desert watering place and an early station between Hot Spring and Cottonwood Well. The station was served by Downeyville post office (TF, p. 17; 1881 Map; HHB, Nev., p. 260; Dir. 1971). A Mr. B. Hyland, the proprietor of the Dead Horse Wells Water Company station, advertised in 1908, "Water delivered to all parts of Rawhide at $2.50 the barrel. The only water that has stood the test" (DM).

DEADMAN. A name usually applied upon encountering a corpse in an area; assigned to a creek heading on the west slope of Buck Mountain, east of Strawberry, and to a wash north of Bald Mountain in the Horse Range, in White Pine County. **DEADMAN GULCH RESERVOIR** is southeast of the wash (GHM, WP 2, 3). Springs so named are a few miles northwest of Sheep Peak, near Mormon Well in Clark County; and south of the former mining camp of Highland in Lincoln County (WA; Dir. 1971). **DEADMANS CANYON** is the possessive name for the upper end of Porter Wash, south of Goodsprings in Clark County; for a wash draining into the Meadow Valley Wash, a mile north of Elgin in Lincoln County; and an alternate name for *Antelope*

Canyon, near Caliente, also in Lincoln County (WA; Dir. 1971).

DEAN (Lander). Formerly a post office (October 18, 1894–November 30, 1905) and a mining camp; named for the **DEAN MINING DISTRICT**, also known as *Lewis*, located near the head of **DEAN CANYON** in 1867, on the north side of the Shoshone Range, about fourteen miles southeast of Battle Mountain (NM; VPG, p. 87). The name commemorates James Dean, pioneer cattleman of the region and owner of the old **DEAN MINE** (OPN, p. 40; M&M, p. 103). See **LEWIS**. **DEAN RANCH** (Eureka) is at the southern end of Crescent Valley near the Lander County boundary. The ranch was served by Palisade post office in the early days (TF, p. 17; GHM, EU 2). **DEAN SPRING VALLEY** (Nye), two miles west of Rawhide Mountain, is "named for Dean Spring located in the eastern part of the valley" (USGB 6903).

DEATH VALLEY NATIONAL MONUMENT (Nye). Death Valley, in Nevada, consists of an area of approximately two-hundred square miles in western Nye County and the southern tip of Esmeralda County, and includes the north end of the Amargosa Desert and almost all of the east slope of the Grapevine Mountains (Furn. Cr. Quad.; OPN, p. 69). The name was given by some members of the Jefferson Hunt party that started southwest over the Mormon Trail in 1849, but broke away from the experienced leader in southwestern Utah, and formed the Manly-Bennett party. Of the one hundred wagons that cut west from Mountain Meadows, all returned to the guidance of Hunt except two families with children and a group of young men called the Jayhawkers. Before reaching Death Valley, they followed the approximate route of U.S. 93 through Delamar Valley. Most of the party reached the coast, though all had despaired before finding a pass in the Panamint Mountains (Nev. Guide, pp. 36, 176; JGS, I, p. 106). William Lewis Manly, one of the survivors, is quoted in Roberts' *History of the Mormon Church* as follows:

> Just as we were ready to leave and return to camp (after having climbed a ridge near their camp where they overlooked the Mohave Desert) we took off our hats, and then overlooking the scene of so much trial, suffering, and death, spoke the thought uppermost, saying: "Goodbye, Death Valley!" Then faced away and made our steps toward camp. Ever after this, in speaking of this long, narrow valley over which we had crossed into its nearly central part, and on the edge of which the lone camp was made for so many days, it was called "Death Valley." Many accounts have been given to the world as to the origin of the name, and by whom it was

thus designated, but ours were the first visible footsteps; and we the party which named it, the saddest and most dreadful name that came to us first from its memories. (JGS, I, pp. 584–85)

The first official mention of the name was on Minard H. Farley's map of 1861 (Gudde, p. 81).

DECKER (Nye). A creek rising on the east slope of the Toiyabe Range, north of Gendron Creek, and flowing into Big Smoky Valley (GHM, NY 2). **DECKER BOB CREEK**, rising south of Toiyabe Range Peak and flowing into Big Smoky Valley, was named for "Decker Bob," a Shoshone Indian who owned a ranch at the creek (SG Map 6; MM).

DECOY (Elko). The name for a manganese mining district twenty miles west of Wendover in the Toano Range; a station on the NN RR eight miles west of the district. Circumstances of the naming are unknown (VPG, p. 39; EP, p. 25; GHM, EL 5).

DEEP CREEK (Elko). The settlement on State Route 11, formerly an old stage station, is named for **DEEP CREEK** which flows through **DEEP CREEK CANYON**, east of the Bull Run Mountains (Nev. Guide, p. 168; GHM, EL 2). Another creek so named and **EAST DEEP CREEK** are northeast of Rowland near the Idaho boundary (GHM, EL 3). The name process involved is illustrated by Capt. James H. Simpson's reason for applying the name to Fish Creek (q.v.). "Mr. Faust (mail) represents the valley of Deep Creek (by Beckwith called Fish Creek. . .), as quite large and fertile. The creek is narrow and so deep (from 6 to 12 feet) as to drown animals, and 1,500 acres of good land can be profitably irrigated by it" (JHS, p. 53).

DEEPHOLE (Washoe). The mining district of this name, north of the Smoke Creek Desert, about ten miles north of Reynard, was named for deep springs (VPG, p. 170; NHS, 1911, p. 91). **DEEP HOLE** post office, established in old Roop County on July 13, 1866, and discontinued on August 6, 1867, was reestablished in Washoe County and operated from February 12, 1894, until October 2, 1911 (FTM, p. 7).

DEEP WELLS (Elko). An old stage station between Wells and Cherry Creek in the valley opposite Spruce Mountain (NHS, 1924, p. 334). The station was named for a number of springs in the valley, called wells by the emigrants. See **WELLS** and **LUNING**.

DEER. The largest member of the deer family in the West, the mule deer, roams through all of the mountain forests of Nevada. **DEER CREEK** is the name of a creek, tributary to the Bruneau River; of a stream, tributary to Bull Run Creek, south of Sugar Loaf Hill; and of a creek, tributary to the Jarbidge

River, all in Elko County. **DEER CREEK CAVE,** the site of recent archaeological explorations, was named by Dr. Richard Shutler, in 1960, for its location north of Jarbidge at the junction of Deer Creek with the Jarbidge River (NK 11-9; Nev. Guide, p. 17; JWC). **DEER CREEK CAMPGROUND** (Clark) is named for **DEER CREEK,** a short year-round stream which flows northeast from Charleston Peak, by which the campground is situated. **DEER CREEK SPRING** is also near the creek (Freese, Map 1; WA; Nev. Guide, p. 234; Dir. 1971).

DEERING CREEK (Elko). A mountain stream at the north end of the Ruby Mountains, tributary to Lost Creek, southeast of Deeth; named for John Deering, an early settler on the creek (SG Map 10; EP, p. 25).

DEERLODGE (Lincoln). The name for a canyon about fifteen miles east of Pioche (WA, Freese, Map 2), and for a former settlement (Census, 1900) and post office, established March 22, 1898, and discontinued October 15, 1900, when Stateline, Utah, became the mail address for its patrons (FTM, p. 8).

DEETH (Elko). A town on the SP RR, between Wells and Elko, which serves as a shipping point for ranches in the area. Deeth was settled in 1868, with the building of the CP RR, and was named by a railroad official for the first settler (OPN, p. 23; Nev. Guide, p. 118). The post office was established on November 2, 1875 (FTM, p. 8). **DEETH MINING DISTRICT** was named for the town (VPG, p. 39).

DELAMAR (Lincoln). The broad **DELAMAR VALLEY,** one of the most striking in the state, is west of the **DELAMAR MOUNTAINS** (formerly called the Meadow Valley Range), bounded on the south and east by Kane Springs Wash and Meadow Valley Wash, and separated from the Highland Range to the north by a pass northwest of Caliente (USGB 6002; Gen. Land Off. Map). **DELAMAR MINING DISTRICT,** also called *Ferguson,* is thirty miles westsouthwest of Caliente (VPG, p. 94) and **DELAMAR SUMMIT,** a local name for *Oak Spring Summit,* is west of Caliente on U.S. 93 (WA; Dir. 1971). The name commemorates Captain John R. De Lamar, a Dutch immigrant, who purchased the group of mines later named for him, in 1893 (Nev. Guide, p. 177; Hulse, Nev., p. 53; OPN, p. 43; JGS, I, pp. 618-19; WA). Before the establishment of **DELAMAR** post office on August 6, 1894, the name of the mine was spelled *De La Mar,* that of the town *De Lamar.* The post office, discontinued on June 15, 1914, was reestablished March 1, 1933, and operated until February 28, 1941, during which time leasers were active in the area and the old dumps were being re-

processed by the Caliente Cyaniding Company (FTM, p. 8; WA).

Ferguson, the alternate name for the district, is honorific of John and Alvin Ferguson, who made the first strike of record in 1891. Using a monkey wrench found in a small ravine, they broke a small piece of quartzite, which proved to be ore, from a ledge and named their claim the *Monkey Wrench* for the incident (WA). The same legend is told in connection with a family named Riggs, said to have made the discovery in 1889 (JGS, I, pp. 618-19). Subsequent to the discovery of the April Fool Mine, on April 1, 1892, by Frank Wilson and D. A. Reeves, a town was laid out below the mine and named *Reeves,* later changed to De Lamar (Delamar) when Captain De Lamar bought the mines (WA; JGS, I, p. 619). The Delamar Mine, up to 1908, had an estimated production of $25,000,000. Although the town was one of the leading gold camps of southern Nevada, nothing remains at the site except old stone walls, a crumbling mill, and a large cemetery. A high mortality rate in the old camp had been caused by the high percentage of silica dust from the Cambrian quartzite in which the gold occurred (NM, pp. 194-99; WA). See **HELENE.**

DELANO (Elko). A mining district, also known as *Delno* (q.v.), discovered thirty-five miles north of Montello, in the extreme northeastern corner of the county near the Utah line. The district is included in the report of the state mineralogist for 1873 and 1874 (SM, 1875, p. 26) and named for either Alanzo Delano, who made first mention of the mineralized area in his 1849 Journal (EP, p. 25), or an early trapper in the county, not further identified (OPN, p. 23; SFH, p. 10; VPG, p. 39). Features named for the early camp include **DELANO WELL,** northeast of the district, and **DELANO PEAK** in the **DELANO RANGE** (GHM, EL 4).

DELAPLAIN (Elko). This station, thirteen miles north of Contact on a branch line of the UP RR from Twin Falls, Idaho, to Wells, Nevada, was named for an employee of the railroad (NK 11-9; EP, p. 26).

DELAWARE (Carson City). The name denotes a mining district on the east side of the Carson River, four miles east of Carson City, and ultimately commemorates an early governor of Virginia, Lord de la Ware (VPG, p. 147; GRS, Names, p. 35). *Sullivan* is the alternate name for the district.

DEL BONDIDO (Esmeralda). A former mining camp on the Tule Canyon road, near Pigeon Springs and twenty-eight miles from Silver Springs; named for Charles Del Bondido (DM).

DELKER (Elko). **DELKER BUTTES** and **DELKER MINING DISTRICT,** twenty-five miles northeast of Currie, are named for a

Mr. Delker who discovered the copper district in 1894 (VPG, p. 39; EP, p. 26; GHM, EL 5).

DELMUE(S) (Lincoln). A non-agency station on the Pioche branch of the UP RR, about nine miles southeast of Pioche near **DELMUES RANCH. DELMUES** also designates a spring, east of the Ely Springs Range, and a well, west of Stampede Gap. The name commemorates Joseph D. Delmue and his brothers, who bought the ranch on March 3, 1871 (GHM, LN 1; WA; DM; OPN, p. 43).

DELNO (Elko). Another name for the Delano Mining District, thirty-five miles north of Montello. **DELNO** post office was established by an order of May 5, 1927, which was later rescinded (VPG, p. 39; FTM, p. 8).

DELPHI SPRINGS (Lyon). The name for a spring on the east side of Smith Valley, near the former route of the NCB RR (DM); commemorative of the seat of the Delphic oracle in ancient Greece.

DENIO (Humboldt). The town and **DENIO SUMMIT,** southeast of the town, were named in honor of Aaron Denio, a native of Illinois, who migrated to the Winnemucca area in the 1860s, and later to the site at the Oregon boundary of present-day Denio. The **DENIO** post office was established in the late 1890s in Harney County, Oregon, and reestablished in Humboldt County, Nevada, January 1, 1951. Aaron Denio, who died in 1907, is buried in the Denio cemetery (LAM, p. 179; GHM, HU 3; FTM, p. 8).

DENTON. The pass, east of Delamar, and at the head of Helene Wash in Lincoln County, was so named in honor of the Denton family, historically prominent in Lincoln County during the early twentieth century (WA). **DENTON CANYON** (Elko) is northwest of Currie in the Cherry Creek Mountains (GHM, EL 5).

DERBY. The station on the SP RR, twenty-seven miles east of Reno and nineteen miles west of Hazen in Washoe County, was established "during the construction of the United States reclamation work and named by the railroad company for an employee of the company named Derby," according to Major G. W. Ingalls (SPD, p. 1030). The small settlement which grew up there became notorious for saloon shooting scrapes which occurred in the "Derby Dives." Abandoned November 3, 1929, the station was four miles east of **DERBY DAM** (Washoe-Storey). The dam, completed by the reclamation service in 1905, diverted the water of the Truckee River eastward by canal to the Carson River, thus decreasing the flow to Pyramid Lake, with the resulting fall of its level (VPG; DM; M&S, p. 23). **DERBY** post office was established to serve the area on May 3, 1906, and discontinued on June 30, 1922, when Wadsworth became the mail address for its patrons (FTM, p. 8). **DERBYS,** a settlement southeast of Summit Lake in old Humboldt County, was served by Humboldt House post office (HHB, Nev., p. 264; TF, p. 17; 1881 Map). **DERBY LAKE** was an early name for a lake southeast of Mud Lake and is shown on Bruff's 1849 manuscript map (Wheat III, 99).

DESATOYA MOUNTAINS. The mountain range extends north from Nye County to form the southeastern boundary between Churchill and Lander counties and runs north to the New Pass Range. The Shoshone place name contains the generic *toyap,* "mountain" (Kroeber, Shoshonean, p. 80), in final position. The rest of the name is of uncertain meaning, variously interpreted as "short, low" (NHS, 1913, p. 182), "cold" (M&M, p. 6), and "big-black" (GRS, Amer., p. 134). Earlier names for the mountain range were *Lookout* and *Sedaye* (WTJ, p. 142). In his *Report* of 1859, Captain James H. Simpson mentions the Lookout Range, but thereafter refers to it as the Sedaye (JHS, pp. 78–79), reported to be an Indian word meaning "bad" or "no good" (NHS, 1913, p. 182). *Sedave* is an 1867 map spelling.

DESERT. "It is only a side track, rightly named, and passenger trains seldom stop. The winds that sweep the barren plains here heap the sand around the scattering sage like huge potato hills" (FES, p. 199). The station is on the Sparks Subdivision of the SP RR, between Upsal and Parran in Churchill County (T75). Although the name is appropriately descriptive, it probably was shifted from earlier named features nearby. **DESERT PEAK,** perhaps the feature named first, is west of Soda Flat and on the northeast end of the Hot Springs Range (Car. Sink 1908; VPG, p. 12). **DESERT MINING DISTRICT,** lying in the first range of hills west of the Forty Mile Desert, was discovered by James Shay while he was prospecting for Mr. Bateman, the owner of Bateman's Ferry on the Humboldt Slough, by report of the *Gold Hill News* of February 4, 1864 (DM). The district was characterized by an almost entire absence of water, even for domestic use (SM, 1867, pp. 28–29). The **DESERT MOUNTAINS** in the southwest corner of Churchill County form part of the eastern boundary of Lyon County (Dir. 1971). The **DESERT RANGE** (Lincoln, Clark), with its southern end about thirty miles north-northwest of Las Vegas, extends north for about fifty-four miles into Lincoln County (USGB 6002). **DESERT GAME RANGE,** a game refuge especially for mountain sheep and migratory waterfowl, is in northwest Clark and southwest Lincoln counties and takes its name from the Desert Range (Park Map; HWY Map; WA). Also in Lincoln County are two valleys so denominated, one lying between the Pahroc and Highland ranges, and another north of the Desert Range and east of the Pahranagat Range (Freese, Map 2). **DESERT CREEK,** a small stream rising in the Sierra Nevada in California and flowing across southern Lyon County into the West Walker River, is west of **DESERT CREEK PEAK** (Well. Sheet; OPN, p. 47). **DESERT STATION** (Douglas) was in the middle of Carson Valley on the road from Carson City to Rodenbaughs. The station never consisted of more than a well surrounded by sagebrush and sand (NHS, 1913, p. 187). **DESERT WELLS** (Churchill), mentioned by Bancroft (Nev., pp. 261–62), was at Sand Springs, about thirty miles southeast of Fallon. The settlement was named for a well of brackish water (NHS, 1913, p. 173; 1881 Map; Car. Sink 1908). **DESERT WELL STATION** (Lyon) was about fourteen miles east of Dayton and twelve miles east of Nevada Station and took its name from a well at which teams stopped to get water. The name was changed to *Nelsons,* commemorative of the owner of the station (JGS, I, p. 136; NHS, 1913, pp. 206–207).

DESERT ROCK, CAMP (Clark). The name for an army camp constructed about twenty-five miles west of Indian Springs to house the troops serving the Nevada Test Site (WA).

DEVIL (Clark). By decision of USGB–5, a peak in the south end of the Spring Mountains near the California line was named **DEVIL** (not *Big Devil, Diablo Grande, Lookout,* or *Mount Diablo*). The peak, a landmark for early travelers, apparently was so named because of its forbidding aspect (GHM, CL 1; OPN, p. 15). **DEVIL CANYON** lies between Devil Peak and **LITTLE DEVIL PEAK** (WA) in the Spring Mountains.

DEVILS. The fanciful name was often given to land and water features associated with the fallen angel because of their unpleasant or forbidding aspects. **DEVILS GATE** is an opening gorge across a reef of siliceous rock, with rocky walls rising perpendicularly on each side, located between Gold Hill and Silver City on the Storey-Lyon county line (Nev. Terr. Map). J. Ross Browne, writing in 1860, related that upon entering Devils Gate, all combined to give him "a forcible impression of the unhallowed character of the place" (NHS, 1926, p. 64). **DEVILS GATE TOLL HOUSE** was at the lower end of the toll road that operated between Gold Hill and Silver City. **DEVILS GATE MINING DISTRICT,** named for the pass, was organized November 18, 1859, and is on the

southeast slope of the Virginia Range, nine miles northeast of Carson City (NHS, 1913, p. 207; VPG, p. 105). **DEVILS GATE CREEK** (Eureka) is named for a pass on U.S. 50, at the north end of the Fish Creek Range and about three miles northwest of Eureka (Robt. Mts. Quad.). **DEVILS HOLE** (Nye) denotes a cave just east of Ash Meadows, noted for a rare fish, a survivor of the Glacial Age, that lives there, in the Amargosa River, and also in Salt Creek in Death Valley. Devils Hole is undoubtedly one of the springs visited by Manly as he was conducting some of the Death Valley forty-niners through that section (VPG; Furn. Cr. Quad.). **DEVILS THROAT** (Clark) is "a strange, vertical-sided hole in an alluvial fan in St. Thomas Gap, north of Tramp Ridge . . . probably caused by a limestone or salt sink underneath" (WA). A peak in the Dead Mountains of Clark County is called **DEVILS THUMB** (WA). **DEVILS PUNCH BOWL.** See **DIANAS PUNCH BOWL.**

DEWEY (Washoe). Formerly a post office in the valley north of the Virginia Range near Pyramid Lake, established July 18, 1898, a little more than two months after the Battle of Manila Bay, and named in honor of Admiral George Dewey. The post office was discontinued on October 15, 1908 (NHS, 1911, p. 84; FTM, p. 8).

DIAMOND. The Diamond name complex seems to stem from **DIAMOND VALLEY,** a valley in Eureka County, lying between the **DIAMOND RANGE** and the Sulphur Spring Mountains, named by an early emigrant party either for its saline efflorescence, or because arenaceous portions of it glittered with small crystals of quartz. According to Simpson, the members of his party facetiously called such crystals California diamonds, "the appellation, doubtless, as veritable as the epithet of ruby, which seems to belong to the precious stones said to have been found in Ruby Valley" (JHS, p. 68). The mountain range east of the valley forms part of the boundary between Eureka and White Pine counties and extends into southwest Elko County. **DIAMOND PEAK,** altitude 10,626 feet, is northeast of Eureka in White Pine County. **DIAMOND MOUNTAIN** was the name of a White Pine County post office, established by an order dated November 17, 1869, but rescinded before operations commenced (FTM, p. 8). Early settlements in Diamond Valley were **DIAMOND SPRINGS** (1867 Map; Wheeler 1871 Map) and **DIAMOND VALLEY** (Census, 1870). The former was the name of a station on the old Overland Stage road, also on the route of the Pony Express, twelve miles northwest of Sulphur Springs Station (Nev., I, 1961, p. 9). In May, 1864, silver-bearing veins were found on the western slope of the Diamond Range, north and west from Diamond Springs Station, and the **DIA-MOND MINING DISTRICT** was formed (MA, pp. 425, 429; SM, 1875, p. 167; VPG, p. 64; Wheeler, 1872, p. 36). The principal claims were the Champion, Hidden Treasure, Patriot, Curtis, and Keller. The mining camp which grew up there was named **DIAMOND CITY.** Postal authorities adopted the word **DIAMOND** to designate the office, first established in White Pine County on September 3, 1874, then moved to Eureka County the same year, where it remained in operation until July 10, 1884, the official date of discontinuance (Wheeler 1871 Map; 1872, p. 36; FTM, p. 8). When the old wagon road was replaced by the now defunct E and P RR, the way station at this point was **DIAMOND,** the first station north of Eureka (MA, p. 286; HHB, Nev., p. 285; Robt. Mts. Quad.; 1881 Map).

DIAMOND A DESERT (Elko), a flat northwest of Jarbidge at the Idaho boundary, and **DIAMOND A MINE,** southeast of Gold Creek Ranger Station, were named for the cattle brand of the Dan Murphy Ranch, "which ran cattle from Gold Creek to lower Diamond 'A' as early as 1868" (EP, p. 26; GHM, EL 3).

DIAMONDFIELD. The name denoted a former post office of Esmeralda County (November 2, 1904–May 30, 1908), established at a small town about three and one-half miles northeast of Goldfield. The town was the promotion of Jack Davis, nicknamed "Diamondfield," who had come from Idaho to the Tonopah area, in the early 1900s. While in Idaho, Davis, a convicted murderer, had been granted a pardon, as he stood black-hooded on the scaffold with a noose around his neck (FTM, p. 8; NM). **DIAMOND FIELD JACK WASH** (Churchill) trends northwest from the Barnett Hills in the southwest part of the county (NJ 11–1).

DIANAS PUNCH BOWL (Nye). The name for one of a number of hot springs in the Toiyabe National Forest, this particular group being located near State Route 82 in the Monitor Valley, south of Potts (HWY Map). The ancient Roman deity was goddess of springs and brooks. A concavity in the earth containing the hot springs probably explains her punch bowl. The *Devils Punch Bowl,* an earlier, local name, also implies the supernatural, but does not appear on any map consulted.

DIESSNER (Washoe). A former locality in Long Valley, west of Mud Lake in the northwestern part of the county, and a post office, established February 13, 1923, and discontinued October 1, 1933, when Vya became the mail address for its patrons. The name commemorates Oscar Diessner, early settler and first postmaster (OPN, p. 66; FTM, p. 8).

DIKE (Clark). The siding on the UP RR, fifteen miles northeast of Las Vegas, was named for **DIKE MINING DISTRICT** which contains the Lead King Mine. The name of the district derives from a mining term (VPG, p. 24; WA; OPN, p. 15; Freese, Map 1). See **DYKE.**

DILLON (Lander). Formerly a station, at Milepost 14, on the NC RR between Bailey and Lewis; named in 1881 for Sidney Dillon, a railroad executive (Son. R. Quad.; DM).

DINNER STATION (Elko). The station, between Elko and North Fork on State Route 11, is a two-story stone structure, surrounded by ranch buildings, and was named for having been a meal stop for stagecoach travelers en route to ranches and mines in northern Elko County (GHM, EL 3; Nev. Guide, p. 166). See **WEILANDS.**

DISASTER (Humboldt). In May, 1864, a party of prospectors made a temporary halt in a canyon about seventy-five miles northwest of Paradise Valley at a point near the Oregon border, and was attacked by Bannock Indians. Four of the party of seven prospectors were killed, and Colonel Thomas Ewing records that "the locality of this tragedy received the name of Disaster Peak" (SPD, p. 164). Fort McDermitt was the mail address for **DISASTER PEAK** (TF, p. 17; 1881 Map). The **DISASTER MINING DISTRICT,** organized in 1914 in the area, took its name from the peak (OPN, p. 36; VPG, p. 71).

DISIGUOY (Elko). A name on which decision has been deferred by the United States Board on Geographic Names (DL 29) for a creek and a hill in the Duck Valley Indian Reservation. **DISIGUOY CREEK,** heading on the west slope of Mount Nagaha Wongops and flowing northwestward to Sheep Creek below Lamb Reservoir, "is reported to be a Shoshone Indian name, *Disiguoy Honops,* meaning 'grassy hill creek.'" **DISIGUOY HILL** is on the south edge of Duck Valley about five miles southwest of Owyhee.

DIVIDE, The **DIVIDE MINING DISTRICT** (Esmeralda), seven miles south of Tonopah on the road to Goldfield, was named for the highest summit on the road, known as **THE DIVIDE,** that marked the center of the district. **DIVIDE MINING DISTRICT** (Elko), eight miles northwest of Tuscarora at the head of Dry Creek, was named because of its location on the divide between the Humboldt and Snake River basins (OPN, pp. 30, 23). **THE DIVIDE** (Storey) separates Gold Hill and Virginia City. Mark Twain described this desolate place as it appeared to him on the night he was the victim of a fake holdup, staged there by his friends. "The 'divide' was high, unoccupied ground, between the towns, the scene of twenty midnight murders and a hundred robberies. As we climbed up and stepped out of this eminence, the Gold Hill lights dropped out of sight at our backs, and the night closed down gloomy and dismal. A sharp wind swept the place, too, and chilled our perspiring bodies through" (RI, II, p. 298). During the heyday of the Comstock Lode, the place was populous, and the *Gold Hill News* of October 11, 1875, notes that the people of The Divide now call their place *Middletown*.

DIVISION. A peak lying west of the Black Rock Desert in southwest Humboldt County was so named for its position near the Washoe and Pershing county boundary (HWY Map). **DIVISION SPRING** was the name given to *Coyote Spring*, west of Hoya and south of Maynard Lake in Lincoln County, by the C. C. Rich party "because of dividing the party here on November 16, 1849" (LRH, II, p. 160, n. 28).

DIXIE. Most of the features in Nevada bearing this favorite name of Southern sympathizers were so denoted in the early 1860s. **DIXIE,** formerly a community at the head of **DIXIE VALLEY** on the east slope of the Stillwater Range in Churchill County, was settled in 1861 (OPN, p. 10; Car. Sink 1908). The valley trends between the Stillwater Range on the west end and the Augusta Mountains and Clan Alpine Mountains on the east (Churchill and Pershing counties), and was called *Osobb* by Federal surveyors of the Fortieth Parallel. It contains the **DIXIE MARSH DISTRICT**, organized in 1861 and active until 1868. The marsh, a producer of salt, borax, and potash, covers about nine square miles and was formed by the desiccation of a shallow lake (USGB 5904; HPS, 1/29/56; VPG, p. 13; OPN, p. 10). **DIXIE VALLEY**, located in the valley for which it was named, is a settlement about thirty-five miles northeast of Fallon and was formerly a post office, established in Churchill County March 7, 1918, and discontinued on December 30, 1933 (FTM, p. 8). **DIXIE MEADOWS,** on the northwest edge of the Humboldt Salt Marsh, and **DIXIE HOT SPRINGS,** on the east slope of the Stillwater Range, are about forty-five miles northeast of Fallon in Dixie Valley. **DIXIE** was the earlier name of *Unionville* in Pershing County, the latter name being given because of loyalty of the settlers during the Civil War (M&S, p. 148). In Elko County, **DIXIE CREEK,** a branch of the south fork of the Humboldt, is east of Bullion, and **DIXIE PASS** is at the north end of the Bullion Mountains (Freese, Map 3; Wheeler 1871 Map; ECN Map). **DIXIE NATIONAL FOREST**, originally designated as the *Charleston Forest Preserve,* is in the Spring (Charleston) Mountains (Guide Map;

Park Map). The forest has yellow pine from 7,500 to 11,000 feet, and juniper (locally called cedar) and nut pine below 7,500 feet (NHS, 1926, p. 418). It is also known as the *Toiyabe National Forest* (Gen. Land Off. Map) and the *Nevada National Forest* (HWY Map).

DOBE (Elko). A canyon and summit, north of Elko, presumably named by early freighters or stagecoach drivers for rain-slick, heavy clay (Nev. Guide, p. 166). See **ADOBE.**

DODGE (Washoe). The station between Wadsworth and Numana on the Wadsworth Subdivision of the SP RR (T75), at the southwest edge of the Pyramid Lake Indian Reservation, probably commemorates Major Frederick Dodge, Indian agent in the 1860s.

DOHERTY MOUNTAIN (Clark). This mountain, at the north edge of Searchlight, was so named in honor of Frank A. Doherty, one of the founders of *The Searchlight Bulletin* (WA).

DOLLY VARDEN (Elko). An early settlement and a mining district, located in 1872, east of Sprucemont and sixteen miles northeast of Currie (SM, 1875, p. 24; VPG, p. 39; HHB, Nev., p. 277; GHM, EL 5). The name could have been given to the mining camp because of the Dolly Varden, or red-spotted trout, in nearby Nelson Creek, or for the lively character created by Charles Dickens in *Barnaby Rudge* (1841). The date of the organization of the district, however, coincides with a tide of liberalism in 1872, one manifestation of which was the formation of the "Dolly Varden Party," a group of independents in revolt against political rings and bossism. In 1874, there was a partial fusion between the Democrats and the "Dolly Vardens," and Adolph Sutro campaigned under their banner for a seat in the United States Senate (JGS, I, pp. 288–89). The early locators and first settlers presumably were members of the independent political group, which is commemorated by the name.

DOME MOUNTAIN (Nye). This mountain, at the head of Beatty Wash just west of Fortymile Canyon, and about two and one-half miles north-northeast of Vent Pass in Yucca Mountain, was so named because its smooth profile is dome-shaped (USGB 6303; DL 58).

DON–DON PASS (Elko). A name of undetermined origin for a pass east of Dolly Varden and on the west side of the Goshute Range, about thirty miles south-southeast of Wendover (1881 Map; ECN Map). See **ALLEGHENY.**

DONNA SCHEE (Humboldt). The isolated hill at the south end of Desert Valley, east of the Jackson Mountains, may have been named by Scotch settlers because of its resemblance to "an eminently beautiful little conical hill, near the extremity of the valley of Aberfoil." Scotch people held these hills to be *Dun Shie,* or fairy mound haunts of the elfin people of Celtic superstition, fancifully named to indicate possession by the *Daoine Shie,* the elfin men of peace (SWS, p. 265; Scott's note 9, NK 11–7).

DORIS MONTGOMERY PASS (Nye). A divide between Beatty and Rhyolite, traversed by the former LV and T RR; named for a member of the family of E. A. ("Bob") Montgomery, one of the discoverers of the Montgomery-Shoshone Mine north of Rhyolite, in 1905 (WA; DM).

DORSEY (Elko). **DORSEY CREEK,** northwest of Columbe(r)t Creek in northern Elko County, commemorates "John Dorsey a horse raiser and brother-in-law of Pete Columbert" (EP, p. 28; GHM, EL 3). A second creek so named and **DORSEY RESERVOIR** are in the north end of the Adobe Range southeast of Dinner Station (GHM, EL 3).

DOUBLE. A name sometimes given, instead of *Two* or *Twin,* to indicate the twofold or paired aspects of land and water features. **DOUBLE SPRINGS.** An early settlement on **DOUBLE SPRINGS FLAT,** southeast of Carters and at the south end of the Pine Nut Mountains, in Douglas County; named for two springs near each other on the summit of Walkers Pass between Carson and Walker River valleys, where the settlement, served by Wellington post office, grew up (1881 Map). At one time a toll road ran from Double Springs to the Kingsbury Road (HHB, Nev., pp. 254–55; NHS, 1913, p. 188; Mark. Sheet). The station on the toll road at Double Springs was also known as *Round Tent Ranch* and *Spragues* (SHM 126). A mining district of Mineral County, called **DOUBLE SPRINGS MARSH,** is named for a dry lake, seven miles east of Schurz (Haw. Quad.; VPG, p. 113). **DOUBLE CANYON** (Clark) is a local name for *Arrow Canyon* and an alternate name for *Split Canyon,* which lies west and north of Arrow Canyon (WA).

DOUBLE UP MOUNTAIN (Clark). Formerly a local name for Potosi Mountain in the Spring Mountains, stemming from the **DOUBLE UP MINE** on the east flank of the mountain (WA).

DOUGLAS. The county was created on November 25, 1861, and named for Stephen Arnold Douglas, an American political leader and chairman of the Committee on Territories, who died the same year. The first settlement in Nevada, Mormon Station (now Genoa), was within the present boundaries of the county. The county seat was moved from Genoa to Minden in 1916. **DOUGLAS** denoted a station on the former V and T RR on the Carson Valley Branch, between Stewart and Minden in Douglas County (V&T Map).

DOUGLASS (Esmeralda). The post office was established July 25, 1898, to serve the mining camp so named, about five miles southwest of Mina, in that portion of old Esmeralda County presently within the boundaries of Mineral County. The post office was discontinued July 31, 1905, when Sodaville became the mail address for its patrons (FTM, p. 8; NM; Census, 1900).

DOUTRE (White Pine). The settlement between Aurum and Bassett, east of the Schell Creek Range, was named for the Doutre brothers, early sheepmen in Spring Valley (GHM, WP 2; NHS, 1924, p. 307).

DOVER SIDING (Mineral). Formerly a siding on the Mina Branch of the SP RR between Thorne and Kinkaid, west of the Gillis Range and northeast of Hawthorne (Haw. Quad.).

DOWNEYVILLE (Nye). An early mining district and former post office (March 31, 1879–October 15, 1901) in Gabbs Valley, west of the Paradise Range; named for P. Downey, the first postmaster (Tono. Quad.; OR, 1879; SM, 1875, pp. 107–109; FTM, p. 8).

DRESSLERVILLE (Douglas). The settlement is southeast of Gardnerville and west of Sheridan (GHM, DO 1). "On March 16th [1917] William F. Dressler gave the Washo tribe, 'in trust' with the U.S. Government, the 40 acres that today constitutes the colony of Dresslerville. The deed provides that the gift will become null and void if the tribe quits residing at Dresslerville with the property reverting to the heirs of Dressler" (JAP, p. 18).

DRIPPING SPRINGS (Clark). A canyon west of Davis Dam in the Newberry Mountains; named for the springs in it (Davis Quad.).

DROWN (Elko). Fred Drown, an early settler, is commemorated by **DROWN CREEK,** which rises on the north side of **DROWN PEAK** in the Ruby Mountains and flows to **DROWN RESERVOIR** (EP, p. 28; SG Map 10; GHM, EL 1).

DRY. The name has been given to many creeks and lakes in the state which are dry all, or most, of the year. **DRY CREEK.** In Elko County, an intermittent stream, heading in the Duck Valley Indian Reservation and flowing generally southwestward to Indian Creek, reported to have been named *Dirdui Panguipa Honops* by the Shoshone (USGB 6103); a creek, rising on the west slope of the Ruby Mountains, east of Jiggs; **DRY CREEK** post office (February 24, 1874–March 26, 1879), moved to Mound Valley (1881 Map; FTM, p. 8); and a creek in the East Humboldt Range, north of Secret Valley (GHM, EL 2, 4). Other streams so named are east of Smith Valley in the Shoshone Mountains in Lander County, and south of Copper Canyon in Mineral County (GHM, MI 1; LA 1). **DRY CREEK STATION** (Eureka), on both the Overland Mail and Pony Express lines, twenty-five miles southwest of Roberts Creek Station, was the scene of an Indian massacre in the 1860s. Gosiute Indians shot through crevices in the station, newly built with cottonwood logs and not yet chinked with mud (Nev., I, 1961, p. 9; JGS, I, p. 136; SPD, p. 180; 1867 Map).

DRY LAKE. A lake between the Clan Alpine Mountains and the New Pass Range in the eastern part of Churchill County; a lake in Smith Creek Valley in Lander County; a lake along U.S. 6, east of Blair Junction in Esmeralda County; a lake east of the Diamond Range and a string of lakes along the east edge of the Schell Creek Range, in White Pine County; lakes on the Elko-White Pine boundary and also in southwest Washoe County; and a valley bounded by the Pahroc Range on the west and by the Highland and Bristol ranges to the east, in Lincoln County (OPN, pp. 10, 40, 31, 43, 72; Gen. Land Off. Map; Freese, Maps 2, 3; SG Maps 1, 2, 9). **DRY LAKE** (Clark), about thirty miles north of Las Vegas, is the center of a name complex: **DRY LAKE VALLEY,** containing the lake, east of the Las Vegas Range and north of Apex; **DRY LAKE STATION,** just east of the lake on the main line of the UP RR; **DRY LAKE RANGE,** between Dry Lake Valley and California Wash; and the former **DRY LAKE** post office, in operation from December 3, 1925, until June 30, 1945, and again from January 31, 1950, until December 31, 1955 (WA; Freese, Map 1; FTM, p. 8).

DRY VALLEY denoted an early mining camp in the Pioche district in Lincoln County (Census, 1870), named for the valley so described on the southwest edge of Pioche, and a settlement in old Roop County, presently Washoe County (HHB, Nev., p. 262). **DRY FLAT VALLEY** (Wheat IV, 137; 1867 Map) was a name given by Simpson to an area between Middle Gate and Westgate "which I call Dry Flat Valley, on account of the whitish clay flat we cross, and which is as smooth and as hard as a floor" (JHS, pp. 13–84). **DRY WELLS STATION** (Lander) was twenty-five miles southeast of Smith Creek Station and west of Jacobsville on the route of the Pony Express (Nev., I, 1961, p. 8).

DRYTOWN. See **WADSWORTH.**

DUANE BLISS PEAK (Douglas). The peak southwest of Spooners Summit commemorates Duane L. Bliss, a prominent lumberman of Lake Tahoe in the late nineteenth century (Tahoe Map). See **BLISS.**

DUCK. Numerous features of Nevada are named for the wild duck. Varieties found in many parts of the state include mallards, mergansers, pinheads, teal, redheads, scaups, widgeons, shovelors, and canvasbacks, some of which rest in certain areas, protected by the thick cattails and attracted to the nut grass and sago pondweed. A portion of western Nevada is in line with the Pacific Flyway route taken by waterfowl migrating south to Mexico (Nev., II, 1960, pp. 25–31). **DUCK CREEK** (White Pine) denotes a creek near Steptoe in Steptoe Valley for which were named **DUCK CREEK DAM,** east of Glenn; **DUCK CREEK MINING DISTRICT,** in the Schell Creek Range near the head of Duck Creek; the **DUCK CREEK RANGE** east of Steptoe Valley; and **DUCK CREEK** post office, established June 10, 1872, and discontinued March 17, 1874 (1881 Map; NJ 11–3; Ely Quad. 1952; VPG, p. 178; FTM, p. 8). In Clark County, a creek so named runs northwest from Whitney Mesa toward Whitney, about midway between Las Vegas and Henderson (WA). **DUCK FLAT** (Washoe). The name for the flat, also called *Duck Lake,* on the dry lake bed of Lake Warner which occupied northeastern California and northwestern Nevada in Pleistocene times and for a former settlement west of Fox Mountain, in old Roop County, served by Buffalo Meadows post office (VPG; TF, p. 17). **DUCK VALLEY.** A valley which extends from the northern portion of Elko County into Idaho and is the site of the **DUCK VALLEY INDIAN RESERVATION** (established in 1877), also called the *Western Shoshone Indian Reservation* (NK 11–9; Gen. Land Off. Map); a Lincoln County valley extending from north of Pioche to the Geyser Ranch near the White Pine County line, with Pony Springs situated midway. *Dry Valley* is an alternate name for the portion lying south of Pony Springs. Alternate names for Duck Valley are *Geyser Valley* and *Lake Valley* (Freese, Map 2; WA).

DUCKWATER (Nye). The post office, first established January 6, 1873, operated, except for a few days in May, 1876, until January 29, 1941, and was reestablished May 16, 1950 (1881 Map). The ranch and locality, which serve sometimes as a base for hunters seeking mule deer, are located in and named for **DUCKWATER VALLEY** which begins seven miles south of the north line of the county and runs south into Railroad Valley. The valley consists almost entirely of meadow land, being well watered by **DUCKWATER CREEK.** Marshy areas in the valley furnish good feeding ground for wild ducks that winter there. **DUCKWATER MOUNTAIN** is northeast of the post office, and within the White Pine County line (SPD, p. 962; OPN, p. 53; HWY Map; Cad. Map).

DUFFER PEAK (Humboldt). A name of unknown origin for a mountain, northwest of Quinn River Crossing on the east side of the Pine Forest Mountains in the west-central portion of the county (GHM, HU 3).

DULUTH (Nye). A former mining district, organized subsequent to discoveries made in July, 1906, about forty-five miles northeast of Mina and forty miles southwest of Austin (DM); a short-lived post office (April 27, 1907–December 14, 1907), established to serve the district; probably named to commemorate the city in Minnesota (FTM, p. 8).

DUN GLEN (Pershing). The settlement in Nevada Territory dates from 1862, at which time ranching was the principal occupation in the area (Nev. Terr. Map). In 1863, United States soldiers were stationed there to hold the Indians in check. During the same year the Sierra Mining District was organized in the north end of the East Range, ten miles northeast of Mill City, and Dun Glen was the business point for the district (SPD, p. 899; SM, 1867). The community, which the *Nevada State Journal* of September 26, 1954, notes was first called *Derbys Dun Glen*, later became known as *Chafey*, for the Chafey Mine located there, with the variant *Chaffey* (Gen. Land Off. Map; 1910 Map). The original settlement name, commemorating Angus Dun(n), who settled there in 1862, has had an unstable orthography: *Dunn Glenn* (SPD, pp. 889, 907) and the composite *Dunglen* (1860 Map; Nev. Terr. Map). *Dun Glen* apparently became official with its adoption by postal authorities for the office which was established in Humboldt County July 18, 1865, and except for a period of six months, continued to operate until April 7, 1894. The name of *Chafey* post office (August 4, 1908–March 4, 1911) was changed to *Dun Glen;* it operated from the latter date until April 15, 1913, when Mill City became the mail address for its patrons (SM, 1867, p. 53; Census, 1870; FTM, p. 8). Features named for the early settlement are **DUN GLEN CREEK** (Dir. 1971), **DUN GLEN PEAK** to the north of it, and **DUN GLEN CANYON** (Son. R. Quad.). **DUN GLEN RANGE** (Churchill). See **CARSON SINK RANGE.**

DUN GLEN, CAMP (Pershing). Camp Dun Glen was first established in 1863 and again in March, 1865, in Paradise Valley in the East Humboldt Range, north of Unionville. Settlers of Dun Glen, for which the camp was named, asked for protection against attacks by hostile Indians. Occupied until April 1866, the camp served as a depot for troops protecting travelers along the Humboldt River, through the Black Rock Range, in Paradise Valley, and on Quinn River (Son. R. Quad.; SPD, p. 907; Ruhlen).

DUNPHY (Eureka). A station on the WP RR, ten miles west of Beowawe; named for the **DUNPHY RANCH** on the Humboldt River (T54).

DUPLEX (Clark). A hill in Searchlight, in the southern part of Clark County; named for the **DUPLEX MINE** located on it (WA).

DUTCH CREEK. A creek so designated, west of Walker Lake in Mineral County, was named for the old Dutchman Mine, located in 1865 by a German named Schnitz who was killed in 1867 by Indians. **DUTCH-CREEK** post office, named for the creek, was established April 8, 1907, and discontinued June 30, 1909, when Copper Hill became the mail address for its patrons. When the Walker Indian Reservation was opened to mining in 1906, Major Falkenberg relocated the old Dutchman Mine. The site of the former boom camp is within the boundaries of the U.S. Naval Ammunition Depot (Haw. Quad.; DM; NM). In Elko County, **DUTCH CREEK** is a stream northeast of Mountain City (SG Map 11).

DUTCH FLAT (Lincoln). This early name for the area surrounding Caliente served as an alternate for *Culverwell,* along with *Clover(dale) Junction* (WA; DM). See **CALIENTE.**

DUTCH JOHN (Lincoln). **DUTCH JOHN PEAK,** on the northwest of the Schell Creek Range, bounded on the east by Lake Valley, and on the south by Grassy Mountain, is about thirty-seven miles north-northwest of Pioche (DL 60); **DUTCH JOHN WELL** is east of the peak (GHM, LN 1).

DUTCHMAN PASS. See **ELDORADO PASS.**

DUTCH NICKS. See **EMPIRE CITY.**

DUTTON (Elko). Formerly a post office in the western portion of the county, established June 20, 1907, and discontinued September 30, 1913, when Midas became the mail address for its patrons (FTM, p. 8).

DYER (Esmeralda). The Nevada post office on State Route 3A near the California line, was established October 16, 1889, and named for Alex P. Dyer, the first postmaster (OR, 1899; FTM, p. 9). **DYER MINING DISTRICT,** east of the town for which it was named and on the west flank of the Silver Peak Range, twenty-eight miles south of Coaldale, was first prospected in 1863 (FCL, p. 66; OPN, p. 31; HWY Map).

DYKE (Churchill). Formerly a settlement between Miriam and Ocala on the west edge of the Humboldt Sink (SG Map 1). The town, new in 1906, according to report of the *Goldfield News* of September 29 of that year (DM), was named for a natural dike, "a lake bar of gravel formed through the action of currents in ancient Lake Lahontan"

(VPG). In times of high water, the water escaped through a vent in this dike to the Humboldt Sink (AEH). See **DIKE**.

EAGLE. The golden eagle and the southern bald eagle (the American eagle) are found in Nevada. Although most name stories relate that the toponym was given because of an incident—the killing of an eagle, the finding of an eagle's nest or feathers—or because of a land feature's resemblance to the eagle, the name givers probably had mixed motives and were perhaps consciously patriotic or even mindful of the $10 gold coin in applying the name. In Churchill County, **EAGLE CANYON CREEK** and **EAGLE SPRINGS** are in the northeast portion of the county in the Clan Alpine Range (GHM, CH 2; NHS, 1913, p. 182). **EAGLE ROCK,** a mountain peak and **EAGLE SALT MARSH,** a mining district, are in the northwest corner of the county. In 1871, B. F. Leete established **EAGLE SALT WORKS** in the district. A post office so named existed from July 10, 1871, to September 21, 1871, and from June 7, 1877, until December 20, 1899, when the name was changed to *Leete* (OPN, p. 10; 1881 Map; HHB, Nev., pp. 261–62; OR, 1879, 1899; FTM, p. 9). **EAGLEVILLE** denotes a locality, about eleven miles northeast of Rawhide, and a former post office (June 3, 1889–March 13, 1913), both in Churchill County. **EAGLEVILLE MINING DISTRICT,** named for the former settlement, but also called *Hot Springs,* is in Mineral County, sixty-four miles southeast of Fallon and eight miles northeast of Rawhide (VPG, p. 113; FTM, p. 9; USGB 5904; NHS, 1913, p. 201; SM, 1867, p. 20). **EAGLE MOUNTAIN** is near the eastern boundary of Douglas County, and **EAGLE MINING DISTRICT,** better known as *Gardnerville,* is fourteen miles southeast of Minden in the Pine Nut Mountains (VPG, p. 33). **EAGLE** also denotes a peak in the Hot Creek Range near Belmont in Nye County; a creek on the west slope of the Santa Rosa Range in Humboldt County; and a mining district in White Pine County, in the Kern Mountains near the Nevada-Utah boundary (OPN, p. 53; Dir. 1971; VPG, p. 186). **EAGLE FLAT** (Elko), a flat north of Wilkins and east of U.S. 93, was named for the large flocks of eagles seen there in the early days (EP, p. 29; GHM, EL 4). **EAGLE VALLEY** (Lincoln), a portion of Ursine Valley, about nineteen miles northeast of Panaca, is said to have been named by first settlers, who shot an eagle upon entering the valley in the

early 1860s (WA). The former settlement so named took its name from the valley (Census, 1870), as did **EAGLE VALLEY MINING DISTRICT,** also called *Fay* and *Stateline,* discovered twenty-one miles northwest of Modena, Utah (VPG, p. 93). For **EAGLE VALLEY** (Carson City), see **CARSON**. **EAGLE WASH** (Clark), south of Eldorado Canyon and parallel to it, takes its name from a large rock in the wash called *The Eagle* (WA). **EAGLE PICHER,** a name recently brought in from the Kansas-Oklahoma-Missouri lead and zinc district, is the designation for a mine south of Vernon and northwest of Lovelock, in southwest Pershing County (VPG; HWY Map). **EAGLE SPRINGS UNIT NO. 1,** in Railroad Valley, Nye County, is the name of Nevada's first oil well (Black Gold, p. 12; GHM, NY 4).

EAST. Among river forks named for their position in relation to the main stream is the **EAST WALKER RIVER,** which rises in the Sierra Nevada in California and joins the West Walker River in Lyon County. It furnished a name for the mining district so denoted, ten miles northwest of Hawthorne on the west slope of the Wassuk Range and east of the East Walker River. Mason Valley was the mail address for the early camp (1881 Map; 1867 Map; TF, p. 17). The district is also named *Mount Grant,* for the mountain of that name in the southern part of the district (VPG, p. 114). **EAST FORK QUINN RIVER** heads on the northeast slope of Eightmile Mountain, Humboldt National Forest, and joins the South Fork to form the Quinn River, in Humboldt County (USGB 6202; Dir. 1971). **EAST FORK** (Douglas), a former settlement and township was named for the **EAST FORK CARSON RIVER,** which flows northwest from Bryant Creek to meet the Carson River, northwest of Gardnerville and Minden (Census, 1870, 1900, 1950; OPN, p. 19; Mark. Sheet). The compass-point name also denotes **EAST CREEK,** one of a group of small streams, east of Prescio on the west slope of the Schell Creek Range in White Pine County (Dir. 1971). **EAST DEEP CREEK** (Elko). See **DEEP CREEK**. A number of orographic features are named for their relation to other peaks or ranges. Two mountain peaks named **EAST** are in Elko County, one northeast of Wells and the other northeast of Elko (OPN, p. 23). **EAST PEAK** (Douglas) is southeast of Tahoe Village near the California boundary (GHM, DO 1). **EAST RANGE** (Pershing, Humboldt) is terminated on the north by the Humboldt River and separated from the Stillwater Range by McKinney Pass on the south (USGB 6002; Dir. 1971). **EAST DESERT RANGE** (Clark, Lincoln) lies between the Desert Range to the west and the Sheep Range to the east, about forty-seven miles north of Las Vegas (USGB 6002). The **EAST MORMON MOUNTAINS** (Lincoln) are approximately twenty-five miles northeast of Moapa and separated from the Mormon Mountains to the west by a narrow valley. The **EAST PAHRANAGAT RANGE** (Lincoln), forty-three miles southwest of Caliente, is bounded on the east by Pahranagat Valley and separated from the Pahranagat Range by a narrow valley on the west (USGB 6002, 6001). The **EAST HUMBOLDT RANGE** (Elko) is south and east of the Humboldt River, for which it is named, and joins the north end of the Ruby Mountains (GHM, EL 1). Cadwalader's Map of the White Pine Range, published in 1869, delineates the **EAST** (or *Eshack*) **RANGE,** separated from the White Pine Mining District by Indian Valley on the west and from the Piowan, or Steptoe, Mountains by Piowan Valley on the east. **EASTGATE** (Churchill). The settlement, once a station on the Overland Road, is about four miles east of Westgate on the west slope of the Desatoya Range near the Lander County line. Captain James H. Simpson named it in 1859 for a conformation of the hills at this point which forms a pass into the valley (OPN, p. 10; NHS, 1913, p. 173; HHB, Nev., pp. 261–62). **EASTGATE MINING DISTRICT**, also on the west slope of the Desatoya Range at the extreme east border of the earthquake center, adjoins the Westgate Mining District (HPS, 1/26/56), sixty miles east-southeast of Fallon (VPG, p. 13). Ellsworth post office served the early settlement (TF, p. 17; 1881 Map). Communities named for their position in relation to a larger settlement include early **EAST BELMONT** (Nye), served by Belmont post office (TF, p. 17); **EAST ELY** (White Pine), a town, post office (established September 15, 1908), and station on the NN RR, named for their situation northeast of Ely; earlier the site of *Georgetown Ranch*. When the NN RR was being built, the yards were at *Ely City*, the first station name adopted, but because the citizens of Ely objected, the name was changed to East Ely in 1908 (DM; Dir. 1971). **EAST LAS VEGAS.** See LAS VEGAS. **EAST RENO.** See SPARKS.

EASTER MINE (Lincoln). The early name for a mine and the canyon in which the mine was located, eight miles below Caliente, was derived from the **EASTER GOLD MINING COMPANY** (WA). See **TAYLOR MINE.**

EASTERN SLOPE. In 1859 the part of Utah Territory in which the Comstock Lode was discovered was called the Eastern Slope, "the name by which this trans-Alpine region had come to be known immediately upon the announcement being made of this rich

metaliferous find over there" (HDG, CP, 8/19/76).

EASTERN TENNESSEE. See **GALENA.**

EASTMAN MILL (Washoe). A former sawmill, located on the south side of the Truckee River about halfway between Glendale and Reno; named for C. H. Eastman, owner (NHS, 1920, pp. 31, 32).

EASTON (Washoe). A non-agency station between Zenobia and Flanigan on the Wadsworth Subdivision of the SP RR and near the California line (T75).

EBERHARDT (White Pine). A former boom camp and post office (June 19, 1871–July 11, 1893), thirty miles west of Ely and five miles southeast of Hamilton, on the south slope of the White Pine Range at the junction of Applegarth and Mazeppa canyons; named for the **EBERHARDT,** a rich mine on Treasure Hill located by T. E. Eberhardt in December, 1867 (SPD, p. 1042; FTM, p. 9; RRE; Census, 1880; SM, 1875, pp. 164–65; NM). In 1869, both the camp and the canyon of location were designated **EBERHARDT** (Cad. Map; GHM, WP 1; 1881 Map).

ECCLES (Lincoln). The name of the UP RR siding between Minto and Caliente in Clover Creek Canyon, was perhaps transferred from an Idaho station of that name on the same railroad (OG, p. 1321).

ECHO. A lake on the east slope of Ruby Dome in the Ruby Mountains, "named for the echo that resounds in the magnificent terrain" (EP, p. 29), and a creek, northwest of Charleston, both in Elko County; a high cliff, south of Charleston Lodge in Clark County (GHM, EL 1; SG Map 11; WA). A mining district so named was located in 1863 in **ECHO CANYON,** four miles east of Rye Patch on the west flank of the Humboldt Range in Pershing County. Principal producers of the district were the Alpha and the Rye Patch mines (GHM, PE 2; SM, 1875, p. 67; VPG, p. 159). A canyon in Clark County so named, also known as **ECHO WASH,** drains eastward from Bitter Springs Valley into Lake Mead and **ECHO BAY** which was named for the canyon. In the early days, the main road from old Saint Thomas to Callville ran through the canyon, and the sounds of teams and wagons echoed strongly from its high walls (WA; GHM, CL 2).

ECLIPSE (Storey). Origin of the mine name on the Comstock is not revealed, but it seems to stem from the mine-naming traditions carried into Washoe from the western slope. Mines in California named Eclipse were in Amador, Inyo, and Monterey counties, at Gibsonville in Sierra County, and at Ophir in Placer County (CSMB, pp. 262–64, 281, 410, 774; CMA, pp. 182–84). Raymond mentions Eclipse mines in White Pine and

Lander counties, Nevada (RWR, pp. 130, 135). The thirty-foot claim on the Comstock was one of the original locations staked in 1859 by Finney, Bishop, Young, Comstock, Rogers, Plato, Bowers, and Knight. Although absorbed by the Consolidated Imperial at an early date, the name remains (IH). The Eclipse is presently controlled by the Sutro Tunnel Coalition, Inc., and Affidavit of Annual Labor is filed (AAL).

EDEN (Humboldt). Early prospectors in Humboldt County came upon a valley hemmed on three sides by mountains, the encircling Santa Rosas, carpeted with red, yellow, and blue flowers in late spring, and named the valley *Paradise*. Eastward is **EDEN VALLEY**, watered by multi-branched **EDEN CREEK**, imaginatively named by prospectors familiar with Genesis. See **PARADISE** (Guide Map).

EDGEMONT (Elko). The composite name, English *edge* + French *mont*, "mountain," was chosen to describe the position of the former boom camp on the west slope of the Bull Run (Centennial) Range, ninety-two miles north-northwest of Elko, and five miles south of White Rock, subsequent to the discovery of gold in the **EDGEMONT MINING DISTRICT** in the 1890s. Slides, which plagued the mining camp nearly every year, were particularly severe in 1906, when a quartz mill was carried away, by report of the *Reno Evening Gazette* of January 16, 1906, and in 1917, when an avalanche destroyed a large mill, assay office, and boarding house. **EDGEMONT** post office was active from October 1, 1901, until October 15, 1918, when White Rock became the mail address for its patrons (DM; NM; VPG, p. 40; FTM, p. 9).

EDGEWOOD (Douglas). A settlement and resort town a few miles south of Glenbrook on U.S. 50, named by a Mr. Averill because of its natural location. *Fridays Station* was the earlier name, commemorating Mr. Friday, the builder of the station, later purchased by Averill. Fridays Station was important in the early days because it was on two heavily traveled routes to Carson Valley, the Kingsbury Grade and the Lake Bigler (Tahoe) Toll Road (NHS, 1913, pp. 188, 194).

EDWARDS CREEK (Churchill). The creek and valley in eastern Churchill County were named by Captain J. H. Simpson in 1859. "I call the stream after one of my assistants, Mr. Edward Jagiello, a Polish gentleman; his surname being difficult of pronunciation, I have preferred his Christian name as the appellation" (JHS, p. 107). A Pony Express and Overland Stage station, named for the creek, was ten miles north of Gold Springs Station (Nev. I, 1961, p. 8; NJ 11–2; 1881 Map; Wheat IV, 137).

EGAN. The mountain range of this name is bounded on the north by the Cherry Creek Range, on the east by Steptoe Valley and Cave Valley, and on the west by White River Valley, Jakes Valley, and Butte Valley, in Lincoln, Nye, and White Pine counties. **EGAN CANYON** denotes a canyon and a mining district, also known as *Cherry Creek*, fifty miles north of Ely. Locations were made in the district in 1863. **EGAN MILL**, run by water power from **EGAN CREEK**, was the first built in Nevada (NJ 11–3; VPG, p. 177; SLC, I, p. 248; Wheat IV, 137; DL 60). The name commemorates Major Howard E. Egan, born in King's County, Ireland, in 1815, who came to Salt Lake City with the pioneer band of 1847. A major in the Nauvoo Legion, he later became an Indian fighter of old Fort Ruby. In the early 1850s Egan rode for George W. Chorpenning's pioneer mail service, between Salt Lake City, Utah, and Sacramento, California. He proved the **EGAN CUT–OFF**, a central route across Nevada, more practicable than the Humboldt River route, and the shorter route was adopted by Chorpenning (Nev. Guide, p. 247; NHS, 1924, pp. 267–272; NM). **EGAN CANYON STATION**, a relay point on both the Overland Stage and the Pony Express routes, was established by Major Egan about four miles south of Cherry Creek and twenty-five miles west of Schell Creek Station (Jackson Map). The post office was first established as **EGAN CANYON** in Lander County on April 13, 1865, moved into Elko County, where it was active from 1869 until June 16, 1873, and was reestablished as **EGAN** in White Pine County on June 19, 1877, and discontinued on March 19, 1878 (FTM, p. 9).

EGLON (Humboldt). A name of undetermined origin for Milepost 428.7, a station northwest of Winnemucca on a spur of the SP RR (T75).

EHRET (Clark). The name of the first post office at Sloan siding, nineteen miles southwest of Las Vegas, commemorated George Ehret, the first postmaster. Established as *Ehret* on May 7, 1919, the post office name was changed to *Sloan* on September 11, 1922 (WA; FTM, p. 9).

EIGHTMILE. The milepost name designates a creek, tributary to Quinn River, south of Two Mile Creek, and **EIGHTMILE MOUNTAIN**, in Humboldt County. Early settlers in the area were served by Fort McDermitt post office (Dir. 1971; SG Map 12; TF, p. 17). **EIGHT MILE STATION** (White Pine) was a mud and log cabin situated on the present site of the *Georgetta Ranch* (Dir. 1971). The Gosiutes, under their war chief, White Horse, burned the station and killed its keeper, initiating the Overland War on March 22, 1863. The war was conducted along a 225-mile route between Schell Creek and Salt Lake City during that year (HPS, 1/29/56; SPD, p. 155). **EIGHT MILE SPRING,** a settlement of the 1870s in the area, was served by Schellbourne post office (TF, p. 17). **EIGHTMILE WELL** (Lincoln), eight miles north of Pioche, was one of a series of wells named for their distance from Pioche (WA).

ELAINE. Formerly a post office established in Elko County May 10, 1880, and discontinued December 9, 1880 (1881 Map; FTM, p. 9); a short-lived mining camp which sprang up about thirty-five miles southwest of Austin in Lander County, in July of 1907 (DM).

ELBOW (Lyon). The early station of old Esmeralda County was at a bend of the East Walker River, southeast of Sweetwater, which served as its mail address (1881 Map; TF, p. 17). Later **ELBOW** post office was established and active for two brief periods in 1881, from March 2 to June 17, and from July 22 to September 5 (FTM, p. 9; GHM, LY 2).

ELBURZ (Elko). A point of connection of the WP RR and the SP RR between Coin and Halleck (T75); perhaps named for the Elburz Mountains in northern Iran.

ELDERBERRY SPRING. Springs named for elderberry bushes growing nearby are situated ten miles west of Indian Springs in Indian Spring Valley, Clark County, and about six miles west of Coyote Spring in Coyote Spring Valley, Lincoln County (WA).

ELDORADO. The word first appears in the early sixteenth century as the Spanish name (meaning "the gilded one") of a legendary Indian Chief of Bogota, whose body was covered with gold during ceremonial rites and whose abode was sought by conquerors of South America (Gudde, p. 94). In time, the name came to mean a paradise of riches and abundance and, as such, was used in Nevada. **ELDORADO CANYON** (Clark) was named in 1857 by a Captain Johnson of Fort Mohave, who was prospecting there (WA). In 1861, upon the discovery in the canyon of the Honest Miner and the Gettysburg mines, among others, the Colorado Mining District was organized (WA). The State Mineralogist notes that "this district takes its name from a remarkable fissure through the rocks made by the Colorado River" (SM, 1875, p. 91). Alternate names for the district are *Eldorado Canyon* and *Nelson* (VPG, p. 24). Among the important claims of the district, the Techatticup Mine, with the Savage vein, and the Wall Street Mine were the principal producers, yielding $3.5 million and $2 million respectively (WA; Nev. Guide, p. 235). Two early, small mining camps, Lucky Jim, active during the Civil War, and **EL-DORADO CITY,** situated near the **ELDO-RADO MINE** (1881 Map), served the district prior to the establishment of **EL-**

DORADO CANYON camp and post office (January 23, 1879–August 31, 1907) about twenty-nine miles southeast of Boulder City (FTM, p. 9; NM). Reputed to be a purely outlaw camp, filled with both Northerners and Southerners who wished to avoid conscription during the Civil War, it was the scene of claim jumping and murder. Mining law was decided by "Winchester's amendment to the Colt statute" (JGS, I, pp. 611–13, 628–31; Nev. Guide, pp. 235–36). Legend accredits first ore discoveries to Spaniards in 1775, who did not stay to develop the claims. One hundred years after the original discovery, an expedition from Mexico came to develop the claims, but found them being worked by the Eldorado Mining Company. Members of the expedition brought with them a map, said to have been drawn at the time of original discovery and to have been found in an old church in Mexico, which unmistakably indicated the site of either the Wall Street Mine (JGS, I, p. 613) or the Techatticup (Nev. Guide, p. 235). The **ELDORADO MOUNTAINS** (Clark), west of the Colorado River and southeast of Boulder City, were named for Eldorado Canyon (USGB 5903; Freese, Map 1). **EL DORADO CANYON** (Lyon), forming a part of the boundary between Douglas and Lyon counties, was named for the supposedly rich ore deposits found there by early miners (NHS, 1913, p. 209). Although the greater part of the area of the **ELDORADO NATIONAL FOREST** lies in California, four hundred acres of it are in Douglas County, Nevada (NHS, 1926, p. 420). **ELDORADO PASS** (Clark), also called *Dutchman Pass,* is about twenty miles south of Las Vegas between Black and Bishop mountains, formerly on the Arrowhead Trail. This was the main road between Las Vegas and Los Angeles and went through Eldorado Canyon (WA). Two early settlements so denoted were **EL DORADO** (Nye), served by Belmont post office, and **EL DORADO CANYON** (Pershing), served by Rye Patch post office (TF, p. 17). The canyon for which the early camp was named is southeast of Valery in the Humboldt Range (GHM, PE 2).

ELDORADO, CAMP (Clark). The temporary camp was established on January 15, 1865, to protect the miners of Eldorado Canyon, for which it was named, against Indian depredations. Until August 24, 1867, soldiers from Fort Mohave were stationed at this camp, situated just north of the mouth of Eldorado Canyon and on the west bank of the Colorado River at the **ELDORADO FERRY** crossing (WCB, p. 142; Ruhlen). The site of the ferry, a suspension type which hung from a cable, is now covered by Lake Mohave (WA).

ELEPHANT ROCK (Clark). The sandstone

feature in the Valley of Fire was named for its resemblance to the elephant (WA).

ELEVENMILE CANYON (Churchill). The canyon heads on the south slope of Table Mountain and extends to the north end of Fairview Valley, about twenty-nine miles east of Fallon (USGB 5904; GHM, CH 2).

ELGIN (Lincoln). A post office, established March 3, 1913, and a station on the UP RR, twenty miles south of Caliente in the Meadow Valley Wash. The name of the town, settled in 1882 in the bottom of the wash and about a mile north of the present site, was perhaps transferred from a city in Scotland of that name, or from Elgin, Illinois, commemorating the Earl of Elgin (HWY Map; HG, p. 116; WA).

ELKO. ELKO COUNTY, created out of Lander County on March 5, 1869, is the second largest county in Nevada, with an area of 17,128 square miles. It was named for the town of **ELKO,** first settled by George F. Paddleford in December of 1868. Officials of the CP RR laid out the townsite (HHB, Nev., p. 276; SPD, 826–27), and the post office was established on January 29, 1869 (FTM, p. 9). Nearby features named for the town include a summit, a peak, and the **ELKO MOUNTAINS** (GHM, EL 1). Elko, now on Interstate 80 and on the SP RR and the WP RR, had been a campsite on the emigrant road. The Kern and Walker party camped there on November 9, 1845, according to Kern's Journal. "About four miles above our camp tonight are some hot springs (Elko) too hot to bear one's hands in" (JGS, I, p. 95). Before the CP RR reached the site in 1868, it was already a freighting point for nearby mining districts: Lone Mountain, Tuscarora, Cope, and Railroad districts, among others (FES, p. 178). The station was a regular breakfast and supper stop, and travelers found of interest one of the hot springs called "Chicken Soup Spring" because the water, seasoned with a little salt and pepper, tasted like chicken broth (FES, p. 177).

It is probable that Charles Crocker, or some other official of the CP RR, named the station, for *Elko* is a typical railroad name, denoting stations in Alabama, Colorado, Georgia, Minnesota, Nevada, South Carolina, Virginia, and British Columbia (GRS, Elko; OG). The meaning of the name remains undetermined. Persistent name legends bear repeating in the interest of their diversity rather than of their credibility. Charles Crocker is said to have named Elko for elk roaming there, or to have given the station the name of the elk, with an *o* added, because he was fond of animals and carried a list of their names in his pocket. *Elk* was the next name on the list (SPD, pp. 826–27; M&S, p. 159). Elko is also said to be Sho-

shone for "white woman," receiving its name because the Indians saw a white woman there for the first time. What appears to be a purely fictive account of the naming occurs in a legend told of an emigrant party of 1850 that found a starving Indian boy near the present site of Elko. They placed him in a bed with a gravely ill, golden-haired white boy and cared for him tenderly. He was found to be the son of a chief when his father and a small band of Indians arrived. The Indians were appreciative of the care given the chief's son by the party and smoked the pipe of peace with them. When the golden-haired white boy died the next day, the grieved Indians chanted death songs, and the chief cried "Elko" again and again. When the father of the white boy returned five years later, he found the carved stones on his son's grave and learned the meaning of the word *Elko* was "beautiful" (TPB, Elko).

ELLENDALE (Nye). A rush to Ellendale occurred in June of 1909, upon the discovery of high grade gold float about thirty miles east of Tonopah. The mining district and camp were named for Ellen Clifford Nay, who located the first claim (VPG, p. 127; NM; DM).

ELLISON (White Pine). The creek, spring, and mine at the north end of the Horse Range were named for George Ellison, a homesteader (NHS, 1924, p. 309; GHM, WP 2).

ELLSWORTH (Nye). The mining district, former mining camp, and canyon so named were about twelve miles west of Ione, on Burnt Cabin Summit road at the north end of the Paradise Range (1881 Map). The district was organized in 1863 subsequent to silver-gold discoveries. **ELLSWORTH** post office was active from March 7, 1866, until December 29, 1884, when Grantsville became the mail address for its patrons (NM; VPG, p. 127; FTM, p. 9; Dir. 1971).

EL PICACHO MINE. See **OAK SPRING.**

ELY. The town of Ely is in southwest-central White Pine County, at the junction of U.S. 50 and U.S. 6 and on the NN RR. The land which included the present townsite of Ely is said to have been first located by George Lamb in 1869 or 1870 and to have been called *Murry Creek Station.* See **MURRY CREEK. ELY** post office was established on November 29, 1878 (FTM, p. 9), and **ELY VILLAGE** was included in the Eleventh Census. The name commemorates Smith Ely who financed the construction of a small copper furnace at the west side of the town in the 1870s. Some accounts credit A. J. Underhill with having named the town for John H. Ely, in return for the latter's having lent him the money to purchase the townsite; however, the establishment of the post office antedates Underhill's arrival in the area (SPD, p. 1049; NHS, 1924, pp. 396–97). Local authority, supplemented by articles in the *White Pine News* of December 25, 1906, and the *Mining and Scientific Press* of January 16, 1909, as well as by the date of the opening of the post office, establishes that the town name honors Smith Ely and his family, thought to have come to Nevada from Ely, Vermont, which may well have been named for his forbears (RRE). David F. Myrick has ascertained that Frederick Thomas of Oakland, California, named the town in 1878 for Smith Ely (DM, RR (I), p. 113). *West Ely* is an early map name and listing (1881 Map; TF, pp. 17, 23). The **ELY MINING DISTRICT** of White Pine County, also known as *Robinson,* is a few miles from Ely in the vicinity of Robinson Canyon in the Egan Range (VPG, p. 182).

ELY MINING DISTRICT in Lincoln County, also called *Pioche,* was visited by Lieut. G. M. Wheeler in the fall of 1868 and again in July of 1871, at which time he described it. "The range, or group of hills occupied by the district [Ely] stands as an island on the eastern foot-slopes of the Ely Mountain Range . . . ," the latter apparently having been named for the district (Wheeler, 1872, pp. 42–43). The name commemorates John H. Ely, a frontiersman, adventurer, and partner of William H. Raymond in the Pioche district. According to Wheeler, the principal companies of the district, first discovered in 1864 and relocated in 1868, were the Meadow Valley, Raymond and Ely, and Pioche. Named for the district are **MOUNT ELY**, also called the Pioche Hills, where the Pioche orebodies were discovered; the **ELY RANGE,** a north-south trending range between the Bristol Range and Patterson Pass; and **ELY SPRINGS,** a group of springs at the head of **ELY SPRINGS CANYON,** in the **ELY SPRINGS RANGE,** mountains bounded by the Highland Range and Bristol Valley. **ELY VALLEY** denotes a mine, about two miles northwest of Pioche on the northern slope of Mount Ely (WA; VPG, p. 98; OPN, p. 43; Freese, Map 2; NJ 11–9, 1881 Map).

EMERALD. A lake of northern Elko County, south of Cougar Peak and west of the east fork of the Jarbidge River; named for the color of its water (SG Map 11). **EMERALD CITY** (Clark) denoted a former townsite, laid out about three miles east of Searchlight at the Summit Springs copper claims, in the first decade of the twentieth century (WA).

EMERSON PASS (Washoe). The pass so named connects the Pyramid Lake basin with the Smoke Creek Desert and is also called *Blue Canyon* (VPG).

EMERYS LANDING (Clark). This possessive name for a boat landing on Lake Mohave at the mouth of Eldorado Canyon, honors Murl Emery, owner (WA).

EMIGRANT. Features of this name honor the early groups of pioneers moving to California or to the Northwest, who found the forbidding land of Nevada an unpleasant barrier. **EMIGRANT PASS** (Elko), a narrow divide on the Humboldt Road, was east of **EMIGRANT SPRING,** a campsite where the travelers had respite from the alkali dust and heat. **EMIGRANT PEAK,** south of Coaldale and at the north end of the Silver Peak Range, and **EMIGRANT PASS** in the range, were on the route to Owens Valley, California (NJ 11–8). **EMIGRANT VALLEY,** on the route taken by the Death Valley forty-niners, is an intermountain valley bounded on the east by the Groom Range, Jumbled Hills, and Chert Ridge and on the west by the Belted and Halfpint ranges, about sixty-five miles north-northwest of Las Vegas, in Lincoln and Nye counties (NJ 11–9; USGB 6301). **EMIGRANT SPRINGS** denoted an early station, west of Patterson in Cave Valley, Lincoln County, and was an early name for Hot Springs in Pershing County. Emigrants also called these hot springs on the Forty Mile Desert the *Spring of False Hope* because their oxen suffered from drinking the water and there was no forage (Nev. Guide, pp. 125, 139; ECN Map; 1881 Map).

EMPIRE. A Nevada post office, on State Route 34 five miles south of Gerlach in Washoe County, established February 16, 1951. The town, settled in 1922, was built by the Pacific Portland Cement Company who named it Empire, a trade name for gypsum products (FTM, p. 9; OPN, p. 66; HWY Map). **EMPIRE MINE** (Storey). A location notice of 1859 contains the following: "The name of the above claim is 'Empire Company'" (GH–A). No further information concerning the name was obtained, other than evidence of its pronounced popularity among the miners. With occasionally justified optimism, prospectors applied this name to mines in nine California counties (CMA, pp. 185, 318; OPJ, p. 8; JRB, Res., pp. 109, 144). The name also designated mines in Esmeralda, Humboldt, and White Pine counties, and a mining district, formerly situated between the Hot Creek and Tyboe districts in the Hot Creek Mountains, Nye County, Nevada, as well as mines located in Owyhee County, Idaho, and in Mesilla County, New Mexico (Wheeler 1871 Map; SM, 1866, pp. 148–151; RWR, pp. 135, 247, 398; JRB, Res., pp. 425, 448). On the Comstock, **EMPIRE NORTH** and **EMPIRE SOUTH,** named because of location, are separately patented claims (AR, No. 56, No. 57). The

Empire is a part of the Consolidated Imperial (IH).

EMPIRE CITY (Carson City). This important territorial town and former station on the V and T RR began as a station established on the Overland Road where it touched the Carson River, three and a half miles from Eagle Ranch, and was called *Dutch Nicks* for Nicholas Ambrosia, the first settler (MA, p. 533). On September 24, 1854, Nicholas Ambrosia was elected justice of the peace of Carson County, Utah Territory (HHB, Nev., p. 76). On March 24, 1855, a land claim was taken by him (MA, p. 38). Territorial records, dated December 4, 1860, state: "Ordered that the survey of 'Empire City' made in May 1860, by Barker & McBride, for Wm. H. Mead, and Nicholas Ambrosia, be approved specially" (WSJ–3). According to Myron Angel, the townsite was laid out in March, 1860, by Eugene Angel and other surveyors, who named it Empire City (MA, p. 562; 1867 Map). Early settlers humorously referred to Empire City as "the seaport town" because of spring floods caused by the Carson River (SPD, p. 979). The town was important for its mills which handled Comstock ore. The first mill, constructed in the spring of 1860, was enlarged as the Mexican Mill, or the Silver State Reduction Works. Meads Mill was built in 1861 (MA, pp. 539, 540). The greatest activity in the area occurred subsequent to the discovery of the "big bonanza." The name of **EMPIRE CITY** post office, established January 22, 1866, was changed to **EMPIRE** September 12, 1895. Operations were discontinued on December 31, 1912 (FTM, p. 9). The town of **NEW EMPIRE** on U.S. 50 is about one and one-half miles west of the site of the territorial settlement (GHM, CC 1).

ENCHANTED FORMATIONS (Clark). A fanciful name for rock forms created by erosion, in the Valley of Fire State Park (WA).

ENDLESS DRAW (Nye). The name for a ravine at the north end of the Cactus Range, about three miles northwest of Cactus Peak and nineteen miles east-northeast of Goldfield (USGB 6303).

ENGADINE (Lincoln). A former post office, established October 11, 1907, in that portion of Ursine Valley designated Round Valley, and discontinued April 15, 1914, when Panaca became the mail address for its patrons (FTM, p. 9); named by the Delmue brothers for the Engadine valley of the Inn River in the eastern portion of their native Switzerland (WA). See **DELMUE(S)**.

ERIE (Clark). A non-agency station on the UP RR, about twenty-five miles southwest of Las Vegas and twenty-two miles north of the California boundary (Freese, Map 1; WA).

ESMERALDA. The Spanish word for "emerald" denotes a Nevada county. Created on November 25, 1861, Esmeralda County has had its boundaries changed by acts of 1869, 1875, 1883, 1911, and 1913, and now has an area of 3,541 square miles. County seats were Aurora, by act of November 25, 1861, and Hawthorne, by act of July 1, 1883. The present county seat is Goldfield, established May 1, 1907 (OPN, p. 4). The name of the county derives from the **ESMERALDA MINING DISTRICT,** discovered August 25, 1860, by J. M. Corey, E. R. Hicks, and James M. Braley and named by Mr. Corey.

> On the 30th of that month they returned with some twenty others, laid out a mining district ten miles square, drew up and signed rules and regulations for the government of the same, and at the suggestion of Corey, christened it Esmeralda Mining District. Esmeralda is the Spanish word for emerald. Probably Corey had in mind some girls with green eyes. Be that as it may, Esmeralda soon became the popular name-word for a territorial empire. There was Esmeralda Hill, Esmeralda Gulch, Esmeralda mines, Esmeralda business houses, Esmeralda County, and later on an effort to have an Esmeralda State instead of Nevada State. The whole region was called Esmeralda in an indefinite sort of way. (SPD, p. 849)

According to J. Wasson, an early writer on Bodie and Esmeralda, Mr. Corey had taken the name from Victor Hugo's *Notre-Dame de Paris* (1831), because the name of the gypsy dancing girl was thought suitable for the Esmeralda Mining District which was to be a "wild dance of death or disappointment to thousands" (RC, p. 38; Nev. Terr. Map).

ESMERALDA post office was transferred from Mono County, California, to Esmeralda County, Nevada, on January 20, 1864, and operations were discontinued on February 27, 1866 (FTM, p. 9; 1867 Map). See **AURORA**.

ESSEX (Washoe). An abandoned coaling station, three miles east of Calvada on the SP RR, formerly the site of an ice house (DM; T1TR), served by Verdi post office (TF, p. 17).

ETNA. A small mill town formerly located in that portion of old Humboldt County presently within the boundaries of Pershing County, on the left bank of the Humboldt River and about three miles north of Oreana. The period of greatest activity was 1866 when **ETNA** post office was active from July 16 until October 19 (NM; FTM, p. 9). **ETNA** is also the designation for a peak, southeast of Wellington in the Mono National Forest of Lyon County, perhaps commemorative of the volcano of northeast

Sicily (Guide Map); for a UP RR station, about four miles southwest of Caliente; and for a cave, formerly called *Wheeler Cave,* an archaeological site at Etna siding, for which it was named (WA). "It is one of three archaeological sites in southern Nevada which establish the earliest date for the presence of man in the region at about 3000 B.C." (M&M, p. 113).

EUREKA. EUREKA COUNTY, created by legislative act of March 1, 1873, is in central Nevada. After boundary changes of February 16, 1875, February 7, 1877, and March 2, 1881, the county now has an area of 4,157 square miles. Since the creation of the county, the seat has been at **EUREKA,** the town from which the name derives (OPN, p. 5; MA, p. 426). The town was named for **EUREKA MINING DISTRICT,** located September 19, 1864. According to G. T. Tannehill, Recorder, a party from Austin consisting of W. O. Arnold, J. W. Stotts, Moses Wilson, W. R. Tannehill, and G. T. Tannehill, found an interesting species of rock and ran a test in their camp fire, "the result being a flow of metal greatly surprising the prospectors." They exclaimed "Eureka," staked their claims, and organized the district (MA, p. 426). The expression derives from a legend concerning Archimedes (287?–212 B.C.), Greek mathematician and inventor, who, upon discovering a method for determining the purity of gold in the crown of King Hiero, his kinsman, is said to have shouted *Eureka* ("I have found it"). The expression became popular as a place name of the Old West, after October 2, 1849, when it was approved as an inscription on the great seal of California (Gudde, p. 99). Although in 1863, the Indians held full sway in the territory of which Eureka County is composed, a few white men in the employ of the Overland Stage Company were there. The discovery of the Ruby Hill mines in 1869 created a rush, and W. W. McCoy and Alonzo Monroe founded a town named for the Eureka Mining District (SM, 1875, p. 6; HHB, Nev., p. 283; Wheeler 1871 Map; 1872 p. 37). The name was adopted for the post office on January 27, 1870, having been changed from *Napias* (January 13–27, 1870), commemorative of Napias Jim, an Indian. The principal mines of the district were those of the Eureka Consolidated Company, the Phoenix, Bull Whacker, Star of the West, and General Lee (FTM, p. 9; Wheeler, 1872, p. 37). *Eureka District* was included in the Ninth Census (1870), *Eureka, Inc.* in the Tenth Census (1880). In December of 1873, Darius O. Mills and W. L. Prichard incorporated the E and P RR, a ninety-mile narrow-gauge road connecting with the CP RR at Palisade. The railroad, later renamed the *Eureka-Nevada,* operated until September, 1938 (GHK, Bonanza, pp. 81, 84, 101).

EUREKA (Lyon). Formerly a small milling settlement on the Carson River and a station between Brunswick and Mound House on the V and T RR; named for the **EUREKA MILL,** built in 1862 (V&T Map; MA, p. 503). According to report, workmen, upon finishing the mill, threw up their hats yelling "Eureka," thus naming the place in a manner prescribed by long tradition (NHS, 1913, p. 216). Lake View was the mail address for the settlement (TF, p. 17).

EVANS. Formerly a station on the E and P RR, between Diamond and Parrys in Eureka County, served by Palisade post office (MA, p. 286; HHB, Nev., p. 285; 1881 Map; TF, p. 17); a creek northeast of Red House in Humboldt County; a creek southwest of Reno and west of the Truckee Meadows in Washoe County (GHM, HU 1; WA 1). **EVANS CREEK MINING DISTRICT,** named for the nearby creek, formerly was about seven miles southwest of Reno. It was organized in August, 1875, when John Poe discovered cinnabar there (SM, 1875, pp. 157–58). See **POEVILLE.**

EVERGREEN FLAT (Lincoln). A flat covered with a stand of creosote (evergreen) brush, in upper Coyote Springs Valley, was the result of an unsuccessful agricultural project started in 1912, when citizens of Mesquite and Bunkerville tried to drain water from Maynard Lake by tunnel and carry it about seven miles down the valley (WA).

EVEY WELL (Clark). An artesian well about seven miles south of Las Vegas; named for the **EVEY RANCH,** on which it was drilled. This first artesian well in Las Vegas Valley was, at the time of drilling in 1908, the third largest in the world (WA).

EXCELSIOR. The name denotes a mountain range extending northeastward from the Toiyabe National Forest to Soda Spring Valley, south of the Garfield Hills and Whisky Flat and north of Huntoon Valley and Teels Marsh in Mineral County (Haw. Quad.); also a former post office, active in Elko County from July 18, 1871, to March 12, 1872 (FTM, p. 9).

EXCHEQUER (Storey). The Comstock Exchequer mining claim is between the Alpha and the Bullion and included among the listings on the county tax roll (JAC, p. 1; AR, No. 66). The property, formerly termed the *Buckeye,* was owned by a London company (VH, p. 90). See **CHERRY CREEK.**

F

AIR. The word, usually in combination with a noun, may be a surname, but is more often chosen to indicate some agreeable aspect of a particular place. **FAIRBANKS SPRING** (Nye), southwest of Amargosa, was named in honor of R. J. ("Dad") Fairbanks, a pioneer of southern Nevada who freighted construction supplies during the building of both the SPLA & SL RR and the T & T RR, and established a tent city at Ash Meadows (GHM, NY 8; DM, RR (I), p. 588). The *Goldfield News* of March 9, 1906, carried an advertisement for town lots being sold in **FAIRFIELD** in Churchill County, by the Fairfield Townsite Company. An order of appointment for a post office, named for the townsite and dated April 5, 1906, was rescinded on November 12, 1906 (DM; FTM, p. 9). **FAIRLAWN**, a post office of Elko County, was active from June 14, 1888, until June 30, 1904 (FTM, p. 10). **FAIR PLAY**, a settlement south of Millers in Ruby Valley, also in Elko County, was served by a post office of the same name from February 7, 1879, until August 10, 1893, when Arthur became the mail address for its patrons (1881 Map; FTM, p. 10). **FAIR-PLAY MINING DISTRICT** (Nye), organized thirty-two miles northeast of Luning in the Paradise Range, is also known as *Atwood* and *Goldyke* (VPG, p. 127). **FAIR-VIEW**, an early settlement of Humboldt County, was south of Golconda, which served as its mailing address (1881 Map; TF, p. 17). The name group of Churchill County stems from **FAIRVIEW PEAK**, south of the Clan Alpine Range and about thirty-eight miles southeast of Fallon, which overlooks **FAIRVIEW VALLEY**, thirty miles southeast of Fallon and south of Dixie Valley, probably named in the 1850s. **FAIR VIEW STATION** was about midway between Middle Gate and Mountain Well on the Overland Mail Route (USGB 5904; 1867 Map; NJ 11-1). **FAIRVIEW**, a mining camp about four miles northwest of Fairview Peak and on the east edge of Fairview Valley grew up as a result of the discovery of the **FAIRVIEW MINE** by F. O. Norton in 1904 or 1905. The mining district, named for the mine, was organized on the western slope of Fairview Peak and is now known as *Bell Mountain* and *South Fairview* (USGB 5904; VPG, p. 13). The mining camp, prosperous from 1907 to 1912, when the ore vein was lost, declined quickly with the closing of the Nevada Hills Mine in 1917 (NM; M&S, p. 121; RRE; Car. Sink 1908). The post office, named for the settlement, was active from April 23, 1906, to May 31, 1919 (FTM, p. 10). In Lincoln County, **FAIRVIEW** is the name of a peak and a wash at the south end of the **FAIRVIEW RANGE**, a range of mountains west of Lake Valley and about twenty miles northwest of Pioche. A mining district so named was discovered in the early 1880s three or four miles from Bristol (NJ 11-6; M&SP, 4/1/82; DM). This silver-nickel district is also called *Silverhorn* (VPG, p. 100). **FAIRVIEW** (Clark) was the name of a salt mine, west of the Virgin River and a mile southeast of the Calico Salt Mine, now under the waters of Lake Mead. This mine, which was a source of supply for Eldorado Canyon in the 1860s and 1870s, had been worked by Indians prior to the coming of white men (VPG; WA). **FAIR VIEW** (Storey) was a claim staked and named in 1859, eliminating the possibility of its having been named in honor of James G. Fair, who arrived in the area several years later. After purchase of the mine by the Bullion, the claim name **FAIR VIEW** was lost on the Comstock (Dir. 1875, p. xxxix).

FALAIS (Churchill). A non-agency station on the Sparks Subdivision of the SP RR between Upsal and Massie; presumably named in commemoration of Falaise in northwest France, the seat of the Dukes of Normandy and probable birthplace of William the Conqueror (T75).

FALCON. A canyon of Nye County so named heads on Split Ridge and extends to its mouth about two miles north-northwest of Ammonia Tanks. The name was applied because "in 1961 a family of prairie falcons nested in the rhyolite cliffs overlooking the canyon" (USGB 6302; DL 54). **FALCON** (Elko) denotes a mine at the north end of the Tuscarora Mountains, and an early settlement served by Tuscarora post office (GHM, EL 2; TF, p. 17). **FALCON HILL** (Washoe) is an isolated hill rising above the desert wash a few miles northwest of the north end of Winnemucca Lake (now dry), lying just to the west of State Route 94 between Nixon and Gerlach; named for the diurnal bird of prey. The hill was named in 1960 by Dr. Richard Shutler, Jr., Curator of Anthropology, Nevada State Museum, Carson City, who had been conducting archaeological explorations in Kramer Cave (q.v.). The cave was reported by William Shinners of Reno and his friends who were exploring the hill for the possibility of capturing falcons (JWC; VPG).

FALL. A name of undetermined origin for a creek rising in the Jarbidge Mountains and flowing to a confluence with the East Fork Jarbidge River; a stream heading in the Sawtooth National Forest of Idaho and flowing to Milligan Creek, east of Jackpot, both in Elko County. **FALL SPRING** (Clark) is southwest of Gold Butte (USGB 6303; NJ 11-9; GHM, CL 2).

FALLON (Churchill). The county seat of Churchill County began as a post office, established July 24, 1896, in a little shack of Michael Fallon in the western part of the county. Fallon grew rapidly as the center of the Truckee-Carson Irrigation

Project, started in 1903 under the Arid Lands Act of 1902 (RRE; M&S, p. 150; FTM, p. 10). The town is a station on the Fallon Branch of the SP RR (T75). The name has been adopted for **FALLON MINING DISTRICT,** also called *Holy Cross,* on the east slope of the south end of the Desert Range, fifteen miles north-northeast of Schurz (VPG, p. 14); **FALLON VALLEY,** the part of Lahontan Valley near Fallon; **FALLON INDIAN RESERVATION** and **FALLON WILDLIFE REFUGE,** said to be the largest public duck-hunting grounds in the United States (NJ 11–1; OPN, p. 11).

FALLOUT HILLS (Lincoln). This group of hills is bounded on the west by Chert Ridge and on the east by the Pintwater Range, about sixty-seven miles northwest of Las Vegas. The name was submitted to the United States Board on Geographic Names by the Geologic Division of the Geological Survey in 1959 in a report stating that the hills were so named because "during 1957–1958 this area was contaminated by radioactive fallout related to A-bomb tests in the Nevada Test Site, a few miles west" (USGB 6001; Kilmartin).

FARRELL (Pershing). Formerly a townsite, laid out about twenty-five miles northwest of Lovelock in that portion of old Humboldt County presently within the boundaries of Pershing County, about seven miles from Vernon; named for William F. ("Bill") Farrell (as noted in the *Reno Evening Gazette* of June 3, 1907, and in the *Lovelock Tribune* of July 19 and 26, 1907), or Jack Farrell, a mine owner. A post office so designated served the town from July 20, 1907, to September 30, 1911, at which time Mazuma became the mail address for its patrons (DM; FTM, p. 10).

FARRIER (Clark). The name of the non-agency station, ten miles north of Moapa on the UP RR, was changed from *Guelph* to Farrier, honorific of Fred Farrier, a railroad official (WA; Freese, Map 1).

FAULKNER CREEK (Eureka). The name of the stream heading in the Toiyabe National Forest and flowing generally eastward to Cedar Creek was established as Faulkner, not *Faulker,* by decision of the United States Board on Geographic Names (USGB 5904).

FAVRE LAKE (Elko). A mountain lake and campsite, four miles from Liberty Lake in the Ruby Range of the Humboldt National Forest; named for Clarence Favre of the Forest Service (SG Map 10; Nev. Guide, p. 161; MM).

FAWN CREEK (Elko). The name, associated with the mule deer which roams the mountain forests of Nevada, occurs less frequently than *Deer Creek* and denotes a tributary of the East Fork of the Owyhee River in the Duck Valley Indian Reservation and a stream

west of the Jarbidge River and near the Idaho line (SG Map 11; GHM, EL 1).

FAY (Lincoln). The name of the former mining camp and post office (September 13, 1900–July 15, 1924) commemorates the daughter of A. W. McCune, a major investor in the district. It was situated twenty-one miles northwest of Modena, Utah, and just inside the Nevada line (FTM, p. 10; WA; Freese, Map 2).

FENELON (Elko). A non-agency station on the Elko Subdivision of the SP RR between Holborn and Pequop; named by railroad officials perhaps in commemoration of Francois Fénelon (1651–1715), tutor to the grandson of Louis XIV (T75; T1SL).

FERBER (Elko). A mining district, forty-eight miles south of Wendover in foothills three miles east of the Toano Range; a flat west of the district; and a wash were so named in honor of the Ferber brothers, who discovered the district in 1880 (EP, p. 32; GHM, EL 5; VPG, p. 40).

FERGUSON. MOUNT FERGUSON (Mineral), a mountain in the Gabbs Valley Range and twenty-eight miles east of Walker Lake, was "named for Henry G. Ferguson (1882–1966), who served with the USGS from 1911–1959, and who spent a large part of his career studying the geology and ore deposits of a broad region in west-central Nevada that included the Gabbs Valley Range" (USGB 6803). **FERGUSON CREEK,** flowing from the Goshute Mountains to the Utah state line, and **FERGUSON SPRINGS,** a settlement on U.S. 50 north of Sugar Loaf Peak and southwest of Wendover (both in Elko County) commemorate the Ferguson family, early settlers in the area (Guide Map; MM). **FERGUSON** (Lincoln). See **DELAMAR.**

FERNLEY (Lyon). A town and trading center in fertile **FERNLEY VALLEY** at the junction of Interstate 80 and U.S. 95; served by the SP RR and settled about 1905 (T75; OPN, p. 47). A post office, named for the town, was established April 21, 1908 (FTM, p. 10).

FIDDLERS GREEN (Lyon). Formerly a small settlement, six miles south of Dayton. "Several shiftless and happy-go-lucky families lived there, who used to spend the day playing and dancing, and so it was dubbed Fiddlers Green" (NHS, 1913, p. 216).

FILBEN. See **JUNCTION.**

FILLMORE (Churchill). A post office of this name was established April 28, 1884, and discontinued December 6, 1886, when Eagle Salt Works became the mail address of its patrons (FTM, p. 10).

FINGER ROCK WASH (Mineral). A wash north of the Cedar Mountains in Stewart Valley; named for a rock formation in the area (Tono. Quad.).

FIRE (Clark). **FIRE BAY,** a bay in the Overton Arm of Lake Mead between Black Point and Stewarts Bay; **FIRE ALCOVE,** part of the Valley of Fire; named for rock coloration in the area (WA). **FIRE CREEK** (Lander) is north of Corral Canyon in the Shoshone Mountains (GHM, LA 2).

FIRST. The name has been applied to a creek, north of Crystal Bay on Lake Tahoe and east of Second Creek and Third Creek in Washoe County; to a stream in Steptoe Valley, north of Kinsey Canyon and south of Second Creek and Third Creek in White Pine County; to a creek running east from Sandstone Bluffs and **FIRST CREEK SPRING,** a spring on First Creek, near Blue Diamond in Clark County. **FIRST CANYON** (Lander) is southwest of Austin in the Toiyabe Range (Dir. 1971; WA).

FISH. The specific term is occasionally applied to fishable streams and lakes. In addition to the many varieties of trout (Elko County alone has over twenty-eight hundred miles of trout streams), large-mouth black bass, crappies, bullheads, catfish, sunfish, white fish, steelhead, salmon, carp, and freshwater shrimp and mussels abound in many areas of the state. See **TROUT** and **SALMON.**

FISH CREEK. A range, extending from southwest of Eureka in Eureka County to northern Nye County; named for **FISH CREEK,** a stream west of the range which was formerly the site of a settlement of workers who made charcoal from the nut pine of the Fish Creek Range for the Charcoal Burners' Association. This was the site of the Fish Creek War between the association and the smelter interests in Eureka, in August of 1879 (Wheeler 1871 Map; JGS, I, p. 320). **FISH CREEK** (Lander), formerly a township with its post office at Austin, was named for a stream which flows from the **FISH CREEK MOUNTAINS** near the Pershing County line, to the Reese River at Watts (Guide Map; Census, 1870).

FISHHOOK RIDGE (Nye). A ridge five miles north of Morey Peak in the Hot Creek Range; "named for the fishhook shape of the crest" (USGB 6903).

FISH LAKE. A group name in western Esmeralda County, stemming from a lake or marsh in **FISH LAKE VALLEY,** five miles east of Dyer and west of the Silver Peak Range (1881 Map). The valley was settled in 1875 when the Pacific Borax Company moved to it (Nev. Guide, p. 222; HHB, Nev., pp. 259–60). **FISH LAKE** post office was active from October 10, 1881, to February 3, 1887, when Columbus became the mail address for its patrons (FTM, p. 10). **FISH LAKE MARSH** denotes a mining district seventy-two miles southwest of Tonopah

(VPG, p. 53). **FISH LAKE CAMP** was a temporary army camp located near Fish Lake and occupied from December 1866 to July 1867 by detachments of troops, sent from Camp Independence, Owens Valley, California, to Nevada to protect mining settlements near the White Mountains from the Indians (Ruhlen). The lake which gave rise to the name group was described by Wheeler when he stopped there in 1871. "The next day the party moved to near Fish Lake, a small body of tepid water, a few rods in extent, in Fish Lake Valley, nineteen miles from Red Mountain Spring" (Wheeler, 1872, p. 79). **FISH LAKE** (Nye) is a lake in the north-central portion of Nye County between the Monitor Range and the Hot Creek Range.

FISH SPRING. The name denotes a flat, five miles east of Gardnerville in Douglas County, named for nearby springs (NHS, 1913, p. 191; Mark. Sheet); a spring in Washoe County at the south end of Honey Lake Valley (1881 Map; VPG); and a valley in Nye County between the Monitor Range and the Hot Creek Range (Wheeler, 1871 Map). Tybo post office served early settlers there (TF, p. 17).

FITTING. A settlement and a mining district on the west flank of the Humboldt Range in Spring Valley Canyon, fourteen miles east of Oreana and twenty-eight miles south of Mill City in Pershing County, served by a post office so named from March 24, 1905, to November 30, 1915 (Love. Quad.; VPG, p. 163; FTM, p. 10); a mining district on the southeast slope and end of the Gillis Range, four miles north of Acme in Mineral County (VPG, p. 109).

FITZGERALD, MOUNT (Elko). The peak is in the Ruby Mountains, twenty-four miles southeast of Elko, and was "named for President John Fitzgerald Kennedy (1917–1963)" (USGB 6601).

FIVE MILE. A station east of Aurora in old Esmeralda County; served by Aurora post office (1881 Map; TF, p. 17); a spring five miles south of Stone Cabin Ranch in Nye County; and a creek north of Nine Mile Ranch in Kings River Valley in Humboldt County (GHM, NY 1; HU 3). **FIVEMILE DRAW** and **FIVEMILE DRAW WELL** are east of Wilkins in northern Elko County (GHM, EL 4).

FLAGSTAFF. The name of one of the principal mines of the Cherry Creek Mining District in White Pine County; and of a mountain in north-central Nye County, in Hot Creek Valley, east of the Monitor Range; probably commemorative of Flagstaff, Arizona (Guide Map).

FLAMING FIRE (Clark). A state recreation ground and game refuge near Lake Mead;

named descriptively for the predominately red rock in the area (Park Map).

FLANIGAN (Washoe). The town on the Wadsworth Subdivision of the SP RR at a point of connection with the WP RR, is southwest of Astor and west of Pyramid Lake (T75, T54). Senator P. L. Flanigan donated the right-of-way through his extensive properties to the WP RR, whose officials named the town for him (JGS, II, pp. 73–75). The post office was established February 12, 1914 (FTM, p. 10).

FLAT. A creek joining the Quinn River north of Skull Creek, and **FLAT CREEK RANCH** on the creek; also a creek west of Kings River, in Humboldt County (GHM, HU 4, 3); a creek west of Elk Mountain, between Cherry Creek and Sheep Creek at the Idaho boundary, in Elko County (GHM, EL 3); a canyon across the Lander-Eureka county line north of U.S. 50 (GHM, LA 1); a spring southwest of Tonkin in the Simpson Park Range, in Eureka County (GHM, EU 1); usually named for surrounding level ground.

FLATIRON (Clark). The name selected in 1910 for a mining district, consisting of a group of claims located by R. E. Lake and Joe Kutcher, on the west side of a dry lake in Eldorado Valley (WA).

FLAT TOP MESA (Clark). The name denotes a prominent mesa of northeastern Clark County, lying west of Mesquite and northwest of Bunkerville (WA).

FLEISH (Washoe). A settlement and former post office and station on the SP RR, two miles west of Verdi; named for the Fleishhacker family of San Francisco, who formerly operated a paper mill at nearby Floriston. The settlement, which grew up at the site of a power station on the Truckee River in 1905, was served by the Fleish post office, earlier named *Marmol,* from May 4, 1908, until May 31, 1909. The railroad station was abandoned on December 15, 1938 (OPN, p. 66; FTM, p. 10; DM).

FLETCHER (Mineral). A former stage stop, way station, and post office, located at a crossroads eighteen miles southwest of Hawthorne and six miles north of Aurora; and nearby **FLETCHER SPRINGS** were named for H. D. Fletcher, first postmaster (NM; OR, 1885; GHM, MI 1; HPS, 1/24/54). The post office was established October 24, 1883, in that portion of old Esmeralda County later within the boundaries of Mineral County, and discontinued on November 30, 1918, when Hawthorne became the mail address for its patrons (FTM, p. 10).

FLOKA (Humboldt). A name of undetermined meaning for a station fifty-three miles from Winnemucca between Sulphur and Antelope on the WP RR (T54).

FLORAL SPRINGS (Lincoln). This spring, west of Pioche, along with Lime and Connor springs was for many years the source of water for Pioche. A millsite on the outskirts of Pioche took its name from the spring (WA; GHM, LN 1).

FLOTZ (Humboldt). A former post office of old Humboldt County, established in Spring Valley (Pershing) on March 21, 1892, and discontinued on March 15, 1904; probably a mistake name resulting from metathesis. The Census of 1900 and the Official Register of 1899 list *Foltz,* named for J. B. Foltz, postmaster (FTM, p. 10).

FLOWERY. A grass-covered, spring-fed swamp in Goshute Valley between the Pequop Mountains and the Toano Range, east of Jasper in Elko County, is called **FLOWERY LAKE.** The area also contains **FLOWERY SPRINGS,** so named "because of the peculiar variety of flowers that grow along its margin at certain times of the year" (OPN, p. 24; Nev. Guide, p. 115; NK 11–12). In 1845 Frémont camped at springs about twelve miles west of Flowery Springs and named them *Whitton Springs* for one of his men. Whitton Springs was known as *Mound Springs* by many emigrant parties and is now shown on some maps as *Chase Spring* (q.v.). **FLOWERY** (Storey). A canyon, east of Virginia City, was named for abundant wild flowers which grow there in the springtime, watered by melting snow from the **FLOWERY RANGE,** northeast of Virginia City, north of Six-Mile Canyon and southeast of Long Valley. **FLOWERY PEAK** is in the south end of the range and north of **FLOWERY RIDGE,** which extends south to Gold Canyon. **FLOWERY MINING DISTRICT** is named for the range in which it was discovered (VPG, p. 168; NHS, 1913, p. 188; 1867 Map; Car. City Quad.). **FLOWERY CITY** was a short-lived settlement in Flowery Canyon (NHS, 1913, p. 188).

FLUORINE (Nye). Formerly a mining camp northeast of Beatty, by report of the *Rhyolite Herald* of April 22, 1908, and a post office, established May 26, 1908, and discontinued July 15, 1909; named for the **FLUORINE MINING DISTRICT,** located at the north end of Bare Mountain, which is immediately east of Beatty. Fluorine is the gas which combined with sodium forms fluorite (DM; FTM, p. 10; VPG, p. 127).

FLYING MACHINE SPRING (Lincoln). The spring, high on a steep slope southwest of Boyd, was so named to indicate the difficulty of access (WA).

FOLTZ. See **FLOTZ.**

FOREMAN CREEK (Elko). The creek rises north of Independence Mountain in the Humboldt National Forest and flows generally southeastward to the North Fork

Humboldt River, and was "so named because it was headquarters for Phillipe Corrilo, foreman for the Dan Murphy Ranch" (Freese, Map 3; SG Map 11; EP, p. 32).

FORLORN HOPE SPRING (Clark). A spring northeast of Nelson; El Dorado Canyon post office was the mail address for early settlers at the spring (1881 Map; TF, p. 17; GHM, CL 3).

FORMANVILLE (Storey). An active town on the Comstock in the 1880s; named for Charles Forman, superintendent of the Forman Shaft (DM). Fire destroyed the town in 1903, by report of the *Reno Evening Gazette* of October 23 of that year.

FORT. Military reservations are entered under the specific term of the name. For Fort Churchill, see **CHURCHILL.**

FORTIFICATION RANGE. A short mountain range about forty-five miles north of Pioche and east of Cave Valley, extending from northern Lincoln County into southern White Pine County; so named because its wall-like appearance, from the western view, and its almost flat top cause the range to resemble a constructed fortification wall (NJ 11–6; JWH).

FORTY MILE. The **FORTY MILE DESERT** (Churchill) is a waterless area of shifting sands between the Humboldt Sink and the Carson River; named for its length by an emigrant party of the 1840s or early 1850s. (The accuracy of the pioneers in determining mileage was made possible by the use of such instruments as the rodometer, invented by the Mormons in Nauvoo and attached to Addison Pratt's wagon to measure the distance to Salt Lake Valley, in 1847.) "The route was first traveled by the Walker-Chiles Party in 1843, with the first wagon train" (SHM 26). Many emigrants and animals died from thirst, hunger, heat, and fatigue during the dreadful crossing of the Forty Mile Desert. According to the diary of one of these emigrants, at least a thousand wagons had been deserted in that short distance. Interstate 80 goes to the west of the present Forty Mile Desert. The name was also applied earlier to the route from the Humboldt to the Truckee River. Later the name was used solely for the Humboldt-Carson River route, as it is today (AEH; M&S, pp. 49–50; Nev. Guide, p. 137; VPG; LRH, XV, p. 321). **FORTYMILE** (Nye) denotes a wash and a canyon extending northward from a point west of Lathrop Wells and southeast of Yucca Mountain (GHM, NY 6, 8).

FORTY–NINE (Washoe). The name for a lake southeast of Vya, for a canyon, a creek, a mountain, and a former camp in the Hays Canyon Range, all in northern Washoe County and appearing on early maps; named by emigrant parties on their way to California in 1849 (OPN, p. 67; VPG, NK 11–7).

FOSSIL. Features named for fossiliferous rock formations include **FOSSIL HILL** in the West Humboldt Range, Pershing County, and **FOSSIL RIDGE** at the southern extremity of the Sheep Range, northwest of Gass Peak in Clark County (VPG; WA).

FOURMILE. The milepost name indicates the distance of **FOURMILE SPRING** east of Las Vegas (WA; Vegas Quad.). **FOURMILE FLATS** (Nye) denotes a valley, seven miles west-southwest of Morey and in the Hot Creek Range; named for nearby **FOURMILE CANYON** (USGB 6903; NJ 11–5). **FOURMILE HILL** (Lyon) is the designation for a range and a creek southeast of Wellington near the Douglas County boundary (GHM, LY 2).

FOURTH OF JULY MOUNTAIN (Clark). The name of the ridge, about three miles southeast of Searchlight (WA), probably signifies the day of the naming, which usually is coincident with the time of discovery or first observation. See **APRIL FOOL MINE** and **NEW YEAR LAKE.**

FOX. The name may commemorate an early settler, or refer to the red fox found in the Sierra Nevada and in eastern Nevada, or to the swift, or desert fox. **FOX CREEK** (Elko) is the name for a creek, tributary to the Jarbidge River, south of Jarbidge, and for a peak, northeast of Copper Basin (Dir. 1971; NK 11–9). **FOX MOUNTAIN** denotes a peak in Washoe County at the north end of the Granite Range (the highest peak in this part of Nevada), also called *Mahogany Peak* from the large groves of mountain mahogany growing on the northeastern slopes (VPG; 1881 Map; NK 11–7). **FOX MOUNTAIN** (Nye) is about three miles northwest of the White River near the Lincoln County line (DL 60; GHM, NY 5). The **FOX MOUNTAINS** (Washoe), between the Smoke Creek and San Emedio deserts, continue northward from the Lake Range (VPG).

FRANCIS (Washoe). A former settlement and a station on the NCO RR, northwest of Cedar and at the California line, served by **FRANCIS** post office from September 23, 1915, until November 10, 1919, when Reno became the mail address for its patrons (N–C–O Map; FTM, p. 10).

FRANKLIN. A lake in Ruby Valley, east of the Ruby Mountains in Elko County, with broad expanses of marsh and tule where wild ducks and geese nest; a river emptying into the north end of the lake. The lake was named by E. G. Beckwith in 1854, in honor of Franklin Pierce (1804–1869), the fourteenth president of the United States. The names **FRANKLIN LAKE** and **FRANK-**

LIN VALLEY appear on Beckwith's 1855 map (Wheat IV, 74). The Rogers and Johnston 1857 Atlas Map shows the **FRANK-LIN RIVER** (Wheat IV, 63). **FRANKLIN** (Lander) denoted a short-lived post office, established February 20, 1900, and discontinued May 2, 1900, when Newpass became the mail address for its patrons (FTM, p. 10). Early **FRANKLIN MILL** (Lyon) was served by Gold Hill post office (TF, p. 17).

FRANKTOWN (Washoe). The town was one of the earliest settled places in western Utah Territory (SPD, p. 1006; DDQ, p. 7). It was laid out by Elder Orson Hyde in Washoe Valley in 1856, and named for Frank Poirier, a resident (SPD, p. 1030). Two 1860 maps of the Washoe mines, prepared by Henry De Groot and R. M. Evans, show the town name (Wheat IV, 189; V (I), 16). Franktown was the terminus of a wood flume, owned by the Virginia and Gold Hill Water Company, and a station on the V and T RR, as well as a territorial post office, established April 22, 1862. Except for brief suspensions of service in 1871 and in 1881, the post office was active until March 15, 1927 (MA, p. 642; C&C, p. 588; FTM, p. 10). **FRANKTOWN CREEK** flows into the northwest corner of Washoe Lake, north of the old site of Franktown (GHM, WA 1).

FREDELLEN (Clark). A blend name designating a short-lived copper camp, active in 1909 and located near Hemenway Pass at the north edge of Boulder City; named by Fred J. Siebert, a mining man, and containing his Christian name (DM).

FREIBURG (Lincoln). This silver-gold-lead mining district, first discovered in 1865 by Messrs. Didlake and Aikens and named *Worthington* (1867 Map), was reorganized as the *Freyberg* district in 1869, by George Ernst and a group of prospectors (WA). Wheeler locates the *Freiburg* district seventeen miles northwest from Silver Canyon, at the eastern base of the mountains (Wheeler 1871 Map; 1872, p. 42). The post office was first named *Fryberg* and established June 6, 1889, with operations being transferred to Hiko on November 1, 1895. Reestablished as *Freiburg*, the post office was active from August 29, 1900, until November 30, 1903 (FTM, p. 10). The district is presently called Freiberg, or Worthington and is located seventy-five miles west of Pioche (VPG, p. 94).

FRENCH BRIDGE. See **WINNEMUCCA**.

FRENCHMAN. FRENCHMAN FLAT (Nye), a dry lake north of Indian Springs and south of Groom Lake, is now an atomic test site. The flat, crossed by the Death Valley forty-niners, was named for a Frenchman, "named La Quinta or Naquinta, who reportedly guided some men of the Mormon Battalion over the Spanish Trail in 1847" (WA; Vegas Quad.). **FRENCHMAN MOUNTAIN** (Clark), also known as **FRENCHMANS** and *Sunrise,* is the southernmost of twin peaks, about fifteen miles east of Las Vegas (OPN, p. 15; WA). **FRENCHMAN MINE,** on the southwest flank of Frenchman Mountain, was developed as a stock-promotion scheme by Paul Watelet and C. W. Hillegas following reports of a gold strike in 1912. The name commemorates Watelet, a native Belgian, who was mistakenly thought to be French (WA). **FRENCHMAN CREEK** (Lander) rises on the east slope of the Toiyabe Range, northeast of Bunker Hill, and flows generally southeastward into Big Smoky Valley. **FRENCHMAN** (Churchill). By decision of the United States Board on Geographic Names, *Frenchman* (not *Bermond, Frenchman Station,* or *Frenchmans Station*) is the official designation of the settlement in Fairview Valley, on U.S. 50 between West Gate and Sand Springs Pass, about thirty miles southeast of Fallon (USGB 5904; Dir. 1971).

FRENCHMANS FORD. See **WINNEMUCCA**.

FRIDAYS STATION (Douglas). The last stop in Nevada (as presently defined) on the Pony Express and Overland Mail routes before entering California; named for the builder of the station (Jackson Map). J. W. Small and M. K. Burke owned the station in 1860 (M&M, p. 52). See **EDGEWOOD**.

FRIEDMAN TUNNEL (Pershing). The low-level tunnel so named commemorates L. A. Friedman, who was president of the Rochester Mines Company and an active mining man at Seven Troughs (DM).

FRISBIE (Lander). The principal mining camp, in 1883, of the Campbell (Bullion) Mining District, twenty-five miles southwest of Beowawe on the east slope of the Shoshone Range. A post office, named for the camp, was in operation from July 16, 1883, to October 29, 1885 (FTM, p. 10; DM; M&SP, 12/8/83).

FROST CREEK (Elko). A creek, tributary to Bull Run Creek northeast of Deep Creek (GHM, EL 2); a creek south of Jiggs in Huntington Valley, named for a Mr. Frost, an early settler who ran a dairy (EP, p. 36, GHM, EL 1).

FRYBERG. See **FREIBURG**.

FULLERS CROSSING. See **RENO**.

FURLONG (Elko). A creek, tributary to the South Fork Humboldt River, south of Lee; "named for N. Lawrence Furlong who came to the South Fork country in the early 1870s and settled near the stream that bears his name" (EP, p. 36). Features named for the creek are **NORTH FURLONG CREEK** and **NORTH FURLONG LAKE,** southwest of

Favre Lake in the Ruby Mountains (NK 11–12; GHM, EL 1).

GABBARD HILLS (Nye). The group of hills just north of Coyote Cuesta, eight miles northeast of Mount Helen and thirty-seven miles east-southeast of Goldfield, was named for "John Gabbard who, with Hermann Trappman, discovered gold in the vicinity in 1904" (USGB 6303).

GABBS (Nye). A town in northwest Nye County on State Route 23, northeast of Luning in **GABBS VALLEY**. The valley extends into eastern Mineral County, east of **GABBS VALLEY RANGE**, north of the Pilot Mountains. A creek so named flows through the valley. The name of the post office, established as *Toiyabe* on December 18, 1942, was changed to Gabbs on June 1, 1943, and is commemorative of Professor E. S. Gabbs, an engineer (HWY Map; Guide Map; FTM, p. 11; OPN, p. 49).

GALENA. The mining camp, a station on the NC RR in 1880, and on the BM and L RR during its brief existence (HHB, Nev., p. 239; DM), was eleven miles from Battle Mountain. It served the **GALENA MINING DISTRICT**, located in 1867 in the Battle Mountains of Lander County. The district was named for its chief ore, argentiferous galena, produced principally in the Avalanche, Buena Vista, Butte, Trinity, and White mines (Wheeler, 1872, p. 40, 1871 Map). With few interruptions, the post office operated from 1871 to 1907. The name of Galena Station was changed to *Lewis,* then to *Lewis Junction.* **GALENA CREEK** and **GALENA CANYON,** also in the northwest corner of Lander County and north of Copper Canyon, were named for the district (GHM, LA 2). **GALENA** (Washoe). A creek, hill, campground, and a settlement of the 1860s that sprang into life to produce timbers for the Comstock. In the early days, there had been a good deal of prospecting on Galena Hill, and a mining district was so named "from the abundance of galena ores within its limits" (SM, 1867, p. 21). The organizers of the district, A. J. and R. S. Hatch, laid out the town of Galena in the spring of 1860 on the east foot of the Steamboat Hills about fourteen miles south of Reno (MA, p. 643; 1867 Map; NM). According to the Davis *History,* the settlement, of which hardly a trace of its graveyard remains, was referred to frequently as the "Eastern Tennessee" of Washoe County because of its radically pro-Union sympathies (SPD, pp. 1010–1012).

GALLAGHERS GAP (White Pine). A gap in the Duck Creek Range, east of Steptoe Valley; named for W. C. Gallagher, the father of former state senator Charles Gallagher (RRE; GHM, WP 4).

GALT (Lincoln). The non-agency station, ten miles south of Carp on the UP RR, may ultimately commemorate John Galt, a Scottish writer for whom Galt, a city in southeast Ontario, Canada, was named by Scottish settlers (Freese, Map 2).

GARDEN. A valley in northwest Lincoln County, in an angle formed by the Worthington and the Golden Gate ranges and extending into Nye County; named for its contrast to the surrounding mountains (OPN, p. 43; GHM, LN 4); a creek north of Bassett Creek in the Schell Creek Range of White Pine County; a canyon extending southwest from Dalzell Canyon, west of Black Mountain, and **GARDEN CANYON SPRING** in Lyon County; a spring northeast of Gold Butte and **GARDEN SPRING WASH** around Azure Ridge running to Grand Wash (GHM, WP 4; LY 2; CL 2; NJ 11–12; WA). **GARDEN PASS** (Eureka) denotes a summit northwest of Eureka on State Route 20, and a former station on the E and P RR; named for **GARDEN VALLEY.** Early settlers of Garden Pass were served by Diamond post office (1881 Map, TF, p. 17; MA, p. 286; HHB, Nev., p. 285; OPN, p. 33; ECN Map).

GARDNER CREEK (Elko). The creek rises in the Ruby Mountains, south of Secret Peak, and flows generally northeastward into Secret Valley. William Gardner, an early rancher, is commemorated (SG Map 10; EP, p. 37).

GARDNERVILLE (Douglas). A town eight miles southeast of Genoa on the East Fork of the Carson River. In 1879, Lawrence Gilman bought a portion of the homestead of John M. and Mary Gardner and moved a hotel to the site. The building, formerly on the emigrant trail between Genoa and Walleys Hot Springs and known as Kent House, was renamed **GARDNERVILLE HOTEL** by Gilman in honor of the Gardner family. **GARDNERVILLE** post office was established June 28, 1881 (GD, CV, p. 98; SHM 129; FTM, p. 11; 1881 Map).

GARFIELD (Mineral). A creek, east of Lucky Boy Pass in the Wassuk Range and southwest of Hawthorne; a mining district, six miles south of Acme in the central portion of the **GARFIELD HILLS; GARFIELD FLAT** and **SPRINGS** and **GARFIELD MILL** site, southeast of Garfield Hills and west of Mina (SG Map 4; GHM, MI 2). The mining district was organized in 1881, shortly after the assassination of James A. Garfield, twentieth president of the United States, and presumably named for him (VPG, p. 114; DM). **GARFIELD** post office was active from November 21, 1883, until November 28, 1884 (FTM, p. 11).

GARNET (Clark). The name of the station on the main line of the UP RR in Dry Lake Valley, between Dry Lake and Apex, is commemorative of a railroad official named Garnet*t* (Freese, Map; WA).

GARRETT BUTTE (Clark). The name of this butte lying north of Bonelli Peak and near Gold Butte commemorates Bill Garrett who lives in the area (WA).

GASKELL (Humboldt). A non-agency station on the main line of the WP RR between Jungo and Raglan and twenty-four miles west of Winnemucca (T54); perhaps named for the English novelist, Elizabeth Cleghorn Gaskell (1810–1865).

GASS (Clark). A spring so named is on the north flank of **GASS PEAK,** eighteen miles north of Las Vegas at the south end of the Las Vegas Range. **GASS PEAK MINING DISTRICT,** a silver-gold-zinc district, is named for the peak on which it is located and is the site of the June Bug Mine (Freese, Map 1; Wheeler 1871 Map; VPG, p. 25; WA). The name honors Octavius D. Gass, owner of the Las Vegas ranch and fort in the late 1860s (SPD, p. 219).

GATES STATION (Lyon). An early desert station between Desert Wells and Dayton; named for its owner (NHS, 1913, p. 213).

GEDDES (Eureka). The post office so named was established southwest of Pinto on March 17, 1882, and discontinued June 18, 1885, when Eureka became the mail address for its patrons (FTM, p. 11; TF, p. 17).

GEIGER. A summit and a lookout on the **GEIGER GRADE,** a famous steep grade in the Virginia Range, extending from Steamboat Valley up over the summit to the Comstock Lode at Virginia City. The original Geiger Grade was built by a Mr. Geiger, who ran the tollhouse at the top of it in 1861 and 1862. In the early days stagecoach holdups were ordinary occurrences on the grade, which became a veritable racetrack to Virginia City with the completion of the CP RR to Reno in 1868. Population figures were taken for Geiger Grade in the 1870 Census (NHS, 1913, p. 194; Nev. Guide, pp. 275–77; GHM, ST 1; VPG). **GEIGER GAP** (Churchill) denotes a pass in the Louderback Mountains about six miles northwest of Wonder (USGB 5904).

GELLER LEDGE AND HARRISON COMPANY (Storey). A location notice under the date of June 17, 1860, gives the name of the ledge as follows: "The said Ledge known as the Geller ledge & Harrison Co" (VMR–E). It appears that Geller's name was Solomon. The oath of Solomon Geller is contained in the *County Book of Carson County Court* (WSJ–2). Davis mentions that "Sol" Geller of Washoe County was elected

to Nevada's lower house (SPD, p. 1008). *Virginia Mining Records* contain the names of C. H. Harrison and J. H. Harrison, but no information indicates that the company name honored either. It seems more likely that a man indirectly responsible for the rush to Washoe, B. A. or Augustus Harrison, gave his name to the company. "B. A. Harrison carried a piece of the black ore to Grass Valley and gave it to James Walsh, who gave it to Melville Atwood to be assayed on June 27. It contained $3000 in silver and $876 in gold" (FCL, p. 223; TAR, p. 95; VMR–A, pp. 170, 281, 312). The location notices for the Utah Mine and the Sierra Nevada Mine include B. A. Harrison, James Walsh, and Melville Atwood among the claimants (GH–A). On November 19, 1863, the Geller Ledge and Harrison Company was consolidated with the Burning Moscow which was purchased by the Ophir in 1865 (HHB, Nev., p. 124; EL, p. 143). The name exists now only in early records and later accounts of the period.

GEM CITY (Pershing). The early settlement, also known as **GEMVILLE,** was southeast of Barbersville and served by Dun Glen post office (1881 Map; TF, p. 18; HHB, Nev., p. 264).

GENERAL THOMAS HILLS (Esmeralda). The group of hills just east of the head of Paymaster Canyon, about six miles southeast of Lone Mountain and nineteen miles northwest of Goldfield, was "named for a mining camp, reported in 1907 to be located in these hills" (DL 60). **GEN. THOMAS MINE** appears east of the north end of Paymaster Ridge on an Esmeralda County map (GHM, ES 1).

GENEVA (Lander). A small settlement on Birch Creek in the Toiyabe Range, started in 1863 (HHB, pp. 16, 269; MM; 1881 Map); a post office named for the settlement and active from June 20, 1867, until September 28, 1868 (FTM, p. 11).

GENOA (Douglas). A town on the west side of the Carson River, the oldest settlement in Nevada. In 1850, a party of Latter-Day Saints, led by Captain DeMont with Hampden S. Beatie as clerk, arrived in Carson Valley from Salt Lake City and found no other white men there. Beatie and Abner Blackburn built a roofless, floorless trading post at a site later called *Old Mormon Station.* The first permanent settlement was established by Colonel John Reese in 1851 and situated one mile south of the earlier trading post. The place was known as *Mormon Station* (q.v.) until 1855. "Genoa was given its name by Elder Orson Hyde of Salt Lake City, who, in 1855, became the first Probate Judge in western Utah when Nevada was Carson County, Utah Territory" (Dangberg, CV, p. 9). It is said that Elder

Hyde renamed the place after the birthplace of Columbus because the cove in the "mountain" reminded him of the Genoa harbor (NHS, 1913, p. 202; 1917, p. 189; M&S, p. 56; Dangberg, CV, p. 8). Perhaps in an effort to enhance the credibility of the name story, some recent accounts have changed the setting of the cove from the mountain to Lake Tahoe, which is not visible from Genoa. The town (altitude 4,700 feet) is in the eastern foothills of the Carson Range of the Sierra Nevada; the lake (altitude 6,300 feet) is on the west side of the range. The lowest elevations of the mountains between Genoa and Lake Tahoe are a little under 8,000 feet. When Captain James H. Simpson arrived at Genoa on June 12, 1859, he found twenty-eight dwelling houses, two stores, two hotels, one electric telegraph office, and one printing establishment. The name appears on Simpson's Map of Wagon Routes in Utah Territory, dated 1859 (JHS, p. 93; Wheat IV, 140). The first newspaper published in Nevada, the *Daily Territorial Enterprise,* started in Genoa as a weekly on December 18, 1858 (SPD, p. 459). Genoa was a regular stop for mail stage drivers and Pony Express riders. The post office, established as *Carson Valley* on December 10, 1852, in Carson County, Utah Territory, was transferred into Nevada Territory in 1861, into Ormsby County (now Carson City) on August 20, 1863 (?), and finally into Douglas County, later that same year (FTM, pp. 5, 11). Nearby features named for the town include **GENOA CANYON** and **GENOA CREEK** which rises south of **GENOA PEAK** and flows generally southeastward into Carson Valley, north of Genoa. Early settlers at **GENOA HOT SPRINGS,** two miles south of the town, were served by Genoa post office (Nev. Terr. Map; 1881 Map; NJ 11–1; TF, p. 18).

GENNETTE CREEK (Elko). A creek rising in the Ruby Mountains northeast of Jiggs; named for Pete Gennette whose home ranch was on the creek (EP, p. 37; GHM, EL 1).

GERALD (Eureka). A locality, former post office (July 24, 1882–June 18, 1885), and non-agency station on the SP RR between Barth and Palisade (T75; FTM, p. 11).

GERLACH (Washoe). A Nevada post office, established October 27, 1909, and township on the main line of the WP RR and on State Route 34, between the Black Rock and Smoke Creek deserts. Emigrants taking "the Noble Road left the Applegate-Lassen Trail at Black Rock Springs, went past this site, and southwestward through Smoke Creek Desert toward Susanville" (SHM 152). The town was settled in 1906 and named for the Gerlach Land and Cattle Company on the nearby Gerlach and Waltz Ranch. The firm was founded before the turn of the

century by Louis Gerlach (HPS, 1/24/54). **GERLACH MINING DISTRICT,** a gypsum district also called *Hooker* and *Washoe County,* is in the Selenite Range, twelve miles south of Gerlach, for which it is named (VPG, p. 151); **GERLACH HOT SPRINGS** are northwest of the town (Dir. 1971).

GETCHELL MINE (Humboldt). A large and notable producer of gold and tungsten is located on Kelly Creek, twenty-eight miles from Golconda in the eastern foothills of the Osgood Mountains. It was discovered in 1934 by Emmett Chase and Ed Knight, and named for Noble H. Getchell, the late mining man (Nev. Guide, p. 129; M&S, p. 149; VPG; NK 11–8).

GEYSER (Lincoln). An old ranch and locality on U.S. 93 about seventy miles north of Pioche, just south of the White Pine County line and east of the Schell Creek Range; a former post office, in operation from February 20, 1889, to October 31, 1913; named for **GEYSER SPRING,** a hot spring of intermittent flow in the upper end of Lake (Duck) Valley, earlier called **GEYSER VALLEY** (FTM, p. 11; WA; NJ 11–6). Geyser was an overnight stopping place on early stage lines between Pioche and Osceola (DM).

GIBBS LAKE (Elko). A mountain lake, high in the East Humboldt Range, southwest of Winchell Lake and east of East Fork Boulder Creek (NK 11–12); named for W. B. Gibbs who settled in the area in 1869 (EP, p. 37). See **STEELE.**

GILBERT. The mining district and former boom camp (Esmeralda County) so named commemorate the three Gilbert brothers, prospectors who located the district twenty-five miles west of Tonopah in the Monte Cristo Range in 1924. The boom lasted until the vein of the Black Mammoth Mine was lost by faulting. The name of McLeans Station on the now dismantled T & G RR, at the southeast edge of the Monte Cristo Range in Big Smoky Valley, was changed to **GILBERT JUNCTION** in 1925. **GILBERT** post office (Esmeralda) was active from April 9, 1925, until November 14, 1942 (NJ 11–5; NM; VPG, p. 53; OPN, p. 31; DM). **GILBERT CREEK** (Elko), named for an early rancher, Gilbert Henry (EP, p. 37), rises on the west flank of Green Mountain in the Ruby Range and joins McCutcheon Creek southeast of Jiggs in Mound Valley (NK 11–12).

GILBERT, MOUNT (Elko). A peak, twenty-two miles southeast of Elko, in the Ruby Mountains; "named for Grove Karl Gilbert (1843–1918), geologist, with United States Geological Survey for 39 years, and best known for papers on the Henry Mountains and Lake Bonneville" (USGB 6601).

GILLIS (Mineral). A stark, barren range, east of Walker Lake. **GILLIS MOUNTAIN MINING DISTRICT**, named for the range, was located prior to 1880, thirty miles north of early Belleville (M&SP, 1/3/80). **GILLIS CANYON**, on the west slope of the range, is south of **GILLIS**, a non-agency station on the Mina Branch of the SP RR (NJ 11–4; T75; Haw. Quad.).

GILPIN (Washoe). The non-agency siding so named, between Fernley and Thisbe on the Sparks Subdivision of the SP RR, was abandoned May 15, 1959. During the summer of 1905, a townsite was laid out here by Captain Matt Barach and a six-mile wagon road to Olinghouse was proposed but never built (T75; DM).

GILSON (Eureka). A mountain in the Diamond Range at the White Pine County boundary, named for the Gilson brothers, old settlers of Newark Valley. **GILSONS RUN** is south from Jacobs Well and north of the Newark district in **GILSONS VALLEY** (OPN, p. 34; ECN and Cad. Maps).

GIROUX WASH (White Pine). The wash so named, south of Kimberly and west of U.S. 6, commemorates Joseph L. Giroux who developed an important copper mining property southwest of Ely in 1899 (NJ 11–3; NHS, 1924, p. 401).

GLENBROOK (Douglas). The town on the east-central shore of Lake Tahoe at **GLENBROOK BAY** began as a lumber camp, but is now a summer resort (MA, p. 380; NJ 11–1). The name derives from old **GLENBROOK HOUSE**, a hotel named for its location by a brook in a glen (NHS, 1913, p. 188). The name of Lake Tahoe post office, established August 7, 1871, was changed to **GLENBROOK** on August 16, 1872 (FTM, pp. 16, 11), with Captain A. W. Pray as postmaster (OR, 1877–1881). The LTNG RR was built in 1876 from Glenbrook on the Nevada side of Lake Tahoe to the eastern summit of the Sierra Nevada, for hauling cord wood and mining timber to a flume for conveyance to Carson City (OPN, p. 5).

GLENCO (White Pine). This early post office southeast of Egan (1881 Map) was established September 2, 1891, and discontinued October 17, 1894, when Aurum became the mail address for its patrons (FTM, p. 11).

GLENDALE. A settlement southeast of Reno on the Truckee River in Washoe County. The site was first known as *Jamisons Station*, named for a Mormon who established a station there in 1852, the only settlement on the Truckee for several years (MA, pp. 623–24). In 1857, the post on the Truckee was called *Stone and Gates Crossing* for John F. Stone and Charles C. Gates. Prior to 1866, John Larcombe of Weymouth, England, came to Stone and Gates Crossing and opened a store which also served as a post

office. Mr. Larcombe, as postmaster, suggested the name *Glendale* (NHS, 1911, p. 93; 1926, p. 304). **GLENDALE** post office was active from October 4, 1867, to July 27, 1868 (FTM, p. 11). **GLENDALE** (Clark) is a locality at the junction of U.S. 91 and U.S. 93 east of Moapa, settled in 1855 (OPN, p. 15; HWY Map). Both mid-century settlements were probably named by ardent Anglophiles who, according to George R. Stewart, found a charm in names containing the words *glen* and *wood* because they were reminded of English country estates (GRS, Names, p. 273).

GLEN HAMILTON (Nye). This short-lived post office was established May 18, 1866, and discontinued October 15, 1866 (FTM, p. 11).

GLOBE (Lander). A canyon heading on the east slope of the Toiyabe Range and extending into Big Smoky Valley, south of Crooked Canyon and north of Santa Fe Creek. An early, small settlement in the canyon was supported chiefly by a sawmill located there (NJ 11–2; NM).

GOAT. The name for a tributary of South Canyon Creek, west of Buckhorn Pasture and north of North Fork Cottonwood Creek in the Humboldt National Forest in northern Elko County; for a lake north of Silver Peak in central Esmeralda County; and for a peak in the Shoshone Range, south of Mount Lewis and west of Indian Creek in Lander County (NK 11–9; Guide Map; NK 11–11).

GOAT ISLAND. See **ALCATRAZ**.

GOBLIN KNOBS (Nye). Hills in the Reveille Range and five miles north of Reveille were so named because "local tuff weathers into hoodoos and weird knobs" (USGB 7103).

GODFREY MOUNTAIN (Humboldt). The mountain, about seventy-five miles from Paradise Valley and twenty miles beyond Quinn River, was the scene of a battle fought on May 20, 1865, between the First Nevada Cavalry and a combined force of Paiutes, Bannocks, and Shoshones. Isaac W. Godfrey of Company D was one of the soldiers lost in the engagement. "The place where the battle was fought is called Godfrey Mountain by the Adjutant General of Nevada" (SPD, pp. 169–70).

GODS POCKET (Elko). The name denotes a peak northeast of Marys River Peak in a picturesque area of the Humboldt National Forest, and a creek rising on the north flank of Gods Pocket Peak and joining Slide Creek, northwest of Hummingbird Springs (SG Map 11; NK 11–9).

GOLCONDA (Humboldt). The name for a town, a mining district three miles southeast of the town, and a summit on Edna Mountain (NK 11–11; VPG, p. 91). The settlement, seventeen miles from Winnemucca on

Interstate 80, is a station on the SP RR and the WP RR and was built in 1868. It was first known as *Greggsville*, having been named for W. C. Gregg, the discoverer and organizer of the **GOLCONDA MINING DISTRICT** in 1866 (SM, 1875, pp. 61–62). Since hot mineral springs are in the area, the early town was famous as a watering place (FES, p. 190). **GOLCONDA** post office was established December 23, 1869 (FTM, p. 11; Census, 1870). Renewed mining activity in the late 1890s prompted the construction of the short-lived Golconda and Adelaide Railroad for hauling copper ore from the Adelaide Mine, which was twelve miles south of Golconda (DM, RR (I), p. 65; SHM 138). See **ADELAIDE**. The name derives ultimately from a town in India, capital of the kingdom ruled by the Kutb Shahi dynasty, 1512 to 1687, and famous for its diamonds.

GOLD. A place name of continuing popularity in Nevada, "The Silver State," occurring in most counties, alone or in combination with Acres, -banks, Bar, -bud, Butte, Canyon, Center, Circle, Crater, Creek, Cross, -dyke, Eagle, -field, Flat, Hill, Hitt, Horn, Meadows, Mountain, Net, Park, Pitt, Plate, Point, -range, Reed, Run, Spring, and Summit. The name was first applied to a canyon in Lyon and Storey counties, when placer gold was discovered there in the spring of 1849. Among the places recently named for the characteristic metal are Gold Acres in Lander County and Gold Meadows Valley in Nye County. **GOLD** (Lincoln) denoted a former mining camp which grew up subsequent to discoveries in State Line Canyon in the White Rock Mountains, east of Pioche, in August, 1914 (DM).

GOLD ACRES (Lander). The gold mining camp so named is at the west edge of Crescent Valley, seven miles southwest of Tenabo on State Route 21 (NK 11–11).

GOLDBANKS (Pershing). A mining district on the east slope of the East Range, south of the divide between Grass and Pleasant valleys, forty miles south of Winnemucca; and a former mining camp, established upon the discovery of gold by A. P. Smith in the spring of 1907 (VPG, p. 150; DM; NM).

GOLD BAR (Nye). The 1907 boom camp was located about three miles northwest of Rhyolite (Furn. Cr. Quad.) and named for the **GOLD BAR MINE,** discovered by Benny Hazeltine in August, 1904, shortly after the strike at Bullfrog made by Shorty Harris and Eddie Cross. **GOLD BAR SWITCH** was the side track on the LV & T RR for this camp (DM). **GOLDBAR** post office was active from May 20, 1907, until July 15, 1909, when its operations were transferred to Rhyolite (FTM, p. 11).

GOLD BASIN. In Churchill County, a mining district so named is on the east base of

Fairview Peak, forty-five miles southeast of Fallon (VPG, p. 14). An Elko County mining district of the same name and also called *Rowland* was discovered in 1889, ninety miles north of Elko (OPN, p. 24; VPG, p. 41).

GOLD BELT (Nye). A gold-silver mining district, located fifty-five miles east of Tonopah, also known as *Eden* and *Eden Creek* (VPG, p. 126).

GOLDBUD (Pershing). The gold camp of the early twentieth century was named facetiously for the rival camp of *Rosebud,* by report of the *Reno Evening Gazette* of April 11, 1907; both camps were in the northern portion of the county.

GOLD BUTTE. The peak in the southern portion of the Virgin Mountains in Clark County apparently took its name from **GOLD BUTTE MINING DISTRICT** when gold was discovered there in 1905. Mica had been discovered in the area in 1873 by Daniel Bonelli. A mining camp, named for the district, was laid out west of Voigt Well, and **GOLD BUTTE** post office served the district from March 19, 1906, until February 28, 1911, when old Saint Thomas became the mail address for its patrons. Mines in the district include the Tramp, Bonelli, Azure Ridge, and Big Thing. **GOLD BUTTE WASH** trends generally northward from near Gold Butte, through the division between Lime Ridge and Tramp Ridge, to Mud Wash (WA; FTM, p. 11; VPG, p. 25; OPN, p. 15; NJ 11–12). **GOLD BUTTES** formerly denoted a mining camp near Lovelock in Pershing County, active in the early twentieth century, according to the *Reno Evening Gazette* of March 11, 1907 (DM).

GOLD CANYON. The canyon extends from the south slope of Mount Davidson in Storey County, through Gold Hill and Silver City to the Carson River at Dayton in Lyon County (NJ 11–1). Discovery of placer gold in this canyon led to the discovery of the Comstock Lode. In 1849, either William Prouse or John Orr discovered gold at the mouth of the canyon. Orr, in charting the progress of his wagon train, named the place Gold Canyon (GDL, Saga, pp. 3–8). Although John Orr named the canyon, a Mr. Blackburn of the party of Hampden S. Beatie had made a prior discovery, having found gold in Gold Creek (q.v.) earlier the same year. **GOLD CANYON** (White Pine). A mining district, fifty miles north of Ely in the Egan Range, and also called *Cherry Creek* and *Egan Canyon* (VPG, p. 177); formerly an Overland Stage station, fifteen miles west of Schell Creek Station, according to the Root and Connelley list (JGS, I, p. 136). **GOLD CANYON MINING DISTRICT** (Lyon), on the southeast slope of the Virginia Range, nine miles northeast of

Carson City, is also called *Silver City, Chinatown, Dayton,* and *Devils Gate* (VPG, p. 105). **GOLD CANYON FLAT DIGGINGS.** See **DAYTON.**

GOLD CENTER (Nye). A former town, established 1905, five miles south of Beatty (Furn. Cr. Quad.); the junction of the T & T RR and the BG RR; also a station on the LV & T RR (NM; DM). **GOLD CENTER** post office served the area from January 21, 1905, until November 30, 1910, when its operations were transferred to Beatty (FTM, p. 11).

GOLD CIRCLE (Elko). The mining district was discovered in 1907 near Midas, forty-eight miles east-northeast of Golconda, and on the Owyhee bluffs just inside of the Humboldt watershed. The Elko Prince was one of the principal producers (VPG, p. 41; OPN, p. 24; SFH, p. 9). The gold mines formed a circle around the town (EP, p. 37).

GOLD CREEK. The creek so named, in Lyon and Storey counties, flows out of Gold Canyon to the Carson River near the present site of Dayton and was named by John Orr when he named Gold Canyon in the spring of 1849 (RRE; M&S, pp. 58, 65). **GOLD CREEK STATION.** See **DAYTON.** In Elko County, **GOLD CREEK** denoted a settlement, seventy-five miles north of Elko at the confluence of Penrod Creek and **GOLD CREEK.** According to legend, in 1873 several $50 nuggets were found in Gold Creek, and the camp "sprang up on the theory that every sagehen in the region had gold nuggets in its craw from feeding on gravel in the stream" (Nev. Guide, p. 169; NK 11–9; NM). The camp was the most active one in the Island Creek Mining District in 1896, and was served by a post office of the same name, established February 24, 1897, and discontinued February 15, 1929, when North Fork became the mail address for its patrons (FTM, p. 11; NM; DM). **GOLD CREEK RANGER STATION** takes its name from the creek on which it is located (NK 11–9). Other shift names in the area are **GOLD CREEK RESERVOIR** (Freese, Map 3; SG Map 11), **GOLD CREEK CAMPGROUND,** seventy-eight miles north of Elko by way of North Fork, and the **GOLD CREEK RANGE,** near Jarbidge (NP, p. 71).

GOLD CROSS PEAK (Clark). The name of the highest peak in the Hiller Mountains, southeast of Bonelli Peak and west of Delmar Butte (WA; NJ 11–12).

GOLDEN. A post office so named operated in Nye County from February 26, 1906, until December 14, 1907, when its operations were transferred to Austin (FTM, p. 11). **GOLDEN ARROW** (Nye). The townsite was incorporated in 1906, about forty miles southeast of Tonopah, and named for the Golden Arrow Company (NM). **GOLDEN CITY** denoted an early town in Elko County laid out at the confluence of Bull Run and Deer creeks; a short-lived settlement which sprang up in 1892 on the west side of the Meadow Valley Range, a few miles north of the later site of Delamar, in Lincoln County (EP, p. 38; JWH, Nev., p. 52). In Nye County, **GOLDEN MOUNTAIN** is a peak north of Gold Flat; **GOLDEN SPRING** is west of Cloverdale Creek and east of **GOLDEN WASH** (GHM, NY 7; SG Map 5).

GOLDEN GATE (Lincoln). The **GOLDEN GATE RANGE** denotes a mountain range which forms an angle with the Worthington Mountains (NJ 11–6). The range took its name from **GOLDEN GATE,** a pass named by a party of Mormons "from its being composed of high ledges of gold bearing quartz" (Wheat IV, 131). J. H. Martineau, the historian of the party, indicated that the pass was in *Gray Head Mountain.* On May 6, 1858, the Mormon party "camped on the slope of the snow mountain which we called Gray Head" (Wheat IV, pp. 130, 131).

GOLDFIELD (Esmeralda). A twentieth-century boom town which sprang into existence as a result of a rich strike on the Sandstorm, near Rabbit Springs, made by William A. Marsh and Harry C. Stimler in December of 1902 (SPD, pp. 360, 863). Goldfield began as a tent town, but by 1903 the demand for buildings was so great that carpenters worked twenty-four hours a day, with small boys holding lanterns to light their work by night (M&S, p. 116). The mining camp and the district were officially named **GOLDFIELD** by resolution of October 20, 1903. W. H. Harris, one of the signers of the resolution, had suggested Goldfield*s,* for his former residence, Goldfield, Colorado, implying more than one field of gold. Claude M. Smith, District Recorder, agreed to the name without the pluralizing. The post office was established December 5, 1903 (FTM, p. 11). The rock at Goldfield was so richly encrusted with gold that the miners called it "jewelry ore" (SPD, pp. 866–67; DRL, p. 10). Goldfield was formerly a station on the LV and T RR and a terminus for the T and G RR. **GOLDFIELD SUMMIT** on U.S. 93 is southeast of the town.

GOLD FLAT (Nye). The name denotes a flat and a well west of Quartzite Mountain, north of Pahute Mesa, and formerly designated a camp in the Kawich Range, its name being changed from *Nixon* to Gold Flat in February, 1905 (NJ 11–8; DM).

GOLD HILL. The town, at the south end of the Comstock Lode in Storey County, was settled as a result of the Johntown prospectors striking surface diggings on a little hill at the north end of the site in 1859. According to Dan De Quille, "Big French

John" Bishop and James "Old Virginia" Fennimore named the town. "After we had measured the ground we had a consultation as to what name was to be given the place. It was decidedly not Gold Cañon, for it was a little hill; so we concluded to call it Gold Hill. That is how the place came by its present name" (DDQ, p. 23). The name is included on two 1860 maps of the Washoe mining region, prepared by Henry De Groot and by R. M. Evans (Wheat IV, 189; V (I), 16). The town was first organized under the laws of Utah Territory and then reorganized under Nevada law on February 20, 1864. It was bounded by the south line of Virginia City on the north, by the Storey-Lyon county line on the east, and by the Storey-Washoe county line on the south (MA, p. 589; NHS, 1913, p. 188). The principal mines of the **GOLD HILL MINING DISTRICT** were the Belcher, Crown Point, Yellow Jacket, Imperial, Empire, and Kentuck. "Dutch Nick" Ambrosia built the first house in the town (SPD, p. 1000). Prior to the building of the now defunct V and T RR, Gold Hill and Virginia City were connected by a line of omnibuses, making four trips every hour (FES, pp. 208–209; Nev. Terr. Map). **GOLD HILL** post office was active from July 13, 1862, to February 27, 1943, when its operations were transferred to Virginia City (FTM, p. 11). **GOLD HILL** (Nye) was formerly situated southeast of Grapevine Peak and north of Boundary Canyon (Wheeler 1871 Map).

GOLD HITT (Esmeralda). A mining camp of the Oneota Mining District, active in 1906 and situated six miles from Basalt in the north end of the White Mountain Range (NM; VPG, p. 111).

GOLDHORN (Esmeralda). A mining camp of the early twentieth century, established at the lower end of Palmetto Valley in March, 1906 (DM).

GOLD MEADOWS (Nye). The name denotes a crescent-shaped valley, at the northern base of Rainier Mesa, about ninety-two miles northwest of Las Vegas (USGB 6002; NJ 11–8).

GOLD MOUNTAIN (Esmeralda). An early mining camp, named for **GOLD MOUNTAIN MINING DISTRICT,** discovered in 1864 by Thomas J. Shaw and relocated in 1865 and sold to Joggles Wright (HHB, Nev., pp. 260–61). The camp was situated on the northern slope of **GOLD MOUNTAIN,** west of Sarcobatus Flat and south of Slate Ridge, about seventy miles south of Tonopah. The chief mines of the district included the Evening Star, Golden Eagle, Boomerang, Little Bell, and Borneo (Wheeler, 1872, p. 47; 1871 Map; NJ 11–8). **GOLD MOUNTAIN** post office (February 15, 1881–May 9, 1891) was to have been reopened

by an order dated November 30, 1907, rescinded before operations commenced (FTM, p. 12). All names were derived from the mountain which is said to have been so named because gold nuggets were found there (OPN, p. 31).

GOLD NET (Esmeralda). The early settlement so named was served by Lida post office (HHB, Nev., p. 260; TF, p. 18).

GOLD PARK. A mining district, also called *Jackson,* forty-four miles southeast of Austin, partly in Lander County and partly in Nye County; named for **GOLD PARK BASIN** on the west slope of the Shoshone Range, in which the district was located (OPN, p. 54; VPG, p. 129). **GOLD PARK** post office was active in Lander County from December 14, 1897, to January 27, 1899, and again from February 14, 1921, to February 28, 1925, when Austin became the mail address for its patrons (FTM, p. 12).

GOLD PIT(T) (Douglas). A former mining camp fourteen miles northwest of Yerington. The name was changed to *Buckskin* in 1906 (M&SP, 5/19/06). See **BUCKSKIN.**

GOLD PLATE (Pershing). The name for a former silver camp about twelve miles southeast of Lovelock, by report of the *Goldfield News* of April 8, 1911 (DM).

GOLD POINT (Esmeralda). A Nevada post office, established October 16, 1932, and a town settled in 1872, ten miles southeast of Lida and thirty miles southwest of Goldfield on State Route 71 (NJ 11–8). The name derives from the **GOLD POINT MINING DISTRICT,** located twenty-five miles southwest of Goldfield and also called *Hornsilver.* The name of Hornsilver post office, established May 16, 1908, was changed to **GOLD POINT** in 1932 (VPG, p. 55; FTM, pp. 12, 13). See **HORNSILVER.**

GOLD RANGE. A mining district in the Excelsior Mountains, southwest of Mina in Mineral County, also called the *Silver Star, Silver Dyke,* and *Marietta* (VPG, p. 18); a gold mining district, active in 1932, in the Groom area of western Lincoln County (WA).

GOLD REED (Nye). A locality and a gold-mercury mining district in the Kawich Range, five miles north of Quartzite Mountain and fifty-four miles east of Goldfield, the site of a boom from 1904 to 1906; named for "O. K. Reed, supt. of the Goldreed Mines Co. at Kawich," by report of the *Mining and Scientific Press* of March 10, 1906 (DM; NJ 11–8; VPG, p. 131). See **KAWICH.**

GOLD RUN (Humboldt). A township named for **GOLD RUN MINING DISTRICT,** also called *Adelaide,* lying on the east slope of the Sonoma Range, fifteen miles south of Golconda. The district took its name from **GOLDRUN CREEK,** which rises just east of Adelaide on the eastern slope of the Sonoma Range and flows into Pumpernickel Valley (NK 11–11).

GOLD SPRING (Nye). By decision of the United States Board on Geographic Names, **GOLD SPRING,** not *Crystal Spring,* denotes a spring on the northeast slope of Mount Stirling, at the north end of the Spring Mountains about eight miles northeast of Johnnie (USGB 6002; Vegas Quad.).

GOLDYKE (Nye). The mining camp of the early twentieth century took its name from **GOLDYKE MINING DISTRICT,** also known as *Fairplay* and *Atwood.* It was at the south end of the Paradise Range, thirty-two miles northeast of Luning. Although the district was discovered in 1901, the first ore was not shipped out until 1906. **GOLDYKE** post office, established on January 9, 1906, was discontinued October 15, 1910, when its operations were transferred to Luning (VPG, p. 127; DM; NM; FTM, p. 12; Tono. Quad.). The blend name combines *gold* with the geological term *dyke,* or dike, meaning a hardened tabular mass of igneous rock that has been forced into a fissure while in a melted state, representing to the prospector a vein of gold. *Dyke* also may stand alone as the name for a mining district and is sometimes combined with *Silver.* See **SILVER DYKE.**

GOLLAHER MOUNTAIN (Elko). By decision of the United States Board on Geographic Names (USGB 6303), **GOLLAHER MOUNTAIN** (not *Gollyer Mountain* [NK 11–9] or *Gollyer Peak* [GHM, EL 4]) is the designation for a peak, approximately eight miles south of the Idaho-Nevada boundary and fourteen miles southeast of Jackpot. Another variant is *Golliher Mountain;* named for "a man by the name of Golliher who ran horses on the mountain at the time it was open land" (EP, p. 38).

GOOD HOPE (Elko). The nineteenth-century settlement and post office (March 24, 1884–February 3, 1887) were named for the **GOOD HOPE MINING DISTRICT,** situated on Chino Creek, fifty-five miles northwest of Elko (HHB, Nev., p. 277; FTM, p. 12; VPG, p. 41).

GOODSPRINGS (Clark). The town, post office, valley, and junction were named for the former **GOOD SPRINGS,** which commemorate a prospector, Joseph Good, who settled at the springs in 1868. In the 1870s, Good built a small hand smelter to test ores. **GOODSPRINGS MINING DISTRICT** (also called *Potosi* and *Yellow Pine*), eight miles northwest of Jean, was named for the settlement which was organized as a town about 1885. **GOODSPRINGS** post office was established April 6, 1899. **GOODSPRINGS JUNCTION,** or **SIDING,** on the Salt Lake Route, UP RR, was renamed *Jean,* with the establishment of that post office on June 28, 1905 (FTM, pp. 12, 14). The *Lincoln County Record* of February 10, 1905, makes a reference to Goodsprings Junction, and the *Las Vegas Age* of August 26, 1905, mentions Goodsprings Siding (DM). **GOODSPRING(S) VALLEY** is a valley between the south end of the Spring Mountains and the Bird Spring Range (NI 11–3; WA; OPN, p. 15; RC, pp. 54–55; JGS, I, p. 404; VPG, p. 26). See **POTOSI.**

GOOSE CREEK (Elko). The creek, in which are found steelhead and Pacific Ocean salmon, is in the northeast corner of Elko County and flows north into the Columbia River. The Goose Creek road from Idaho, used by many forty-niners, cut southwest to the headwaters of the Humboldt River (Nev. Guide, p. 19; M&S, p. 159). The creek, named for Canada geese and snow geese, was delineated on the Topographical Map of the Road from Missouri to Oregon, prepared by Charles Preuss in 1846 (Wheat III, 24–27). Nearby features named for the creek include **GOOSE CREEK MINING DISTRICT,** discovered in 1871, thirty miles north of Tecoma in the **GOOSE CREEK RANGE.** The range separates **GOOSE CREEK VALLEY** from Thousand Spring Valley (SM, 1875, p. 24). **GOOSE CREEK GAME PRESERVE** is in the northeast corner of Elko County (NK 11–9; Guide Map).

GORDON. The name of **GORDON** post office (Nye), established June 28, 1906, was changed to *Round Mountain* (q.v.) on March 4, 1907. The post office, on the west slope of the Toquima Range, about sixty miles north of Tonopah, was named for Louis Gordon, who located the Round Mountain mines in 1906 (FTM, p. 12; SHM 96). **GORDON CREEK** denotes a stream rising on the east slope of the East Humboldt Range and flowing into Clover Valley, in Elko County; and a creek flowing from the east slope of the Schell Creek Range into Spring Valley in White Pine County (SG Maps 10, 9; Dir. 1971).

GOSHUTE. The **GOSHUTE MOUNTAINS** lie in the southeast corner of Elko County and extend into northern White Pine County. **GOSHUTE VALLEY** lies between the Toano Range and the Pequop Mountains in Elko County. A dry lake earlier described as a brackish pond with two small tributaries and no outlet (GAC, p. 128), at the Elko-White Pine county line is so named. **GOSHUTE CREEK** (White Pine) rises on the eastern slope of the Cherry Creek Mountains and flows into Steptoe Valley south of **GOSHUTE LAKE.** In Elko County, **GOSHUTE PASS** is a low divide on U.S. 93 south of Wells, and **GOSHUTE PEAK** is on the west slope of the north part of the Goshute Mountains, across the valley from Dolly

Varden. The **GOSHUTE INDIAN RESER-VATION** is partly in Utah and partly in northeastern White Pine County. "In the period of western migration, the Overland Trail passed through what is now the Goshute Reservation" (M&M, p. 209). **GOSHUTE STATION** (Elko) is south of Currie on the NN RR and northeast of Goshute Lake (NK 11–9; 11–12; GHM, EL 5; WP 4).

The name commemorates the Gosiute Indians, a Central Numic (Shoshonean) tribe that lived in the area. The Gosiute vocabulary obtained in 1873 by John Wesley Powell includes the noun *Go-shup*, "Ashes" (Fowler, p. 253). Early historian Myron Angel records that the Ash-Utes dealt with the Pahranagats and "supplied the latter with much dried meat, buckskins, etc." (MA, p. 186). According to R. V. Chamberlin the name derives from *kutsip*, or *gutsip*, "ashes," "parched or dry earth" (FWH, I, p. 496). Captain James H. Simpson called the range the *Go-shoot*, or *Tots-arrh*, and gave his guide's explanation of the tribal name. "The Go-shoots, according to Mr. Bean, my guide of last fall, who has lived in this country for the last ten years, and professes to be well acquainted with the various tribes inhabiting the Territory, are an offshoot from the Ute Indians, and left their tribe about two generations ago, with their leader or chief, Goship, a disaffected leader. Their proper name, therefore, is probably Goship-utes, which has been contracted to Go-shoots" (JHS, p. 54). *Goshoot* is the designation for the mountains and the lake on Lieutenant E. G. Beckwith's 1855 map of his explorations for a Pacific Railroad Route (Wheat IV, 74).

GOSIUTE (Elko). The former post office at the north end of Goshute Valley was established January 22, 1907, and discontinued September 30, 1907, when Cobre became the mail address for its patrons (FTM, p. 12). **GOSIUTE** is an alternate spelling for *Goshute* (q.v.) Lake (1881 Map).

GOULD AND CURRY (Storey). Aside from being the first mine on the Comstock to uncover a large body of rich ore in 1862, the Gould and Curry has a remarkable history and association with famous people and events. Artemus Ward made a descent into the Gould and Curry during a visit to Virginia City in 1863 (GHS, p. 26; GDL, Saga, p. 259). After the fire of 1875, John W. Mackay lived in two rooms in the office of this mine (EM, pp. 22, 128; OL, Silver, p. 162). According to Mark Twain, the Gould and Curry's "streets of dismal drifts and tunnels were five miles in extent" (SLC, II, p. 94) and since the mine employed six hundred and seventy-five men, "in the matter of elections the adage was, 'as the Gould & Curry goes, so goes the city' " (SLC, II,

p. 13). Joseph T. Goodman wrote that Confederate sympathizers held military maneuvers in the mine during the Civil War. The claim of organization of the Gould and Curry, a patented claim on the Comstock, was 1,200 feet; however, it presently includes 608 feet lying between the Best and Belcher and the Savage mines (AR, No. 62; JJP, p. 102; IH).

The name honors the original locators in 1859 who consolidated their claims, Alvah (or Alva) Gould and Abram (or Abraham) V. Z. Curry. Both men sold their interests in the great mine at an early date. Gould went to Reese River in 1862 and to several other pioneer mining camps in Nevada, then to California (HDG, CP 12/23/76). Mark Twain credits his arresting and largely facetious account of the disposition of the claim to Abe Curry in *Roughing It*.

> Mr. Curry owned two-thirds of it—and he said that he sold it out for twenty-five hundred dollars in cash, and an old plug horse that ate up his market value in hay and barley in seventeen days by the watch. And he said that Gould sold out for a pair of second-hand government blankets and a bottle of whisky that killed nine men in three hours, and that an unoffending stranger that smelt the cork was disabled for life. Four years afterward the mine thus disposed of was worth in the San Francisco market seven millions six hundred thousand dollars in gold coin. (SLC, II, pp. 34–35)

Sam P. Davis called Abram Curry the most prominent of all the early pioneers of Ormsby (presently Carson City) County. In addition to being one of the founders of Carson City, he was owner of the Warm Springs Hotel where Nevada's First Territorial Legislature met in 1861; was elected to represent former Ormsby County in the lower house on September 3, 1862; was one of the founders of the first Masonic Lodge in Nevada, organized in Carson City on February 3, 1863; was warden of the territorial prison; and was the recipient of the government contract for building the United States Mint in Carson City, as well as the mint's first superintendent (DDQ, p. 50; MA, p. 58; HHB, Nev., p. 103; GHS, p. 44; WD, p. 102; SLC, I, pp. 177–78; SPD, pp. 254, 673, 975–76; SHM 180).

GOVERNMENT. The peak, southeast of Ursine between Deerlodge and Stateline in Lincoln County, was named for the government signal station once situated on it. **GOVERNMENT WASH** (Clark) is an incident name for a wash which drains east into the Virgin River above Riverside. A government party, camping in the wash sometime prior to 1900, lost their equipment during a cloudburst (Dir. 1971; WA).

GRANDPA MINING DISTRICT. See **GOLDFIELD** and **COLUMBIA.**

GRANITE. Features in at least ten Nevada counties are named for granite, the hard, coarse grained igneous rock, usually gray or pink, and consisting essentially of quartz, feldspar, and mica. **GRANITE** (Mineral) designated a mining camp and post office, active from May 5, 1908, to May 15, 1909, named for the **GRANITE MINING DISTRICT.** The district, also known as *Mountain View* and *Reservation,* was eight miles northwest of Schurz and northeast of the Wassuk (Walker River) Range (NM; FTM, p. 12; VPG, p. 114). **GRANITE** also denotes a mining district organized in 1875 on the west flank of the Paradise Range, forty-five miles north-northeast of Luning in Nye County; and a mining district, six miles southwest of Granite on the east flank of the Egan Range in White Pine County (NM; VPG, pp. 132, 179).

GRANITE CREEK. The **GRANITE CREEK DESERT,** extending from eastern Washoe County across the northwest portion of Pershing County, between the Smoke Creek Desert and the Black Rock Desert, was named for granite predominant in the area (NK 11–10). **GRANITE CREEK** also designated an early way station on the Honey Lake Road, where the station keeper and expressman were killed by Indians in March, 1865 (SPD, p. 165); a post office active in old Roop (Washoe) County from July 13, 1866, until August 6, 1867 (FTM, p. 12); and a former gold mining district, located in May, 1902, by James Raiser and James D. Murray of Granite Creek. In August, 1902, the name of the district was changed to *Donnelly,* and the town of *Raiser City* was laid out (DM).

GRANITE MOUNTAIN. The name for a mountain, east of Buena Vista Valley and at the south end of the East Range in Pershing County (Son. R. Quad.); for a mining district, ten miles northwest of Reno (also called *Peavine, Reno,* and *Crystal Peak*) in Washoe County (VPG, p. 172); and for a mining district also known as *Dolly Varden* or *Mizpah,* sixteen miles northeast of Currie in Elko County (VPG, p. 39).

GRANITE PEAK. A peak, southeast of Red Rock Valley and west of Dogskin Mountain in southwest Washoe County; a peak at the south end of the Granite Range in northern Washoe County; a mountain, northwest of Black Canyon in the southern portion of the Snake Range in southeast White Pine County (NK 11–1, 11–10; NJ 11–6); a peak, about eight miles north-northeast of Santa Rosa Peak in the Santa Rosa Range in Humboldt County (USGB 6002; NK 11–8).

GRANITE POINT (Pershing). A non-agency station on the main line of the SP RR between Perth and Toulon and eight miles

west of Lovelock (T1TR; T75). The station is named for **GRANITE POINT,** a nearby protrusion of granite. "On the right of the station, which is merely a side track, there is a ragged, broken mountain, which undoubtedly gives the place its name. It is the only curious or interesting thing to be seen from the cars" (FES, p. 198; 1881 Map; NK 11–10).

GRANITE RANGE (Washoe). The mountain range so named trends generally northwest from Gerlach in northern Washoe County (NK 11–10; Guide Map).

GRANITE SPRING. Springs so named are situated at the north end of the Toano Range in Elko County, west of Buck Mountain in Eureka County, northwest of Carp in Lincoln County, and at Gold Butte, and in the Dead Mountains in Clark County (GHM, EL 5; EU 1; WA). **GRANITE SPRING VALLEY** (Pershing) extends north from Copper Valley to Adobe Flat and is bounded on the east by the Trinity Range and on the west by the Sahwave Mountains; **GRANITE SPRING WASH** runs north of the valley; and **GRANITE SPRING RIDGE** is west of the northern Sahwave Mountains. The early settlement at **GRANITE SPRING** in the south end of the valley was served by White Plains post office (GHM, PE 1; 1881 Map; TF, p. 18).

GRANT. A mountain in the Clan Alpine Mountains of Churchill County, named for Ulysses S. Grant (1822–1885), the eighteenth president of the United States (NHS, 1913, p. 184); the highest peak in the Wassuk Range in Mineral County (altitude 11,303 feet), north of Cory Peak (NJ 11–4). **GRANT GAME REFUGE** in northeast Nye County is named for the **GRANT RANGE,** which extends north of the Quinn Canyon Range and between Railroad Valley and White River Valley (NJ 11–6).

GRANTSVILLE (Nye). An early mining camp and a post office (*Grantville*), active from February 3, 1879, to October 31, 1901, three miles southeast of Union in **GRANTS-VILLE CANYON** and north of **GRANTS-VILLE MOUNTAIN** on the west slope of the Shoshone Mountains (NJ 11–5). The camp and mining district date from 1864 and coincide with the discovery and naming of the Union and North Union districts, also in the Shoshone Mountains. **GRANTSVILLE MINING DISTRICT,** which enjoyed a period of renewed activity in 1880 and 1881, when the Alexander and the McMahon mines were producing, is presently better known as *Union.* The group name honors General Ulysses S. Grant and was given by loyal Unionists in the area who also named the two Union districts and nearby Sherman Peak (JGS, I, p. 177; SM, 1867, p. 56; 1881 Map; VPG, p. 144; DM).

GRAPEVINE. A name applied principally in southern Nevada to places where wild grape vines were found in profusion. The **GRAPEVINE RANGE** extends from southwestern Nye County into northwestern Esmeralda County along the California line. **GRAPEVINE PEAK** is at the north end of the range and northeast of **GRAPEVINE SPRING** (NJ 11–8; Wheeler 1871 Map). Springs so named are also west of Carp in Lincoln County; about two miles east of the Johnnie Mine in Nye County; southeast of Las Vegas, east of Gold Butte in Cedar Basin, and four miles south of Sheep Spring in Clark County (WA). **GRAPEVINE CANYON** denotes a canyon in Lincoln County between Elgin and Boyd and on the east edge of the Meadow Valley Wash, and a canyon extending eastward from the Dead Mountains and north of Davis Dam (WA; Wheeler 1871 Map). By decision of USGB–5, **GRAPEVINE** (not *Bethune*) is the designation for a canyon and a pass in the Amargosa Range.

GRASS SPRING CANYON (Nye). A canyon extending from Pahute Mesa just west of Dead Horse Flat to Gold Flat, about seven miles south-southwest of Quartzite Mountain; named for a spring in the canyon (DL 53).

GRASS VALLEY. A valley in Lander County, northeast of Austin near the Eureka County line, extending to the south end of the Cortez Mountains, between the north end of the Toiyabe Range and the Simpson Park Mountains (NJ 11–2; NK 11–11); named for the abundance of grass (OPN, p. 40). Another valley so named is between the Sonoma Range and the East Range, extending from north of Pleasant Valley in northeast Pershing County to south of the Humboldt River in southern Humboldt County. A small settlement in this valley, named for the plentiful supply of forage, was near Winnemucca (Census, 1870; Nev. Guide, p. 132). In Washoe County, **GRASS VALLEY** denotes a meadow with a small lake below the top of Mount Rose (Nev. Guide, p. 194) and a small valley, north of the Granite Range on a tributary to Cottonwood Creek (VPG). A Lander County post office of this name was established November 23, 1911, and discontinued February 15, 1913, when Austin became the mail address for its patrons (FTM, p. 12).

GRASSY. Features named for abundant grass in an area include a canyon southeast of Jefferson in the Toquima Range in Nye County; springs on an old stage road, north of Delamar in Lincoln County; and springs east of the Spring Mountains in Clark County (SG Map 6; WA). **GRASSY MOUNTAIN** denotes a mountain just south of Dutch John Mountain and north of the

Fairview Range, about thirty miles north-northwest of Pioche in Lincoln County (DL 60); and a peak southwest of Jackpot in Elko County (GHM, EL 4).

GRAVELLY FORD (Eureka). This famous campsite and emigrant crossing of the Humboldt River was east of the present site of Beowawe. It was here that James A. Reed of the Donner Party killed John Snyder. A quarrel developed while members of the party were doubling up their teams in order to haul their wagons up the steep inclines. Upon stabbing Snyder with his hunting knife, Reed was banished to the desert. He reached California and organized the first rescue group sent to aid the remaining members of his train, snowbound and starving in the Sierra Nevada (SPD, p. 224; Nev. Guide, p. 126). The name is included on W. Wadsworth's Map of the Overland Route, published in *The National Railroad Guide* in 1858 (Wheat IV, 106). **GRAVELLY FORD** post office was in operation from February 22, 1869, to January 31, 1870 (FTM, p. 12). Beowawe later served its patrons (TF, p. 18).

GRAVEL PIT. A townsite of Mineral County, promoted in 1907 and named for a nearby ballast pit on the N and C RR. The railroad siding, milepost 378.6, was first named *Walker Pit*, later *Walker* (DM). **GRAVEL PIT SIDING** (Clark), a siding on the UP RR for loading borax, twelve miles northeast of Las Vegas, probably was the early name for *Dike* (WA).

GRAY CONE (Lincoln). The name for a conically shaped peak, of predominantly gray coloration, lying about three miles southeast of Pioche in the west-central portion of the county (WA; Dir. 1971).

GRAY EAGLE MINE. See **CHERRY CREEK.**

GREASEWOOD BASIN (Clark). The depression at the head of Black Wash and east of Saint Thomas Gap is named for greasewood (*Sarcobatus vermiculatus*), a plant of the alkali desert growing there (WA; NJ 11–12).

GREAT BASIN. A plateau between the Sierra Nevada and the Wasatch Mountains, covering western Utah, most of Nevada, and eastern California; rivers and streams flow into it, forming lakes, but with no ultimate outlet to the sea; "this country known since the date of the explorations of Frémont, 1843 and 1844, and by his appellation, as the Great Basin . . ." (JHS, p. 13). Frémont wrote as follows: "The contents of this Great Basin are yet to be examined" (JCF, Report, p. 276; Wheat III, 56).

GREAT CALIFORNIA MOUNTAIN. See **SIERRA NEVADA.**

GREAT EASTERN (Clark). The mining district (also known as *Copper King, Key West,* and *Bunkerville*), fifteen miles south of Bunkerville, took its name from the **GREAT EASTERN MINE,** located about 1902 by Samuel W. Darling and Alvin M. Thompson (VPG, p. 23; WA).

GREAT QUARTZ MOUNTAIN (Lincoln). The early, descriptive name for Mount Irish, which lies sixty miles west of Caliente (NJ 11–9; Freese, Map 2). "Great Quartz Mountain is a mass of uplifted and somewhat altered strata, with a general dip to the west. The quartzite, 500 to 600 feet thick, that caps the ridge, are of slight inclination, exposing their edges on both sides of the mountain, and they contain an interstratified bed of black limestone. Below them is an almost uninterrupted exposure of limestone, to the eastern base of the mountain, and in these are the mines" (Wheeler, 1872, pp. 43–44; 1871 Map).

GREENFIELD. See **YERINGTON** and **MASON.**

GREEN MONSTER. A fanciful name for a canyon (Nye County) heading on the east slope of the Monitor Range south of Danville Canyon, and extending into Little Fish Lake Valley; for a creek in this canyon; and for a mine of Clark County, one of the principal producers of the Goodsprings Mining District (NJ 11–5; WA).

GREEN MOUNTAIN. A mining district organized in 1869 near Tule Canyon, northwest of Gold Mountain, and twelve miles southeast of Oasis, California; presently better known as *Sylvania* and named for the Sylvania Mountains. Presumably *Green Mountain* was the earlier name for the mountains and was adopted for the mining district (Wheeler, 1872, p. 47; 1871 Map; VPG, p. 61). **GREEN MOUNTAIN** (Elko). A mountain east of Jiggs in the Ruby Mountains and **GREEN MOUNTAIN CREEK,** rising on the mountain and joining Toyn Creek west of Harrison Pass; "named for the genus Ceanothus, an evergreen shrub [commonly called chaparrel or buck brush] that covers the south and western slopes" (EP, p. 39; GHM, EL 1).

GREEN SPRINGS. The large spring on the eastern edge of Railroad Valley, at the western foot of the White Pine Range in White Pine County, is an oasis in the desert (NJ 11–3; VPG). **GREEN SPRINGS** (Nye) formerly denoted a short-lived boom town forty-five miles southeast of Fairview, active in 1906; and its post office, established July 23, 1907, and rescinded by order of March 19, 1908 (DM; FTM, p. 12).

GREENVILLE (Lyon). Formerly an agricultural community of Mason Valley, prosperous in the early 1880s, served by Mason Valley post office; named for the deep blue-green alfalfa fields in the valley (NM; Nev. Guide, p. 211).

GREGGSVILLE. See **GOLCONDA.**

GREGORY'S MILL (Carson City). The name of the first steam mill erected in western Utah Territory, three miles west of Carson City on Mill Creek, in 1859; named for the proprietor, a Mr. Gregory (NHS, 1913, p. 194; MA, p. 541).

GREY HILLS. See **CHALK MOUNTAIN.**

GREYS (Elko). The possessive name for a stream which empties into **GREYS LAKE,** west of Angel Lake at the north end of the East Humboldt Range. Enoch Grey, a homesteader in early Starr Valley, is commemorated (SG Map 10; EP, p. 39).

GRIFFITH PEAK (Clark). The peak, southeast of Charleston Peak in the Spring Mountains, was named for Senator E. W. Griffith, who developed the Charleston Park resort in Kyle Canyon (WA).

GRIMES CANYON. See **COPPER KETTLE.**

GRIMY GULCH (Nye). This ravine, which extends from the east end of Pahute Mesa to the south end of Kawich Valley, about sixty-two miles southeast of Goldfield, was so named for the reason that "on windy days the finely weathered rock in the ravine makes one grimy" (DL 53; USGB 6302).

GRISWOLD (Elko). A creek south of Robinson Lake, and a lake north of Ruby Dome at the north end of the Ruby Mountains; named for Chauncy W. Griswold who came to Elko County from Missouri in the 1870s. His son, Morley, was once governor of Nevada (JGS, II, pp. 4–5; GHM, EL 1).

GRITTY GULCH (Nye). A ravine heading on the east end of Pahute Mesa and extending to the south end of Kawich Valley, about sixty-two miles southeast of Goldfield; named descriptively for "eroded rock debris in the valley" (USGB 6302; DL 53).

GRIZZLY HILL (Lyon). A hill at the mouth of American Ravine. Hosea and Allen Grosch, who are included among the possible original discoverers of the Comstock Lode, occupied a cabin at the base of this mountain. In 1858, Allen Grosch cached his library and his chemical apparatus somewhere about Grizzly Hill. The name presumably commemorates some feature so designated in California and was named by the brothers who came to Nevada from California in the early days (NHS, 1913, p. 218). See **OPHIR.**

GROOM. A mountain range (Lincoln) bounded on the north by Sand Spring Valley, on the northeast by the Timpahute Range, on the east by Tikaboo Valley, on the southeast by the Jumbled Hills, and on the south by **GROOM LAKE,** a dry lake at the northwest end of Emigrant Valley. The name derives from the **GROOM MINING DISTRICT,** organized in Lincoln County in 1870, which was named for the **GROOM**

MINE and probably worked as early as 1850. The district is about thirty miles from Yucca Flat, the present site of atomic tests (NJ 11-9; USGB 6002; VPG, p. 95; WA; Wheeler, 1872, p. 45; 1871 Map). **GROOM PASS** (Nye), a pass in the divide between Emigrant Valley and Yucca Flat, about eleven miles southwest of Groom Lake, is so named because the "pass is crossed by Groom Lake Road" (USGB 6301; DL 50).

GROUP SPRINGS (Clark). The name for a group of springs about seven miles south of Las Vegas, southwest of Mesquite Spring, and northeast of Arden (Vegas Quad.; WA).

GROUSE CANYON (Nye). A canyon on the west edge of Yucca Flat, about eighty-five miles northwest of Las Vegas; named for the indigenous sage hen, or sage grouse (USGB 6002).

GRUBBS WELLS. See **CAMP STATION.**

GUANO VALLEY. The valley, which lies principally in Harney County, Oregon, and takes its name from bird deposits, heads in Washoe County, Nevada, and trends northward along Catnip and Fish creeks, by which it is watered, into Oregon (NK 11-7; OPN, p. 67; VPG).

GUELPH (Clark). A station north of Moapa on the SPLA and SL RR, renamed *Farrier* on the UP RR. The name commemorates either a member of a German royal family, or a member of the Guelph family or political party in medieval Italy (NJ 11-12).

GYPSUM (Clark). **GYPSUM CAVE** is a great dry cavern, twenty miles east of Las Vegas, overlooking the site of Hoover Dam. In it were found the remains of extinct Pleistocene animals, as well as traces of Basket-Makers, early Pueblos, and Paiutes (JGS, I, p. 6). Before the excavations of 1930 and 1931, the cave was known merely for its gypsum deposits, for which it was named (Nev. Guide, p. 22). A wash, named for the cave, drains southeastward from the Dry Lake Range into the Colorado River, east of Las Vegas Wash (NK 11-12; WA).

HAAS (Humboldt). A post office, established January 5, 1885, and discontinued November 5, 1887, when the name was changed to *Norths Ranch* (FTM, p. 12).

HACKBERRY SPRING (Lincoln). Springs named for the nearby hackberry are west of Meadow Valley Wash, near Vigo Canyon, and on the southeast slope of the Mormon Mountains (WA). Wheeler's Map of 1871 shows **HACKBERRY SPRING** in Grapevine Canyon, the name he gave to the Meadow Valley Wash.

HACKSAW CANYON (Nye). A canyon five miles northeast of Morey Peak; "named for

the nearby Atomic Energy Commission's drill hole" (USGB 6903).

HAFED (Washoe). A station between Patrick and Vista, milepost 253.1 on the Sparks Subdivision of the SP RR (T1TR; T75). A variant spelling is *Hayfed* (SPD, p. 1031).

HALE AND NORCROSS (Storey). Another leading mining company on the Comstock that adopted the names of the men who located the claim in 1859. Calvin Hale, a fifty-year-old carriage maker from New Hampshire, came overland with his wife and small son and daughter to Hangtown (Placerville), California. After being wounded when Indians raided their wagon train, he went to Franktown, Nevada, and with Jim Norcross located the Hale and Norcross Mine. Hale furnished the money and Norcross did the work. After disposing of his mine, Hale went to Austin and Treasure Hill, Nevada, and is buried in the old Austin cemetery (HHR). The Hale and Norcross is an officially patented claim of four hundred feet between the Chollar and the Savage mines (AR, No. 42).

HALFPINT RANGE. A range of hills bounded on the east by Emigrant Valley and Nye Canyon, on the south by Frenchman Flat, on the west by Yucca Flat, and on the north by Groom Pass and part of Emigrant Valley; so named in 1962 not only "because of its relatively low and broken relief in contrast to many nearby ranges," in Lincoln and Nye counties, but also because the toponym "is in keeping with other names in the area, e.g. Pintwater Range" (USGB 6301; DL 50).

HALFWAY. A station midway between Carson City and Virginia City, through which ran the dividing line of Lyon and Ormsby (Carson City) counties, was named **HALF-WAY HOUSE.** The station was later moved to Mound House (NHS, 1913, p. 207). **HALFWAY WASH** (Clark) drains from Mormon Mesa into the Virgin River, about ten miles southwest of Riverside (NJ 11-12; WA).

HALLECK (Elko). A settlement, a station on the SP RR and WP RR between Elburz and Deeth, thirty-five miles west of Wells, and a post office (active from April 24, 1873, until October 31, 1949, reestablished January 16, 1950) (NK 11-12; T75; T54; FTM, p. 12). The names stem from **CAMP HAL-LECK,** established July 26, 1867, for the purpose of protecting construction workers on the Central Pacific Railroad, and travelers over the Hastings Cutoff road and the Humboldt River route against Indian forays. This largest military reservation in Nevada was situated at the west foot of the East Humboldt Range and on the east bank of Cottonwood (Soldier) Creek. The post was in the southeastern part of the reserve and about twelve miles southeast of present Halleck Station and was "delightfully located, well watered, and surrounded with thriving groves of cottonwood trees" (FES, p. 176). Captain S. P. Smith, with Company H of the Eighth United States Cavalry, established the post in compliance with the orders of Major General Henry W. Halleck (1815–1872) for whom the camp was named. On April 5, 1879, the name was changed to **FORT HALLECK,** and on October 11, 1886, the military reservation was ordered relinquished (Ruhlen; Wheeler 1871 Map).

HALLIGAN MESA (Nye). The mesa, ten miles southeast of Morey Peak and in the Pancake Range, was "named for Colonel Edward G. Halligan (died 1967), U.S. Army" (USGB 6901).

HALLSVALE (Lander). A station on the NC RR, between Ravenswood and Silver Creek; named for R. L. Hall of New York City, vice-president of the Nevada Central Railroad Company formed September 2, 1879 (MA, p. 283; HHB, Nev., p. 169).

HAMBLIN. A mountain between Callville Wash and Boulder Wash, near **HAMBLIN BAY** in Lake Mead, Clark County; a valley of northern Lincoln and southern White Pine counties, on the Utah boundary, south of the Snake Range and northwest of the Wilson Creek Range; and **HAMBLIN VALLEY WASH,** extending southeastward into Utah, north of the White Rock Mountains (WA; NJ 11–12; NJ 11–6). The name commemorates William Hamblin, a Mormon missionary who, with the help of the Indians, located and claimed the Panacker Lode in White Pine County (JGS, I, pp. 601, 614).

HAMILTON (White Pine). A mining camp on the north slope of the White Pine Range, east of **MOUNT HAMILTON** (altitude 10,-742 feet) the site of silver mines which were heavy producers in 1865–1874 (NJ 11–3; 1881 Map). The Federal Census of 1870 gives the population of Hamilton as 3,913; the area is presently listed as a township (Census, 1870, 1960). **HAMILTON MINING DISTRICT,** also known as *White Pine,* is thirty-six miles west of Ely, near Treasure Peak. **HAMILTON** post office was established August 10, 1868, and discontinued March 14, 1931, when Ely became the mail address for its patrons (FTM, p. 12). The name commemorates W. A. Hamilton who surveyed the townsite in May, 1869.

HAMLIGHT (Lincoln). The name was applied to a canyon, which drains north into **HAMLIGHT FLAT,** the mouth of Patterson Wash, two miles east of Pioche, and to a former station on the P and B RR, to commemorate Ham Light, an early stage station operator and mining man in Pioche (WA; DM; GHM, LN 1).

HANCOCK SUMMIT (Lincoln). The summit so denoted is in the Pahranagat Range, southwest of Hiko on State Route 25, and takes its name from John Hancock. Hancock, who was traveling with a woman companion, murdered a doctor and his driver at the summit in the 1890s. Some years later, the woman told police of the murders; Hancock was tried and convicted at Pioche and hanged in Carson City (GHM, LN 3; WA).

HANKS CREEK (Elko). The possessive name for a stream, tributary to Marys River, northeast of Stag Mountain and south of Marys River Ranch; named for Caleb Hank who ranged cattle in the creek area (NK 11–9; EP, p. 40).

HANNAPAH (Nye). A gold-silver-mercury mining district, also called *Silver Zone* and *Volcano,* and a former mining camp, fifteen miles northeast of Tonopah, south of Cedar Coral Spring in the southern end of the Monitor Range, which was active in the first decade of the twentieth century. Hannapah, a name of undetermined meaning, is perhaps a variant of Shoshonean *hanaupah* (Kroeber, Handbook, p. 895). The *Wadsworth Semi Weekly Dispatch* of December 5, 1902, reporting the new strike and duly noting the name, furnished its own droll etymology: "The name is the Japanese word for 'hang on tight' " (GHM, NY 1; VPG, p. 129; DM).

HANSEN (Washoe). The post office so named was established April 28, 1898, and discontinued July 21, 1903, when Eagleville, California, became the mail address for its patrons (FTM, p. 12).

HAPPY CREEK (Humboldt). A creek rising on the northeast slope of the Jackson Mountains and flowing into Quinn River Valley, south of Quinn River Crossing; and **HAPPY CREEK RANCH,** on State Route 8A, named for the creek. An early mining district, named for the creek, was on the northeast slope of the Jackson Mountains (NK 11–7; OPN, p. 36).

HAPPY JACK (Clark). The name for an old mine, located about a mile north of the Tramp Mine, in the Gold Butte Mining District of southern Clark County (WA).

HARBOR CREEK (Carson City). A stream in Bliss Meadows, east of Secret Harbor, Lake Tahoe; named for the harbor (SG Map 3).

HARDIN CITY (Humboldt). A short-lived mining camp and mill town in the Black Rock Range about forty-five miles north of Gerlach, organized in 1866 on the basis of a report that James Allen Hardin, a member of an emigrant party of 1849, had discovered silver float there (NM). Peter Lassen was killed several miles northeast of Hardin City on the southwest slope of Pahute Peak, while he and his party were looking for this reported silver ore (VPG). The post office established in old Roop (Washoe) County as Harden City on July 13, 1866, was renamed *Harveyville* on October 4, 1866, indicating a change in the mining camp name, and was discontinued on August 6, 1867 (FTM, p. 12; M&M, p. 93).

HARE CANYON (Churchill). A canyon heading on the east slope of the Stillwater Range and extending to Dixie Valley near Dixie Hot Springs, about forty-two miles northeast of Fallon; named for the ubiquitous jack rabbit (NJ 11–1; USGB 5904).

HARLAN PEAK (Esmeralda). A mountain in the southern part of the Silver Peak Range; presumably named for Harlan Acree who was killed by a high voltage wire while working near Silver Peak for the power company (OPN, p. 31; MM).

HARLEQUIN HILLS. See **CALICO MOUNTAINS.**

HARNEY (Elko). A non-agency station on the main line of the SP RR, milepost 517.0 between Cluro and Barth (T75).

HARRIMAN (Washoe). The name of a post office, established on September 15, 1903, at a division point on the SP RR just east of Reno, honored Edward H. Harriman, the president of the railroad. On May 27, 1904, the name was changed to *Sparks* (FTM, p. 12; NHS, 1926, pp. 349–50). See **SPARKS.**

HARRINGTON CREEK (Elko). A creek, tributary to South Fork Owyhee River northeast of Tuscarora; named for Jack Harrington, the first settler, who came to this area in 1868 (GHM, EL 2; OPN, p. 25; EP, p. 45). See **JACK(S).**

HARRISON PASS (Elko). This pass over the Ruby Mountains south of Jiggs was used by Frémont in 1845 and by some of the early emigrants bound for California (GHM, EL 1; VPG). The name is honorific of Thomas Harrison, an early rancher who came to Ruby Valley in 1865 (EP, p. 41).

HARVEYVILLE. See **HARDIN CITY.**

HASKELLS SAW MILL (Carson City). A water-power mill built in 1861 on Clear Creek, about eight miles southwest of Carson City; named for the owner of Haskell and Company (NHS, 1913, p. 194, 1926, p. 390).

HAT PEAK. A peak just west of the Duck Valley (Western Shoshone) Indian Reservation in northern Elko County (NK 11–8); a peak on the western slope of the Monitor Range, southeast of Sheep Mountain in Nye County; named for the shape of the mountains.

HAVEN, FORT (Washoe). An earthwork thrown up on the Truckee River, approximately one mile from Pyramid Lake, by soldiers of the "Carson River Expedition," around June 6, 1860. The expedition, under command of Captain Joseph Stewart, had fought with the Paiute Indians led by Young Winnemucca on June 2, 1860. They remained at the temporary fort until July 15, 1860, when they marched to the Carson River and established Fort Churchill. The fort was named for Major General J. P. Haven of the California Militia, who had served as a volunteer aide on the staff of Colonel Hays's Washoe Regiment of Nevada, which participated in the battle (Ruhlen). See **CHURCHILL.**

HAVILAH (Humboldt). A name of undetermined meaning for a mining camp of the early twentieth century, twenty-five miles northwest of Winnemucca, east of Silver State Valley in the Silver State Range, as noted by the *Goldfield Daily Tribune* of September 26, 1907 (DM).

HAWS STATION (Lyon). Formerly a station on the Twelve-Mile Desert about thirty-five miles from Dayton; named for Bert Haws, the proprietor (NHS, 1913, p. 213).

HAWTHORNE (Mineral). The county seat and trading center for a wide area, seven miles southwest of **THORNE STATION,** whose name, shortened from the town's designation, exemplifies the preference of the railroad builders for brief names (NJ 11–4). **HAWTHORNE MINING DISTRICT** is also called *Lucky Boy,* for the Lucky Boy Mine, three miles southwest of Hawthorne, and *Pamlico,* for an early mining camp so named in the west end of the Garfield Hills (VPG, p. 115). Hawthorne was settled in the early 1880s with the building of the C and C RR, of which it was a main division point below Walker Lake. The post office, established in old Esmeralda County on May 16, 1881, was transferred to Mineral County in 1911 (FTM, p. 12). An article in the Virginia City *Evening Chronicle* of April 1, 1881, predicts "the new town of Hawthorne, on the line of the Carson and Colorado Railroad at Walker Lake, will in the near future, give employment to a great many workingmen of all classes" (MA, p. 421). The town is presently the site of a United States Naval Ammunition Depot. The name commemorates William Hawthorn, a cattleman and early justice of the peace, who had formerly served as constable at Carson City. His advertisement in the first thirty-three issues of the *Walker Lake Bulletin* shows his name without the letter *e*; however, beginning with the issue of November 7, 1883, his name appears as W. A. Hawthorne (MM; OPN, p. 50; DM). The early community was also known as **HAWTHORNE CITY** (1881 Map; TF, p. 18).

HAYES, CAMP (Lyon). A temporary camp about twenty miles east of Carson City, at Reeds Station. It was occupied by volunteers, who assembled there in May, 1860, and formed the Nevada Militia to fight in the

Pyramid Lake Indian War. The camp, vacated May 26, 1860, was named for Colonel John ("Jack") C. Hays, an Indian fighter, in command of the Washoe Regiment (Ruhlen). See **BUCKLANDS.**

HAY RANCH (Eureka). Originally a station on the stage road to Austin (M&SP, 7/31/69); later on the E and P RR. The station was named for a hay ranch at which it was situated. Nevada historian Myron Angel described the ranch and explained the need of the E and P RR for the hay. "Eighteen miles southwest from Palisade is the hay ranch of the Eureka and Palisade Railroad Company . . . from which 1,000 tons of hay are cut annually. The company runs a line of freight teams from the terminus of their road at Eureka, to Pioche and all intermediate points, employing from 300 to 400 mules, each team hauling from 30,000 to 40,000 pounds. The hay cut at the ranch is for the partial subsistence of these teams" (MA, p. 428; 1881 Map).

HAYS CANYON (Washoe). A canyon heading in the **HAYS CANYON RANGE,** southwest of Boulder Lake and north of **HAYS CANYON PEAK,** and extending into Surprise Valley; named for Colonel John C. Hays who commanded the Washoe Regiment in the Pyramid Lake Indian War of 1860 (NK 11–7; SPD, p. 63). See **HAYES.**

HAYSTACK. A peak near the Humboldt County line in western Elko County, south and east of Milligan Creek and north of old Gold Circle; named for its resemblance to a haystack (Freese, Map 3; OPN, p. 24); a former mining camp (noted by the Goldfield *Weekly Post* of June 6, 1914), south of Jungo and named for **HAYSTACK BUTTE,** at the south end of Desert Valley in northern Pershing County (NK 11–10; DM).

HAYWARDS (Lyon). Formerly a station on the V and T RR, just beyond Mound House; named for an adjacent mill (NHS, 1913, p. 213). The name probably commemorates either Joseph L. Hayward, United States Marshal for Utah Territory, who arrived with Orson Hyde at Mormon Station on June 15, 1855 (MA, p. 38), or Alvinza Hayward, one of the charter members of the Union Mill and Mining Company (SPD, p. 413; 1881 Map).

HAZEN (Churchill). A settlement, a station on the SP RR twenty-three miles northwest of Fallon, and a post office established April 25, 1904. The town was first settled in 1869 and named for William Babcock Hazen, an American army officer and aide to William Tecumseh Sherman (FTM, p. 12; NHS, 1913, p. 184).

HEALY (Churchill). Formerly a post office in the Clan Alpine Range, on the east side of Dry Lake; named for Mary A. Healy, postmaster, of the Healy Ranch (OR, 1883,

1885; NHS, 1913, p. 179). The name of the post office, first established as *Healey* on June 7, 1882, was changed to Healy on August 6, 1883. Operations were transferred to Alpine on March 30, 1899 (FTM, p. 13).

HEELFLY CREEK (Elko). A creek rising on the northwest slope of the Ruby Mountains and flowing to Dennis Flats to join Secret Creek; "named for the heelflies that attack cattle at their hooves and lay eggs which eventually hatch into grubs and emerge through the hide on the back of the animal in this form" (SG Map 10; EP, p. 41).

HELEN, MOUNT (Nye). A mountain in western Nye County, south of the Cactus Range, east of Stonewall Mountain, and north and west of Pahute Mesa and Gold Flat (NJ 11–8).

HELENA. Formerly a station in Lander County, on the NC RR between Silver Creek and Ledlie (MA, p. 284; HHB, Nev., p. 269); a post office of Nye County, established December 8, 1908, and discontinued July 15, 1909, when its operations were moved to Tonopah (FTM, p. 13).

HELENE (Lincoln). The wash so named drains into Delamar Valley, past the Magnolia Mine north of old Delamar. The name derives from the former mining camp and post office at the Magnolia Mine, active from June 30, 1892, until December 22, 1894, when Delamar became the mail address for its patrons. According to the *Pioche Weekly Record* of April 7, 1892, the mining camp was named for Helene Cohn, the wife of one of the original partners of John Ferguson, who discovered the Magnolia in the Ferguson (Delamar) Mining District (WA; DM; FTM, p. 13; GHM, LN 2).

HELLS KITCHEN (Washoe). The name, descriptive of intense heat, denotes a canyon draining from the Lake Range into Pyramid Lake (VPG).

HENDERSON. An industrial center producing chlorine, steel alloys, titanium, rocket fuel, and chemicals, situated eleven miles southeast of Las Vegas on U.S. 95; a station between Las Vegas and Boulder City on a branch line of the UP RR; a post office established January 1, 1944; named to commemorate State Senator A. S. Henderson (NJ 11–12; WA; FTM, p. 13). The town, laid out in 1942, for several years was called *Basic* locally, for Basic Magnesium, Inc., the first plant built there. Victory Village, Carver Park, and Pittman are now a part of the Clark County city, which was incorporated June 8, 1953 (WA). In Eureka County, **HENDERSON CREEK** rises northwest of **HENDERSON SUMMIT** on the west slope of the Roberts Mountains, and flows through Garden Valley and into Pine Valley to join Pine Creek east of the Cortez Mountains (NJ 11–2; NK 11–11).

HENDRYS CREEK (White Pine). The mountain stream, rising in the Snake Range southeast of Mount Moriah, and flowing into Snake Valley, was named for early **HENDRIES MILL**, whose owner remains unidentified (NK 11–9; TF, p. 18).

HENRY (Elko). A station on the UP RR between Contact and Shores and west of White Peaks on Salmon Falls Creek; named for Henry Harris who was a foreman for the Sparks–Harrell Ranch (NK 11–9; EP, P. 41).

HEPLY (Washoe). A short-lived post office established June 23, 1891 in the southern portion of the county, and discontinued on December 4, 1891, when its operations were transferred to Reno (FTM, p. 13).

HERCULES. A canyon in Churchill County, heading at Badger Flat and extending as far as Dixie Valley. The site of the former **HERCULES** mining camp is in the valley about two miles north of Wonder and was named for the **HERCULES MINING DISTRICT** (also called *Wonder*) on the west slope of the Clan Alpine Range, seventeen miles by road northeast of Frenchman. The district was served by **HERCULES** post office from December 18, 1906, to October 31, 1908 (USGB 5904; VPG, p. 21; FTM, p. 13). **HERCULES GAP** or **GATE** (White Pine) denotes a gap in the Egan Range and a former mining camp in the early Lake Mining District, north of Ely and northeast of former Mineral City. The geological feature was named by Simpson in 1859. "I call the place the Gate of Hercules, on account of its stupendous walls" (JHS, p. 117). The camp grew up as a result of mineral discoveries in 1873 in the Egan Range (NHS, 1924, p. 291; 1881 Map; JHS Map). **HERCULES CREEK** (Nye) rises north of North Twin River and southwest of Toiyabe Range Peak in the Toiyabe Range and flows into Big Smoky Valley (SG Map 5). Hercules was the most illustrious hero of Greek mythology.

HERON ISLAND (Clark). An island in a group known as the Overton Islands, in the lower part of the Overton Arm of Lake Mead (WA); named for the indigenous bird.

HERRIN (Humboldt). A non-agency station on the Winnemucca Subdivision of the SP RR, milepost 452.7, between Iron Point and Valmy (T75).

HERSTIN (Churchill). Formerly a station three miles northeast of Wadsworth on the old line of the SP RR through northwest Churchill County (T1TR).

HESLIP (Washoe). A station on the Wadsworth Subdivision on the SP RR, milepost 299.4, between Numana and Sutcliffe and west of Pyramid Lake (T75).

HESSES CAMP (Clark). The camp was maintained as a mining promotion by King C. Gillette and John B. Stetson at the mouth of Las Vegas Wash during the 1920s. It was named for J. Fred Hesse, who was the surveyor and who later became the mayor of Las Vegas (WA).

HEUSSER MOUNTAIN (White Pine). The mountain, east of Smith Valley and on the west edge of Steptoe Valley, across from McGill, was named for Albert Heusser, a rancher and cattleman. Heusser came to Nevada in 1871, was the first blacksmith at Ely, and erected the second building there (JGS, II, p. 436; NJ 11–3).

HICKERSON SUMMIT (Lander). A summit southeast of Austin on U.S. 50 in the Toiyabe National Forest, west of Stoneberger Creek; named for John Hickerson of Austin because it was on the road to his ranch. A variant spelling is *Hickison* (MM; GHM, LA 1).

HICKS. A creek rising on the south flank of **HICKS MOUNTAIN**, south of Alder Mountain in the Humboldt National Forest, joining the Bruneau River, east of Mustang Butte (NK 11–9), and an early mining district ten miles from Island Mountain, both in Elko County (SM, 1876, p. 24; HHB, Nev., p. 277). The district was "named for 'Cap' Hicks, a Cherokee Indian scout" (EP, p. 41) and served by Mountain City post office (TF, p. 18). **HICKS STATION** (Nye) was a stop on the old stage route between Warm Springs and Eureka, east of Long Canyon. **HICKS SPRING** at the station site "was formerly named Shoshone *sap:ava*, meaning 'scum water'" (M&M, p. 149; GHM, NY 3). **MOUNT HICKS** (Mineral) commemorates E. R. Hicks, an early prospector in the old Esmeralda region. The mountain, east of the Anchorite Hills and north of Alkali (Aurora) Valley, is near the mine discovered by Hicks (NJ 11–4; SPD, p. 855; Haw. Quad.).

HIDDEN. The name for a small, enclosed valley between the Arrow Canyon Range and the Las Vegas Range, in Clark County; for a ranch, also called **HIDDEN HILLS**, below Manse in Pahrump Valley, in southern Nye County; and for a spring northwest of Carp, in Lincoln County, presumably named by C. L. Averett, who developed it for stock-watering purposes (NJ 11–12; WA). **HIDDEN CLIFF** (Nye). A cliff on the east slope of Black Mountain, just northwest of the head of Yellow Cleft, and about twenty-six miles north-northeast of Beatty; named for its partly concealed position (USGS 6302; DL 56). **HIDDEN FOREST** (Clark) denotes a secluded stand of saw timber on the west slope of Sheep Mountain in the Sheep Range, for which was named **HIDDEN FOREST CAMP**, between Hayford Peak and Sheep Peak (NJ 11–12; WA). **HIDDEN TREASURE** (White Pine), the famous mine located in 1867 on the upper slope of Treasure Hill, south of Hamilton, was staked and apparently named by an Austin prospector, A. J. Leathers, who was led to the site by an Indian on January 4, 1868 (Nev. Guide, pp. 252–53). **HIDDEN VALLEY** (Washoe) is the name for a small settlement about five miles southeast of Reno, at the west base of the Virginia Range and northeast of the Huffaker Hills (VPG; GHM, WA 1).

HIGHLAND (Lincoln). A mountain range, west of the Meadow Valley Wash, extending north from near Caliente; a peak in the Highland Range, about thirteen miles northwest of Panaca; a spring about a mile southwest of the old mining camp so named (NJ 11–9; Wheeler 1871 Map; NM; USGB 6002; WA). The names stem from the **HIGHLAND MINING DISTRICT**, seven miles north-northwest of Pioche, discovered and named in 1868, as recorded by a Nevada pioneer, Charles Gracey.

> On the first of August Mr. Cavence returned from prospecting, and with him came a man called Allen McDougal. They told big stories about what they had found, and the samples when assayed proved to be rich in silver. As silver ore was the only thing desired in those days . . . I at once . . . bought an outfit and wagon. I remember the outfit cost me seven hundred and thirty dollars. We loaded it up and started for Lincoln County, Highland District, the latter named by Mr. McDougal, who was Highland Scotch. (NHS, 1909, p. 105)

HIGHLAND CHIEF. A popular mine name placed by Scottish prospectors, designating a mine in the Echo district of old Humboldt County; the **HIGHLAND CHIEF 2** and the *Scottish Chief* in the same district; a mine in the Lewis district of Lander County, owned by J. A. Blossom in 1880 (SM, 1866, pp. 49–50; DM). A mine and a district in the Highland Range (Lincoln) were denoted simply *Chief*. See **CHIEF**.

HIGH ROCK. HIGH ROCK CANYON (Washoe) was so named from its being an imposing cleft with narrow high rock walls. Petroglyphs on the walls, as well as rockshelters and campsites in the area, prove the presence of man from as early as 3000 B.C. "Northern Paiute Indians roamed these lands when John C. Frémont first journeyed through High Rock Canyon in 1843. The Applegate brothers blazed their trail from Oregon through the canyon to the Humboldt in 1846. Peter Lassen partially followed this route in 1848, and gold seekers crowded the trail in 1849" (SHM 149). The name of the canyon appears on an 1849 manuscript map included in the Diaries of J. Goldsborough Bruff (Wheat III, 99). The last attack by Indians on white men in Nevada took place here. In 1911, four sheepmen passing through **LITTLE HIGH ROCK CANYON** on their way to their camp in the Black Rock Desert were killed by Indians, who were, in turn,

hunted down and killed east of Golconda (M&S, p. 82; VPG; JWH). **HIGH ROCK CREEK**, with its tributaries, **LITTLE HIGH ROCK** and **EAST FORK HIGH ROCK**, rises in the Calico Mountains in Washoe County and flows into **HIGH ROCK LAKE**, in western Humboldt County. In years of very heavy precipitation, the lake overflows into Fly Creek which discharges into the Black Rock Desert (NK 11–7; VPG).

HIKO (Lincoln). A settlement in the north end of Pahranagat Valley, on State Route 38, established in the late 1860s and named in 1867. The name of Pah Ranagat post office, established March 25, 1867, was changed to **HIKO** on June 24, 1867. The report of the State Mineralogist for 1867 states that the name of *Hiko,* then the county seat, was a Shoshone Indian word signifying "white man's city." It is also said to mean "white man" because at this point the Indians saw the first white man (MA, p. 490; Wheeler, 1879, p. 470; JGS, I, p. 261; OPN, p. 44). **HIKO RANGE**, named for the settlement, is a north-south trending range east of Pahranagat Valley and west of the South Pahroc Range (USGB 6001). Variants are *Hyco* and *Hyko* (Wheeler 1871 Map; WA; NJ 11–9; Freese, Map 2; FTM, pp. 13, 21).

HILINE SIDING (White Pine). A junction on the NN RR east of Ely in Steptoe Valley where the high line to the McGill smelter takes off from the main line of the railroad (NJ 11–3; DM).

HILL. An early station on the old emigrant road, eleven miles southeast of Fallon in Churchill County; named for William Hill, who kept the **HILL**, or Slough, **RANCH**. **HILL** post office was established May 18, 1882, and discontinued in 1912 (?), when its operations were transferred to Fallon (NHS, 1913, p. 179; FTM, p. 13; OR, 1883, 1885, 1899). The place was also called **HILLS STATION** (HHB, Nev., pp. 261–62; TF, p. 18). **HILLS CREEK** (Elko) rises southeast of California Mountain on the east slope of the Independence Mountains and flows generally eastward to join Malhala Creek, south of Jim Creek (SG Map 11).

HILLER. The name for a low range of mountains on the north side of the Colorado River, west of Temple Mesa, in Clark County, and a former post office of Lander County, active from August 14, 1919, until January 15, 1921, when Beowawe became the mail address for its patrons (NJ 11–12; WA; FTM, p. 13).

HILLTOP. Features descriptively named for their position near the top of a hill or mountain are a mining district, camp, and former post office (February 17, 1909–March 14, 1931), about eighteen miles southeast of Battle Mountain on the northwest slope of Shoshone Peak in the Shoshone Mountains,

Lander County; and a mine in Clark County, at the top of Gold Butte (VPG, p. 85; FTM, p. 13; WA). **HILLTOP CANYON** (Lander), north of Maysville Summit, takes its name from the **HILLTOP MINING DISTRICT** (NK 11–11).

HIMIX (Clark). The coined name for a former concrete mixing plant, in operation on the Nevada side of the canyon during the construction of Hoover Dam; named for its high-level location (WA). See **LOMIX.**

HINDS HOT SPRINGS (Lyon). Formerly a resort (because of the supposed medicinal value of the springs) situated at the north end of Smith Valley, southwest of Alkali Flat and north of Wellington; named for John C. Hinds who located the springs at the foot of the Pine Nut Mountains in 1858 (Well. Sheet; JGS, II, p. 414; NHS, 1913, p. 213).

HOBART. The name was applied to a creek and reservoir, north and east of Marlette Peak in the Carson Range in Washoe County, and to a former post office (July 22, 1889–November 16, 1901) near Glenbrook in Douglas County, to commemorate W. S. Hobart, one of the owners of the Hobart Lumber Company at Crystal Bay on Lake Tahoe in the late 1870s (GHM, WA 1; MM; DM, RR (I), p. 425).

HOBSON (White Pine). A settlement south of Ruby Lake in Ruby Valley, established in 1898 at the site of old Fort Ruby; named for Admiral Richmond P. Hobson, famed for sinking the *Merrimac* in Santiago Harbor during the Spanish-American War. A post office, named for the town, was first established August 2, 1902, and discontinued for the last time November 30, 1936, when Ruby Valley became the mail address for its patrons. The former townsite is presently the headquarters for the Fort Ruby Ranch (GHM, WP 3; NM; FTM, p. 13).

HODGES CANYON (Eureka). The canyon heads east of Summit Mountain, on the northeast slope of the Monitor Range, and extends into Antelope Valley north of Cedar Creek (SG Map 6). The name commemorates the Hodges family who owned a ranch nearby (MM).

HOGPEN SHOOT (Lincoln). An incident name for a famous ore-shoot in the Lucky Bar Mine in the Delamar Mining District. "A hogpen had been built on the side of the hill, and the story goes that one day it was found that the hogs had rooted the dirt off a rich outcrop of gold. The ore shoot was promptly named in accord with the circumstances of its discovery" (WA).

HOGS BACK (Esmeralda). This early, short-lived settlement was served by Aurora post office and presumably named for a sharp, steeply sloping ridge in the area (HHB, Nev., p. 260; TF, p. 18).

HOLBORN (Elko). A non-agency station on the Elko Subdivision of the SP RR, milepost 624.1, between Anthony and Fenelon and fourteen miles east of Wells (T75).

HOLBROOK (Douglas). The mining district, also known as *Mountain House,* is southeast of Minden in the Pine Nut Range on the California border (VPG, p. 34). The district's name was derived from **HOLBROOK STATION** (or Mountain House Station), named for its proprietor, Charles E. Holbrook (OPN, p. 19), who was also postmaster of **HOLBROOK** post office, established January 28, 1863, and discontinued March 31, 1915 (FTM, p. 13).

HOLE IN THE MOUNTAIN (Elko). The highest peak (altitude 11,276 feet) in the East Humboldt Range, east of Halleck; "so named because of a natural stone 'window' near its apex which can be seen from Starr Valley to the west and Clover Valley to the east" (EP, p. 42; NK 11–12). *Lizzie's Window* is a local variant.

HOLLIDAYS STATION (Douglas). Ben Holliday established a temporary store and station, in 1854, about three miles down the Carson River from Mormon Station, now Genoa (NHS, 1913, p. 194).

HOLY CROSS. See **FALLON** and **TERRELL.**

HOME (Clark). A mistake name for an old ranch near Moapa, once owned by the *Holm* family, and for nearby springs which supplied water to the ranch (WA).

HOMESTAKE (Clark). The name for a mine in the Alunite district, twenty-two miles from Las Vegas and two miles west of Boulder City, a mine discovered by soldiers from Fort Mohave in the 1860s, near Bullhead Canyon and about forty-five miles southeast of Searchlight (WA).

HOMESTEAD (Storey). A fort on the heights between Gold Hill and Virginia City in the 1860s, where people gathered on April 19, 1865, to mourn the death of President Abraham Lincoln; a tunnel so named beneath the fort (Ruhlen; DM).

HONEST MINER (Clark). The first claim staked in the Eldorado Canyon Mining District, twenty-four miles northeast of Searchlight in the Opal Mountains, is said to have been the **HONEST MINER,** discovered in 1861 (WA; VPG, p. 24).

HONEY LAKE (Washoe). A valley west of Flanigan, extending into Washoe County, Nevada, from Honey Lake in California; named for the lake which had been so denoted by members of the Peter Lassen Party in 1850, because of the honeydew which they found on the heads of wild oats in the basin (NK 11–10; Gudde, p. 136; VPG).

HONEY LAKE SMITHS (Lyon). An early trading post, ten miles from Fort Churchill, was so named for the owner, who had originally come from Honey Lake, California. The site of this trading post, which was known in 1860 as Williams Station (q.v.), is now under the waters of Lake Lahontan Reservoir. Mark Twain described his arrival at this way station, where he had to remain for eight days because the Carson River flooded. "We rode through a snowstorm for two or three days, and arrived at 'Honey Lake Smith's,' a sort of isolated inn on the Carson River. It was a two-story log house situated on a small knoll in the midst of the vast basin or desert through which the sickly Carson winds its melancholy way. Close to the house were the Overland stage stables, built of sun-dried bricks. There was not another building within several leagues of the place" (SLC, II, p. 209).

HONEYMAN CREEK (Elko). The stream flows into Johnson Creek six miles south-southwest of Tobar and was "named for Captain Francis Honeyman, U.S. Army, who homesteaded in the area" (USGB 7004). *Hunneman* Creek is a variant spelling (SG Map 10).

HOOVER DAM (Clark). Boulder Dam was called Hoover Dam in honor of Herbert Clark Hoover, the thirty-first president of the United States, during 1932 and 1933, and was officially renamed so in 1947. See **BOULDER.**

HOPE, MOUNT (Eureka). A peak, south of Henderson Summit in the southern part of the Sulphur Spring Mountains, west of Garden Pass Creek, and **MOUNT HOPE MINE,** on the eastern slope of the mountain; named for Samuel J. Hope (NJ 11–2; OPN, p. 34). An earlier name *Coopers Peak* was given by Captain James H. Simpson in 1859. "Immediately to our north is a conical peak, which, as we found afterward, in our journey westward, continued for days a most notable landmark, and which I call Cooper's Peak, after Adjutant General Cooper of the Army" (JHS, p. 71).

HORNET SPRING (Clark). The spring, about twenty miles southwest of Indian Springs, on the old road to Pahrump Valley, probably was named for the yellow jacket wasp. In the 1880s the settlers at the spring were served by Mesquite post office (1881 Map; TF, p. 18).

HORNSILVER. In Esmeralda County, a mining district twenty-five miles southwest of Goldfield; a former mining camp, established in the early twentieth century; and a post office (May 16, 1908–October 16, 1932). The place has also been called *Lime Point* and *Gold Point*. "Originally it was Limepoint, named for a pointed lime hill southwest of the townsite; later, when high grade ore rich in hornsilver was mined, and the first name sounded quite barren it became Hornsilver, a correct and more attractive label. When silver lost some of its favor for the mining public, Goldpoint seemed to offer more promising title, for there are many gold prospects in this district" (CHL, p. 180). **HORNSILVER** (Nye) denotes an old mine at Wahmonie, twenty miles north of Lathrop Wells on U.S. 95; named for hornsilver (cerargyrite), a silver chloride containing seventy-five percent silver (Lida Quad.; VPG, p. 55; NM; FTM, p. 13; WA). See **SILVERHORN.**

HORN SPRING (Lincoln). Mr. I. J. Horn, an early resident of Delamar, is commemorated by this spring near the former mining camp (WA).

HORSE. The wild horse has given names to over forty natural features in fourteen Nevada counties. Canyons so named are southeast of Mount Tenabo in the Cortez Mountains, and southeast of Diamond Springs in the Diamond Mountains (GHM, EU 1, 2); in Lander County west of Mount Lewis in the Shoshone Mountains (GHM, LA 2); in Lincoln County west of Camp Valley Creek in the Wilson Creek Range; in Nye County east of Peavine Creek in the Toiyabe Range, and west of Willow Creek in the Monitor Range; in Pershing County northeast of Oreana in the Humboldt Range; in Washoe County north of Fish Springs in the Fish Creek Mountains, and east of Buffalo Slough in the Buffalo Hills; in White Pine County north of **LITTLE HORSE CANYON,** east of Mount Moriah in the Snake Range (GHM, LN 1; NY 2, 3; PE 2; WA 2, 3; WP 1). **HORSE CREEK.** An intermittent stream rising north of Wonder in the Louderback Mountains and flowing into Dixie Valley, in Churchill County (USGB 5904); creeks between Beaver and Cottonwood creeks and east of Arthur in the East Humboldt Range, both in central Elko County; a tributary of Peavine Creek in the southern end of the Toiyabe Range and a creek in the Monitor Range, south of Clover Creek, both in Nye County; and a creek east of Cortez in Eureka County (Dir. 1971). **HORSE MOUNTAIN** designates a peak southwest of Mill Creek in the Shoshone Mountains in Lander County, and a mountain northeast of Lamoille on the west slope of the Ruby Mountains in Elko County (GHM, LA 2; EL 1). **HORSE SPRING.** Springs so named are southeast of Carp and about six miles northeast of Gold Butte in Clark County; east of Caliente in Lincoln County; northeast of Ramsey in Lyon County; east of Pahrump Valley in Nye County; west of Tule Ridge in the Virginia Mountains, and on Petersen Mountain in Washoe County (WA; GHM, LY 1; WA 1). **HORSE SPRING CANYON** lies southeast of Kyle in the Sawmill Range in Lincoln County (GHM, LN 2). **HORSE SPRING WASH,** named for nearby Horse Spring in Clark

County, trends northerly from Gold Butte to Saint Thomas Gap on the east side of Tramp Ridge (WA; NJ 11–12).

HORSE HEAVEN. The name has been applied in central and northern Nevada, especially to the well-watered areas where large herds of wild horses earlier roamed. In northern Nye County, **HORSE HEAVEN CANYON** heads on **HORSE HEAVEN MOUNTAIN**, just south of the Eureka County boundary, and extends into Monitor Valley, northeast of Potts. **HORSE HEAVEN FLAT** is southeast of the mountain (GHM, NY 3; Nev. Guide, p. 17). Other flats so denoted are northeast of Mountain City in Elko County, and south of Whirlwind Valley in Lander County. In White Pine County, **HORSE HEAVEN** is the name of a hill northeast of Granite Basin in the Snake Range (GHM, EL 3; LA 2; WP 1).

HORSESHOE. In Douglas County, **HORSE-SHOE BEND** describes the Big Bend of the Carson River. **HORSESHOE GULCH** denotes a small canyon, southeast of Porphyry Gulch, in the Goodsprings Mining District, Clark County. **HORSESHOE BASIN** is a valley in Lander County (GHM, DO 1; Dir. 1971). **HORSESHOE STATION** (Eureka) was a former way station on the E and P RR (MA, p. 286; WA). See **BIG BEND**.

HORSESHUTEM SPRING (Nye). The springs so named are about five miles northeast of the former Johnnie townsite and south of Grapevine Spring (Furn. Cr. Quad.; WA).

HORSE THIEF. For a number of years after 1865, Luther Canyon (q.v.) south of Genoa in Douglas County was known as **HORSE THIEF CANYON** because John and Lute Olds, who had a ranch and station nearby, rustled horses from emigrants and sent them up the canyon and into **HORSE THIEF MEADOWS**. After the horses had fed and rested, they were sold to new emigrants on the trail (SHM 118). **HORSE THIEF GULCH CAMPGROUND** is near Ursine in northeast Lincoln County (GHM, LN 1).

HOT CREEK. A name group in Nye County stems from a creek "so called because a volume of hot water, issuing from a series of springs, makes a creek of respectable proportions, at least in a county where every little rivulet is so named, and where an extraordinary creek is called a river" (SM, 1867, p. 62). **HOT CREEK**, a former townsite and post office (established August 7, 1867, discontinued March 13, 1881, and reestablished May 5, 1897, to operate until January 26, 1912), was west of the creek and named for **HOT CREEK MINING DISTRICT**. The district was organized subsequent to rich ore discoveries in 1865, on the eastern slope of the **HOT CREEK RANGE**, which is composed of croppings from a volcanic forma-

tion. The creek flows from the Hot Creek Range into **HOT CREEK VALLEY**. The valley runs nearly parallel with Railroad Valley and its insufficient water supply is obtained from small creeks and springs. **HOT CREEK RANCH**, at the west edge of the valley, occupies the site of the former mining camp (NJ 11–5; NM; FTM, p. 13; SPD, p. 962; Wheeler, 1872, p. 39, 1871 Map). The Hot Creek Mining District, also called *Tybo* and *Keystone*, is seventy miles northeast of Tonopah (VPG, p. 143). **HOT CREEK** (Elko) denotes both a creek rising on the north end of Table Mountain and flowing to Wild Horse Reservoir, and a tributary of Wildcat Creek, north of Currant Creek and east of the Gibbs Ranch (NK 11–9; NJ 11–9).

HOT LAKE (Humboldt). The lake, southwest of Denio and north of Continental Lake, is named for the hot springs that feed it (NK 11–7; OPN, p. 36).

HOT SPRINGS. A station between Desert and Mirage, fifty miles northeast of Wadsworth, on the old line of the CP RR through northwest Churchill County (T1TR; 1881 Map). "The station is in the midst of a desert, and is named from the Hot Springs, whose rising steam can readily be seen about half a mile from the track on the left. There are quite a number of them boiling hot. They formerly extended along the base of the hill, still farther to the left, and nearer to the track, but while they seem to have dried up in one locality, they have broken out in another" (FES, p. 199). The Churchill County post office so named was active from March 26, 1873, to October 24, 1874 (FTM, p. 13). Also in northwest Churchill County are the **HOT SPRINGS MOUNTAINS**, trending northeastward from Hazen to the Mopung Hills, and **HOT SPRINGS MARSH**, a mining district, fifteen miles northeast of Fernley. They were named for a salt marsh, shown on current maps as **HOT SPRINGS FLAT** (NJ 11–1), which lies northwest of Hot Springs Mountains and near **HOT SPRINGS STATION** (VPG, p. 16) (also called *Bradys Hot Springs*). **HOT SPRINGS RANGE** (Humboldt) is bounded on the west by Paradise Valley and on the east by Eden Valley. **HOT SPRINGS PEAK** is at the northern end of the range and about thirty-two miles northnortheast of Winnemucca (NK 11–8; USGB 6002). In Elko County, **HOT SPRINGS** denotes a locality at natural hot springs, near **HOT CREEK**, just east of the Owyhee River and northwest of Table Mountain (NK 11–9). Additional mining districts so named were organized in Mineral County, eight miles northeast of Rawhide (SM, 1867, p. 56; VPG, p. 113); in early Esmeralda, in 1865 (HHB, Nev., p. 260; SM, 1867, p. 37); and in early Douglas County (HHB, Nev., pp. 254–55; OPN, p. 20). **HOT SPRINGS STATION** (Lander) on the NC RR between Mound Springs and Bridges, was named for nearby hot springs described as follows: "About 25 miles south of Battle Mountain, are some very fine hot springs. There are nearly 60 of them, covering about half a section of land. The largest one is about 60 feet long by 30 feet wide, and at times rises and falls from three to five feet. These springs are on the stage road to Austin, and are something of a wonder to travelers in that direction" (FES, p. 187). The name of Spring City post office, of old Roop County, was changed to **HOT SPRINGS** on October 4, 1866, and operations were discontinued August 6, 1867 (FTM, p. 13).

HOT SULPHUR SPRINGS (Elko). The springs on Hot Creek, a tributary of South Fork Owyhee River southwest of Jack Creek, were named for their hot sulphurous water (GHM, EL 2).

HOYA (Lincoln). A siding on the UP RR about twenty miles north of Moapa, and **HOYA PIT,** an abandoned railroad gravel pit, about two miles north of the station in Meadow Valley Wash (NJ 11–12; WA).

HOYE. A canyon in Douglas County, northwest of Wellington, on the West Walker River between Antelope and Smith valleys; a settlement, formerly at the west edge of Smith Valley, north of Wellington in Lyon County (Well. Sheet; VPG). The old settlement, called **HOYES STORE** by Bancroft, was built by and named for John Hoye, who came to Smith Valley in 1863 or 1864 and kept a station at the mouth of the canyon on the edge of Alkali Flat (NHS, 1913, p. 194; HHB, Nev., p. 254).

HUALIPI (Humboldt). A post office so named was established June 30, 1915, and discontinued April 15, 1919, when Gerlach became the mail address for its patrons (FTM, p. 13).

HUBBARD (Elko). A locality between Harney and Shores Siding in northern Elko County; named for nearby **HUBBARD CREEK,** which flows generally westward to **HUBBARD BASIN** (SG Map 2; NK 11–9). An early rancher, not further identified, is commemorated (EP, p. 43).

HUDSON (Lyon). A locality at the extreme end of Wilson Canyon, nine miles from Ludwig, formerly a station on the NCB RR (NCB Map). **HUDSON** post office was active from April 17, 1911, to July 14, 1917, and again from January 5, 1918, to January 30, 1943, when its operations were transferred to Smith (FTM, p. 13).

HUFFAKERS (Washoe). The name for a community, seven miles south of Reno on U.S. 395, commemorates Granville W. Huffaker, a native of Wayne County, Kentucky, who drove cattle from Salt Lake City to the Truckee Meadows in the late 1850s and sold beef to the miners in the early days of the Comstock. Mr. Huffaker bought a ranch near Steamboat Springs, and in 1871, the place was made a regular station on the V and T RR. A bonanza V-flume, constructed by the Pacific Wood, Lumber and Flume Company to bring lumber from the Sierra Nevada, ended at this point (MA, pp. 628, 632, 643; 1881 Map; HHB, Nev., p. 248, n. 13, p. 86, n. 53; GHK, V&T, p. 17). **HUFFAKER HILLS,** in the Truckee Meadows, are west of the Virginia Range (NJ 11–1).

HUGHES STATION (Lyon). In the early days, two brothers, James and Harvey Hughes, kept a trading post (which was named for them) about four miles from Honey Lake Smiths Station (NHS, 1913, p. 213).

HULSE (Lincoln). **HULSE CANYON** and **HULSE CREEK,** rising in the Wilson Creek Range and emptying into Patterson Wash north of Pioche, were named for James Madison Hulse and Delora Elmira Craw Hulse, who settled on the creek in the late 1880s (GHM, LN 1; JWH).

HUMBOLDT. The Humboldt name complex commemorates Baron Friedrich Heinrich Alexander von Humboldt (1769–1859), German naturalist, traveler, and statesman, and stems from the Humboldt River and Humboldt Mountains, named by John Charles Frémont during his explorations of 1845–1846. Both names appear on the 1848 map drawn by Charles Preuss, Frémont's topographer (Wheat III, 56). The Humboldt is a river almost three hundred miles long, formed by the confluence of its north fork and east fork about thirteen miles northeast of Elko, and flowing west of the West Humboldt Range, through the Humboldt Sink to the western part of the Carson Sink. The river now is impounded behind Rye Patch Dam, completed in 1936 by the Bureau of Reclamation. Prior names for the Humboldt were *Marys* or *Marias, Unknown, Pauls, Swampy, Barren,* and *Ogdens.*

Before 1845, the river probably was best known as *Marys.* There are conflicting accounts of the naming. One asserts that Mary was the wife of Peter Skene Ogden, an explorer for the Hudson's Bay Company (HMC, p. 784), who named the river for her in 1825 (HHB, Nev., p. 36; HMC, p. 84). However, it is doubtful that Ogden saw the Humboldt before 1827 (VPG), or in 1828 (FNF, p. 56), or in 1831 (MA, p. 22). Others state that Mary was the wife of one of Ogden's men (GG, p. 32), or of Jedediah Strong Smith, an independent trapper, who named the river for her in 1825 (MA, pp. 20–21). The best authenticated accounts, however, agree that

Jed Smith had no wife (VPG; RRE; JGS, I, p. 45).

In his notes, Ogden called the river *Unknown* when he discovered it near the mouth of the Little Humboldt, about three miles north of present Winnemucca, and thought it was a branch of the Sandwich Island (Owyhee) River (GG, p. 31; EMM, Nev., pp. 67–68; JGS, I, pp. 40–41). *Unknown River* and *Unknown Lake* are the designations for the river and the sink on the manuscript map which illustrates Ogden's *Journal of Snake River Expedition 1828–29* (Wheat II, 116). When Joseph Paul, one of Ogden's men, died on December 18, 1828, and was buried on the banks of the Humboldt, Ogden recommended, in his report of 1829, that the river be called "Paul's River, as he must remain here till the great trumpet shall sound" (FNF, p. 60; JGS, I, p. 42, n. 3; Nev. Guide, p. 129). On Ogden's return route after May 29, 1829, he noted "Unknown River is known as Swampy River or Paul's River."

Among the small bands of "free trappers" in 1829, the stream was known as *Ogdens River*. The Joseph Walker party, following roughly the old route of the SP RR from Ogden, gave the appellation of *Barren* to the river in 1833 (JGS, I, pp. 43, 45; JHS, pp. 18, 20; ZL, p. 153). The river was known to Washington Irving as both *Marys* and *Ogdens*. In the early 1860s Mark Twain camped for two days in the vicinity of the "Sink of the Humboldt," traveled a short distance along the river, and later described it in *Roughing it*.

> People accustomed to the monster mile-wide Mississippi, grow accustomed to associating the term "river" with a high degree of watery grandeur. Consequently, such people feel rather disappointed when they stand on the shores of the Humboldt or the Carson and find that a "river" in Nevada is a sickly rivulet which is just the counterpart of the Erie canal in all respects save that the canal is twice as long and four times as deep. One of the pleasantest and most invigorating exercises one can contrive is to run and jump across the Humboldt River till he is overheated, and then drink it dry. (SLC, I, pp. 193–194)

The **HUMBOLDT TRAIL**, through **HUMBOLDT VALLEY**, generally followed the course of the river; the valley is now traversed by the SP RR, WP RR, and Interstate 80. The **HUMBOLDT SINK**, a marsh containing a lake into which the waters of the river, now impounded behind Rye Patch Dam, formerly emptied, is in southern Pershing and northern Churchill counties. The John A. Dreibelbis 1854 manuscript map of a proposed route for a Pacific Railroad across the Sierra Nevada includes the name of the valley and the sink (Wheat III, 167).

The **WEST HUMBOLDT RANGE** (Pershing), whose Indian name was *Tac-a-roy*, meaning "Snow Mountains," according to Captain James H. Simpson (JHS, p. 64), is a north-south trending mountain range with its south end about seventeen miles east-southeast of Lovelock (USGB 6002; Car. Sink 1908, 1951). In Churchill County are the **HUMBOLDT SALT MARSH**, forty-six miles northeast of Fallon, in Dixie Valley, and the **HUMBOLDT SLOUGH**, in the desert about twenty-nine miles from old Ragtown. **HUMBOLDT WELLS**, a station on the CP RR, was named for some springs about one-half mile west of the station, which had been a mecca of emigrants on the Humboldt Trail (SM, 1875, pp. 27–28). Population figures for the settlement were included in the federal census of 1870. The **HUMBOLDT NATIONAL FOREST** (Elko, Humboldt, Lincoln, Nye, White Pine) has its chief value in grazing land and watershed protection (NHS, 1926, p. 424; Dir. 1971), and the **HUMBOLDT GAME REFUGE** (Elko) was created chiefly for the protection of waterfowl and sage chickens (Nev. Guide, p. 168).

In Pershing County, **HUMBOLDT** is the name for an SP RR station thirty-three miles northeast of Lovelock, on the Salt Lake Division of the main line, and for a mining district between Prince Royal and Eldorado canyons, at the north end of the West Humboldt Range. A post office so denoted served the district from October 11, 1912, until May 15, 1919, when its operations were transferred to Imlay (VPG, p. 151; T75; T1TR; FTM, p. 13). **HUMBOLDT CITY** (Humboldt) was settled in 1860 in **HUMBOLDT CANYON** (Nev. Terr. Map). Its post office was active from April 18, 1862, until November 30, 1869 (FTM, p. 13). The camp was situated in the center of the **HUMBOLDT MINING DISTRICT**, discovered in 1862 (SM, 1867, pp. 45–55), and was about two miles distant from the station on the transcontinental railroad, named for **HUMBOLDT HOUSE**, a regular breakfast and supper station. A post office so designated existed from June 3, 1872, until November 15, 1909 (FTM, p. 13; OR, 1877, 1885).

HUMBOLDT COUNTY, created by act of November 25, 1861, is in the northwest part of the state. Winnemucca is the county seat, by authority of an act of February 14, 1873 (1867 Map).

HUMBUG. See **BATTLE MOUNTAIN**.

HUMMINGBIRD SPRING. Springs northeast of Gods Pocket Peak in the Humboldt National Forest of Elko County, and a spring east of Boyd Siding on the UP RR in Clark County; named for the bird, several species of which are found all over Nevada (Dir. 1971; WA; Nev. Guide, p. 18).

HUMP, THE (Nye). A hill in the northeast end of the Halfpint Range; "so named in 1962 because of its smoothly rounded hump shape" (USGB 6301; DL 50).

HUNGRY (Washoe). A name of undetermined origin for a valley bounded on the southwest by Lemmon Valley and on the northeast by Warm Springs Valley; a spring and a mountain at the western edge of the valley (Reno Quad.; NJ 11–1).

HUNTER. The station on the main line of the WP RR about nine miles southwest of Elko, presumably commemorates Thomas and William Hunter who took up a ranch near Elko in 1869 (Freese, Map 3; T54; EP, p. 44; SPD, p. 1224). **HUNTER MINING DISTRICT** (White Pine) is on the west side of the Egan Range, fifteen miles south of Cherry Creek. A post office so named served the district from June 19, 1877, until February 19, 1878 (NHS, 1924, p. 388; VPG, p. 179; FTM, p. 14).

HUNTERS (Washoe). A lake in the Carson Range, west of Huffaker, and a creek, northeast of the lake and south of Mogul; named for John M. Hunter, who owned a toll bridge at **HUNTERS CROSSING** (NHS, 1911, pp. 62, 88; SG Map 3). The CP RR tracks reached John M. Hunter's station on the Truckee River on April 26, 1868; their bridge across the Truckee was completed about the end of April, 1868. Effective May 5, 1868, Virginia City stages met regular trains at Hunters Crossing for a short time (DM). **HUNTERS** post office was active from March 19, 1867, until January 31, 1870 (FTM, p. 14).

HUNTINGTON (Elko). A name applied by Simpson to "a spring just discovered by Lott Huntington, of the mail party, and which therefore I have called after him" (JHS, p. 62). The name was adopted for **HUNTINGTON,** a former settlement and post office, first established March 17, 1873, discontinued July 15, 1904, and reestablished December 7, 1923, to operate until January 31, 1931, when Jiggs became the mail address for its patrons (1881 Map). **HUNTINGTON VALLEY** extends from north of Newark Valley (White Pine) into Elko County, and **HUNTINGTON CREEK,** a tributary of the South Fork Humboldt River flows through the valley (HHB, Nev., p. 277; Dir. 1971; Wheeler 1871 Map; Freese, Map 3; NJ 11–3; NK 11–12).

HUNTOON VALLEY (Mineral). A small valley northwest of Basalt and bounded on the north by the Excelsior Mountains and on the west by the Anchorite Hills; the site of mineral discoveries in the early twentieth century, by report of the *Reno Evening*

Gazette of April 12, 1901 (NJ 11–4; Haw. Quad.; DM).

HUNTS CANYON (Nye). The canyon so named heads in the Monitor Range near **HUNTS CANYON RANGER STATION,** and extends into the north end of Ralston Valley. The name derives from **HUNTS RANCH,** located at the northeast edge of the valley (NJ 11–5).

HUPTON (Clark). A post office in operation from December 8, 1922, to December 15, 1925, at the White Star plaster mill, southeast of Moapa; named for A. C. Hupp, a company official (FTM, p. 14; WA).

HUXLEY (Churchill). A station west of the Carson Sink, on the main line of the SP RR between Ocala and Parran (T75); probably named for Thomas Henry Huxley, English biologist and writer.

HYKO. See **HIKO.**

HYLTON (Elko). A short-lived post office, established May 1, 1911, and discontinued November 30, 1913, when Lee became the mail address for its patrons; named for John J. Hylton who was a prominent citizen of the Jiggs (q.v.) area (FTM, p. 14; EP, p. 44).

ICARUS (Elko). The name, which designates a non-agency station between Loray and Pequop on the Elko Subdivision of the SP RR (T75), ultimately commemorates the son of Daedalus of Greek legend who, by means of waxen wings, flew too near to the sun; the wax melted and Icarus sank into the sea.

ICE (Lincoln). The post office so named was active from October 9, 1888, to May 2, 1890 (FTM, p. 14).

ICEBERG (Clark). The narrows in Lake Mead between Greggs Basin and Grand Wash; named by Major J. W. Powell, in 1871. A reef so denoted is at the mouth of the canyon (VPG; Wheeler 1871 Map; WA).

ICHTHYOSAUR FOSSIL AREA (Nye). A state park in the Toiyabe National Forest, south of Ione and west of Toiyabe Dome; named for the fossils discovered there (HWY Map).

IKES CANYON (Nye). A canyon extending from the eastern slope of the Toquima Range, southeast of White Rock Mountain, into Monitor Valley, southwest of Dianas Punch Bowl (NJ 11–2); presumably named for Ike McMonigal, a rancher of Monitor Valley (MM).

ILLINOIS CREEK (Nye). A creek rising on the west slope of the Toiyabe Range and joining the Reese River, south of Stewart Creek; named by settlers from Illinois for their native state (NJ 11–5).

ILLIPAH (White Pine). The name for a creek

rising at the north end of the White Pine Range and flowing generally northeastward into Jakes Valley; for a former settlement, north of Moorman Ridge on U.S. 50 at the west edge of the valley; and for its post office, established March 22, 1898, and discontinued November 30, 1913, when its operations were transferred to Kimberly (NJ 11–3; FTM, p. 14). An earlier spelling appears in the name of **ILLAPAH SPRINGS,** three miles east of Hamilton (MA, p. 660). The name is from Shoshone *illa,* "rock" (?) and *pah,* "water" (GRS, Amer., p. 219).

IMLAY (Pershing). The town, also a division point on the SP RR between Mill City and Humboldt, commemorates Mr. Imlay, a civil engineer who surveyed the town about 1908 for the SP RR (RC, p. 56). A post office so named was established October 3, 1908 (FTM, p. 14). **IMLAY MINING DISTRICT,** also known as *Humboldt,* at the north end of the West Humboldt Range, was named for the town (VPG, p. 151).

INCLINE (Washoe). A town **INCLINE VILLAGE** on the northeast shore of Lake Tahoe, established in 1882 on **INCLINE CREEK** near Crystal Bay, and a post office active from February 7, 1884, to September 21, 1895 (NJ 11–1; FTM, p. 14). The town, which supplied lumber to the Sierra Wood and Lumber Company, "received its name from the steep incline of sixteen hundred feet up which the lumber was hauled by a continuous car affair on the hydraulic plan to a flume whence it was flumed to Lakeview, where it was dumped and loaded, and sent to the mines around Virginia City and Carson" (NHS, 1911, p. 91). **INCLINE CAMPGROUND** and **INCLINE LAKE** are north of the town (Park Map).

INDEPENDENCE (Elko). Two mountain ranges, one east of Carlin and bounded on the west by the Tuscarora Mountains, the other extending north from Tobar and lying between Clover and Independence valleys; two valleys, one between the Independence and Tuscarora ranges, south of the Bull Run Mountains in western Elko County, the other between the **INDEPENDENCE RANGE** and the Goshute and Pequop ranges in eastern Elko County (NJ 11–8, 11–11; NK 11–9, 11–12). **INDEPENDENCE STATION,** formerly on the CP RR west of Moor, was named for **INDEPENDENCE VALLEY** in eastern Elko which, in turn, derived its name from **INDEPENDENCE SPRINGS,** which furnished water for the valley and the station (GAC, p. 127; 1881 Map; FES, p. 174). The **INDEPENDENCE MOUNTAINS** in western Elko were named for the broad valley north of Elko. According to Davis, "this valley is named Independence from the fact that it was first discovered by a scouting

party of United States soldiers on the Fourth of July" (SPD, p. 824).

INDIAN. The name occurring in eleven of Nevada's seventeen counties commemorates the various tribes, or individual Indians, associated with the state. The Paviotso or Northern Paiute, the Shoshone, the Southern Paiute, the Washo, the Gosiute, and a few of the Bannock once occupied the present state area, while the Mono and the Mohave roamed through it.

INDIAN CREEK. A creek rising on the east slope of the Ruby Mountains north of Pearl Lake; a creek flowing from the Pequop Mountains into Steptoe Valley southwest of Dolly Varden; a creek flowing from Sulphur Spring Range into Huntington Valley; and an intermittent stream rising just inside the Duck Valley Indian Reservation and flowing to Bull Run Creek and **INDIAN CREEK HILL** within the reservation, all in Elko County. The Shoshone Indian name for the latter creek is reported to be *Nayantovoy,* meaning "standing Indian" (NK 11–12; NK 11–8; USGB 6103; SG Maps 10, 2). Creeks so named are also found in Esmeralda County, rising in the White Mountains south of Davis Creek, and flowing northwest of Dyer (Dir. 1971); in White Pine County, one flowing from the Schell Creek Range into Steptoe Valley, north of Clear Creek; and **BIG INDIAN CREEK,** rising in the Schell Creek Range and joining Duck Creek; with **LITTLE INDIAN CREEK,** south of the larger creek in the range (NJ 11–3). A Nye County creek so denoted is a southern tributary of the Reese River and flows through **INDIAN VALLEY,** between Mahogany Hill and the Shoshone Mountains. **INDIAN CANYON** (Lander) heads on the western slope of the Toiyabe Range, southwest of Austin, and extends into Reese River Valley (GHM, LA 1). **INDIAN MINING DISTRICT** (Pershing) is in **INDIAN CANYON** on the east flank of the Humboldt Range, east of Oreana and near **INDIAN PEAK** (VPG, p. 152; NK 11–10).

INDIAN GARDEN (Nye). A stream so named rises from **INDIAN GARDEN SPRINGS** on the eastern slope of the Monitor Range and flows into Little Fish Lake Valley north of Fish Lake. The features were named for Indian gardens near the springs, southeast of Burnt Cabin Flat Spring (SG Map 7; DIR. 1971). Early settlers at **INDIAN GARDENS** were served by Tybo post office (TF, p. 18).

INDIAN HILL (Clark). An early name for Wells Siding on the UP RR near Logandale, and a wash running eastward through **INDIAN HILL;** descriptive of nearby Indian gardens (WA).

INDIAN MIKE CREEK (Elko). The name for a creek flowing into Idaho at a point about twelve miles east of Jackpot; commemorative of "Indian Mike" (Shoshone), the leader of a renegade group that murdered four stockmen in California in 1911. He was killed by a posse near Golconda, Nevada (GHM, EL 5; EP, p. 45).

INDIAN QUEEN. See **SHOSHONE.**

INDIAN SPRING(S). A settlement on U.S. 95, forty-four miles northwest of Las Vegas, in Clark County, formerly a station on the now defunct LV and T RR between Owens and Charleston; a post office active from April 28, 1917, to January 15, 1919, reestablished April 16, 1953; an Air Force Base and a Gunnery Range, all in **INDIAN SPRINGS VALLEY,** a valley west of the Pintwater Range and east of the Spotted Range (NJ 11–12). The name derives from an old Indian ranch formerly at the site, sold by the last Indian owner "Old Ben" to Charles Towner in 1876. **INDIAN SPRINGS STATION** on the former LV and T RR, prior to 1906, was named Indian Creek for the Indian Creek Ranch owned at that time by George Latimer. Forty-niners, seeking a route shorter than the Spanish Trail, camped at the springs before going west into Death Valley. The J. H. Martineau party of Mormons named the place *Willow Springs* in 1858 (Wheat IV, 132). The old trail to Pahranagat Valley crossed the area, also the Goldfield-Las Vegas stage route (NHS, 1913, p. 218; FTM, p. 14; DM; WA). Among numerous other springs so named are a spring in the Bullfrog Hills, four miles north of Rhyolite (one of the town's three sources of water); a spring in the Spotted Range northwest of Johnnie Water, Nye County; and a spring on the northwest flank of Magruder Mountain southwest of Lida, the site of a former mining camp in Esmeralda County (Furn. Cr. & Lida Quads.; 1881 Map; DM). **INDIAN SPRINGS MINING DISTRICT** (Lyon), also called *Palmyra* and *Como,* is in the north-central part of the Pine Nut Range ten miles southeast of Dayton and three miles north of Lyon Peak (VPG, p. 103), and was a flourishing gold-silver camp in 1865 (NHS, 1913, p. 218).

INDIAN TRAIL WASH (Clark). The wash so named extends southward from Azure Ridge, east of Gold Butte (WA), and presumably formed a portion of an old Indian trail.

INDRA (Nye). The name of a post office established November 17, 1898, by an order rescinded April 25, 1899, probably before operations commenced (FTM, p. 14).

INGERSOLL CANYON (White Pine). A canyon extending from the Egan Range to Robinson Canyon, four miles west of Ely; named for the nearby **INGERSOLL MINE** (DL 29).

INMAN (Mineral). The former camp located about fifteen miles west of Walker Lake was named for W. M. Inman and Claude Inman, a fire chief of Goldfield, by report of the *Goldfield News* of July 21, 1906 (DM).

INYO NATIONAL FOREST (Esmeralda). Named for the **INYO MOUNTAINS** of California. *Inyo* is said to mean "dwelling place of a great spirit" (Gudde, p. 143).

IONE (Nye). A settlement and post office, active from September 2, 1865, to April 3, 1882 (at which time it was called **IONE CITY**), reestablished as **IONE** July 16, 1912, discontinued April 30, 1914, and reestablished December 18, 1918 (FTM, p. 14). The settlement was named for **IONE MINING DISTRICT,** also called *Union, Berlin,* and *Grantsville,* organized sixty miles southwest of Austin on the west slope of the Shoshone Mountains and named by P. A. Haven in 1863 for a mining district so named in California (VPG, p. 144; 1881 Map; OPN, p. 54; Nev. Terr. Map). Features named for the old camp, the first county seat, are **IONE SPRING,** northwest of Ione, and **IONE CANYON,** which trends southwestward from the west slope of the Shoshone Mountains into **IONE VALLEY** (NJ 11–5).

IRETEBA PEAKS (Clark). The peaks south of Eldorado Canyon in the Opal Mountains, were named for Ireteba, a Mohave Indian guide with the Ives expedition (WA; NI 11–3).

IRISH, MOUNT (Lincoln). A peak northwest of Hiko and sixty miles west of Caliente; named for O. H. Irish, an Indian agent for Utah Territory in 1865, and earlier called *Great Quartz Mountain* (NJ 11–9; OPN, p. 44; WA).

IRON POINT (Humboldt). On the SP RR, Winnemucca Subdivision between Preble and Valmy, "this station is near the point of a low ridge, with barren sides and rocky summit; the rocks a little reddish, indicating the proximity of iron" (T75; 1881 Map; FES, p. 190). The pass at Iron Point was used by an estimated thirty thousand emigrants in 1849. **IRON POINT** post office, except for brief intervals, was active from February 7, 1878, until January 15, 1919, when its operations were transferred to Red House (VPG; FTM, p. 14; AEH).

IRVING (Eureka). A post office so named was established June 17, 1904, by an order rescinded January 5, 1905, probably before operations commenced (FTM, p. 14).

IRWIN CANYON (Nye). A canyon, north of Troy Canyon on the west slope of the Grant Range, and a former mining camp; named for F. L. Irwin, who staked claims in the canyon in 1905 (WA; NJ 11–6).

ISLAND CITY (Churchill). The order of establishment for a post office of this designation, dated July 24, 1915, was rescinded because the postmaster declined the appointment (FTM, p. 14).

ISLAND MOUNTAIN (Elko). This silver-gold mining district, seventy-five miles north of Elko, was discovered in 1873 (SM, 1875, p. 22; VPG, p. 42). Emanuel Penrod, who had been the partner of Henry Comstock at Virginia City, was the first postmaster of ISLAND MOUNTAIN post office, established May 5, 1884, and discontinued February 28, 1887 (OR, 1885; FTM, p. 14). The district took its name from ISLAND MOUNTAIN, a peak east of the confluence of Penrod and Hay Meadow creeks (NK 11–9).

ISLEN (Lincoln). A siding on the main line of the UP RR in Clover Creek Canyon between Minto and Barclay, sixteen miles northeast of Caliente (Freese, Map 2; WA).

ITALIAN. A creek, rising on the west slope of the Toiyabe Range and flowing to the Reese River, south of Silver Creek, in Lander County; and ITALIAN SPRING CREEK, tributary to Burns Creek in the Independence Mountains, in Elko County; named for Italian settlers (NJ 11–2; SG Map 11).

IVANPAH. The name, probably Southern Paiute (Kroeber, Handbook, p. 895), meaning "good water" (Wheeler, 1879, p. 470), or "good (or clear, white) water" (Gudde, p. 145), denotes springs in Pahrump Valley in Nye County; and a silver mining district in southwest Clark County and in California. The mining district took its name from the original Ivanpah mining camp located at a clear spring at the base of Clark Mountain, San Bernardino County, California (Wheeler 1871 Map; Gudde, p. 145).

I X L. This name signifying excellence denotes a ranch in northern Washoe County, south of Round Mountain, and a copper mine, renamed *Duplex*, in the Searchlight Mining District of Clark County (NK 11–7; WA). I X L CANYON (Churchill), heading on the east slope of the Stillwater Range and trending generally southeastward for about two miles to Dixie Valley, about thirty-four miles northeast of Fallon, was named for the I X L MINING DISTRICT, discovered in 1878 and also known as *Silver Hill* (Car. Sink 1908; NJ 11–1; MA, p. 364; VPG, p. 15).

J ACK(S). JACK CREEK (Elko), also known as JACK STATION, is situated north of North Fork on State Route 11 at the confluence of Harrington Creek and Jack Creek, which has its source in the Independence Mountains. The name commemorates Jack Harrington, an early rancher on Jack(s)

Creek, which appeared on earlier maps as *Harrington Creek* (q.v.). Population figures for Jack Creek were included in the Twelfth Census (1900). Features named for the creek include JACK CREEK CAMPGROUND, at the head of Independence Valley, and JACK CREEK NORTH FORK SUMMIT, named for both the creek and North Fork Humboldt River. The summit is east of JACK CREEK GUARD STATION. In the northern end of the Independence Mountains, SOUTH JACKS denotes a peak named for its position relative to JACKS PEAK, also known as *Pewaket Mountain*. The peak is said to be named for either Indian Jack, not further identified, or Jack Harrington. Additional creeks in Elko County so named are JACK CREEK, a tributary of the Jarbidge River north of Jarbidge, and JACKS CREEK, a tributary of the Owyhee River south of Wild Horse. JACKS VALLEY, one of the principal valleys of Douglas County, was settled as early as 1857. Lying at the eastern base of the Sierra, the valley borders on Clear Creek and extends several miles south. One of two early settlers, Jack Winter, or Jack Redding, is commemorated. JACKS SPRINGS CANYON (Mineral) denotes a canyon east of Huntoon Valley and northwest of Basalt (Guide Map; NK 11–8; GHM, EL 2, 3; MI 2; NP, p. 72; OPN, pp. 20, 25; NHS, 1913, p. 210).

JACKASS. Features named for the desert burro include a creek southeast of Tonkin Summit in Eureka County, a creek in the southeast tip of Douglas County, and a spring at the north end of the Dogskin Range in Washoe County (GHM, EU 1; DO 1; WA 1). JACKASS FLATS (Nye) designates a flat northwest of Skull Mountain on the Las Vegas Bombing and Gunnery Range (GHM, NY 8).

JACKPOT (Elko). A community on U.S. 93 about one mile south of the Idaho-Nevada boundary; named for winnings at the slot machines. Earlier referred to as *Unincorporated Town No. 1*, the gambling center was officially named *Jackpot* by Elko County Commissioners on April 7, 1959 (NK 11–9; DL 57; EP, p. 45). Nevada has had legalized gambling since 1931.

JACKRABBIT. The Jackrabbit Mining District, also called *Bristol*, is about twenty miles northwest of Pioche in Lincoln County. The district, named for the JACKRABBIT MINE, was located in 1876 by Isaac Newton Garrison about ten miles north of Pioche on the east side of the Bristol Range. Local legend attributes the discovery to serendipity: Garrison picked up a rock to throw at a jack rabbit and found himself holding high grade silver (JWH; SPD, p. 356; VPG, p. 96). JACK RABBIT KNOB (Nye) is the name for a hill about six miles east of Cactus Flat

Playa and thirty-eight miles east of Gold-field (USGB 6303).

JACKSON. The **JACKSON MOUNTAINS,** sometimes referred to as the **JACKSON CREEK MOUNTAINS,** are bounded on the east by Desert Valley and on the west by the Black Rock Desert, in Humboldt County. **JACKSON CREEK,** which flows from the western slope of the range into the Black Rock Desert, also denotes a ranch and a township (NK 11–7; Census, 1950). **MOUNT JACKSON** (Esmeralda) is a peak east of Lida and north of Gold Point (NJ 11–8). **MOUNT JACKSON RIDGE** is the designation for hills extending east-northeast from Mount Jackson, fifteen miles south of Gold-field (USGB 7202). A post office of Elko County so named was ordered established on June 25, 1890, and discontinued April 10, 1891, apparently without operations ever having commenced (FTM, p. 14). **JACKSON SIDING** (Clark) on the UP RR at the narrows of the Muddy River near Anderson Wash, also has been called *Jackman,* presumably for Fred Jackman, a Hollywood director who was on location in the area in the early 1920s (WA).

JACOBSVILLE (Lander). On May 2, 1862, William M. Talcott, former Pony Express rider, discovered rich ore in Pony Canyon when cutting wood for **JACOBS STATION,** on the old route of the Pony Express and a maintenance point on the transcontinental telegraph line. The rush to Reese River resulted, and Jacobs Station, situated near some springs and also known as *Jacobs Well* and *Jacobs Spring,* increased in importance, being the settlement nearest the Reese River mines. The Overland Mail station at this point was sometimes denoted *Reese River Station.* In December, 1862, Lander County was created, and Jacobs Station, renamed **JACOBSVILLE,** was made county seat. **JACOBSVILLE** post office was active from March 3, 1863, until April 9, 1864 (Nev. Terr. Map; 1881 Map; C&C, p. 588; JGS, I, p. 136). The name commemorates George Washington Jacobs, who was agent for the Overland Mail Company at Jacobs Station (M&S, p. 151; Nev. Guide, pp. 258–59).

JACOBS WELLS (Eureka). A station on the Overland Stage and the Pony Express routes, midway between Ruby and Diamond Springs stations (Nev. I, 1961, p. 9; JGS, I, p. 136; 1867 Map).

JAGGERSVILLE (Mineral). A mining camp of the late nineteenth century, located about eleven miles south of Hawthorne and re-named *Oroville* in 1906, when gold was discovered there, by report of the *Reno Evening Gazette* of June 18, 1906. The name commemorates Thomas Jaggers, who built an arrastre near his rock cabin where he crushed the ores from his mine named the *Dark Secret.* The prospector, said to have usually worn a Prince Albert coat and a tall, silk hat, was accustomed to introducing himself as "Honest Tom Jaggers, from Jaggersville, with a jag on" (NM, p. 97; DM). See **ORO–VILLE.**

JAKES. The Jakes family, early settlers of Steptoe Valley (White Pine) are commemorated by **JAKES VALLEY,** a valley bounded on the west by the Egan Range and on the east by the White Pine Range. **JAKES POND RESERVOIR** in the center of the valley, and **JAKES WASH** and **JAKES WASH WELL** at its south end are named for the valley (GHM, WP 2; OPN, p. 73). **JAKES CREEK** is the name for a western tributary of Salmon Falls Creek, south of Henry in Elko County (NK 11–9), and for a creek flowing from McConnell Peak to the South Fork Quinn River, east of Fort McDermitt Indian Reservation in Humboldt County (NK 11–8).

JAMES CREEK (Douglas). This creek which rises north of Genoa Peak in the Carson Range, east of Lake Tahoe, probably commemorates Lee James who fought with the Genoa Rangers in the Pyramid Lake Indian War of May, 1860 (SG Map 3).

JAMESTOWN. A former Nye County mining camp and post office (June 13, 1908–August 31, 1910), twelve miles south of Antelope. According to the *Goldfield News* of October 26, 1912, the principal mine in the area was the Golden Chariot No. 1 (FTM, p. 14; DM). **JAMESTOWN** (Clark) denoted a former Indian camp, situated about four miles below the mouth of Las Vegas Wash at the Colorado River crossing, in the first decade of the twentieth century. The *Rhyolite Daily Bulletin* of March 9, 1908, reported that the place was named for Al James, of the Arizona Club in Las Vegas. The townsite is presently under the waters of Lake Mead (DM; WA).

JAMISONS STATION. See **GLENDALE.**

JANUARY. The name designates a wash, heading on Knob Hill and draining into Eldorado Canyon in Clark County (WA); and an important claim in the Goldfield district in Esmeralda County. The property, "one of the big discoveries . . . in the annals of Nevada mining," was located in the first decade of the twentieth century by John Jones, who discarded his given name for that of the great mine and signed his checks "January Jones" (JGS, II, pp. 273–74).

JARBIDGE (Elko). A Nevada post office, established March 5, 1910, and town (the most isolated mining camp in the state), surrounded by the **JARBIDGE MINING DIS–TRICT** on the Snake River watershed, are in a "rough mountainous region of intrusive and extrusive andesite and rhyolites of Tertiary age" (SFH, p. 8; FTM, p. 14). The district came into prominence in 1908, with its rich gold deposits controlled by the Guggenheim interests. In 1919, the Long Hike Mine was the largest single gold producer in the state. In 1935, the mines were closed (JGS, I, p. 487; M&S, p. 128; SFH, p. 8). **JARBIDGE PEAK** is southeast of Jarbidge and north of Matterhorn in the **JARBIDGE MOUNTAINS** near the Idaho state boundary. The **JARBIDGE RIVER** flows through **JARBIDGE CANYON**, an eroded gorge, cut down by the action of water through solid rock. Along the river, **JARBIDGE CAMPGROUND** is in a grove of aspen and mountain laurel. "As early as 10,000 years ago, native hunting parties camped in nearby caves to hunt game. Sometime after 1150 A.D., Shoshone speaking people entered the region, camping and hunting here until the beginning of historic time" (SHM 69). According to Jarbidge legend, the name of the canyon, from which the complex stems, comes from a Shoshone Indian word *Jahabich,* meaning "devil" (OPN, p. 25), or from *Tswhawbitts,* the name of a mythical crater-dwelling giant who roamed the Jarbidge Canyon for many years. Preying only on Indians, he tossed his victims into a basket, which he wore strapped to his back, and returned to his crater to feast on them. Since the giant was difficult to escape, being able to cross creeks with one step and to climb steep mountains with a few strides, the Indians avoided the canyon (NHS, 1924, pp. 235–36).

JASPER (Elko). The former settlement, forty miles southeast of Wells and south of Spruce Siding at the eastern edge of Independence Valley, was the site of a smelter for the Sprucemont mines in 1885. **JASPER WELL** takes its name from the settlement (NK 11–12; GHM, EL 5; DM). **JASPER CREEK,** flowing from the eastern slope of the Ruby Mountains into Ruby Valley, was named for an early settler, John Jasper (EP, p. 48).

JEAN (Clark). A post office, established June 28, 1905, and a station on the UP RR, thirty-three miles southwest of Las Vegas, between Sutor and Borax (NI 11–3). The town was settled in 1905, with the completion of the SPLA and SL RR, and named for Jean, the wife of George Fayle who lived in the area. **JEAN MINING DISTRICT** was named for the siding (OPN, p. 15; WA; VPG, p. 28).

JEFFERSON (Nye). A former boom camp about seventy miles northeast of Tonopah and fifteen miles northeast of Round Mountain and a post office, active, except for two brief intervals, from October 22, 1874, until August 13, 1890; named for **JEFFERSON CANYON.** The canyon furnished a name for **JEFFERSON CANYON MINING DISTRICT** (also known as *Concordia* and *Green Isle*), on the west side of the Toquima Range.

JEFFERSON CREEK rises on the west slope of the Toquima Range and flows through the canyon into Big Smoky Valley, and **MOUNT JEFFERSON** is northeast of the old camp and district. All names stem from the **JEFFERSON MINING COMPANY** which owned the important mines of the district (NJ 11–5; FTM, p. 14; SM, 1875, p. 102; Wheeler, 1872, p. 14, 1871 Map; VPG, p. 130).

JERICHO HEIGHTS (Clark). The name for a townsite laid out at a ranch which is presently the site of Pittman. It was chosen by the ranch owner, B. R. Jefferson who was one of the discoverers of the Three Kids Mine (WA).

JERSEY (Pershing). A valley heading southwest of Buffalo Valley and extending to Dixie Valley, about five miles north-north-west of Cain Mountain; a mining district in the Fish Creek Mountains, forty-three miles southwest of the town of Battle Mountain; a former post office named **JERSEY CITY** which served the district from August 31, 1876, until April 10, 1877 (USGB 6302; VPG, p. 152; FTM, p. 15).

JESSUP (Churchill). A mining district discovered in 1908 on the east slope of the south end of the Trinity Range, thirty miles southwest of Lovelock, a former mining camp, and a post office, established March 18, 1908, and discontinued July 31, 1912, when its operations were transferred to Parran. During the rush to Jessup, the SP RR stopped all passenger trains at White Plains, from which two stage lines ran daily to the mining camp (FTM, p. 15; DM; NHS, 1913, p. 183; VPG, p. 15).

JETT (Nye). A creek so named rises north of Pablo Creek in the Toquima Range and drains into Big Smoky Valley. **LITTLE JETT CREEK** empties into the Reese River, north of Mahogany Mountain in the Toiyabe Range (NJ 11–5; SG Map 5). The name was perhaps bestowed by John Davenport who discovered the **JETT MINING DISTRICT** on May 1, 1866, on the east flank of the Toiyabe Range, in **JETT CANYON,** fifty miles north of Tonopah (SM, 1875, p. 106; VPG, p. 130). **JETT** post office was active from March 16, 1880, to April 21, 1881, and from June 6, 1890, to March 25, 1891, when Belmont became the mail address for its patrons (FTM, p. 15).

JIGGS (Elko). A town on State Route 46, in Mound Valley, west of the Ruby Mountains. The site was formerly a year-round camp for Indians gathering the pine nut harvest and, more recently, served as the headquarters for "King Fisher," a fictional character created by Zane Grey (Nev. Guide, p. 162; HWY Map). Prior names for the settlement had been *Mound Valley, Skelton,* and *Hylton.* The name controversy led to postal authorities selecting the name **JIGGS** from a list submitted by local ranchers for the post office established December 18, 1918 (RC, p. 57; FTM, p. 15). The name commemorates the comic-strip character, created by George McManus and noted for squabbling with his cartoon wife Maggie.

JOB (Churchill). A canyon extending from the east slope of the Stillwater Range to Dixie Valley, about thirty-four miles northeast of Fallon; a peak, the highest point in the Stillwater Range, about thirty miles eastnortheast of Fallon (NJ 11–1; USGB 5904). "The peak gets its name from the fact that Moses Job scaled its height in 1855 to plant the American flag on its very top" (GD, CV, p. 3).

JOBS (Douglas). The station so named was one of the earliest in the territory and was located a few miles below Mormon Station (Genoa). John Reese wrote "then there was a man by the name of *Job* who started a store 10 miles west of me" (NHS, 1917, p. 188). **JOBS STORE** was also a post office, established in Carson County, Utah Territory, July 1, 1858, and discontinued October 21, 1858, when the name was changed to *Motts Ranch*. The name honors Moses Job who settled in the valley in 1852 and who is also commemorated by Job Peak and Job Canyon in the Stillwater Range, where he operated a toll road (FTM, p. 15; SPD, p. 817; NHS, 1913, p. 195).

JOE BILLY BASIN (Elko). The valley, west of Ruby Valley Maintenance Station, is named for an early settler, Joe Billy Smith (GHM, EL 1; EP, p. 48).

JOHN DAY (Elko). A peak in the northern Ruby Mountains; a creek flowing generally northward into Lamoille Valley from the northwest slope of the Rubies; a reservoir south of Halleck; named for John Day, an early rancher in the Lamoille area (GHM, EL 1; EP, p. 48).

JOHNNIE (Nye). The name commemorates "Ash Meadows Johnnie," an Indian for whom the **JOHNNIE MINE** was named. The mine was worked in the late 1890s under the auspices of the Church of the Latter-Day Saints, who also operated a small mill there. In May, 1905, a townsite was laid out at the **JOHNNIE MINING DISTRICT**, just west of Mount Shader at the west end of the Spring Mountains, when the Johnnie Consolidated Mining Company was formed. Railroad service was provided when the LV and T RR, in 1906, reached Amargosa Station (also known as **JOHNNIE SIDING**), twelve miles from the mining camp. The Johnnie Consolidated Mill opened up large ore bodies and shipped bullion by 1908. As a result of their activity, as well as that of other mining companies, the boom at Johnnie lasted for several years. The district con-

tinues to be worked, since it is said that some properties have considerable rich ore showing. The townsite, which was a number of miles southwest of the Johnnie Mine, is now marked by the misnomer **JOHNNIE WATER** (Kaw. Quad.). Walter Averett states that the mining camp received its water from Horseshutem Spring, four miles to the east. The order to establish *Johny* post office, dated June 28, 1898, was rescinded April 18, 1899. **JOHNNIE** post office, except for a short interval, was active from May 27, 1905, to November 1, 1935. It was reestablished as *Johnnie Mine* on September 14, 1936, and was discontinued on July 1, 1942, when its operations were transferred to Pahrump (WA; NM; VPG, p. 130; FTM, p. 15; OPN, p. 54).

JOHNSON. The name for a creek rising on the west slope of the Toiyabe Range, south of Austin (Lander County), and flowing westward through **JOHNSON CANYON** into Reese River Valley; and for a creek flowing from the East Humboldt Range (Elko County), southeast of Steele (Gibbs) Lake, into Clover Valley. The latter creek was named for William Johnson, a rancher (Nev. Guide, p. 262; SG Maps 6, 10; EP, p. 48).

JOHNS PEAK (Clark). The mountain north of Hayford Peak in the Sheep Range, known locally by this name, commemorates John Thomas who formerly operated a sawmill there (WA).

JOHNTOWN (Lyon). A small settlement of mill hands, located in a canyon three miles north of Dayton. Chinese placer miners worked there in the 1850s, causing others to name it Johntown, after an old term "John Chinaman" (NHS, 1913, p. 216). See **EM-PIRE CITY**. According to Dan De Quille, Johntown from 1856 to 1858 "was the 'big mining town' of Western Utah—at least was the headquarters of most of the miners at work in the country" (DDQ, p. 10). The settlement name appears on Dr. Henry De Groot's Map of the Washoe Mines dated 1860 (Wheat IV, 189).

JOKER MINE (Clark). A traditional name for a mine discovered southeast of Gold Butte, on the edge of Scanlon Wash, near the Colorado River (WA; Dir. 1971). Similar mine names, associated with luck in card playing, are Big Casino, Black Jack, Four Aces, and Solo Joker.

JOSECO (Lincoln). A settlement southeast of Caliente, near Barclay in Clover Valley; a post office which, except for one brief interruption, operated from August 10, 1916, to April 30, 1943, when Caliente became the mail address for its patrons. This form of the name Joseph perhaps commemorates Joseph Smith, the Prophet of the Church of Jesus Christ of Latter-Day Saints (FTM, p. 15; WA; Freese, Map 2).

JOY (White Pine). A former settlement at the

south end of the Ruby Range in a pass between Bald Mountain and South Bald Mountain; a post office active from May 6, 1897,
to June 21, 1899, and from March 22, 1906,
until October 15, 1918, when operations
were transferred to Simonsen (NM; FTM,
p. 15).

JULIA. The name denoted a series of mines
on the Comstock Lode: Julia, Julia Lateral
Lode, Julia Lode, and Julia Sarah Ann. The
original Julia, located about 1860, had 2,000
lineal feet, and was mined at a low level,
as were nearly all the leading mines on the
Comstock, where the rock was very hot.
Nevada pioneer, B. F. Miller, wrote that "in
the Julia mine the heat was so intense that
the water was scalding hot and even with
the use of revolving fans miners were known
to drop dead from heat" (NHS, 1924, p.
267). During bonanza days in April, 1876,
a poem (a medley of the Comstock mines)
entitled "Julia" appeared in the Stock Report
(NHS, 1917, pp. 104–105). Although the
origin of the name is undetermined, presumably Julia Bulette, famous courtesan of the
Comstock, is commemorated. She joined the
early rush to Washoe and, a few years later,
was murdered and robbed of her furs and
jewels. In spite of the protests of the Comstock wives, the men of the Virginia Engine
Company, of which she had been an honorary member, assisted in the funeral pro-
cession to the isolated cemetery which is still
to be seen in the hills at some distance east
of Virginia City (Dir. 1875, pp. xlv–xlvi; SP,
pp. 157–161; GDL, Saga, p. 58).

JUMBLED. JUMBLED ROCK GULCH
(Nye). The ravine, a half mile north of
Moores Station, was so named because "it
drains a faulted area characterized by a series
of fault blocks" (USGB 6903). JUMBLED
HILLS (Lincoln). A group of hills about nine
miles long, between the Groom Range to the
north and the Desert Range to the southeast,
about eighty miles north-northeast of Las
Vegas (USGB 6002; NJ 11–9).

JUMBO. A settlement in Humboldt County,
south of Sod House and thirty miles northwest of Winnemucca; named for the JUMBO
MINE, discovered in 1935 in the Awakening
Mining District of the Slumbering Hills and
named for its supposed size. The mine proved
to be a small producer (Guide Map; VPG,
p. 70; Nev. Guide, p. 214; OPN, p. 37).
JUMBO (Washoe) denoted an early twentieth-century camp, on the Ophir Grade from
Washoe Valley to Virginia City (DM), and a
post office active from April 16, 1908, to
November 30, 1910. JUMBO (Clark) is the
designation for a pass southeast of Gold
Butte, between Wild Burro Wash and Scanlon Wash; for a peak about five miles southeast of Gold Butte; and for a spring on the
south slope of the peak. JUMBO BASIN

(Clark) is the name for the valley south of
Jumbo Peak (WA; HWY Map).

JUNCTION. The post office so named in Nye
County was active from March 20, 1873,
until July 31, 1906, and was situated north
of Blue Springs in Big Smoky Valley (FTM,
p. 15; 1881 Map; MM). JUNCTION was an
earlier name for *Filben* on the SP RR, named
for its location at the junction of the railroad's branch to former Candelaria (DM).

JUNCTION CITY (Clark). Formerly a railroad camp and switching point on the Six
Companies Railroad, which operated during
the construction of Hoover Dam. At Junction City, now covered by Lake Mead, the
railroad forked, with one line to Arizona
gravel pits and the other to Black Canyon
(WA). See RIOVILLE.

JUNE BUG MINE (Clark). An insect name
for a lead-silver mine discovered on the
southwest flank of Gass Peak, by Milton J.
West and J. W. Lockett, on June 5, 1915
(WA).

JUNGO (Humboldt). A name of obscure origin for a town and station on the WP RR
between Antelope and Gaskell (T54). The
settlement at the edge of a vast dry lake,
called JUNGO FLAT, is said to have been
named for JUNGO POINT, an old survey
peak about thirteen miles distant (NK 11–
10; OPN, p. 37). JUNGO post office was
active from January 31, 1911, until May 31,
1952, when its operations were transferred
to Winnemucca (FTM, p. 15).

JUNIPER (Pershing). A mining camp of the
early twentieth century so denoted was located on the eastern slope of the Sahwave
Mountains, twenty miles west of Toy, near
JUNIPER SPRING. The name derives from
the JUNIPER RANGE MINING DIS-
TRICT, discovered in February, 1908 (NK
11–10; VPG, p. 153; DM). The district was
named for a belt of western juniper (*Juniperus utahensis* and *Juniperus menosperma*)
in the range.

K

KAMMA MOUNTAINS (Pershing).
A range in the northwestern part of the
county, north of Seven Troughs Range and
extending into Humboldt County (NK 11–
10). The name was placed by the Fortieth
Parallel Survey and derives from Northern
Paiute *ka-mu*, "jackrabbit" (Fowler, p. 211;
GRS, Amer., p. 233).

KAOLIN. A wash, also called *Waterpocket
Wash*, running westward from Mead Lake
Station on the UP RR, through Overton
Ridge, and a former settlement and post
office (May 7, 1914–August 31, 1932), in
Clark County (NJ 11–12; FTM, p. 15; WA).
KAOLIN (Lincoln) denotes a canyon trend-

ing eastward from the **KAOLIN MINE** into the Meadow Valley Wash, and a spur line on the UP RR between Boyd and Stine, built to serve the American Clay Company whose kaolin deposits were located about 1919 on a peak east of the railroad (WA). The name for this white clay used in making porcelain derives from Chinese *kao,* "tall," + *ling,* "hill," the name of the mountain where it was first mined in China.

KARO (Lincoln). The post office so named was established March 8, 1917, and discontinued August 31, 1918, when Pioche became the mail address for its patrons (FTM, p. 15).

KASOCK. See **BIG KASOCK.**

KAWICH (Nye). The **KAWICH RANGE** extends southward from the Hot Creek Range to Pahute Mesa and forms a divide between Cactus Flat and Gold Flat on the west and Reveille Valley and **KAWICH VALLEY** on the east. **KAWICH CANYON** heads just west of Gold Meadows and trends along the west side of the Belted Range to Kawich Valley (USGB 6302; 6303; Kaw. Quad.; NJ 11–8). **KAWICH PEAK** is midway of the Kawich Range, and **KAWICH MINING DISTRICT,** also known as *Gold Reed,* is on the eastern slope of the mountains, five miles north of Quartzite Mountain. A post office so denoted served the district from April 10, 1905, to June 15, 1908. The name commemorates an Indian chief whose name is said to have meant "mountain" in Shoshone (VPG, p. 131; FTM, p. 15; OPN, p. 54).

KEEGAN (White Pine). A locality between Bassett and Robinson, east of the Schell Creek Range in Spring Valley; named for Pat Keegan, one of the first sheepmen to settle in the valley in the 1870s (SG Map 9; NHS, 1924, p. 307).

KELLY CREEK (Humboldt). A valley east of the Osgood Mountains and a mining district, also known as *Potosi,* discovered in 1887, thirty miles north of Golconda on the east slope of the mountain range. The district includes the Getchell Mine. **KELLY CREEK** post office was active from February 28, 1887, to July 12, 1888, when its operations were transferred to Fairlawn. The features were named for **KELLY CREEK** which rises on the east slope of the Osgood Mountains and is tributary to Evans Creek (NK 11–8; OPN, p. 37; FTM, p. 15; VPG, p. 75).

KENNEDY (Humboldt). A gold-silver-lead mining district on the east slope of Granite Peak in the East Range, fifty-two miles by road southwest of Winnemucca; a former mining camp, fifty-eight miles by road east-northeast of Lovelock; a post office, established January 15, 1892, and discontinued December 15, 1917. Kennedy was strongly shaken and suffered some damage during the strong earthquake of November, 1915. The name commemorates Charles E. Kennedy who discovered the Imperial Mine about 1891 and was also an early postmaster in old Humboldt, presently Pershing, County (VPG, p. 153; NM; FTM, p. 15; OR, 1899).

KENT (White Pine). A post office so denoted was established June 20, 1899, and discontinued January 15, 1907, when its operations were transferred to McGill (FTM, p. 15).

KENTUCK (Storey). J. A. ("Kentuck") Osborne (Osborn, Osburn, Orsburn) was one of the early locators on the Comstock. "John Osborne . . . went to Western Utah at an early day, having been engaged in placer mining along Gold canyon for several years prior to the discovery of the Comstock lode. Being a native of Kentucky, he was known among his companions as "Kentuck," the claim at Gold Hill so named having been called after him" (HDG, Cp, 10/14/76). The claim is patented and includes ninety-five feet along the lode between the Crown Point and the Yellow Jacket (IH; AR, No. 69, No. 195).

KERN (White Pine). A mountain range near the Utah line and north of the Snake Range; named for Kern County, California, which was created and named on April 2, 1866, in commemoration of Edward M. Kern, Frémont's topographer and artist (OPN, p. 73; Gudde, p. 154). A mining district, discovered in 1859 by employees of the Overland Mail Company and named *Eagle,* was later named for the mountains in which it was located. Since the discovery of tungsten in 1910, the best known designation for the district has been *Tungstonia* (VPG, p. 186; NJ 11–3).

KERSHAW (Lincoln). An early post office (October 29, 1892–December 31, 1904) and settlement, south of Caliente in **KERSHAW CANYON;** named for Samuel and Amity Kershaw, settlers there in 1870 (FTM, p. 15; WA; NJ 11–9). A pump station power plant so named was on the Salt Lake Route and due east of Delamar. The station where coal was dumped to run the power plant was renamed *Stine* (DM). **KERSHAW CANYON–RYAN STATE PARK,** a short distance south of Caliente along U.S. 93, was first opened to the public as a state park in June, 1926, and covers approximately 250 acres, 40 of which were given to the state by Mr. and Mrs. James Ryan of Caliente, who are commemorated by the name (NP, p. 60).

KEYSTONE. A popular mine name chosen by prospectors to signify that the claim would be of first importance in a district. **KEYSTONE** (Nye) denotes a mining district (also known as *Tybo* and *Hot Creek*), named for the **KEYSTONE MINE** (SM, 1866, p. 215) in the Hot Creek Range, about seventy miles northeast of Tonopah (VPG, p. 143).

The post office which served the district, formerly denoted *Hot Creek,* was renamed Keystone on January 26, 1912, and was discontinued March 12, 1927 (FTM, p. 15). In Clark County, **KEYSTONE SPRING** on Shenandoah Peak, west of Goodsprings, and **KEYSTONE WASH** which drains westward from Shenandoah Peak (WA), take their names from a mine located in the early 1890s. **KEYSTONE MILL,** built at Taylors Well in 1893, and **KEYSTONE** post office, established June 23, 1893, and discontinued July 15, 1895 (when Sandy became the mail address for its patrons), also were named for the mine (FTM, p. 15; WA). Until the creation of Clark County in 1908, the features were within the boundaries of Lincoln County. **KEYSTONE** (Eureka), a post office active from April 14, 1898, to September 23, 1898, took its name from the Keystone Mine, discovered in the 1860s (SM, 1866, p. 100). **KEYSTONE** (White Pine), formerly a small townsite near present-day Ruth, was the headquarters of the New York-Nevada Copper Company before Ruth was established (RRE).

KIERNAN (Lincoln). A Canadian, John Kiernan, who came to Pioche in 1870 and moved into the Meadow Valley Wash in 1876, is commemorated by a ranch and locality about five miles south of Elgin at Kyle Siding on the UP RR. He was owner of the old Cherokee Mine in the early days of the twentieth century, and the mine was designated Kiernan as late as 1908 (WA). **KIERNAN** post office, located at the Conaway Ranch from December 23, 1891, to May 14, 1904, took its name from P. Kiernan, postmaster, presumably a descendent of John Kiernan (OR, 1899). The post office was reestablished December 14, 1908, and discontinued January 15, 1912, when its operations were transferred to Caliente (WA; FTM, p. 15).

KILN CANYON (Nye). A canyon, six miles west of Tybo; "named for two old kilns located near the head of the canyon" (USGB 6903).

KIMBALL (Lander). The short-lived post office was established April 25, 1910, and discontinued October 31, 1911, when Hilltop became the mail address for its patrons (FTM, p. 16).

KIMBERLY (White Pine). A town west of Ruth in the rich copper district in the Egan Range; also the terminus of the NN RR, 150 miles southwest of Cobre. The post office, established July 24, 1905, so named at the suggestion of Joseph L. Giroux of Giroux Consolidated Mines, honors Peter L. Kimberly who acquired a fortune in mines in the Lake Superior region and in the West (RC, pp. 57–58; OPN, p. 73; RRE) and was a principal stockholder of the Giroux Copper

Company and pioneer in the district (DM; FTM, p. 16).

KING LEAR PEAK (Humboldt). The peak in the southern portion of the Jackson Mountains, overlooking the Black Rock Desert, is named for the legendary King Lear of Britain, the main character of the famous tragedy by Shakespeare (NK 11–7).

KING PEAK (Elko). A peak in the Ruby Mountains, about one mile northwest of Overland Lake; "named for Clarence King (1842–1901), leader of the Fortieth Parallel Survey and first Director of the United States Geological Survey" (USGB 7002).

KINGSBURY ROAD (Douglas). This principal toll road in Douglas County in the early days extended from Carson Valley to Lake Tahoe and was named for the Kingsbury brothers, who built it. "The trail was opened as a wagon road in 1860 by D. D. Kingsbury and John M. McDonald" (SHM 117). A. B. Kingsbury, one of the brothers, was killed in a snowslide in the mountains in 1861. **KINGSBURY CANYON** was named for the toll road which traversed it (NHS, 1913, pp. 195, 201; 1922, p. 121). See **EDGEWOOD.**

KINGS CANYON (Carson City). A canyon, west of Eagle Valley and in the Carson Range; named for Dr. B. L. King, who came to Carson County, Utah Territory, in 1852 and ran a public resort. **KINGS CANYON ROAD** connects Carson City to Spooners Summit (Car. C. Quad.; SPD, p. 979; VPG).

KINGSLEY(S). See **KINSLEY.**

KINGS RANCH. See **CARSON CITY.**

KINGS RIVER (Humboldt). A river, rising in Oregon and flowing through **KINGS RIVER VALLEY,** between the Jackson Mountains and the Quinn River Range, and emptying into the Quinn River northeast of Happy Creek Ranch (NK 11–7). The valley probably was settled near the end of the nineteenth century, with the discovery of the gold mining district named for the river and is located forty-five miles northwest of Orovada (Census, 1900; HHB, Nev., p. 264; VPG, p. 73). Early settlers in the valley were served by Willow Creek post office (TF, p. 18).

KINGSTON (Lander). A creek rising in the Toiyabe Range and joining Santa Fe Creek in Big Smoky Valley; a ranger station and a ranch so named situated on the creek; a mining district, twenty miles south of Austin on the eastern flank of the Toiyabe Range (NJ 11–2; Wheeler 1871 Map). In the 1860s **KINGSTON CANYON** was the location of a number of flourishing mining camps (Nev. Terr. Map). A post office which served the mining camp for which it was named was established four times between January 11, 1865, and July 11, 1906, and discontinued January 31, 1907, when Austin became the mail address for its patrons (FTM, p. 16).

The name derives from the **KINGSTON MINE** discovered in 1863 (NM).

KINNEY. This fifty-foot claim on the Comstock, along with the old California, the Central No. 1 and the Central No. 2, is a part of the present California. The name honors George W. Kinney who purchased the ground on September 16, 1859, from Joseph Webb for $200, left the Comstock area in 1865, and sold his interest in 1872. He brought suit against the Consolidated Virginia in 1874, but the suit was rejected. Kinney may have been in the area several years prior to the Comstock discovery since *First Records of Carson Valley Utah Ter 1851* show a Barber and Kinney land claim under date of September 30, 1853 (WSJ–1). **KINNEY PEAK** is in north-central Nye County in the Monitor Range (SG Map 6).

KINSLEY (Elko). An early settlement, south of Toano, was named **KINSLEYS SPRINGS** (HHB, Nev., p. 277). The name shifted from **KINSLEY MINING DISTRICT** discovered in 1860 on the east slope of the Antelope Range, twenty-eight miles southeast of Currie (SM, 1866, p. 103, 1875, p. 25; VPG, p. 42). **KINSLEY DRAW** is a wash west of the **KINSLEY MOUNTAINS**, a range west of Antelope Valley (GHM, EL 5). A variant name for the settlement, served by Schellbourne post office, was *Kingsleys Spring* (1881 Map; TF, p. 19); for the mining district *Kingsley.* "In 1865 George Kingsley, a soldier, came to the country and the area was given his name" (EP, p. 50).

KIT CARSON (Elko). A mining district, discovered in 1872 fifty miles north of Wells, and also known as *Porter, Salmon Falls,* and more recently *Contact.* The name honors Christopher ("Kit") Carson, American trapper, scout, and Indian agent (SM, 1875, p. 27; VPG, p. 38).

KITTREDGE (Elko). The name for a canyon and a creek, rising in the Adobe Range northeast of Elko; named for C. B. Kittredge, who settled on the creek in 1871 (GHM, EL 1; EP, p. 50).

KLECKNER CREEK (Elko). The stream so denoted flows between the South Fork Humboldt River below Lee, to Favre Lake, north of North Furlong Creek in the Ruby Mountains. C. H. Kleckner, an early rancher, is commemorated (GHM, EL 1; EP, p. 50).

KLONDIKE (Esmeralda). A mining district discovered in 1898 by James Courts and called, at that time, **SOUTHERN KLONDIKE;** an early mining camp and former station on the T and G RR, fourteen miles south of Tonopah; a former post office which served the area from March 26, 1901, until March 14, 1903, when Butler became the mail address for its patrons. Jim Butler was on his way to Klondike when he discovered Tonopah. The name, with its variant *Klon-*

dyke, commemorates the Klondike region in Yukon Territory (1910 Map; NJ 11–8; VPG, p. 56; FTM, p. 16).

KNOB HILL (Clark). A mountain in the Eldorado Canyon Mining District, southwest of Nelson; named for its knob-like contours (WA).

KNOLL (Elko). An early prospector and "squaw man" named *Noll* is commemorated by **KNOLL CREEK,** south of Contact, and a prominence denoted **KNOLL** and situated east of Bloody Run Gulch (EP, p. 50; GHM, EL 4).

KOBEH VALLEY (Eureka). The name from Shoshone *ko-vi,* "face" (Fowler, p. 265), denotes a valley along Roberts Creek between the Roberts Mountains and the Sulphur Spring Mountains and was recorded by Captain James H. Simpson in 1859. "The valley in which we are encamped differs from any we have seen. Heretofore they have ranged north and south, and averaged a breadth of probably only one-fourth their length. This one, however, has no particular form, and while branching out laterally in different directions, shows a form as long as it is broad. The Digger Indians that have come into our camp call it Ko-bah, or Face Valley, a very good name" (JHS, p. 71).

KODAK (Pershing). A siding on the SP RR, milepost 348.7, between Colado and Lovelock (T75).

KONIGSBERG (Douglas). A mining camp of the 1860s, later called *Silver Mountain,* and its post office, established May 12, 1863, and transferred into California the same month. The mining camp name also was spelled Koenigsberg (JAP, p. 17; FTM, p. 16).

KRAMER CAVE (Washoe). The largest cave of the Falcon Hill series, located a few miles northwest of the northern end of Winnemucca Lake (now dry), the site of recent archaeological explorations. The cave was named in 1960 by Dr. Richard Shutler, Jr., Curator of Anthropology, Nevada State Museum, Carson City, for "Dr. Fritz Kramer who was interested in the work and at that time Chairman of the Nevada Park Commission" (JWC).

KUMIVA (Pershing). A name of unknown origin for a peak on the east side of the Selenite Range, in the west-central portion of the county (Guide Map).

KYLE. Kyle Canyon (Clark) drains generally eastward from Charleston Peak in the Spring Mountains into Las Vegas Valley and was named for the Kyle brothers who operated a sawmill in the canyon in the 1870s. The brothers were murdered in 1883 (?) at the Kyle Ranch, presently known as the *Boulderado Guest Ranch,* about a mile north of Las Vegas Ranch (WA; JGS, I, p. 591; Vegas Quad.). **KYLE** (Lincoln) denoted a former siding on the UP RR about four miles south of Elgin in the Meadow Valley Wash. The siding was abandoned in 1949 (Freese, Map 2; WA).

LABOU FLAT (Churchill). A salt basin in Fairview Valley, east of the Sand Springs Range and about thirty miles southeast of Fallon (USGB 5904; NJ 11-1). Captain J. H. Simpson gave the name *Dry Flat Valley* to the flat in 1859 "on account of the whitish clay flat we cross, and which is as smooth and as hard as a floor" (JHS, p. 84).

LABYRINTH CANYON (Nye). A canyon extending from the north slope of Black Mountain to Thirsty Canyon, north-northeast of Beatty; "named for the labyrinthine appearance of the weathered rock formations in the canyon" (USGB 6302; DL 56).

LAGOMARSINO PETROGLYPH SITE (Storey). An extensive petroglyph site in the Virginia Range, north of Virginia City; named for a local rancher. It "has had the most detailed documentation and analysis of all Nevada petroglyph sites" (M&M, p. 180).

LAHONTAN. A dam so named was completed in 1915 forming **LAHONTAN RESERVOIR** to store the waters of the Truckee and Carson rivers for use on the lands of the Newlands project, in southwest Churchill and eastern Lyon counties (NJ 11-1; VPG). **LAHONTAN GAME REFUGE** is in Churchill County (Park Map). A former post office named for the dam was established November 15, 1911, and discontinued May 31, 1916 (FTM), p. 16). The features were named for ancient **LAKE LAHONTAN**, which received its name in the reports of the exploration of the Fortieth Parallel and commemorates Baron de Lahontan, French officer and traveler. **LAHONTAN BASIN** was once occupied by the ancient lake (ICR, Geol., p. 18; NP, p. 20).

LAKE. Former **LAKE COUNTY,** created in 1861, was a narrow area of land above old Washoe County. Among a number of lakes contained in the county were Honey, Pyramid, and Winnemucca. On December 2, 1862, the county was renamed *Roop* for Isaac Roop, the governor of the provisional Territory of Nevada in 1859. Later surveys proved part of the area to be in Plumas County, California, and the remaining section of Roop County was added to Washoe County (M&S, p. 147). **LAKE RANGE** (Washoe) is named for its position between Pyramid Lake and Winnemucca Lake (NK 11-10). A peak on the northwest shore of Walker Lake and a valley at the south end of the lake are so named for their proximity

to Walker Lake, in Mineral County (OPN, p. 50). **LAKE VALLEY** was the name derived from Lake Tahoe, of an early settlement in Douglas County, represented at the Constitutional Convention of November, 1863 (MA, p. 81; Census, 1870); and also denotes a valley in the northern part of Lincoln County between the Ely Range and the Fortification and Wilson Creek ranges, named for a fresh water lake at its north end (NJ 11-6).

LAKES CROSSING. See RENO.

LAKEVIEW. Formerly a station on the now defunct V and T RR, two miles from Mill Station, in Washoe County, at a point where Washoe and Eagle valleys almost join (GHK, V&T, p. 30). The station was founded by the Virginia and Gold Hill Water Company and received lumber flumed from Incline on the northeast shore of Lake Tahoe (SPD, p. 1031). The station was named for its view of Washoe Lake, now on U.S. 395. A Washoe County post office named **LAKE VIEW** (1881 Map) was established April 5, 1881, and discontinued August 13, 1883, when its operations were transferred to Carson City. In old Ormsby (Carson City) County, the name denoted a hill north of Carson City and a former post office active from July 17, 1890, to October 17, 1894. **LAKEVIEW** was also the name for a settlement of the early twentieth century in Mineral County on Reservation Hill, named for its view of Walker Lake, and for a post office which existed in Lander County from July 11, 1910, to April 15, 1915 (OPN, p. 59; DM; FTM, p. 16).

LA MADRE (Clark). The Spanish name for "mother" denotes a mountain on the east side of the Spring Mountains and a spring on the mountain (Vegas Quad.; NJ 11-12).

LAMB SPRING (Lincoln). An alternate name for *Elderberry Spring,* about six miles west of Coyote Spring in the southern portion of the county (WA).

LAMBS CANYON (Nye). A canyon extending from the eastern end of Pahute Mesa to Kawich Valley, about thirteen miles southsoutheast of Quartzite Mountain; "named for a weathered wooden sign identifying Lamb's Camp, a camp which was at one time located in the canyon" (USGB 6302; DL 53).

LAMOILLE (Elko). **LAMOILLE CREEK** flows into the East Fork Humboldt River from the **LAMOILLE LAKES,** high in the Ruby Mountains. **LAMOILLE VALLEY** provided forage for the livestock of many emigrants who temporarily left the main (grass-denuded) Humboldt River Route near Starr Valley and returned to it near the present site of Halleck. The valley was settled in the 1860s, with Camp Halleck as its post office. **LAMOILLE** post office, except for two intervals, has operated since August 27, 1872. **LAMOILLE CANYON,** forming a crescent in the most rugged portion of the Ruby Mountains, has stands of mountain mahogany and aspen blended with pine and stunted willow and many varieties of wild flowers covering its floor. Two versions of the naming are extant. Lamoille Creek is said to have been named for a French Canadian trapper who built a cabin there in the 1850s. Lamoille Valley is reported to have been named in 1865 by settler Thomas Waterman for his native Vermont. Variant map spellings are *Lemoille* for the valley, *La Moile* for the creek, and *La Moille* for the settlement. In 1868, the settlement begun by John P. Walker was known as *The Crossroads* (Census, 1870; 1881 Map; FTM, p. 16; OPN, p. 25; Nev. Guide, p. 161; SHM 109).

LANDER. At the time of its creation on December 19, 1862, **LANDER COUNTY** embraced a third of the state and was referred to as the "Great East" and later as the "mother of counties" because so many counties were created from it. The county seat was removed from Jacobsville to Austin, by general election of the voters in September of 1863. The name honors Frederick W. Lander, chief engineer for a Federal wagon route, the Central Overland Route, from Fort Kearny to Honey Lake, via the South Pass. He had been appointed Special Indian Agent and arranged a year's truce with Young Winnemucca in 1860, for the Paiutes had determined to fight for ten snows until the whites quit trespassing on their domain (WTJ, p. 216). "For services thus and subsequently rendered, Colonel Lander was honored by having his name given to a county created soon after the organization of the Territory of Nevada" (MA, p. 164). Lander, a brigadier general in the Civil War, died from wounds received in battle at the age of forty at Paw Paw, Virginia, on March 2, 1862 (MA, p. 462; HHB, Nev., p. 265). Other places named to commemorate Colonel Lander are **LANDER SPRING** on the emigrant road through the Kamma Mountains; a former post office (October 15, 1906– October 15, 1909); and **LANDER CITY** (Lander), a former mining camp twelve miles southwest of Austin at the mouth of Big Creek, active in the late 1860s (VPG; FTM, p. 16; NM).

LANE CITY (White Pine). The community, four miles northwest of Ely on the NN RR and U.S. 50, occupies the site of former Mineral City in Robinson Canyon. **LANE** post office was active from October 21, 1902, to September 30, 1903, and again from May 12, 1906, to July 31, 1911, when its operations were transferred to Ely. The name commemorates Charles B. Lane, who pur-

chased the famous Chainman Mine in 1896 (NJ 11–3; OPN, p. 73; FTM, p. 16; DM).

LA PLATA (Churchill). A canyon extending from the south slope of the Stillwater Range to Fairview Valley; a mining district, also known as *Mountain Wells;* a former mining camp and post office, denoted La Pla*t*ta City, and active from April 13, 1865, until November 25, 1867, in **LA PLATA CANYON,** about twenty-five miles east of Fallon. By report of the *Gold Hill News* of December 19, 1863, **LA PLATA** was being laid out in the new Mountain Wells district. From 1864 to 1868 it was the county seat of Churchill. The descriptive name from Spanish, meaning "silver," was given by association with the silver mines of the district (VPG, p. 16; NHS, 1913, p. 174; M&S, pp. 149–150; JGS, I, p. 172; Nev. Terr. Map; NJ 11–1; FTM, p. 16; USGB 5904; DM).

LASSENS. The possessive name commemorates Peter Lassen, Danish pioneer, who had a residence on the Humboldt River about four miles west of Humboldt House in Humboldt (Pershing) County. The place, named **LASSENS MEADOWS,** was situated where the overland route divided, the main travel going on down the Humboldt past old Fort Churchill, and via the Carson River to Hangtown, or via the Truckee River route to Sacramento. The lesser travel crossed the Humboldt and moved west through Cedar Springs Pass to the Black Rock Desert and through the Sierra Nevada to the California gold fields. The latter route was called the **LASSEN ROAD** or **CUT–OFF** (Trails Map; SPD, p. 889; RRE; EWH; MM). The name of the meadows is included on an 1865 map of North Pacific States and Territories, by Captain John Mullan (Wheat V (I), frontispiece). Peter Lassen was killed by Bannock Indians in March, 1859, on the southwest flank of Pahute Peak in the Black Rock Range, about twenty miles north of Black Rock (VPG; NHS, 1924, p. 5).

LAST CHANCE. A creek in Nye County, rising on the east slope of the Toiyabe Range, north of Toiyabe Range Peak, and joining Ophir Creek in Big Smoky Valley (NJ 11–5). **LAST CHANCE HILL** was the site of the celebrated Wild West Ledge, discovered in 1860 in the western portion of old Esmeralda County (SPD, p. 236; JGS, I, p. 172).

LAS VEGAS (Clark). The city, situated in the southeast corner of the state, has one of the oldest place names of record in Nevada. Traders on the Old Spanish Trail camped in the meadows of wild grass watered by springs. In 1829, the Antonio Armijo caravan from Santa Fe crossed southern Nevada and camped near some springs where Las Vegas is now situated (M&S, p. 38). J. C. Frémont camped at the site on May 3, 1844. "After a day's journey of 18 miles, in a northeasterly direction, we encamped in the midst of another very large basin, at a camping ground called *las vegas*—a term which the Spanish use to signify fertile or marshy plains, in contradiction to *llanos,* which they apply to dry and sterile plains" (JCF, Report, p. 266). The name of the camping ground appears on the 1848 map drawn by Charles Preuss, Frémont's topographer (Wheat III, 57). The journals of the forty-niners contain some of the various Spanish names for this patch of meadows with good water. Joseph P. Hamelin, Jr. reached "Las Vegas or Meadow Springs" on December 30, 1849, and Heap described the place as "Ojo del Gaetan (Spring of Gaetan) or Vega Quintana as this meadow is sometimes called" (LRH, XV, p. 90, VII, p. 239). In his advertisement in the *Deseret News* of December 14, 1854, Lt. Colonel Steptoe mentions Las Vegas as a station on a proposed road (JGS, I, p. 118). Missionaries from the Church of Jesus Christ of Latter-Day Saints out of Salt Lake City began permanent settlements at Las Vegas in 1855. The Mormons, under the leadership of William Bringhurst, built an adobe fort called *Las Vegas Mission* in order to Christianize the Indians and to establish a trading station on the Salt Lake-Los Angeles Trail. Under date of February 28, 1856, the *History of Las Vegas Mission* recounts that "a post office is established at Vegas and is named Bringhurst by the Department because there was already one named Vegas in New Mexico." Although the Mormons were recalled to Salt Lake City in 1857, they re-returned in the 1860s to attempt a second settlement. **LAS VEGAS VALLEY,** located in the Rio Virgin district, is included in the *Ninth Census* (1870). Early owners of the Las Vegas Ranch which, along with the old fort, is presently located on Fifth Street between Washington Street and Cashman Field, were Albert and William Knapp, Octavius D. Gass, and Archibald and Helen Stewart (WA). Census figures for *Las Vegas* were thirty according to the *Twelfth Census* (1900). The name of the post office, established at Los Vegas on June 24, 1893, was changed to Las Vegas on December 9, 1903 (FTM, pp. 16, 17). The real growth of the city began with the building of the SPLA and SL RR, in 1905, when Senator William A. Clark purchased the Stewart (Las Vegas) Ranch to gain water and land for the new town. When the railroad was near completion, a tent town called *McWilliamstown* was established on the west side of the railroad by J. T. McWilliams. It was also called *Old Town* or *Ragtown,* and is now named *Westside.* The LV and T RR, constructed in 1906 and 1907, made Las Vegas the outlet for the Groom and the Johnnie mining districts and the gateway to booming Goldfield and Ton-

opah (WA). The railroad was formally dissolved on October 31, 1918. Las Vegas, now the heart of an expanding industrial center, is renowned as a resort area and is the largest city in Nevada.

The old Spanish descriptive term, denoting the luxuriant meadows of the early campsite, has been applied to the fifty-mile valley in which the city is located, drained by **LAS VEGAS WASH,** which runs generally southeast, then northeast, to **LAS VEGAS BAY,** on Lake Mead. The name also designates two communities, **EAST** and **NORTH LAS VEGAS;** a mountain range, north of Las Vegas and east of the Sheep Range; a national forest, also known as *Toiyabe;* a mountain pass in the Spring Mountains west of Goodsprings, also named *Columbia;* a mining district, twelve miles southeast of the city; a beach; a game range; and a bombing and gunnery range (NJ 11–12; WA; VPG, p. 28; Park Map; Cane Spr. Quad.).

LATHAM. A farming area east of Riverside and south of Toquop Wash in Clark County, is named **LATHAM BOTTOM** for the man who first farmed there (WA). **LATHAM CREEK** (Elko). A stream so named rises east of Spruce Mountain Ridge and flows generally northward into Independence Valley, west of Cole Creek (NK 11–12).

LATHROP WELLS (Nye). A locality twenty-nine miles southeast of Beatty at the junction of U.S. 95 with State Route 29, in the Amargosa Desert (HWY Map).

LAUREL (Humboldt). The name for a short-lived post office of southern Humboldt County, established June 26, 1911, and discontinued July 31, 1913, when its operations were transferred to Winnemucca (FTM, p. 16).

LAVA. LAVA RIDGE (Nye) is a ridge at the northern end of the Belted Range, eight miles north-northwest of Belted Peak, about sixty-one miles east of Goldfield (USGB 6303). **LAVA BUTTE** (Clark), a large, black butte, southeast of Las Vegas, also known locally as *Black Peak* or *Gyp Peak* (NJ 11–12; WA), is named for its vesicular lava capping.

LAVON (White Pine). A locality and a siding on the NN RR between Adverse and Hiline, in Steptoe Valley (NJ 11–3; GHM, WP 1).

LAWTON (Washoe). The station on a spur of the SP RR, Sacramento Division, is named for **LAWTONS HOT SPRINGS,** about five miles west of Reno. The name commemorates Sam L. Laughton, who is listed in an 1884–1885 Directory of the Truckee Basin and Lake Tahoe as proprietor of *Granite Hot Springs,* the earlier designation for the springs now denoted by the orthographic variant *Lawtons* (T187; SPD, p. 1031; DM).

LEADVILLE (Washoe). A mining district, thirty-eight miles north of Gerlach; named for a former mill town and lead mining camp located on State Route 34, west of the Black Rock Range, and active from 1909 to 1920 (Guide Map; VPG, p. 171; NM).

LEDLIE (Lander). The settlement, formerly a station, with a warehouse, corrals, and a wye track, on the NC RR seven miles north of Austin, was named for James H. Ledlie of Utica, New York, who was one of the directors of the Nevada Central Railroad Company, formed September 2, 1879 (MA, p. 284; HHB, Nev., p. 238; DM).

LEE. The town, situated between Jiggs and Lamoille in Elko County, was settled in 1863 and later named by J. L. Martin for **LEE CREEK,** the east tributary of the South Fork Humboldt River on which it is located (NK 11–12; OPN, p. 25). Martin, a native of Maine, is also credited with having named the creek in 1869 for General Robert E. Lee (EP, p. 51). A post office so named was established February 14, 1882 (FTM, p. 16). **LEE CANYON** (Clark) heads in the Spring Mountains and trends generally northeastward, twenty-eight miles northwest of Las Vegas. **LEE SPRING CANYON** (Clark) extends from the Spring Mountains to Peak Spring Canyon, thirteen miles east of Pahrump. The canyon takes its name from **LEE SPRING** located therein, southwest of Charleston Peak (USGB 6103; WA; NJ 11–3; Vegas Quad.). In Eureka County, **LEES SPRING** was an early settlement north of Eureka, which served as its mail address (1881 Map; TF, p. 19).

LEELAND (Nye). The station on the former T and T RR, milepost 144.01, was named for Lee, California, the camp for the Lee Mining District which was situated about one mile west of the Nevada line (DM). **LEELAND** post office was established November 23, 1911, and discontinued November 14, 1914, when Death Valley, California, became the mail address for its patrons (FTM, p. 16).

LEETE (Churchill). A mining district, fifteen miles northeast of Fernley in northwest Churchill County; named for B. F. Leete who established the Eagle Salt Works there in 1871. The name of *Eagle Salt Works* post office was changed to **LEETE** on December 20, 1899. Fernley became the mail address for the patrons of Leete post office on January 15, 1912 (FTM, p. 16). See **EAGLE.**

LEETEVILLE (Churchill). The community, formerly a post office (January 28, 1895– June 15, 1907), ten miles west of Fallon was named for James Leete (NHS, 1913, pp. 179–180). Esther M. Leete was the first postmaster (OR, 1899). The site, known to old settlers as *Ragtown,* was the point on the Carson River where all the emigrants arrived after crossing the dread Forty Mile Desert (VPG; AEH). Ragtown is shown southwest of Leeteville on the 1908 Carson Sink Quadrangle. See **RAGTOWN.**

LEHMAN (White Pine). Caves, which had been used by Indians as a burial site, were discovered by Absolom S. Lehman in 1869 (Nev., I, 1963, p. 15; M&M, p. 212). An area of one square mile overlying the caves was made a federal reservation in 1922 and **LEHMAN CAVES NATIONAL MONUMENT** in 1933. Consisting of large chamber galleries and passages formed in limestone, the spectacular caves are on the east flank of Wheeler Peak (NJ 11–6; NP, pp. 68–69). **LEHMAN CREEK** rises north of Stella Lake in the Snake Range and flows into Snake Valley near Baker (NJ 11–3). An early settlement **LEHMANS** was served by Osceola post office (1881 Map; TF, p. 19).

LEITH (Lincoln). The non-agency station on the main line of the UP RR so named is ten miles south of Elgin in the Meadow Valley Wash (NJ 11–9).

LEMMON VALLEY (Washoe). The valley, north of Reno and northeast of Peavine Mountain, and the site of Stead Air Force Base (phased out in 1965), was named for the Fielding Lemmon family, who had a ranch there. In 1861, Mr. Lemmon's ranch was an overnight stopping place for teamsters and travelers. He apparently was a member of the first convention called to frame a state constitution in 1863 (HNS, p. 89; OPN, p. 67; 1893 Map; NJ 11–1).

LEONARD CREEK (Humboldt). The creek so denoted runs southward in the central part of the south end of the Pine Forest Range. Before losing its waters in the Black Rock Desert, it is used to irrigate a large acreage of alfalfa (NK 11–7; VPG).

LEWIS. A mining town, fourteen miles southeast of Battle Mountain in Lander County; named for the **LEWIS MINING DISTRICT,** which was organized when ore was discovered in **LEWIS CANYON** in 1874, by Jonothan Green and E. T. George. Principal producers in the district were the Eagle and Defiance in 1875, and the Starr and Grove and the Betty O'Neal, discovered in 1880 (SM, 1876, p. 210). The town was built in three sections along Lewis Canyon. Lowertown or **LEWIS STATION** was on the BM and L RR; Middletown was about a mile and a half up the canyon; and Uppertown was the small settlement at the Starr and Grove Mine, about a mile beyond Middletown. See **BATTLE MOUNTAIN** and **GALENA.** **LEWIS** post office was established April 5, 1878, and survived until August 31, 1901, after the mill was torn down and after the BM and L RR had been sold (FTM, p. 16; 1881 Map; GHK, Bonanza, pp. 127–28; BLK, pp. 85–86; SM, 1875, p. 76; DM).

LEWIS CANYON heads on the north flank of **MOUNT LEWIS** and extends into Reese River Valley (NK 11-11). It has not been determined that the name honors J. F. Lewis who was elected Supreme Court Judge of Nevada in 1864 (SPD, p. 194). In Clark County, a group of springs west of Piute Valley are named **LEWIS HOLES,** and an area east of Overton in the Virgin River Valley is designated **LEWIS BOTTOM** (WA).

LEXINGTON (White Pine). A creek rising east of Granite Peak in the Snake Range and flowing into Snake Valley; a silver-wolfram mining district on the west flank of the Snake Range, fifty-five miles southeast of Ely; probably named by prospectors who were natives of older places so denoted, such as those in Massachusetts and Kentucky (NJ 11-6; VPG, p. 184).

LIBERTY. The name for a lake east of Kleckner Creek and between Lamoille and Favre lakes in the Ruby Mountains, Elko County; and for a former mining camp, twenty miles north of Tonopah in Nye County, and active in the first decade of the twentieth century (Freese, Map 3; DM). **LIBERTY PIT** (White Pine) is an east-west trending, open-pit copper mine six miles west of Ely (NJ 11-3). Alternate names are *Copper Pit* and *Ruth Pit* (DL 29).

LIDA (Esmeralda). A settlement on State Route 3, about thirty miles southwest of Goldfield; a summit southwest of the town; and a small valley east of the Palmetto Mountains, in which the town is situated (NJ 11-8; Lida Quad.; HWY Map). The **LIDA VALLEY MINING DISTRICT** was discovered by William Scott in 1869 and joined the Silver Peak District on the southeast (SPD, p. 857; SM, 1875, p. 36). A post office, named for the settlement, was transferred from Inyo County, California, into Esmeralda County, Nevada, on April 25, 1873, and except for two brief intervals, served the area until July 30, 1932. The valley and district, also known as *Alida,* commemorate the wife of David Buel of Austin (FTM, p. 17). See **ALIDA.** The large springs at Lida Valley once supplied water to Goldfield.

LIMA (Pershing). A former mining camp, earlier known as *Williamsburg,* in the Sacramento Mining District on the west flank of the Humboldt Range, about eighteen miles northeast of Lovelock. The camp was founded in the early 1860s and a post office so named was established in old Humboldt (Pershing) County on December 3, 1866, and discontinued on December 16, 1867 (NM; FTM, p. 17).

LIME. The name is applied to land features with exposed limestone beds and to water features when this sedimentary rock is found in the banks of a stream or near a spring.

LIME (Elko). A creek northeast of White Elephant Butte in the Elk Mountains (GHM, EL 3); and **LIME MOUNTAIN,** a mining district located on a ridge extending from Bull Run Creek to Deep Creek, near Bull Run Mountain (also referred to as Lime Mountain) in the Bull Run Range (VPG, p. 43; OPN, p. 25). **LIME** (Clark) denotes a ridge, south of Bitter Ridge and east of the Overton Arm of Lake Mead; and a canyon heading at the south end of Lime Ridge and trending generally northwestward, its lower portion called **LIME WASH,** which drains into Lake Mead (NJ 11-12; WA). **LIME** (Lincoln) is the name for a hill, east of Pioche, for a spring on the west slope of the Highland Range near Pioche (WA), and for a mountain east of Leith (GHM, LN 2).

LIMESTONE PEAK (White Pine). The name of the mountain on the west side of the White Pine Range, north of Circle Wash, is descriptive of the rock in the area (NJ 11-3).

LINCOLN. LINCOLN COUNTY in southern Nevada, once part of New Mexico Territory and later in Arizona Territory, was created February 25, 1866, with Crystal Springs as the first county seat. The seat was moved next to Hiko and finally, in 1871, to Pioche. The name commemorates Abraham Lincoln, the sixteenth president of the United States. **LINCOLN CREEK** (Douglas) flows between Genoa Peak and Lake Tahoe (SG Map 3). **MOUNT LINCOLN** (Churchill) is a peak in the Stillwater Range, about twenty-eight miles east of Fallon (USGB 5904). **LINCOLN PEAK** (White Pine) lies southeast of Mount Washington in the Snake Range. **LINCOLN MINING DISTRICT,** discovered on its west slope in 1869, is also called *Tungsten* for ore deposits located in 1900 (VPG, p. 185; OPN, pp. 5, 74; NJ 11-6; NJ 11-1). **LINCOLN CANYON** heads on the east flank of Lincoln Peak and extends into Baking Powder Flat. A former settlement, about a mile west of Sandy in Lincoln (Clark) County, was founded about 1901, by report of the *Lincoln County Record* of March 31, 1905, and named **LINCOLN CITY,** taking its name from the county (NJ 11-1; WA; DM).

LINDSAY CREEK (Elko). A creek rising south of Rattlesnake Mountain in the Ruby Mountains and flowing into Huntington Valley; named for Joseph Lindsay, an early settler (GHM, EL 1; EP, p. 52).

LITTLE. The term is often applied to land features to show a relationship to larger features. Included among hydrographic features so named relative to their larger counterparts (q.v.) are **LITTLE BITTER WASH** in southern Clark County; **LITTLE FISH LAKE** at the northwest end of the valley so named and earlier called *Fish Spring Valley,* in Nye County (NJ 11-5; Wheeler 1871 Map); **LITTLE SODA,** a lake northwest of Fallon in Churchill County (NJ 11–1); **LITTLE CHERRY** and **LITTLE JETT** creeks in Nye County; **LITTLE COTTONWOOD** and **LITTLE SALMON** creeks in Elko County; **LITTLE FORK,** South Fork Owyhee River (not **LITTLE OWYHEE RIVER**) in Elko and Humboldt counties (USGB 5904); **LITTLE HIGH ROCK CREEK** and **CANYON** and **LITTLE WASHOE LAKE** in Washoe County. **LITTLE TRUCKEE RIVER** is included on Dr. Henry De Groot's 1860 map of the Washoe Mines (Wheat IV, 189). Among the orographic features so denoted are **LITTLE SKULL MOUNTAIN** (Nye), a mountain group just southwest of Skull Mountain at the northeastern end of the Amargosa Desert (USGB 6103), and **LITTLE DEVIL PEAK** (Clark), lying near the California boundary, southwest of Jean, west of Devil Canyon and northwest of Devil Peak (NI 11–3). **LITTLE PILOT PEAK** (Mineral) in the north end of the Cedar Range is so named to distinguish it from Pilot Peak (OPN, p. 50). **LITTLE SMOKY VALLEY,** east of the Fish Creek Range in Eureka County and extending south into Nye County, between the Pancake and Antelope ranges, probably was named subsequent to the discovery of Big Smoky Valley, for the mist over the valley. Additional features so named are **LITTLE VALLEY** (Washoe), a beautiful, intermountain valley in the Carson Range between Lake Tahoe and Washoe Valley, once noted for its gold placers and served by Franktown post office (TF, p. 19); **LITTLE MEADOWS,** a meadows and a creek west of Troy Peak in the Grant Range; and **LITTLE ANTELOPE,** a summit on U.S. 50, north of Hamilton and between Pancake and Robinson summits in White Pine County (VPG; Dir. 1971). The *First Directory of Nevada Territory* named the country between Dayton and "Dutch Nicks" the "Little, or Ten-Mile Desert." Early maps show the land east of Dayton as the "Little Desert," also termed the Twelve-Mile Desert. Comparison was made with the Twenty-six-Mile Desert (NHS, 1913, p. 209). **LITTLE BANGOR** (Washoe) was a lumber camp established in 1863 and inhabited largely by people from Bangor, Maine. It is said to have been "so named because of the large sawmills operating there" (NHS, 1911, p. 93; JGS, II, p. 207). **LITTLE GIANT** (Lander) denoted a silver mine, discovered in 1867 a few miles from Battle Mountain, and one of the principal mines of the Battle Mountain district (Nev. Guide, p. 128). **LITTLE WINNEMUCCA. See WINNEMUCCA.**

LIZARD HILLS (Nye). A group of hills just northeast of Gold Mountain, thirty-nine miles east-southeast of Goldfield; named for the presence of the reptile. Both the scaly and the smooth-skinned lizard are found throughout the state; the Gila lizard lives in the Virgin River Valley near the Colorado (USGB 6303; Nev. Guide, p. 20).

LOBDELL(S) (Douglas). An early settlement in Smith Valley, served by Walker River post office and named for J. B. Lobdell, a rancher who settled on Desert Creek in 1861 and raised hay, grain, and vegetables, which he sold to old Fort Churchill (1867 Map; HHB, Nev., p. 260; NHS, 1913, pp. 195, 227; TF, p. 19).

LOCKES (Nye). The settlement on U.S. 6 southwest of Currant, was once known as *Ostonside* (OPN, p. 55; Guide Map). Eugene and Sarah Locke, who owned a ranch at the site, are commemorated (MM).

LOCOMOTIVE MINE. See CENTRAL.

LODI. LODI VALLEY, west of the Paradise Range in northwest Nye County (NJ 11–5), was once the site of a town named for the valley, but also called **LODIVALE,** near the Churchill County line (OPN, p. 55). The name of **LODIVALE** post office, established July 23, 1909, was changed from *Phonolite*. Upon its discontinuance August 15, 1910, Luning became the mail address for its patrons (FTM, p. 17). **LODI MINING DISTRICT,** probably named for the valley, was located in 1863 on the west flank of the Paradise Range, forty-five miles north-northeast of Luning (VPG, p. 132). **LODI** (Eureka) was a station on the former E and P RR (LRB, p. 35).

LODIVALE. See LODI.

LOGAN CITY (Lincoln). An early village ten miles west of Hiko, and south of the Pahranagat mines in a wide pass and near a spring of water; a flourishing community in 1866 (JGS, I, p. 261; 1881 Map; M&S, p. 155). A post office named **LOGAN SPRINGS** served the area from July 2, 1868, until August 1, 1871 (FTM, p. 17), when Hiko became its mail address.

LOGANDALE (Clark). A town and post office, eleven miles from Moapa on the Moapa-Mead Lake Branch of the UP RR (NJ 11–12). The site was first settled in 1864 by Latter-Day Saints and named *Saint Joseph*. In 1881 another group of Mormons migrated to Muddy Valley, and "St. Joseph was renamed Logan (Logandale) after the principal settlers of the new migration" (JGS, I, p. 601). Robert Logan is listed by Indian Agent G. W. Ingalls as one of the prominent settlers of Moapa Valley (SPD, p. 114). *Logan* post office, established March 16, 1895, was changed to **LOGANDALE** June 30, 1917, to avoid confusion with Logan, Utah (FTM, p. 17). **LOGAN MINING DISTRICT,** twenty-six miles southeast of Moapa, and **LOGAN WASH,** at Logandale, were named for the early settlement (VPG, p. 28; WA).

LOGAN SPRINGS. See LOGAN CITY.

LOMA (Esmeralda). The name of **LOMA**

post office, established June 26, 1907, was changed to *Reservation* May 15, 1909 (FTM, p. 17).

LOMIX (Clark). A blend name for the low-level concrete mixing plant located in the bottom of Black Canyon and operated during the construction of Hoover Dam (WA). See **HIMIX**.

LONE. The term denotes isolated, or otherwise distinctive, features in the state. **LONE MOUNTAIN** (Elko) is a peak in the Independence Range. A mining district, located on its west slope in 1869 and named for the mountain, is noted for the Sleepy Hollow and Rip Van Winkle mines. The latter is also known as "The Rip" (SM, 1875, p. 25; GHM, EL 3; Nev. Guide, p. 167). The mountain, the most distinctive feature of the region, was so named because it rises above the main axis of the range (OPN, p. 26). A variant is *Nannies Peak* (GHM, EL 3). **LONE MOUNTAIN** (Esmeralda) denotes a range in the north-central portion of the county (NJ 11–5); a peak at the north end of the range; and a mining district on the peak (OPN, p. 31; VPG, p. 57). **LONE MOUNTAIN,** south of Kobeh Valley and west of Hay Ranch in Eureka County, was described and named *Lowry* by Simpson (NJ 11–12). "Mr. Lowry says that in California thunder and lightening are scarcely known. I call the isolated mount just to the west of north of our camp after this last-mentioned gentleman" (JHS, p. 112). **LONE PEAK** in southeast Pershing County is near the Lander County line and west of the Augusta Mountains (NK 11–11). **LONE PINE** is the name for a canyon north of Dutch Canyon, on the west slope of the Pine Nut Range in Douglas County (Mark. Sheet), and for a spring south of Charleston Peak in the Spring Mountains and on the old Red Rocks road, in Clark County (WA).

LONG. A specific term applied usually to valleys or canyons, notable for their length in the areas in which they appear, and occasionally adopted for adjacent features. **LONG CANYON** (Elko) extends from the north end of the Adobe Range to North Fork Humboldt River, northwest of Rasid Siding (NK 11–9). **LONG DRY CANYON** is southeast of Topaz Lake in Douglas County (SG Map 4B). **LONG VALLEY.** A long, narrow valley between the east and west forks of the Carson River, extending into California from Douglas County (NHS, 1913, p. 191). Other valleys so named for length are in northwest Washoe County, northwest of the Calico Mountains and southwest of the Shelton National Antelope Refuge (NK 11–7); in White Pine County, west of the Butte Mountains and north of the White Pine Mountains, and formed by **LONG VALLEY WASH** (NJ 11–3); in Lincoln

County, that portion of the Meadow Valley Wash which lies between Carp and Leith (WA); and in Storey County, northeast of Virginia City. **LONG VALLEY CREEK** (Storey), with its source in the Washoe Range northeast of Virginia City, is joined by Lousetown Creek and runs north to the Truckee River in wet seasons (NJ 11–1; OPN, p. 65). Settlements were named for the valleys in Washoe County (HHB, Nev., p. 256; TF, p. 19; Census, 1870), and in Storey County (MA, p. 75). **LONG PEAK** (Lander) denotes a mountain peak on Battle Mountain, northeast of Antler Peak, named for its position at the head of **LONG CANYON** (USGB 6003; NK 11–11).

LONGSTREET (Nye). The short-lived camp of the early twentieth century, located forty miles east of Tonopah, was named for its founder, Jack Longstreet, a squaw man reputed to have been a desperado (NM). **LONGSTREET MINING DISTRICT,** also called *Bellehelen,* is in the north end of the Kawich Range (VPG, p. 122).

LOOKOUT. A name sometimes given to orographic features to signify that they afford a good view or prospect of the surrounding area. **LOOKOUT** (Clark). Formerly a point near Hoover Dam from which visitors watched the construction, and a name for a peak south of Goodsprings (WA). The **LOOKOUT RANGE** and *Sedaye* were names given by Captain James H. Simpson to mountains now called *Desatoya,* in Churchill and Lander counties (JHS, p. 79; WTJ, p. 142). The Lincoln County mountain on which the Delamar Mine was discovered was earlier so denoted. The former Ormsby (Carson City) County settlement so named and mentioned by Bancroft was at a quartz mill, two and a quarter miles from Carson City (WA; HHB, Nev., p. 225; FES, p. 208; GHK, V&T, p. 31).

LORAY (Elko). A non-agency station on the SP RR between Montello and Cobre. Formerly wood and timber cut in the mountains for the use of the road were delivered there (T75; FES, p. 173; GAC, p. 126). **LORAY MINING DISTRICT,** organized in 1883 on the north end of the Toano Range, is five miles southeast of Loray, and **LORAY WASH** drains northeastward from the north end of the Toano Range (NK 119; 1881 Map; VPG, p. 43).

LORENA (Mineral). The townsite was platted in the summer of 1908, about a mile from Bovard on the northeast flank of the Gabbs Valley Range, northeast of Hawthorne. Settlers were forced to leave the camp because of lack of water (NM).

LORING (Pershing). The mining district, ten miles northeast of Lovelock at the west end of Coal Canyon in the Humboldt Range, was named in 1919 for W. J. Loring, who financed work in the district. The *Lovelock Review Miner* of July 11, 1919, notes that this district includes the older Willard district, said to have been named for Jess Willard, the prize fighter (VPG, p. 167; DM; DB, p. 57).

LOST. Reported to be among the lost mines of Nevada are the **LOST BREYFOGLE** (thought to be the Johnnie Mine); named for Charles C. Breyfogle, who found gold somewhere east of Death Valley in the summer of 1864, while escaping from an Indian massacre; the **LOST MORMON,** alleged to be somewhere in the McCullough Range; and the **LOST GUNSIGHT,** said to be near Indian Springs, all in Clark County (WA). Creeks so named include a deep creek rising in the north end of the Granite Range and flowing to Duck Flat, Washoe County; a creek rising on the northeast slope of the Ruby Mountains, south of South Fork Ackler Creek, and tributary to Deering Creek in Starr Valley; a creek east of Jackpot, both in Elko County (VPG; NK 11–7; GHM, EL 4). **LOST MEADOW CREEK** (Elko) is a northern tributary of the Owyhee River, west of Wild Horse Reservoir and De Long Ridge, southeast of Mountain City (SG Map 11). **LOST CABIN SPRING** (Clark) is west of Roses Spring and southeast of Charleston Peak in the Spring Mountains (WA). **LOST CITY** (Clark). A mingling of a prehistoric band of early Pueblo Indians (who came from what is now northern Arizona) with Basket-Makers living in pit dwellings in Moapa Valley, resulted in a busy, prehistoric center called *Pueblo Grande de Nevada,* or the *Lost City of Nevada,* archaeological sites lying along both sides of the lower sixteen miles of the Muddy River. "These sites, several hundred in number, are composed of pithouses, pueblo ruins, campsites, rockshelters, salt mines and caves" (RS). The straggling community was probably built some time after A.D. 600. Decline set in either because of a succession of dry years or, more likely, because of attack by nomadic wild tribes. The last Pueblo settlements in Moapa Valley, one of which is dated by Dr. Richard Shutler as A.D. 700 to 1100, were placed on mesa tops and in other easily defended places. The archaeological remains from Lost City, doomed again by submersion under Lake Mead, have been preserved in the museum at Overton, Nevada (JHS, I, p. 3; NP, pp. 61–62; Park Map).

LOUDERBACK MOUNTAINS (Churchill). A group of mountains, bounded on the west by Fairview and Dixie valleys and separated from the Clan Alpine Mountains on the east by Hercules Canyon and Badger Flat; named for George D. Louderback, a geologist in the field of seismology, formerly of the University of Nevada, who made studies of the Basin ranges and the gypsum deposits (USGB 5904; SPD, p. 349; NJ 11–1).

LOUSETOWN (Storey). **LOUSETOWN CREEK,** northeast of Virginia City and tributary to Long Valley Creek (NJ 11–1), was named for a former settlement. The old station was situated on Lousetown Creek north of Virginia City and one and a half miles northeast of Castle Peak, a site northeast of the Geiger Grade (VPG; 1881 Map).

LOVELL (Clark). A wash heading in **LOVELL CANYON** in the Spring Mountains and extending to where it disperses into several small distributaries, about thirty-two miles west-southwest of Las Vegas (USGB 6201). **LOVELL SUMMIT** is southeast of Charleston Peak between Trout Canyon and Lovell Canyon. **LOVELL** also denotes a wash which drains into Callville Wash near West End Wash, and a siding on the UP RR between Dike and Valley, northeast of Las Vegas (NJ 11–12; WA; USGB 6201).

LOVELOCK (Pershing). The county seat of Pershing County was once the site of the emigrant camping ground called *Big Meadows* on the Humboldt River. See **BIG MEADOWS.** The first settlers on the meadows were James Blake and his family in 1861. Blake had a 312-acre claim and ran a stage station. In 1866, George Lovelock, a native of England, moved to the Big Meadows and purchased the Blake properties and secured the oldest water right on the river. From this property, he donated about eighty acres to the CP RR for a townsite (JGS, II, p. 106). The early station was called *Lovelock's* (T1TR). "At this point, we observe a comfortable farm-house on the borders of extensive meadows. Long ricks of hay, and trains loaded with the same article, attest the richness of the moist bottom land known as Lovelock's Ranch" (GAC, p. 154). The early post office name was Lovelock*s*, established February 8, 1875, but changed to **LOVELOCK** on March 24, 1922 (FTM, p. 17). The population of *Lovelocks Village* is included in the 1890 Census, but of **LOVELOCK** at the turn of the century (Census, 1900). Lovelock (not *Lovelocks*) was the decision of the United States Geographic Board in its Fifth Report. Shift names are **LOVELOCK VALLEY,** in which the town is located, also designated as *Upper Valley* and *Lower Valley* (NJ 11–12; Love. Quad.); **LOVELOCK INDIAN COLONY,** an area covering twenty acres just west of the town; and **LOVELOCK MINING DISTRICT,** a niter district located ten miles south of the town (VPG, p. 154; M&S, p. 280; OPN, p. 61). Nearby **LOVELOCK CAVE,** in which University of California archaeologists made important discoveries, is an exceedingly dry cave which has yielded clothing, implements, and mummies of the ancient people of northern Nevada (VPG, JGS, I, p. 4).

LOWER EMIGRANT CROSSING. See **WADSWORTH.**

LOWER ROCHESTER (Pershing). A locality and former mining camp, southeast of Oreana on the west slope of the Humboldt Range; named for its position west and slightly south of Rochester (NK 11–10).

LOWER WHITE BLOTCH SPRING (Clark). A spring, south of Fossil Ridge and west of Gass Spring (WA); probably named for its position in relation to White Spot Spring. *Blotch Springs* (NJ 11–12) may be the designation for both White Spot and Lower White Blotch springs.

LOWRY PEAK. See **LONE.**

LUCCA (Lander). The post office, also denoted *Lacca*, existed from March 24, 1869, to July 19, 1869 (FTM, p. 17).

LUCIN (Elko). The mining district, six miles southeast of Tecoma in the Pilot Range near the Utah line, was named for Lucin, an SP RR station in Utah just across the boundary line (T75; SM, 1875, p. 26; VPG, p. 43). See **BUEL.**

LUCKY BOY (Mineral). A gold mine and a mining district, the west section of the Hawthorne district, on the east slope of the Wassuk Range, discovered in 1906 by men repairing a stage road over a pass; the mine named for the mining district (NJ 11–4). **LUCKYBOY** post office was established March 19, 1909, and discontinued October 31, 1913, when Hawthorne became the mail address for its patrons (FTM, p. 17). The city of Hawthorne has prospered because of several mining booms in the Lucky Boy (VPG, p. 115; M&S, pp. 126, 140; OPN, p. 50; 1910 Map).

LUCKY STRIKE (Clark). A canyon heading northeast of Angels Peak on the west side of the Spring Mountains and extending into Las Vegas Valley, south of Deer Creek; presumably named for a lead mine so designated in the canyon (NJ 11–12; WA).

LUCY GREY (Clark). A mountain range east of Jean, extending south to the California line, west of the McCullough Range; a mining district, better known as *Sunset* or *Lyons*, fifteen miles southeast of Jean in the range; named for the principal mine of the district the **LUCY GREY,** discovered by T. L. Bright, in 1905 (WA).

LUDWIG (Lyon). The mining district so named is in the central portion of the Singatse Range, four miles southwest of Yerington, and is also called *Mason* and *Yerington.* John D. Ludwig, an early California Indian fighter who discovered the principal mine in the district, is commemorated. The NCB RR was completed to the mine on November 1, 1911, and the station, serving the Nevada-Douglas Copper Company, was named **LUDWIG.** The name of *Morningstar* post office was changed to **LUDWIG** on November 24, 1911. Postal operations were transferred to Hudson on July 19, 1932 (NCB Map; NJ 11–4; VPG, p. 107; NM; FTM, p. 17).

LUND (White Pine). A town on State Route 38 west of the Egan Range in southern White Pine County; settled in 1898 and named in honor of Anthony C. Lund, one of the presidency in control of the Church of Jesus Christ of Latter-Day Saints. The post office so named was established October 1, 1898 (OPN, p. 74; FTM, p. 17; NJ 11–6).

LUNING (Mineral). A station on the SP RR in Soda Springs Valley between Thorne and Mina, a supply center and shipping point for the Nevada Brucite quarry, thirty-five miles to the north; named for Nicholas B. Luning of California, a heavy bondholder of the C and C RR which was later purchased by the SP RR (NJ 11–4; T75; Nev. Guide, p. 221; DM). Earlier at the site, a stage station on the route to Grantsville was called *Deep Wells.* The town was started late in 1881 when the C and C RR reached Deep Wells, and the name was changed to **LUNING.** The Santa Fe Mining District, organized in 1879 upon the discovery of silver, lead, and copper on the west slope of the Gabbs Valley Range, is also called the **LUNING DISTRICT** and is a few miles east of the town for which it is named (VPG, p. 118). **LUNING** post office was established January 16, 1882 (FTM, p. 17).

LURLINE (Elko). A post office (May 28, 1915–September 30, 1919) established to serve Ruby City, a Mormon promotional venture; named for Lurline Gleen, a sister of one of the promoters (FTM, p. 17; EP, p. 53).

LUTHER CANYON (Douglas). The canyon, south of Genoa, "takes its name from Ira M. Luther who from 1858–1865 had a sawmill there. . . . In 1861, he was a delegate to the Second Nevada Territorial Legislature" (SHM 118). See **HORSE THIEF CANYON.**

LUX (Lyon). A non-agency station, milepost 331.9, east of Wabuska in Mason Valley, on the Mina Branch of the SP RR (T75); probably named for a Mr. Lux, co-owner of the Pacific Livestock Company in the valley (DM, RR (I) p. 227).

LYNDON GULCH (Lincoln). The canyon so denoted is in the Comet Mining District, southwest of Highland Peak in the Highland Range, fourteen miles southwest of Pioche, and is the type location for the Lyndon limestone formation (WA).

LYON. LYON COUNTY, created by the act of November 25, 1861, is in west-central Nevada. Myron Angel wrote that the name honored General Nathaniel Lyon, who died near Springfield, Missouri, in the battle of

Wilson's Creek, on August 10, 1861 (MA, p. 494). However, Nevada historians Davis, Mack, and Sawyer record that the name commemorates a hero of the Indian wars, Captain Robert Lyon, who came to Nevada in June of 1850 by wagon train, an opinion supported by early Nevada families (SPD, pp. 22, 37; M&S, p. 144; MM). **LYON PEAK**, in the western part of the county for which it was named, is south of Rawe Peak and west of Churchill Canyon (Wab. Sheet). An early mill located on a hillside on the southwest edge of Dayton in Lyon County, was built in 1865 and so named. Having been built by Fred Birdsall and a man named Carpenter, it was also known as the *Birdsall and Carpenter,* and later *Douglas(s)* for J. M. Douglas of Virginia City who purchased it in 1882 (DM; SM, 1866, p. 148). **CAMP LYON** apparently was a temporary military camp twenty miles north of Battle Mountain, shown on the Railway Survey Map of 1883 and on Wheeler Survey Maps Index, 1880 (Ruhlen). **LYON(S)VILLE**, a former settlement in Ursine Valley in Lincoln County, was north of Panaca. Pioche post office served the community (WA; Wheeler 1871 Map; TF, p. 19).

McAFEE (Elko). **McAFEE CREEK** rises on the east slope of **McAFEE PEAK** and flows to a confluence with North Fork Humboldt River, near North Fork. The name honors the early McAfee family (NK 11–9; EP, p. 55).

McCABES (Nye). The possessive name for a sawmill situated in 1869 on Currant Creek, west of the White Pine Mountains, commemorates its owner (Cad. Map; TF, p. 19). A variant is *McCubes* (1881 Map).

McCANN CREEK (Elko). A creek rising west of Mount Blitzen and joining the South Fork Owyhee River, north of Boulder Creek; named for Hamilton McCann, the first settler on the creek (NK 11–8; EP, p. 55).

McCLANAHAN SPRING (Clark). The spring so named in the McCullough Range honors John McClanahan, who lived in the Goodsprings area from 1880 until his death in 1908 (WA; Dir. 1971).

McCLANESBURG (Washoe). The mining camp, later renamed *Olinghouse* (q.v.), grew up about four miles north of Wadsworth when F. Plane and Brooks McLane, for whom the camp was named, discovered ore deposits on Green Hill in 1897 (DM).

McCLELLAN. McCLELLAN CREEK (Elko), named for a family that settled on the creek, rises north of Lone Mountain in the Independence Mountains and joins Dorsey Creek southwest of Tule Valley (NK 11–9; EP, p.

55). **McCLELLAN PEAK** is in the Washoe Mountains on the Storey-Washoe line (OPN, p. 65).

McCONNELL (Humboldt). Thomas McConnell, a rancher, is commemorated by **McCONNELL CREEK** which rises in the Santa Rosa Range south of Antelope Creek and flows into Quinn River Valley (GHM, HU 3; M&S, p. 189). **McCONNELL PEAK** is about three miles north of Granite Peak and eleven miles southeast of McDermitt in the Santa Rosa Range (NK 11–8).

McCOY (White Pine). A creek rising on the east slope of the Schell Creek Range and flowing into Spring Valley; a settlement near the creek and south of Robinson; presumably named for Thomas McCoy, a trapper (NJ 11–3).

McCULLOUGH (Clark). A mountain range extending from southwest of Henderson and east of Whitney Mesa to a few miles northeast of the Nevada-California boundary line; **McCULLOUGH MOUNTAIN** in the south end of the range northwest of Searchlight; **McCULLOUGH SPRING** north of McCullough Mountain (NI 11–3; WA).

McCUTCHEON CREEK (Elko). An intermittent stream rising north of Green Mountain in the Ruby Mountains and flowing into Mound Valley below Jiggs to join Huntington Creek; "named for J. M. McCutcheon, a native of Missouri who settled in Mound Valley in 1869" (NK 11–12; EP, p. 55).

McDERMIT(T). A town on U.S. 95, partly in Malheur County, Oregon, and partly in Humboldt County, Nevada; a creek rising north of Disaster Peak and joining the Quinn River below the town, and in **FORT McDERMITT INDIAN RESERVATION;** a mercury mining district, also known as *Opalite* and located seventy-seven miles north of Winnemucca near the Oregon-Nevada line; and a post office first established October 24, 1866; all named for old **FORT (CAMP) McDERMITT** (NK 11–7, 11–8; VPG, p. 173). The post was turned over to the Interior Department on July 24, 1889, its reconstructed buildings serving as headquarters for the Indian reservation (Ruhlen). The first military camp in the vicinity was established as *Quinn River Camp No. 33* in the summer of 1865 by Captain J. C. Doughty, in compliance with the orders of Lieutenant Colonel Charles McDermit, of the Second Cavalry, California Volunteers, Commander of Fort Churchill and of the Military District of Nevada. In February, 1865, an Indian uprising commenced in Humboldt, and Colonel McDermit, with his scouting troop of cavalry, had several skirmishes with the Indians later in the year. On August 7, 1865, while on his way to the camp, Colonel McDermit was killed from ambush by Indians near the creek which was later named for him. On

August 14, 1865, the name of the post was changed to **CAMP McDERMIT,** in honor of the murdered officer. The name of the camp, located on the north bank of East Fork Quinn River near the mouth of a canyon heading in the Santa Rosa Mountains, was changed to **FORT McDERMIT** on April 5, 1879. Established to protect travelers on the stage route and wagon road from Virginia City, Nevada, to Boise City, Idaho, this military installation also served to keep the Indians living in the area under control. During the 1870s, Sarah Winnemucca, the daughter of the Paiute chieftain Poito Winnemucca, was hospital matron of the post (Ruhlen; JGS, I, p. 237; M&S, p. 79; LAM, p. 393; 1860 Map).

Camp McDermit post office was established four times before May 7, 1879, when the name was changed to *Fort McDermitt.* On March 14, 1891, **McDERMITT** post office became the name (FTM, pp. 5, 10, 18). Bancroft gives the spelling of the fort name as *McDermit,* which spelling also appears for the town name on some highway maps (HHB, Nev., p. 264; HWY Maps 1958, 1961–62). It is probable that postal authorities were responsible for the double *t,* the usual spelling of the name.

McDONALD (White Pine). The name for a stream rising on the west slope of the Schell Creek Range and flowing to Duck Creek, south of Worthington Canyon; and for an old salt marsh, north of Mud Flat and west of the White Pine Mountains; commemorates Angus B. McDonald, a blacksmith from Prince Edward Island who, having been attracted by the mineral discoveries, settled in the area in 1876 (SG Map 9; Cad. Map; SPD, p. 1137; NHS, 1924, pp. 322, 423).

McGARRY, CAMP (Humboldt). On November 25, 1865, a field camp was established at Summit Lake, northeast of Soldier Meadow on the Applegate Cut-off to Oregon, by Companies D and I, Sixth Infantry, California Volunteers, to protect the mail road from Chico, California, to the Owyhee River settlements of Oregon. Designated a post on September 9, 1867, and declared a reservation on September 19, 1867, the installation was named to commemorate Brevet Brigadier General Edward McGarry of the United States Volunteers, a native of New York, who died December 31, 1867. Camp McGarry, garrisoned by one company each of cavalry and infantry, was included along with Camp Bidwell, Surprise Valley, California, in the District of Summit Lake which was organized in 1867. On March 25, 1871, the post was turned over to the Interior Department for a Paiute and Shoshone Indian reservation named Summit Lake. Numerous mounds of dirt and rock cairns today mark the graves of those emigrants and soldiers

killed by the hostile Indians of this High Rock Canyon country (Ruhlen; Wheeler 1879 Map; M&S, p. 80; NK 11–7).

McGIBBON (Esmeralda). A mining camp of the early twentieth century; named for a prospector, Sherwin McGibbon, who made ore discoveries at the site, by report of the *Goldfield News* of June 2, 1905 (DM).

McGILL (White Pine). A town on U.S. 93, a station, and a junction southwest of the station, eight miles north of East Ely in Steptoe Valley; the site of the largest copper smelter in Nevada (NJ 11–3). The name of **McGILL** post office, established April 28, 1891, was officially *Smelter,* from September 7, 1907, to August 14, 1908, at which time it was again changed to McGill (FTM, p. 18). The town is on land which was formerly the McGill Ranch. William N. McGill, born in Cincinnati, Ohio, in 1853, first went to western Nevada where "his first employment was running lines into Sutro's 'big bore' into the Comstock Lode, and known today as the Sutro Tunnel." In the early 1870s, while engaged in making surveys for the United States Government, he came to White Pine County. Associated with the Adams-McGill Land and Cattle Company, he became one of the great landowners of the state (NHS, 1911, p. 80, 1924, pp. 408–411; SPD, p. 1152).

McKEE, CAMP (Humboldt). In consequence of the Indians killing the operators of Granite Creek stage station (situated on Granite Creek, forty-five miles northeast of Smoke Creek Station) on April 1, 1865, military detachments were sent to all the stage stations on the Susanville-Humboldt River Road. Camp McKee, established in the following December and named for a person as yet unidentified, was at the Granite Creek Station. After the post's abandonment in October, 1866, its stores were moved to Camp McGarry at Summit Lake (Ruhlen).

McKEEVERSVILLE (Clark). The name identifies the old section of Boulder City (now the location of government warehouses) about a mile north of Boulder City airport, and commemorates the McKeever family who operated a tent store in 1930 near the site (WA).

McLEANS (Esmeralda). The name of the station at the southeast edge of the Monte Cristo Range in Big Smoky Valley, on the now dismantled T and G RR, was changed to *Gilbert Junction* in 1925. The earlier station name may commemorate David McLean who came to White Pine County, Nevada, in the 1870s from Nova Scotia. In 1891, he took up ranching near Tonopah in Nye County, and later removed to Esmeralda (SPD, pp. 1154–55). See **GILBERT.**

McLEOD (Nye). A creek rising southwest of Toiyabe Range Peak and flowing into **Mc-**

LEOD RESERVOIR in Big Smoky Valley; named for John McLeod, a rancher and cattleman of the valley (MM; GHM, NY 2).

McMARLINS STATION. See **DAYTON.**

McWILLIAMS (Clark). The summer-home area at the head of Lee Canyon in the Spring Mountains was named for J. T. McWilliams who developed it (WA; Vegas Quad.).

MACHADO (Elko). **MACHADO CREEK** rises in the Wild Horse Range and flows to the Owyhee River, east of Wild Horse Crossing. The significance of the Spanish word, meaning "hatchet," as applied to the creek is unknown (SG Map 11).

MACKAY AND FAIR (Washoe). A lumber camp established in 1863 and named for John W. Mackay and James G. Fair, bonanza kings on the Comstock. An alternate name was *Mayberry Camp,* commemorating James Mayberry who founded the camp (NHS, 1911, p. 88).

MACKS CANYON (Clark). A canyon, west of Lees Canyon and north of Charleston Peak in the Spring Mountains (WA).

MADELIN (Washoe). A name given by E. G. Beckwith in 1854 for a pass west of Lassens Meadows and north of Lassens Road (PRR–3 Map; Wheat IV, 74).

MAGEE (Churchill). Formerly a station and settlement southwest of Fallon, near Saint Clair (Car. Sink 1908). The name honors William Magee, one of the principal residents (NHS, 1913, p. 180).

MAGGIE (Elko). The creek so named, which rises in the Independence Mountains in Elko County, flows southwestward into Eureka County, and empties into the Humboldt River about one mile above Carlin in Elko County, commemorates the daughter of an early emigrant. According to one account, it was one of four creeks named by a man for his four daughters. A guide book explains the naming as follows: "The stream is named for a beautiful Scotch girl, whose parents stayed here for a time, while recruiting their stock, in the old times when the early emigrants toiled up [sic] the river" (GAC, p. 137). **MAGGIE PEAK,** in the Independence Mountains, was named for the creek (OPN, p. 26; Wheeler 1871 Map; NK 11–8; NK 11–11).

MAGNESITE WASH (Clark). The wash which drains eastward between Kaolin and Overton washes into the Muddy River Valley, is named for its magnesite deposit. The alternate name *White Wash* is descriptive of the white beds formed by the magnesite (WA).

MAGNUSON (White Pine). A settlement on U.S. 93 between Cherry Creek and McGill (Guide Map); named to commemorate John Magnuson, who came directly from Sweden to the area in 1881 and secured employment driving oxen and hauling wood (NHS, 1924, pp. 321–22).

MAGRUDER MOUNTAIN (Esmeralda). The mountain, southwest of Lida and northwest of Gold Point at the south end of the Palmetto Mountains, is named for J. Bankhead Magruder, an officer of the Confederate Army (OPN, p. 32).

MAHOGANY. Features named for stands of mountain mahogany include **MAHOGANY MOUNTAIN** and **MAHOGANY HILL,** south of Toiyabe Dome in the Toiyabe Range, and **MAHOGANY PEAK,** three miles north-northwest of Morey Peak in the Hot Creek Range, all in Nye County; **MAHOGANY MOUNTAIN** (Lincoln) is east of Serviceberry Canyon and northeast of Pioche (USGB 6903; NK 11–5; Freese, Map 2). **THE MAHOGANIES** is the designation for a mountain range east of Mountain City in Elko County (GHM, EL 3). The specific also denotes creeks in Elko, Humboldt, and Washoe counties; a flat in Washoe County; and a spring in White Pine County (Dir. 1971).

MAJESTIC LOOKOUT (Clark). The name for an observation point overlooking the weird formations of blood-red Jurassic sandstone in the Valley of Fire State Park, northeast of Las Vegas (WA).

MAJUBA (Pershing). **MAJUBA MOUNTAIN,** south of Antelope Range in the Trinity Range, earlier called Majuba *Hill,* was given its name in sympathy with the Boer victory over the British at Majuba Hill in South Africa on February 27, 1881. **MAJUBA HILL MINING DISTRICT** is also known as *Antelope.* A mine here produced the most tin of any deposit in the United States. **MAJUBA CANYON** is a northeast trending canyon, heading south of the mountain for which it is named (VPG; NK 11–10).

MALTBY (Washoe). The early stage station, east of Verdi in the western portion of the county, was named for its owner, J. S. Maltby (NHS, 1911, p. 87).

MAMMOTH. A settlement noted by Bancroft (HHB, Nev., pp. 254–255), eighteen miles from Genoa on the road from Carson City to Aurora in Douglas County, and also known as *Mammoth Ledge.* The name derived from a large silver-bearing quartz vein cutting across the Pine Nut Range at Walkers Pass, discovered in 1859 and called the **MAMMOTH LEDGE.** The Eagle Mining District, also known as the **MAMMOTH EAGLE DISTRICT,** was organized in 1860, north of the road leading into the Walker River region, and contained the Mammoth Ledge. In 1860, the valley was also named *Mammoth Eagle.* **MAMMOTH LEDGE** post office was active from February 6, 1863, to February 4, 1867, and from November 24, 1868, to August 13, 1869, when its operations were transferred to Wellington (MA, p. 75; NHS, 1913, p. 189; FTM, p. 17). The place was later known as *Carters Station* q.v.) (SHM 126). **MAMMOTH** denotes a mining district discovered December, 1863, on the west flank of the Paradise Range, with Ellsworth as its center, forty-five miles north-northeast of Luning in Nye County (1867 Map); and one of the important mines of the Trinity Lode in the Battle Mountain district in Lander County (SM, 1875, pp. 107–109; VPG, p. 132). **MAMMOTH CITY** (White Pine) was laid out in April, 1869, in Pleasant Valley where Fossil Canyon and the gentle slope of Treasure Hill meet. It enjoyed a brief existence (DM).

MANGANESE (Clark). Features named for manganese deposits are a wash lying south of Cleopatra Wash and the Cleopatra Mine and draining eastward from Black Mountain to Miners Cove in the Overton Arm of Lake Mead; and a former mining district, located fifteen miles southwest of Las Vegas, by report of the *Las Vegas Age,* of November 17, 1917 (WA; DM).

MANHATTAN (Nye). A town forty-five miles north of Tonopah in **MANHATTAN GULCH,** which extends from the west slope of the Toquima Range into Big Smoky Valley (SG Map 7); and a mining district, located in the 1860s immediately south of the Jefferson Canyon district on the west side of the Toquima Range (Wheeler, 1872, p. 41). The name derives from the old **MANHATTAN MINES** located southwest of Belmont (MA, pp. 342, 518; MM). Although Wheeler found the district abandoned in 1871, it was rejuvenated in the early twentieth century. In April, 1905, John C. Humphrey and his partners, said either to have been returning from Belmont to the Seyler Ranch, or to have been herding cattle in Manhattan Gulch, discovered gold near the base of April Fool Hill about one hundred feet from the old Belmont-Cloverdale wagon road. The resulting gold rush brought an influx of prospectors who settled in the area (NM, p. 51; SHM 97; SPD, p. 968; M&S, p. 120). **MANHATTAN** post office was established December 26, 1905 (FTM, p. 17).

MANSE (Nye). The settlement at the junction of State Routes 16 and 52 in the extreme southeastern portion of the county, near the Clark County line, is known also as the *Manse Ranch* (NJ 11–12). The ranch was settled by Joseph Yount and his family in 1875, since, it is said, the Indians killed their horses and prevented them from moving further. The place was known later as *Whites Ranch,* having been purchased by Harsha White, who operated a sawmill on Charleston Peak in partnership with Nehemiah Clarke, as noted in the *Las Vegas Age* of September 30, 1905, and of October 30, 1915. Joseph

Yount took up land southeast of the Manse Ranch (Vegas Quad.). **MANSE** post office was active from July 15, 1891, to March 31, 1914, when Johnnie became the mail address for its patrons (FTM, p. 17). The name is said to be an Indian name for "brush" or "bushes," descriptive of the bushes that had grown around the spring before the ranch was settled (OPN, p. 55). Hodge gives *Manses* as a variant of *Mansos,* from Spanish *manso,* "mild." The term denoted a former semi-sedentary tribe on the Mexican frontier and also was applied by the Spaniards as a designation for subjugated Indians (FWH, pp. 801–802). See **YOUNTS RANCH.**

MANSEAUS HALF–WAY HOUSE (Lyon). A former way station named for its proprietor, a Mr. Manseau, and for its position half way between Virginia City and Carson Lake on the road to the Reese River mines (NHS, 1913, p. 214).

MANZANITA LAKE (Washoe). A shallow lake on the campus of the University of Nevada at Reno; named for the manzanita (*Arctostaphylos nevadensis*), an evergreen shrub, the Spanish diminutive of *manzana,* meaning "apple."

MARA WASH (Nye). An intermittent watercourse heading about one mile north of Hampel Hill and trending generally eastward to Frenchman Flat, north of Mercury (USGB 6201). The name is from Uto-Aztekan *metla-(tli),* "metate, grinding stone," which appears in Southern Paiute as *mara-tsi-,* according to Professor Edward Sapir (ES, p. 451).

MARBLE (Mineral). A mining district, also called *Lodi,* on the west flank of the Paradise Range, north-northeast of Luning (VPG, p. 132). The district is located at **MARBLE FALLS CANYON,** which heads in the Paradise Range and extends into Lodi Valley (NJ 11–5; VPG, p. 132). **MARBLE** post office was established March 2, 1906, and discontinued December 15, 1917, when its operations were transferred to Luning (FTM, p. 17).

MARDIS (Elko). An early mining district, discovered in 1876 near the Jarbidge district and named for George Washington Mardis (OPN, p. 26). See **ALLEGHENY.** Population figures for the mining camp there were included in the *Twelfth Census* (1900).

MARIETTA (Mineral). **MARIETTA MINING DISTRICT,** also known as *Silver Star,* is located in the Excelsior Mountains southwest of Mina. The former mining camp and post office (June 29, 1877–July 11, 1881) serving the district were ten miles northwest of Belleville (HHB, Nev., pp. 259–60; 1881 Map; Census, 1880; VPG, p. 118; FTM, p. 17).

MARKER DAM (Pershing). The dam existing near Lovelock in the latter part of the nineteenth century took its name from P. N. Marker (DM), not further identified.

MARLETTE (Washoe). A creek east of Lake Tahoe, and a mountain peak in the Sierra Nevada were named for **MARLETTE LAKE** (GHM, WA 1). The artificial lake was created to provide a permanent water supply for Virginia City; the pipe line was completed in 1875. General S. H. Marlette, who surveyed the lake, is commemorated (NHS, 1913, p. 195).

MARMOL (Washoe). A former post office (June 20, 1891–May 4, 1908) and a station, two miles east of Calvada on the SP RR, abandoned July 15, 1920 (FTM, p. 18; SPD, p. 1031; DM). The community, settled about 1890, was given the Spanish name meaning "marble" for the Inyo Marble Works there, operated by Israel Luce (DM; NHS, 1911, p. 91).

MARSHALLS STATION (Elko). This station of the early 1880s was served by Tuscarora post office (HHB, Nev., p. 277; TF, p. 19).

MARSHLAND (Lyon). The post office so named was established December 13, 1886, and discontinued March 9, 1888, when Dayton became the mail address for its patrons (FTM, p. 18).

MARTIN. In Humboldt County, **MARTIN CREEK** rises in the Santa Rosa Division of the Humboldt National Forest and flows through Paradise Valley. **MARTIN CREEK RANGER STATION AND CAMPGROUND** is north of Paradise Valley and serves as a base for trout fishermen and deer hunters (GHM, HU 4; NP, p. 72; Nev. Guide, p. 216). **MARTIN** (Washoe) is a station on the WP RR, west of Black Springs (GHM, WA 1). **MARTIN CANYON** (Elko), near Gold Creek, commemorates Hugh Martin who settled in the area in 1867 (EP, p. 54). **MARTINS FORK.** See **MAGGIE.**

MARY CREEK. See **CARLIN.**

MARYS RIVER (Elko). A tributary of the Humboldt River rising in the Humboldt National Forest and flowing southward into the Humboldt near Deeth; named for the Indian wife of an explorer. **MARYS LAKE** is an early name for Humboldt Lake (JCF, Report, pp. 196, 211, 213–14). **MARYS RIVER** is an alternate name for the Humboldt River on the western portion of Ensigns and Thayer's 1849 Map of United States (Wheat III, 69). See **HUMBOLDT.** Features named for the river include a valley denoted **MARYS RIVER BASIN** and **MARYS RIVER PEAK** (GHM, EL 3).

MASON. The name group in Lyon County commemorates Henry ("Hock") A. Mason, who, in 1859, settled **MASONS RANCH.** The ranch formed part of the boundary line of Douglas County, beginning at the Walker River and running west to the mouth of Clear Lake. Mason built the first house in **MASON VALLEY,** constructing the walls of willows and adobe and the roof of tules (MA, p. 502). The town of **MASON,** surveyed and built in 1909, was the headquarters of the NCB RR, also called the Mason Valley Line, and formerly a station on the C and C RR, one mile south of Yerington (SPD, p. 954). The post office was established December 8, 1908. An early settlement denoted **MASON VALLEY** (1881 Map) and once called *Greenfield* was sixteen miles from Wabuska. A post office named for this settlement was established August 15, 1871, and discontinued February 6, 1894 (FTM, p. 18). **MASON MINING DISTRICT,** also known as *Yerington,* is in the central portion of the Singatse Range, southwest of Yerington (VPG, p. 107). **MASON MOUNTAIN** (Elko) is a peak southeast of Mount Ichabod. **MASON CREEK** rises on the north flank of the mountain and flows northeastward to Charleston Reservoir (NK 11–9; NJ 11–1). "Hock" Mason, the owner of Masons Ranch in Lyon County, ran cattle in the Charleston area and is also commemorated by the Elko County features (EP, p. 54).

MASSACRE LAKE (Washoe). Some small lakes, or dry sinks, also called Massacre Lake*s*, east of Vya, in the northern portion of the county (NK 11–7). A large and well-equipped wagon train was attacked near here in 1850 by Indians of the High Rock Canyon country. Forty men of the emigrant party were killed in the battle and interred in a common grave (Nev. Guide, p. 216; OPN, p. 68). A creek which empties into the south end of the lake and a ranch on the creek also are named **MASSACRE** for the lake.

MASSIE (Churchill). The non-agency station on the Sparks Subdivision of the SP RR, milepost 292.5, between Hazen and Falais, was so named in March, 1903 (T75; DM).

MATTERHORN (Elko). A mountain south of Jarbidge Peak in the Jarbidge Mountains, Humboldt National Forest; named for a peak in the Pennine Alps on the Swiss-Italian border (NK 11–9).

MATTESON (Humboldt). The post office of early Humboldt County was active from February 17, 1868, to July 27, 1868 (FTM, p. 18).

MAVERICK SPRINGS RANGE. A mountain range in northern White Pine and southern Elko counties, bounded on the west by Ruby Valley and on the east by Long Valley; named for springs, which in turn were named for unbranded or orphaned cattle. The term derived from Samuel A. *Maverick* (1803–70), a Texas lawyer who did not brand his cattle (NK 11–12).

MAYBERRY CAMP. See **MACKAY AND FAIR.**

MAZEPPA (White Pine). **MAZEPPA CAN–**

YON, thirty miles west of Ely and five miles southeast of Hamilton on the south slope of the White Pine Mountains, took its name from the **MAZEPPA MINE**. The mine probably was named for the play *Mazeppa,* performed at Virginia City in February, 1863, with Adah Isaacs Menken in the title role (HNS, p. 75).

MAZUMA (Pershing). This slang word for money derived from the Yiddish *m'zumon,* "the ready necessary," denoted a former mining camp and post office about twenty-five miles northwest of Lovelock. The townsite was announced in the *Lovelock Tribune* of February 15, 1907, and the post office was established on the following August 28. In July, 1912, a flash flood from the Seven Troughs Range washed away the town, except for a few buildings on the upper walls of the canyon, and killed at least eight people. The post office was discontinued and operations moved to Seven Troughs on November 30, 1912 (NM; DM; FTM, p. 18).

MEAD, LAKE (Clark). The lake, formed by Hoover Dam, is 115 miles long, with a shoreline distance of 550 miles, in Nevada and Arizona. The **LAKE MEAD NATIONAL RECREATION AREA** was set up under the Department of the Interior in 1936 and comprises more than 3,000 square miles, with headquarters at Boulder City, Nevada. **MEAD LAKE STATION**, sixteen miles southwest of Moapa, is also known as *Nepac* (Freese, Map 1) and is the terminus of the Moapa-Mead Lake Branch of the UP RR. **MEAD LAKE** post office, earlier called *Nepac,* was established October 15, 1939, and discontinued December 31, 1942, when its operations were transferred to Overton (Nev., I, 1961, pp. 19, 24; NJ 11–12; FTM, p. 18). The name commemorates Elwood Mead, Commissioner of the Bureau of Reclamation, who recommended the awarding of the bid for the construction of Boulder (Hoover) Dam in 1931 (JGS, I, p. 558).

MEADOW CANYON (Nye). A canyon extending from the west slope of the Toquima Range into Monitor Valley north of Belmont; named for wild hay meadows there. **MEADOW CANYON GAME REFUGE**, named for the canyon, is southeast of Jefferson (Park Map; MM; Wheeler 1871 Map).

MEADOW CREEK (Elko). A tributary of the Bruneau River in **MEADOW CREEK CANYON**, a miniature of Jarbidge Canyon; and **MEADOW CREEK CAMPGROUND**, located approximately nine miles from Gold Creek on the Gold Creek-Rowland-Jarbidge road (GHM, EL 3; Park Map; NP, p. 71).

MEADOW VALLEY. A mountain range extending northeast from Clark County into Lincoln County, separated from the Delamar Mountains by Kane Springs Wash, on the west, and from the Mormon Mountains by

the **MEADOW VALLEY WASH,** on the east. See **PROVIDENCE.** The wash, which extends from Cap Valley southward to Moapa, was named for **MEADOW VALLEY**, which is that portion of the wash in which Panaca is located, and was named for natural grasslands along the river. J. H. Martineau, historian of a Mormon exploring party of 1858, described the valley as "a large meadow of wire and broad-leaf grass" (Wheat IV, 128). Apparently the wash and its continuation, the Muddy River, were the *Adams River* so named by Jedediah Strong Smith. The major divisions of the wash are Mormon Canyon, between Rox and Carp; Long Valley, between Carp and Leith; and Rainbow Canyon, between Elgin and Caliente. Wheeler denoted the entire distance between Caliente and Moapa *Grapevine Canyon* (NJ 11–12; NJ 11–9; Wheeler 1871 Map; JGS, I, pp. 27–28; WA). Meadow Valley in the Panaca district is included in the *Ninth Census,* Meadow Valley Wash in the *Twelfth Census* (1870, 1900).

MEADS MILL (Carson City). A former mill constructed near Empire for handling Comstock ore; named for its owner (SPD, p. 981).

MEDICINE (Elko). The **MEDICINE RANGE**, about forty miles west-southwest of Currie, takes its name from **MEDICINE SPRINGS**, at the end of the range (GHM, EL 5). The springs were so named because Indians used the spring water as a medicinal aid (EP, p. 55). Medicine Springs and Mud Springs are alternate names for the mining district in the range (VPG, p. 45). See **MUD.**

MELANDCO (Elko). The UP RR siding north of Wells has "a coined name representing the Metropolis Land Company that was a going concern at the time of the construction of the railroad" (EP, p. 55; GHM, EL 4).

MELVIN (White Pine). A town laid out thirty-three miles north of Ely, in 1907, by report of the *Lovelock Tribune* of June 21, 1907; a post office active from March 20, 1907, to January 31, 1913, when Steptoe became the mail address for its patrons (DM; FTM, p. 18).

MENDHA (Lincoln). A siding on the Prince Railroad, four miles northwest of Pioche; an alternate name for the old mining camp of the Highland Mining District located on the east side of the Highland Range, about six miles west of Pioche. The names derive from the **MENDHA MINE,** one of the principal producers of the Highland district, also commonly called Mendha (WA; DM; GHM, LN 1).

MERCURY (Nye). The town, begun in 1953 by the Atomic Energy Commission, is just south of Frenchman Flat in the Las Vegas Bombing and Gunnery Range. It derives its name, according to air force personnel, from the **MERCURY MINE** a few miles north of the town (RC, pp. 64–65; Vegas Quad.; NJ 11–12). Features named for the town are **MERCURY VALLEY,** a basin bounded on the northeast by **MERCURY RIDGE** and the Spotted Range and on the southwest by the Specter Range and the Spring Mountains (USGB 6103); and **MERCURY** post office, established March 1, 1952 (FTM, p. 18).

MERRIMAC (Ormsby). The early settlement and former station on the V and T RR two miles below Empire, was named for the **MERRIMAC(K) MILL** on the west side of the Carson River, which was built about 1861 for the crushing of Comstock ore (FES, p. 208; GHK, V&T, p. 31; SPD, p. 981; MA, p. 540). **MERRIMAC CANYON,** for which the mill was named, presumably was named by New Englanders in the area for the Merrimack River, or for some older, Eastern settlement (NHS, 1913, pp. 202–203).

MESQUITE (Clark). The name of the town on Interstate 15, in the Virgin River Valley near the Utah line, is descriptive by association with mesquite in the area. The pods of the mesquite (*Prosopis chilensis* and *Prosopis glandulosa*) were stored by the Indians in the early days as a food reserve for the winter. Although Mormons were in the area prior to the exodus of 1857, Mesquite was established in 1880 when a company of ten families from St. George, Utah, settled on the north side of the Virgin River, near Bunkerville (NHS, 1924, p. 248; OPN, p. 16; NJ 11–12). The post office name, first spelled *Mesquit* (July 19, 1880–August 5, 1887) was changed to Mesquite on July 27, 1897, the date of resumption of service (FTM, p. 18). **MESQUITE** is also the name for a valley southeast of Pahrump Valley in both California and Clark County, Nevada; for a spring west of Whitney; and for a former well on the road between Las Vegas and Whitney (WA). See **BUNKERVILLE.**

METALLIC (Esmeralda). The official name for a former mining camp, located in a canyon about midway between Columbus and Candelaria, about fifteen miles south of Mina, and its post office, established January 4, 1880, and discontinued July 7, 1881 (HHB, Nev., p. 260; FTM, p. 18). The camp was known also as *Metallic City* and familiarly as *Pickhandle Gulch,* the latter name having been given because miners are said to have frequently settled their differences with flailing pickhandles (NM; MM). See **AXHANDLE** and **PICKHANDLE.**

METROPOLIS (Elko). A town eleven miles northwest of Wells, near Bishop Creek, settled by the Metropolis Land Company for which it was named; formerly a station on a now dismantled spur line built by the SP RR (OPN, p. 26; NM; NK 11–9). A post office so denoted served the area from November 24, 1911, to December 10, 1942, when its operations were transferred to Wells (FTM, p. 18).

MEXICAN. According to most accounts, the Comstock mine was named for Gabriel Maldarnardo (variants are *Meldonado* and *Maldonado*), a Mexican miner, who purchased the Comstock ground from Emanuel Penrod for $3,000 on November 30, 1859 (DDQ, p. 43; HHB, Nev., p. 107). Angel cites a letter written by Penrod in October, 1880. "After it was known to be lead, our company gave Comstock and myself 100 feet of it, joining our work on the north, for staking off the claim and saving it to the company. This 100 feet was the original 'Mexican'" (MA, p. 56). This ground was also known as the *Spanish* (DDQ, p. 43; GHS, p. 17). "This piece of ground went for a long time by the name of the Spanish claim, and is so designated on the earlier maps, the Mexicans being indifferently called Spanish, referring to the nationality of their ancestors and the language they speak" (HDG, CP, 12/16/76). There is reason to believe that the mine was known as the Mexican even before its purchase by Maldarnardo. Mexicans who had worked in silver mines of their native country were in the area. Frank Antonio, or "Old Frank," who may have told the Grosch brothers about the silver ledges was a Mexican (M&S, p. 66). "The Mexicans had an arastra [sic] at work on the croppings of what is now known as the Comstock lode and worked ore from the Mexican mine. These claims were worked as late as 1857" (Dir. 1875, p. iv). The original Mexican was consolidated with the Ophir, and the present Mexican, which takes its name from the first, has six hundred feet along the lode, acquired from the North Ophir (IH; HDG, CP, 8/12/76). A tenacity in preserving mine names is apparent in Storey County tax rolls which show the patented claim as the *Spanish and Mexican* (AR, No. 4028). The **MEXICAN MILL,** named for the mine and located at Empire City, was also known as the *Silver State Reduction Works.* **MEXICAN SPRING** denotes a spring in Clark County, northwest of Potosi Mountain in the Spring Mountains (WA).

MICA PEAK (Clark). The mountain so named is east of Gold Butte and north of Jumbo Peak in the southeastern portion of the county (NJ 11–12; WA). The name is descriptive of the mica slate in the rock.

MIDAS. The mining camp on State Route 18, west of Tuscarora in Elko County, has been the scene of several gold rushes, the first a result of the location of the Elko Prince Mine in 1907 by Paul Ehlers. The post office so named was established November 16,

1907, and discontinued September 30, 1942, when its operations were transferred to Golconda. **MIDAS MINING DISTRICT,** named for the mining camp, is also known as *Gold Circle* and *Summit* and is on the southeast slope of the Owyhee Bluffs, forty-eight miles east-northeast of Golconda (HWY Map; M&S, p. 160; NM, p. 126; VPG, p. 41). The name of **MIDAS** post office, in Nye County, was changed from *Ione City* on April 8, 1882. The post office was discontinued December 10, 1942, but the name survives in **MIDAS SPRING,** north of Ione and on the west edge of the Shoshone Mountains (FTM, p. 18; GHM, NY 2). **MIDAS CANYON** (Lander) is a canyon in the Toiyabe Range, northwest of Mount Prometheus and north of Austin (SG Map 6). The name is derivative of *Midas,* the Phrygian king of Greek legend, to whom Dionysus granted fulfillment of his wish, that all he touched might turn to gold.

MIDDLE. MIDDLE GATE (Churchill) denoted a station forty miles east of Carson Lake on the road to the Reese River mines via the Twenty-six-Mile Desert; named by Simpson, who wrote under date of June 4, 1859, "On reaching our camping-place, which I call the Middle Gate . . ." (JHS, p. 83). See **EAST GATE** and **WEST GATE**. The station, listed in the Root and Connelley tabulation of stage stops on the Overland Trail, was fifteen miles east of Cold Springs Station and thirteen miles west of Fairview. **MIDDLE LAKE** (Washoe) is between Massacre Lake and West Lake (NK 11–7). **MIDDLE CREEK** (White Pine), on the west slope of the Schell Creek Range, is named for its position between Little Creek and East Creek northeast of Prescio (Dir. 1971). Mountain peaks so named are **MIDDLE PEAK,** in the southwest corner of Clark County in the Dead Mountains, and **MIDDLE STACK,** ten miles east-northeast of Contact in Elko County (OPN, pp. 16, 26). The latter peak took its name from **MIDDLE STACKS RANCH,** "the only place between the Vineyard and San Jacinto Ranches where there were stacks of hay" (EP, p. 56).

MILL. Nevada features of this designation were named for nearby mills. **MILL CITY** (Pershing). The town on Interstate 80 (also a station), twenty-eight miles southwest of Winnemucca on the SP RR between Imlay and Cosgrave, was started in 1862 in anticipation of the Humboldt, or French, Canal. The ninety-mile canal was planned to carry water from east of Winnemucca at the Humboldt to Mill City and to transport ore from the Humboldt Mining District to the mills. It was started by J. A. Ginacca of French Ford (Winnemucca) but never completed. Mill City, however, was fortunate in being located on the transcontinental railroad, and

a foundry built in 1875 by A. B. Gould did work for Winnemucca, Unionville, Cornucopia, Bull Run, Oreana, and Rye Patch mining camps (M&S, p. 203; SM, 1875, p. 62; MA, p. 455; T1TR). The **MILL CITY** post office, established in Nevada Territory on June 22, 1864, was discontinued on December 31, 1948, and Imlay became the mail address for its patrons (C&C, p. 589; Nev. Terr. Map; FTM, p. 18). **MILL CITY MINING DISTRICT,** seven miles southwest of Mill City on the southeast slope of the Eugene Mountains, is one of the largest producers of tungsten ore in the United States (OPN, p. 62; VPG, p. 154). **MILL CANYON** (Eureka). A mining district organized in 1863 in the Cortez Mountains, twenty-five miles south of Beowawe; named for a mill erected in the canyon in 1864 (VPG, p. 67; OPN, p. 34). **MILL CREEK** (Elko). A creek west of Rio Tinto was so named for a nearby quartz mill of the 1870s; a creek east of Gold Creek "was named for the mill constructed there in 1876 by Henry and Bob Catlin" (SG Map 11; GHM, EL 3; EP, p. 56). **MILL CREEK** (Lander). The name for a creek west of Tenabo and a summit in the Shoshone Mountains. The early settlement named for the creek was served by Battle Mountain post office (GHM, LA 2; TF, p. 19). Additional creeks so named include a stream northwest of Baker in the Snake Range of White Pine County; a creek at the northeast extremity of Lake Tahoe in Washoe County (Dir. 1971). **MILL CREEK SETTLEMENT** (Carson City), three miles west of Carson City, was noted for two sawmills, Ashe's and Gregory's. The rapid fall of the creek made it valuable for propelling machines (NHS, 1913, p. 198). **MILL STATION** (Washoe), a lumber station on the road between Carson City and Washoe City was the site of several mills (1881 Map; NHS, 1911, p. 91). **MILL POINT** (Clark), one of the original Muddy River settlements between Overton and Saint Joseph, was named for a grist mill erected at the site by James Leithead. The name was changed to *Simonsville,* for Orrawell Simons who built another mill there (WA).

MILLER. MILLER MOUNTAIN is north of Basalt in southern Mineral County near the Esmeralda line (GHM, MI 2). An early mining district so named was organized in 1881 about seventy-five miles north of Wadsworth and fourteen miles west of the Washoe-Humboldt boundary, and named for its discoverer H. B. Miller (DM). See **BRUNSON. MILLER GRADE** (Clark) is the name for a steep hill several miles above Nelson, on the road to Searchlight near the Wall Street Mine (NI 11–3).

MILLERS. A town fifteen miles west-northwest of Tonopah in Esmeralda County, where thousands of tons of Tonopah ores were treated; formerly a station on the T and G RR; named for Charles R. Miller, a director of the railroad (VPG; NM; DM, RR (I), p. 261). A post office so named was active from January 17, 1906, to September 12, 1919, and from February 16, 1921, to December 31, 1931, when its services were transferred to Tonopah (FTM, p. 18). **MILLERS** (Douglas) was first named **MILLERS- VILLE** and so appears on United States Geological Survey maps of 1893. The name honors Elizabeth, the wife of a Scotch blacksmith, Alexander Miller. The survey party, camped near the Miller home, named the place for Mrs. Miller in appreciation for pies and biscuits she baked for them (Dangberg, CV, p. 101). **MILLERS STATION** (Lyon) was on the Carson River and named for its proprietor (NHS, 1913, p. 214). The name is included on an 1859 map of the Overland and Ocean Mail Routes, prepared by Dixson and Kasson (Wheat IV, 149). See **REEDS**. **MILLERS** (Humboldt) denoted a short-lived post office, established December 20, 1889, and discontinued April 23, 1892, when Kennedy became the mail address for its patrons (FTM, p. 18).

MILLETT (Nye). A locality and former stage station, townsite, and post office, west of Alkali Flat on State Route 8A, in Big Smoky Valley at a site earlier known as the Scheel Ranch which was named for its owner Charles Scheel. The name was changed to Millett in the middle 1890s, when Albion Bradbury Millett married the widow of Charles Scheel and moved from his Twin River ranch to her ranch. During a mining boom in the early 1900s, Mrs. Millett opened a store at the ranch, and **MILLETT** post office was established on May 3, 1906. New strikes made at old mines west of the ranch in the Toiyabe Range precipitated the laying out of Millett townsite. Although the small settlement did not last long, the post office continued to operate from the ranch store until July 3, 1930, when its services were transferred to Round Mountain (MM). **MIL- LETT MINING DISTRICT,** named for the ranch and also known as *North Twin River,* is on the east flank of the Toiyabe Range (SG Map 6; VPG, p. 133).

MILLION HILLS (Clark). A group of hills, about fifteen miles east of Gold Butte, on the Nevada-Arizona boundary; and **MIL- LION HILLS WASH,** which drains southward from Azure Ridge into Lake Mead, west of the hills for which it is named (WA).

MINA (Mineral). The town on U.S. 95 is the terminus of the Mina Branch of the SP RR, formerly a station on the C and C RR (T75). A post office so named was established September 25, 1905 (FTM, p. 19). **MINA MINING DISTRICT,** also known as *Silver Star,* is in the Excelsior Mountains, southwest of the town. The Spanish word meaning "mine," or "ore," is descriptive of the mining area (NJ 11–4).

MINDEN (Douglas). The county seat on U.S. 395, south of Gardnerville in Carson Valley. The town was established in 1905 by the H. F. Dangberg Land and Livestock Company (operated by the sons of Henry Fred Dangberg, Sr.) and the V and T RR, which built a short line from Carson City to Minden, in order to give Carson Valley railroad connection (M&S, p. 236; NJ 11– 4). "It was in the village of Halle near the Prussian town of Minden, Westphalia, that H. F. Dangberg, Sr., who settled in Carson Valley in 1857 was born; hence the name Minden" (GD, CV, p. 120). A post office named for the town was established October 3, 1906 (FTM, p. 19).

MINERAL. MINERAL COUNTY was created from the northern part of Esmeralda County on February 10, 1911, and Hawthorne was named county seat. The name was given because the county is a highly mineralized area (SPD, p. 957; OPN, p. 6). **MINERAL BUTTES** is the denotation for buttes in southeastern Clark County, north of Garrett Butte and near Gold Butte (WA). **MINERAL CITY** (White Pine). Upon the discovery of silver, lead, and copper, four miles northwest of Ely in 1869, a mining camp so named sprang up. After a decline, the district was revived because of the gold strikes in the Chainman and Emma mines, the principal producers in the area. **MINERAL CITY** post office served the camp for which it was named from August 9, 1870, until December 28, 1876 (NM; 1881 Map; FTM, p. 19). See **LANE CITY. MINERAL HILL** (Eureka), an early mining camp, former station on the E and P RR, and post office which, except for brief intervals, served the area from May 9, 1871, to April 15, 1914; named for **MINERAL HILL MINING DISTRICT,** discovered in June, 1869, on the west slope of the Sulphur Springs Range. The region was inhabited by Shoshones, who worked to a limited extent for the miners. The principal mines worked in the early days were the Austin, Mary Ann, Rim Rock, Grant, Star of the West, Vallejo, and Pogonip (GMW, 1872; pp. 35–36, 1871 Map; FTM, p. 19; M&SP, 7/17/69; SPD, p. 839; VPG, p. 67; NM; Census, 1870). Additional mining districts using this general descriptive term are **MINERAL BASIN** (Pershing), near the Churchill County line, twenty-five miles southeast of Lovelock, and **MINERAL RIDGE** (Esmeralda), twenty miles south of Blair Station and also called *Silver Peak* and *Red Mountain* (VPG, pp. 155, 59). **MIN- ERAL RAPIDS** was the name for a post office established in Carson County, Utah

Territory, April 17, 1860, and discontinued February 13, 1861 (FTM, p. 19). See **DAYTON.**

MINERS. The possessive, occupational name denotes a cove at the mouth of Manganese Wash and a spring, north of Eldorado Canyon, in southern Clark County (WA). **MINERS HOPE.** See **BATTLE MOUNTAIN.**

MINIUM STATION (Lander). Formerly a stage stop on the Austin-Belmont route, in Big Smoky Valley north of Millett and near the Kingston Mining District; operated from the 1860s until about 1890 and named for its owner (Wheeler 1871 Map; MM).

MINNEHAHA CANYON (White Pine). A canyon on the east slope of the Diamond Range in the Newark Mining District, the site of the old Centenary Mill; named for *Minnehaha*, the Indian maiden who becomes the wife of Hiawatha in Henry Wadsworth Longfellow's *The Song of Hiawatha* (1855) (Cad. Map).

MINTO (Lincoln). This somewhat popular name for railroad stations in the western United States and Canada is the designation for a siding on the UP RR between Islen and Eccles, possibly derived ultimately from Lake Minto in northwest Quebec. The siding earlier was named *Dutch Flat*, by report of the *Lincoln County Record* of December 16, 1904 (OG; DM).

MIRAGE (Churchill). A station on the old line of the CP RR between Hot Springs and White Plains, twenty-six miles northeast of Wadsworth (GAC, p. 156; T1TR). "It is simply a side track with no habitation near it but a section house. . . . This place, like many others, is named from some peculiarity of location or from some characteristic of the country. . . . It is reported that many a weary emigrant in the days of old, was deceived by the optical illusions that here seemed so real, and wondered why he did not reach the cooling lakes and spreading shade that seemed so near and yet so far away" (FES, pp. 198–99).

MIRIAM (Churchill). A non-agency station on the Sparks Subdivision of the SP RR, milepost 324.2 between Ocala and Toy, west of the Humboldt Sink (T75).

MITCHELL CREEK (Elko). A creek heading on the west slope of the Ruby Mountains and joining Tenmile Creek, southeast of Elko; named for James Mitchell, an early settler (NK 11–12; EP, p. 57).

MIZPAH. The richest producer of all the claims, located when Jim Butler made his rich strike in 1900 at Tonopah, in Nye County; it initiated the twentieth-century mining boom throughout Nevada. According to Butler, Mrs. Butler staked the **MIZPAH CLAIM** and named it. The Biblical place name, associated with fidelity and trust, was engraved on her wedding ring (VPG; Nev. Guide, p. 225). **MIZPAH MINING DISTRICT** (Elko), also called *Dolly Varden,* sixteen miles north of Currie, was organized in December, 1906. A post office so named served the camp from May 20, 1907 to November 15, 1912, when its operations were transferred to Currie. Another active camp of this name was near Ely in White Pine County, according to the *Reno Evening Gazette* of May 23, 1907 (VPG, p. 39; FTM, p. 19; DM).

MOAPA. A station on the UP RR, fifty miles north of Las Vegas and about one mile west of U.S. 93, and a post office established July 22, 1889, in **MOAPA VALLEY,** or *Muddy Valley,* in Clark County. The valley was settled in 1865 by Mormons of Utah who farmed the land, planted cottonwood trees, and established the towns Saint Joseph, Saint Thomas, Overton, and West Point. Also in the vicinity are **MOAPA MINING DISTRICT,** a gypsum district south and east of Moapa, and **MOAPA INDIAN RESERVATION** (SPD, p. 102; WA; VPG, p. 29; NJ 11–12; Park Map). **MOAPA PEAK** (Lincoln) at the south end of the Mormon Mountains and sixteen miles north-northeast of Moapa is "named for the Moapa Indian Reservation" (USGB 7102). The name is from *Moapariats,* "mosquito creek people," which denoted a Southern Paiute band living in or near Moapa Valley (FWH, p. 915). John Wesley Powell noted the name "Mo-a-pats: the people who live on the Muddy [River]" (Fowler, p. 161). See **MUDDY.**

MOCKINGBIRD (Clark). The name for a spring west of Gold Butte and south of Quail Spring, and for a mine in Eldorado Canyon, both in southern Clark County (NJ 11–12; WA).

MOGUL (Washoe). A non-agency station on the Sacramento Division of the SP RR, on the Truckee River, seven miles west of Reno between Verdi and Lawton; perhaps named for a type of steam locomotive (T1TR; T187).

MOHAVE, LAKE (Clark). The lake created by Davis Dam on the Colorado River in the Lake Mead National Recreational Area, in Arizona and Nevada; named for the Mohave Indians from their name for themselves *hamok,* "three," + *avi,* "mountain" (Kroeber, Handbook, p. 896).

MOHAWK CANYON (Nye). A canyon heading on the west slope of the Toiyabe Range and extending to Reese River Valley between New York and Crane Canyons; named in commemoration of the most easterly of the Iroquois Five Nations, formerly resident along the Mohawk River in New York (GHM, NY 2). *Mohawk* is cognate with Narragansett *mohowaicuck,* "they eat animate things," hence "eaters of human flesh."

MOKOMOKE (White Pine). A name of undetermined origin for a mountain group at the north end of the White Pine Mountains (Cad. Map; NJ 11–3).

MOLEEN (Elko). A non-agency station on the Elko Subdivision of the SP RR, eleven miles east of Carlin between Avenel and Vivian (T1TR; T75). The community was settled in 1869 and named by railroad officials for nearby turrets, peaks, and domes standing in irregular order and called **MOLEEN ROCKS** (FES, p. 180; 1881 Map).

MONARCH. The traditional mining name was selected for a town laid out in 1906 on the Ralston Desert, northeast of Manhattan in Nye County. The Reverend Benjamin Blanchard sold town lots and mining claims and ranch sites of dubious value. The WP RR located an alternate line there and considered Monarch to be a prospective division point. On October 15, 1906, the post office was established by official order, and three days later, the *Reno Evening Gazette* predicted that the town was on its way to being a mere memory. Leaving $73,000 in debts, the Reverend Blanchard had absconded with $75,000 of the investors' money. The citizens formed an exodus to Manhattan, and the order to establish a post office was rescinded on March 25, 1907 (FTM, p. 19; NM; DM). Mark Twain and Mr. Ballou recorded, but apparently never worked, a claim located near Unionville, in Humboldt County. "Then we named the mine 'Monarch of the Mountains' (modesty of nomenclature is not a prominent feature in the mines)" (SLC, I, p. 202). **MONARCH** (Lincoln) denotes a mine, north of Highland Peak in the Highland Range (HWY Map).

MONITOR. A range in north-central Nye County, extending across southeast Lander County into Eureka County; a valley between the Toquima and Monitor ranges. **MONITOR PEAK** is in the Monitor Range in Nye County (NJ 11–2; NJ 11–5). These features are said to have been so named for a hill which resembled the battleship *Monitor* used by the Union forces against the *Merrimac* in 1862 (OPN, pp. 34, 41). **MONITOR** also designated mills constructed in the early 1860s, one in Lyon County and another in Kings Canyon, Carson City County, as well as a mine in the Echo district of old Humboldt County and a mine on Middle Hill in early Esmeralda County (SM, 1866, pp. 151, 49–50, 34; NHS, 1926, p. 390).

MONKEY WRENCH WASH (Lincoln). The wash draining into Delamar Valley past the **MONKEY WRENCH MINE** was named for the mine, which was discovered either by a family named Riggs in 1889, or by John and Alvin Ferguson in 1891. The prospectors are said to have discovered rich ore upon breaking a piece of quartzite from a ledge in a small ravine with a monkey wrench, and

to have named the mine for the incident (WA; JGS, I, pp. 618–19). See **DELAMAR.**

MONTANA (Nye). The early name for a station on the now defunct BG RR, later changed to *Bonnie Claire* (q.v.).

MONTE CRISTO. A mountain range in northwest Esmeralda County, southeast of the Pilot Mountains and west of Big Smoky Valley; mills formerly located west of Treasure City in White Pine County, and in Lincoln, Lyon, and Carson City counties (NJ 11–5; Cad. Map; NHS, 1909, p. 105). Wheeler's map of 1871 shows the variant *Christo* in the name for the mountain range. The name was probably chosen for the reason suggested by Gudde (p. 199), because of the influence of *The Count of Monte Cristo* (1844), by Alexandre Dumas. The **MONTE CRISTO OIL CORPORATION WELL** is named for the range (Dir. 1971).

MONTELLE (Mineral). A post office so named was established April 18, 1900, and discontinued November 30, 1911, when Pine Grove became the mail address for its patrons (FTM, p. 19).

MONTELLO (Elko). A terminal agency on the Elko Subdivision of the SP RR; named by railroad officials in 1869 perhaps for an older station of this name in the East. **MONTELLO** post office was established February 27, 1912, the name being changed from *Bauvard* (SPD, p. 829; 1881 Map; FTM, p. 19; T75).

MONTEZUMA. An early mining camp and post office (February 24, 1880–December 11, 1888), a station on the former T and G RR, in Esmeralda County; named for the **MONTEZUMA MINING DISTRICT,** seven miles west of Goldfield (FTM, p. 19; 1881 Map; HHB, Nev., p. 260). The mining district was discovered in May, 1867 by Thomas Nagle, Matthew Plunkett, and a Mr. Carlyle, on Mount Nagle (Wheeler, 1872, p. 46), which was later renamed **MONTEZUMA PEAK** (SPD, p. 857). Ores from the mines which included the Savage, Mountain Queen, Osceola, and Burchard, were worked at Benton and Columbus (Wheeler 1871 Map; NJ 11–8). A mining district so named was organized in Nye County in 1865 and was served briefly by a post office named for the camp and active from August 5, 1872, to May 19, 1873 (SM, 1875, pp. 107–109; FTM, p. 19). **MONTEZUMA MINE,** in the Arabia district of Pershing County, was a great producer of silver, lead, and antimony before 1875 (HPS, 1/29/56). Montezuma, or Moctezuma, II (1480?–1520), the Aztec emperor of Mexico at the time of the Spanish conquest, is honored by the name. It is believed that slaves of Montezuma sought turquoise all the way from Searchlight to Tuscarora (HPS, 1/24/54; NM).

MONTGOMERY. A mining district, later renamed *Johnnie,* located in 1890 or 1891 in Nye County, Nevada, eighty miles from Ivanpah, California. By report of the *Nevada State Journal* of May 1, 1891, the mines were discovered by George Montgomery and five men from San Andreas, California, who were searching for the Lost Breyfogle Mine. The location of the townsite and post office (August 7, 1891–March 17, 1894) may have been at the later Johnnie townsite. The exceedingly rich Chispa Mine was the principal producer of the district (WA; FTM, p. 19; DM). Another mining district so denoted was at the north end of the White Mountains and west of Fish Lake Valley, in Mineral County. It is now known as the *Buena Vista* or *Mount Montgomery* district (Wheeler 1871 Map; VPG, p. 111). **MONTGOMERY-SHOSHONE** (Nye) denoted the prominent mine of Rhyolite, first located in 1904 by E. A. Montgomery (SPD, p. 36), or by Bob Montgomery (with a Shoshone Indian named Mike(?)), for whom it was named (DM).

MONUMENT. MONUMENT PEAK, twenty-three miles northwest of Elko in Elko County, was named for stone markers, or monuments, used to fix the locations of mining claims (OPN, p. 26). Canyons of this name are located north of Patterson Peak in the Fortification Range in Nye County, and on the east side of Bristol Valley, eight miles west of Chief Mountain in Lincoln County (ECN Map; WA).

MOONSHINE (Nye). A peak in the Antelope Range, three miles northwest of Crested Wheat Ridge; named for nearby **MOON-SHINE CREEK** (USGB 6903).

MOOR (Elko). A non-agency station with telegraph on the SP RR between Wells and Anthony (T75). The station name on the CP RR was **MOORS** and commemorated the boss of a woodchoppers' crew during the construction of the railroad (1881 Map; HHB, Nev., p. 277; M&SP, 10/30/80). **MOOR SUMMIT** is southeast of the station at the north end of the Wood Hills (NK 11–9).

MOORES STATION (Nye). An old stage station in Hot Creek Valley east of the Morey Mine; named for its proprietor (GHM, NY 3). The Shoshone name for the site was *dzicava,* "dried-juniper water," according to Julian Haynes Steward (M&M, p. 149).

MOOR HEN MEADOW (Nye). The meadow in an unnamed valley, approximately two miles east-northeast of Mouse Meadow and four and one-half miles west-northwest of Oak Spring Butte, was "named after the Moor Hen, a common visitor to the area" (USGB 6302; DL 53).

MOORMANS RIDGE (White Pine). The ridge in the White Pine Range, south and east of Illipah Creek and west of Jakes Valley, is named for Captain W. M. Moorman,

who had served in the Confederate Army. He settled in White River Valley in the 1880s, later moving to Illipah where he bought the Dutch Jake Ranch and raised stock (NHS, 1924, p. 390; NJ 11–3).

MOOSE CREEK (Elko). A map name for a creek flowing from the east slope of the Rubies into Ruby Valley, north of Wines Creek. The variant name *Mose Creek* commemorates "the Indian couple, Brownie and Maggie Mose, who with their family lived upon this stream" (EP, p. 59; GHM, EL 1).

MOREY (Nye). **MOREY PEAK** is at the east edge of the Hot Creek Range. It was named for the **MOREY MINING DISTRICT,** discovered in 1865 about thirty miles northeast of Tybo in the eastern foothills of the Hot Creek Range. Most of the principal mines, which included the Magnolia, Bay State, Cedar, American Eagle, Mount Airy, and Black Hawk, were worked by the Morey Mining Company (Wheeler, 1872, p. 38; VPG, p. 134; NJ 11–5). A post office named for the district was active from November 15, 1872, to April 15, 1905, at which time its operations were transferred to Eureka (FTM, p. 19).

MORGAN. A station on the former V and T RR in old Ormsby (Carson City) County at the **MORGAN MILL** (GHK, V&T, p. 31; FES, p. 208); a post office in Lander County, active from November 23, 1881, to February 2, 1885, when its operations were transferred to Kingston (FTM, p. 19); a well on one of the early trails between Tule Springs and Las Vegas in Clark County (WA); a creek rising on the western slope of the Monitor Range in Nye County and flowing generally westward into Monitor Valley, north of South Fork Mosquito Creek (NJ 11–5).

MORIAH, MOUNT (White Pine). The peak in the Snake Range in eastern White Pine County near the Utah line, was named by Latter-Day Saints for the Palestine hill on which Solomon's Temple was built (NJ 11–3; OPN, p. 74).

MORMON. Several Nevada place names commemorate the missionaries and traders of The Church of Jesus Christ of the Latter-Day Saints, founded in 1830 at Manchester, New York, by Joseph Smith, with headquarters at Salt Lake City, Utah. Their religious faith is based on the *Book of Mormon,* written on gold tablets by a fourth-century prophet *Mormon* and found and translated by Joseph Smith near Palmyra, New York, and published in 1830. The word, as well as its derivatives *Mormondon, Mormonism,* and *Mormonite,* gained currency from 1833 to 1837. The Mormons settled in Nevada in the 1850s, and the earliest settlement in the state, presently Genoa, began as a trading post on the west side of the Carson River.

It was first established by Hampden S. Beatie in 1850 and reestablished by Colonel John Reese in 1851, both Mormons from Salt Lake City. Colonel Reese recorded that the place was called **MORMON STATION.** The name of the station is included on an 1855 Map of the Mining Region of California, drawn and compiled by George H. Baker (Wheat IV, 38). See **GENOA.** Southern Nevada places named honorifically for Mormon settlers of the 1850s are in Clark and Lincoln counties. The **MORMON MOUNTAINS** lie east of the Meadow Valley Wash, west of the **EAST MORMON MOUNTAINS,** and north of **MORMON MESA. MORMON PEAK,** the highest in the range, is within the boundaries of Lincoln County. **MORMON WELL** (Clark) is an intermittent spring, located north of Yucca Forest in the valley between the Las Vegas and Sheep ranges, first filed on by Daniel Bonelli in 1896 (NJ 11–12; Vegas Quad.; WA). Mormon Well was also the early name for *Nyala,* a settlement on the west slope of the Quinn Canyon Range in Nye County (NJ 11–6; WA). **MORMON CANYON** denotes that portion of the Meadow Valley Wash between Rox and Carp in Lincoln County, and **MORMON GREEN SPRINGS** is the designation for springs located northwest of Blue Diamond in Clark County (Blue D. Quad.; WA).

MORNINGSTAR (Lyon). Formerly a town, four miles from Buckskin, and a post office, active from June 12, 1908, to November 24, 1911. The name of the town and the post office was changed to *Ludwig* (NHS, 1913, p. 214; FTM, p. 19; DM). Freeman Morningstar, who was in the region when the townsite was laid out, is commemorated (NHS, 1913, p. 214).

MORRISTOWN (Nye). The name of this post office, established August 29, 1904, was changed to *Reveille* on June 15, 1905 (FTM, p. 19).

MORTON (Elko). A short-lived post office, established August 5, 1890, and discontinued April 23, 1892, when Wells became the mail address for its patrons (FTM, p. 19).

MOSE CREEK. See **MOOSE CREEK.**

MOSES, MOUNT (Lander). A mountain peak in the south end of the Fish Creek Mountains, west of Cottonwood Creek; named for the son of Amram and Jochebed, in the Old Testament, who led the Israelites out of Egypt (NK 11–11).

MOSQUITO (Washoe). A valley in the northwestern portion of the county, north of Long Valley and west of Mud Lake, takes its name from **MOSQUITO LAKE** in the valley (NK 11–7). The lake might have been named by early emigrants who encountered the dipterous insect there. Dan De Quille described such a mosquito-infested lake, near which he camped in 1861, in *Washoe Rambles.* "At night the mosquitos came off from the lake and bordering marshes, in clouds, causing us to pass a most restless night— even fire and smoke would not cause them to cease their persecution" (REL, p. 42).

MOSS SPRING (Clark). The spring so named and located on the south side of Mount Newberry apparently commemorates Johnny Moss, a prospector of the early days in southern Nevada (WA).

MOTE (Humboldt). A non-agency station, milepost 466.3 between Piute and Valmy on the Winnemucca Subdivision of the SP RR (T75).

MOTT (Douglas). A canyon heading in the Carson Range southeast of East Peak, and extending into Carson Valley (Tahoe Map). The name honors the Mott family, who arrived in Carson Valley on July 14, 1851. Hiram Mott and his son Israel founded **MOTTSVILLE** about six miles south of Genoa. The post office named **MOTTS RANCH,** earlier *Jobs Store,* was established on October 21, 1858, and discontinued February 1, 1860. In 1854, Eliza Ann, the wife of Israel Mott and the first white woman settler, opened the first school of Carson County, Utah Territory, in her kitchen (NHS, 1913, p. 195; HHB, Nev., pp. 254–55; SPD, pp. 227–28; Dangberg, CV, p. 8; SHM 121). The settlement name *Mottsville* appears on Dr. Henry De Groot's 1860 map of the Washoe Mines (Wheat IV, 189).

MOUND HOUSE (Lyon). Formerly a milling and railroad center six miles southwest of Dayton; the junction of the C and C RR (built from Mound House to Hawthorne and on to Keeler, in California, in the early 1880s) and the V and T RR (MA, p. 502; 1881 Map). The post office so named was established three times from January 29, 1877, to July 20, 1907, and was discontinued on July 15, 1929, when its operations were transferred to Carson City (FTM, p. 19). Formerly a tollhouse on the road owned by Mackay and Fair, the place had been known as *Mound Station,* situated between Carson City and Dayton and named for the mounds of gypsite abounding in the area (NHS, 1913, p. 207; VPG).

MOUND SPRINGS. The name for a former station in Lander County between Artesian Well and Hot Springs on the NC RR. The station, named for springs in the area, was served by Galena post office (1881 Map; TF, p. 20). Springs in Elko County, named *Whitton Springs* by Frémont on November 1, 1845, to honor one of his men (VPG, JGS, I, p. 89; MA, p. 284; GHM, EL 5). The name *Mound Spring* appears on an 1849 Map of the Emigrant Road from Independence, Missouri, to San Francisco, California, prepared by T. H. Jefferson (Wheat III, 94).

MOUND VALLEY (Elko). The valley, north of Huntington Valley and west of the Ruby Mountains, took its name from low hills in the area which resemble ruined pyramids. Early settlers were served by Dry Creek post office (1881 Map; TF, p. 20; Nev. Guide, p. 162; NK 11–12).

MOUNTAIN. The name, chosen because of the natural setting, is found in combination with Chief, City, House, Lake, Springs, View, and Wells. **MOUNTAIN CHIEF** (Nye). An early mining district on the eastern slope of the Toquima Range, named for the **MOUN-TAIN CHIEF MINE,** located north of early Northumberland Mill (Wheeler, 1872, p. 41; 1871 Map). **MOUNTAIN CITY** (Elko). A town settled in the 1860s at the southeast corner of the Duck Valley (Western Shoshone) Indian Reservation, on the Owyhee River, about thirty miles west of Jarbidge (1881 Map; NK 11–9; M&S, p. 130). Features named for the town are **MOUNTAIN CITY MINING DISTRICT** in the northwest portion of the Bull Run Mountains, ninety miles north of Elko, whose principal mines are the Resurrection, Protection, Nelson, and Old Mountain City; and **MOUNTAIN CITY CAMPGROUND,** above Mountain City on the Owyhee River (SFH, p. 8; VPG, p. 44; HP, p. 72; Park Map). **MOUNTAIN CITY** post office was established February 21, 1870 (FTM, p. 19). **MOUNTAIN HOUSE** (Douglas). A mining district and, formerly, a mining camp in the Pine Nut Range, southeast of Minden on the California border. Before the establishment of Holbrook (q.v.) post office, the mining camp was served by Walker River post office (HHB, Nev., pp. 254–55; VPG, p. 34; TF, p. 20). **MOUNTAIN OF HIEROGLYPHICS** (Lyon). A mountain of solid rock formation, covered with petroglyphs, on the west end of the Dead Camel Mountains and about three miles southeast of Silver Springs (NHS, 1913, p. 210; VPG). **MOUNTAIN LAKE.** See **TAHOE. MOUN-TAIN SPRINGS.** A Pony Express station in White Pine County, twenty-five miles east of Ruby Station (Nev., I, 1961, p. 9; 1867 Map); a settlement in the western part of early Humboldt County, served by Sheepshead post office (HHB, Nev., p. 264; 1881 Map; TF, p. 20); a settlement in the Spring Mountains of Clark County, named for springs that were formerly a campsite on the Old Spanish Trail; and nearby **MOUNTAIN SPRINGS PASS.** The name *Mountain Springs* appears on an 1855 map of a land route from Salt Lake City to San Francisco, prepared by Captain Rufus Ingalls (Wheat IV, 29). The campsite was also known to early travelers as *Piute Springs* (LRH, II, p. 92; WA; Vegas Quad.; SHM 32). **MOUNTAIN VIEW** (Mineral). A mining camp, consisting of a large and airy townsite laid out in May,

1906, near Buckskin; a mining district, also called *Granite,* at the north end of the Wassuk Range, eight miles northwest of Schurz. A post office so named was active from April 28, 1908, to November 30, 1908, when its operations were transferred to Granite (VPG, p. 114; DM; FTM, p. 19). **MOUNTAIN WELLS** (Churchill). A canyon and a silver mining district, also known as *La Plata,* discovered in 1862 on the east slope of the Stillwater Range, twelve miles north of Frenchman and thirty miles east of Fallon; a station on the Overland Mail route midway between Fairview and Stillwater stations; named for **MOUNTAIN WELL,** a spring in the Stillwater Range, about ten miles southeast of Stillwater, a watering place on the old road to Stillwater (VPG, p. 16; OPN, p. 12; 1867 Map; USGB 5904; GHM, CH 2).

MOUNT AIR(E)Y STATION (Lander). A stop on the Pony Express and on the Overland Mail about midway between Reese River and Castle Rock stations; named for **MOUNT AIRY** (1867 Map; Jackson Map; JGS, I, p. 136). See **AIRY, MOUNT.**

MOUNT MONTGOMERY (Mineral). The settlement on U.S. 6, seventeen miles east of the California line, was a station on the former C and C RR (NJ 11–7). A mining district so named, but earlier called *Montgomery* (Wheeler 1871 Map), was discovered in 1864 at the north end of the White Mountains, near the Esmeralda County boundary (VPG, p. 111; OPN, p. 50; SM, 1867, pp. 30–37). **MOUNT MONTGOMERY** post office was established September 22, 1916, and discontinued September 30, 1945, when Tonopah became the mail address for its patrons (FTM, p. 20).

MOUSE MEADOW (Nye). The meadow in an unnamed valley south of the Belted Range and north-northeast of Gold Meadows, was named for the field mice and rodents commonly seen there (USGB 6302; DL 53).

MOUSES TANK PICNIC AREA (Clark). A recreation area in the Valley of Fire; named for a natural open tank, hollowed out by the force of water in soft sandstone. The rocks above the tank once afforded a hiding place for *Mouse,* a Southern Paiute. In 1896, Mouse while drunk shot up some Indians at the Daniel Bonelli ranch. He evaded pursuers for two years. Fellow tribesmen had so named him because of his shy and silent movements and his habit of hiding out (WA; JGS, I, p. 621; Cronkhite; GHM, CL 2).

MUD. The name usually signifies, in Nevada, marshy tracts of land and stagnant pools, in general the conditions of drying streams and lakes. **MUD FLAT** (Washoe) is a remnant of the lake bed of ancient Lake Lahontan, between the Lake Range and the Selenite Range, south of Gerlach (NK 11–10). **MUD LAKE** designates a small lake in northern

Washoe County, east of Mosquito Lake and west of Bald Mountain, and a lake in northwest Humboldt County (GHM, WA 3; HU 3). **MUD MEADOW CREEK** (Humboldt), also known as *Soldier Meadows Creek*, rises on the west slope of the Black Rock Range and flows southwestward to Soldier Meadows, then southward to the Black Rock Desert (1881 Map; NK 11–7). **MUD MEADOWS** was the name of a short-lived post office in former Roop County, established February 12, 1867, and discontinued August 6, 1867 (FTM, p. 20). **MUD SPRING** denotes a spring northeast of Elgin, in Lincoln County; a spring west of Blue Diamond, in Clark County; and a spring on the northern slopes of the Sylvania Mountains, about one mile northeast of the Nevada-California boundary and twelve miles west-southwest of Lida, in Esmeralda County (WA; Blue D. Quad.; USGB 6002). **MUD SPRINGS.** The name for a station on the former LV and T RR between Original and Petersgold, nine miles west of Rhyolite, in Nye County; for a summit between the Amargosa Desert and Sarcobatus Flat, also in Nye County and formerly used by the LV and T RR; for springs on the east slope of the Stillwater Range, at the mouth of Willow Canyon and south of Job Canyon, about thirty-four miles east-northeast of Fallon (Churchill County); for a canyon, draining westward into the Meadow Valley Wash, at the east end of Stine Siding, in Lincoln County; for a canyon north of Aurora, in Mineral County; for a wash at the northwest end of the Snake Range, in White Pine County; for a creek and a former settlement north of Elko, near Bull Run Basin, in Elko County; and for two mining districts, one located in 1910 by Fred Martin, Sam Bachman and Garfield Bardamus forty miles west-southwest of Currie, in Elko County, and the other located twenty miles southeast of Battle Mountain (Lander), near **MUD SPRING GULCH,** which heads on the east slope of the Shoshone Range and trends generally southeastward into Crescent Valley (WA; Blue D. Quad.; DM; USGB 5904; NJ 11–1; SG Maps 1, 4, 10, 11; VPG, pp. 45, 87; SFH, p. 9). **MUD WASH** (Clark) drains westward from Bitter Ridge into the Overton Arm of Lake Mead (NJ 11–12).

MUDDY (Clark). The southern Nevada name group derives from the **MUDDY RIVER,** which heads in an area of springs, called Warm Springs and flows to Lake Mead, southeast of Overton (USGB 6001; NJ 11–12). The name probably was applied by the Jedediah S. Smith party, whom Harrison G. Rogers, clerk for Smith, locates on "Muddy River" on October 1, 1826 (JGS, I, p. 28). According to pioneers, the name was an Indian word which sounded like "muddy" but meant "fertile soil" (OPN, p. 44). Edward

Sapir determined that the word was Southern Paiute *mo-ri,* "bean." Later investigations have yielded terms meaning "deceitful water, the river looks shallow, but is not" and "foolish water, mo-ha-pa." A Southern Numic vocabulary obtained by John Wesley Powell contains the geographical term *Mo-op* for the Muddy River (Fowler, pp. 133–34, 154). See **MOAPA.** Spanish names for the river were known to early emigrants. *Rio de los Angeles,* mentioned in Lewis Granger's letter of April 8, 1850, appears as *River of the Angels* in Shearer's *Journal* of 1849. Heap knew the Muddy as *Rio Atascoso* and described it. "Rio Atascoso is a narrow stream, but in many places quite deep; its water is clear and it derives its name from the slimy and miry nature of its banks and bed" (LRH, XV, pp. 37, 61, VII, p. 238). The **MUDDY MOUNTAINS** lie northwest of the Black Mountains, west of the Overton Arm of Lake Mead, and south of the **NORTH MUDDY MOUNTAINS.** The highest peak in the Muddy Mountains is designated **MUDDY,** as is a spring northwest of Moapa and about a mile north of Warm Springs. The fertile Moapa Valley is known locally as **MUDDY VALLEY,** separated into Upper and Lower valleys by The Narrows, and was first settled by the Mormons in 1855, with the arrival of the members of the **MUDDY MISSION.** Early towns established by the Mormons in the valley were Saint Joseph, Mill Point, West Point, and Saint Thomas, abandoned in 1871 by all except Daniel Bonelli and his family. With the return of the Mormons in 1880, the old towns were reestablished and others were founded (WA; NJ 11–12). **MUDDY MOUNTAINS MINING DISTRICT,** a copper-silver district, named for the range, is also known as *Saint Thomas* and *Logan* and is located twenty-six miles southeast of Moapa (VPG, p. 28).

MUMMY MOUNTAIN (Clark). The mountain about two miles northeast of Charleston Peak and southwest of Deer Creek in the Spring Mountains is named for its resemblance to an Egyptian mummy in profile, when viewed from the northwest (WA).

MUNCY (White Pine). A town and early post office on **MUNCY CREEK,** which rises on the east slope of the Schell Creek Range and flows eastward into Spring Valley (OR, 1883; ECN Map; NJ 11–3). The settlement, also known as *Muncy Creek,* gave promise of being a great copper camp in the late 1870s (NHS, 1924, p. 303). **MUNCY CREEK MINING DISTRICT,** also called *Aurum,* is in the northern part of the Schell Creek Range, eighteen miles southeast of Cherry Creek (VPG, p. 176).

MUNEY (White Pine). The post office so named probably served the Muncy Creek district. It was established on July 24, 1882, with operations being transferred to Aurum on March 21, 1898, and reestablished on February 20, 1909, to operate until April 22, 1911, when McGill became the mail address for its patrons (FTM, p. 20).

MURPHY(S). An early station in Churchill County, nine miles from the Humboldt Slough and one mile from the foot of Humboldt Lake; named for its proprietor (HHB, Nev., pp. 261–62; NHS, 1913, p. 180; TF, p. 20; 1881 Map). The surname also designates a canyon west of Big Creek in the Toiyabe Range, in Lander County; a creek tributary to Secret Creek southeast of Halleck (Elko), named for John F. Murphy, a rancher who had served at old Fort Halleck; a wash southeast of Minerva (White Pine) in the Snake Range; a wash near Gold Creek (Elko), named for the Dan Murphy Ranch (EP, p. 60; GHM, LA 1, WP 1; SG Map 10).

MURRY (White Pine). The creek in Steptoe Valley, on which Ely is situated, was named by Captain Simpson. "The road leaves this gate (Hercules) to the left about 0.5 miles, and 1.7 miles further down Spring Canon brings us to Steptoe Valley, which we follow on its western side for four miles in a southeasterly direction, and encamp on a noble creek, which I call after Lieut. Alexander Murry, the energetic officer in command of the escort of my party" (JHS, pp. 117–18). **MURRY CREEK** was the early name for Ely (q.v.). A canyon southwest of Ely in the Egan Range was called, also by Simpson, "Murry's Canon, after Lieut. Alexander Murry, the commanding officer of the escort" (JHS, p. 63). The canyon name is no longer possessive (NJ 11–3). **MURRY SUMMIT** on U.S. 6 southwest of Ely, is a shift name.

MUSTANG. Features named for a type of wild horse first introduced by the Spanish in the American West include **MUSTANG BUTTE** and **MUSTANG DRAW**, a mountain and a canyon in Elko County, northeast of Mountain City near the Idaho boundary; **MUSTANG MOUNTAIN**, a peak in Esmeralda County, near the Mineral County boundary and northeast of Boundary Peak in the White Mountains; **MUSTANG SPRING**, a spring southeast of Mill City in the East Range in Pershing County, and a spring east of Shoshone in the Snake Range in White Pine County (GHM, EL 3; ES 1; PE 2; WP 1).

NACHE. A peak at the south end of the Nightingale Range, near the junction of Pershing, Churchill, and Washoe counties; a former settlement, also spelled *Nach*, southeast of Gerlach in Pershing County; named for *Naches*, a peaceable chief of the North-ern Paiutes of tall and commanding appearance. Naches, who was a brother, or "possibly classificatory brother" of Sarah Winnemucca Hopkins, was John Wesley Powell's principal Northern Paiute informant in 1873 (MA, p. 186; Fowler, p. 16). *Natches* is a graphic variant of the chief's name (SPD, p. 129), and the designation of a former gold camp in Barber Canyon in the East Range of Pershing County. Natchez Pass, south of Barber Canyon, took its name from the early camp, which was so named in honor of the Northern Paiute chief (NK 11–11; DM). *Natchez* (Elko) denoted an early station on the Salt Lake Division of the SP RR between Deeth and Halleck. The station was served by Deeth post office (T1SL; 1881 Map; TF, p. 20).

NAGOMINA CREEK. See **BREAKNECK CREEK.**

NAPIAS (Lander). The name of the shortlived post office, established January 13, 1870, and discontinued January 27, 1870, when it was renamed *Eureka*, commemorates an Indian, Napias Jim. Frank Drake and Ed Applegarth were led to a rich ore body by an Indian who had brought them rock samples, remarking "Mebbe so napias" (Powell lists Gosiute *Nap-i-as*, "Money, paper"). The claim was filed as the South Aurora, for its position below the North Aurora; however, both mines were incorporated later as the Eberhardt and Aurora Mining Company, Limited, White Pine County (NHS, 1924, pp. 282–84; FTM, p. 20; Fowler, p. 253).

NARINO HONGUY HILL (Elko). A hill on the north side of the Owyhee River, in the Duck Valley Indian Reservation, about three miles northwest of Mountain City; said to be a Shoshone Indian name meaning "back of a saddle," which is descriptive of its shape (USGB, DL 29; Decision Deferred). By decision of the United States Board on Geographic Names, *Reservation Hill* remains the official designation, not *Narino Honguy*, the Shoshone name used by people living on the reservation (USGB 6103). Powell lists a noun *Nar'-i-no-tsi*, "Saddle," in the Shoshone vocabulary he gathered in 1873 (Fowler, p. 266).

NARROWS (Clark). A railroad siding on the St. Thomas Branch of the UP RR; named for its position at **THE NARROWS** of the Muddy River (NJ 11–12; WA).

NASHVILLE (Washoe). The former townsite of the 1906 promotional era was named for Charles H. Nash who located the Nash Mine. The *Reno Evening Gazette* of July 23, 1906, noted that Nashville was on Freds Mountain northwest of Reno, in a mining district denoted *Esmeralda*, but earlier *Dogskin* (DM; NJ 11–1).

NATCHEZ. See **NACHE.**

NATIONAL (Humboldt). A mining district

and former mining camp on the west slope of the Santa Rosa Range, northwest of Buckskin Mountain, about seventy-four miles north of Winnemucca. J. L. Workman, who discovered the district in 1907, named it for his *National* automobile. He also named other geographic features for automobile parts, for example, *Radiator Hill* (VPG; NK 11–8). The National vein, uncovered in 1909 by the Stall brothers, yielded almost pure electrum, "an alloy composed of about half-and-half gold and silver," which averaged about $30,000 per ton (NM, p. 220). **NATIONAL** post office was active from August 7, 1908, to December 31, 1919, when its operations were transferred to McDermitt (FTM, p. 20).

NATIONAL CITY. See **BRISTOL CITY.**

NAYANTOVOY CREEK (Elko). The Shoshone Indian name for a creek heading within the Duck Valley (Western Shoshone) Indian Reservation, reported to mean "standing Indian" (USGB, DL 29; Decision Deferred), officially designated *Indian Creek* (q.v.) (USGB 6103).

NELLIS AIR FORCE BASE (Clark). The base, nine miles north of Las Vegas at the site of former *McCarran Field*, was named in 1950 in honor of Lieutenant William H. Nellis of Las Vegas, who was killed over Germany in the second World War (NJ 11–12; WA).

NELSON. A settlement in Clark County on State Route 60 in Eldorado Canyon, twenty-nine miles south of Boulder City. The camp was platted in March, 1905, and named for Charles Nelson, a prospector who was murdered at his mine in May, 1897, by an Indian named Ahvote. Nelson, a business center for the Eldorado Mining District, was served by a post office, established June 17, 1905, discontinued February 15, 1929, reestablished January 27, 1938, and again discontinued on July 25, 1944, when Searchlight became the mail address for its patrons (NI 11–3; OPN, p. 17; WA; FTM, p. 20). **NELSON CREEK** (Elko). A creek rising in the Currie Hills and flowing generally northeastward into Steptoe Valley (NK 11–12; GHM, EL 5); a tributary of Willow Creek, southwest of Tuscarora, "named for Thomas Nelson of Stone House who owned large bands of sheep that ranged in the area" in the 1880s (EP, p. 60; GHM, EL 2).

NELSONS. See **DESERT.**

NENZEL HILL (Pershing). **NENZEL HILL,** at the head of Rochester Canyon, was named for Joseph F. Nenzel, a prospector and mine owner in the Rochester Mining District (NK 11–10). Nenzel, a native of La Crosse, Wisconsin, came to Limerick Canyon, in 1907, from the Black Hills of South Dakota. On June 25, 1912, he located his monuments at Rochester, and the boom began seven months

later. **NENZEL** was the name given to *Oreana* for a short time in 1913 because freight on the SP RR was being missent to Oceano, California (SPD, pp. 901, 920; DM; OPN, p. 62).

NEPAC (Clark). An alternate name for *Mead Lake Station* on the UP RR; the name of a short-lived post office, earlier called *Saint Thomas,* established June 16, 1938, and discontinued October 15, 1939, when the name was changed to *Mead Lake* (Freese, Map 1; NJ 11–12; WA; FTM, p. 20).

NEVADA. On August 8, 1857, James M. Crane was selected to represent the people of the proposed new territory at the Federal capital (AJM, p. 16). The bill for the organization of *Sierra Nevada Territory* was presented to the Committee on Territories early in 1858 by Delegate Crane, but the committee shortened the name to *Nevada,* a Spanish word meaning "snow-covered" (OPN, p. 2; JHS, p. 91; GRS, p. 304). The region had been known generally as the *Eastern Slope,* or *Washoe.* California newspapers referred to the new government as *Carson Territory,* or *The Territory of Sierra* (SPD, p. 203, n. 7). The Enabling Act of March 21, 1864, began "To enable the People of Nevada . . ." During the Constitutional Convention, which started on July 4, 1864, and lasted until midnight on July 27, delegates suggested a number of names for the state: *Humboldt, Washoe, Esmeralda, Sierra Plata, Oro Plata,* and *Bullion.* When a decision was reached, however, the Preamble began "We, the people of the State of Nevada, . . ." (AJM, pp. 25–26; GRS, p. 304).

NEVADA CITY (Churchill). A cooperative colony founded in 1916 by the Nevada Colony Corporation (organized April 28, 1916) principally through the efforts of socialist promoter C. V. Eggleston. Although the property of the corporation was scattered throughout the county, the acreage officially designated *Nevada City* was on the J. Scott Harmon ranch four miles east of Fallon. "Almost three dozen houses were constructed over the next two years and the community assumed the name of Nevada City" (WSS, p. ix). The colony went into receivership on May 1, 1919, and Nevada City was soon deserted (WSS, pp. xi, 16, 108, 113). **NEVADA CITY** (Lyon). See **DAYTON.**

NEVADA HILL. The peak so named is northwest of Topaz Junction in Douglas County (GHM, DO 1). **NEVADAHILLS** (Churchill). The order to establish **NEVADAHILLS** post office dated October 9, 1907, was rescinded March 19, 1908, perhaps before operations commenced (FTM, p. 20). The name derived from the **NEVADA HILLS MINE** on the western slope of Fairview Peak. See **FAIR.**

NEVADA NATIONAL FOREST. See **DIXIE.**

NEVADA PROVING GROUND (Nye). The area in the south-central portion of the county, including Frenchman Flat, Yucca Flat, and the old Wahmonie townsite, used for testing atomic weapons and also called the *Nevada Test Site* (NJ 11–12; WA).

NEVADA STATION (Lyon). An Overland Stage station, also on the line of the Pony Express, the stop between Bisbys and Desert Wells; named by the Overland Stage Company for the State of Nevada (JGS, I, p. 136; NHS, 1913, p. 218; Jackson Map).

NEVIN (Eureka). An early settlement west of Tonkin on State Route 21 (GHM, EU 1). An order to establish **NEVINS** post office, dated October 31, 1906, was rescinded May 18, 1907 (FTM, p. 20).

NEWARK (White Pine). **NEWARK VALLEY,** south of Huntington Valley and east of the Diamond Range, was one of the first settled areas in the county. **NEWARK LAKE** is a large dry lake bed in the valley. **NEWARK CAVE,** on the east side of the valley, "is a small, wave-cut cavern, on the uppermost Pleistocene lake terrace of Newark Lake" (M&M, pp. 212–13). **NEWARK MINING DISTRICT,** also known as *Strawberry,* was discovered by Stephen and John Beard in 1866 on the east slope of the Diamond Range, twenty-nine miles northeast of Eureka. A settlement which grew up around **NEWARK MILL** was about fifteen miles southeast of Eureka on Pancake Mountain and was served by Eureka post office. **NEWARK SUMMIT** (Eureka, White Pine) is a pass in the Diamond Mountains, about fifty-five miles west-northwest of Ely (NJ 11–3; Census, 1870, OPN, p. 74; NM; VPG, p. 180; Wheeler 1871 Map; TF, p. 20).

NEWBERRY MOUNTAINS (Clark). A mountain range on the west side of the Colorado River, in the southern tip of Nevada; named for Dr. Newberry, a geologist with the Ives expedition of 1858. The name earlier applied to a group of peaks in the north end of the Dead Mountains, given wide berth by the Indians who called them *Spirit Mountains* and believed them to be the dwelling places of departed chieftains (NI 11–3; USGB 6002; WA; Wheat IV, 98; OPN, p. 17; Wheeler 1871 Map). The southern part of the range, within the California boundary, is still named Dead Mountains.

NEW BOSTON (Esmeralda). An early settlement in old Esmeralda County, mentioned by Bancroft (HHB, Nev., p. 261); its post office active from April 22, 1879, to June 5, 1879 (FTM, p. 20); named by settlers for their native city, Boston, Massachusetts. After 1879 Belleville post office served the community (TF, p. 20).

NEW JERUSALEM (Lyon). The ranch at the settlement three miles east of Dayton, according to report, formerly was owned by an atheist. New Jerusalem was a term of derision for the ranch and the surrounding area, and was mentioned as a place on the route taken by Dan De Quille, in 1861, in *Washoe Rambles* (REL, pp. 129, 133; NHS, 1913, p. 216).

NEWLAND (Lincoln). An early settlement and post office (February 1, 1896–May 15, 1912), established between Pioche and Stateline, at Eagle Valley. John J. Bristow, who was in charge of establishing the mail route, thought the name *Eagle Valley* was too long for the post office. He suggested *Newlands* in honor of Francis Griffith Newlands who framed the Newlands Reclamation Act, passed in 1902, and who was United States Senator from Nevada from 1909 to 1915 (JGS, I, p. 363; M&S, p. 305; NHS, 1924, p. 474; FTM, p. 20).

NEW MOUNTAINS (Clark). A former, local name for the Sheep Range northwest of Las Vegas; applied by J. F. Spurr in 1903 (WA).

NEW PASS. The **NEW PASS RANGE** in Churchill and Lander counties is separated, on the north, from the Clan Alpine Mountains by a pass and, on the south from the Desatoya Mountains by **NEW PASS** (NJ 11–2). The name, which is shown on a map of the Fortieth Parallel Survey, apparently was given by a pioneer who felt that he had discovered a new pass through the mountains. This road was a principal one across central Nevada until the late 1920s (VPG). **NEW PASS MINING DISTRICT,** located prior to 1866 (SM, 1867, p. 28) and named for the mountain range, is twenty-seven miles west of Austin at the Churchill County line (VPG, p. 87). A post office designated **NEWPASS** (having been changed from *Franklin*) was established in Lander County on May 2, 1900, and discontinued on February 28, 1903, when its operations were transferred to Austin (USGB 5904; FTM, p. 20).

NEW RIVER (Churchill). The locality and canal in Churchill County are named for the Carson River.

New River and Old River were caused by the overflowing of Carson River in January, 1862. Before this the waters of the Carson emptied into the Upper Sink and passed through Carson and Stillwater Sloughs into the Lower Sink. The dry river bed through which Old River now flows could be seen plainly in 1861, but after this flood it was no more. The same flood also cut the channel where New River now runs past the west side of the town of Stillwater. (NHS, 1913, p. 177)

NEW TRUCKEE (Washoe). A former mining district, located in May, 1869, about six miles from Hot Springs, an early station on the CP RR a few miles east of Wadsworth; named for the Truckee River (q.v.) (DM).

NEW VIRGINIA MOUNTAINS (Churchill). Mountains in the western portion of the county; presumably named either because of association with the Virginia Mountains of southern Washoe County, or with reference to the state of Virginia (NHS, 1913, p. 185).

NEW YEAR LAKE (Washoe). The lake in the summit area of the Hays Canyon Range, in northwestern Washoe County near the California boundary, first appears, unnamed, on Frémont's Map of 1845. An unknown name-giver apparently first sighted it on January 1 (NK 11–7; VPG).

NEW YORK. A canyon in the Toiyabe Range between San Francisco Canyon and Austin, in Lander County; a canyon heading on the west slope of the Toiyabe Range between Marysville and Mohawk canyons, in Nye County; a former mining district on the western slope of the south end of the Spring Mountains, in Clark County (Dir. 1971; Wheeler, 1872, p. 53); named for the native state of the name-givers.

NICKEL (Churchill). Formerly a community on the west side of the Humboldt Salt Marsh, forty-five miles southeast of Lovelock; named for the nickel mines near the head of Cottonwood Creek (NHS, 1913, p. 175). Nick*le* post office, except for two interruptions, was active from March 21, 1890, to March 20, 1906 (FTM, p. 20).

NIGHTINGALE. The **NIGHTINGALE MOUNTAINS** extend from southwest Pershing County across the northern boundary of Washoe County. The name is a product of folk etymology, having been corrupted from *Nightengill*, to *Nightengale*, to the present designation (NHS, 1913, p. 182; NK 11–10; GHM, PE 1; WA 3). The range was named in honor of Alanson W. Nightengill, who was Captain of Company C, Truckee Rangers, of the Washoe Regiment in the 1860 Indian war, and also the first State Controller of Nevada (SPD, p. 72; HNS, pp. 100–102). A mining district and camp so named, active in the late 1920s, are on the east slope of the Nightingale Mountains in Pershing County (GHM, PE 1).

NINEMILE. NINEMILE PEAK, situated on the Nye-Eureka county line in the Antelope Range, and also known as *Sharp Peak,* takes its name from **NINEMILE CANYON** which extends from the north side of the peak in Eureka County into Antelope Valley (NJ 11–2). **NINE MILE HOUSE** (Esmeralda) was an early station north of Aurora, served by Elbow post office (1881 Map, TF, p. 20).

NIVLOC (Esmeralda). A mine discovered in 1907 on the east slope of the Silver Peak Range, southwest of the town of Silver Peak, by Tom Fisherman, a Shoshone Indian; named for the mine owner, Colvin, with the letters of his name inverted (NJ 11–8; DM). The post office was established as Nivloc*k* on October 11, 1940, and discontinued on November 15, 1943, when Silver Peak became the mail address for its patrons (FTM, p. 20).

NIXON (Washoe). A town and post office established August 22, 1912, formerly the site of an Indian village described by Frémont as "a collection of straw huts" (JHS, Report, p. 218) when he camped there on January 15, 1844. The settlement, center of the Pyramid Lake Indian Reservation, was named for George Stuart Nixon, United States Senator from Nevada from 1905 to 1911. Nixon came to Nevada from Placer County, California, and worked as a telegrapher at Brown's Station and at Humboldt House. During the Tonopah-Goldfield mining excitement, he rose to great fortune and political eminence (JGS, II, p. 111).

NOLAN (Mineral). A non-agency station east of Walker Lake on the Mina Branch of the SP RR, milepost 369.3, between Gillis and Thorne (T75).

NORDYKE (Lyon). The early settlement at the edge of Mason Valley, eighteen miles from Wabuska, was the site of a flour mill and a quartz mill erected by the Wilson brothers. They named the place for a Mr. Nordyke who installed Nordyke and Marmon machinery in the flour mill (NHS, 1913, p. 214). **NORDYKE** post office was active from June 13, 1892, to January 15, 1914, when its operations were transferred to Mason (FTM, p. 20). **NORDYKE PASS** is south of Delphi (GHM, LY 2).

NORTH. The compass-point name denotes a peak in Clark County, in the extreme southwest corner near the California boundary, north of Middle Peak; a creek in the Schell Creek Range, northwest of Doutre in White Pine County; and a peak at the north end of Battle Mountain in Humboldt County (OPN, p. 17; SG Map 9; NK 11–11). Additional peaks and mountain ranges named for their positions relative to a similar feature include **NORTH SCHELL PEAK,** north of South Schell Peak in the Schell Creek Range; **NORTH SHOSHONE PEAK,** north of South Shoshone Peak in the Shoshone Mountains; **NORTH MUDDY MOUNTAINS,** a mountain range north of the Muddy Mountains; and **NORTH PAHROC RANGE,** the north part of the Pahroc Range, separated from South Pahroc Range by Pahroc Summit pass (USGB 6001; NJ 11–3; NJ 11–2; NJ 11–12). Among the hydrographic features are **NORTH FURLONG CREEK,** a north tributary of Furlong Creek, on the west slope of the Ruby Mountains (NK 11–12), and **NORTH TWIN RIVER,** north of South Twin River, in the Toiyabe Range (NJ 11–5). The latter also denotes a mining district on the eastern flank of the Toiyabe Range, named for the river. The **NORTH OPHIR**

MINE swindle on the Comstock was a fraud perpetrated during Mark Twain's stay at Virginia City. The mine, said to be an extension of the original Ophir and to be yielding pure silver, was selling for sixty-five dollars a foot before it was discovered that the ground had been "salted" with half-dollar coins (SLC, II, p. 22).

NORTHAM (Churchill). The post office so named was established October 28, 1908, and discontinued October 15, 1928, when Fallon became the mail address for its patrons (FTM, p. 20).

NORTH FORK (Elko). The settlement and former post office (January 17, 1889–June 30, 1944) were named for the North Fork Humboldt River (Guide Map; FTM, p. 20).

NORTH LAS VEGAS (Clark). The city, adjoining Las Vegas on the northeast, was founded by Thomas Williams in 1919 and earlier denoted *Vegas Verdes,* the Spanish name for "green meadows." Vegas Verd*i* post office, established July 23, 1932, became NORTH LAS VEGAS on October 1, 1932, operations being discontinued on February 15, 1951, but reestablished on September 1, 1957 (NJ 11–12; WA; FTM, p. 20).

NORTHS RANCH (Humboldt). An early settlement and post office named for Orlando North, postmaster (OR, 1899; Census, 1900). Earlier named *Haas,* the post office was established as Norths Ranch November 5, 1887, and discontinued February 28, 1911, when its operations were transferred to Golconda (FTM, p. 20).

NORTHUMBERLAND (Nye). The name, commemorative of an English county north of the Humber River and near the Scottish border, denotes a cave sixty miles southeast of Austin, not fully explored but known to be of considerable size (M&S, p. 19; Nev. Guide, p. 9); a former mill and mining district, located in 1866 in the north end of the Toquima Range, about thirty-eight miles southeast of Austin. A short-lived post office so denoted served the district from February 24, 1885, to July 16, 1886 (VPG, p. 135; SM, 1867, pp. 56–66; FTM, p. 20; NM).

NUMANA (Washoe). A non-agency station, south of Pyramid Lake on the Wadsworth Subdivision of the SP RR between Dodge and Heslip, in the Pyramid Lake Indian Reservation; named for Numana, a Northern Paiute chief. Numana was also called Captain Dave (MA, p. 144). In his list of Northern Paiute chiefs, John Wesley Powell places Captain Num*u*na with the *Ku yu-i-di ka* ("Black sucker eaters") at Wadsworth on the Truckee (Fowler, p. 230). According to Chief Harry Winnemucca of the present-day reservation, Numana ("father"), who was chief after Numaga, died in July, 1919 (Hermann, pp. 159, 165).

NUT PINE CANYON (Nye). A creek rising on the east slope of the Shoshone Mountains south of Barrett Canyon, and flowing generally southeastward to the Reese River; named for the characteristic nut-pine tree (*Pinus edulis, Pinus monophylla*) (SG Map 5).

NYALA (Nye). The settlement (presently Sharp Ranch) at the west edge of the Quinn Canyon Range and about ninety miles southwest of Ely was known earlier as *Mormon Well.* NYALA post office, except for a brief interval, was active from February 5, 1914, to January 15, 1936, when its operations were transferred to Currant (NJ 11–6; WA; FTM, p. 20). The name appears to be a derivative of Nye, the name of the county in which it is located.

NYE, CAMP (Washoe). The former military camp was established in June, 1862, in Washoe Valley, five miles north of Carson City. The camp was abandoned in late 1865, having operated during the Civil War as a base and depot for volunteers serving in Nevada. The name was given to commemorate James W. Nye, Governor of Nevada Territory from 1861 to 1864 (Ruhlen).

NYE COUNTY. Nye County, with 18,294 square miles, is the largest county in Nevada; it was organized in 1864 out of Esmeralda County. The county seat, formerly at Ione and at Belmont, was moved to Tonopah by act of May 1, 1905. James Warren Nye, Governor of Nevada Territory and a United States Senator from Nevada, is honored (HHB, Nev., p. 269; SPD, p. 960; OPN, p. 6). Mark Twain considered him to be a seasoned politician, whose "eyes could out-talk his tongue, and this was saying a good deal, for he was a very remarkable talker, both in private and on the stump" (JGS, I, pp. 146–47).

OAK. Features named for the scrub oaks growing there are found in the southern portion of the state. OAK BUTTE denotes a butte at the north edge of Yucca Flat, in Nye County. OAK CREEK is the name for a creek rising in the Sandstone Bluffs near Blue Diamond, and flowing generally eastward; for a canyon trending northward from a point near Eldorado Canyon to Lonesome Wash; and for a spring near Oak Creek which flows generally eastward from the Spring Mountains, all in Clark County (WA; Blue D. Quad.). OAK SPRINGS (Nye) designates a mining district in the Belted Range, twenty miles north of Yucca Pass at Oak Butte; named for nearby springs so denoted. OAK SPRINGS SUMMIT on U.S. 93 west of Caliente, in Lincoln County, is named for springs so named and located south of the summit (VPG, p. 135; WA; HWY Map).

OASIS. The town at the junction of U.S. 40 and State Route 30, southwest of Cobre in Elko County, took its name from the OASIS RANCH, owned by E. C. Hardy in the late 1880s (GHM, EL 5; EP, p. 61). In Nye County, OASIS denotes a peak north of Beatty, so named because its green appearance is in contrast with the surrounding terrain, and a valley east of the Amargosa River northeast of Beatty (Guide Map; GHM, NY 8). OASIS VALLEY was visited by Wheeler in 1871. "The objective point was a place since called Oasis Valley, known at the time to be sensibly to our westward, and containing good grass and water. This locality was reached after three days of the most severe marching, and was found to be a narrow valley, surrounded by low rolling mesas, from which broke, in many places, a large number of springs of good, clear water, but of varying thermal conditions" (Wheeler, 1872, p. 16).

OCALA (Churchill). The name of OCALA STATION, in the Humboldt Sink (Forty Mile Desert) between Miriam and Huxley on the Salt Lake Division of the SP RR, perhaps was transferred from Ocala, Marion County, Florida, or from some other older station so named (OG, p. 1411). OCALA INDIAN CAVES lie southeast of the station for which they were named (GHM, CH 1).

OCHER RIDGE (Nye). A ridge running along the west side of the Belted Range, immediately south of Cache Cave Draw, about sixty-three miles southeast of Goldfield; named for the distinct colors of the rocks (DL 53).

ODDIE, MOUNT (Nye). A steep mountain, just north of Tonopah and near Mount Butler; named for Tasker Lowndes Oddie, twelfth governor of Nevada and former United States Senator (NJ 11–5). Oddie, with Jim Butler and W. Brougher, developed the Tonopah Mining District (VPG; FCL, p. 184). See TONOPAH.

OGDENS RIVER. See HUMBOLDT.

OLD COX STATION (Churchill). Formerly a station southeast of Carson Lake near the southern boundary of the county; presumably named for the proprietor (NHS, 1913, p. 180).

OLD RIVER STATION (Churchill). An Overland Stage station in 1862, fourteen miles southeast of Stillwater Station. Old River and New River resulted from an overflow of the Carson River in January, 1862 (1867 Map; JGS, I, p. 136). See NEW RIVER.

OLDS HOTEL (Douglas). The station, about twelve miles south of Genoa and named for its owner, Lute Olds, was distinguished for being the scene of the killing of Sam Brown, desperado and scourge of the Comstock, by Henry Van Sickle on July 6, 1861 (SPD, pp.

248–49; Dangberg, CV, p. 140). The name is shown on an 1860 Map of the Washoe Mines, prepared by Dr. Henry De Groot (Wheat IV, 189). See VAN SICKLE STATION.

OLINGHOUSE (Washoe). OLINGHOUSE CANYON, heading on the east flank of the Pah Rah Range and trending generally eastward into Dodge Flat, was named for OLINGHOUSE MINING DISTRICT in the canyon, nine miles west of Wadsworth. The area had been prospected in 1860 and first locations were made in 1864. In the late 1890s, the camp was called McClanesburg, for Brooks McClane who with F. Plane, found deposits on Green Hill in 1897, and was served by Ora post office (June 28, 1898–October 31, 1902). In March, 1905, a proposal was made to name the district Ingalls for Buck Ingalls, owner of the Buster group of mines; however White Horse became the official designation and still serves as an alternate name for the district. OLINGHOUSE post office was established October 1, 1903, and discontinued July 31, 1923, when Wadsworth became the mail address for its patrons. The name commemorates Elias Olinghouse who, after having freighted from Denver to Salt Lake City, settled at Wadsworth and ran a freight line of six-mule teams and ox teams to Belmont, before the building of the transcontinental railroad. His death in Reno on December 5, 1913, was noted by the Churchill County Eagle. In 1906–07, the Nevada Consolidated Mining Company built a railroad, since dismantled, from OLINGHOUSE JUNCTION, on the CP RR west of Wadsworth, to a point near the mining camp. The Cabin No. 2 Mine was the principal producer of the district (NJ 11–1; NM; DM; NHS, 1911, p. 87; VPG, p. 172; JGS, I, p. 447; FTM, p. 21).

OMAR. See COBRE.

OMCO (Mineral). A mining district on the northern part of the Cedar Mountains, twenty-two miles northeast of Mina and near the Nye County boundary; a former post office, established April 26, 1917, and discontinued March 15, 1921, when its operations were transferred to Simon. The manufactured name was derived from the Olympic Mines Company (VPG, p. 112; FTM, p. 21; OPN, p. 51).

O'NEIL (Elko). The former settlement, north of Wells, took its name from O'NEIL post office which, except for a brief interval, was active from August 17, 1894, to January 15, 1925, when its operations were transferred to Metropolis. The name commemorated James O'Neal, the first postmaster (FTM, p. 21; OR, 1899; Census, 1900). O'NEIL BASIN, thirteen miles west of Contact, extends north into Idaho and was "named for the O'Neils, the first settlers in this area in the early 1880's" (USGB 7104).

O'NEILS CROSSING. See **VERDI.**

ONEOTA. A locality at the junction of the Pioche-Hiko-Cherry Creek roads northwest of Hiko in Coal Valley, Lincoln County, served by a post office so named from July 19, 1909, to April 30, 1912, when its operations were transferred to Sharp (WA; FTM, p. 21); a former post office in Esmeralda County, active from June 1, 1906, to February 15, 1907, when Buena Vista became the mail address for its patrons (FTM, p. 21).

ONION VALLEY (Carson City). A valley about four miles east of Carson City; named for wild onions found growing there (NHS, 1913, pp. 191–92).

OPAL MOUNTAIN (Clark). A mountain north of Copper Mountain and southeast of Ireteba Peaks in the Eldorado Mountains; named for stones resembling the opal found there. Dr. Newberry, with the Joseph C. Ives expedition of 1858, reported finding "opalescent chalcedony" in the **OPAL MOUNTAINS,** an early alternate name for the *Eldorado Mountains* (q.v.). The name appears on the Ives map of the Rio Colorado of the West (Wheat IV, 98; NI 11–3; WA; OPN, p. 17; Wheeler 1871 Map).

OPHIR. The discovery of the outcrop of the Ophir bonanza has been linked to the original discovery of the Comstock Lode and leads to the conflicting stories regarding the identity of the original locator, or locators, and the date of the discovery and the naming. The problem remains largely unresolved.

Among the possible original discoverers were Hosea Ballou and Ethan Allen Grosch, brothers who were engaged in placer mining in Gold Canyon as early as 1853. According to an old directory of Storey County, the Grosch brothers staked a claim and named it *Pioneer*. "In 1853 Allen and Hosea Grosch reported they had discovered silver ledges. The first location was named 'Pioneer' and was made where Virginia now stands, and was the very claim afterward jumped by Comstock, and which has since given his name to the lode" (Dir. 1875, p. *iv*). When the Grosch Consolidated Gold and Silver Mining Company incorporated in 1863, filed against the Ophir and the Gould and Curry, claiming the rights of the heirs of the brothers, the company was unsuccessful in establishing its claim that the brothers made the original discovery (SPD, pp. 389–390; EL, pp. 27, 133). Although the consensus today is that the Grosch brothers did not discover the Comstock Lode, the following account asserts their prior claim and explains away other contenders for the honor of the original discovery of the lode.

The claim was afterwards enlarged by the addition of other claims, and had several owners, among whom were Penrod, Comstock, Finney (Old Virginia), Reilly and McLaughlin, and was at one time run by Penrod, Comstock & Co. The name was several times changed, till at last the name 'Ophir' was given it. This is the claim which gave the name of Comstock to the lode. . . . If the lode had been called after the first discoverer it should have been named the 'Grosch lode,' for the brothers located claims for themselves and others thereon long before the days of Virginia and Gold Hill were known. (Dir. 1875, p. *xxi*)

The brothers were unable to do anything about their discovery, for Hosea died in the fall of 1857 and Allen died the following winter (SPD, p. 385).

On October 21, 1859, the first indictment for murder on the Comstock was found against William Sides, the brother of Richard Sides for whom the Sides Claim was named, for a homicide committed at Gold Hill a short time after the discovery (HDG, CP, 12/23/76; SPD, p. 277). The victim was John Jessup, reported to have been the original locator of the Ophir. "After the death of Jessup, and while the majority of the inhabitants of Gold Hill were over in Eagle Valley with his murderer, Reilly and McLaughlin jumped his claim, and have received the credit of first discovering the Comstock" (Dir. 1875, p. *x*). In 1864, the Ophir gave John Jessup's mother $30,000 for his claim (AEH, pp. 15, n. 16, 38–40).

Peter O'Riley and Patrick McLaughlin are usually credited with having discovered the Ophir. According to Smith, in 1859 they "dug into a layer of rich black sand that proved to be a concentrate from the hidden Ophir bonanza" (GHS, pp. 2–3). Lincoln mentions Henry Comstock's connection with it. "In June, 1859, two Irish miners named Peter O'Riley and Patrick McLaughlin, were working at the head of Six-Mile Canyon to the N. of Gold Hill. In digging a water hole, they uncovered the top of the Ophir bonanza, located it, and washed gold from it. Henry Comstock happened along that evening, and by putting up a bluff secured a place for himself and a friend on the location notice" (FCL, p. 223). Dan De Quille's account of the naming of the mining camp seems to confirm the 1859 date, insofar as the application of the name *Ophir* is concerned. The camp had been spoken of and placed upon the records as *Pleasant Hill* and *Mount Pleasant Point*. In August, 1859, it was designated as *Ophir,* in September as *Ophir Diggings* (DDQ, p. 32). Patrick McLaughlin sold out, and it was his one-sixth interest that started the Hearst fortune (HDG, CP, 9/30/76; EL, p. 413). Peter O'Riley sold his interest in the Ophir in the fall of 1859 to John

O. Earl and Judge James Walsh (HDG, CP, 9/2/76).

James Finney (Fennimore), known as "Old Virginia," was a resident of Johntown in the early days, having settled in Carson Valley in 1852, and contends with the Grosch brothers for the distinction of having made the first quartz location in the area (DDQ, p. 10; SPD, p. 807; Dir. 1875, p. vi). "The Ophir claim was the first that was located as a quartz claim at any point on the Comstock Lode, though as early as February 22nd, 1858, Old Virginia made a location on a large vein lying to the westward of the Comstock. This vein is known as the Virginia lead or Virginia croppings" (DDQ, p. 53).

Henry Comstock is accused of having secured a place for himself on the Ophir either by outmaneuvering O'Riley and McLaughlin (VPG, CL, p. 23; FCL, p. 223), or by trading a horse and a bottle of whisky for "Old Virginia's" stake in the Ophir, after which trade he immediately formed the firm of Penrod, Comstock, and Company. He wanted to call the property the Comstock, but compromised on the Ophir (GDL, Saga, p. 35). See COMSTOCK and PENROD.

Ophir could be another instance of direct transfer of names from California. Professor Gudde mentions Ophir in Placer County, California, as the only survivor of five mining towns named Ophir, and further, includes information about Mount Ophir, Mariposa County, and Ophir City as the original name of Oroville (Gudde, p. 217). The name of Ophir was applied to individual mines as well as to mining camps and districts (JRB, Res., p. 154; CMA, pp. 318, 359; CSMB, pp. 408–410; OPJ, p. 66). The traditional and prevalent name *Ophir* derives from the Judaic tradition and refers to a Biblical region famous for its gold.

The Ophir has 675 feet and is located between the Mexican and the California, being made up of the original Mexican, the Burning Moscow, the North Ophir, and the South Ophir (EL, p. 177; IH; JAC, p. 1). The claim is patented (AR, No. 171). Shift names in the area, stemming from the Ophir Mine, are numerous. OPHIR CREEK is north of old Franktown and south of Slide Mountain, in Washoe County. OPHIR HILL (Storey) is near Mount Davidson. OPHIR GRADE (Storey, Washoe) extended from the Ophir Mine to the OPHIR MILL in Washoe Valley. The town of OPHIR was settled three miles below Washoe City and one mile above Franktown, when the Ophir Mining Company erected a quartz mill and reduction works at that point in 1861 (MA, pp. 643–44). OPHIR post office, earlier named *Washoe*, was established in Nevada Territory July 3, 1862, and discontinued June 19, 1871 (Nev. Terr. Map; FTM, p. 21). OPHIR

was also the name of a station on the former V and T RR (1881 Map).

OPHIR (Nye). OPHIR CREEK, rising on the east slope of the Toiyabe Range and flowing generally southeastward into Big Smoky Valley, was named for OPHIR CITY, situated in OPHIR CANYON, forty-five miles south of Austin. First ore discoveries were made in 1863. Ophir City mining camp was laid out with the discovery of the Murphy Mine, the chief mine in the area, and the building of the Murphy Mill (NM; MM; NJ 11–5).

ORA (Washoe). A short-lived post office west of Wadsworth, at the eastern foot of the Pah Rah Range, established June 28, 1898, and discontinued October 31, 1902, when its operations were transferred to Wadsworth (FTM, p. 21). See OLINGHOUSE.

ORANGE LICHEN CREEK (Nye). A stream northwest or Moores Station; "named for the orange lichens which cover the exposed welded tuff" (USGB 6903).

OREANA. A non-agency station on the SP RR between Lovelock and Rye Patch in Pershing County (T75), formerly a "mill, whistle-blowing town" on the Humboldt River. It was the site of the Montezuma Smelting Works built in 1867 for treating ores from the Arabia and Trinity districts and said to be the first smelter in the United States to ship lead to the commercial market. Other smelters in the West previously retained their output for local use (M&SP, 3/27/80; HPS, 1/29/56; SPD, p. 893; NM). Population figures for Oreana were included in the 1870 Census, and the post office, established February 26, 1867, was discontinued five times, the last being February 15, 1951, when its operations were transferred to Lovelock (FTM, p. 21). Recently the principal producer in the area was the Champion Spark Plug Mine (q.v.). See NENZEL. OREANA PEAK is in the east-central part of the Pine Nut Range, in Douglas County (OPN, p. 20). The name may be manufactured from "ore" + Greek *ana*, "greatly" or "excessively," or corrupted from Spanish *orejano* meaning "unbranded" (cattle). The word *oreana* is used in cattle country to indicate a young, unbranded calf (MM; LAM, p. 460).

ORIENTAL (Esmeralda). ORIENTAL WASH, a watercourse heading near Gold Mountain and draining westward into Death Valley, is named for the rich ORIENTAL MINE, discovered by Thomas Shaw on Gold Mountain and developed by him in 1871. According to the *Carson City News* of November 6, 1908, the discoverer of the Oriental was an Indian. ORIENTAL post office served the area from June 21, 1887, to October 15, 1900, when its services were transferred to Lida. ORIENTAL WASH

MINING DISTRICT, thirty miles southwest of Goldfield, is also called *Tokop* and *Old Gold Mountain* (NM, p. 144; DM; FTM, p. 21; VPG, p. 61).

ORIGINAL (Nye). The station on the former LV and T RR, three miles west of Rhyolite, took its name from the Original Buckskin Mine nearby (Furn. Cr. Quad.; DM).

ORMSBY, CAMP (Washoe). The temporary military camp was established on the Truckee River ten miles from Pyramid Lake after the second battle of the Indian War, fought on June 2, 1860. Captain Joseph Stewart of "The Carson River Expedition" was in command of the camp named in honor of Major William M. Ormsby, who was killed in the battle of May 12, 1860, at Pyramid Lake (Ruhlen).

ORMSBY COUNTY. The former county was created by the act of the Territorial Legislature, approved November 25, 1861, and Carson City was made the county seat. This smallest county of the state had a land area of 168 square miles, twelve of which were under water (Lake Tahoe). The name commemorated Major William M. Ormsby, a pioneer and prominent citizen who, as chief of the "Carson City Rangers," met his death in the Pyramid Lake Indian War of 1860 (SPD, pp. 51, 52, 58; MA, pp. 527–28). When the county and Carson City were consolidated into one municipal government named *Carson City*, by legislative fiat in 1969, the commemorative name was lost from the nomenclature, except for **ORMSBY BOULEVARD** in Carson City and **ORMSBY HOUSE,** a hotel-casino named for a nineteenth-century hostelry so denoted. See **CARSON.**

ORO. See **OROVILLE.**

OROVADA (Humboldt). The town so named, on U.S. 95 south of Rebel Creek and forty-one miles north of Winnemucca, was settled in 1918, and its post office was established September 25, 1920. The name was manufactured from Spanish *oro*, "gold" + *vada* from Nevada (NK 11–8; FTM, p. 21).

OROVILLE (Mineral). Gold discoveries made in June, 1906, about ten miles south of Hawthorne, prompted the sale of building lots, the platting of a townsite, and the construction of a stamp mill at a site formerly known as Jaggersville. Names chosen to signify the mineral were *Oroville, Oro City,* and *Oro.* The order to establish **ORO** post office, dated March 7, 1907, was rescinded October 23, 1907, probably before operations had begun. The mining camp at the east edge of Whisky Flat on the west flank of the Garfield Hills was abandoned by 1909 (NM; DM; FTM, p. 21; Haw. Quad.).

OSCEOLA (White Pine). The camp, known principally for placer mining and situated on the west flank of the Snake Range, about forty miles southeast of Ely, was named for the **OSCEOLA LEDGE,** discovered by George P. Blair (SM, 1875, pp. 170–71) or by Joseph Watson and Frank Hicks (NHS, 1924, p. 360), in 1872. Extensive work in the placer fields did not begin until 1877. **OSCEOLA** post office was established March 26, 1878, and existed until December 15, 1920, when Baker became the mail address for its patrons (1881 Map; FTM, p. 21). The name honors the noted Seminole chief *Osceola,* properly *Asi-yahola,* and is from *asi,* "black drink" and *yaholo,* a drawn-out cry made by an attendant while each man drinks in turn (FWH, p. 159).

OSGOOD MOUNTAINS (Humboldt). A mountain range trending northeastward from north of Golconda on the Humboldt River, east of the Hot Springs Range and Eden Valley, in the southeastern portion of the county (NK 11–8).

OSINO (Elko). A non-agency station nine miles northeast from Elko, on a spur line on the SP RR running into **OSINO CANYON** which heads on the east slope of the Adobe Range (T75; T1SL).

OSOBB VALLEY. See **DIXIE.**

OSTONSIDE. See **LOCKES.**

OTEGO (Elko). A former telegraph station on the early CP RR five miles west of Pequop, which was used only in winter to give notice of snow-blocked trains (HHB, Nev., p. 277; GAC, p. 127; FES, p. 174).

OTTS CREEK (Douglas). The name of the small stream in Pine Nut Valley commemorates Henry Ott, an early settler (NHS, 1913, p. 201).

OVEREND, CAMP (Humboldt). The temporary military camp was south of Golconda in the Sonoma Range and occupied during June, 1865, by Company B, Second Cavalry, California Volunteers, while on a scout after hostile Indians who had been on a rampage in Paradise Valley. The camp was named for Second Lieutenant W. G. Overend of the company, by First Lieutenant R. A. Osmer, in command (Ruhlen).

OVERLAND (Elko). The name commemorates the **OVERLAND MAIL COMPANY** which served settlers in the south end of Ruby Valley in the 1860s. **OVERLAND FARM** supplied grain for the horses of the stage line for which it was named. Ruby Valley post office was the mail address for the farm. The name of the farm was applied to **OVERLAND CREEK** and **OVERLAND LAKE.** The lake, altitude 9,000 feet, has tepid surface waters. It is below the rough scarp of Ruby Mountain summits and drains into Ruby Valley. Clarence King, in the Fortieth Parallel Survey, named the lake *Marian* for his sister (EP, pp. 54, 62; 1881 Map; TF, p. 20; Nev. Guide, p. 162; GHM, EL 1).

OVERTON (Clark). A town, fifteen miles from Moapa near Lake Mead; a station on the UP RR, two miles northwest of Mead Lake station; a post office established in Pah Ute County, Arizona, April 25, 1870, and discontinued December 16, 1872, re-established in Lincoln County, Nevada, on May 24, 1883, and transferred into Clark County, upon its creation in 1909 (NJ 11–12; 1881 Map; FTM, p. 21). Overton Museum contains the relics from Lost City, now under the waters of Lake Mead. The Mormon settlement was laid out originally on the east side of the Virgin River. "In fact the name of Overton is said to have been derived from the term Over-town as applied by the residents of the Hill town to the new settlement over the river" (JGS, I, p. 594). The present townsite was selected for Overton with the re-settlement after 1880. Features named for the town are a beach and boat landing several miles below the town, on the west side of the **OVERTON ARM** of Lake Mead; a magnesite district in Magnesite Wash, southwest of Overton; a group of islands (Bighorn, Gull, Heron, Ramshead), also called *Virgin Islands,* in the Overton Arm of Lake Mead; a mesa and a ridge south and west of Overton; and a wash, which drains westward from Overton into Moapa Valley, also called *Box Wash.* **SOUTH FORK OVERTON WASH** is north of Kaolin Wash (NJ 11–12; WA; VPG, p. 30).

OWENS (Clark). A station established in June, 1907, on the former LV and T RR; named for John J. Owens of Tonopah. The *Las Vegas Age* of April 14, 1907, notes that Owens, who had a saw mill in the Spring Mountains on Charleston Peak, was building a road over which to haul lumber from his mill to the railroad, twelve miles distant (Vegas Quad.; DM; WA).

OWYHEE (Elko). The town on State Route 11 is the headquarters of the Duck Valley (Western Shoshone) Indian Reservation and takes its name from the **OWYHEE RIVER.** The river heads in Elko County east of Spring Creek Ranch, and flows to the Snake River, about five miles south-southwest of Nyssa, in Malheur County, Oregon (USGB 5904; NK 11–9). "The Owyhee River was known to Ogden and the early trappers as Sandwich Island River, so called because some natives of those islands were killed by Indians at its mouth. When the Sandwich Islands became known as Hawaii on the maps the name of the river was changed accordingly, but the spelling followed phonetic methods" (JGS, I, p. 39 n. 1). The name appears on an 1849 Map of the Oregon Territory, by Charles Wilkes (Wheat III, 97). *Owhyhee* was an early variant (Wheat IV, frontispiece). Principal branches of the Owyhee are **EAST FORK OWYHEE RIVER,**

SOUTH FORK OWYHEE RIVER, and **LITTLE FORK SOUTH FORK OWYHEE RIVER,** in Elko and Humboldt counties in Nevada. **OWYHEE** post office, active from July 13, 1889, to December 31, 1890, was re-established December 15, 1899 (FTM, p. 21).

OX CORRAL CREEK (Lander). An intermittent stream heading south of Mount Callaghan in the Toiyabe Range and flowing into Grass Valley south of Skull Creek; named for an ox corral located nearby in Grass Valley (NJ 11–2).

PABLO (Nye). A creek rising on the east slope of the Toiyabe Range and flowing generally southeastward into Big Smoky Valley; a settlement on the creek and at the west edge of the valley; said to have been named for an early settler, a Mexican named *Pablo* (NJ 11–5; MM).

PACKARD (Pershing). A wash draining from the south end of the Humboldt Range, across **PACKARD FLAT** and southward to the Carson Sink; named for former **PACKARD** mining camp, located about two miles south of Rochester in December, 1912, by Henry Lund. Discoveries in May, 1913, by R. Ray, led to a major development, and the Nevada *Packard* Mines Company built a 100-ton cyanide plant in 1915 (NK 11–10; DM).

PACTOLUS (Nye). The order to establish **PACTOLUS** post office, dated August 27, 1904, was rescinded December 13, 1904, probably before operations commenced (FTM, p. 21).

PAH RAH (Washoe). A wishbone-shaped mountain range, a part of the Virginia Mountains, northeast of Reno, extending from the Truckee River northward to Mullen Pass. **PAH RAH MOUNTAIN** is south and west of Pyramid Lake in the Pah Rah Range (NJ 11–1). A. S. Gatschet recorded that *Pah-Rah* was a Shoshone name for "river," *Pa-rha* meaning "river" in the language of the Chemehuevi (Wheeler, 1879, pp. 446, 441; USGB 5903).

PAHRANAGAT (Lincoln). The **PAHRANAGAT RANGE** extends northwestward from the Sheep Range, bounded on the west by Tikaboo Valley and separated from **PAHRANAGAT VALLEY** by the **EAST PAHRANAGAT RANGE** on the east. **UPPER PAHRANAGAT** and **LOWER PAHRANAGAT** lakes are in lower Pahranagat Valley (NJ 11–9). The name, a variant of *Paraniguts,* commemorates a Southern Paiute band that inhabited the valley, apparently the first named of the land features. Interpreters of the name agree that the initial element *pah* means "water," but vary widely in the meanings attached to the rest of the word. Major G. W. Ingalls, who took a census of the Indians in 1873, reported that the Indians who lived in this valley tilled the soil, their principal crop being squash. "The Pah-ran-a-gat Indians are a branch of the Ute family and derive their tribal appellation from the cultivation of the watermelon, which in their language is called pah-ran-a-gat (pah meaning water, and ran-a-gat melon or vine-growing)" (SPD, p. 187). A. S. Gatschet in Wheeler (1879, p. 444) records that the name is from Southern Paiute *pa rangar* meaning "squash." According to Hodge *Pa-ran-i-guts* means "people of the marshy spring" (FWH, II, p. 202). Isabel T. Kelly has determined that the Southern Paiute name means "put their feet in the water" (M&M, p. 115). The first white people to pass through the valley were probably the ill-fated forty-niners of Death Valley fame. White settlers first came into the valley in 1864 and 1865. Now extensively cultivated, the valley meadows were used for a number of years as grazing land for stolen horses, while the canyons and washes served as good hideouts for the thieves. Upon the discovery of silver in March, 1865, by John H. Ely, Ira Hatch, and others, the **PAHRANAGAT MINING DISTRICT**, ten miles west of Hiko, was organized. The Green Monster, Black Warrior, and Montezuma were among the principal mines. **PAH RANAGAT** post office was established March 25, 1867, and discontinued June 24, 1867, most of the mines having been abandoned when the rush to White Pine County began (WA; FTM, p. 21). "The district of Pahranagat Lake, once the scene of great activity and excitement, is now comparatively deserted, except by a few persons known as 'chloriders,' who here and there coyote little pockets of rich ore, and take it to the Crescent mill, where it can be worked by the wet process" (Wheeler, 1872, p. 44).

PAHROC(K) (Lincoln). The **PAHROC RANGE** is about forty miles long, with a pass about twenty-seven miles west of Caliente creating two distinct units, **SOUTH PAHROC RANGE** and **NORTH PAHROC RANGE** (USGB 6001). **PAHROC SUMMIT** is east of Hiko on U.S. 93, and **PAHROC SPRING** is at the south end of the range. Hiko was the mail address for early settlers at Pahrock Spring (1881 Map; TF, p. 20). The creosote bush is the chief plant life in the high **PAHROC VALLEY,** a valley lying between the Hiko Range and the Pahroc Range, about thirty-two miles west of Caliente. Recent maps give the spelling *Pahroc* for the summit and *Pahrock* for the mountains, spring, and valley (GHM, LN 4). The name is said to mean "underground water" in Southern Paiute (OPN, p. 45).

PAH–RUM (Washoe). **PAH–RUM PEAK** is at the north end of the Lake Range, west of Rattlesnake Canyon. The name may commemorate the Parumpats (Pa-room-pats), a Paiute band living at Parum (Pa-room) Spring, when J. W. Powell and G. W. Ingalls took a census of Indians in Nevada in 1873 (SPD, p. 98). See **PAHRUMP.**

PAHRUMP. A settlement and a post office, established five times since July 27, 1891. the last time being July 1, 1942 (FTM, p. 21), on State Route 16, north of Manse in **PAHRUMP VALLEY,** which extends from California into Nye and Clark counties (NJ 11–12). The name was established as Pahrump (USGB–2), earlier having been *Pah-rimp.* "I then moved southward and crossed a low range into another sandy and gravelly desert, (Pah-rimp Desert,) which extends south for miles, and skirts the Spring Mountain Range. This desert contains several beautiful little oases, the principal one being at Pah-rimp Springs, at which point are located quite a number of Pah-Ute Indians, very friendly and quite intelligent. These Indians raise corn, melons, and squashes. Great quantities of wild grapes were found around these springs" (Wheeler, 1872, p. 84). Meanings suggested are "water-stone" from Southern Paiute *pa* ("water") and *timpi* ("stone"), modified phonetically to *rimpi* or *rumpi* (Gudde, p. 221); "people of the meadows" from *Parumpaiats,* a Southern Paiute Indian band from in or near Moapa Valley (FWH, p. 204; SPD, p. 98). Local tradition favors "great spring" or "water mouth" (MM), "big flow of water," "big orifice," or "cave from which water flows" from Southern Paiute (OPN, p. 17).

PAHUTE. The large mesa, south of the Cactus Range, west of Gold Flat and east of Sarcobatus Flat, is in Nye County and within the Las Vegas Bombing and Gunnery Range (NJ 11–8). **PAHUTE PEAK** (Humboldt) is near the north end of the Black Rock Range and south of *Piute* Creek (NK 11–10). **PAHUTE MOUNTAINS** (Lincoln) was the former designation of the Worthington Mountains (WA). From linguistic data he had gathered, John Wesley Powell learned that *Pai-yu-ti* was the English name, *Pa-vi-ot-so* the Shoshoni name, and *Nu-mu* the true name of this Indian tribe. There is some disagreement among specialists concerning the meaning of Paiute. According to John P. Harrington, "talk about Paiute meaning 'water Ute' or 'true Ute' is nonsense, because no such word as 'Ute' occurs in the language" (Fowler, p. 283 n. 9). Others maintain that *Pah-Ute,* "water Ute" or "Ute who lives near water," was the original name of the Paiute Indians, a branch of the Ute, a division of the Shoshonean Indians (FWH, p. 186; Kroeber, Handbook, p. 986). See **PAIUTE** and **PIUTE.**

PAINTED PEAK (Washoe). The name of this peak, lying on the east side of Long Valley and west of Massacre Lakes, is derived from its multi-colored rock (NK 11–7; VPG).

PAIUTE. PAIUTE RIDGE (Nye) is the name for a mountain northeast of Yucca Flat. **PAIUTE SPRING** (Mineral) is a spring northwest of Schurz and south of Weber Reservoir (GHM, NY 6; MI 1). The name, commemorating the Paiute Indians, is more often spelled *Pahute* or *Piute* (q.v.) in Nevada nomenclature.

PALISADE (Eureka). A township, post office (established May 2, 1870), and non-agency station on the SP RR and the WP RR, ten miles west of Carlin; named for rock formations in **PALISADE CANYON**, in which it is located (FTM, p. 21; NK 11–11; T75). In 1833, Zenas Leonard described the Palisades of the Humboldt as a "cluster of hills or mounds, which presented the appearance, from a distance, of a number of beautiful cities (citadels?) built up together" (JGS, I, 50). The name appears as *Pallisade Rock* on an 1855 Map of the Mining Region of California, drawn and compiled by George H. Baker (Wheat IV, 38). A traveler of 1869 wrote as follows: "Just before reaching the station named Palisade in the region of the Humboldt, we passed a genuine palisade, whose columnar structure reminds one very much of the Giant's Causeway" (M&SP, 8/28/69). Palisade was the northern terminal of the E and P RR, built to transport base bullion from Eureka and other points on the road to the CP RR. Palisade*s* was an early variant (Wheeler 1871 Map; OR, 1877).

PALMETTO (Esmeralda). A mountain range extending from the south end of the Silver Peak Range, east of the Sylvania Mountains; a wash draining northwestward from the west slope of the Palmetto Mountains; a mountain peak in the range, west of Lida; a mining district on the west slope of the range; and a former mining camp on Palmetto Wash. The mining district was formed on April 9, 1866, discoveries having been made by T. W. McNutt, H. W. Bunyard, and Thomas Israel (HHB, Nev., pp. 260–61; SPD, p. 857; 1881 Map; NJ 11–8; Wheeler, 1872, p. 47). **PALMETTO** post office was active from April 24, 1888, to June 7, 1894, and from December 16, 1905, to December 31, 1907 (FTM, p. 21). The name apparently stems from the **PALMETTO MINE,** a principal mine of the district (adjoining the Carolina Mine) named by the prospectors for their native state, South Carolina, whose nickname is the *Palmetto State.*

PALMYRA (Lyon). An early settlement, now abandoned, twelve miles southeast of Dayton, whose post office was established in Nevada Territory on May 5, 1865, and operated until July 31, 1866 (FTM; p. 21; Nev. Terr. Map). Myron Angel recorded that the population of the camp was eighty in 1860 (MA, p. 75). **PALMYRA MINING DISTRICT** is in the north-central portion of the Pine Nut Range, three miles north of Lyon Peak and ten miles southeast of Dayton (VPG, p. 102). The name is probably commemorative of Palmyra, New York, near Hill Cumorah where Joseph Smith is said to have unearthed the gold plates that were the source of the Book of Mormon.

PALOMINO RIDGE (Elko). The ridge named for its coloration is about three miles long and rises to an elevation of 7,383 feet, about nine miles north-northwest of Currie (NK 11–12; USGB 5902).

PAMLICO (Mineral). A mining district three miles south of Hawthorne, including the east slope of the Wassuk Range and the west end of the Garfield Hills; a former mining camp that flourished in the late 1880s (Haw. Quad.; VPG, p. 115; M&SP, 7/7/88). The name derives from the Pamlico Indians, an Algonquian tribe formerly living on the Pamlico River in North Carolina and incorporated as slaves of the Tuscarora in 1711 (FWH, p. 197).

PANACA (Lincoln). A community fifteen miles from Caliente on State Route 25, in the Meadow Valley Wash, with a siding on the Pioche Branch of the UP RR; a flat in the upper part of present-day Pioche; a mining district, midway between Pioche and Caliente (RRE; VPG, p. 97). The town, founded in May, 1864, was named for the *Panacker Ledge.* Earlier the same year, William Hamblin, a Mormon missionary to the Indians, had for a small consideration induced the Indians to lead him to a place where *panacker* was to be found in abundance. After the Panacker Ledge (Panaca Claim) was staked, the surrounding area became known as **PANACA FLAT** (JGS, I, pp. 601, 614; SPD, p. 930; RRE). *Pa-na-ka* is a Southern Paiute word meaning "metal" and was in the Las Vegas vocabulary of the Southern Numa, gathered by John Wesley Powell. *Pan-nuk kir,* "metal, money, wealth," appears in Powell's vocabulary of the Utes of White and Uintah rivers, also a subdivision of the Southern Numa (Fowler, pp. 156, 168). **PANACA** post office, except for a brief interruption, has been in operation since September 24, 1867 (FTM, p. 22; NJ 11–9; Wheeler 1871 Map).

PANCAKE. The low, flat **PANCAKE RANGE** extends north from the Reveille Range of eastern Nye County into southwest White Pine County to south of Newark Valley and is named for its "various outcroppings which resemble stacks of pancakes" (S&H, III, p. 44). **PANCAKE SUMMIT,** named for the range, is fifteen miles west of Little Antelope Summit on U.S. 50 in White Pine County (NJ 11–3).

PANGUIPA CREEK (Elko). An intermittent stream heading in the Duck Valley (Western Shoshone) Indian Reservation and flowing to Indian (Nayantovoy) Creek; reported to be a Shoshone Indian name, *Dirdui Panguipa Honops,* meaning "little fishes creek" (USGB). *Dry Creek* is the official designation of the stream by decision of the Geographic Board (USGB 6103).

PAPOOSE (Lincoln). The **PAPOOSE RANGE** is southwest of the Jumbled Hills, south of Groom Lake and north of **PAPOOSE LAKE,** near the Nye County boundary. The Algonquian name derives from Narranganset, *papoos,* "child" (NJ 11–9).

PARACHUTE CANYON (Nye). A five-mile canyon extending from North Timber Peak on Timber Mountain to an unnamed canyon approximately twenty-one miles northeast of Beatty; "named for the parachute found in the canyon" (DL 61).

PARADISE. The town of **PARADISE VAL-LEY** on State Route 8B was established in 1866 in Humboldt County by C. A. Nichols and became the business center of the valley for which it was named. The settlement was called **PARADISE CITY** at first (SPD, p. 910), but very soon was recorded as Paradise Valley (Census, 1870). **PARADISE VALLEY** post office was established February 6, 1871 (FTM, p. 22). **PARADISE HILL SUMMIT** is a pass on State Route 8, and **PARADISE WELL** is southeast of the pass. The early settlement **PARADISE HILL** was served by Winnemucca post office (HHB, Nev., p. 264; GHM, HU 4; TF, p. 20). Paradise Valley, one of the principal agricultural areas of Nevada, sometimes called an oasis of northern Nevada, was named by a group of prospectors who explored it in June, 1863. Myron Angel relates that one of the men, W. B. Huff, exclaimed "what a paradise" upon seeing the valley, thus naming the place (MA, p. 445; JGS, I, p. 239). The euphemistic name was belied for a time, when Indian hostilities in 1865 and 1866 precipitated the building of a fort, Camp Winfield Scott, at the north end of Paradise Valley and the temporary establishment of Camp Overend in the Sonoma Range, south of Golconda (SPD, p. 176; Ruhlen; 1881 Map).

PARDO (Elko). A name of undetermined meaning for a siding on the WP RR, about eight miles northeast of Elko and ten miles west of Elburz (T54).

PARK. A canyon heading on the eastern slope of the Toiyabe Range, northwest of Millett in Nye County. **PARK CANYON,** an early mining camp in the canyon was the site of the La Plata Mill, built in 1867. A post office so named was active from January 25,

1886, to November 11, 1886, when its operations were transferred to Junction (NM; FTM, p. 22; 1881 Map). The **PARK RANGE,** seven miles north of Moores Station in Nye County, was "named for Park Mountain, the highest peak in the range" (USGB 6903).

PARK CREEK (Lander) rises on the west slope of the Shoshone Mountains, west of North Shoshone Peak, and flows into Smith Valley to join Rock Creek, north of Gold Park (GHM, LA 1).

PARKER (White Pine). A locality, west of Uvada and near the Utah boundary; named for Amasa L. Parker who came to Nevada in 1862 and drove stages for the Overland Mail Company from Salt Lake City to the Reese River, until the railroads were built (SPD, p. 1124; OPN, p. 74). **PARKER** post office was established in White Pine County January 13, 1910 (having been transferred from Juab County, Utah), and operated, with brief interruptions, until April 1, 1929, when the name was changed to *Uvada* (FTM, p. 22).

PARRAN (Churchill). A telegraph station on the SP RR between Huxly and Desert in the Humboldt Sink (Forty Mile Desert); a post office established January 29, 1910, and discontinued July 31, 1913, when Hazen became the mail address for its patrons (FTM, p. 22).

PARRYS (Eureka). The name of a way station, mentioned by Myron Angel, on the former E and P RR (MA, p. 286).

PATNA (Lyon). Patna Siding, milepost 284.4, on the Sparks Subdivision of the SP RR between Argo and Hazen, was renamed *Darwin* on January 1, 1943 (DM).

PATRICK (Washoe). A non-agency station on the Sparks Subdivision of the SP RR, milepost 257.3 between Hafed and Clark, at the McCarran Ranch; named for the late Patrick A. McCarran, the first Nevada-born United States Senator to represent the state (DM; T75; M&S, p. 297).

PATSY CANYON (Nye). The canyon, heading on the east slope of the Shoshone Mountains southeast of Mount Berlin, and extending into Reese River Valley, may have been named for Patsy Bowler whose family lived on Reese River (SG Map 5; MM).

PATSVILLE (Elko). The settlement, formerly a mining camp serving the Rio Tinto Mining District in the northwest portion of the Bull Run Range, is two miles south of Mountain City on State Route 43 (NK 11–9; NM, p. 184). The town is "named for Pat Maloney, a dance hall proprietor" (M&M, p. 69).

PATTERSON. A gold-lead mining district at **PATTERSON PASS,** fifty miles south-south-east of Ely at the south end of the Schell Creek Range in northern Lincoln County; a former post office, established July 20, 1887, and discontinued September 19, 1910, when its operations were transferred to Geyser. The name honors Robert G. Patterson to whom an Indian pointed out the district in 1869 (VPG, p. 97; 1881 Map; OPN, pp. 45, 74; FTM, p. 22). **PATTERSON WASH** runs through Dry Valley, near Pioche, in Lincoln County (HWY Map; NJ 11–6). The name also denoted, in the 1870s, a ranch in the vicinity of present-day Overton in Clark County (WA), and an early settlement of Nye County (Census, 1870).

PAVLAK (Elko). A former post office, active from December 14, 1915, to January 15, 1921, when its operations were transferred to Jarbidge; named for Mike Pavlak, one of the discoverers of the **PAVLAK MINE,** two miles north of present-day Jarbidge. **PAV-LAK FOREST CAMP** is south of Jarbidge (FTM, p. 22; EP, p. 63; GHM, EL 3).

PEAK SPRING CANYON (Clark). This canyon in the Spring Mountains heads on the south slope of Charleston Peak and trends generally southwestward about eight miles (USGB 6201). The name appears to signify the location of the canyon's head on the highest peak (Charleston) in the *Spring* Mountains.

PEARL. A small lake in the high Rubies (Elko County), lying about one mile north-northwest of **PEARL PEAK** and southeast of **PEARL CREEK** which rises in the Ruby Mountains and joins Huntington Creek. Evidence concerning the naming and its order remains inconclusive. The lake, about one-tenth of a mile long, is said to have been named for its resemblance to a pearl. "Grandma" Pearl Toyn, who lived a few miles distant, may be commemorated by the creek name. The name *Pearl* may have been selected to fit into the gemstone pattern created by the *Diamond* and *Ruby* name groups (USGB, DL, 4/13/61; NK 11–12; EP, p. 63). **PEARL SPRING** (Clark) is an old name for *Cottonwood Springs,* situated just south of Blue Diamond (WA).

PEASLEE CANYON (Lincoln). The canyon heading on the west slope of the Highland Range is the type location for the Peaslee Limestone formation (WA; GHM, LN 1).

PEAVINE. A small mining camp and district in Washoe County, organized in 1863 upon the discovery of the Lucky Bill Mine ten miles northwest of Reno on the slopes of **MOUNT PEAVINE;** named for wild pea-vines growing near **PEAVINE SPRINGS.** *Peavine Springs* is shown on two 1860 maps of the Washoe region, one prepared by Dr. Henry De Groot, the other by R. M. Evans (Wheat IV, 189; V (I), 16). Shift names in the area are **PEAVINE CREEK,** an intermittent stream, and **PEAVINE SUMMIT,** a pass between Granite Mountain and **PEA-VINE PEAK** (NJ 11–1; SM, 1866, pp. 21–25; 1875, pp. 159–60; VPG, p. 172; Census,

1870). See **POEVILLE. PEAVINE** (Nye). A settlement and former post office (August 25, 1890–October 5, 1895) on **PEAVINE CREEK,** which has its source on the south slope of the Toiyabe Range south of Mahogany Mountain, and flows into Big Smoky Valley, then southwest to below Millers and east of Coaldale in Esmeralda County. The name derives from **PEAVINE CANYON,** the site of several green ranches, and is descriptive of the wild peavines found growing there (NJ 11–5; 1881 Map; FTM, p. 22; MM, Toiyabe, p. 9).

PECK (Lincoln). The name for this two-car siding on the Pioche Branch of the UP RR, about six miles north of Caliente, honors Tom Peck who was the General Freight Agent for the railroad at Los Angeles in the 1920s (Freese, Map 2; WA).

PEDRO. The short-lived post office, apparently near the Nye-Lander county boundary, was established in Nye County on January 20, 1882, transferred into Lander County on October 4, 1882, and discontinued on November 8, 1883, when Grantsville became the mail address for its patrons (FTM, p. 22).

PEKO (Elko). Formerly a side track station and section house on the SP RR, four miles west of Halleck at the head of Humboldt Canyon (Wheeler 1879 Map; HHB, Nev., p. 277; T1SL). According to Crofutt's *Guide,* officials of the CP RR named the station for the pekoe tea enjoyed by Chinese laborers on the railroad (EP, p. 63).

PENNSYLVANIA (Lincoln). An old mining district discovered by Philip Klingensmith about ten miles east of Elgin, in 1871; a mill built in the district about 1890; presumably named by Klingensmith, who is reported to have come into southern Nevada a short time after the Mountain Meadows Massacre of September 10, 1857 (WA). The Klingensmith Mine was the chief producer of the district.

PENOYER. The former name for *Sand Spring Valley* (q.v.), in northwestern Lincoln and eastern Nye counties; commemorative of H. H. Penoyer, a legislator in 1881 (Freese, Map 2; OPN, p. 45; USGB 6001).

PENROD CREEK (Elko). The name commemorates Emanuel Penrod, a partner of Henry Comstock on the Comstock Lode. The creek rises north of Island Mountain and empties into Wild Horse Reservoir (NK 11–9). Emanuel Penrod was postmaster at Island Mountain in 1885. The Federal Census of 1870 identifies E. Penrod as a farmer from Illinois, forty-four years of age. See **OPHIR** and **ISLAND MOUNTAIN.**

PEQUOP (Elko). A mountain range, west of Independence Valley in eastern Elko County; a summit in the range on U.S. 40; a non-agency station on the Elko Subdivision of the SP RR between Fenelon and Icarus. The name is said to be Shoshone and applied to a band of Indians (OPN, p. 27; NK 11–9). Bancroft gives the variant Peoquop for the range (HHB, Nev., p. 9). The early residents of Pequop were served by Toano post office (TF, p. 20; 1881 Map).

PERSHING COUNTY. The county, in the northwestern part of the state, was created by an act of March 18, 1919, from southern Humboldt County, with Lovelock as county seat, and named for General John Joseph Pershing, commander in chief of the American Expeditionary Force (1917–1919) (M&S, p. 164; OPN, p. 6).

PERTH (Pershing). A non-agency station on the Sparks Subdivision of the SP RR between Granite Point and Lovelock (T75). The name may derive from a county of central Ireland, or from a seaport of western Australia.

PETE HANSON CREEK (Eureka). The intermittent stream rising on the west slope of Roberts Creek Mountain in the Roberts Mountains and flowing circuitously to Henderson Creek; named for an early settler in Denay Valley (USGB 6002; NJ 11–2).

PETERSON (Lander). A creek flowing from the west slope of the Shoshone Mountains into Smith Creek Valley; a ranch in the valley; and **PETERSON STATION** on U.S. 50; named for Pete Peterson who owned the ranch (NJ 11–2; OPN, p. 41).

PETES (Lander). A canyon heading at the north end of the Toquima Range, east of Clipper Gap Canyon, and extending into Big Smoky Valley; a summit west of Toquima Cave, near the head of the canyon; and a nearby spring; named by Captain Simpson in 1859. "This spring, creek, and canyon I call after Pete, the Ute Indian, who has been of so much service to us in our explorations" (JHS, p. 116; GHM, LA 1).

PETROGLYPH BUTTE (Nye). A butte, one mile south of Moores Station; "named for the Indian writings found on the butte" (USGB 6903).

PHIL (Washoe). **PHIL SIDING** on the WP RR is six miles west of Gerlach in the north end of the Smoke Creek Desert (T54; NK 11–10).

PHILLIPSBURG (Esmeralda). A former mining camp, eighteen miles northwest of Goldfield in the southwest foothills of Lone Mountain; named for G. H. Phillips who discovered rich ore there in May, 1906 (NM).

PHONOLITE (Nye). A gold-silver mining district and a former townsite laid out at the north end of the Paradise Range, forty-five miles southwest of Austin, in 1906. A post office so named served the area from January 26, 1907, to July 23, 1909, when its name was changed to *Lodivale* (VPG, p. 124; NM; FTM, p. 22; SG Map 5). The district was named for a fine-grained igneous rock also known as clinkstone.

PHYSIC SPRING (Clark). The spring about midway between Boulder and West End washes is named for the presence of a hydrous magnesium sulfate, Epsom salts (WA).

PICKHANDLE GULCH (Mineral). Pickhandle Gulch or "The Gulch" popularly denoted old *Metallic City*, about fifteen miles south of Mina in the Candelaria Hills, formerly in Esmeralda County. The mining community, in a steep canyon and surrounded by rich mines, was well known for its all-night poker games and kindred activities. An American authority on ghost towns, Nell Murbarger, found evidence of an enterprising citizenry in a sturdy cabin constructed of "native stone and wooden whiskey cases," stenciled endboards showing the date of shipment and the vintage year (NM; DM; HHB, Nev., pp. 260–61; MM). A variant listing is *Pick Handle* for this mining community served by Candelaria post office (TF, p. 20). See **METALLIC CITY.**

PIE CREEK (Elko). The creek north of Dinner Station was so named because "an old German baker had a place on the creek and attracted customers with a sign which read, 'Piecake'" (EP, p. 64; GHM, EL 3). The easy substitution of *creek* for *cake* provided a name for the stream.

PIGEON SPRING. Springs named for the domestic pigeon or rock dove are south of Gain Spring on the east flank of the Black Rock Range, in Humboldt County; and at the north end of the Sylvania Mountains near Palmetto Wash, in Esmeralda County (NK 11–7; NJ 11–8; Wheeler 1871 Map). **PIGEON SPRINGS** is an alternate name for *Palmetto Mining District,* forty-two miles southwest of Goldfield, in Esmeralda County (VPG, p. 58).

PILOT. Lying just inside the Nevada boundary in Elko County, and northwest of the Salt Lake Desert, **PILOT PEAK** was a landmark for emigrants. The Bartleson-Bidwell party camped there in 1841 "after two or three fatiguing days—one day and night without water—the first notice we had of approach to any considerable mountain was the sight of crags dimly seen through the smoke, many hundred feet above our heads" (JGS, I, p. 63). Frémont named the peak in October, 1845, during his third expedition. "Nearly upon the line of our intended travel, and at the farther edge of the desert, apparently fifty to sixty miles away, was a peak-shaped mountain. . . . To the friendly mountain I gave the name of Pilot Peak" (JGS, I, p. 89). Flowing down the eastern slope of the mountain, **PILOT CREEK,** also named by Frémont, saved the lives of the Donner party after their terrible crossing of the Salt Lake Desert in 1846. The **PILOT RANGE,** named for the peak, trends northwestward from north of Wendover, along the Nevada-

Utah line. **PILOT MINING DISTRICT,** an early district which included the mountain, and **PILOT STATION** on the WP RR between Clifside and Ola, complete the Elko County name group (NK 11–9; VPG; AEH). In Mineral County, **PILOT PEAK** lies at the south end of the **PILOT MOUNTAINS,** a mountain range west of the Cedar Mountains in the southeastern portion of the county, while **LITTLE PILOT PEAK** is at the north end of the Cedar Mountains. **PILOT CONE** is a cone-shaped peak west of Rawhide in the northern part of the county (NJ 11–5; HWY Map). **PILOT** (Lander). The post office so named was active from May 28, 1906, to April 30, 1909, at which time Austin became the mail address for its patrons (FTM, p. 22).

PINE. The descriptive name is associated with the sugar pine (*Pinus lambertiana*) and the lodge-pole pine (*Pinus contorta*), which grow in the Yellow Pine Belt, and with the single-leaf piñon, the nut pine (*Pinus monophylla*), which grows at lower elevations. **PINE CANYON** (Clark) is an amphitheater in the Spring Mountains, across Kyle Canyon from the mouth of Fletcher Canyon (WA). **PINE CREEK** (Nye) denotes a creek near Mount Jefferson in the Toquima Range and a former settlement on the creek, served by a post office from May 9, 1873, to January 4, 1875, and from September 29, 1879, to January 18, 1881 (1881 Map; FTM, p. 22). Other creeks so named are south of Jarbidge in Elko County; southeast of Orovada in Humboldt County; west of Wheeler Peak on the west slope of the Snake Range in White Pine County; south of Palisade and in **PINE CREEK VALLEY** in Eureka County; and between Sandstone Bluffs and Blue Diamond Hill in Clark County, with **PINE CREEK SPRING** near the creek (SG Maps 5, 6, 10, 11; Blue D. Quad.; WA). **PINE FOREST** (Humboldt) was the name of an early settlement (HHB, Nev., p. 264) named for its location in the **PINE FOREST RANGE,** which extends northeastward from the Black Rock Range (NK 11–7). The settlement was served by Mill City post office (TF, p. 21). **PINE GROVE** (Lyon). An early settlement in **PINE GROVE CANYON;** a flat northeast of the canyon; a summit in the **PINE GROVE HILLS,** where Frémont, in 1844, first encountered the nut pine tree; and a mining district, discovered in 1865 on the east slope of the Pine Grove Hills, twenty-three miles south of Yerington. See **WILSON.** A post office served the former camp (which was northwest from Rockland and northeast of Lobdell Summit), except for one interruption, from September 7, 1868, to November 30, 1912, when its operations were transferred to Yerington (1881 Map; NJ 11–4; SM, 1875, pp. 37–38; VPG,

p. 103; FTM, p. 22). **PINE NUT. PINE NUT VALLEY** (Douglas), watered by **PINE NUT CREEK,** is a depression in the foothills of the **PINE NUT MOUNTAINS,** a mountain range lying east of Carson and Eagle valleys in Ormsby (Carson City), Lyon, and Douglas counties; named for the numerous forests of the nut pine (NJ 11–1; NHS, 1913, p. 192). Dr. Henry De Groot included the name of the valley on his 1860 Map of the Washoe Mines (Wheat IV, 189). Former settlements named for the pine tree include **PINE STATION,** an early way station of Eureka County, served by a post office from May 7, 1886, to February 14, 1888 (Census 1880; 1881 Map; MA, p. 285; FTM, p. 22), and **PINE VALLEY,** settled near Carlin (Elko) in the late 1860s (Census, 1870). **PINE VALLEY** (Eureka) denotes a mining district six miles west of Palisade, also called *Safford* (VPG, p. 68).

PINK HOLES HILL (Nye). The hill, about three miles east-southeast of Hampel Hill and six miles north-northwest of Mercury, was named for its color and its numerous wind-eroded holes (USGB 6103).

PINNACLES RIDGE (Nye). The name for a ridge containing many sharp pinnacles and forming the crest of the northeast portion of Yucca Mountain, between Vent Pass on the east, and Pinyon Pass on the west (USGB 6303; DL 58).

PIÑON PEAK (Nye). The Spanish word for "pine nut" denotes a mountain south of Longstreet Canyon and northeast of Rocky Peak, in the southern portion of the Monitor Range (SG Map 7; Guide Map). Variants are *Pinion* and *Pinyon*, indicating the Spanish pronunciation (NJ 11–5; HWY Map). See **PINE.**

PINTO. In Eureka County, **PINTO SUMMIT,** southeast of Eureka on U.S. 50, is named for **PINTO MINING DISTRICT,** discovered in the late 1860s in the eastern foothills of the Diamond Range, its principal producers being the Mountain Chief, Michigan, Uncle Sam, and Our Own mines. The early camp and post office (September 9, 1870–February 15, 1871) were at the entrance to a wide canyon a short distance southeastward from Eureka (FTM, p. 22; Census, 1870; VPG, p. 64; Wheeler 1871 Map). The post office was reestablished on August 6, 1875, and active until November 14, 1884, when Eureka became the mail address for its patrons. **PINTO CREEK** rises on the east slope of the Diamond Range and flows into Newark Valley (NJ 11–3). **PINTO VALLEY** (Clark), a valley trending northeastward from Hamblin Mountain west of the Black Mountains, is named for the spotted bean (*Phaseolus vulgaris*), the word deriving ultimately from Latin *pingere*, "to paint" (NJ 11–12). **PINTO RIDGE** is north of Pinto Valley for which it was named (USGB 7103).

PINTWATER RANGE. A mountain range extending from northwest Clark County into southwest Lincoln County; humorously named due to the sparseness of springs and streams on the slopes of the range (NJ 11–12; NJ 11–9).

PINYON (Nye). Features named for nearby stands of pinyon pine include **PINYON BUTTE** in the Eleana Range south of Rainier Mesa and east of Stockade Wash; and **PINYON PASS** in the northeast portion of Yucca Mountain at the head of Yucca Wash (USGB 6002; 6303; DL 58; GHM, NY 6). See **PINE** and **PIÑON.**

PIOCHE (Lincoln). As a result of the discovery of the Panacker Ledge in 1864 by William Hamblin, on the northeast side of Ely Mountain, the Meadow Valley Mining District was organized. Because of Indian hostilities around Panaca, prospecting was discontinued for a time. In 1868, E. M. Chubard and Joseph Grange reorganized the district and renamed it *Ely,* in honor of John H. Ely who had arrived late in 1868. Shortly thereafter, F. L. A. Pioche, a French banker of San Francisco, purchased the properties. In 1869, or 1870, the new town which had been laid out by P. McCannon, L. Lacour, and A. M. Bush was named Pioche at the suggestion of Mrs. Carmichael Williamson (MA, pp. 484, 487; HHB, Nev., pp. 272–73; SPD, pp. 930–31; WA; JWH). **PIOCHE** post office was established August 17, 1870 (FTM, p. 22). Two mining companies, the Raymond and Ely, owned by William Raymond and John H. Ely, and the Meadow Valley, with which F. L. A. Pioche was associated, together produced more than half of the total silver in the district during the early boom period. In 1873, the Pioche and Bullionville Railroad was completed for the purpose of transporting ores from the Ely district to the mills at Bullionville. Two thousand claims had been located in the district by 1875. In addition to the Raymond and Ely and the Meadow Valley, principal mines included the Mazeppa, Prince, Newark, American Flag, Panaca, Abe Lincoln, and Caselton, among others. Early Pioche, estimated to have had a population of 15,000 people, is reported to have been one of the wildest towns of the Old West. It is distinguished for its cemetery, said to have contained the bodies of from sixty to seventy-five men slain before anyone in town died a natural death (DRL, p. 10; Nev. Guide, pp. 173–74; WA). During a second production boom period between 1939 and 1956, the Pioche district produced over $70,000,-000, mainly in lead and zinc (RRE). Pioche, the county seat, is presently the terminal of a branch of the UP RR. The **PIOCHE**

HILLS, a low ridge of which Mount Ely is the highest point, are also called the **PIOCHE RANGE** (NJ 11–9; Freese, Map 2).

PIONEER (Nye). A former mining camp in the Bullfrog Mining District; named for the **PIONEER MINE,** discovered in 1907 (NM; VPG, p. 124). The name also denoted a station on the T and T RR and the BG RR (DM). **PIONEER** post office was established March 2, 1909, and discontinued February 19, 1931, when Beatty became the mail address for its patrons (FTM, p. 22). **PIONEER CLAIM.** See **OPHIR.**

PIPER PEAK (Esmeralda). The peak, midway of the Silver Peak Range on the west slope, was named for N. T. Piper who owned the Oasis Ranch in Fish Lake Valley (NJ 11–8; MM).

PIROUETTE MOUNTAIN (Churchill). The name for a mountain with three peaks having elevations over 5,000 feet, in the Louderback Mountains about four miles west of Wonder and thirty-five miles east of Fallon (NJ 11–1; USGB 5904).

PITTMAN (Clark). The town, about a mile west of Henderson, of which it is now a part, and its post office established July 3, 1942, were named honorifically for Key Pittman, former United States Senator from Nevada (NJ 11–12; WA; MM).

PITTSBURG. The former Lander County camp, situated in the **PITTSBURG MINING DISTRICT,** fifteen miles southeast of Battle Mountain, on the north flank of Mount Lewis between Maysville and Dean canyons, is named for the **PITTSBURG MINE.** A post office named for the camp was established as Pittsburg*h* on October 11, 1888, and changed to Pittsburg on March 5, 1892. The last discontinuance of operations took place on May 15, 1900. An old manganese mine of Clark County, first located by Daniel Bonelli between Boulder Wash and the Colorado River, was also named **PITTSBURG.** The mines were named to commemorate the Pennsylvania city so denoted in honor of William Pitt (1708–1778), the English statesman called "the Elder Pitt" (NM; VPG, p. 87; FTM, p. 22; WA; CO, p. 526).

PIUTE. The name, an alternate spelling for *Pahute* and *Paiute* in Nevada nomenclature, denotes a valley in Clark County, west of Searchlight and extending from south of Crescent Mountain to San Bernardino County, California (NI 11–3); a wash in Piute Valley; a ridge at the north end of the Muddy Mountains, between Dry Lake Siding and Atlatl Rock (NJ 11–12), also in Clark County, as are **PIUTE SPRINGS,** north of Potosi Pass in the Spring Mountains. The springs, called *Pa'ash* by the Indians in the area (Kroeber, Handbook, p. 596), were known to emigrants and early settlers as

Piute. See **MOUNTAIN SPRINGS. PIUTE CANYON** heads on Battle Mountain, in Humboldt County, and trends northeastward to **PIUTE SIDING** on the SP RR, in Lander County, northwest of Battle Mountain Station (USGB 6003; NK 11–11; 1881 Map). **PIUTE CREEK,** a variant for *Pahute Creek,* in Humboldt County, denotes an intermittent stream heading in the Black Rock Range north of Pahute Peak and trending southeastward into the Black Rock Desert (NK 11–7; SG Map 1). **PIUTE MEADOWS** and **PIUTE MEADOWS RANCH** are named for the creek. Early settlers of Piute Meadows were served by Mill City post office (GHM, HU 2; TF, p. 21). See **PAHUTE** and **PAIUTE.**

PLACERITES (Pershing). A mining district in the low hills on the east slope of the Kamma Mountains, forty-seven miles north of Lovelock, discovered in the 1850s; named for the placer gold found there. The first placer mining was done by hand methods in the 1870s (VPG, p. 156; GHM, PE 1; OPN, p. 62).

PLACERVILLE (Elko). The early mining district and camp in Elko County (Census, 1870), may have been named for Placerville, California.

PLATINA (Clark). The Spanish word for "platinum" denoted a former townsite and post office (January 3, 1916–May 31, 1917), near Sandy in Mesquite Valley. The town sprang into existence when H. K. Riddall, in March, 1914, discovered platinum in the old Boss Mine. The mine was first located by Joseph Yount on January 1, 1886, on the edge of Mesquite Valley and near the site of the Keystone Mill. Although the boom at Platina lasted only about a year, mining continued until late 1918 or early 1919 (DM; WA; FTM, p. 22).

PLATO (Storey). Joseph Plato was the locator and owner of this ten-foot claim on the Comstock which was absorbed by the Consolidated Imperial (IH). Affidavit of Annual Labor on the Plato is filed by the Sutro Tunnel Coalition, Inc. (AL; HDG, CP, 11/25/76).

PLATORA (Humboldt). The blend name, derived from Spanish *plata,* "silver" + *oro,* "gold," designated a post office established May 7, 1909, and discontinued September 30, 1925, when Rebel Creek became the mail address for its patrons (FTM, p. 23).

PLEASANT HILL. See **OPHIR.**

PLEASANT VALLEY. A small valley, southwest of Steamboat Valley in Washoe County, through which Galena Creek runs from the slopes of Mount Rose, traversed by U.S. 395, and formerly, by the V and T RR. The valley was settled by the Mormons in 1856 and named for its pleasant aspects. The name appears on the 1859 map of Captain James H. Simpson's explorations across the Great Basin of Utah (Wheat IV, 137). In Elko County, the name designated an early settlement in a valley of the same name, west of the Ruby Mountains. The settlement was served by Elko post office (Census, 1900; TF, p. 21). **PLEASANT VALLEY CREEK** (White Pine) is named for a valley in the Kern Mountains, extending to the southeast across the Utah boundary. Hamilton was the mail address for early settlers there (OPN, p. 75; TF, p. 21). **PLEASANT VALLEY** post office was in operation from March 15, 1892, until April 26, 1894, when Aurum became the mail address for its patrons (FTM, p. 22). Additional early settlements of this designation were in Eureka and Humboldt counties, and mail service was provided by post offices at Alpha and Winnemucca (HHB, Nev., pp. 264, 285; TF, p. 21). **PLEASANT VALLEY** (Pershing), between the East Range and the Tobin Range, was the scene of violent earthquakes on October 2, 1915, created by the **PLEASANT VALLEY FAULT,** with a vertical displacement of fifteen feet (OPN, p. 62; Nev. Guide, p. 132; NK 11–11).

PLUTONIUM VALLEY (Nye). A valley extending from just northeast of French Peak (west of Scarp Canyon) in the Nevada Proving Grounds; named for a radioactive element (symbol Pu) (USGB 6201).

PLUTO VALLEY (Nye). A valley heading about one and a half miles southeast of Lookout Peak and following the course of Nielson Wash eastward, is about fourteen miles northwest of Mercury and in the Nevada Proving Grounds; named for the prince of the underworld in Roman and Greek mythology (USGB 6201).

POCKETS (Lincoln). The old watering place about fifty-five miles south of Caliente, on the stage and mail route down the Meadow Valley Wash, was named for water pockets in a narrow wash entering the Meadow Valley Wash from the east. The pre-railroad settlement was known also as *Angle City* during 1903 and 1904, for a big bend in the wash between Carp and Rox (DM; WA).

POEVILLE (Washoe). The mining camp on the slopes of Peavine Mountain and nine miles northwest of Reno was called *Peavine* until 1863 when John Poe discovered a rich claim there. In honor of this man (who was said to be a cousin of Edgar Allan Poe), the camp was called *Poe City, Podunk,* and **POEVILLE,** which was the name of the post office, active from September 1, 1874, to March 22, 1878 (1881 Map; FTM, p. 23; Nev. Guide, p. 193; HHB, Nev., p. 256; NHS, 1911, p. 84; SM, 1875, p. 157). See **PEAVINE.**

POGONIP (White Pine). An early town on the west side of the White Pine Range just below the crest of the ridge; named for *pogonip,* a heavy winter fog containing ice particles, from Shoshonean (Paiute) and meaning "white death," according to report, since it caused pneumonia (SM, 1875, pp. 164–65; MM).

POINT OF ROCKS (Nye). The name for a ridge on the south side of a gap in the Specter Range, through which U.S. 95 passes west into the Amargosa Desert north of Johnnie (Furn. Cr. Quad.; WA).

POINT, THE (Elko). A hill in the Duck Valley Indian Reservation on the south edge of Duck Valley and about five miles southwest of Owyhee (USGB 6103; NK 11–8). See **DISIGUOY.**

POISON. A creek flowing northward from Cougar Point, east of East Fork Jarbidge River and west of Spring Creek, in Elko County; a spring at the south end of the Palmetto Mountains, one mile northwest of Alum Creek and near Walker Spring, in Esmeralda County; presumably named for undrinkable water (SG Map 11; Lida Quad.).

POISON SWITCH. See **YERINGTON.**

POKER BROWN (Pershing). A name of undetermined origin for a gap south of Majuba Mountain, at the north end of the Trinity Range, and for a canyon extending from the Trinity Range into Seven Troughs Valley (NK 11–10).

POLE. Canyons and creeks in five Nevada counties (Elko, Humboldt, Pershing, Washoe, White Pine) were so named because poles were cut there (Dir. 1971). **POLE CREEK RANGER STATION** (Elko), northeast of Jarbidge, is near the source of **POLE CREEK** which was named for "a fine stand of pole quality aspen" (EP, p. 66). The specific occurs with three generics in **POLE CANYON CREEK SUMMIT**, north of Deeth on the northern edge of the Great Basin (Nev. Guide, p. 118; GHM, EL 3).

POLLOCK, CAMP (Washoe). The temporary military camp was established in Smoke Creek Valley near Smoke Creek Camp, for occupation by Company D, First Cavalry, Nevada Volunteers. The company was under the command of Captain A. B. Wells, on an expedition from Fort Churchill to the Humboldt River, Smoke Creek, and Surprise Valley, California, during June and July, 1864. Colonel Robert Pollock, Third Infantry, California Volunteers, presumably is commemorated (Ruhlen).

PONDERERS REST. See **DAYTON.**

PONY. Features so named commemorate the Pony Express, a postal system by which mail was relayed from Missouri to California by riders mounted on swift ponies. (The service was inaugurated April 3, 1860, and discontinued October 24, 1861.) It followed the Simpson route and covered 407 miles in Nevada; similar "pony lines" operated in other areas of the state. In Lander County,

the **PONY LEDGE** and **PONY CANYON** were near Austin (q.v.). **PONY SPRING** (Lincoln) was a former pony stop at a spring about twenty-five miles north of Pioche. The wells lying between Pioche and Pony Spring were given milepost names (WA). **PONY ROAD** (Churchill) was so named because it was used by riders of the Pony Express (NHS, 1913, p. 180).

POOR AND COSSITTS (Washoe). The former name for islands in the Truckee River near Reno, noted by the *Gold Hill News* and the *Nevada State Journal* of August 20, 1874; apparently commemorating early ranchers in the area. Mr. Poor operated a ranch just west of Reno (DM).

POORMAN (Elko). **POORMAN PEAK,** southeast of Gold Creek, took its name from **POORMANS CREEK,** so named by a Major Switzer, who was unsuccessful when he tried "to placer in the creek" (EP, p. 66; GHM, EL 3).

PORCUPINE CREEK (Humboldt). A creek rising on the west flank of the Santa Rosa Range and joining Chimney Creek in the valley northeast of the Bloody Run Hills; named for the porcupine which lives in the timbered areas of the state (NK 11–8).

PORPHYRY. A peak in the Louderback Mountains, about two miles northwest of Wonder, in Churchill County; a hill in Elko County, the site of the ore discoveries that led to the Tuscarora boom; a gulch in the Goodsprings Mining District (Clark), the location of the Yellow Pine Mine; named for the characteristic igneous rock (USGB 5904; EP, p. 66; WA).

POTOSI. A mountain, pass, spring, and wash in the Spring Mountains, Clark County, about thirty-five miles southwest of Las Vegas in the **POTOSI** (Goodsprings, Yellow Pine) **MINING DISTRICT;** named for the **PO-TOSI MINE** (NK 11–3). On May 9, 1856, an Indian told Mormons at Las Vegas Mission of ore deposits on the west side of a mountain, and Brigham Young sent Nathaniel V. Jones to develop them. Work began in December, 1856, and the first ore was smelted by Jones. The project was abandoned, however, when the ore proved generally poor (DM). Jones is thought to have named the lead mine for the Potosi lead-zinc district of his native state, Wisconsin (WA; OPN, p. 17). Traces of silver discovered in 1861 led to the establishment of a mining camp. An article in the *Deseret News* of April 3, 1861, concerning Las Vegas Silver Mines, reported the location of the mining camp.

> The mines of silver recently discovered on the Las Vegas directly on or not far from the road to San Bernardino, are attracting considerable attention. Several companies have been organized at Marysville and other places in California, and

gone thither to make fortunes in the mines. A town has been laid out some 30 miles west of the Colorado River and about the same distance from Las Vegas, called Potosi, where the Colorado Mining Company are engaged in the erection of a smelting furnace for the reduction of the argentiferous galena, of which their mine is composed. The claims of this company are situated about a mile from town, in a steep mountain side, and the lead is said to be of vast size and undoubted richness. (NHS, 1926, pp. 281–82)

In a letter of January 26, 1866, Ira Hatch wrote of his visit to the deserted camp. "From here [Cottonwood Spring] we journeyed to the old Las Vegas lead mines, leaving the California road about 5 miles to the right. Here I found that an old city which had been deserted two years ago had been built by the miners and was called Potosi; it had been built since I was here" (NHS, 1926, p. 283).

Zinc became the principal product of the district in 1905, and the discovery of platinum in the Boss Mine in 1914 created a short-lived boom town Platina (q.v.). In addition to lead, silver, zinc, and platinum, other minerals worked to a degree in the district include copper, gold, palladium, cobalt, nickel, radium, and antimony (WA; VPG, p. 26). Among the many claims are the Accident, Addison (named for Addison Bybee), Christmas, Columbia, Dawn, Green Monster, Kirby (named for John A. Kirby), New Year, Ninetynine, and Shenandoah (WA).

Alternate, sometimes older, names for the features are *Silver Buttes* (1861) for that portion of the Spring Mountains in which the mine was located; *Double Up* for Potosi Mountain, from the Double Up Mine on its east slope; *Comet* (1870) for the Potosi Mine; *Yellow Pine* (1882) and *Goodsprings*, in later years, for the mining district (WA; DM; VPG, p. 26).

POTOSI (Storey). The original Potosi on the Comstock was a four-hundred-foot claim that overlapped the surface or placer claim belonging to Billy Chollar (q.v.). The present Potosi consists of seven hundred feet lying between the Chollar and the Bullion (IH). The name on the Comstock could have been transferred from earlier-named mines in California, located in Amador, El Dorado, Mariposa, and Placer counties (JRB, Res., pp. 19, 106; CSMB, p. 42; CMA, p. 318; OFJ, p. 47), from the Potosi lead district in Missouri (TAR, pp. 151, 155), or from the silver mining district at San Luis Potosi in Central Mexico. Ultimately, the name in both Clark and Storey counties commemorates the famous silver mines of Bolivia on Cerro Rico de Potosi. These mines, discovered in 1545, poured forth about $1,400,000,000 in gold

and silver in three and a half centuries (CHS, Mine, p. 4; JRB, Res., p. 617).

POTT HOLE VALLEY (Nye). A ravine, west of Morey Peak in the Hot Creek Range; named by the United States Board on Geographic Names in 1969 for nearby **POT HOLE SPRING** (USGB 6903).

POTTS (Nye). A settlement in Monitor Valley between the Toquima and Monitor ranges, on State Route 82 northeast of Dianas Punch Bowl; a ranger station and hot springs; named for William Potts, a rancher and sheep man whose home was the location of a post office active from August 12, 1898, to October 31, 1941 (NJ 11–2; HWY Map; MM; OR, 1899; FTM, p. 23).

POWELL (Mineral). A. Powell, a miner and proprietor of a toll road, is commemorated by a mountain, springs, and a canyon heading on the east slope of the Wassuk Range and trending southeastward to Whisky Flat (NJ 11–4; SG Map 4; OPN, p. 51).

PRAIRIE GATE (White Pine). The name of the Overland Mail station on the eastern border of Nevada, thirteen miles northeast of Antelope Springs; listed in Root and Conelley's *The Overland Stage to California* (JGS, I, p. 136).

PREBLE. A non-agency station on the WP RR and on the SP RR, four miles east of Golconda in Humboldt County (T75; T54). **PREBLE MOUNTAIN** (Nye), near the Esmeralda boundary and a little south of east of Goldfield, was named for Charles S. Preble, surveyor general from 1877 to 1880 (OPN, p. 56; NJ 11–8).

PRESTON (White Pine). A town and ranching community at White River in the southern part of the county, on State Route 38; named for William B. Preston, presiding Bishop in 1897 when the town was established by Mormons who migrated from Moroni, Utah (NJ 11–6; RC, p. 72; OPN, p. 75). A post office so named served the community from September 7, 1899, until 1951 (FTM, p. 23).

PRICES LAKE (Washoe). Two small lakes on Ophir Creek, west of old Franktown and south of Slide Mountain. They were named Upper Prices Lake and Lower Prices Lake for a sawmill operator, W. E. Price, who was also an assemblyman for Washoe County in 1873 (DM; VPG).

PRICHARD (Nye). The order to establish **PRICHARD** post office in Nye County, dated February 5, 1894, was rescinded April 14, 1894, perhaps before operations began (FTM, p. 23).

PRINCE (Lincoln). The terminus of the Prince Consolidated Railroad built from Pioche in 1912; named for the **PRINCE MINE** (Freese, Map 2; NJ 11–9).

PRINCE ROYAL (Pershing). A settlement of Nevada Territory; a mining district on the west flank of the north end of the Humboldt Range between **PRINCE ROYAL CANYON** and Eldorado Canyon (Nev. Terr. Map; VPG, p. 151; SM, 1866, p. 47; NK 11–10).

PRINCETON (Lincoln). A short-lived post office established June 8, 1909, and discontinued January 31, 1910, when its services were transferred to Pioche (FTM, p. 23).

PROMETHEUS, MOUNT (Lander). A mountain east of Austin in the Toiyabe Range. In Greek mythology, *Prometheus* taught mankind the use of fire, which he had stolen from heaven for their benefit, and was punished by Olympian Zeus by being chained to a rock where a vulture came each night to eat away his liver (NJ 11–2).

PROSPECT. PROSPECT PEAK, south of Eureka in the Fish Creek Range (Eureka County), was named in the early 1860s because of numerous prospect holes. Rich ore discoveries in 1864 resulted in the organization of **PROSPECT MINING DISTRICT** (M&S, p. 160; VPG, p. 64). A post office so named served the area from March 3, 1893, to April 30, 1918 (FTM, p. 23). **PROSPECT SPRING** (Clark) is at the south end of La Madre Mountain and north of Willow Spring in the Spring Mountains (Vegas Quad.).

PROVIDENCE (Lincoln). The name given the Meadow Valley Wash by the Flake-Rich party, when they reached it at a point between Carp and Leith in 1849. The wash was called "Providence Creek on account of finding it so Providentially," according to the diary of William Farrar (LRH, II, p. 207). Under date of November 10, 1849, Henry W. Bigler recorded in his journal "this Creek the Camp called Providence Creek" (LRH, II, p. 157). The wash is also referred to as **PROVIDENCE CANYON** (LRH, II, p. 207).

PROW (Nye). A point of land near the center of Yucca Mountain, is named **THE PROW** "for its resemblance to the prow of a ship." **PROW PASS** is near the center of Yucca Mountain and north-northwest of The Prow (USGB 6303; DL 58).

PUEBLO. The **PUEBLO MOUNTAINS,** a mountain group northwest of the north end of the Pine Forest Range, and **PUEBLO VALLEY,** east of the mountains, in northern Humboldt County, Nevada, but largely in the State of Oregon, may have been named for a former mining camp so denoted, possibly the present Ashdown Mine (1881 Map; NK 11–7). **PUEBLO MINING DISTRICT** was discovered in 1863 on the west slope and near the north end of the Pine Forest Range, twelve miles south of Denio. A post office named for the district was in operation from February 13, 1867, to August 6, 1867. **PUEBLO MILL** was burnt by the Bannock Indians in the 1860s (VPG, p. 78; SM, 1866, pp. 45–55; Census, 1900; FTM, p. 23).

PUEBLO (Clark) is the name for a railroad siding on the Moapa Valley Branch of the UP RR between Logandale and Arrowhead (WA; Freese, Map 1). *Pueblo,* the Spanish word for "village," derives from latin *populus,* "people."

PUEBLO GRANDE. See **LOST CITY.**

PUNY DIP CANYON (Washoe). The canyon, heading in the Carson Range west of Big Meadows and southwest of Verdi, apparently was named for its relative shallowness when compared with Deep Canyon which lies just northeast of it (GHM, WA 1).

PURDYS (Washoe). A post office transferred from Sierra County, California, into Washoe County, Nevada, on March 4, 1911, and discontinued on October 15, 1913, when Reno became the mail address for its patrons (FTM, p. 23).

PURGATORY. PURGATORY HOLE is a fanciful name for a deep canyon heading on the south side of Bunker Peak in the Clover Mountains, east of the Meadow Valley Wash (WA). **PURGATORY PEAK** (Pershing) is north of Limbo Peak in the Selenite Range (GHM, PE 1).

PUSSY WILLOW WASH (Clark). A watercourse running southwest from Whitney Ridge to Mud Wash (WA); named for the small American willow (*Salix discolor*) found growing there.

PYRAMID (Washoe). A desert lake of unusual beauty about thirty-three miles north of Reno; the largest remnant of ancient Lake Lahontan. The surface of the lake stretches over 125,000 acres, at an elevation of 3,700 feet. Frémont discovered the "sheet of green water" that "broke upon our eyes like the ocean" on January 10, 1844, and named it on January 13.

> . . . we encamped on the shore, opposite a very remarkable rock in the lake, which had attracted our attention for many miles. It rose, according to our estimate, 600 feet above the water; and, from the point we viewed it, presented a pretty exact outline of the great Pyramid of Cheops. . . . This striking feature suggested a name for the lake; and I called it Pyramid Lake; and though it may be deemed by some a fanciful resemblance, I can undertake to say that the future traveller will find a much more striking resemblance between this rock and the pyramids of Egypt, than there is between them and the object from which they take their name. (JCF, Report, p. 217)

The rock, the home of the lake's owls and loons, is a quarter of a mile around the base. An estimated two hundred gallons of boiling water gush from its crevices each minute (HPS, 1/24/54; VPG). **PYRAMID LAKE INDIAN RESERVATION,** comprising 322,808 acres, surrounding and including the lake, was withdrawn from settlement on November 29, 1859, on the recommendation of Major Frederick Dodge, Indian Agent for Utah Territory, and was established on March 23, 1874, by presidential proclamation, signed by Ulysses S. Grant (Nev. Terr. Map; OPN, p. 69; NJ 11–1; NK 11–10). **PYRAMID CITY,** a former mining camp twenty-six miles northeast of Reno, was laid out in 1876, as a result of the organization of the **PYRAMID LAKE MINING DIS-TRICT** on April 12, 1876, in the Virginia Range, about six miles west of the south end of Pyramid Lake (SM, 1875, pp. 158–59; MA, p. 644; M&SP, 7/31/80; VPG, p. 173). The camp was divided into **UPPER PYRA-MID** and **LOWER PYRAMID** (1881 Map). **PYRAMID** post office served the district from February 28, 1879, to October 7, 1879 (FTM, p. 23). **PYRAMID** station on a branch line of the SP RR, milepost 319.6 south of Big Canyon Station and west of Pyramid Lake, except for one interruption, has been served by a post office so named since April 20, 1880 (FTM, p. 23; NK 11–10; T75).

QUAIL SPRING (Clark). A spring east of Fossil Ridge and north of Gass Spring in the Las Vegas Range; a spring north of Mockingbird Spring and south of Lime Canyon; presumably named for the game bird. **QUAIL SPRINGS WASH** is a watercourse draining generally westward from the spring for which it is named to Lake Mead, east of the Overton Islands (NJ 11–12).

QUARTET DOME (Nye). A mountain with four peaks in the Belted Range just west of Summit Bench, approximately one mile east of Ocher Ridge (DL 56).

QUARTETTE (Clark). The name for a famous mine in the Searchlight Mining District, fifty miles south of Las Vegas, east of Piute Valley; a former mill and a post office, which served the company from September 15, 1900, to September 15, 1902 (WA; NHS, 1924, pp. 377–78; FTM, p. 23).

QUARTZITE (Nye). A mountain between Kawich Valley on the east, and Gold Flat on the west, named for the the quartzite rock found in the area; a ridge at the northern end of Yucca Flat, about a mile southwest of Oak Spring (DL 53; NJ 11–8; Kaw. Quad.).

QUARTZ MOUNTAIN. A mountain in Nye County, near the Mineral County boundary and fifteen miles north of Gabbs, the site of mineral discoveries in the early 1920s which resulted in the organization of **QUARTZ MOUNTAIN MINING DISTRICT.** A post office so named served the district from June

7, 1927, to January 15, 1929, when its operations were transferred to Broken Hills (NJ 11–2; VPG, p. 136; NM). Quartz Mountain is also the alternate name for *Quartz Peak,* a mountain in the Pintwater Range, and for Mount Irish and Great Quartz Mountain (q.v.) northwest of Hiko in Lincoln County (Freese, Map 2; NJ 11–9). The name is descriptive of the geological formation of the mountains.

QUEEN. The name of a locality southwest of Mount Montgomery in Mineral County, a former station on the C and C RR, and a mining district at the north end of the White Mountains, also known as *Oneota* and *Buena Vista;* believed to have derived from the prominent old Indian Queen Mine, in the mining district and about five miles east of the former railroad station (NJ 11–7; DM; VPG, p. 111). **QUEEN** post office was active in Mineral County from October 26, 1912, to January 15, 1914, when its operations were transferred to Benton, California (FTM, p. 23). **QUEEN CITY,** a former mining camp established in 1907, by report of the *Reno Evening Gazette* of August 27, 1907, furnished a name for the summit so denoted at the north end of the Belted Range on State Route 25, just west of the Lincoln County boundary, in Nye County (HWY Map; DM). **QUEEN CITY** (Humboldt), mentioned by Bancroft (HHB, Nev., p. 264), was a mill town of the 1870s for former Spring City, north of Paradise Valley (NM). **QUEEN PEAK** (Churchill) is a peak on the west slope of the Clan Alpine Mountains, about two miles north of Wonder (USGB 5904). **QUEEN SPRINGS.** See AURUM.

QUINCY (Nye). A former camp in the Royston Mining District, twenty-five miles north of Tonopah in the San Antonio Mountains, active in the early 1920s (VPG, p. 138; NM).

QUINN. The **QUINN RIVER** rises east of the summit of the Santa Rosa Range near the Oregon line, flows westward cutting a deep gorge through these mountains, and then southwestward through **QUINN RIVER VALLEY** to its sink in the Black Rock Desert, northeast of Gerlach, in Washoe County. Peter Skene Ogden called the Quinn River, in 1828, the *River of the Lakes* for the series of small lakes through which the river flows (JGS, I, p. 40). **QUINN RIVER CROSSING,** formerly a small settlement on State Route 8A that served scattered ranches and mining districts in the area, is now a ranch headquarters (NK 11–8; Nev. Guide, p. 215; AEH). Queens River (Humboldt), included in the Federal Census of 1870, and Queen River Valley, mentioned by Bancroft (HHB, Nev., p. 264) may be variants. **QUINN RIVER CAMP 33.** See McDER-MITT. **QUINN CANYON RANGE** is a short mountain range in northeast Nye

County, passing through the northwest corner of Lincoln County (NJ 11–6).

QUO VADIS MINE (Clark). A gold mine discovered by the Catlin brothers in 1905 in the Alunite Mining District, in Eldorado Pass and southwest of Bishop Mountain (WA), may have been so named because of the popularity of the novel *Quo Vadis,* by Henryk Sienkiewicz.

RABBIT. Features named for wild rabbits in the area include **RABBIT CANYON** on the east flank of the Pah Rah Range north of White Horse Canyon, in Washoe County; **RABBIT CREEK** west of Lamoille Creek, in Elko County; **RABBIT SPRING(S)** southwest of Alpha in the Roberts Mountains, in Eureka County; in the Gabbs Valley Range, in Mineral County; and southeast of Panaca, in Lincoln County (GHM, WA 1; EL 1; EU 1; MI 1; LN 1). **RABBIT SPRINGS** (Esmeralda) denoted a camp near the mineral discovery in December, 1902, which started the rush to Goldfield (M&S, p. 115).

RABBIT HOLE (Pershing). **RABBIT HOLE SPRINGS,** found and named by the Applegates in 1846, on the east slope of the Kamma Mountains. These springs (on the Applegate Cutoff) provided the last water on the emigrant trail before the twenty-one-mile drive across the Black Rock Desert to Black Rock Spring. The name appears on two sketch maps accompanying the 1849 diaries of J. Goldsborough Bruff (Wheat III, 95, 99). **RABBIT HOLE CREEK** and **RABBIT HOLE MINING DISTRICT,** located about fifty miles north of Lovelock, were named for the springs (VPG, p. 156; 1881 Map).

RADIO CRYSTAL (Clark). A mine at the east edge of Cedar Basin and south of Mica Peak; named for rock crystal (NJ 11–12).

RAGGED TOP (Pershing). Near the Humboldt Sink in Pershing County, a peak which has a columnar structure resembling ruins is named **RAGGED TOP MOUNTAIN.** A mining district, named for the mountain, is on the west slope of the Trinity Range, ten miles by road west of Toulon (NK 11–10; OPN, p. 62; VPG, p. 157).

RAGLAN (Humboldt). The station on the main line of the WP RR between Gaskell and Winnemucca, may have been named by railroad officials for Baron Fitzroy Raglan, who commanded British troops in the Crimean War and ordered the charge of the "Light Brigade" in the battle at Balaklava, in 1854 (T54; CO, p. 687).

RAGTOWN (Churchill). **RAGTOWN STATION,** about twelve miles northwest of present-day Fallon, was on a farm owned by Asa L. Kenyon in 1854. Exhausted and thirsty emigrants recuperated here at the Carson River after their trip across the Forty Mile Desert. The station was so named because of the many rags cast off by the travelers at this point, for the tattered garments of the emigrants which, after being washed in the Carson River, were hung in the bushes to dry, or for the structure that served as a station. In 1855, Jules Remey and Julius Brenchley stated that it consisted of "three huts, formed of poles covered with rotten canvas full of holes" (JGS, I, p. 123). The station name appears on an 1855 map by Lt. Col. E. J. Steptoe showing overland routes from Salt Lake City to San Francisco Bay (Wheat IV, 28). During his *Rambles* in 1861, Dan De Quille visited Ragtown. "We were now heading for the ancient and well-known city of Ragtown, situated on the north bank of the Carson, some sixteen miles above Redman's. . . . It was long after dark when we passed through Ragtown, and we could not exactly make out the 'lay of the land,' but did not [sic] succeed in counting the buildings. We found two to be the correct number, one of which appeared to be a stable. The whole town is owned by Mr. Asa Kenyon—including 'dips, spurs and angles' " (REL, p. 42). **RAGTOWN** post office was active from May 14, 1864, to May 29, 1867, and from May 5, 1884, to April 19, 1887, when Saint Clair became the mail address for its patrons. Ragtown Monument now marks the site of the old station, and **RAGTOWN PASS** is on U.S. Alt. 95 west of Hazen (NJ 11–1; FTM, p. 23). See **LEETEVILLE.**

RAILROAD. A valley, between the White Pine, Grant, and Quinn Canyon ranges to the east, and the Pancake Range to the west (NJ 11–3; NJ 11–6; SPD, p. 963). The name may have been chosen because in 1871 a franchise was granted for a narrow-gauge railroad through Elko, Lander, Nye, White Pine, and Lincoln counties, and a survey of the valley could have been made; or a natural gravel bar in the long valley could have suggested the name (OPN, p. 75). Shift names in the area are **RAILROAD VALLEY MARSH** and a mining district named for the marsh, eighteen miles southwest of Currant, in Nye County (VPG, p. 124); **RAILROAD VALLEY MIGRATORY BIRD REFUGE** is in the southeast corner of Nye County (Park Map; Nev. Guide, p. 16). **RAILROAD PASS** denotes a low gap in the Shoshone Mountains, in Lander County, once the scene of many Indian attacks (Nev. Guide, p. 262); a low divide, two miles west of Boulder City and twenty-two miles from Las Vegas, traversed by the UP RR, in Clark County; and a pass through the north end of the

Diamond Range, between White Pine and Eureka counties, the latter pass used by Frémont in 1845 (WA; VPG). See **CHOKUP PASS**. **RAILROAD MINING DISTRICT** (Elko) was organized in 1868 and is twenty-seven miles southwest of Elko (SM, 1875, p. 22; VPG, p. 45). The district was named for the transcontinental railroad then under construction. **RAILROAD CITY,** the mining camp for the district, was laid out in 1870, about one mile from Bullion City (NM; Census, 1870; 1900). **RAILROAD SPRINGS** is the designation for springs in the McCullough Range, west of the UP RR, in Clark County; for springs and a mining district named for the springs, in the north end of the Silver Peak Range, twenty-five miles southwest of Goldfield near the former T and G RR, in Esmeralda County (VPG, p. 59).

RAINBOW. Features named for their multi-colored rock include **RAINBOW CANYON,** which designates a portion of the Meadow Valley Wash between Caliente and Leith, in Lincoln County, and a canyon draining north into Kyle Canyon, near Charleston Park in the Spring Mountains, Clark County; **RAIN-BOW GARDENS,** a valley between Las Vegas Wash and Sunrise Mountain, in Clark County; and **RAINBOW VISTA,** an area in the Valley of Fire State Park, in Clark County (WA). **RAINBOW HILLS** (Washoe). The hills in the Virginia Range near Pyramid Lake so named, although predominantly brown, are sometimes streaked with rose and purple (VPG, Nev. Guide, p. 143).

RALSTON (Nye). **RALSTON VALLEY,** which begins sixty miles south of the northern line of Nye County near Belmont and runs to the southern line, was described by Wheeler (1872, p. 77) as being "from eight to twelve miles wide, a sandy, gravelly, stony desert, with no vegetation except wild sage." The name commemorates Judge James Harvey Ralston who lost his life through starvation and exposure on the edge of the valley in May, 1864. **RALSTON** was also the name of a station in Nye County, on the former LV and T RR in Stonewall Valley (SPD, p. 962; TF, p. 21; NJ 11–5; NJ 11–8; Lida Quad.).

RAMSEY (Lyon). The former mining town, eleven miles northwest of old Fort Churchill and twenty-eight miles north of Dayton, was named for Tom and Bladen Ramsey. They staked 150 claims in the **RAMSEY MINING DISTRICT,** in 1906, on the southeast flank of the Virginia Range on the boundary line between Lyon and Storey counties. A post office so named was active from October 26, 1906, to July 31, 1913 (NJ 11–1; VPG, p. 104; M&SP, 8/11/06; NHS, 1913, p. 214; FTM, p. 23).

RAND (Mineral). The station so denoted on the former C and C RR was named for **RAND MINING DISTRICT,** on the northeast slope of the Gabbs Valley Range in the northeastern portion of the county. *Rand* is a shortened surname and commemorates R. J. Randall, the owner of several claims in the district. A post office named for the district was established March 9, 1915, and discontinued July 6, 1935, when its operations were transferred to Rawhide (OPN, p. 51; FTM, p. 23).

RAPPELJE SIDING (Lincoln). The name, from 1920 to about 1928, for former *Cloud Siding,* thirty-four miles south of Caliente on the UP RR, commemorates a railroad official (WA). See **CLOUD.**

RASID (Elko). A non-agency station on the Elko Subdivision of the SP RR, milepost 581.2, between Halleck and Deeth (T75).

RASPBERRY CREEK (Humboldt). A creek rising on the west slope of the East Range; formerly a station on the CP RR between Rose Creek and Mill City (NJ 11–11). "The creek from which this station derives its name rises in the hills about six miles south of the road and affords but little water in the summer. Why this station is called Raspberry Creek and the one we last passed Rose Creek we never understood. We saw no indications of roses or raspberries at either place" (GAC, p. 151). A short-lived post office named **RASPBERRY** was in operation from May 19, 1870, to July 20, 1870 (FTM, p. 23; 1881 Map).

RATTLESNAKE. Several species and so called sub-species of the rattler are found in the state. The western diamondback lives in the ledgy canyons along the Colorado River. Horned rattlesnakes, or sidewinders, are found south of Goldfield along the edge of Death Valley. The prairie rattler inhabits central Nevada, the Pacific rattlesnake the northern and western sections, the tiger rattlesnake the desert mountains. Panamint and Great Basin rattlers are all over the state. **RATTLESNAKE CREEK** (Elko) is south of Lee on the west slope of the Ruby Mountains. **RATTLESNAKE CANYON** denotes a canyon in the Egan Range west of McGill, in White Pine County (RRE), and a canyon southeast of Rowland in the Humboldt National Forest, Elko County (GHM, EL 3). On the west slope of the Ruby Mountains, in Elko County, are **RATTLESNAKE MOUNTAIN** and a lake so named, north of the mountain (NK 11–12). **RATTLESNAKE HILL** (Churchill). A red butte, formerly an Indian burial ground and the site of an inter-tribal battle in 1867 between the Pit River (California) Indians and the Pyramid Lake Paiutes, lies northeast of Fallon and south of Old River (Car. Sink 1908). In Clark County, features named for the rattlesnake include a peak, north of Bonelli Peak; a spring on the west side of Rattlesnake Peak, east of Garrett Butte; and a wash, the upper end of Twin Springs Wash (NJ 11–12; WA). THE RATTLESNAKE. See BLUE EAGLE.

RAVENSWOOD (Lander). RAVENSWOOD STATION on the former NC RR between Reese River Canyon and Hallsvale stations, thirty-three miles north of Clifton, was named for the RAVENSWOOD MINING DISTRICT. The district was on the east slope of the Shoshone Mountains, twenty-five miles north-northwest of Austin, and was active in the early 1880s (MA, pp. 284, 475; HHB, Nev., p. 269; DM; 1881 Map). Austin post office served the area (TF, p. 21).

RAWE PEAK (Lyon). The name of the mountain peak in the Pine Nut Mountains, southeast of Dayton, was originaly *Raw* Peak, having been named for R. S. Raw, Assistant Superintendent of the Sutro Tunnel Company (NJ 11–1; NHS, 1913, p. 210; OPN, p. 47). The mistake name *Rawe* probably was introduced by mapmakers.

RAWHIDE (Mineral). A town south of Big Kasock Mountain in northern Mineral County; a mining district named for the town at the south end of the Sand Springs Range, near the southern boundary of Churchill County. Charles Holman, a rancher and prospector, is credited with naming the settlement in 1903 by reason of his nailing a steer's tail to a mail box on a post and instructing, by a sign, "Drop mail for Rawhide here." It is more likely, however, that the settlement name is descriptive of the rawhide color of the hills (NJ 11–1; Census, 1960; OPN, p. 51; M&S, p. 125; VPG, p. 117). During the Rawhide boom of 1907 and 1908, an estimated 10,000 people swarmed into the area, attracted by great strikes such as the Grutt Hill Mine, by Stingaree Gulch (Rawhide's row, said to have rivaled San Francisco's Barbary Coast), and by the camp's ninety saloons, which existed along with a single church (NM, pp. 223–32). The grade was completed and rails and ties laid for the proposed short-line Rawhide Railroad. On September 4, 1908, a fire destroyed most of the town. RAWHIDE post office was active from October 11, 1907, to August 31, 1941 (FTM, p. 23).

REBEL CREEK (Humboldt). The settlement at the west foot of the Santa Rosa Range in Quinn River Valley was named for REBEL CREEK, an intermittent stream, tributary to the Quinn River (NK 11–8). It is said that a Confederate soldier met a Union soldier at the creek and that they fought to determine who would name it. The victorious Southerner named the creek (OPN, p. 38). A post office so denoted was established April 19, 1902, and discontinued December 15, 1947, when its operations were transferred to Orovada (FTM, p. 23); Early

REBEL CREEK STATION was served by Paradise Valley post office (TF, p. 21; 1881 Map). See WILLOW.

RED. Geographical features in the state so named have a predominance of red mineral coloring, or are associated with other features so characterized. RED BLUFF SPRING denotes a spring in Nye County, near the Lincoln County line, northeast of the Reveille Mining District (Wheeler 1871 Map), and a spring southwest of Bitter Ridge near Mud Wash, in Clark County (NJ 11–12; Wheeler 1871 Map). RED BUTTE (Humboldt) is the name for a mining district organized in 1908 on the west slope of the Jackson Range, fifteen miles north of Sulphur (VPG, p. 77). RED CANYON (Douglas), a mining district also known as *Silver Lake*, is eighteen miles southeast of Minden, on the east slope of the Pine Nut Range, west of Smith Valley (VPG, p. 34). RED HILL (Lincoln) is the name for a peak about two miles south of Pioche (WA). RED MOUNTAIN is the name for a mercury mining district (also called *Castle Peak*), ten miles north of Virginia City in Storey County, near the Washoe County line, which was discovered in the early 1860s, according to a report of the *Gold Hill News* of February 24, 1864, and March 21, 1864 (VPG, p. 168; DM). The name also designates an iron mining district on the southeast slope of the Virginia Range on the boundary line between Lyon and Storey counties, twelve miles northeast of Dayton (VPG, p. 104); and a gold-silver-lead district discovered January 26, 1864, on RED MOUNTAIN in the Silver Peak Range, Esmeralda County (Wheeler, 1872, pp. 48, 79; VPG, p. 59; NJ 11–8). RED MOUNTAIN SPRING issues from the foot of the peak. Additional peaks denoted RED MOUNTAIN are (1) north of Tonopah in the San Antonio Mountains, Nye County (NJ 11–5), (2) in the north end of the Monitor Range, Nye County, (3) northeast of the Nye County line in the White Pine Mountains, White Pine County (NJ 11–6). RED MOUNTAIN CREEK (Washoe) flows from the Granite Range to Alkali Flat (NK 11–10). RED NEEDLE (Clark) is the name for a pinnacle in Rainbow Gardens, east of Las Vegas (WA). RED ROCK is the name for a canyon heading northeast of Mount Jefferson in the Toquima Range, in Nye County (Dir. 1971), and for the canyon at the head of RED ROCK WASH, which drains from an area of red sandstone, southeast of Charleston Peak in the Spring Mountains, Clark County. RED ROCKS denotes an area, also in the Spring Mountains of Clark County, named for the strongly colored formations (VPG). A hill of red rock in Washoe County, called RED ROCK, furnished a name for a valley in the same area (NJ 11–1) and for an early settlement (Census, 1870). **RED ROCK** (Esmeralda) denoted a station on the former LV and T RR south of Goldfield. **RED SPRING** designates a spring east of Charleston Peak in the Spring Mountains, Clark County (Blue D. Quad.), and a spring near Red Canyon in the Goshute Range, White Pine County, mentioned by Simpson. "This cañon I call Red Cañon, on account of its red-colored rocks. The Spring is called by the Indians Un-go-pah, or Red Spring" (JHS, p. 121; 1867 Map; 1881 Map). **RED TOP GULCH** (Churchill) heads on the northwest slope of Driscoll Peak in the Louderback Mountains and extends to Dixie Valley (USGB 5904). **RED WASH CREEK** (Mineral), between Sweetwater and Rough creeks, rises on Dome Hill and flows to the East Walker River (GHM, MI 1).

RED COW CREEK (Elko). An intermittent stream rising in the Tuscarora Mountains and flowing to the South Fork Owyhee River, west of Big Cottonwood Canyon; perhaps named for a domestic cow seen nearby (NK 11–8).

RED HOUSE (Humboldt). A station on the main line of the WP RR, twenty-five miles northwest of Battle Mountain (T75); a post office active from October 5, 1914, to April 30, 1936, and from April 18, 1939, to June 30, 1955, when Golconda became the mail address for its patrons (FTM, p. 23).

REDLICH (Mineral). The post office so named was established May 17, 1907, and discontinued August 15, 1912, when its operations were transferred to Sodaville (FTM, p. 23).

REDMANS STATION (Churchill). The station and toll bridge, on the emigrant road at the Carson Slough, were sixteen miles southeast of Ragtown and twenty-five miles from Sink Station, at the Upper Sink of the Carson. Dan De Quille wrote of the station in 1861. "A mile ahead we could see the house of Doctor Redman and we laid our course toward it, as there we expected to camp for the night. This station is on a slough (called a slough but it is the Carson river), which empties into the Lower Sink some fifteen miles below, running northeast. Mr. Redman has a toll-bridge on this stream for the accommodation of emigrants taking the cut-off from Sand Springs to Ragtown" (REL, p. 32).

RED POINT (Elko). A station on the UP RR west of Wilkins, a shipping point for cattle; "named by Archie Bowman at the request of railroad officials . . . after the noticeable red formation on the hill" (EP, p. 67). The hill so designated is northeast of the station (GHM, EL 4). **RED POINT** also denotes a peak on Elk Mountain near the Idaho boundary (GHM, EL 3).

RED RING MOUNTAIN (Nye). A mountain, eight miles northeast of Moores Station; named by the United States Board on Geographic Names in 1969 "for the iron-stained rocks on the mountain" (USGB 6903).

REED (Elko). **REED CREEK** heads in the Humboldt National Forest and flows into the Duck Valley (Western Shoshone) Indian Reservation to the Owyhee. *Yandai,* meaning "groundhog holes," is reported to be the Shoshone Indian name for the creek (USGB 6201; NK 11–8). **REED STATION,** a stage station on the road to Tuscarora; named for Henry Reed, a homesteader in 1865 (EP, p. 68).

REEDERVILLE (Washoe). Formerly a community beyond Duck Lake and near the California line; named for Bill Reeder, who operated a business there (HPS, 1/29/56).

REEDS STATION (Lyon). An early station on the emigrant road, west of Fort Churchill and seven miles down the Carson River from Dayton; named for the proprietor, G. W. Reed. Dan De Quille rested in a grove outside the station on July 4, 1861 (REL, p. 161). The earlier name of the station was *Millers.*

REESE RIVER (Lander). A river, rising in the Toiyabe Range in Nye County and flowing northward to meet the Humboldt River at Battle Mountain in flood years; a valley through which the river flows (NJ 11–5; NJ 11–2). Captain Simpson named the river and the valley for John Reese, in 1859.

> The valley in which we are encamped, as well as its creek, I call after Mr. Reese, our guide, who, with two other men, discovered it some years since in their peregrinations between Salt Lake City and Carson Valley. They gave it the name of New River; but as Mr. Reese has been of considerable service, and discovers very laudable zeal in examining the country ahead in our explorations, I have thought it is but just to call the river and valley after him. The Indian name of the river is Pang-que-o-whop-pe, or Fish Creek. (JHS, p. 78)

John Reese, with his brother Enoch, established Mormon Station. See **GENOA.** "He started the first trading-post, and also fed the hungry emigrants for a consideration. But he did not stop at this. He put up a blacksmith shop and shod their animals and repaired their wagons, and later erected a flouring and saw-mill" (MA, p. 378). According to the manuscript which he prepared for Bancroft, Reese "went with Capt. Simpson taking 10 wagons right through the country to Genoa" (NHS, 1917, pp. 189–90). Early emigrants had named the valley *Whirlwind* for the columns of dust frequently seen ascending skyward (GAC, pp. 146–47). **REESE RIVER BUTTE** is at the Nye-Lander county line, east of the river, and **REESE RIVER GAME REFUGE** is in northwestern Nye County (NJ 11–2; Park

Map). See **CAÑON**. For the discovery of the Reese River mines, see **AUSTIN. REESE RIVER** post office was active from June 5, 1946, to August 7, 1951, in Nye County (FTM, p. 23).

REEVES. See **DELAMAR.**

REGAN (White Pine). A mining district in the Kern Mountains near the Nevada-Utah boundary, sixty-five miles east-southeast of Cherry Creek; a former post office, established August 20, 1906, and discontinued November 30, 1907, when Trout Creek, Utah, became the mail address for its patrons (VPG, p. 186; FTM, p. 24).

REGENT (Mineral). A mining district organized February 17, 1907, on the south end of the Sand Springs Range, twenty-eight miles east of Schurz, and also known as *Rawhide*. First locations are said to have been made in December, 1906, by Schaedler and Wassen, ranchers who lived near Fairview (VPG, p. 117; DM).

REIPETOWN. See **RIEPETOWN.**

RENNOX (Lander). A station on the WP RR at the south edge of the Sheep Creek Range, southeast of North Battle Mountain and west of Kampos (T54; NK 11-11).

RENO (Washoe). Reno, on the Truckee River, is at the junction of U.S. 395 and U.S. 40 and is served by the WP RR and the SP RR, also formerly by the V and T RR. The county seat was moved from Washoe City to Reno in 1871. The site was first known as *Fullers Crossing*, having been named for C. W. Fuller, from Susanville, who built a hotel and the first bridge across the Truckee in 1859. His log toll bridge was washed away in 1862. In 1863, he sold his rebuilt bridge to Myron C. Lake, a veteran of the Mexican War, and in time, the place became known as *Lakes Crossing*. The name survived as late as 1890 in Lake House, a hotel on the south bank of the Truckee, on the original Fuller location and at the site of the present Riverside Hotel (MA, p. 634; HHB, Nev., p. 256; NHS, 1920, p. 59). By 1868, the CP RR had finished construction to a point across the river from Lake's hotel. Lake deeded forty acres of land to Charles Crocker in consideration of his causing a station to be established there. Some wanted to call the new station *Argenta* because of the silver ore to be transported there from the Comstock Lode. The *Gold Hill Daily News* had favored this name, but commented in 1868 "Reno is more easily written and the Railroad officials had sense enough to omit city, a term which was usually a burlesque" (NHS, 1924, pp. 99–100). The town was officially established on May 9, 1868, the post office on May 13, 1868. At the suggestion of men who had served in the Mexican War, railroad officials named the place for Jesse Lee Reno, an American army officer who was killed in action at South Mountain (a ridge in southern Pennsylvania and western Maryland) on September 14, 1862 (OPN, p. 69; 1867 Map; MA, p. 635; NHS, 1911, p. 85; Nev. Guide, p. 148). The University of Nevada, opened in Elko on October 12, 1874, was moved to Reno and reopened on March 31, 1886.

RENO BELL (Washoe). The mine so named in the Wedekind Mining District, four miles northeast of Reno, commemorates the city and C. B. Bell, a prospector and mine owner (DM; VPG, p. 175).

RESERVATION. A mining district, also known as *Granite*, at the north end of the Wassuk Range, eight miles northwest of Schurz; a former post office (May 15, 1909–November 15, 1909); a hill, south of Weber Reservoir and west of the Walker River; a non-agency station on the Mina Branch of the SP RR between Lux and Schurz; all named for being in or near the Walker River Indian Reservation which is mainly in Mineral County (NJ 11-1; T75; VPG, p. 114; FTM, p. 24). **RESERVATION HILL** (Elko). A hill on the north side of the Owyhee River, about three miles northwest of Mountain City in the Duck Valley Indian Reservation, from which it takes its name (USGB 6103). See **NARINO HONGUY.**

REVEILLE (Nye). A mountain range, extending south from the Pancake Range; a peak in the south end of the range; a valley lying between the Reveille and Kawich ranges; a mining district located in 1866 in the Reveille Range, seventy miles east of Tonopah; a former mining camp; a post office active, but with numerous interruptions, from September 24, 1867, to December 31, 1911 (NJ 11-5; NJ 11-8; Wheeler, 1872, p. 42; 1867 Map; SM, 1867; pp. 56–66; VPG, p. 136; Census, 1870; SM, 1875, p. 102; FTM, p. 24). A member of the prospecting party that discovered the mineral deposits, Editor Fairchild of the *Reese River Reveille*, named the district to commemorate the newspaper, which first appeared in 1863 and which is the oldest continuously published paper in Nevada (MM; Nev. Guide, pp. 84–85; NM).

REYNARD (Washoe). The station on the WP RR so named is on the east edge of the Smoke Creek Desert and thirty-two miles northeast of Flanigan (T54).

RHODES (Mineral). The locality at the junction of State Route 10 and U.S. 95, eight miles south of Mina, took its name from **RHODES SALT MARSH**, just east of the former settlement and three miles south of Sodaville. The name originally was spelled Rho*a*des, in honor of A. J. Rhoades who worked the salt marsh (MA, p. 419; HHB, Nev., p. 260). *Rhodes* was the name of the post office, established in Esmeralda (Mineral)

County on October 2, 1893, and discontinued October 14, 1911 (FTM, p. 24). At one time, prior to the establishment of **RHODES MARSH STATION** on the former C and C RR, salt was transported from the marsh to Virginia City by a train of camels (Haw. Quad.; NJ 11–4; MM).

RHYOLITE (Nye). The boom town of 1906 was founded by the Busch brothers in 1904 on the northeast flank of Bonanza Mountain in the Bullfrog Hills, about five miles west of Beatty and not far from the north end of Death Valley. The mining district so denoted and also known as *Bullfrog,* was named for rhyolite, the predominant rock in the area. The site of the mining camp, once served by three railroads, the former LV and T RR, T and T RR, and BG RR, is marked by the old railroad depot and by the Rhyolite Bottle House which, according to Nell Murbarger, was constructed of "51,000 quart liquor containers laid in adobe-mud mortar, their bottom ends to the outside" by Tom Kelly, a saloonkeeper of bonanza days (HWY Map; Bull. Quad.; NM, p. 218; VPG, p. 124). **RHYOLITE** post office was established May 19, 1905, and discontinued September 15, 1919, when its operations were transferred to Beatty (FTM, p. 24). **RHYOLITE HILLS** denotes a group of hills bounded on the north and east by Emigrant Valley, on the south by Groom Pass and the Halfpint Range, and on the west by the northeast end of Yucca Flat (USGB 6302). **RHYOLITE KNOB** is a hill at the north end of Kawich Valley, fifty-six miles east of Goldfield (USGB 6303).

RIBBON CLIFF (Nye). The cliff on Pahute Mesa, about four miles east of the top of Black Mountain, is "named for the ribbon-like appearance of a prominent thin bed of rock which runs in an undulating manner along the cliff face" (USGB 6302; DL 56).

RIEPETOWN (White Pine). The mining settlement on the east edge of Kimberly, about seven miles west of Ely, was named for Richard A. Riepe (1848–1918), who was born in Herstelle, Westphalen, Germany. He came to Nevada in the early 1870s, served as an assemblyman for Lincoln County in 1883 and for White Pine County in 1889–1891, and was appointed postmaster of Ely on August 27, 1887 (NHS, 1920, pp. 271, 272; DM; USGB 6301; NHS, 1924, p. 407). Variants are *Reipetown* (Ely Quad. 1916; GHM, WP 1; NJ 11–3) and *Reifetown,* the name of the post office established May 1, 1909, and discontinued April 30, 1912, when Kimberly became the mail address for its patrons (FTM, p. 24).

RIGGS SPRING (Lincoln). The spring in the mountains about eight miles southeast of Delamar commemorates the Riggs family who may have been the first locators of the

Delamar district, with their discovery of the Monkey Wrench Mine in 1889 (JGS, I, pp. 618–19; GHM, LN 2; WA). See **DELAMAR.**

RILEY, FORT (Storey). After the defeat of the Nevada volunteers by the Paiute Indians in the Battle of Pyramid Lake, May 12, 1860, the women and children of Virginia City were sheltered in a half-finished stone house, which had been barricaded for defense and denoted **FORT RILEY.** The name commemorates its builder, Peter O'Riley, a Johntown miner, who with Patrick McLaughlin, is credited with having discovered the Ophir bonanza on the Comstock (GHS, pp. 2–3; FCL, p. 223; Ruhlen). See **OPHIR.**

RINGBOLT RAPIDS (Clark). The name for former rapids in the Colorado River, about three and one-half miles below present Hoover Dam. When the river was low, the rapids made boat travel difficult, with the result that "a heavy ringbolt, with a ring 12' in diameter and 1¾" thick, was set in an 80-ton andesite boulder subsequently known as Ringbolt Rock, so that the steamer 'Esmeralda' could winch itself up and down over the rapids" (WA).

RIO TINTO (Elko). The town, just south of Mountain City and on the Owyhee River, was named for a nearby mine. The immense Rio Tinto (Spanish "dyed [tinted] river") copper deposits were discovered by S. Frank Hunt, who named the mine for the *Minas de Riotinto,* rich copper mines of southwest Spain on the Tinto River (NK 11–9; OPN, p. 27; Nev. Guide, p. 170). A biographical sketch of Hunt written by John A. Fulton describes the discovery.

> About three and one-half miles south of Mountain City, he [S. Frank Hunt] discovered a large gossan outcrop, and later a float boulder showing green copper stain, in the bed of Copper Gulch. In November, 1919, he located the Nevada Rio Tinto group of mining claims covering the outcropping . . . and early in 1931 the Rio Tinto Copper Company was organized. . . . The Company sold enough stock to sink an incline shaft through the oxidized zone and struck the top of the rich Rio Tinto sulphide ore body at a depth of 227 feet below the surface on February 26, 1932. . . . The Rio Tinto Copper Company sold out to the International Smelting and Refining Company in 1932. (SFH, Intro.)

The operations of **RIO TINTO** post office, established December 7, 1936, were transferred to Mountain City on February 29, 1948 (FTM, p. 24).

RIOVILLE (Clark). A former town that grew up at the site of Bonellis Ferry, at the junction of the Virgin and the Colorado rivers; also called *Junction City* and *Junctionville* (WA; JGS, I, pp. 594–95). **RIOVILLE** post office was active from November 2, 1881, to June 30, 1906, when Saint Thomas became the mail address for its patrons. The sites of both towns are now under the waters of Lake Mead (FTM, p. 24).

RIO VIRGIN. See VIRGIN.

RIO VISTA (Lyon). A station on the former C and C RR, fifty-four miles from Mound House and sixteen miles from Wabuska; named for the view of the Carson River (NHS, 1913, p. 208).

RIPLY (Clark). The name of **RIPLY** post office, changed from *Sandy* on September 23, 1910, became *Platina* on January 8, 1916 (FTM, p. 24).

RIP VAN WINKLE (Elko). The **RIP VAN WINKLE MINE,** also known as "The Rip," and the Sleepy Hollow Mine (both of the Lone Mountain district) were located in 1869 and named to commemorate two short stories by Washington Irving, *Rip Van Winkle* (1819) and *The Legend of Sleepy Hollow* (1820).

RISSUE (Douglas). **RISSUE ROAD** was a toll road down the valley of the Walker River, built by a man named *LaSue* or *Lasue,* who also maintained a ferry on the Walker River (NHS, 1913, p. 196). **RISUE,** a variant of the mistake name, denotes a canyon heading in the Pine Nut Mountains, south of Long Dry Canyon, and a spring in the canyon (GHM, DO 1).

RIVER BED STATION (Churchill). An early station on the road from Virginia City to the Reese River mines, via the Twenty-Six-Mile Desert; named for its location on an old river bed, presumably the Carson (NHS, 1913, p. 175).

RIVERSIDE (Clark). A settlement, southwest of Bunkerville and just north of the Virgin River in the northeastern portion of the county; named for its position near the river (NJ 11–12).

ROACH (Clark). A locality and a station on the UP RR south of Borax and five miles north of the California line; named at the time of settlement in 1905 (NI 11–3; OPN, p. 17).

ROBBERS ROOST. Features so named were known, or thought likely, to have been good hideouts for thieves. A settlement of early Elko County, served by Toano post office, and a ranch in the Meadow Valley Wash are so denoted. The latter received its name shortly before 1900 when two peddlers who stopped at the ranch were robbed during the night by two men living there, Hardy who escaped, and Pippin who was imprisoned for the crime (HHB, Nev., p. 277; TF, p. 21; WA). **ROBBERS ROOST CAVE** (Clark) is a cave on the northeast side of Mummy Mountain, two miles northeast of Charleston Peak in the Spring Mountains (WA). **ROBBERS ROOST RIDGE** (White

Pine) is a ridge between the lower end of Butte Valley and Queue Valley, about thirty-two miles northwest of Ely (USGB 5902). **ROBBERS ROOST SPRINGS** and **ROBBERS ROOST WELL** are southwest of the ridge for which they are named (GHM, WP 3).

ROBERTS (Eureka). The **ROBERTS MOUNTAINS** of central Eureka County are north of Kobeh Valley and east of the Simpson Park Mountains. **ROBERTS CREEK** flows from the Roberts Mountains into Kobeh Valley where it joins Coils Creek. **ROBERTS CREEK MOUNTAIN** is north of the creek and south of Western Peak. **ROBERTS CREEK STATION,** a station on both the Overland Stage and Pony Express lines, was attacked by Indians in April, 1860. The stop was twenty-five miles southwest of Diamond Springs Station (Nev. I, 1961). A mining district, located on the Roberts Mountains for which it is named, is thirty miles northwest of Eureka. The name group honors Bolivar Roberts, a division superintendent of the Pony Express (NJ 11–2; Robt. Mts. Quad.; 1881 Map; VPG, p. 68; OPN, p. 34).

ROBINSON. **ROBINSON CANYON** and **SUMMIT,** west and north of Ely in the Egan Range of White Pine County, were named for the **ROBINSON MINING DISTRICT,** located in the canyon in 1869. Thomas Robinson, who had been an assayer at Pahranagat, was one of the locators and operators of the Trench Mine and a leading rancher in the Ely country. The settlement of **ROBINSON,** between Keegan and McCoy in Spring Valley, was included in the Federal Census of 1870 (NJ 11–3; NHS, 1924 p. 282; DM; SPD, p. 1048; Ely Quad. 1952). **ROBINSON** (Elko) denotes a lake east of Lamoille and north of Green Mountain, in the Ruby Mountains, and a creek rising near **ROBINSON LAKE** on the east slope of the Rubies and flowing into Ruby Valley; named for George Robinson, an early rancher (NK 11–12; EP, p. 74).

ROCHESTER (Pershing). In the early 1860s, a party of prospectors in the West Humboldt Range started operations on the lime contact where it cut through a canyon. They named the canyon for their native city, Rochester, New York (SPD, pp. 889, 900, 920). However, it was not until ore discoveries in 1911 that the camp became very productive. Activities in **ROCHESTER MINING DISTRICT,** about twenty miles northeast of Lovelock, brought about the establishment of a mining camp so named, which became a small feeder town for Oreana. A narrow gauge railway (1913–1920) connected the mining district with the main line of the SP RR at Oreana and was familiarly known as the "Silver Belt Railroad" (DM, RR (I), pp. 57–62). The camp was divided into three parts: **LOWER ROCHESTER,** near the Rochester Mill on Lincoln Hill, **CENTRAL ROCHESTER** to the east, and **ROCHESTER,** also called *Upper Rochester* and *East Rochester* (HPS, 1/29/56; DM; VPG, p. 157; NK 11–10). See **NENZEL** and **LOWER ROCHESTER.**

ROCK. The name usually occurs as a specific term with single generics for water features. **ROCK CREEK** denotes creeks in Elko, Esmeralda, Eureka, Humboldt, and Lander counties. **ROCK CREEK MINING DISTRICT** (Elko) was discovered at the head of Rock Creek and ten miles west of Tuscarora in August, 1876. The district was served by Tuscarora post office (VPG, p. 46; TF, p. 21). A mining district of Lander County so named (also called *Bateman Canyon*) is fifteen miles south of Battle Mountain (VPG, p. 81; NK 11–11; NK 11–8; Dir. 1971). **ROCK LAKE** is south of Ophir Creek and east of Prices Lake in Washoe County (GHM, WA 1). **ROCK SPRING(S)** designates springs in Churchill, Elko, Eureka, Humboldt, Lander, Washoe, and White Pine counties. More than one generic term occurs in **ROCK SPRING TABLE,** a flat in northwest Humboldt County, and **ROCK SPRING TABLE RESERVOIR.** Early settlers at Rock Spring, for which the features were named, were served by Buffalo Meadows post office (1881 Map; TF, p. 21). **ROCK SPRINGS COW CAMP,** a ranch on **ROCK SPRINGS CREEK,** is situated at Rock Springs in northeast Elko County. Early settlers at the springs were served by Tecoma post office (1881 Map; TF, p. 21; GHM, EL 4). **ROCK SPRINGS CANYON** (Lincoln) heads in the Delamar Mountains and trends eastward to the Meadow Valley Wash, near Stine Siding (WA). **ROCK VALLEY** and **ROCK VALLEY WASH** are northeast of Lathrop Wells in Nye County (GHM, NY 8).

ROCK POINT MILL (Lyon). The former mill, one of the largest on the Carson River, was built about 1861 a mile northeast of Dayton, by Hugh Logan, J. R. Logan, James Holmes, and John Black. The mill later was known as the *C. C. Stevenson,* for its owner, who was Governor of Nevada, 1887–1890 (DM; NHS, 1922, p. 34).

ROCKLAND (Lyon). An early mining camp in **ROCKLAND CANYON** on the east slope of the Pine Grove Hills, twenty-three miles south of Yerington; a mining district in the canyon; a former post office, active during three different periods, from January 9, 1871, to January 31, 1909; named for the **ROCKLAND MINE** discovered in 1866. An order to establish **ROCKLAND MINE** post office, dated December 12, 1916, was rescinded June 5, 1917 (NJ 11–4; 1881 Map; Census, 1870; HHB, Nev., pp. 260–61; NM; VPG, p. 103; FTM, p. 24).

ROCKY. Peaks named for heavy rock outcroppings are northeast of Virginia City in the Flowery Range in Storey County, and north of the Smoke Creek Desert in the Granite Range in Washoe County (Car. C. Quad.; OPN, p. 69). **ROCKY BLUFF** denotes a peak southwest of Wild Horse Reservoir in Elko County (GHM, EL 3). Canyons so named are in Eureka, Humboldt, Lander, and Pershing counties (Dir. 1971). **ROCKY GAP SPRING** (Clark) is a spring southeast of Charleston Peak in the Spring Mountains, between Red Rocks and the Roberts Ranch (WA).

RODENBAUGHS STATION. See **DESERT.**

RODEO CREEK. The name from Spanish *rodear* ("to go around") is descriptive of a creek in northern Eureka County, which flows circuitously from the Tuscarora Mountains into Boulder Valley (NK 11–11). A creek so named in Washoe County rises on the east slope of the Lake Range and flows into Mud Flat, south of Bull Creek (NK 11–10). The latter creek may have been the site of a cattle "roundup," an event known in Spanish as a "rodeo."

RODERICK (Washoe). A former post office established October 5, 1929, and discontinued April 30, 1936, when its operations were transferred to Wadsworth (FTM, p. 24).

ROE PEAK (Lincoln). A peak north of Broad Canyon, northwest of Pioche, in the Bristol Range; named for the Roe brothers who operated a copper smelter in Bristol, about 1888 (NJ 11–6; WA).

ROGERS. The Rogers claim on the Comstock was purchased by Eilley Orrum and became a part of the Sandy Bowers claim. See **BOWERS.** The name honored James F. Rogers, one of the early locators, a quiet young man who "one morning in the summer of 1860 . . . was found dead in his room in Virginia City, shot through the head by a pistol ball. Whether it was a case of suicide or assassination never was ascertained" (HDG, CP, 11/25/76; HHB, Nev., p. 109). **ROGERS** (Clark) denotes a wash draining eastward from the Muddy Mountains into **ROGERS BAY,** in the Overton Arm of Lake Mead, and a spring in Rogers Wash (NJ 11–12; WA).

ROLLER COASTER KNOB (Nye). A hill on the east side of the Cactus Range, about twenty-eight miles east-southeast of Goldfield; "named after the 'Roller Coaster' project of the Atomic Energy Commission," in 1963 (USGB 6303).

ROMANO (Eureka). A post office of this name was active from February 24, 1902, to August 31, 1914, and from February 3, 1919, to February 15, 1929. Its operations were transferred to Palisade in 1914 and to Eureka in 1929 (FTM, p. 24).

RONDA (Pershing). A station on the main

line of the WP RR, at the south edge of the Black Rock Desert and four miles west of Sulphur; perhaps so named for a commune in southern Spain (T54).

ROOP. Formerly a settlement of central Washoe County at the western boundary line; established about 1860 and named for **ROOP COUNTY,** now a part of Washoe County. **ROOP** post office (Washoe) was established July 6, 1894, and discontinued August 30, 1924, when it was transferred to Wendel, California (FTM, p. 24). The county name commemorated Isaac Roop, who was elected governor under the Provisional Territorial Government established by the people of western Utah in 1859 (NHS, 1911, p. 85). See **WASHOE** and **LAKE.**

ROOSEVELT (Esmeralda). The former mining camp was about seventeen miles south of Lida and may have been named in honor of Theodore Roosevelt (1858–1919), twenty-sixth president of the United States (DM). **ROOSEVELT WELL** is east of the site of the mining camp (GHM, ES 2).

ROOT (Clark). S. C. Root, a miner, is commemorated by the name of an old mining camp of the Goodsprings district, on the north side of **ROOT** (Bonanza) **HILL** (WA).

ROSE. Jacob H. Rose, who put up one of the first mills on the Eastern Slope, at Franktown, built a house in **ROSE CANYON** in 1852. According to Davis, the canyon in Ormsby (Carson City) County had been named for Richard Rose, who came to western Utah, also in 1852. Jacob Rose, a prominent pioneer, was honored by having his name applied to a mountain north of Lake Tahoe and southwest of Reno in Washoe County (SPD, p. 228; NHS, 1926, p. 394). Features named for **MOUNT ROSE** include a summit, a relay station, **ROSE KNOB,** and **ROSE KNOB PEAK,** west of Incline Lake (NJ 11–1; SPD, p. 228; NHS, 1926, p. 394). Another story of the naming of Mount Rose relates that H. S. Ham, an editor of a Washoe City newspaper, named the peak for a Miss Rose Hickman (NHS, 1911, p. 89). **ROSE CREEK** (Humboldt). A side track station on the CP RR (now on the SP RR) eleven miles from Winnemucca; named for **ROSE CREEK,** which flows from north of Dun Glen Peak in the East Range. "You will have to look sharp to see the creek, or the roses, and, by way of variety, you will discover plenty of sage brush. It is a staple article in this country" (FES, p. 193; GAC, p. 151; NK 11–11; T1TR). **ROSE CREEK** (Mineral) rises on the west slope of the Wassuk Range and empties into the southwest end of Walker Lake (NJ 11–4). **ROSE SPRING** (Clark) denotes a spring southeast of Charleston Peak in the Spring Mountains (Vegas Quad.). On May 23, 1858, J. H. Martineau, historian of a Mormon exploring party, noted in his Journal that they "found a good cool spring near the edge of the bench which we named Rose Springs" (Wheat IV, 135). **ROSE TANK** is the name for a water hole on the Arden-Pahrump road, in southwest Clark County (WA). **ROSE VALLEY** (Lincoln), an early settlement served by Pioche post office, was named for its position in that portion of Ursine Valley so denoted (Census, 1870, 1900; WA; 1881 Map; TF, p. 21).

ROSEBUD (Pershing). A peak and a canyon in the Kamma Mountains were named for the rose-colored hills there (NK 11–10; VPG). **ROSEBUD MINING DISTRICT** organized at the site ten miles southeast of Sulphur, and resulting in the platting of a townsite so named, was active in 1906 and 1907 (VPG, p. 158; NM; DM). A post office named for the camp was active from January 19, 1907, to July 31, 1909 (FTM, p. 24). See **GOLDBUD.**

ROSEMAY (White Pine). A short-lived post office, in operation from May 15, 1899, to July 31, 1900, when Strawberry became the mail address for its patrons (FTM, p. 24). The Official Register of 1899 lists a variant Rosemary.

ROSEWELL (Nye). A former station on the now defunct LV and T RR between Cañon and Chlorine, in the Amargosa Desert about eighteen miles southeast of Beatty. The name commemorates G. W. Rose who, with E. E. Palmer, put down a 210-foot well which produced approximately one hundred barrels of water a day. The station was known also as *Roses Well,* and the well was called both *Palmers* and *Roses.* The well was dug by the two men to serve their freight line between Las Vegas and Beatty (Furn. Cr. Quad.; WA; VPG).

ROUGH CREEK (Lyon). This creek, upon which Frémont camped in January, 1844, flows northward from Aurora, north of Bodie Creek, and discharges into the East Walker River (NJ 11–4; VPG).

ROUNDED RIDGE (Nye). The ridge in the Halfpint Range two miles southwest of The Hump was so named for "its smoothly rounded but steep sides" (USGB 6301; DL 50).

ROUND MOUNTAIN. A town, mining district (discovered by Louis Gordon in 1906), and post office (established March 4, 1907) sixty miles north of Tonopah and twenty miles north of Manhattan, on the west slope of the Toquima Range (VPG, p. 137; SHM 96; FTM, p. 24; NJ 11–5). "Round Mountain, after which the district and its leading company take their name, is a low, round top mountain of porphyry and rhyolite, on the east side of Smoky Valley, near the base of the Toquima range" (SPD, p. 971).

ROUND MOUNTAIN (Churchill) is the descriptive name for a knob in the Clan Alpine Mountains, about one and a half miles northeast of Wonder (NJ 11–1; USGB 5904).

ROUND SPRINGS (White Pine). An early settlement eight miles east of Hamilton on the Ely-Hamilton stage route (NHS, 1924, p. 450).

ROWLAND (Elko). Rowland Gill, a stockman and settler of 1889, is commemorated by the name of this town between Jarbidge and Mountain City and near the Idaho line, and its post office, active from March 5, 1900, to November 14, 1942 (OPN, p. 27; FTM, p. 24; NK 11–9).

ROX (Lincoln). A siding and pumping station settled in 1902 on the UP RR in the Meadow Valley Wash, fifteen miles north of Moapa; named to describe the rocky nature of the surroundings (NJ 11–12; WA; OPN, p. 45). A post office so named was established May 20, 1921, and discontinued August 15, 1949, when its operations were transferred to Carp (FTM, p. 24).

ROYAL CITY (Lincoln). The name of a mining camp established about 1877, and a post office active from October 15, 1878, to January 26, 1879, in the Jackrabbit (Bristol) Mining District which was discovered in 1876 (1881 Map). The name of the camp was changed later to *Jackrabbit* for the mine so denoted (WA; FTM, p. 24; DM).

ROYSTON (Nye). A mining district, also called *San Antone*, twenty-five miles north of Tonopah in the San Antonio Mountains; a mining camp, active in the early 1920s (VPG, p. 138; NM).

RUBY. The Ruby complex of Elko and White Pine counties stems from **RUBY VALLEY,** apparently named by an emigrant party of the late 1840s, or 1850s, for red garnets (commonly referred to as "ruby garnets") which they found there. See **VALLEY OF FOUNTAINS.** The valley's name was known to Captain James H. Simpson, who in 1859 established two wagon routes between Camp Floyd, Utah, and Genoa. "Ruby Valley takes its name from the circumstance, so I am informed, of rubies having been picked up in it on the west side, a few miles north of the mail-station. However this may be, it is very certain we could not find any, and the probabilities are that it is no more a ruby valley than the others we have crossed" (JHS, p. 64). Red garnets from the mountains were panned by a soldier with Colonel P. E. Connor, in 1862, from the gravel from their camp near the south end of the range. **RUBY VALLEY** post office, established in Utah Territory April 30, 1862, and active until 1869, "was probably the station on the overland stage route generally called Camp Ruby or Fort Ruby, which was the military

headquarters of the troops guarding the mail route in the Fall of 1862" (C&C, p. 593; Nev. Terr. Map; VPG). **FORT RUBY** (White Pine) was established on the west side of Ruby Valley, a half-way point on the six-hundred-mile mail route from Salt Lake City to Carson Valley, on September 4, 1862. Troops had previously patrolled the road because of the Pyramid Lake Indian War of 1860 and, after the establishment of the fort, had numerous skirmishes with Indians, both along the mail route and the Humboldt route. The name of the adobe and log encampment was changed to *Camp Ruby* on January 1, 1867. Its garrison was moved to Camp Halleck on March 10, 1869, and the camp was abandoned September 20, 1869 (Cad. Map; 1860 Map; 1867 Map; Ruhlen; HPS, 1/29/56). **RUBY VALLEY** is also the name for an Indian reservation; for a mining district on the east slope of the **RUBY MOUNTAINS,** forty-five miles southwest of Tobar and thirty-five miles south of Halleck, in Elko County; and for a former station, between Mountain Springs and Jacobs Well, on the line of the Pony Express (VPG, p. 47; Jackson Map). The highest point in the Ruby Mountains, a north-south trending mountain range west of the valley, is **RUBY DOME,** elevation 11,349 feet. **RUBY RANGE** denotes a mining district, fifteen miles west of Tobar. Some lakes in the high Rubies retain small icebergs throughout the summer. **RUBY LAKE** is south of Franklin Lake in Ruby Valley and the site of **RUBY LAKE NATIONAL WILDLIFE REFUGE** and **RUBY MARSH.** The name of the lake appears on Britton and Rey's Map of the State of California, published by George H. Goddard in 1857 (Wheat IV, 60). On the main line of the WP RR, **RUBY** is the designation for a station ten miles southeast of Wells (NK 11–12; NJ 11–3; VPG, p. 47; T54). **RUBY PASS.** See **CHOKUP PASS.**

RUBY HILL (Eureka). In 1865, Owen Farrell, M. G. Clough, and Alonzo Monroe, were led to a site about two and a half miles west of Eureka by an Indian. There, they located the Buckeye and Champion mines on a northwesterly spur of Prospect Mountain, which they called **RUBY HILL.** The mining camp "took its name from the fact that large pockets of ruby silver were uncovered there" (NHS, 1924, p. 302). In July of 1870, San Francisco capitalists formed the famous Eureka Consolidated Mining Company (MA, pp. 426, 434). A post office named for the mining camp served the area from September 23, 1873, to November 30, 1901, and the RH RR (built from Eureka) for a time served the **RUBY HILL MINING DISTRICT,** which is also known as *Eureka* (1881 Map; VPG, p. 64; FTM, p. 24).

RUTH (White Pine). At the town of **RUTH,**

west of Ely on the NN RR, is one of the world's largest open-pit copper mines—an east-west trending pit, about a mile long and a half mile wide, known as the Liberty Pit (q.v.). One of the claims which opened the ore deposit was the **RUTH**, named by D. C. McDonald for his daughter. The town and post office, established February 8, 1904, were named for the Ruth Claim (RRE; NJ 11–3; FTM, p. 25).

RYE PATCH (Pershing). The station on the CP RR (now on the SP RR, between Humboldt and Oreana) was named for wild rye grass growing there. In 1873, "on the moist ground around this place, patches of wild rye grow luxuriantly" (GAC, p. 153). By 1879, according to Williams' Guide, "the increase, however, in the herds of the stockmen has destroyed its [wild rye's] native growth, and it is now seldom seen" (FES, p. 196). Because an English company erected a ten-stamp mill at **RYE PATCH** railway station in 1870, a small settlement grew around it, and a post office established as *Rye Valley* on June 3, 1872, was renamed Rye Patch on November 11, 1872, and discontinued November 4, 1916 (MA, p. 450; 1881 Map; FTM, p. 25). Shift names in the area are **RYE PATCH MINE** in the Echo district; **RYE PATCH MINING DISTRICT,** four miles east of the station on the west flank of the Humboldt Range; **RYE PATCH DAM,** completed on the Humboldt River in 1936 by the Bureau of Reclamation; and **RYE PATCH RESERVOIR,** created by the dam for irrigating land in the Lovelock area (MA, p. 450; OPN, pp. 62–63; T75; SPD, p. 897; NK 11–10; VPG, p. 159).

RYNDON (Elko). The name denotes a non-agency station on the Elko Subdivision of the SP RR between Elburz and Osino, and a former post office, active from January 22, 1903, to March 31, 1904, when Elko became the mail address for its patrons (T75; FTM, p. 25).

SACATONE (Clark). The name of a wash which drains generally southeastward from the Newberry Mountains to Grapevine Canyon; descriptive of the coarse grass in the area of the watercourse (Davis. Quad.).

SACRAMENTO. A mining district so named was located on the west flank of the Humboldt Range in **SACRAMENTO CANYON** (Pershing), in the early 1860s (Nev. Terr. Map; Love. Quad.; VPG, p. 160). In 1924, a dumortierite deposit was discovered in the district. See **OREANA** and **CHAMPION.**
SACRAMENTO (White Pine) denotes a mining district on the west slope of the Snake Range at **SACRAMENTO PASS,** on U.S.

50 between Baker and Ely. The Spanish name for "Holy Sacrament" may have been transferred by prospectors from California, thus commemorating a city so denoted in that state (VPG, p. 182; NJ 11–3).

SADLER (Elko). **SADLER BASIN,** a small valley east of the Diamond Hills, lies southwest of the **SADLER RANCH** for which it is named. The ranch, formerly a stage stop in Huntington Valley, was named for Governor Reinhold Sadler (1899–1902) who once owned it (GHM, EL 1; EP, p. 70).

SADLER, CAMP (Ormsby). A name of undetermined origin for a temporary military camp, established near Carson City during the Civil War (Ruhlen; DM).

SAFFORD (Eureka). Ben C. Safford was a veteran prospector and the discoverer of the **SAFFORD MINING DISTRICT** six miles west of Palisade in **SAFFORD CANYON.** The district was also known as *Barth* and *Pine Mountain.* A former mining camp, laid out in September, 1881, and a post office, active from July 31, 1882, to May 7, 1883, took their names from the district they served (VPG, p. 68; DM; FTM, p. 25; GHM, EU 2).

SAGE. The name denotes a station on the WP RR ten miles southwest of Shafter, and a spring northwest of Jack Creek, in Elko County; a creek rising north of Windy Canyon and joining Weaver Creek southeast of Osceola, in White Pine County; a flat east of Salt Wells, in Churchill County (T54; SG Map 9; GHM, EL 2, 6; CH 2). Of the many species of sagebrush in the state, the three-dented leaf sagebrush (*Artemisia tridentata*) is the most common and, under good conditions, may grow to a height of ten feet.

SAGEBRUSH. Water features named for an abundance of sagebrush in the area include **SAGEBRUSH CREEK,** east of Rock Spring Table Reservoir in Humboldt County, and **SAGEBRUSH SPRING,** northeast of Stony Point in the Sheep Creek Range in Lander County (GHM, HU 3; LA 2). See **SAGE.**

SAGE HEN. In the southwest corner of Pershing County, **SAGE HEN VALLEY** lies between the Nightingale and Sahwave ranges and extends into the northeast part of Churchill County. **SAGE HEN WASH** traverses the valley, and **SAGE HEN SPRING** is at its west side. **SAGE HEN CREEK** is a small stream east of the valley. Another wash in Pershing County so named runs north of Copper Valley (NHS, 1913, p. 177; NJ 11–1; GHM, PE 1). **SAGE HEN** also designates a flat in Esmeralda County north of Boundary Peak; a creek in Lyon County northwest of Sweetwater; and springs in Mineral County west of Mount Montgomery, and in White Pine County on Shellback Ridge (GHM, ES 1; LY 2; MI 2; WP 2). **SAGEHEN SPRING** denotes springs north of La Plata in Churchill County, and

southeast of Elk Mountain in northern Elko
County. **SAGEHEN BASIN** (Elko) is a
valley south of Horse Heaven Flat. **SAGE-
HEN WASH** (Lincoln) runs west of Buck
Wash in the Wilson Creek Range. A range in
the northwest corner of Humboldt County is
named **SAGEHEN HILLS** (GHM, CH 2;
EL 3; LN 1; HU 3). All features were named
for the indigenous sage grouse.

SAGUNDAIS (Mineral). A spring south of
Walker Lake; named by Frémont on November 21, 1845, for his Delaware chief guide
who found it (JGS, I, p. 94). *Sagundai* is a
variant spelling (GHM, MI 2).

SAHWAVE (Pershing). A short range bounded
on the west by Sage Hen Valley and on the
east by Granite Spring and Copper valleys.
The name, placed by the Fortieth Parallel
Survey, is from Northern Paiute *sai-wav,*
"sage" and is contained in the Paviotso
vocabulary given by Naches to John Wesley
Powell in 1873 (Fowler, p. 211; NK 11–10).

SAINT CLAIR STATION (Churchill). A post
office established at a way station (consisting
of a bridge and store) on the Carson River
southeast of old Ragtown. The station was
owned by James A. St. Clair(e), by report
of the *Lyon County Sentinel* of May 27,
1865. The name of the post office, active
from April 13, 1865, to November 30, 1869,
was changed to *Saint Clair* when the office
was reestablished February 16, 1877, to
serve the agricultural community that grew
up around the station. Upon its discontinuance on November 30, 1907, Fallon became
the mail address of its patrons (1881 Map;
M&M, p. 18; FTM, pp. 25, 38).

SAINT JOSEPH (Clark). A Mormon village,
originally settled north of Mill Point in the
Moapa (Muddy River) Valley in 1865, and
its post office, established in Pah Ute County,
Arizona, August 26, 1867, and discontinued
October 6, 1871. After a great fire in 1868,
a new town of Saint Joe, or Saint Joseph,
was started at the present site of Logandale,
and later renamed Logan (q.v.). The post
office was reestablished and active in Lincoln (Clark) County from May 4, 1876, to
November 13, 1883, when its operations
were moved to Overton (JGS, I, p. 261;
FTM, p. 25; WA; Wheeler 1871 Map).
"SAINT JOSEPH (Moapa Stake), Lincoln
County, Nevada, was settled by Latter-Day
Saints in 1865 and named Saint Joseph in
honor of Joseph W. Young (son of President Brigham Young) who took an active
part in the colonization of the Muddy Valley" (AJ, January, 1921, p. 46).

SAINTS REST (Carson City). The former
station on the road to Lake Tahoe presumably was named by Latter-Day Saints in the
early days (NHS, 1913, p. 198).

SAINT THOMAS (Clark). A former settlement near the confluence of the Virgin and

the Muddy rivers; named for Thomas S.
Smith, who led a Mormon migration to the
Muddy Valley in January, 1865. Since June
11, 1938, the townsite has been under the
waters of Lake Mead. Former **SAINT
THOMAS** post office was established July 23,
1866, and discontinued June 16, 1938. The
name is perpetuated in **SAINT THOMAS
MINING DISTRICT**, also called *Muddy
Mountains* and *Logan,* twenty-six miles southeast of Moapa; **SAINT THOMAS GAP,** a
saddle in the Virgin Range east of the former site of the town; and **SAINT THOMAS
WASH,** which heads near the Valley of Fire
and trends eastward to the Overton Arm of
Lake Mead (AJ, January, 1921, p. 46;
Wheeler 1871 Map; VPG, p. 28; WA; NJ
11–12; JGS, I, p. 593; FTM, p. 25).

SALERATUS CREEK. See **AMARGOSA.**

SALINAS (Churchill). An early settlement,
mentioned by Bancroft, and its post office,
active from April 15, 1880, to October 4,
1882; apparently named for old **SALINA
MINING DISTRICT**, located at a Churchill
County salt flat (HHB, Nev., pp. 261–62;
FTM, p. 25; 1881 Map; SM, 1867, pp. 28–
29).

SALMON FALLS CREEK (Elko). A tributary of the Snake River, also called **SAL-
MON RIVER,** which flows north from the
divide between the Humboldt and Snake
River basins to join the Snake River in Idaho,
and finally reaches the Columbia River;
named for the Pacific Ocean salmon which
come upstream from the Columbia. **NORTH
FORK SALMON FALLS CREEK** is its principal tributary (NK 11–9). **LITTLE SALMON**
is a tributary of the Humboldt River.
SALMON MINING DISTRICT was organized in 1872, sixty miles north of Toano on
Salmon Falls Creek (SM, 1875, p. 24).
Salmon River is now an alternate name for
the Contact Mining District (VPG, p. 38). An
early mining camp at the district was called
both **SALMON CITY** (TF, p. 21; HHB, Nev.,
p. 277) and **SALMON RIVER** (Census,
1900).

SALMON TROUT RIVER. See **TRUCKEE.**

SALT. A name group in Clark County stems
from **SALT POINT,** a small ridge extending
into Lake Mead, about three miles south of
the former site of Saint Thomas. Indians
operated a salt mine here from ancient times.
The mine, described by Jedediah Smith who
visited it in 1826, was the earliest mentioned
mineral deposit in Nevada. *Salt Cave* is
shown on the map of Frémont's 1843–44
expedition on which George Gibbs drew
Smith's material, and *Rock Salt Cavern* appears on an 1833 Map of North America,
prepared by A. H. Brué, who also shows the
influence of Jedediah Smith's names (Wheat
II, pp. 128, 144). Before Lake Mead was
formed by the impounding of water behind

Hoover Dam in 1938, the point was known as **SALT MOUNTAIN,** or *Big Salt Cliff,* so named to describe a cliff of salt, half a mile long and one hundred to one hundred and fifty feet high, west of the Virgin River. An early map erroneously shows the mountain of salt to be northwest of West Point and gives its dimensions as five miles long and six-hundred feet high (1881 Map). Shift names include **SALT BAY,** between Salt Point and Black Point in the Overton Arm of Lake Mead; **SALT COVE,** a cove above Salt Point; and **SALT RAVINE,** a watercourse running along Salt Point (Wheeler 1871 Map; VPG; WA). **SALT MARSH VALLEY** (Churchill) was an early name for Dixie Valley, west of the Clan Alpine Range, chosen because of its position near the Humboldt Salt Marsh (NHS, 1913, p. 177). **SALT VALLEY** (Churchill) was an early name for the valley fronting former La Plata (q.v.) in the Stillwater Range, so denoted for the quantity of salt taken from it (NHS, 1913, p. 177). **SALT WELL** (Clark) was a sinkhole of unknown depth, about two miles west of former Rioville, thought to be the deepest spot in Lake Mead (1881 Map; WA). **SALT WELLS** (Churchill), an early settlement, was so named for its position just north of Sand Springs Salt Flat and north and west of the Sand Springs Range.

SAMS CAMP (Lincoln). The designation for a wash and a well, about twenty miles east of Leith, may have been chosen to honor one of two early settlers, Sam Reveal or Sam Beal (WA; GHM, LN 2).

SAN ANTONIO (Nye). A short mountain range, north of Tonopah; a mining district discovered in the range in 1863 (NJ 11-5; 1867 Map; SM, 1867, p. 61). The name, probably honorific of Saint Anthony of Padua, was applied by J. P. Cortez, who was the owner of La Libertad, the first opened, and the southernmost, mine of the district (Wheeler, 1872, pp. 45-46). **SAN ANTONIO STATION,** also called *San Antone,* was established about thirty miles southwest of Belmont, in the 1860s. The adobe and brick station contained from fifteen to twenty rooms and earlier was known as *Bradleys.* Its nearby springs afforded water for the camels which once carried salt from Columbus Salt Marsh to the mills on Peavine Creek (MM, Toiyabe, p. 7). The station post office was named San Antonia from May 14, 1873, to January 25, 1888, and San Antonio from April 8, 1896, to July 14, 1906, when its operations were moved to Tonopah (FTM, p. 25).

SANBORN (Humboldt). The former camp, the site of an ore mill near Winnemucca, was served by a post office from July 16, 1890, to July 1, 1891 (FTM, p. 25; DM).

SAND HILL STATION (Churchill). The

Pony Express station, between Sand Springs and Carson Sink stations, was named for a mountain of pure white sand near the station, about three miles long, a half-mile wide, and about fifteen-hundred feet high (Nev., I, 1961, p. 8). See **SINGING MOUNTAIN.**

SANDPASS (Washoe). A pass on the summit of the ridge between Honey Lake Valley and the Smoke Creek Desert; a post office named for the pass and established December 11, 1911. When the post office was discontinued February 14, 1916, Sheepshead became the mail address for its patrons (VPG; FTM, p. 25).

SAND SPRING(S). In Churchill County, the name derives from **SAND SPRINGS,** a group of springs on the east side of **SAND SPRINGS VALLEY** and about a half mile north of U.S. 50. **SAND SPRINGS RANGE** denotes a mountain range separated on the north from the Stillwater Range by **SAND SPRINGS PASS** and terminated on the south by Big Kasock Mountain (USGB 5904). **SAND SPRINGS STATION** was fifteen miles east of Carson Lake and twenty-five miles west of Middle Gate in the early days (NHS, 1913, p. 175). **SAND SPRINGS SALT FLAT** and **SAND SPRINGS MINING DISTRICT** extend from Salt Wells to Frenchman along U.S. 50. **SAND SPRINGS** post office served the area from November 23, 1907, to October 31, 1911, when its operations were moved to Fallon (FTM, p. 25; NJ 11-1; VPG, p. 17). **SAND(Y) SPRING,** an early settlement in Esmeralda County, was served by Columbus post office (TF, p. 21; 1881 Map). **SAND SPRING VALLEY,** a valley in western Lincoln County, was named for **SAND SPRINGS** east of the valley. Early settlers were served by Hiko post office. A variant name is *Sand Valley* (USGB 6001; NJ 11-9; TF, p. 21; GHM, LN 4).

SANDSTONE (Clark). A spring between Blue Diamond and **SANDSTONE BLUFFS,** serrated sandstone cliffs forming the eastern edge of the Spring Mountains between Blue Diamond and Red Rocks. The cliffs are also called *Sharktooth Ridge,* for their general outline (Blue D. Quad.; WA).

SANDWICH ISLAND RIVER. See **OWYHEE.**

SANDY (Clark). The former town, about thirty miles west of Las Vegas, was the millsite for the Keystone Mine. The place, earlier known as *Taylors Well,* was served by **SANDY** post office from January 10, 1896, to September 23, 1910, when the name was changed to *Ripley* (WA; NM; FTM, p. 25). **SANDY MILL** is the current designation (NI 11-3). **SANDY VALLEY,** the southeast portion of Mesquite Valley, took its name from its former principal settlement (WA).

SAN JACINTO (Elko). A station on the UP RR eight miles northeast of Contact; named for the **SAN JACINTO RANCH**. The ranch was one of the holdings of Jasper Harrell and John Sparks, Governor of Nevada (1903–1908). The latter, who came to Nevada from Texas, named the ranch in memory of the battle of San Jacinto. This battle was fought April 21, 1836, near the mouth of a Texas river named for San Jacinto (St. Hyacinth), a Silesian nobleman who became a monk. **SAN JACINTO** post office was active from November 17, 1898, to April 15, 1938, when Contact became the mail address for its patrons (OPN, p. 28; NS, p. 83; EP, p. 70; FTM, p. 25; GHM, EL 4).

SAN JUAN (Nye). A peak on the west slope of the Toiyabe Range; a stream at the base of the peak; a mining district, forty miles up the Reese River from Austin. The early mining camp was served by Junction post office. A fairly common Spanish name in the West, these locations were perhaps named by a veteran of the Mexican War for San Juan de Ulloa in Mexico (1881 Map; SG Map 5; GHM, NY 2; DM; TF, p. 21).

SAN LORENZO (Nye). An early mining camp, "a small village among a series of hills in a small valley, altitude 6,600 feet," in the San Antonio district; presumably named by J. P. Cortez, who opened the first mine in the district (Wheeler 1871 Map, 1872, p. 45). See **SAN ANTONIO**.

SANO (Washoe). The station on the WP RR, at the southeast edge of the Smoke Creek Desert and north of Pyramid Lake, may commemorate ultimately Sano de Pietro, an Italian painter of the fifteenth century or is possibly a reference to *sand,* since it is but a few miles north of Sand Pass (T54).

SAN PEDRO (White Pine). The Spanish name for Saint Peter denoted a mining town between Black Horse and Osceola, served by *Sanpedro* post office from November 6, 1911, to September 30, 1912 (DM; FTM, p. 25).

SAN PEDROS (Nye). A little mining camp of the 1870s, which sprang up in the Spanish Belt Mining District, just west of San Pedros castle, and had daily stages to Austin; named for Emanuel San Pedro, a Castillian grandee, who, with a party of Mexicans from California, discovered the Spanish Belt mines in 1870 (SFH, pp. 2, 5).

SANTA CLARA (Pershing). The name of the early mining district and town, located in **SANTA CLARA CANYON** and commemorative of Saint Clare of Assisi, may have been transferred from California or given by Mexican miners. Mill City served the district (1867 Map; SM, 1867, pp. 45–55; HHB, Nev., p. 264; Nev. Terr. Map; Love. Quad.; Gudde, p. 279; TF, p. 21).

SANTA FE. SANTA FE CREEK (Lander) rises on the east flank of the Toiyabe Range and flows eastward to Big Smoky Valley where it joins Kingston Creek. It took its name from **SANTA FE MINING DISTRICT,** discovered by Mexican prospectors in the late 1850s or early 1860s. A mining camp named for the district was also called *Guadalajara* (NM; NJ 11–2; 1867 Map; VPG, p. 86). **SANTA FE** (Mineral) denotes a mining district, on the west slope of the Gabbs Valley Range and seven miles east of Luning, where important copper discoveries were made in the 1880s (VPG, p. 118; DM). The places were named for the capital city of New Mexico which probably commemorates Santa Fe near Granada (founded by Ferdinand and Isabella in 1492). The Spanish name means "holy faith" (Pearce, p. 149).

SANTA ROSA (Humboldt). A mountain range with its southern extremity approximately eight miles north of Winnemucca and north of the Bloody Run Hills; a peak in the Santa Rosa Range, lying northwest of Paradise Valley; named for Saint Rose of Lima, who became the first cannonized saint in the New World and was the most popular saint in the Spanish colonies of America (NK 11–8; USGB 6002; Pearce, pp. 149–50).

SANTIAGO (Carson City). The station on the former V and T RR, seven miles from Carson City, was named for **SANTIAGO MILL.** The name of the mill is probably a transfer name, but derives ultimately from "Santo-Iago, the ancient Spanish rendering of St. James the Greater, one of the Twelve Apostles, who established Christianity in Spain" (Pearce, p. 150; MA, p. 541).

SARCOBATUS FLAT (Nye). The playa so named, traversed by U.S. 95, is east of Pahute Mesa and extends northward from the Bullfrog Hills. Sarcobatus, or greasewood, grows in abundance here (NJ 11–8; VPG).

SAVAGE (Storey). This claim on the Comstock consists of approximately eight hundred feet between the Hale and Norcross and the Gould and Curry (FCL, p. 228). The original location notice claimed 1,800 feet and was dated July 4, 1859 (GH–A). The name honors Leonard Coates Savage, one of the six original locators (S&S). Henry Comstock said that he "staked out" the claim and presented it to Old Man Savage (DDQ, p. 50; GDL, Saga, p. 35). According to De Groot, Savage (a Downieville, California, miner) bought the ground from a party of "jumpers" (HDG, CP, 12/30/76). The Savage is officially patented (AR, No. 51).

SAVORY (Nye). A creek rising on the southern slopes of **SAVORY MOUNTAIN,** south of Butler Basin, in the Monitor Range, and flowing into Little Fish Lake Valley; presumably named for the agreeable taste and odor of the water. **LITTLE SAVORY**

CREEK is a tributary of Savory Creek (NJ 11–2; SG Map 6).

SAWMILL. Features named for the former presence of sawmills include, in Nye County, a creek rising on the east slope of the Monitor Range and entering Little Fish Lake Valley, south of Clear Creek; a canyon north of Jefferson in the Toquima Range; and a canyon on the east side of the Quinn Canyon Range. Early settlers in the latter canyon were served by Duckwater post office (GHM, NY 5; SG Map 5; TF, p. 21). Additional canyons so named are east of Preston in the Egan Range in White Pine County, on the east slope of the Buffalo Hills, northwest of Gerlach, and in the extreme southwestern portion of Washoe County (GHM, WA 2, 1; WP, 1). In Clark County, the name designates a canyon trending eastward from the Sheep Range, about three miles north of Mormon Well, and a spring in the canyon; the site of a sawmill operated in the 1890s by J. M. Thomas (WA; Vegas Quad.). In Lincoln County, SAWMILL CREEK is east of White Rock Peak. The early mill was served by Bristol post office (TF, p. 21); SAWMILL CANYON runs westward from Elly Mountain to the Meadow Valley Wash, about three miles south of Caliente. It is named for a former sawmill owned by Phil Klingensmith. SAWMILL MOUNTAIN is a peak in the SAWMILL RANGE, east of Elgin (WA; NJ 11–5; GHM, LN 1, 2). A range in Elko County, named SAWMILL RIDGE, is southeast of Jarbidge (GHM, EL 3).

SAWTOOTH. SAWTOOTH KNOB (Humboldt), a peak at the north end of the Antelope Range, was so named from its profile which resembles a tooth of a circular saw (VPG, GHM, HU 2). SAWTOOTH MOUNTAIN (Nye) is a peak in the Bullfrog Hills (GHM, NY 7).

SAXTON PEAK (White Pine). The peak in the Egan Range, south of Robinson Canyon, is named for a Mr. Saxton who, with a Mr. Aultman and President William McKinley, was one of the principal stockholders of the Canton Mining Company at Robinson Canyon (NJ 11–3; NHS, 1924, p. 294).

SCALES (Lyon). The station, west of American Flat on the V and T RR (now dismantled), three miles from Silver City and five miles from Virginia City, was so named because railroad scales for weighing ore were at the station. The place was known also as Baltic and Baltic Switch (TF, p. 21; NHS, 1913, p. 216).

SCANLON (Clark). Mike Scanlon is commemorated by a dugway east of Bonelli Peak, and a hill at the mouth of SCANLON WASH, which drains eastward from Bonelli Peak to the former site of SCANLONS FERRY. The ferry was established by Scanlon in 1881, about midway of Bonellis Ferry and

Pierces Ferry crossing the Colorado River (WA).

SCARP CANYON (Nye). A canyon heading about one mile east of Pahute Ridge and five miles west of the southern end of Papoose Lake, extending to Frenchman Flat, twenty-five miles northwest of Indian Springs; named presumably for its abrupt declivity (NJ 11–9).

SCHELL CREEK (White Pine). A small stream on the west slope of the Schell Creek Range was named for Major A. J. Schell, United States commander in charge of a detachment of troops for protection of the Overland Mail. Shift names are SCHELL CREEK RANGE, a mountain range approximately ten miles east of Ely in both Lincoln and White Pine counties; and former SCHELL CREEK STATION, an Overland Stage and Pony Express station between Egan Canyon and Antelope Springs stations (DL 60; NJ 11–3; Nev., I, 1961, p. 9; JGS, I, p. 136). A variant spelling Shell, earlier used interchangeably with Schell, has led to an erroneous explanation for the naming of the mountain range, said to have been "so named because of many fossil clam shells found in the range, and limestone formation of range shows its composition of shells" (OPN, p. 75; 1867, Park, HWY, Guide, Gen. Land Off. Maps). Also included in the name group are NORTH SCHELL PEAK, SOUTH SCHELL PEAK, and SCHELL CREEK GAME REFUGE, all in the Schell Creek Range (Ely Quad. 1952; Park Map).

SCHELLBOURNE (White Pine). A mining community settled in 1869 in the north end of the Schell Creek Range and eighteen miles east of Cherry Creek (M&S, p. 158; HWY Map). SCHELLBOURNE post office was established December 27, 1871, and discontinued October 15, 1925 (FTM, p. 25). The name commemorates Major A. J. Schell. See SCHELL CREEK. The old settlement, also known as Fort Schellbourne, is near SCHELLBOURNE SUMMIT at the northern end of the Schell Creek Range (NM; 1881 Map; NJ 11–3).

SCHLEY (Elko). The post office so denoted was established September 26, 1898, and discontinued July 15, 1903, when Ruby Valley became the mail address for its patrons. The name honors Admiral Winfield Scott Schley, who commanded the American fleet which fought, and defeated, the Spanish fleet at Santiago de Cuba on July 3, 1898 (FTM, p. 25; VPG).

SCHURZ (Mineral). A town at the junction of State Route 3 and U.S. 95 on the Walker River, north of Walker Lake; headquarters for the Walker Lake Indian Reservation, which is predominantly Paiute (NJ 11–4). The name commemorates Carl Schurz, American statesman and author, born near Cologne, Germany. The post office at Schurz, also a station of the SP RR, was established October 21, 1891 (FTM, p. 25).

SCOSSA (Pershing). A mining district and former mining camp, twenty-eight miles west of Imlay on the west slope of the Antelope Range; named for James and Charles Scossa who discovered the gold district in 1930 (VPG, p. 161; GHM, PE 1; OPN, p. 63).

SCOTT CREEK (Elko). A tributary of Salmon Falls Creek west of Contact; "named for Lee Scott, brother of Death Valley Scotty, who camped there and herded between 700 and 1,000 head of bulls for the Sparks-Harrell outfit in the days before they kept their animals under fence" (EP, p. 71; GHM, EL 4). See **SCOTTYS JUNCTION.**

SCOTTSVILLE (Humboldt). A post office so named was active from February 3, 1868, to November 19, 1869 (FTM, p. 25).

SCOTTYS JUNCTION (Nye). The junction of U.S. 95 and State Route 72, which leads to **SCOTTYS CASTLE** in California (GHM, NY 7). The castle was built by "Walter ('Death Valley') Scott, a former champion roughrider in Buffalo Bill's show, and A. M. Johnson of Chicago" (Gudde, p. 286).

SCRUGHAM PEAK (Nye). The name of this peak, south of Buckboard Mesa and northeast of Timber Mountain, commemorates James G. Scrugham, Governor of Nevada, 1923–1926 (NJ 11–8).

SEAMAN (Lincoln). The short mountain range, extending northeast from Mount Irish, east of Coal Valley, is in the northern portion of the county. **SEAMANS WASH** is a watercourse draining southeastward from the Seaman Range to the White River (NJ 11–9).

SEARCHLIGHT (Clark). A town on U.S. 95 at the east edge of Piute Valley, and a post office established October 31, 1898; named for a mine and district discovered about fifty miles south of Las Vegas in 1897. There is no agreement on the origin of Searchlight's name, but one version is that it came from the Lloyd-Searchlight Mining Co. (VPG, p. 30; OPN, pg. 18). A boom in the district took place in the first decade of the twentieth century, as a result of the construction of the Barnwell and Searchlight Railroad which was purchased and operated by the AT and SF RR who sold the spur line in 1911 (M&S, p. 118; SPD, p. 599). Two legends concerning the naming are (1) that one of a group of prospectors remarked that a searchlight would be necessary to find any valuable ore (CHL, p. 214) and (2) that a box of "Searchlight" matches served as an inspiration for the name (RC, p. 76).

SEARVILLE (Nye). A short-lived post office established December 3, 1868, and discontinued March 19, 1869 (FTM, p. 26).

SECOND CREEK. The name for a creek between First and Third creeks and north of Crystal Bay, Lake Tahoe, in Washoe County; and for a stream between First and Third creeks northeast of Steptoe on the west slope of the Schell Creek Range, in White Pine County (GHM, WA 1; WP 4).

SECRET. **SECRET VALLEY** (Elko) may have been named by United States troops that noticed Indians suddenly disappearing in the vicinity, or by emigrants. The valley and **SECRET CANYON** and **SECRET PASS,** dividing the Ruby Mountains to the south from the East Humboldt Range on the north, probably were named prior to 1845, at which time the part of Frémont's party under Kern and guided by Walker went west through Secret Canyon and onto the Humboldt near present Halleck (VPG). Peter Skene Ogden used Secret Pass in 1828 (GGC, p. 118). **SECRET CREEK,** in the area, flows between Halleck and Arthur. **SECRET** post office was active from October 27, 1916, to October 15, 1918 (NK 11–12; JGS, I, p. 65; FTM, p. 26). On the east shore of Lake Tahoe (Carson City), **SECRET HARBOR** denotes a harbor and a creek named for the harbor (Tahoe Map). **SECRET CANYON** (Eureka) is the name for a mining district, also known as *Eureka,* and for a mining camp at the north end of Little Smoky Valley, southwest of Eureka and former Vanderbilt City. Among the early mines of the district were the Geddis, Calico, and **SECRET VALLEY** (Wheeler 1871 Map, 1872, p. 37; VPG, p. 64).

SEDAYE MOUNTAINS. Captain Simpson named a mountain range which forms a part of the Lander-Churchill county boundary (Desatoya Range) the Sedaye, or Lookout Mountains (WTJ, p. 142). See **DESATOYA.** "Limiting Reese Valley, which we are approaching, is a low range trending generally north and south, and beyond them a very high range covered with snow, called by the Indians the Se-day-e or Lookout Mountains" (JHS, pp. 78–79).

SELENITE RANGE (Pershing). A range in the western portion of the county, between Winnemucca Lake and the Granite Creek Desert; named for a kind of gypsum found in crystallized or foliated form. This gypsum deposit is now operated on a large scale (NK 11–10).

SELIGMAN (White Pine). A former settlement founded by Eugene Robinson on the west side of the White Pine Mountains in 1886; a post office established September 19, 1887, and discontinued December 31, 1905, when its operations were moved to Hamilton (NHS, 1924, p. 281; FTM, p. 26).

SENNER (Esmeralda). The post office near Lida was established December 12, 1891, and discontinued January 8, 1895 (FTM, p. 26).

SENTINEL (Humboldt). The name denotes a mesa-like peak at the south end of the Pine Forest Range overlooking the Black Rock

Desert, and a rock on the west side of Quinn River Valley (NK 11–7; OPN, p. 38).

SERVICEBERRY CANYON (Lincoln). A canyon about fifteen miles northeast of Pioche, extending eastward from Ursine Valley and north of Mahogany Peak (Freese, Map 2; WA); named for shrubs growing in the canyon.

SEVEN LAKES MOUNTAIN (Washoe). The mountain, named for the seven lakes on its crest, lies between Dry Valley on the north and Red Rock Valley on the south, about twenty-eight miles north of Reno, and extends into Lassen County, California (USGB 6002).

SEVEN–MILE. A milepost name for a wash extending from the west side of the Antelope Range, south of Ninemile Peak, into Dry Valley in Nye County; and for a canyon which begins at the north end of the Comstock Lode near the Utah Mine, and joins Six-Mile Canyon just north of Sugar Loaf Mountain in Storey County (HPS, 1/24/54; NJ 11–2).

SEVEN SISTERS (Clark). The name for seven formations of Jurassic sandstone in the Valley of Fire State Park, west of the Overton Arm of Lake Mead, northeast of Las Vegas (WA; GHM, CL 2).

SEVEN TROUGHS (Pershing). A mountain range extending north from Granite Springs Valley in western Pershing County; a mining district and a community at the mouth of **SEVEN TROUGHS CANYON,** which heads on the east slope of the range. Tungsten is now mined in the district in which rich gold ore was discovered in 1905, with first ore shipments being made on December 31, 1906, according to the *Lovelock Tribune* of January 4, 1907 (VPG, p. 161; HPS, 1/29/56; NK 11–10). A post office served the district from July 18, 1907, to February 15, 1918 (FTM, p. 26). "It derives its name from a series of seven troughs which had been placed below some springs in the canyon by stockmen for watering stock. The water was brought to the surface by a large black basalt dike which cut through the mountain, crossing the canyon at this point, and along which contact the ore was found" (SPD, p. 903).

SEVENTY–SIX (Elko). The creek, northeast of Charleston and in **SEVENTY–SIX CREEK PASTURE,** was so named for the year of mineral discoveries in the area, 1876 (EP, p. 71; GHM, EL 3).

SEYLER PEAK (Nye). E. Syler, a rancher and prospector who owned Peavine Ranch during the early 1900s is commemorated by this peak in the south end of the Toiyabe Range, east of Peavine Creek. **SEYLER RESERVOIR** is named for the peak (MM; GHM, NY 2).

SHADY RUN (Churchill). A mining district

on the east slope of the Stillwater Range, forty miles northeast of Fallon; a former mining camp, forty-five miles northeast of Fallon, near the old camp of White Cloud; named for a small stream with shade trees along its banks (VPG, p. 18; DM).

SHAFTER (Elko). General W. R. Shafter, a commander in the United States Army in Cuba during the Spanish-American War, is commemorated by this station at the NN RR crossing of the WP RR and by a former post office, active from August 28, 1908, to April 19, 1957 (OPN, p. 28; T54; FTM, p. 26).

SHAKESPEARE CLIFF (Douglas). The cliff, also called *Shakespeare Rock,* is on the southeast shore of Lake Tahoe.

> The Shakespeare Rock, plainly visible from the Glenbrook House on the south shore of the lake, is so called on account of there being in the rugged outlines of its face a striking resemblance to the features of the immortal poet. (DDQ, p. 317)

> Truly extraordinary is the perfect likeness of Shakespeare on the face of Shakespeare Cliff, a few hundred yards from Glenbrook. (SPD, p. 817)

SHAMROCK (Nye). The crescent-shaped canyon, extending from north of Mount Berlin in the Shoshone Mountains to Ione Valley, was named for **SHAMROCK,** an active mining camp in 1898, established by the Nevada Gold Mining Company (DM; GHM, NY 2).

SHANTYTOWN (Elko). The small settlement west of Ruby Lake is chiefly a supply center for hunters and fishermen and is named for its general appearance (GHM, EL 1).

SHARP (Nye). A settlement on the east slope of the Quinn Canyon Range, a short distance north of the Lincoln County line, was named in honor of Thomas C. Sharp, a miner and rancher who settled in Nye County in the 1870s (SPD, p. 1278). A post office so named was active from December 14, 1901, to May 1, 1939 (FTM, p. 26).

SHARP PEAK. Sharp-pointed mountains so named include a peak in Elko County, northeast of Currie in the Dolly Varden Mountains; a peak in Lincoln County, west of Tempiute on the Nye County boundary; a mountain in southern Eureka County, in the Fish Creek Range; a peak in Nye County, also known as *Nine Mile Peak,* in the Antelope Range (VPG; GHM, EL 5; LN 4; NY 3).

SHEEP. Features in the state named for bighorn sheep are the **SHEEP RANGE** (Clark), a mountain range trending northward from Las Vegas Valley, east of the Desert Range, in the Desert Wildlife Refuge for Nelson bighorn sheep (NJ 11–12). **SHEEP PEAK,** the second highest peak of the range and at its south end; **SHEEP MOUNTAIN,** a mountain northwest of Big Ten Peak in the Monitor Range of Nye County, and a moun-

tain south of Jean and at the north end of
the Lucy Grey Mountains (Clark) (NI 11–3;
SG Map 5); **SHEEP CREEK,** a stream heading in the Duck Valley Indian Reservation
and flowing to the South Fork Owyhee River,
in Elko County; a creek east of Mud Springs
on the west slope of the Independence Range,
in Elko County; and a stream northwest of
Sweetwater and at the California line, in
Lyon County; **SHEEP CANYON,** a canyon
southwest of Paradise Peak in the Paradise
Range, Nye County; a canyon heading on
the east slope of the Toiyabe Range, near
Rock Creek, Lander County; and a canyon
on the east slope of the Stillwater Range,
extending to the south end of Dixie Valley
(SG Maps 4, 5, 6; USGB 5904, 6302); and
SHEEP PASS (Washoe), a pass in the Lake
Range and northeast of the north end of the
Pyramid Range (VPG). **SHEEP SPRING**
(Clark), a spring about ten miles southwest
of Coyote Spring and north of Mormon Well,
takes its name from the Sheep Range (WA).

SHEEPSHEAD (Washoe). A ranch in the
Smoke Creek Desert named for **SHEEPS-
HEAD SPRINGS,** about twelve miles distant
(1881 Map). The springs were named so
because the head of a mountain sheep, nailed
to a tree at the site, remained there for several years (NHS, 1911, p. 92). A post office
named for the ranch was established March
28, 1879, and discontinued March 15, 1926,
when Flanigan became the mail address for
its patrons (FTM, p. 26). Variants are *Sheep
Head* (HHB, Nev., p. 262) and *Sheephead*
(OR, 1879, 1885).

SHENANDOAH (Clark). A peak west of
Goodsprings in the Spring Mountains, named
for the **SHENANDOAH MINE** in the range.
The mine name commemorated the Shenan-
doah Valley in Virginia, the scene of several
Confederate victories in the Civil War,
March–June, 1862 (NI 11–3; OPN, p. 18).

SHERIDAN (Douglas). The community near
Job Peak was called *Jobs Store*. With the
establishment of the post office, which was
territorial but first noted in an 1865 list, the
name was changed to Sheridan in honor of
General Philip Henry Sheridan who commanded the Army of the Shenandoah (Nev.
Terr. Map; C&C, p. 589; NHS, 1913, pp.
203–204). **SHERIDAN CREEK,** at the settlement, was named for the post office, which
was discontinued November 15, 1920 (FTM,
p. 26; GHM, DO 1). See **TEMPIUTE.**

SHERMAN. A peak in the Paradise Range of
northern Nye County; a creek northeast of
Elko in Elko County (NJ 11–5; GHM, EL
1). In White Pine County, at the south end
of the White Pine Range, a former settlement
named **SHERMANTOWN** was founded by
Joseph Carothers in 1868, near **SHERMAN
CREEK** and west of **SHERMAN MOUN-
TAIN** (Census, 1870; 1881 Map; NHS, 1924,

p. 375). A post office named for the mining
camp was active from April 30, 1869, to
June 19, 1871 (FTM, p. 26). The date of the
founding and naming of the mining camp
might indicate that the name commemorates
General William Tecumseh Sherman.

SHINGLE BUTTES (Nye). The buttes, about
two miles west of Moores Station and named
by the United States Board on Geographic
Names in 1969, "are capped by layers of
welded tuff that appear as shingles" (USGB
6903).

SHORES (Elko). A siding on the Twin Falls-
Wells branch line of the UP RR between
Henry and Red Point; named for George
Shore, an early rancher (EP, p. 72; NK 11–9).

SHOSHONE. The Shoshone (Shoshoni) Indians, the most northerly division of the
Shoshonean family, lived in northeastern and
central Nevada. The name may mean "grass-
house people" (FWH, p. 557), or refer to
their hairdressing and mean "head," "tan-
gled," or "curly" (Gudde, p. 292). John Wesley Powell referred to these Indians as the
Nu-mas [Central Numa]. *Numa, Num, Num,*
and *Nu-ints* are terms meaning "Indian" in
various Numic vocabularies appearing in the
Powell manuscripts (Fowler, pp. 265, 270,
275). **SHOSHONE MINING DISTRICT** was
organized in 1869 on the west flank of the
Snake Range, fifty-five miles southeast from
Ely in White Pine County (M&SP, 8/7/69;
VPG). The Indian Queen was the principal
mine (SM, 1875, pp. 171–72). **SHOSHONE**
post office, established May 8, 1896, at a
ranch near the district in Swallow Canyon,
was named by George Swallow because a
number of Indians were living in the area
(FTM, p. 26; RC, p. 77; OR, 1899; 1881
Map). **SHOSHONE** (Eureka), a non-agency
station on the SP RR ten miles west of
Beowawe, "was called Shoshone Point by the
people in the valley, because a mountain,
or high ridge, pushes out into the valley, like
a promontory. This is one of the landmarks
on the dividing line between the Shoshone
and Piute tribes of Indians" (Fes, p. 185;
1867 Map). Creeks so named are (1) near
Bunker Hill on the east slope of the Toiyabe
Range in Lander County, (2) near Round
Mountain in the Toquima Range of Nye
County, and (3) in the New Pass Range,
flowing northwestward into Humboldt Salt
Marsh in Churchill County (Dir. 1971; NHS,
1913, p. 182). The **SHOSHONE MOUN-
TAINS** extend from northwest Nye County
into Lander County and are west of Reese
River Valley. **SHOSHONE MINING DIS-
TRICT** (Lander), discovered in 1863 twenty
miles north-northwest of Austin, was named
for the mountain range (NJ 11–2; NJ 11–5;
M&S, pp. 70, 153; VPG, p. 88).

SIDES (Storey). The claim on the Comstock,
sometimes called the *Dick Sides,* or *Sides*

and Company, was named for Richard D. Sides, the original locator (EL, p. 48) who lived in the area prior to the Comstock discovery. On September 20, 1854, he was elected Treasurer of Carson County (SPD, p. 229). The Sides claim of five hundred linear feet, lying between the White and Murphy on the north and the Best and Belcher on the south, is now a part of the Consolidated Virginia (IH; HDG, CP, 12/23/76).

SIEGEL. Former **SIEGEL** post office, active in White Pine County from January 19, 1907, to July 31, 1908, when its operations were transferred to Aurum, took its name from the **SIEGAL MINING DISTRICT** in the northern part of the Schell Creek Range, about eighteen miles southeast of Cherry Creek, and also called *Aurum* (VPG, p. 176; FTM, p. 26). **SIEGEL CREEK** and the **SIEGEL MINES** are north of **MOUNT SIEGAL** in the Schell Creek Range (GHM, WP 4). In Douglas County, **MOUNT SIEGEL** denotes a mountain in the southern part of the Pine Nut Range and a mining district twenty miles east of Minden (1881 Map; VPG, p. 34).

SIERRA CANYON (Douglas). The canyon, extending from the south slope of Genoa Peak to the Carson River, one-half mile north of Genoa, was named for the Sierra Nevada (USGB 5902).

SIERRA NEVADA. The Spanish name meaning "snowy saw-teeth" was applied by Padre Pedro Font on April 3, 1776 (Gudde, p. 294), and appeared on his 1776 map as a designation for the northern end of the mountain range. Although his map of 1845 shows Sierra Nevada of California, Frémont noted in his 1845 Report that the Sierra Nevada had been commonly known as the *Great California Mountain*. In his Journal, Zenas Leonard placed the Joseph Walker party "at the base of the California mountain" on February 27, 1834 (JCF, Report, pp. 165, 227; JGS, I, p. 56). The name appears on the Rufus B. Sage map of 1846 (Wheat III, 41). Those who viewed the lofty mountains from the west named them Sierra Nevada, descriptive of the snow-covered peaks; whereas the free trappers, explorers, and early emigrants who had braved Nevada's alkali deserts and viewed the range from the east, apparently saw it as a great barrier to the less forbidding land they sought and commonly referred to the high Sierra as the California Mountain. **SIERRA NEVADA MINE.** The location notice for this ground on the Comstock, dated June 22, 1859, claimed 3,600 feet between the Union Consolidated and the Utah (GH–A). The mine, named for the mountain range which lies between Nevada and California, is assessed in Storey County (AR, No. 4023).

SILENT (Nye). **SILENT BUTTE** is north of the north end of Basalt Ridge and just northwest of the mouth of **SILENT CANYON**, a canyon on the north side of Pahute Mesa, about fifty miles southeast of Goldfield. **SOUTH SILENT CANYON**, also on the north side of Pahute Mesa, is named for its position relative to Silent Canyon (DL 53; GHM, NY 6).

SILLIMAN, MOUNT (Elko). This peak in the Ruby Mountains, twenty-two miles southeast of Elko was "named for Benjamin Silliman (1779–1864) of Yale University," who was the first professor of geology in the United States and the founder of the *American Journal of Science* (USGB 6601).

SILVER. Although the name has become one of the most popular in Nevada, it is probable that no geographic entity in "The Silver State" bore the descriptive adjective, meaning silver ore, prior to 1859. The discoverers of the Ophir outcrop on the Comstock, who were looking for gold, struck an odd-looking black dirt. The black mineral was various compounds of silver sulfur and other metals, probably argentite, a silver sulfide (VPG). Only subsequent to the assay made at Grass Valley, California, was the value of the silver realized and the name widely used. See **OPHIR** and **GELLER LEDGE**. An early settlement of Eureka County was named **SILVERADO**, a blend of "silver" and "ado" from El Dorado (HHB, Nev., p. 285). Eureka post office served the area (TF, p. 22). Discoverers of **SILVER BEND**, a mining district located in May, 1866, on the southeast flank of the Toquima Range north of Belmont in Nye County, believed its argentiferous veins would be found to be of even greater value than the Comstock. The camp, ten miles south of early Peavine, was served by Belmont post office (SM, 1867, p. 62; Wheeler 1871 Map; TF, p. 22). **SILVER BOW** (Nye) denotes a gold-silver mining district on the west flank of the Kawich Range, where Ed Clifford discovered the **SILVER GLANCE MINE** in 1901 (VPG, p. 138; M&M, p. 159). The former mining camp, situated about fifty-three miles east of Tonopah and active in the early 1900s, had a post office from September 27, 1905, to November 30, 1907, and a newspaper. In 1906, *The Standard* "printed the front page of one entire edition in ink mixed with gold dust assaying $80,000 to the ton" (NM, p. 268). **SILVER BUTTE MINE** (Elko) is east of Ruby Wash (GHM, EL 1). **SILVER BUTTES** was an early name for the Spring Mountains in Clark County (WA). **SILVER CANYON** is the name of a canyon northwest of Hiko in Lincoln County, and formerly designated a mountain range west of Pahranagat Valley, now known as the Pahranagat Range (GHM, LN 4; OPN, p. 45; WA). **SILVER CANYON**

(White Pine) is a canyon east of Aurum on the west slope of the Schell Creek Range (GHM, WP 4).

SILVER CITY (Lyon) was the third most important mining camp of the early days, when it rivaled Virginia City and Gold Hill. Failing to develop any bonanzas, but being on the main line of travel between the Comstock mines and the Carson River mills, Silver City later derived its importance from quartz mills. Its post office has existed since territorial days, having been established in Carson County, Utah, on May 10, 1860 (C&C, p. 588; FTM, p. 26). The name is shown on Dr. Henry De Groot's Map of the Washoe Mines, dated 1860 (Wheat IV, 189). **SILVER CITY MINING DISTRICT** is on the southeast slope of the Virginia Range, nine miles northeast of Carson City (VPG, p. 105). **SILVER CITY** was also the name for a former mining camp south of Hiko and about three miles from Logan City in Lincoln County (1881 Map); and for another camp about six miles west of Overton, in Clark County, that was short-lived since the claims were worthless, the sandstone having been salted with silver ore (WA). **SILVER GLANCE,** meaning argentite, is the name of a mining district (also called *Wellington*) in the Pine Nut Range, Douglas County, thirty miles south-southeast of Minden (VPG, p. 35); and of a former mining camp near former Hannapah and about seventeen miles east-northeast of Tonopah, in Nye County (NM). **SILVER HILLS RANGE,** east of Stillwater in Churchill County, was the location site of an early mining district named for the range and also known as *I X L* (VPG, p. 15; 1867 Map; NHS, 1913, p. 178). **SILVERHORN MINING DISTRICT** (Lincoln), also called *Fairview,* was discovered by J. L. Whipple in 1920 and named for hornsilver, a rich chloride ore, containing seventy-five percent silver (VPG, p. 100; WA). **SILVER KING MINING DISTRICT** was the designation for a district discovered northwest of Bristol Wells (Lincoln) in 1874. **SILVER KING WELL** takes its name from **SILVER KING MINE** (WA; DM; GHM, LN 1). **SILVER LODE,** formerly a mining district in Churchill County, was discovered in the 1860s (SM, 1867, pp. 148–51). In Douglas County, the former mining boom town Konigsberg (q.v.) was renamed **SILVER MOUNTAIN** in 1863. **SILVER PARK** denoted an early settlement in Nye County (Census, 1870) and a mining district north of the settlement, in White Pine County (SM, 1875, pp. 171–72). Atlanta Mining District on the north end of the Wilson Creek Range, about forty miles northwest of Pioche, is also named **SILVER PARK** for one of the principal mines of the district (VPG, p. 92; WA).

SILVER PEAK (Esmeralda). The town,

on the west edge of the **SILVER PEAK MARSH** in the foothills of the **SILVER PEAK RANGE** and in the lowest part of Clayton Valley, was settled in territorial days (Nev. Terr. Map) and has had several revivals because of mining activities. Lithium is now being extracted from under the floor of Clayton Valley (SHM 155). The post office so named, active from April 2, 1866, to December 15, 1913, was reestablished on December 8, 1916, as Silverpeak (FTM, p. 26). In 1906 the Silver Peak Railroad was built to connect with the now defunct T and G RR for the transporting of low-grade ores. Silver was taken from the Mohawk Mine of the **SILVER PEAK MINING DISTRICT,** organized February 1, 1865, until early in 1956 (HHB, Nev. pp. 260–61; SM, 1867, pp. 37–44; OPN, p. 32; HPS, 1/29/56). The district, about twenty miles south of Blair, was located on **SILVER PEAK,** about three miles from Red Mountain, the two peaks being joined by a sharp, comb-like ridge (Wheeler, 1872, p. 79). The township, as well as the post office, is named *Silverpeak* (Census, 1960; NSS, 1973), while the map name appears both as *Silverpeak* (GHM, ES 1; NJ 11–8) and *Silver Peak* (Lida Quad.). The Silver Peak Range extends from a low divide north of Emigrant Peak to Palmetto Wash, and includes Palmetto Mountain just west of Lida (USGB 6201; NJ 11–8). An early settlement of Nye County, situated northwest of Jefferson, was served by Belmont post office and named **SILVER POINT** (1881 Map; TF, p. 22). **SILVER SPUR,** a station on the former V and T RR, was between Haywards and Mound House in Lyon County (V&T Map). **SILVER STATE VALLEY** (Humboldt), east of the Slumbering Hills, takes its name from the **SILVER STATE MINE** which was named for the state and located on the east slope of the Slumbering Hills (NK 11–8). **SILVER WAVE** designated a mining district in early Churchill County (SM, 1867, pp. 148–51). **SILVER ZONE** (Elko), a station on the WP RR between Shafter and Arnold, was named for **SILVER ZONE PASS.** The WP RR follows the same route through this pass in the Toano Mountains that early emigrant parties coming across the Utah salt desert had taken (T54; GHM, EL 5; Nev. Guide, p. 115). The name derives from the **SILVER ZONE MINING DISTRICT,** discovered about 1872, twenty-five miles south of Toano (M&SP, 8/4/88; DM). A post office named for the district was established August 27, 1872, and discontinued September 10, 1873 (FTM, p. 26).

The name *Silver* is also used as a descriptive term for glistening water. **SILVER CREEK** (Elko) is the name for a creek, heading on the west slope of Pennsylvania

Hill and flowing to Indian Creek, and a ranch on the creek (USGB 6103; GHM, EL 2); (Nye) a creek west of Belmont and on the southeast flank of the Toquima Range (GHM, NY 3); (White Pine) a creek rising south of Mount Moriah in the Snake Range (GHM, WP 1); (Lander) a tributary of the Reese River, north of Italian Creek, and **SILVER CREEK RANCH. SILVER CREEK STATION** on the former NC RR between Hallsvale and Caton, twenty-five miles north of Austin, was named for the Reese River tributary (NJ 11–12; 1881 Map; GHM, LA 1). **SILVER LAKE** denotes a lake southeast of Shallow Lake in northwest Elko County, and a mining district of Douglas County, eighteen miles southeast of Minden on the east slope of the Pine Nut Range, named for a small lake on the north side of Mount Siegel (VPG, p. 34; NHS, 1913, p. 189; OPN, p. 28). **SILVER SPRINGS** is the name of a town southwest of Fallon on U.S. 50 and a post office established July 1, 1954, in Lyon County (GHM, LY 1). It is also an alternate designation for the *Silver Park* (Atlanta) Mining District of Lincoln County (VPG, p. 92).

SIMON (Mineral). P. A. ("Pop") Simon is commemorated by a former mining camp and post office (November 11, 1919–June 30, 1938), situated at the north end of the Cedar Range, about twenty miles northeast of Mina (FTM, p. 26; NM).

SIMONSEN (White Pine). The name of **SIMONSEN** post office, changed from *Cold Creek* on March 28, 1913, became *Strawberry* on May 15, 1936 (FTM, p. 26).

SIMONSVILLE (Clark). The old Mormon settlement in the Moapa Valley, between Overton and former Saint Joseph, was named to commemorate Orrawell Simons who operated a grist mill there in 1866 (JGS, I, p. 593; WA).

SIMPSON. A former post office at **SIMPSON COLONY** (Lyon), established November 13, 1913, and discontinued November 30, 1943, when its operations were transferred to Wellington (FTM, p. 26). See **COLONY.** In Lincoln County, springs denoted **SIMPSON** are west of the Bristol Range (WA).

SIMPSON PARK. The **SIMPSON PARK MOUNTAINS** extend east of Grass Valley and northeast of Austin, in Eureka and Lander counties (USGB 5901). **SIMPSON PARK CANYON,** named for the range, is at the north end of Big Smoky Valley and on the east slope of the Toiyabe Range. Former **SIMPSONS PARK STATION** (Lander) was midway between Dry Creek and Jacobsville stations on the Pony Express and Overland Stage routes (Nev., I, 1961, p. 8; JGS, I, p. 136; Jackson Map). The name honors Captain James H. Simpson of the topographical engineers, who, with a party of sixty-

four men, left Camp Floyd, forty miles south of Salt Lake City, on May 2, 1859. They crossed the Great Basin, following a southwest course to Genoa, and returned on August 5, 1859. One of the two wagon routes he established immediately became the route of the Pony Express. The Overland Mail Route, the Overland Telegraph (completed October, 1861, between California and Omaha), and the Lincoln Highway (modern U.S. 50) followed the trail blazed by Simpson (JGS, I, pp. 106, 136, 175; NJ 11–2). See **REESE RIVER.** "The party has given my name to this lake, park, and pass; and also to the creek, but as it has been my rule to preserve the Indian names, whenever I can ascertain them, and Ton-a-ho-nupe is the name of the creek, I shall continue so to call it (JHS, p. 77).

SINGATSE (Lyon). A mountain peak west of Yerington and northeast of Ludwig, in the **SINGATSE MOUNTAINS;** a small mountain range west of Mason Valley and east of the Buckskin Range (NJ 11–1).

SINGING MOUNTAIN (Churchill). A high peak of sand (also called **SAND MOUNTAIN**) near Sand Springs; so named because the constantly shifting pellets of sand make a humming sound (Nev. Guide, p. 264).

SINKAVATA HILLS (Mineral). The name of the hills in northeast Mineral County is said to be derived from an Indian word meaning "sink," an area of sunken land (NHS, 1913, pp. 182–83; GHM, MI 1).

SINK STATION (Churchill). The early station, named for its position on the Upper Sink of the Carson, was visited and described by Dan De Quille in 1861.

We reached the Sink Station a little before sundown, and unsaddling our animals, drove them out to the margin of the lake to graze. The Station consists of a one-story house, surrounded by an adobe wall enclosing a plot of ground some six rods square. This wall is eight feet high, and three feet thick at the bottom by one at the top, with loopholes for muskets. The stables are also within the walls. This Station is on the west side of the lake and within a few rods of the shore. It is a stopping place, both for the Overland Mail Line and the Pony Express. (REL, p. 28)

SISKRON (Humboldt). A short-lived post office established November 18, 1878, and discontinued February 3, 1879, when its name was changed to *Spring City* (FTM, p. 26).

SIX–MILE CANYON. The canyon, in Storey and Lyon counties, was named for its length. The Comstock Lode was discovered in Ophir Ravine near the head of Six-Mile Canyon which, in the early days, formed a valuable roadway between the Comstock and the Carson River country (NJ 11–1; VPG; NHS, 1913, p. 192). See **OPHIR.** The name appears on De Groot's 1860 Map of the Washoe

Mines (Wheat IV, 189). This numeral name also denotes canyons in Lincoln and Nye counties; a flat in Lincoln County; a creek in Elko County; a spring in Nye County; and springs and a wash in White Pine County (Dir. 1971).

SKAGGS (White Pine). An order to establish **SKAGGS** post office, dated September 10, 1906, was rescinded on March 25, 1907, probably before operations commenced (FTM, p. 26).

SKEDADDLE CREEK (Washoe). The creek, presumably named for its swiftness, rises on the northern slope of Hot Springs Mountain, in Lassen County, California, and following a circuitous route, flows through westernmost Nevada, in the hills west of the south end of Smoke Creek Desert, before discharging into Honey Lake (NK 11–10; VPG).

SKELETON HILLS (Nye). A small group of hills west of the Specter Range, south of Skull Mountain, on the east edge of the Amargosa Desert; so named by decision of the United States Geographic Board *Sixth Report* (Furn. Cr. Quad.).

SKELTON (Elko). A post office in Mound Valley, active from November 24, 1884, to May 1, 1911, when the name was changed to *Hylton* (FTM, p. 27). See **JIGGS.**

SKULL. The term, "usually restricted to places where human skulls were noticed" (GRS, Amer., p. 447), denotes three creeks in Nevada. **SKULL CREEK** (Elko), a tributary of the South Fork Owyhee River, southeast of Cottonwood; (Humboldt), a creek rising on the west slope of the Santa Rosa Range, north of Willow Creek; (Lander), a creek rising on the east slope of the Toiyabe Range and flowing into Grass Valley (GHM, EL 2; HU 4; LA 1). **SKULL MOUNTAIN** (Nye) is a mountain joined to **LITTLE SKULL MOUNTAIN** by a low saddle on the southwest, fifteen miles northeast of Lathrop Wells (USGB 6103; Furn. Cr. Quad.).

SKUNKTOWN (Lander). The early settlement in the northern portion of the county was served by Lewis post office (TF, p. 22; HHB, Nev., p. 269).

SLATE. Orographic features so named for geological formations include **SLATE MOUNTAIN,** a peak in the Sinkavata Hills, southsouthwest of Fairview Peak, in Churchill County, and **SLATE RIDGE,** a ridge northwest of Oriental Wash and south of Gold Point in southern Esmeralda County (NJ 11–1; USGB 5904; NJ 11–8).

SLAUGHTERHOUSE. This name was usually given to places where cattle were slaughtered for town butcher shops. **SLAUGHTERHOUSE CANYON.** Canyons so denoted are in Nye County, west of Jefferson and near Indian Creek; in Douglas County, north of Glenbrook and east of Lake Tahoe; in Eureka County, west of Union in the Sulphur Spring Range; and in Lincoln County, north of Pioche and running northeastward from Mount Ely (SG Maps 3, 6; GHM, EU 2; WA). **SLAUGHTERHOUSE CREEK** (Elko) is tributary to the Owyhee River, north of Mountain City (GHM, EL 3).

SLEEPING COLUMN CANYON (Nye). The canyon extends from about one mile west of Cactus Spring in the Cactus Range to its mouth, two miles west of Urania Peak and twenty miles east of Goldfield. The name is descriptive of the "horizontal rock columns in the canyon" (USGB 6303).

SLEEPY HOLLOW MINE. See **RIP VAN WINKLE** and **LONE.**

SLIDE. SLIDE MOUNTAIN, a peak southeast of Mount Rose and twenty-seven miles south of Reno, Washoe County, was named for a huge slide showing on its southeast face and also for a considerable slide occurring there in historical time (NJ 11–1; OPN, p. 69; Nev. Guide, p. 194; VPG). In Elko County, **SLIDE CREEK** is a tributary of the East Fork Jarbidge River, and **SLIDE ROCK RIDGE** is a ridge north of Marys River Peak (GHM, EL 3).

SLIM CREEK (Clark). The wash extending from Blue Point Spring to the Overton Arm of Lake Mead was so named in 1912. Men were employed by the Syphus family to dig a ditch between Blue Point and Rogers springs, for the purpose of increasing the flow of water down the wash to irrigate the land. They were forced to drink the cathartic spring waters, and the resultant and noticeable weight loss among the workers furnished a name for the wash (WA).

SLOAN (Clark). A station on the UP RR between Bard and Erie, about eighteen miles southwest of Las Vegas; named for a limestone-dolomite-carnotite district. The area, first settled about 1912, was served by *Ehret* post office, named for the Ehret family and established May 7, 1919. The name was changed to Sloan on September 11, 1922 (NI 11–3; VPG, p. 30; FTM, pp. 9, 26; WA).

SLOUGH RANCH (Churchill). The ranch and early station on the emigrant road at the Carson Slough were described by Dan De Quille, who camped nearby in 1861. "Just a short distance below where the slough begins to widen out into the Sink, we found the lake bordered by a very extensive meadows of excellent grass, and at the edge of the meadow a new, unfinished, adobe house, built by parties who have located a ranch here" (REL, p. 38). See **HILL.**

SLUMBERING HILLS (Humboldt). The **SLUMBERING HILLS,** northwest of Winnemucca, are the site of the **SLUMBERING HILLS MINING DISTRICT.** Although a second mining district was organized on the western slope and named *Awakening,* the hills continue to slumber undisturbed (VPG,

p. 70; GHM, HU 4). See **AWAKENING** and **AMOS.**

SMELTER. See **McGILL.**

SMILEYS SPUR (Lincoln). The former name for Comet Siding, about three miles southwest of Panaca, commemorates Ed Smiley who was manager of the Silver Comet Mill in 1916 (WA).

SMITH. SMITH VALLEY, on West Walker River in Lyon County, was named by a party of herdsmen who settled there in August of 1859. Timothy B. Smith, R. B. Smith, and Cyrus ("Adobe") Smith were members of the group and "the name of the place was selected on account of the predominance of 'Smith' in the party" (NHS, 1913, p. 224). The post office, established on June 4, 1892, also commemorates the Smith group (RS, p. 78). **SMITH CREEK** (Elko), tributary to the South Fork Humboldt River northwest of Lee, was named for C. E. Smith, an early settler in the area (NK 11–12; Wheeler 1871 Map; EP, p. 73). **SMITH CREEK STATION,** on the line of the Pony Express and of the Overland Stage, was the first station in the Shoshone country, the summit of the Desatoya Mountains west of Smith Creek being the boundary between the Shoshones and the Paiutes. Warren Wassen stopped at the station on December 19, 1861, enroute to Ruby Valley, having been requested by Governor James W. Nye to settle an Indian dispute following the death of the friendly Shoshone Chief Chokup (Wheeler 1871 Map; SPD, p. 155). **SMITH CREEK VALLEY** (Lander). The valley, lying between the Desatoya Mountains to the west and the Shoshone Mountains to the east, and **SMITH CREEK,** rising in the Desatoya Mountains and flowing into the valley, were named for one of Captain Simpson's men on May 30, 1859 (NJ 11–2). "Both the stream and cañon I call after my assistant, Lieut. J. L. Kirby Smith" (JHS, p. 79).

SMITHS (Washoe). The station on the now defunct V and T RR was a short distance from Washoe City and between Steamboat and Commonwealth (V&T Map). The possessive name refers to George Smith, Sr. of Sherrington, England, who lived near Steamboat Springs, as Myron Angel relates, with his eight children and an estimable wife. "Mr. Smith was one of the first, if not the first white man to settle along the eastern base of the Sierra Nevada Mountains. . . . The danger surrounding such an early settlement among the Indians cannot be fully portrayed" (MA, p. 633). A fort, built at the ranch during the Indian war of 1860, was called **FORT SMITH** (JGS, II, p. 464).

SMOKE CREEK (Washoe). The **SMOKE CREEK DESERT,** a vast playa once occupied by an arm of Lake Lahontan, is west and north of Pyramid Lake and of the Lake Range. **SMOKE CREEK** rises in California and enters the desert from the northwest, and **SMOKE CREEK RESERVOIR** extends southeast from the California boundary. The name, which derives from the dust devils that are frequently seen on this desert, appears on an 1854 manuscript map of a proposed route across the Sierra Nevada for a Pacific Railroad, by John A. Dreibelbis (Wheat III, 167). **SMOKE CREEK** was also the name of a temporary camp and depot on Smoke Creek, about five miles east of the California-Nevada line and near **SMOKE CREEK STATION,** between Susanville, California, and the Humboldt River (1881 Map). Because the citizens of the area needed protection from hostile Indians of the Honey Lake region, twenty-five enlisted men under the command of Lieutenant Henry W. Williams, from Fort Crook, California, established a camp at Smoke Creek on December 15, 1862. Nevada volunteers, ordered from Fort Churchill to replace the California troops in October, 1863, were removed to Granite Creek Station, with the abandonment of Smoke Creek in April, 1866 (Ruhlen). A former post office of Roop (Washoe) County, active from July 13, 1866, to August 6, 1867, and a station on the WP RR, south of Reynard Siding and west of Wild Horse Canyon, were named for the desert (NK 11–10; FTM, p. 27; VPG; HHB, Nev., p. 262).

SNAKE (White Pine). **SNAKE VALLEY,** on the Utah border, is bounded on the west by the **SNAKE RANGE,** which extends from south of the Kern Mountains to the southern line of White Pine County. **SNAKE CREEK** and **SNAKE MINING DISTRICT,** organized in February, 1869, and also known as *Bonita*, are on the east slope of the range south of Baker. Although the Snake Range is said to have been named for its sinuous course, early historian Myron Angel refers to the range as the *Snake Creek Range* (p. 648), an indication that the mountains may have been named for the creek. The Snake Indians, who formed one dialectic group with the Paviotso of western Nevada may be commemorated (FWH, p. 606). According to McArthur, the name *Snake* came from the fur trade period (LAM, p. 561).

SNIVELY (Elko). The former mining district, about three miles south of the SP RR and seven miles east of Toano, was named for A. P. Snively who discovered it in late October of 1883, according to the *Mining and Scientific Press* of February 9, 1884 (DM).

SNOW WATER LAKE (Elko). The lake in Clover Valley, east of the East Humboldt Range, is dry except when fed by water from melting snow (NK 11–12; OPN, p. 28). The name appears on Johnson and Browning's 1861 map of Utah Territory (Wheat V (I), 11).

SODA LAKE (Churchill). Two lakes northwest of Fallon are contained in the depressions of two craters. **LITTLE SODA,** covering about sixteen acres, was discovered in 1850. This lake is now nearly dry, but formerly was mined. It was reported that "the waters of the lake, embracing an area of between sixteen and seventeen acres, furnish an almost inexhaustible supply [of soda]" (SM, 1875, p. 6). **BIG SODA** covers about four hundred acres, has a depth of about 150 feet, and is without surface inlet or outlet (OPN, p. 13; Nev. Guide, p. 267; NJ 11–1). The mining district called **SODA LAKES** is six miles northwest of Fallon and about one mile north of U.S. 50 (VPG, p. 18).

SODA SPRINGS (Mineral). A valley south of Gabbs Valley Range and west of the Pilot Range; named for springs in the valley containing natural soda (OPN, p. 51; NJ 11–4). **SODA SPRINGS,** where Martin Brazzanovich once operated baths and a hotel in the valley, was an early name for Sodaville (HHB, Nev., pp. 260–61; DM).

SODAVILLE (Mineral). The locality, once the most important settlement between Reno and Tonopah and a station on the C and C RR, is four miles south of Mina. The post office was active from October 9, 1882, until March 31, 1917, when its operations were moved to Mina (FTM, p. 27). **SODAVILLE MINING DISTRICT,** east of the town for which it was named, is in the south end of the Pilot Range (VPG, p. 116; NJ 11–4).

SOD HOUSE (Humboldt). The settlement, also known as *Sod House Station,* between Amos and Happy Creek on State Route 8A, took its name from a sod house in the vicinity. Peter Skene Ogden passed this point in November of 1828 (EMM, Nev., pp. 67–68; NK 11–7).

SOLDIER(S). A creek, tributary to Rock Creek, in northern Lander County and southern Elko County, southwest of Tuscarora; a creek at the north end of the Ruby Mountains, rising north of **SOLDIER LAKES** (NK 11–12; Guide Map); named for the soldiers of old Fort Halleck (EP, p. 74). **SOLDIERS SPRING** (Churchill). A pass and an early settlement in the northeast portion of the county (HHB, Nev., pp. 261–62). These features were named for troops bivouacking there, as was **SOLDIER MEADOWS** in northern Washoe County, the site of a soldier encampment in the early days. Frémont camped here on December 31, 1843, having come from Long Valley, down High Rock Creek. The meadow became a famous rest area for man and beast in 1849 (NK 11–7; VPG; JGS, I, p. 73). Mud Meadow Creek, which flows through the meadow, is also called Soldier Meadows Creek. **SOLDIER MEADOWS MINING DISTRICT,** a nitrate

district, is fifty-three miles north of Gerlach (VPG, p. 76).

SONOMA (Humboldt). The **SONOMA RANGE** extends from northeast Pershing County into southeast Humboldt County, east of Grass Valley. **SONOMA PEAK,** at the north end of the range, and **SONOMA MOUNTAIN,** a mining district named for the peak, are five miles southeast of Winnemucca. **SONOMA CREEK** is at the base of the mountain and south of Santa Rosa Creek (NK 11–11; VPG, p. 76). The name group may derive from a California feature so named, which in turn "is doubtless derived from the Wintun word for 'nose,'" a word probably applied to an Indian chief with a prominent nose, hence the land or tribe of "Chief Nose" (Gudde, pp. 300–301).

SOUTH. SOUTH FORK (Elko). The early settlement was named for the **SOUTH FORK HUMBOLDT RIVER,** which empties into the Humboldt between Elko and Carlin, and was situated in **SOUTH FORK VALLEY,** in the basin of the stream (Guide Map; OPN, p. 28; JHS, p. 64). The name of **SOUTH FORK** post office, established February 24, 1874, was changed to *Coral Hill* on May 1, 1874 (FTM, p. 27). **SOUTH FORK INDIAN RESERVATION** is an alternate name for *Te-Moak Indian Reservation* (q.v.). **SOUTH AMERICAN CANYON** (Pershing), a district of placer deposits, was named for its location one mile south of American Canyon in the West Humboldt Range, east of Oreana (VPG, p. 162; NK 11–10). **SOUTH FORK OWYHEE RIVER** rises on the eastern slopes of the Tuscarora Mountains, near Independence Valley, and flows to the Owyhee River in Owyhee County, Idaho, and Elko County, Nevada (NK 11–8; USGB 5904). **SOUTH PAHROC RANGE** (Lincoln) is separated from the North Pahroc Range by Pahroc Summit, a pass about twenty-seven miles west of Caliente (USGB 6001; NJ 11–9). **SOUTH SCHELL PEAK** in the Schell Creek Range is named for its position south of North Schell Peak (NJ 11–3). **SOUTH SHOSHONE PEAK** in Nye County, is named for its position relative to North Shoshone Peak, in Lander County, in the Shoshone Mountains (NJ 11–2).

SOUTHEASTERN (Lincoln). A former copper mining district discovered in the spring of 1870, according to Wheeler, "to the southeast from Tim-pah-ute Peak." Apparently the district was named for the **SOUTHEASTERN MINE,** located about twelve miles from Groom and believed by Walter Averett to be the Bluebell Mine, or one near it (Wheeler, 1872, p. 45; WA).

SOUTHERN KLONDYKE. See **KLONDIKE.**

SOUTHERN PACIFIC SPRING (Mineral). The spring so denoted is at the foot of the mountains just east of Soda Spring Valley and about three miles east of the Southern Pacific Railroad, for which it is named. During the faulting at the time of the 1932 earthquake, a fault opened through the spring (VPG; NJ 11–4).

SPANISH. An ethnic name implying possession by Spanish-speaking people for a canyon heading west of Toiyabe Peak in the Toiyabe Range, in Lander County; and for springs near a canyon, so named and heading on the west slope of the Shoshone Mountains, west of Ione, in Nye County (NJ 11–5; GHM, LA 1; NY 2). **SPANISH BELT MINING DISTRICT**, on the southeast flank of the Toquima Range, about fifty miles north-northeast of Tonopah, in Nye County, was named for a Castillian, Emanuel San Pedro, according to S. Frank Hunt.

This doughty pioneer, imbued with that inner impulse or elemental urge of the explorer, organized and equipped a party of Mexicans in California in 1870 for an expedition into the then trackless wastes of Nevada, that resulted in the discovery of these Spanish Belt silver bonanzas. . . . After a sojourn on the Comstock lode he pushed southeast for 200 miles and established a rendezvous at Spanish Springs his winter camp. . . . From this base he divided his company of Mexican miners into parties and sent them forth to prospect the nearby ranges. (SFH, p. 2)

The principal mines of the district, clustered along the southeastern slope of **SPANISH PEAK,** were named the Barcelona, Catalonia, and Mariposa (SM, 1875, p. 104; VPG, p. 122; 1881 Map; SFH, p. 1; NJ 11–5). **SPANISH SPRING** (Washoe), having been used in the early days by Mexican squatters, was so named by those who later took up the land. Alces Blum named nearby **SPANISH SPRING PEAK** and **SPANISH SPRING VALLEY** for the spring. The valley is north of Sparks, and the peak east of the valley, in the Pah Rah Range (NJ 11–1; Reno Sheet). **SPANISH MINE** (Clark), an old lead mine south of Mormon Well in the Sheep Range, was so named because of a legend which relates that Spaniards worked the mine before the settlement of southern Nevada (WA). **SPANISH RAVINE** (Storey), the ravine just south of Ophir Ravine, was worked by Mexican miners in the early days.

SPARKS (Washoe). Sparks, adjoining the eastern city limits of Reno on U.S. 40, was established as a division point on the SP RR when the railroad shops were moved there from Wadsworth, in 1904. A post office had been instituted under the name of *Harriman* on September 15, 1903, in honor of Edward H. Harriman, the president of the railroad, but he requested that the name be changed. Other proposed names were *East Reno* and *Glendale,* which were rejected by railroad officials because they would interfere with the safe dispatching of trains, since confusion might arise because of Reno, Nevada, and Glendale, California, stations. The post office was established May 27, 1904, and the town was incorporated in 1905. The name is honorific of John Sparks (1843–1908), who was governor of Nevada at the time (NHS, 1926, pp. 349–50; 1909, p. 54). See **ANDERSONS.**

SPECTER RANGE (Nye). A short mountain range east of the Amargosa Desert and south of Skull Mountain (Furn. Cr. Quad.).

SPENCER (Lander). The post office, established February 20, 1896, and discontinued in 1908–09(?), was named for Sarah E. Spencer, postmaster (FTM, p. 27; OR, 1899).

SPIRIT MOUNTAIN (Clark). A mountain about nineteen miles north-northwest of the southern tip of Nevada, in the Newberry Mountains; said to have been so named because of the Indians' belief that it was the dwelling place of departed chieftains (NI 11–3). See **NEWBERRY.**

SPOONERS (Douglas). **SPOONERS SUMMIT,** on U.S. 50 northeast of Glenbrook, was named for **SPOONERS STATION,** settled as a wood camp two miles from Glenbrook. The name honors M. Spooner, the owner of the old station. **SPOONER LAKE** is south of Marlette Lake and near the former station site (HHB, Nev., pp. 254–55; NHS, 1913, p. 196; NJ 11–1).

SPOTTED RANGE (Clark). A mountain range west of Indian Springs Valley in the northwestern portion of the county; named for the variety of colors in the mineral deposits (NJ 11–12).

SPRAGUES. See **DOUBLE.**

SPRING. Creeks originating from springs are in Pershing County, in Pleasant and Dixie valleys; in Elko County, one west of Deeth, another near the Idaho line, between Pole and Poison creeks; in Nye County, in the Quinn Canyon Range, west of Garden Valley; and in Churchill County, flowing from the Clan Alpine Range to Dixie Valley. Simpson found five springs in Steptoe Valley, White Pine County, within compass of half a mile from his camp and wrote "I have therefore called this canon Spring Cañon" (JHS, p. 117). Valleys named for the natural springs within them are in Pershing County, on the east side of the Humboldt Range; in Storey and Lyon counties; and in White Pine County, between the Schell Creek Range and the Snake Range. **SPRING VALLEY STATION** (White Pine), on the Overland Stage route, was between Antelope Springs and Schell Creek stations (JGS, I, p. 136). The name of the valley appears on Captain James H. Simpson's 1859 map of his explorations across the Great Basin (Wheat IV, 137). A mining district of the 1880s denoted **SPRING VALLEY** is on the east flank of the Humboldt Range, about fourteen miles east of Oreana, in Pershing County (VPG, p. 163). See **FITTING.** A former mining district of Lander County so named was west of the Eureka district, immediately north of the stage road from Austin to Eureka (Wheeler, 1872, p. 39; 1871 Map). **SPRING CITY** was the name for a post office established in former Roop County on July 13, 1866. Its name was changed to *Hot Springs* on October 4, 1866 (FTM, p. 27). A mining district organized in 1868 on the east slope of the Santa Rosa Range, forty-five miles north-northeast of Winnemucca, took its name from former **SPRING CITY** mining camp and post office, established February 3, 1879, in Humboldt County, the name having been changed from *Siskron.* Postal operations were transferred to Paradise Valley on March 14, 1895 (FTM, p. 27; 1881 Map; VPG, p. 75; NM). **SPRING PEAK** (Mineral) is a peak southwest of Aurora, near the California boundary. **SPRING MOUN-TAINS** (Clark). A mountain range west of Las Vegas and east of Pahrump Valley, the largest and highest mountain mass in southern Nevada (NJ 11–12).

SPRINGDALE (Nye). A settlement on the Amargosa River, north of Beatty, formerly a station on the LV and T RR. A post office so named served the area from February 19, 1907, to January 15, 1912, when it was moved to Pioneer (FTM, p. 27).

SPRING OF FALSE HOPE. See **EMI-GRANT.**

SPRINGER (Lincoln). **SPRINGER HILL,** the site of a group of mining claims located in 1867, about twelve miles above Hiko, and **SPRINGERS CANYON,** in the Pahranagat Range south of Hiko, commemorate J. E. Springer, an early settler and the builder of the first house in Hiko (WA; DM).

SPRUCE MOUNTAIN (Elko). A mountain peak in the southwest end of the Pequop Range; named for mountain spruce. **SPRUCE MOUNTAIN MINING DISTRICT,** about forty-five miles south of Wells, had its first boom in 1871 "at a time when the miners of the west knew how to stage an affair of this kind. . . . Over 2,000 people rushed to this new Eldorado inside of six months" (SFH, p. 10; 1881 Map). The camp, southwest of the mountain and seven miles east of U.S. 93, was served by *Spruce Mount* post office from April 29, 1872, to April 15, 1884; reestablished as *Sprucemont* (September 10, 1886–June 26, 1895); as *Spruce* (June 26, 1895–August 31, 1896); (August 17, 1901–November 29, 1902); and again as *Sprucemont* (November 1, 1929–October 17, 1935). **SPRUCE MOUNTAIN RIDGE** extends northward from the peak, east of Independence Valley (NK 11–12; FTM, p. 27).

SQUAW. The Anglicized spelling of an Indian word meaning "woman," found in Algonquian dialects in the East: Narraganset, *eskwaw;* Delaware, *ochqueu;* Cree, *iskwew* (Gudde, p. 303). **SQUAW VALLEY** (Washoe). A mountain valley west of the Granite Range and opening into the Smoke Creek Desert (OPN, p. 70). **SQUAW CREEK** (Mineral). A creek rising southwest of Hawthorne in the Wassuk Range. **SQUAW LAKE** (Nye). A lake on the east slope of the Monitor Range, northeast of Eagle Peak (Guide Map). **SQUAW VALLEY** (Elko). A valley and a ranch southeast of Midas; "so named because Indian women used to gather seeds and bulbs in the area" (EP, p. 77; GHM, EL 2).

STAG CANYON (Washoe). The canyon leads from the Lake Range into the south end of the San Emidio Desert. In January, 1844, Frémont's party ascended this canyon and descended Sweetwater Creek. From the summit of the pass, they discovered Pyramid Lake (VPG; GHM, WA 2).

STAMPEDE GAP (Lincoln). The name denoted a mining camp at the gap so named, north of the Highland district and northwest of Pioche, active in 1869. Charles Gracey, a Nevada pioneer, built a small furnace for smelting the rich ores there (NHS, 1909, p. 106; NJ 11–9).

STAMPS (Lincoln). The name for an early post office, active from September 10, 1888, to May 25, 1895 (FTM, p. 27).

STANSFIELD (Mineral). A town of the 1880s, about ten miles east of Hawthorne, a former station on the C and C RR; named for William Stansfield, a teamster who hauled copper ore (DM).

STAR. In 1860, rich ore was discovered on the west slope of **STAR PEAK,** in the northern portion of the West Humboldt Range, Pershing County. **STAR MINING DISTRICT** was organized near **STAR CREEK CANYON,** and the small mining camp **STAR CITY,** about ten miles west of Mill City, was the scene of a boom after the discovery of the celebrated Sheba Mine on the lime contact along the base of Star Peak (Nev. Terr. Map; SPD, p. 898). *Star City* is included on an 1865 map of the North Pacific States and Territories, prepared by Captain John Mullan (Wheat V (I), frontispiece). The group name probably derives from the mountain, which was so named because it is the principal peak in the northern end of the range. Star*r* City post office served the area from April 15, 1862, to September 21, 1868 (FTM, p. 27; NK 11–10; Love. Quad.). **STAR CANYON** (Lyon) is a large gulch or ravine separating the Indian Springs Mining District from the Palmyra Mining District, in the Pine Nut Range (DM).

STARR. STARR VALLEY, a north-south trending valley southwest of Wells in Elko County, was named for a Captain Starr of the United States Army. The settlement in the valley was served by Halleck Station post office (Census, 1870). **STARR** post office (Lander), established October 18, 1881, and discontinued May 12, 1882, when its operations were transferred to Lewis, was named for the **STARR AND GROVE MINE.** The *Battle Mountain Messenger* of December 10, 1881, noted that a post office to be established at Uppertown would be named *Starr-Grove,* in honor of A. M. Starr, one of the mine owners, and Sam Groves, a former manager (TFM, p. 27; DM).

STARVATION. STARVATION FLAT (Lincoln). The alluvial fan at the west edge of Coyote Springs Valley "was named by cattlemen who had to drive cattle across the wide, barren flat" (WA). **STARVATION SPRING** (Humboldt) is north of Red Butte in the Jackson Mountains (GHM, HU 2). **STARVATION CAMP** is a vanished name for a campsite southeast of the confluence of the Little Truckee with the Truckee River. The name appears on Dr. Henry De Groot's 1860 Map of the Washoe Mines (Wheat IV, 189).

STATE LINE. Features named for their geographical position include a peak in Washoe County, south of Honey Lake Valley on the Nevada-California boundary; a canyon in Lincoln County, heading in the White Rock Mountains at the Utah border and extending to Spring Valley Wash; a locality in Clark County, just north of the California line, and the **STATE LINE HILLS** lying along the state boundary, northwest of **STATE LINE INTERCHANGE** on U.S. 91 (Guide Map; NJ 11-6; GHM, CL 3). In southern Esmeralda County, **STATELINE SPRING** and **STATE LINE MILL** are near the California boundary (GHM, ES 2). **STATELINE** (Douglas) is a town at the south end of Lake Tahoe, on the California-Nevada boundary. **STATELINE WELL** (Elko) is in the Western Shoshone Indian Reservation, just south of the Idaho line (GHM, DO 1; EL 2).

STEAD (Washoe). **STEAD AIR FORCE BASE** in Lemmon Valley was so named in 1954. **STEAD INTERCHANGE** on U.S. 395 takes its name from the base which was phased out in 1965 (M&M, p. 190; GHM, WA 1).

STEAMBOAT (Washoe). **STEAMBOAT SPRINGS,** eleven miles south of Reno on U.S. 395, is the name for hot mineral springs discovered in 1860 by a Frenchman, Felix Monet. In the early days, when the air was cool and calm, William Wright (Dan De Quille) reported that as many as sixty or seventy columns of steam could be seen rising along the ridge, many ascending to a height of fifty feet (DDQ, pp. 327–28). Mark Twain explained the name in a letter from Steamboat Springs, Nevada Territory, August 23, 1863. "They are natural—the devil boils the water, and the white steam puffs up out of crevices in the earth, along the summits of a series of low mounds extending in an irregular semi-circle for more than a mile . . . From one spring the boiling water is ejected a foot or more by the infernal force at work below, and in the vicinity of all of them one can hear a constant rumbling and surging, somewhat resembling the noises peculiar to a steamboat in motion—hence the name" (HNS, pp. 70–71). The springs are at the north end of **STEAMBOAT VALLEY,** a small valley extending northeast from Pleasant Valley. The name of the valley is shown on Dr. Henry De Groot's 1860 Map of the Washoe Mines (Wheat IV, 189). In 1871, the V and T RR was completed to this point from Reno, and the station was named for the springs (GHK, V&T, p. 29; MA, p. 645). The **STEAMBOAT HILLS** are east of the valley (GHM, WA 1). **STEAMBOAT SPRINGS MINING DISTRICT** was organized December 3, 1875, nine miles south of Reno, when Thomas Wheeler discovered sulfur and cinnabar mines just north of west of the springs (SM, 1875, p. 157; VPG, p. 174). **STEAMBOAT** is the name of the post office established February 12, 1880 (FTM, p. 27).

STEELE (Elko). A stream so designated heads in **STEELE LAKE,** eleven miles west of Tobar, and flows southeast to disappear in Clover Valley. The features were "named for Jim Steele, who settled in the area in the 1860s" (USGB 7004). *Steeles* and *Steels* are variants for the creek and *Gibbs* for the lake (NK 11–12).

STEINER CREEK (Lander). The creek, west of Ackerman Canyon in the Simpson Park Range, was named for the L. Steiner family who owned a big ranch on the creek, now known as the McGee Ranch (SG Map 6; MM).

STEPTOE (White Pine). **STEPTOE VALLEY,** between the Egan Range and the Schell Creek Range, runs the length of White Pine County from north to south. Flowing southwestward from the Duck Creek Range, **STEPTOE CREEK** turns north into Steptoe Valley (NJ 11–3; Ely Quad. 1952). The valley and a town, on the east flank of the Egan Range and on Duck Creek, were settled in 1868 (Nev. Terr. Map; Census, 1870). **STEPTOE,** which existed as a Lander County post office from May 24, 1864, to November 25, 1864, was established in White Pine County on October 14, 1893, and discontinued on October 15, 1940, when McGill became the mail address for its patrons (FTM, p. 27). **STEPTOE** is also a station name on the NN RR. *Steptoe Valley* appears on Captain James H. Simpson's 1859 map of his explorations across the Great Basin (Wheat IV, 137). The name commemorates Colonel E. J. Steptoe, a famous fighter of the Old West and, in 1861, one of Beckwith's aides (OPN, p. 76; NHS, 1924, p. 79; JHS, pp. 24–25).

STERLING (Nye). A former mining camp, established in 1907 about seven miles from the former LV and T RR and near Indian Springs, by report of the *Reno Evening Gazette* of May 3, 1907. The order to establish **STERLING** post office, dated June 3, 1907, was rescinded February 13, 1908 (FTM, p. 27; DM).

STEWART (Carson City). The community, post office, and former station on the Carson Valley Branch of the now defunct V and T RR, between Minden and Carson City, were named for a school for Indians, maintained by the Federal Government on a large farm three and one-half miles south of Carson City. The school was first called *Stewart Institute* for Senator William M. Stewart, through whose efforts it was founded in 1890. Before the establishment of a post office at Stewart on June 2, 1905, it came to be known as the *Carson Indian School,* because Carson City was the nearest post office. The school, which has students from the Navajo, Paiute, Shoshone, and Washoe tribes, is under the jurisdiction of the Carson Indian Agency (M&S, p. 142; RC, pp. 79–80; NHS, 1913, p. 204; V&T Map; NJ 11–1). William M. Stewart was a successful mining lawyer at Virginia City on the Comstock, and on December 15, 1864, was elected United States Senator from Nevada on the first ballot and served in the Senate for twenty-eight years (HHB, Nev., pp. 174, n. 63, 186–87; MA, pp. 540–41; M&S, p. 305).

STEWARTS POINT (Clark). The boat dock and beach at the point of a ridge extending into the Overton Arm of Lake Mead, a few miles below Overton Beach (WA), may commemorate Archibald Stewart, who purchased the original ranch at Las Vegas from Octavius D. Gass in 1882. See **LAS VEGAS.**

STILLWATER (Churchill). The name group derives from the **STILLWATER SLOUGH,** a large, deep slough named for the sluggishness of the water. The settlement of **STILL-WATER** began as a station near the Stillwater Slough and on the Overland Route, in 1862, midway between Mountain Wells and Old River stations, and became the county seat in 1868, losing it to Fallon in 1902. **STILLWATER** post office, was established on January 11, 1865. The **STILL-WATER RANGE** is between Dixie Valley and the Carson Sink, bounded on the north by McKinney Pass and on the south by Sand Springs Pass (NHS, 1913, p. 178; JGS, I,

p. 136; Nev. Terr. Map; NJ 11–1; USGB 5904). **STILLWATER** also denotes a national wildlife refuge, a reservoir, and a canal in the central portion of the county (GHM, CH 1, 2).

STIMLER (Esmeralda). A former mining camp of the Silver Peak district, noted by the *Rhyolite Daily Bulletin* on November 22, 1907, and discontinued January 20, 1909, when the name was changed to *Mary Mine* (FTM, p. 28). The name commemorated Harry Stimler, one of the discoverers of Goldfield (DM).

STINE (Lincoln). A siding on the UP RR, between Etna and Boyd in the Meadow Valley Wash, abandoned in 1949; named for Marcus Stine, one of the owners of the Delamar district in 1901. The *Reno Evening Gazette* of September 7, 1909, reported that the power plant at Stine was being torn down, the Delamar mines having closed permanently (Freese, Map 2; WA; DM).

STIRLING (Nye). **MOUNT STIRLING,** at the northwest end of the Spring Mountains, took its name from the former mining camp on the north side of the mountain, the site of **STIRLING MINE.** *Sterling* (q.v.) was the name of the post office which served the district (NJ 11–12; WA).

STOCKTON (Lyon). **STOCKTON FLAT WELL,** near the junction of U.S. 50 and State Route 1C southwest of Silver Springs, took its name from early **STOCKTON STA-TION.** The former trading post was named for its owners, J. N. North and W. Nicholas, who were from Stockton, California, and were called "the Stockton boys" (GHM, LY 1; NHS, 1913, p. 218).

STOFIEL (Elko). A post office in the Wild Horse area established June 11, 1891, and discontinued June 30, 1899 (FTM, p. 28); named for and operated by the Walter Stofiels (EP, p. 78).

STONE AND GATES CROSSING. See **GLENDALE.**

STONEBERGER. The creek (Nye, Lander, Eureka) heads at **STONEBERGER BASIN** (Nye) in the Toquima Range, west of Dianas Punch Bowl, and flows to Bean Flat (Eureka). The creek took its name from **STONE-BERGERS,** an early ranch station twenty miles east-northeast of Kingston in Lander County, named for its owner. Austin was the mail address for the early station (NJ 11–5; NJ 11–2; USGB 5904; TF, p. 22; HHB, Nev., p. 269; 1881 Map).

STONE HOUSE (Humboldt). A stop on the Overland Stage Route, an early post office (November 26, 1890–March 24, 1915), and a station on the SP RR nineteen miles west from Battle Mountain (1881 Map; T1TR; FAC, p. 149; FTM, p. 28), whose foundation can now be faintly seen among the rocks and brush (MM). "This was not an old trading post, but a station in former times of the Overland Stage Company, and the house, built of stone near some very fine springs, was one of the eating-houses on their line, where travelers could relish square meals of bacon and coffee with safety. . . . Stone House Mountain, as it is now called, rears its head just back of the crumbling ruins" (FES, p. 189).

STONEWALL (Nye). **STONEWALL MOUNTAIN** is on the northwest edge of the Pahute Mesa and south of **STONEWALL FLAT**. A mining district so named is at **STONEWALL SPRING** on the mountain and seventeen miles south-southeast of Goldfield. **STONEWALL** was the name of the station on the LV and T RR between Cuprite and Wagner (NJ 11–8; VPG, p. 139). The name honors General Thomas Jonathan Jackson who gained the sobriquet "Stonewall" because of his stand at Bull Run.

STONY POINT (Lander). A mountain southeast of the town of North Battle Mountain, and an early station west of Shoshone Point (GHM, LA 2; 1867 Map). The name appears on an 1858 Map of the Overland Route, by W. Wadsworth (Wheat IV, 106).

STOREY COUNTY. Storey County was created on November 25, 1861, at which time Virginia City was made the county seat. The name commemorates Edward Faris Storey, Captain of Company K (known as the Virginia Rifles), Washoe Regiment, who was killed June 2, 1860, in the Pyramid Lake Indian War. Both Captain Storey, born in Jackson County, Georgia, in 1828, and his father, Colonel John Storey, fought in the Mexican War. Captain Storey moved to California in 1852 and to Nevada in 1859 (MA, p. 569; SPD, pp. 64, 997; DDQ, p. 80; Ruhlen).

STOREY, FORT (Washoe). The fort, named for Captain Edward Faris Storey, was a temporary earthwork thrown up on the Truckee River about eight miles south of Pyramid Lake, and the same distance north of Wadsworth, by the Washoe Regiment of Nevada Volunteers before their battle with the Paiutes on June 2, 1860. The fort was abandoned on June 6, 1860 (Ruhlen). See **STOREY COUNTY.**

STRAWBERRY. **STRAWBERRY VALLEY** (Nye) is a small valley, traversed by U.S. 95 for about two miles, which opens into the Amargosa Desert at Point of Rocks at the southeast end of the Specter Range. A name legend relates that a prospector's mule, loaded with jars of strawberry jam (a gift from the prospector's parents), bucked off his pack. Broken jars and jam spread at random gave the small valley its name (WA). **STRAWBERRY** (White Pine) is the name for a settlement east of Diamond Peak in the Diamond Range; for a post office active

from September 7, 1899, to November 30, 1938; and for a creek in the Snake Range, southeast of Osceola; presumably named for wild strawberries growing nearby (FTM, p. 28; GHM, WP 1).

STREUBEN KNOB (Nye). The hill, three miles northwest of Reveille in the Reveille Range, was "named for Victor Streuben, who operated the nearby Red Hill Mine" (USGB 7103).

STRIPED HILLS (Nye). The mountain group immediately north of the Skeleton Hills and about four miles east of Lathrop Wells, was "so named because its rock structure appears as alternate dark and light banding" (USGB 6103).

STUMP SPRING (Nye). The Jefferson-Hunt train stopped at this spring on the California emigrant road, in Pahrump Valley between Cottonwood and Pahrump springs (LRH, II, p. 93; Wheeler, 1872, p. 85). Lewis Granger's letter of April 8, 1850, refers to it as *Willow Spring* (LRH, IV, p. 61) and G. Harris Heap as *Agua Escarbada* (LRH, VII, p. 242). An 1855 map by Captain Rufus Ingalls shows *Stump Spring* (Wheat IV, 29). A variant is Stump*s* Spring. Early settlers were served by St. Thomas post office (TF, p. 22).

STURTEVANT (Washoe). An early stage station a few miles from Clarks that was important because travelers from Virginia City and places adjacent went there to catch the overland train; named for its owner, James H. Sturtevant, nicknamed "Farmer Jim." Mr. Sturtevant was included in the personnel of the Constitutional Convention, Carson City, July, 1864, and was elected to the House of Representatives of Nevada Territory, representing Washoe Valley (SPD, pp. 1003, 1007, 194, 197).

SUGAR LOAF. The name for hills and mountain peaks, according to George R. Stewart, spread from Sugar-Loaf Hill, not far from Providence, Rhode Island, which was named when "the sugar that men knew came in the form of a large cake, sticking up to a high rounded point at the end" (GRS, Names, p. 64). In Nevada, peaks named **SUGAR LOAF** are in Storey County, east of Virginia City in Six-Mile Canyon; in southern Lyon County in the Sweetwater Range; in the extreme western part of Esmeralda County on the Mineral County line; and in Elko County, a peak in the northeast portion of the county and a hill just south of the Duck Valley Indian Reservation (OPN, pp. 29, 32, 47; NHS, 1913, p. 193).

SULLIVAN (Carson City). The **SULLIVAN MINING DISTRICT**, also known as *Delaware*, on the east side of the Carson River, four miles east of Carson City, was discovered in 1860, abandoned because of Indian troubles, and relocated in 1862 (VPG, p. 147; DM).

SULPHUR. Places named for native sulfur deposits include a town and a station on the main line of the WP RR between Floka and Ronda (Humboldt); named for **SULPHUR MINING DISTRICT,** located in 1875 on the northwest flank of the Kamma Mountains (VPG, p. 77; OPN, p. 38). **SULPHUR** post office served the area, with interruptions, from January 17, 1899, to May 31, 1953, when its operations were transferred to Winnemucca (FTM, p. 28). Population figures for **SULPHUR MINE,** Humboldt County, were included in the Federal Census of 1900. **SULPHUR SPRINGS RANGE,** extending from east-central Eureka County into Elko County, was named for sulfur springs in the range near **SULPHUR SPRINGS STATION** (Eureka). The station was on the Overland Stage and the Pony Express, thirteen miles east of Roberts Creek Station (JGS, I, p. 136; Nev., I, 1961, p. 9; USGB 6002; 1867 Map; HHB, Nev., p. 285).

SUMMIT. A name given to indicate a point of elevation or a pass through the mountains. **SUMMIT CAMP** (Douglas) was a camp near Spooners Summit, the lowest pass in the vicinity, and a station on the former LTNG RR (HHB, Nev., p. 255; 1881 Map; NHS, 1913, p. 190; VPG). **SUMMIT** (Storey) was a station at the head of the Geiger Grade which served stage travelers, teamsters, and herders in the early days (NHS, 1913, p. 189). The name also designates a peak and a township in northwest White Pine County (Census, 1950; NJ 11–3). **SUMMIT LAKE** (Humboldt) is a lake in the Black Rock Range, at the summit of the road and on the drainage divide between the Black Rock Desert and Virgin Valley. An Indian reservation is named for the lake (NK 11–7; VPG). **SUMMIT** (Eureka) denotes a peak in the southwest portion of the county in the Monitor Range; a peak in the Diamond Range; and a locality, formerly a station on the old E and P RR, west of the Sulphur Spring Mountains (NJ 11–2). **SUMMIT** is also the name for a canyon north of Ophir Canyon, in the Toiyabe Range of Nye County; and for a post office of Elko County on **SUMMIT CREEK,** established February 8, 1908, and discontinued July 31, 1909, when Midas became the mail address for its patrons (NJ 11–5; EP, p. 78; FTM, p. 28; MM). **SUMMIT** (Clark) is the name for a pass between Immigrant Canyon and New Springs Wash and for a nearby spring, east of Gold Butte. Another spring so named is about three miles east of Searchlight (WA). **SUMMIT SPRING** (Lincoln) is southeast of the Groom district and about ten miles west of Hiko (Wheeler 1871 Map; WA; NJ 11–12). A post office of former Roop County, named **SUMMIT SPRINGS,** was active from March 19, 1867, to August 6, 1867.

SUNFLOWER. Features named for an abundant growth of sunflowers in the region include a flat, a summit, and a reservoir southeast of Mountain City in northern Elko County, and a spring west of Carp, in Kane Springs Wash, Lincoln County (Nev. Guide, p. 169; WA; GHM, EL 3).

SUNKIST (Washoe). The post office so named was established April 24, 1916, and discontinued April 15, 1919, when its operations were transferred to Gerlach (FTM, p. 28).

SUNLAND (Mineral). The post office, earlier named *Buena Vista,* was established April 24, 1911, and discontinued July 31, 1912, when Mina took over its operations (FTM, p. 28).

SUNNYSIDE (Nye). An early settlement (presently Whipple Ranch) and post office (July 10, 1890–January 31, 1933) of northeastern Nye County, near the Lincoln County boundary (FTM, p. 28; OPN, p. 57); a wash in the Shoshone Mountains east of Phonolite (SG Map 6; GHM, NY 5).

SUNRISE. **SUNRISE PEAK** (Storey) was an early name which the Johntown miners gave Mount Davidson (q.v.). A former mining district so named was discovered about six miles south of Como, in Lyon County, in September, 1906 (DM). **SUNRISE MOUNTAIN** (Clark) is northeast of Las Vegas (NJ 11–12).

SUNSET (Clark). The **SUNSET MINING DISTRICT,** also called *Lyons* and *Lucy Grey,* is fifteen miles southeast of Jean. Gold was discovered in 1895, and the principal mine of the district, the Lucy Grey, was discovered in 1905 by T. L. Bright (VPG, p. 31; WA).

SUN VALLEY (Washoe). The town, northeast of Reno, takes its name from the valley in which it is situated. **SUN VALLEY** lies west of Spanish Springs Valley (GHM, WA 1).

SURPRISE. The name for a mountain valley on the Nevada-California line, chosen because "emigrants who had just traversed the Black Rock Desert were 'surprised' as they came out of the arid sagebrush hills into the smiling valley" (Gudde, p. 309). **SURPRISE REEF** (Clark) in the Overton Arm of Lake Mead is several miles north of Virgin Basin (WA).

SUSANS BLUFF (Lyon). The bluff, about fourteen miles east of Dayton, overlooks the Carson River and is a short distance west of old Fort Churchill. Susan O'Brien escaped from captivity and committed suicide by jumping from the top of the high bluff; her father, mother, and brother were killed by the Indians (MM).

SUSIE CREEK. A creek, east of Maggie Creek, joins the Humboldt River at a point north of Vivian in Elko County and was named by an early emigrant for one of his daughters (1881 Map). See **CARLIN.** A mining district, named for the creek, is about fifteen miles north-northwest of Carlin in Eureka County (VPG, p. 66; GHM, EL 1).

SUTCLIFFE (Washoe). A trading post and resort, also a station on the Wadsworth Subdivision of the SP RR between Heslip and Bristol, on the west shore of Pyramid Lake; named for James Sutcliffe who owned a ranch in the area (T75; VPG). **SUTCLIFFE** post office was active from July 27, 1929, to August 15, 1940 (FTM, p. 28).

SUTOR (Clark). A locality and a station on the UP RR, formerly on the SPLA and SL RR, north of Jean; named for a radium district two miles to the west (Freese, Map 1; VPG, p. 31).

SUTRO (Lyon). Between June 5 and July 25, 1866, Congress passed a piece of special legislation: "a grant to Adolph Sutro, for the right of way and other privileges to aid in the construction of a draining and exploring tunnel to the Comstock Lode in the State of Nevada" (NHS, 1913, p. 163). Mark Twain saw "Mr. Sutro, the originator of this prodigious enterprise," as "one of the few men in the world who is gifted with the pluck and perseverance necessary to follow up and hound such an undertaking to its completion" (SLC, II, p. 97, n. 1). Because of opposition from the Bank of California, said to have had the controlling interest in the Comstock Lode (M&SP, 9/25/69), Sutro was unable to drive his so called "coyote hole" until after the great fire in the Yellow Jacket Mine on April 24, 1869. He, then, was able to prove how his tunnel could have saved the lives of the miners. On August 25, 1869, miners subscribed $50,000 in gold to the stock of the Sutro Tunnel Company (M&SP, 9/11/69). On October 19, 1869, the first shovelful of earth was turned, and on July 8, 1878, the four-mile Sutro Tunnel made connection with the Comstock Lode at the Savage Mine. The tunnel passed a mile north of Gold Hill and a mile short of the summit of Mount Davidson and drained the entire Comstock ledge (VPG; TS, p. 39; SPD, p. 1001; MA, pp. 504, 511; FCL, p. 223; TW, p. 49). The car track for the Sutro Tunnel Railroad was put down October 30, 1869 (M&SP, 11/6/69). Almost overnight the mushroom town **SUTRO** sprang up at the mouth of the tunnel. "The town of Sutro, at the mouth of the tunnel, though hardly metropolitan in its character, is well laid out, and contains scores of substantial frame dwellings, shops, and other buildings, nearly all belonging to the Company, and used and occupied principally by the families of the men connected with the works" (TS, p. 42). The post office of **SUTRO** was active from March 25, 1872, to October 30, 1920, when its operations were transferred to Dayton (FTM, p. 28).

Sutro moved to San Francisco in 1879 and was later elected mayor of that city (SPD, p. 405). The mouth of the tunnel and the remains of a large mill are visible from U.S. 50 at a point about five miles east of Dayton. **SUTRO SPRINGS,** in the Flowery Range, are northeast of the tunnel site (GHM, ST 1).

SWALES (Elko). The name denotes a mountain southwest of Monument Peak in the Independence Mountains and about fifteen miles north-northeast of Carlin, and a creek tributary to Susie Creek (USGB; NK 11–11; GHM, EL 1). Variants are *Swalls* (Freese, Map 3) and *Swails* (OPN, p. 29). According to report, the mountain "was named by a mining engineer who was a native of England. In the early days that he worked in the district he thought that the low foliage that covered the mountain looked like the English countryside below the old moats. The term swales refers to that type of foliage covering" (EP, p. 79).

SWAN LAKE (Washoe). The name for a lake and a reservoir north of the lake, in the Charles Sheldon Wildlife Refuge, in the northern portion of the county (NK 11–7). Petroglyph sites in the lake area and the Charles Sheldon National Antelope Refuge probably were associated with antelope hunts (M&M, p. 198).

SWANSEA (White Pine). The former town, settled in 1869, was less than a mile north of Shermantown in the White Pine Range. Its mills smelted the ores from Hamilton and Treasure City (1881 Map, M&M, p. 219). The name is commemorative of Swansea, a smelting center in southeastern Wales (NM).

SWEETWATER. The name is sometimes given to hydrographic features and is descriptive of water that is fresh or has a noticeable absence of hydrominerals. **SWEETWATER** (Lyon). **SWEETWATER FLAT,** a valley flat between the **SWEETWATER MOUNTAINS** and the Bald Mountains, trends generally northwestward from **SWEETWATER CANYON** (USGB 6002; Well. Sheet). An early settlement and post office (January 26, 1870–December 26, 1925) were at the site of a former station on the way to Aurora and Bodie in the early 1860s (FTM, p. 28; Census, 1870; OPN, p. 47). The name derives from **SWEETWATER CREEK** in the canyon (GHM, LY 2). **SWEETWATER CREEK** (Washoe) rises in the Lake Range south of the San Emidio Desert and drains westward into the north end of Pyramid Lake (VPG; NK 11–10).

SWIFTS STATION (Carson City). The early station on the road to Lake Tahoe was named for its owner, Mr. S. T. Swift, formerly the sheriff of Ormsby (Carson City) County (NHS, 1913, p. 196). Carson City post office served *Swifts Springs,* an alternate name for the station (TF, p. 22).

SYLVANIA (Esmeralda). The **SYLVANIA MOUNTAINS,** west of the Palmetto Mountains and on the California border, were named for the **SYLVANIA MINING DISTRICT** and its former camp, discovered in 1870 about fifty miles southwest of Goldfield, Nevada, and twelve miles southeast of Oasis, California (VPG, p. 61). The mountains, earlier named *Green Mountain,* furnished a name for the mining district which was organized in 1872. In 1873, the name was changed to *Sylvania* for sylvanite, a telluride of silver, in the district (NJ 11–8; SPD, p. 857; HHB, Nev., p. 261; SM, 1875, pp. 35–36).

TABLE MOUNTAIN. Peaks and mountains so named for their table-like tops are in Churchill, Clark, Elko, Eureka, Lincoln, Lyon, Mineral, Pershing, and White Pine counties (Dir. 1971; ECN Map; NJ 11–1; NI 11–3). Two ranges named **TABLE MOUNTAIN** are northeast of Paradise Valley, in Humboldt County, and north of Garden Valley and west of the Sulphur Spring Range, in Eureka County (GHM, HU 4; EU 1). **TABLE MOUNTAIN MINING DISTRICT,** named for the Churchill County peak, is at the north end of Dixie Valley (VPG, p. 19). **TABLE MOUNTAIN** also denoted an early settlement in Esmeralda County (Census, 1870). **TABLE TOP MOUNTAIN** (Elko) is a peak west of Contact (GHM, EL 4).

TAFT (White Pine). The name designates a peak north of South Schell Peak, in the Schell Creek Range, and a creek flowing into Spring Valley. **TAFT** post office was established February 23, 1909, and discontinued April 19, 1917, when the name was changed to *Cleveland Ranch* (GHM, WP 1; FTM, p. 28). The name may commemorate William Howard Taft, the twenty-seventh president of the United States, 1909–13.

TAHOE, LAKE. A mountain lake in the Sierra Nevada in both Nevada and California was viewed by Captain Frémont on February 14, 1844, who wrote: "With Mr. Preuss, I ascended today the highest peak to our right, from which we had a beautiful view of a mountain lake at our feet, about fifteen miles in length, and so entirely surrounded by mountains that we could not discover an outlet" (JCF, Report, p. 234). Although *Mountain Lake* appeared on his 1845 map, in a letter written from Prescott, Arizona Territory, on February 29, 1881, Frémont said "what is now called Lake Tahoe I named Lake Bonpland upon my first crossing of the Sierra in 1843–44" (MA,

p. 25). The naming was honorific of Aimé Jacques Alexandre Bonpland, the French naturalist. Professor John Le Conte wrote that in 1851, one of the Indian expeditions organized by the state of California had named the lake *Bigler,* in honor of Governor John Bigler. The name was legalized by the California legislature during the session of 1869–70 and appears on three 1855 maps prepared by George H. Baker, J. H. Colton, and Colonel E. J. Steptoe (Wheat IV, 38, frontispiece, 28). There was a very strong tendency, nevertheless, to call the lake *Tahoe* (1867 Map). Maps of 1874, 1876, and 1881 of California and Nevada had the double designation (M&SP, 9/11/80; 1881 Map). Dr. Henry De Groot published an article on the origin and meaning of the term *Tahoe* in 1880. He had employed one of the leading men of the Washoe tribe to accompany him on a visit to the lake.

> Inquiring of my guide the Indian name for this water, he told me that they call it "Tah-hoe-ee," meaning big lake or water. . . . the foregoing is the correct and only meaning of the word in the Washoe language, and the above is a true version of the time and manner in which it came to be applied to this lake. As used by the Washoes it is a word of three syllables with the chief accent on the last, as set forth above; and since it is likely to be retained in our vocabulary, I suggest that we adopt this pronunciation as being more analogous to the Indian tongue and likely to work in a uniformity in the popular method of pronunciation which now vibrates between "Tay-hoe," "Tah-hoe," and "Ta-hoe". (M&SP, 9/18/80)

In 1862, William Henry Knight, on the advice of De Groot, caused the United States Land Office to approve the name (Nev. Guide, p. 194; Gudde, p. 312). According to Simpson *Ta-hou* means "sea" in the Washo language (JHS, p. 370). From the findings of Kroeber and De Groot, Professor Gudde has deduced that *ta* is the Washo root for "water" and that *tah-oo* or *ta-au* means "lake water," "sheet of water" (Gudde, p. 312).

TAHOE VILLAGE, a town in Douglas County, **TAHOE MEADOWS,** a flat in Washoe County, and **TAHOE NATIONAL FOREST** were named for the lake. Former **LAKE TAHOE** post office (August 7, 1871, to August 16, 1872) was in Douglas County. The Lake Tahoe Narrow-Gauge Railroad, built by H. M. Yerington and D. L. Bliss in 1875 for transporting timber and cordwood to the Comstock, was eight and three-quarters miles long, running from Glenbrook on the Nevada side of the lake to the eastern summit of the Sierra Nevada where a "V" shaped flume was located (OFM, pp. 3–7).

TALAPOOSA (Lyon). A mining district on

the east slope of the east extension of the Virginia Range, eleven miles south of Fernley, and a former mining camp; named for the **TALAPOOSA MINE** discovered in 1864. The toponym is commemorative of a Creek tribe formerly on the Tallapoosa River in Alabama (VPG, p. 106; DM; FWH, p. 677).

TAMBERLAINE CANYON (White Pine). The canyon so named heads on the west slope of the Duck Creek Range and extends into Steptoe Valley, above Steptoe Creek. The name may commemorate Joseph Thompson, a prospector known as "Tamerlane Joe," one of the locators of *Tamerlane*, a camp of the early 1870s (NJ 11–3; NHS, 1924, pp. 291, 298).

TATES STATION (Nye). A former station in Big Smoky Valley, about two miles south of Millett and a half mile east of State Route 8A, on the Austin-Belmont mail and passenger route, from 1886 to 1901. Thomas Tate, who operated the stage line from the late 1870s until about 1903, selected the site as a halfway place between Austin and Belmont. In 1886, he built a house and stables there and a branch stage line to Ophir Canyon, about five miles southwest in the Toiyabe Range, where a mining camp was enjoying a lively revival at the time. A variant of the station name is *Tate* (MM).

TAYLOR. Silver ore discoveries made in 1873 about sixteen miles southeast of Ely in the Schell Creek Range, White Pine County, led to the organization of the **TAYLOR MINING DISTRICT.** The first propecting was done by representatives of the Martin White Company, one of whom was named Taylor. The town came into prominence in the early 1880s through the output of the Monitor and Argus mines, the principal producers of the district. A post office so named served the area from May 9, 1883, to September 9, 1893, when its operations were transferred to Ely (VPG, p. 185; NM; NHS, 1924, p. 370; FTM, p. 28). **MOUNT TAYLOR** (Elko) is a peak southwest of Currie in the Cherry Creek Mountains. **TAYLOR MINE** (Clark) is the name for a canyon (once traversed by the Bamberger Road to Delamar) which drains eastward into the Meadow Valley Wash about eight miles below Caliente. The canyon was named for the **TAYLOR MINE**, located on the south side of the canyon and approximately three miles west of the Meadow Valley Wash by Joseph Taylor (for whom it was named) in company with Ben Henkle and Clyde Bailey (WA). See **EASTER. TAYLORS WELL**. See **SANDY.**

TEALS MARSH (Esmeralda). A salt marsh thirty miles southeast of Aurora and ten miles northwest of Basalt; named for William E. Teal, who was a member of the House of Representatives of Nevada Territory for Aurora in 1861 (SPD, pp. 192, 197;

SM, 1867, p. 37). A variant is Teels Marsh (NJ 11–4; HHB, Nev., p. 260).

TECHATTICUP (Clark). **TECHATTICUP WASH** drains eastward from the **TECHATTICUP MINE,** for which it is named, through Eldorado Canyon to the Colorado River. There is a persistent rumor that the mine was worked by Spaniards in very early times. Opened in 1863 in the Eldorado Canyon Mining District, the mine proved to be the richest in the canyon, producing about $3.5 million in gold and silver. The name, of uncertain meaning, is said to be Southern Paiute from *tecahenga* ("hungry") and *tosoup* ("flour") and to mean "hungry, come and eat some flour" (WA; JGS, I, p. 611, n. 17).

TECOMA (Elko). A non-agency station on the Ogden Subdivision of the SP RR, ten miles east of Montello (T1SL; T75); a post office, first established December 1, 1871, and discontinued August 31, 1921 (FTM, p. 28); a mining district near the Utah border and ten miles north-northeast of the station (VPG, p. 48). The town was settled in 1869 with the building of the transcontinental railroad (Census, 1870) and named for the "celebrated Tecoma Mines, one owned by Howland and Aspinwall of New York, and the other owned by a London company, both mines bearing the same name" (FES, pp. 172–73; 1881 Map).

TECOPA CHARCOAL OVENS (Clark). The three ovens in Wheeler Wash on the west side of the Spring Mountains were built in 1875 by Nehemia ("Red") Clark for J. B. Osbourne, who was operating a smelter at Tecopa, a mining camp in Inyo County, California. The camp was named by Osbourne for Chief Tecopa, a leader of the Southern Paiute tribes. "Chief Tecopa is honored for the peaceful relations he maintained between the Southern Paiute Indians and the white men who came to live among them" (WA; SHM 171). According to Professor Gudde (p. 315), the chief's name is derived from *tecopet*, "wildcat."

TELEGRAPH. TELEGRAPH CANYON, where a considerable amount of free gold was mined in the 1870s and 1880s, heads on **TELEGRAPH HILL,** about twelve miles south of Cherry Creek, on the west slope of the Egan Range in White Pine County. **TELEGRAPH PEAK** (Lander) is seven miles north-northeast of Austin in the Toiyabe Range. These features presumably were named in 1861 for the Overland Telegraph (NHS, 1924, p. 388; GHM, WP 3; OPN, pp. 41, 76).

TELEPHONE. A canyon heading on the northeast side of Mummy Mountain in the Spring Mountains and trending northeastward to Kyle Canyon, in Clark County; a former mining district organized in September, 1885 at **TELEPHONE CREEK** about eight miles from Mountain City in Elko County; a canyon heading south of Pilot Peak and extending into Rhodes Salt Marsh, in Mineral County; perhaps named for telephone lines passing through them (VPG; WA; GHM, WP 3; EL 3; DM).

TELLURIDE (Nye). A mining district, also called *Flourine,* organized on Bare Mountain, immediately east of Beatty; named for *telluride,* a compound of tellurium (VPG, p. 127).

TE-MOAK INDIAN RESERVATION (Elko). The reservation, south of the Humboldt River, west of the Ruby Mountains and east of State Route 46, commemorates a Shoshone chief *Tim-oak.* Special Indian Commissioners J. W. Powell and G. W. Ingalls reported in 1873 that Tim-oak was a Chief of Alliance for the Pagantso band of Ruby Valley; the Nogaie band of Spring Valley, White River Valley, the Robinson district, and the vicinity of Duckwater; and the Kaidatoiabie band in the vicinity of Hamilton, Halleck, Elko, Mineral Hill, Palisade, and Carlin (Fowler, p. 105; NK 11–12). It is said that "the name Temoak means rope and he was so called because he braided rope" (EP, pp. 79–80). See **SOUTH.**

TEMPEST (Lincoln). A post office, established August 30, 1922, and discontinued January 22, 1929, when its operations were transferred to Bristol Silver; named for the **TEMPEST MINE** in the Bristol Mining District (FTM, p. 28; WA).

TEMPIUTE. See **TIMPAHUTE.**

TENABO. A peak in the southwest end of the Cortez Mountains on the Lander-Eureka county line; a mining district northwest of Mount Tenabo in Lander County; and a former mining camp, twenty-five miles southeast of Battle Mountain in Eureka County. New Mexicans in the area may have named the mountain for an ancient pueblo of the Piros, probably at the Siete Arroyos, northeast of Socorro and east of the Rio Grande in New Mexico (FWH, p. 727; OPN, p. 41). The name, however, is of uncertain meaning and also said to be a Paiute word meaning "dark colored water" (OPN, p. 35). The post office so named was established December 7, 1906, its operations being transferred to Cortez on July 31, 1912 (FTM, p. 28).

TEN MILE (Humboldt). The name for a mining district, also called *Winnemucca,* on Winnemucca Mountain, four miles northwest from Winnemucca (VPG, p. 79). **TEN-MILE DESERT.** See **LITTLE.**

TENNESSEE FORREST (White Pine). A mining claim so named was staked by B. F. Miller and Al Forrest north of the canyon at Ward, in May, 1875. The name was a combination of Miller's nickname "Tennessee," for his native state, and his partner's surname. The claim was relocated in later

years by Ben and Granville Mitten, who sold the Tennessee Forrest as a tunnel site for the Martin White interests (NHS, 1924, pp. 348, 349).

TENNESSEE GULCH (Elko). The mining district, also known as *Alder,* and **TENNESSEE MOUNTAIN,** eight miles north of Gold Creek, were named by early miners for W. G. Atkinson of Genoa, Nevada. Writing under the name of "Old Tennessee," Atkinson furnished California newspapers with mining predictions about Nevada. "Wanting to advertise their mines in this area of Elko County they named the mountain and gulch for him and left it to Tennessee to tell the world of their fabulous strikes" (EP, p. 80; VPG, p. 36; GHM, EL 3).

TERRELL (Churchill). A mining district, also called *Holy Cross,* and a former mining camp, on the east slope of the south end of the Desert Range, fifteen miles north-northeast of Schurz; located in August, 1911, and named for V. B. ("Jud") Terrell, who made the discovery (VPG, p. 14; DM). A variant spelling occurs in Terrill Mountains, a range in the extreme southwest portion of the county, named for the district (GHM, CH 1).

TESORA (White Pine). The name Tesora (from Spanish *tesoro,* "treasure") for a post office established April 23, 1869, was changed to *Treasure City* on June 15, 1869 (FTM, p. 29).

THIRD CREEK. A creek north of Lake Tahoe and between Second and Incline creeks, in Washoe County; a creek northeast of Steptoe, between Second and Fitzhugh creeks in the Schell Creek Range, White Pine County (GHM, WA 1; WP 4).

THIRSTY CANYON (Nye). A canyon extending from Pahute Mesa to Oasis Valley, about six miles northeast of Springdale and fifty-three miles southeast of Goldfield; officially designated in the *Fifth Report* of the United States Geographic Board. **EAST THIRSTY CANYON,** also heading on Pahute Mesa and extending to Thirsty Canyon about eleven miles northeast of Springdale, is named for its position relative to Thirsty Canyon (USGB 6302; NJ 11–8).

THISBE (Washoe). A non-agency station on the Sparks Subdivision of the SP RR, between Clark and Gilpin. The name derives from the story of the Babylonian lovers Pyramus and Thisbe in Ovid's *Metamorphoses.* Before the relocation of the CP RR, in 1902, Thisbe was four miles east of Wadsworth, from which it is now seven miles west (T75; DM).

THOMAS CANYON (Elko). **THOMAS CANYON CAMPGROUND,** at the intersection of **THOMAS CANYON** with Lamoille Canyon in Elko County; named for Raymond Thomas, "an Elko school teacher who lost his life [October, 1916] rescuing members of a school outing from a sudden blizzard which struck the area" (EP, p. 75; NP, p. 69; GHM, EL 1).

THOMPSON. In Lyon County, formerly a station on a branch line of the NCB RR, which extended north from Wabuska about three miles to the smelter of the Mason Valley Mines Company at **THOMPSON**, and a post office active from June 28, 1911, to June 30, 1920, when Wabuska became the mail address for its patrons. The name commemorates William B. Thompson who, with George Gunn, was one of the principal owners of the mining company (NCB Map; FTM, p. 29; DM). **THOMPSON CREEK** (Elko), a creek rising on the west slope of the Ruby Mountains north of Moose Creek, named to commemorate Henry Thompson, who diverted the creek water to irrigate his ranch (EP, p. 80; GHM, EL 1).

THORNE (Mineral). A station on the Mina Branch of the SP RR, southeast of Walker Lake; a former post office established July 1, 1912, and discontinued September 30, 1921, when its operations were transferred to Hawthorne. The name derives from *Hawthorne*, the town south of the station (NJ 11–4; FTM, p. 29).

THORNTON (Douglas). The former settlement about twelve miles east of Genoa at Clear Creek was named for a Mr. Thornton, who had a ranch there. The place was also known as *Thorntons* and was served by Genoa post office (HHB, Nev., p. 255; NHS, 1913, p. 197; TF, p. 22).

THORP(E). In Nye County, **THORP** post office established June 15, 1905, and discontinued July 13, 1909, when its name was changed to *Bonnie Clare;* named for a settlement so called, and also known as *Thorps Well,* on the western edge of Sarcobatus Flat. The name commemorates Guy Thorp, who had arrastras at Gold Mountain, by report of the *Walker Lake Bulletin* of April 23, 1883 (FTM, p. 29; DM). **THORPE CREEK** (Elko). A creek flowing from the east slope of the Ruby Mountains into Lamoille Valley; named for John P. Thorpe who settled on the creek in 1869 (EP, p. 81; GHM, EL 1).

THOUSAND CREEK (Humboldt). A ranch on State Route 8A in northwestern Humboldt County; named for **THOUSAND CREEK,** which drains from Virgin Valley eastward toward Denio and receives its name from its numerous channels through a broad flat (NK 11–7; VPG).

THOUSAND SPRING (Elko). A creek which rises in the mountains in northeastern Nevada, runs southward and eastward, and is lost in a sink at the Utah boundary; a valley in this region; named for many hot, cold, and mineral springs in the valley (NK 11–9; M&S, p. 48; OPN, p. 29). The valley is so named on Lieutenant E. G. Beckwith's 1855

map of Explorations and Surveys for a Rail Road Route. An earlier name *Hot Spring Valley* is shown on the sketch map accompanying the 1849 Diaries of J. Goldsborough Bruff (Wheat IV, 74; III, 95).

THREE KIDS MINE (Clark). Manganese deposits discovered in the Las Vegas district, twelve miles southeast of Las Vegas, in September, 1917, by R. H. Edwards, B. R. Jefferson, and J. F. Marrs. Being middle-aged men, they called the strike the *Three Kids* (WA; GHM, CL 2).

THREE MILE. A milepost name for a creek in the Quinn River Valley of northern Humboldt County; for a canyon heading south of Wildcat Peak in the Toquima Range of Nye County; and for an early station three miles west of Wadsworth in Washoe County (SG Map; GHM, HU 4; 1881 Map; HHB, Nev., p. 256). **THREEMILE SPRING** (Clark) is an alternate name for *Cow Spring* (WA).

THURMAN (Clark). A gold mining district and former mining camp, sixteen miles southeast of Searchlight in the Newberry Mountains; named for John Thurman who discovered ore there about 1906 (WA).

TIKABOO VALLEY (Lincoln). The valley is bounded on the north by the Timpahute Range, on the south and west by the Groom Range, Jumbled Hills, and Desert Range, and on the east by the Pahranagat and North Pahranagat ranges (USGB 6002; NJ 11–9). A variant name is *Tickapoo* (GHM, LN 3).

TIMBER. The name associated with heavily wooded areas designates an intermittent stream, tributary to Duck Creek and north of Berry Creek, in White Pine County (NJ 11–3). **TIMBER MOUNTAIN.** A mountain southwest of Buckboard Mesa and east of Springdale, in Nye County; a mountain northwest of Troy Peak in the Grant Range, northeastern Nye County (Dir. 1971); and an old mining district, discovered in 1869 in the Spring Mountains (Nye), which at that time included the north end of the mountain range and extended into the Amargosa Desert. Mount Stirling and the present Johnnie district thus were within its boundaries. According to Wheeler, galena, sulfide of silver, and large deposits of low-grade base metal silver ores were distributed over a large, heavily timbered area (Wheeler 1871 Map; 1872, p. 52). In Clark County, **TIMBER MOUNTAIN** also denoted a mining district organized by P. H. Bendixsen in 1910, about seventeen miles west of Searchlight on Timber Mountain, apparently in the McCullough Range, and was an alternate name for the area around the Potosi Mine, in the south end of the Spring Mountains (WA).

TIMPAHUTE (Lincoln). The **TIMPAHUTE RANGE** extends thirteen miles northeastward from Coyote Summit pass, at the north end of Tikaboo Valley (USGB 6002; NJ 11–9). The *Sheridan* Mining District (renamed **TEM PAH–UTE**) was discovered in December, 1868, by D. Service and William Plumb. According to Wheeler (1872, p. 44; 1871 Map) the *Tem Piute* Mining District was supposed at one time to have an immense vein of ore, the Inca Lode, running through it. The area was first important for lead and silver in the 1870s, and a post office denoted *Tem Piute* was active from February 20, 1879, to January 16, 1883. The region was almost deserted until 1950 when the Wah Chang Trading Company of New York City, tungsten buyers and importers, incorporated the entire district under the name of the Black Rock Mining Company. *Tempiute* post office was operative from February 1, 1953, to October 18, 1957, when its operations were transferred to Caliente (MA, p. 486; WA; VPG, p. 100; Census, 1870; TF, p. 22; FTM, p. 28). The name commemorates a Southern Paiute band and is derived from *timpi*, "stone, rock," *pa*, "water" + Ute, hence "rock-water-people." Myron Angel records that "in December, 1874, a party, supposed to belong to Tem-pah-Ute Bill's band of Indians, attacked and killed two white men about seven miles from Hiko" (MA, p. 187).

TIOGA (Elko). The name for a former settlement south of Loray in Elko County; an Iroquois Indian name (meaning "at-(the)-forks") that "spread to many states, usually without thought of its meaning" (GRS, Amer., p. 484; SG Map 2).

TIPPECANOE (Lyon). A post office established October 18, 1887, and discontinued July 25, 1890, when Mason Valley became the mail address for its patrons; presumably named by Hoosiers for the Tippecanoe River in central Indiana, the scene of General William Henry Harrison's victory over Tecumseh's Indians in 1811. The name provided a nickname for Harrison and became a part of a presidential campaign slogan "Tippecanoe and Tyler too" in 1840. The Miami Indian name *Kitapkwanunk* or *Kitapkwanunka,* "buffalo-fish place," denoted the place at the mouth of a river occupied by the Miami before the Shawnee took possession (FWH, p. 759).

TIPPETT (White Pine). The name of a town on the west side of Antelope Valley, and a pass on State Route 2 southwest of the town (GHM, WP 4). **TIPPETT** post office, active from May 11, 1896, to December 15, 1913, and from June 4, 1914, to June 30, 1926, was named for a Mr. Tippett, a wealthy sheepman in the area (FTM, p. 29; NHS, 1924, p. 307).

TIPPIPAH (Nye). **TIPPIPAH SPRING,** an early camping site for Indian groups, west of Yucca Flat and north of **TIPPIPAH**

POINT on Shoshone Mountain, in the Nevada Test Site (NJ 11–8; M&M, p. 159); named from Bannock *tipi,* "rock," *ba,* "water," to indicate a spring flowing from rocks (Kroeber, Shoshonean, p. 80).

TISDELL (Douglas). A name, with altered spelling, for an early settlement ten miles southeast of Genoa; named for James or Jack Teasdale (HHB, Nev., p. 255; SHM 125; NHS, 1913, p. 197; TF, p. 22; 1867 Map).

TIVA CANYON (Nye). A canyon extending from the southeastern part of Shoshone Mountain to a point about two miles southeast of Topopah Spring. The name is from Southern Paiute *tewa,* "pine" (USGB 6201). John Wesley Powell found Numic terms for the piñon pine to be *ti-wap* in the western area, *tu-wop* in the southern area, and *ti-va-wo-pi* in the Gosiute vocabulary of the central area (Fowler, pp. 211, 155, 173, 252).

TOANO (Elko). A mountain range north of the Goshute Range and near the Utah line; a valley between the Toano and the Pequop ranges, also known as *Goshute Valley;* formerly a post office active from August 9, 1869, to January 11, 1870, and again from January 10, 1872, to March 12, 1906, when its name was changed to *Cobre* (FTM, p. 29); and a terminal base of the SP RR between Pequop and Loray, thirty-six miles east of Wells (TISL; B&H, p. 121; ELS, Pacific, pp. 254–56; JGS, I, p. 313). **TO–A–NO MOUNTAINS** appears on a map of the Pacific Railroad Survey, prepared by Beckwith (PRR–2). *Toana* is a graphic variant (TF, p. 23; 1881 Map; FTM, p. 29; Freese, Map 3; NK 11–9; NK 11–12). The name from Gosiute "is probably 'pipe-camping-place,' from some association with a tobacco pipe" (GRS, Amer., p. 485).

TOBAR (Elko). A station on the WP RR between Ventosa and Wells; said to have been named by railroad officials for a directional sign in the area reading "To Bar." The post office at the site was established as *Clover City,* the name being changed to **TOBAR** December 20, 1911, and renamed Clover City on December 11, 1918. Tobar post office was again active from January 18, 1921, to September 17, 1942, at which time Wells took over its operations (FTM, p. 29; NK 11–12).

TOBIN (Pershing). A mountain range near the eastern boundary of the county, south and west of the Sonoma Range; a peak in the center of the range; a former mining camp, active in 1907, presumably named for the Clement L. Tobin family of Winnemucca (Son. R. Quad.; DM; OPN, p. 63).

TOHAKUM PEAK (Washoe). The name for this peak in the Lake Range, east of the north end of Pyramid Lake, is from Northern Paiute *To-ha-kum,* "large, white rabbit," listed by John Wesley Powell in the vocabulary given by Chief Naches (Fowler, p. 211; NK 11–10).

TOIYABE. The **TOIYABE RANGE,** extending from northern Nye County into Lander, is a unit of the **TOIYABE NATIONAL FOREST,** whose net area includes 1,883,862 acres lying in Nye, Eureka, and Lander counties. The highest mountains in the range are **TOIYABE DOME,** a name variant for the official designation *Arc Dome* (USGB 7002), **TOIYABE DOME SOUTHEAST SUMMIT,** and **TOIYABE RANGE PEAK,** all in Nye County, and **TOIYABE PEAK** in Lander County (NJ 11–2; NJ 11–5). **TOIYABE CITY** (Nye) was a mining camp serving the Murphy Lode mines in Ophir Canyon (MM). **TOIYABE** denoted a post office in Nye County, established December 18, 1942, and discontinued June 1, 1943, when its operations were moved to Gabbs (FTM, p. 29). The name is from Shoshone *toyap,* "mountain" (Kroeber, Shoshonean, p. 80). See **ARC DOME.**

TOKOP (Esmeralda). The name for a mining district and a former mining camp, fifteen miles west of Bonnie Clare, on Gold Mountain, reported to be from Shoshone *takav,* "snow" (VPG, p. 61; DM).

TOLICHA (Nye). A mining district, also called *Monte Cristo,* in the Pahute Mesa, twenty-six miles north of Beatty, organized as a result of gold-silver discoveries on **TOLICHA PEAK,** south of Obsidian Butte and west of Quartz Mountain (NJ 11–8; VPG, p. 139). A mining camp so named was active in the 1920s (DM).

TOM CAIN CREEK (Elko). A stream of northern Elko County, tributary to Marys River, south of Stoney Creek and northeast of Deeth; named to commemorate an early settler of Clover Valley, Tom *Kane* (NK 11–9; EP, p. 81). See **CAIN** and **CANE.**

TONGUE WASH (Nye). A wash which heads between the Eleana Range and Rainier Mesa and extends to the north end of Yucca Flat; probably named for its tongue-shaped outline visible from an aerial view (USGB 6002; NJ 11–8).

TONKA (Elko). The station is at a point of connection of the SP RR and WP RR, just east of Carlin, and said to be named for the tonka bean which flavored the snuff used by construction workers on the SP RR (T54; T75; EP, p. 82). A tributary of the Humboldt River at this point is named **TONKA CREEK** for the station (GHM, EL 1).

TONKIN (Eureka). An early settlement at the foot of Roberts Creek Mountain; a spring and a summit, south of the settlement; a post office, active from December 9, 1898, to March 14, 1931; named for John G. Tonkin, who was postmaster at the time the station

was established (FTM, p. 29; OR, 1899; GHM, EU 1).

TONOGOLD (Nye). The name of a mining camp which flourished about 1913. Apparently it is a blend of *Tono* from Tonopah (the camp four miles to the south and in bonanza at the time) and *gold* from the gold ore discoveries (DM).

TONOPAH (Nye). Tonopah, at the junction of U.S. 6 and U.S. 95 near the Esmeralda County line, was the site of Nevada's second great silver bonanza and is the county seat, by act of the legislature in 1905. The report of the surveyor-general of Nevada in 1902 states that "the Tonopah mines were discovered by James L. Butler, Esq., an old resident and ex-District Attorney of Nye County" (JGS, I, p. 399). Butler may have been told of the ledges by the Indians, for he is said to have spoken the Shoshone dialect and to have been looked upon by the Indians as a friend (SPD, p. 966). Butler's account of the discovery, written by him on November 19, 1902, explains his interpretation of the name and tells of the discovery.

> Tonopah is an Indian name, which, I learned when a boy, signifies a small spring. The Indians, on their periodical trips from the Cowich [Kawich] and other places to Rhodes' Salt Marsh, camped at this spring. . . . I passed over the Manhattan Mountains, left Rye Patch and traveled all day [May 19, 1900] to the spring known by the Indians as Tonopah, near which I found quartz. . . . My first location [on August 25, 1900] was the Desert Queen, next the *Burro,* and then I told my wife to name one, which she did, naming it the *Mizpah,* which at that time did not look any better than the others, but since has proved to be the richest on record. (JGS, I, p. 399, n. 3)

During the boom days of the early twentieth century, Tonopah was served by the C and C RR and by the T and G RR, which operated until after the Second World War. **TONOPAH** post office was established March 3, 1905, the name being changed from *Butler* (FTM, p. 29). An early, local name for a southern prolongation of the Toquima Range was the *Tonopah Hills* (SFH, p. 1; NJ 11–5).

The local Indian word *tonopah* has been interpreted as "hidden spring," "brush water springs," "greasewood spring," "little water," and "water brush," the last being accepted by old-timers in the area (CBG, Gold, p. 19; B&C, US West, p. 239; OPN, p. 58; Nev. Guide, pp. 225–26; FCL, p. 184; TW, p. 149; MM). The name appears to mean "greasewood water (spring)" and to derive from either Shoshone (Central Numic) *to-nuv,* "greasewood," or Northern Paiute (Western Numic) *to-nav,* "greasewood," and *pa,* "water," in both dialects (Fowler, pp. 267, 211; GRS, Amer., p. 488).

TOPAZ LAKE (Douglas). The lake, southwest of Yerington, in southern Douglas County, Nevada, and in Mono County, California, may have been named for the color tones of the water (NJ 11–4).

TOQUIMA RANGE. A mountain range with its south end about twenty-five miles northnortheast of Tonopah in Nye County, extends between Big Smoky Valley on the west and Monitor Valley on the east, into Lander County; a unit of the Toiyabe National Forest (USGB 6002). The *Toquimas,* "black backs," were a Mono band formerly living in the lower Reese River Valley, Lander County (FWH, p. 785).

TOQUOP WASH. The wash drains generally southeastward from Tule Flat in Lincoln County and enters the Virgin River about one and a half miles southwest of Bunkerville in Clark County. The name from Southern Paiute *to-kwop,* "black tobacco," is descriptive of a weed growing in the wash, used as tobacco by the Indians (Wheeler, 1879, p. 436; WA; NJ 11–12; Fowler, pp. 156, 181).

TOULON. A non-agency station on the Sparks Subdivision of the SP RR between Toy and Granite; a peak in the Trinity Range northwest of the station, both in Pershing County. **TOULON LAKE** extends from a point just east of the station into northern Churchill County. The name may ultimately commemorate Toulon, a Mediterranean seaport in southern France (T75; GHM, PE 1; CH 1).

TOWN CREEK (Elko). A creek and a flat northeast of Wells; named for their proximity to that town (NK 11–9).

TOY (Pershing). The non-agency station with part-time telegraph, on the SP RR and south of Toulon, was known earlier as *Browns,* which in the 1860s was a terminal of the CP RR (NK 11–10; SPD, p. 894). See **BROWNS.** A tungsten district so named and also known as Browns is on the west slope of the Trinity Range, two miles south of **TOY** section house (VPG, p. 20).

TOYLAND (Humboldt). A short-lived post office, active from December 19, 1916, to November 30, 1918, when its operations were moved to Lovelock(s) post office (FTM, p. 29).

TRAPPMAN HILLS (Nye). The group of hills one mile south of Wilsons Camp, four miles east of Mount Helen, and thirty-five miles east-southeast of Goldfield, was named to commemorate "Hermann Trappman who, with John Gabbard, discovered gold in the vicinity in 1904" (USGB 6303).

TREASURE. On January 4, 1868, A. J. Leathers and others, led by an Indian guide, located the celebrated **HIDDEN TREASURE**

MINE on an isolated peak, **TREASURE HILL,** on the middle ridge of the White Pine Range of western White Pine County. The peak, which was also the site of the famous Eberhardt Mine, was named for the rich ore discoveries (SM, 1875, pp. 164–65; Nev. Guide, p. 253; JGS, I, p. 257). The mining camp which grew up near the summit of Treasure Hill was named **TREASURE CITY** (1881 Map) as was a post office established June 15, 1869, and discontinued December 9, 1880 (FTM, p. 28). See **TESORA** and **HIDDEN TREASURE. TREASURE HILL** (Lincoln), one of the mountains on which Pioche is situated, probably took its name from Treasure Hill (White Pine), the site of the mining camp of Hamilton. The rush to Pioche started at about the same time as Hamilton's decline; Hamiltonians were among the first to reach Pioche in number (JWH). **TREASURE HILL** (Esmeralda). The mining camp so denoted was established in 1908 in the south extension of the Silver Peak Range, about thirty-five miles southwest of Goldfield (DM).

TREATY HILL (Humboldt). A hill north of Valmy between U.S. 40 and the tracks of the WP RR; so named because Indians are believed to have settled territorial disputes there (HWY Map).

> For generations hard battles were fought between the different Indian tribes over the springs and hunting grounds of the Battle Mountains and the Humboldt Valley. The legend is that after one battle centuries ago the chiefs decided to settle their problems by compromise. A stone wall was built on the brow of the hill, and in the peace treaty it was agreed that all land on "the side of the rising sun" belonged to one group and all on "the side of the setting sun" to the other. (Nev. Guide, p. 129)

TREGO (Pershing). A station on the main line of the WP RR; located at the foot of **MOUNT TREGO** and at the south edge of the Black Rock Desert (RT, p. 10; GHM, PE 1).

TRIDENT PEAK (Humboldt). The peak, lying in the Jackson Mountains southeast of Denio and west of Kings River Valley and not far from the Oregon line, was named for its natural outline (OPN, p. 38). An alternate name is *Obrian Peak* (GHM, HU 3).

TRINITY. A three-peaked mountain range extending from northwest Churchill County into Pershing County, west of the Humboldt River. **TRINITY MINING DISTRICT,** also known as *Arabia,* was discovered by George Lovelock, in 1859, in **TRINITY CANYON** on the east flank of the mountain range and eleven miles north of Lovelock (HPS, 1/29/56; HHB, Nev., p. 264; SM, 1866, p. 55; 1881 Map; OPN, p. 63; VPG, p. 165).

TROUT CREEK. A name chosen because of

trout inhabiting the waters: silver trout (Lake Tahoe), rainbow trout (Truckee River), cutthroat (a species of land-locked salmon), or black-spotted trout (Pyramid Lake and Topaz Lake), and Loch-Leven trout; found principally in the places indicated, but also in many other streams of the state. Creeks so named are north of Goose Creek, in northeast Elko County, and south of Bishop Creek, west of Wells, also in Elko County; northwest of Mount Tenabo and between Lewis and Mill creeks in Lander County; east of Cottonwood Creek (Humboldt) and near the Lander County line; west of the Pine Forest Range in **TROUT CREEK VALLEY** of northern Humboldt County; and on the east side of the Jackson Range, also in Humboldt County (SG Maps 1, 2, 12; Nev. Guide, p. 19; Dir. 1971; VPG).

TROY (Nye). **TROY PEAK** is northeast of Nyala, on the west side of the Grant Range near the south end, and was named for a mining district, also called *Nyala*, located in 1867. **TROY** post office was active from February 18, 1873, to August 7, 1876, and again from April 24, 1908, to February 28, 1913 (NJ 11–6; NM; VPG, p. 141; 1881 Map; FTM, p. 29).

TRUCKEE. The **TRUCKEE RIVER** flows out of Lake Tahoe at a point near Tahoe City, California, through **TRUCKEE CANYON**, crosses the Nevada line southeast of Verdi, and continues northeast from Reno across the **TRUCKEE MEADOWS**. It forms part of the boundary between Washoe and Storey counties and flows into Pyramid Lake. Frémont camped on the Truckee near Pyramid Lake in 1844. On January 15, he wrote that "an Indian brought in a large fish to trade, which we had the inexpressible satisfaction to find was a salmon trout" and on January 16, "this morning we continued our journey along this beautiful stream, which we naturally called the Salmon Trout river" (JCF, Report, pp. 218–19). This name also appeared on the profile maps of the Pacific Railroad Survey. According to Myron Angel, the river was named *Truckee* by a party of men (perhaps the Stevens-Murphy party) who left Council Bluffs, Iowa, on May 20, 1844, enroute to California. When they reached the Humboldt River, an Indian guide named Truckee joined them and offered to guide them. He became a great favorite with the group, and when they reached the lower crossing of the Truckee (Wadsworth), they named the river for him (MA, pp. 24–25). According to Princess Winnemucca (Mrs. Sarah Hopkins), Truckee was her grandfather and had been the chief of the entire Paiute nation and also a guide for Frémont, who called him Captain Truckee. *Truckee*, according to the Indian princess, means "all right," or "very well" (SWH, pp. 5–9). Cap-

tain Truckee, whose daughter was one of the wives of Winnemucca, died October 8, 1860, in the Pine Nut Mountains, south of Como in Lyon County (MA, p. 165). The valley in which Sparks and Reno are situated is called the **TRUCKEE MEADOWS,** which extend on both sides of the Truckee River. The name of the meadows appears on Dr. Henry De Groot's 1860 Map of the Washoe Mines (Wheat IV, 189). **TRUCKEE MEADOWS** post office was active in Washoe County from September 22, 1862, to September 13, 1872 (FTM, p. 29). The **TRUCKEE MOUNTAINS,** in southeastern Washoe County, are on the east side of the Truckee River.

TUCK RANCH (Clark). The ranch, formerly at the site of Whitney (q.v.) near Las Vegas, was named for Jack Tuck, who took up the land later purchased by Stowell Whitney in 1900 (WA).

TUGSTONIA. See **TUNGSTONIA.**

TULE. Features named for an abundant growth of tule or for nearby tule marshes include **TULE CANYON** (Esmeralda), the site of a mining district, also called *Lida*, thirty miles southwest of Goldfield, served by **TULE** post office (September 20, 1905– June 15, 1906). **TULE PEAK** (Washoe) is the highest peak in the northern part of the Virginia Range. **TULE SPRINGS** (Clark), is the name for a group of springs in the Las Vegas Wash, ten miles northwest of Las Vegas; for an archaeological site recently explored near **TULE SPRINGS RANCH;** and for a former station on the now defunct LV and T RR, between Las Vegas and Corn Creek. **TULE FLAT** (Lincoln), a wide valley east of the Meadow Valley Wash, extends from the Mormon Mountains to the Clover Mountains (JWC; VPG, p. 56; WA; FTM, p. 29). **TULE** (Humboldt) is a station east of Weso on the SP RR (1881 Map; GHM, HU 1). The name derives from Nahuatl *tollin* ("bulrush").

TUNGSTEN (Pershing). A former settlement and post office (established May 26, 1944) in the Eugene Mountains, northwest of Mill City; named for **TUNGSTEN MINE,** once an important producer there (Guide Map; FTM, p. 29).

TUNGSTEN MINES (White Pine). The post office so named was active from October 14, 1916, to June 30, 1917, when its operations were moved to Ely (FTM, p. 29). **TUNGSTEN QUEEN MINE** is southeast of Minerva in the Snake Range (GHM, WP, 1).

TUNGSTONIA (White Pine). The name for a tungsten mining district (also called *Kern*), in the Kern Mountains near the Nevada-Utah boundary, about sixty-five miles east-southeast of Cherry Creek (VPG, p. 186). A short-lived post office denoted *Tugstonia* and active from January 4, 1917, to August

3, 1917, may have served this district (FTM, p. 29).

TUPAPA SEEP (Nye). The name for a spring about one mile southeast of Hampel Hill and seven miles northwest of Mercury; reported to be Southern Paiute and to mean "emerging water" (USGB 6201).

TUSCARORA (Elko). The **TUSCARORA MOUNTAINS** are west of the Independence Mountains and Independence Valley in western Elko County. The first quartz ledge discovered in the **TUSCARORA MINING DISTRICT** was the Young America, located by W. O. Weed in 1871. Other principal producers of the district were the Dexter, Navajo, Nevada Queen, and Grand Prize (SM, 1875, p. 17; 1881 Map; NM). Wheeler reported that Chinese placer miners worked the southern slope of the hills facing Independence Valley, washing the gold-bearing gravels in sluices with water brought from two to six miles (Wheeler, 1872, p. 35). The town of **TUSCARORA**, at the junction of State Routes 11 and 18, about forty-five miles northwest of Elko, began as a mining camp for the district on Mount Blitzen and had a post office by July 18, 1871 (FTM, p. 29). The name was chosen by John Beard, a settler in the area who had come from North Carolina, where the important confederation of tribes, the Tuscarora "hemp gatherers" lived (FWH, p. 842; OPN, p. 29).

TWAIN (Pershing). A former townsite in Black Canyon on the northwest slope of the Humboldt Range, east of Valery on the SP RR, was named for Mark Twain, according to the *Carson City News* of March 24, 1909. Mark Twain prospected in and around Unionville, southeast of Black Canyon, in December of 1861 (DM; NM).

TWELVE–MILE DESERT. The land east of Dayton (Lyon) was also called *Little Desert*, in comparison with Twenty-Six-Mile Desert (NHS, 1913, p. 209). The R. M. Evans map of the Washoe mining region, dated 1860, shows *12 Mile Little Desert* (Wheat V (I), 16).

TWELVE MILE HOUSE (Douglas). The station was built by Thomas Wheeler in 1859, at a site twelve miles from Genoa and also about twelve miles from Cradlebaugh Bridge (SHM 125; HHB, Nev., p. 255; 1881 Map). **TWELVE MILE HOUSE** post office operated from June 17, 1879, to November 17, 1879 (FTM, p. 29).

TWENTY–SIX–MILE DESERT (Churchill). The stretch of desert was west of Ragtown and was named for its length. The name appears on an 1855 map of the mining region of California, by George H. Baker (Wheat IV, 38). Because their horses were used up from fatigue and from the effects of the alkali water they had drunk, Dan De Quille

and his fellow prospectors crossed this desert on foot on July 3, 1861 (REL, pp. 155–57).

TWIN. The name is usually given for two features that resemble each other. **TWIN PEAKS** (Churchill) denotes a mountain with two peaks in the south end of the Clan Alpine Mountains, about two miles south of Wonder (NJ 11–1; USGB 5904). **TWIN RIVER** (Nye). The gold mining district on the east slope of the Toiyabe Range, about fifty miles south of Austin, was named for two streams rising in the Toiyabes and flowing into Big Smoky Valley, presently denoted **NORTH TWIN RIVER** and **SOUTH TWIN RIVER** (NJ 11–5). The district was the scene of a rush, between 1865 and 1869, when 1,500 locations were made there after Henri Boulerond and a group of Frenchmen made the first ore discoveries at the mouth of Ophir Canyon. The district enjoyed a revival in the 1880s. The most celebrated mine was the Murphy (SM, 1866, p. 65; 1875, pp. 107–109; MM, Toiyabes, p. 6). **TWIN RIVER** post office was active from June 18, 1867, to December 5, 1893, when Belmont became the mail address for its patrons (FTM, p. 29). See **TATES STATION**. **TWINRIDGE HILL** (Nye). A hill with two parallel ridges, about two miles west of The Hump in the Halfpint Range (USGB 6301). **TWIN SPRING(S)** denotes springs in Elko, Eureka, Lander, Lyon, Nye, Pershing, and Washoe counties; a range **TWIN SPRING HILLS** east of Willow Creek Ranch in Eureka County. **TWIN SPRINGS RANCH** (Nye) is east of Warm Springs in Hot Creek Valley. The early settlement was served by Tybo post office (GHM, EU 1; NY 5; 1881 Map; TF, p. 23; Dir. 1971). **TWIN PIÑON GULCH** (Nye). The ravine, fifteen miles north-northeast of Moores Station, was so named by the United States Board on Geographic Names in 1969 because "the most prominent trees in the ravine are twin piñon pines" (USGB 6903).

TWIN FLAT (Lyon). An early settlement on a flat on the north side of Gold Canyon at the upper end of Silver City; named because two sets of twins were born there in 1864 (NHS, 1913, p. 217).

TWO TIPS (Washoe). A mountain in the Truckee Range, north of Fernley on the Churchill County line; named for its physical aspect (Nev. Guide, p. 139; OPN, p. 71).

TYBO (Nye). A mining district so named was discovered near **TYBO CREEK** in the Hot Creek Range in 1866, fourteen miles from Hot Creek Station (Wheeler, 1872, p. 40; SHM 172; VPG, p. 143). The mining camp, named for the district, grew rapidly. A post office was established September 3, 1874, discontinued July 14, 1906, and reestablished February 11, 1929, with its operations transferred to Tonopah on October 15, 1937 (SM,

1875, pp. 102, 104–105; Census, 1880). The name is from Central Numic (Gosiute and Western Shoshone) *tai-vu,* "white man," as listed in the John Wesley Powell manuscripts (Fowler, pp. 250, 265). A variant is *Tyboe,* shown on Wheeler's map of 1871.

TYROL (Eureka). A non-agency station on the SP RR between Palisade and Carlin; perhaps named for the Tyrol region in the Alps of western Austria and northern Italy and referring to the mountainous terrain surrounding the station (T75).

UNION. A township in **UNION CAN-YON** on the west slope of the Shoshone Range in Nye County, eight miles southeast of Ione (NJ 11–5). The Storm King and the Berlin mines were the principal producers of the **UNION MINING DISTRICT**, located in 1863 (SM, 1867, pp. 64–66). A post office in Nye County so named was established January 20, 1896, by an order rescinded on July 25, 1896 (FTM, p. 30). **UNION MINES** (Eureka) was the name of a post office, about fifty miles north of Eureka, serving the **UNION MINING DISTRICT** from April 27, 1916, to November 27, 1918 (VPG, p. 69; FTM, p. 30). **UNION CONSOLIDATED** (Storey). A claim on the Comstock Lode, staked June 10, 1859, between the Mexican and the Sierra Nevada (MA, p. 58; FCL, p. 228). A variant is *Mexican-Union* (AR, No. 136). *Union,* "the most popular of the abstract terms in U.S. place-naming," was chosen frequently during the Civil War times (GRS, Amer., p. 503).

UNIONVILLE (Pershing). A territorial town, established with the discovery of the **UNION-VILLE MINING DISTRICT**, also known as Buena Vista, in Buena Vista Valley and on the east slope of the West Humboldt Range, twenty-five miles by road south of Mill City. The mining camp, first named *Buena Vista* for the canyon, later was called *Dixie,* until Northern sympathizers outnumbered Confederates in the area and changed the name to Unionville, on July 4, 1861 (1867 Map). The most illustrious, but one of the least successful, of the prospectors in old Humboldt was Mark Twain. He participated in the "beggar's revel" and later wrote that of all his experiences "this secret search among the hidden treasures of silver-land was the nearest to unmarred ecstasy" (SLC, I, pp. 205, 196). He was twenty-six when he and his three companions "entered Unionville, Humboldt County, in the midst of a driving snowstorm. Unionville consisted of eleven cabins and a liberty pole. Six of the cabins were strung along one side of a deep cañon, and the other five faced them. The rest of the

landscape was made up of bleak mountain walls that rose so high into the sky from both sides of the cañon that the village was left, as it were, far down in the bottom of a crevice" (SLC, I, p. 194). See **MONARCH** and **TWAIN**. The town was the county seat of Humboldt County from the time of its creation in 1861, until 1873 (Nev. Terr. Map; MA, pp. 81, 459; HHB, pp. 263–64; Census, 1870). UNIONVILLE post office was active from April 15, 1862, until October 1, 1956, when Imlay became the mail address for its patrons (FTM, p. 30). See **DIXIE**.

UNKNOWN RIVER. See **HUMBOLDT**.

UPPER. The term is mostly used in Nevada to show the relative position of water features, especially springs and canals. Its use may create a double specific with a single generic **UPPER MAGGIE SPRING** (Elko), a double specific with a double generic **UPPER RISUE CANYON SPRING** (Douglas), or a triple specific with a single generic **UPPER NEW VIRGINIA CANAL** (Douglas). **UPPER INDIAN CREEK** (Pershing) is north of Indian Creek in the Tobin Range. **UPPER PAHRANAGAT LAKE** (Lincoln) is northwest of Lower Pahranagat Lake. Variant names may occur for the related features. Lower White *Blotch* Spring is so named for its position south of White *Spot* Spring (GHM, CL 1); it is also known as *Blotch* Springs (NJ 11–12) and **UPPER WHITE BLOTCH SPRING** (WA). Valleys so denoted include **UPPER DRY VALLEY**, north of Dry Valley, west of Pyramid Lake in Washoe County; **UPPER VALLEY**, that portion of Lovelock Valley north and west of Lower Valley in Pershing County. **UPPER TOWN**, an early settlement in Hot Creek Valley (Nye), was northwest of Lower Town. Tybo post office served both (1881 Map; TF, pp. 19, 23; Dir. 1971). See **ROCHESTER**.

URANIA (Nye). The name for a peak in the Cactus Range, about two miles southwest of Cactus Spring and twenty-two miles east of Goldfield, "derived from the Urania Mine located nearby" (USGB 6303).

URSINE (Lincoln). A farming community, thirteen miles northeast of Pioche, settled by a small colony of Mormons in 1863 in the section of **URSINE VALLEY** known locally as Eagle Valley. Early settlers wanted the post office (established April 17, 1895) to be named *Eagle Valley,* but to avoid confusion with Eagle Valley in Ormsby (Carson City) County, Eagle Salt Works, and Eagleville in Churchill County, postal officials chose the name *Ursine,* for reasons unknown (JWH; RC, p. 82). **URSINE VALLEY**, the upper thirty miles of the Meadow Valley Wash, is divided into five valleys locally named Dry, Eagle, Rose, Spring, and Camp valleys (NJ 11–9; Freese, Map 2; WA).

UTAH (Storey). The **UTAH MINE**, the northernmost claim on the Comstock Lode proper, consisted of 1,000 feet lying north of the Sierra Nevada Mine. The name was included in the original location notice, dated July 4, 1859, and commemorates *Utah* Territory which in turn derives from that of the *Ute* or *Uta* tribe (GH–A; AR, No. 37; JAC, p. 1).

UVADA (White Pine). The post office, established on May 9, 1928, in White Pine County, near **UVADA SIDING**, forty-one miles northeast of Caliente and just inside the Utah boundary, was transferred to Trout Creek, Utah, on June 30, 1944 (FTM, p. 30; WA; NJ 11–9). The coinage is from the two state names.

V

VALERY (Pershing). A siding on a spur line of the SP RR between Humboldt and Rye Patch stations and east of Rye Patch Reservoir (NK 11–10; T75).

VALLEY (Clark). **VALLEY SIDING**, between Lovell and Wann on the UP RR, is named for its position in Las Vegas Valley (NJ 11–12).

VALLEY OF FIRE (Clark). The **VALLEY OF FIRE STATE PARK**, northeast of Las Vegas and west of the Overton Arm of Lake Mead, is a basin about six miles long and three miles wide, with rough floor and jagged walls. Rocks of grotesque shape are covered with well-preserved petroglyphs. The valley was named for its blood-red Jurassic sandstone. **VALLEY OF FIRE WASH** runs through the valley for which it is named and enters Lake Mead about five miles below Overton Beach (NP, p. 61; WA; NJ 11–12).

VALLEY OF FOUNTAINS (Elko). T. H. Jefferson's name for Ruby Valley (q.v.) on his 1849 Map of the Emigrant Road (Wheat III, 94).

VALLEY PASS (Elko). A settlement and non-agency station with telegraph, on the SP RR northwest of Cobre; named for a pass connecting two valleys (T75; OPN, p. 29).

VALLEY VIEW. The early settlement in Douglas County so named was about ten miles south of Genoa and on a stream north of Olds Hotel, overlooking Carson Valley (HHB, Nev., p. 255; TF, p. 23; NHS, 1913, p. 190). A mining district of this name is eighteen miles northeast of Austin on the east slope of the Toiyabe Range in Lander County (VPG, p. 80; Dir. 1971).

VALMY (Humboldt). A settlement and a station on the SP RR between Iron Point and Mote Siding. **VALMY** post office, earlier named *Stone House* (q.v.), was established March 24, 1915 (NK 11–11; FTM, p. 30).

VANDERBILT (Lander). The post office, ac-

tive from August 24, 1871, to August 8, 1873, served a mining camp called **VANDERBILT CITY** (Wheeler 1871 Map; FTM, p. 30).

VANDERWATER (Pershing). A settlement in the southern portion of old Humboldt County (presently Pershing), northeast of Oreana; a post office active (except for brief interruptions) from June 7, 1880, to July 23, 1883 (1881 Map; FTM, p. 30).

VAN DUZER (Elko). **VAN DUZER CREEK**, south of Rio Tinto, commemorates F. C. Van Duzer who owned a dairy ranch on the creek during the 1870s. **VAN DUZER MINING DISTRICT**, in the northwest portion of the Bull Run Range (also known as *Cope, Rio Tinto,* and *Mountain City*), takes its name from the creek (EP, p. 84; VPG, p. 44; GHM, EL 3).

VAN SICKLE STATION (Douglas). An early trading station south of Walley Hot Springs in Carson Valley; named for Henry Van Sickle who owned it from 1857 to 1885. Name variants were *The Station* and *Van Sickles* (Dangberg, CV, p. 40; SHM 117; TF, p. 23). See **OLDS HOTEL.**

VARYVILLE (Humboldt). A gold mining district, also called *Columbia* and *Leonard Creek,* discovered in the 1870s on the east slope of the south end of the Pine Forest Range, twelve miles west of Quinn River Crossing. Winnemucca post office was the mail address for the early camp (VPG, p. 77; TF, p. 23).

VAUGHN (Lander). Formerly a station on the NC RR, twenty-nine miles north of Austin, between Silver Creek and Ravenswood stations; named for L. S. Vaughn, who owned adjoining land (DM).

VEGAS VERDI. See **LAS VEGAS.**

VELVET (Pershing). The name for a gold-opal-diatomite district ten miles west of Lovelock on the east slope of the Trinity Range (VPG, p. 167; FHM, PE 1).

VENTOSA (Elko). The station so named is southeast of Ruby Station on the WP RR (GHM, EL 5).

VENT PASS (Nye). A pass at the head of Paintbrush Canyon in the northeast end of Yucca Mountain; so named for the vent of a lava flow exposed by erosion in the pass (DL 58).

VERDI. In Washoe County, the site on the Truckee River ten miles west of Reno, known earlier as *O'Neils Crossing,* was named for a man who built a bridge there in 1860. The lumber town grew up at the point with the arrival of the CP RR, whose officials named the place for the Italian operatic composer, Giuseppe Verdi. On November 4, 1870, the Central Pacific's Train No. One, upon reaching Verdi, was held up by seven robbers who carried away the payroll of the Yellow Jacket Mine on the Comstock, later recovered by Sheriff Jim Kinkead (MA, p. 647;

EH, pp. 124–32; T1TR). **VERDI** post office was first established November 30, 1869, its name having been changed from *Crystal Peak* (FTM, p. 30; 1881 Map). **VERDI** (Elko). A peak and a lake east of Thomas Canyon in the Ruby Mountains; named by the United States Forest Service for vibrant green vegetation in the area (EP, p. 85; GHM, EL 1).

VERNON (Pershing). A former settlement and post office (October 31, 1906–July 31, 1913), the southernmost camp of the Seven Troughs Mining District, thirty miles northwest of Lovelock (FTM, p. 30; GHM, PE 1).

VERZAN CANYON (White Pine). A canyon heading on Willard Hill northeast of Ruth and extending to Robinson Canyon; named for John Verzan, who came into the area in the early 1880s (Ely Quad. 1916; DM).

VICTOR (Churchill). A locality and site of a former mining camp on the north slope of the Louderback Mountains, about thirty-six miles east of Fallon; served by a post office so named from April 8 to December 31, 1907 (USGB 5904; FTM, p. 30).

VICTORIA (Mineral). A former mining district near Hawthorne, active in the middle 1880s; presumably named by an English prospector for Queen Victoria (DM).

VICTORINE (Lander). The mining district and its former camp so named were located in May, 1908, twenty-four miles south of Austin on the west flank of the Toiyabe Range. The district is also known as *Kingston* (VPG, p. 86; DM). **VICTORINE MINE.** See **CHERRY CREEK.**

VIGO (Lincoln). A siding on the UP RR between Galt and Carp; a canyon heading near Hidden Spring in the Meadow Valley Mountains and extending into the Meadow Valley Wash, a little south of Vigo Siding; a manganese district twenty-four miles east of Vigo in the Mormon Mountains (NJ 11–9; WA; VPG, p. 100).

VINCENT (Clark). A mining district, also known as *Alunite* and *Railroad Pass,* on State Route 98 two miles west of Boulder City; named for Robert Vincent, one of the owners of the Quo Vadis Mine in 1909 (VPG, p. 22; WA).

VIRGIN (Clark). A river rising in Utah and entering Clark County in the northeast corner, flowing through the **VIRGIN MOUNTAINS** and **VIRGIN VALLEY** west of the mountains. The mountain group extends from the north end of the Overton Arm of Lake Mead, in Nevada, into Mohave County, Arizona, to the Virgin River. **VIRGIN CANYON**, in Nevada and Arizona, is a narrows in Lake Mead formed in a drowned canyon of the Virgin River. **VIRGIN PEAK**, a mountain peak in the Virgin Mountains, about eleven miles southeast of Riverside, is on **VIRGIN PEAK RIDGE. SOUTH VIR-**

GIN PEAK RIDGE extends southward from Virgin Peak Ridge to Whitney Pass. Mining districts so named are **VIRGIN PEAK,** south-southeast of Bunkerville; and **VIRGIN RIVER,** also called *Saint Thomas,* lying along the Virgin River, south of its junction with the Muddy River (USGB 6203; VPG, p. 31). The name group stems from the Virgin River, a name of unknown origin, but thought to be a corruption of Spanish *Rio Virgen* or *Rio de la Virgen,* "River of the Virgin," which appears in early documents. Whether this name originated with Spanish traders in the area or with early Spanish explorers is undetermined. A map of the Dominguez-Escalante expedition of 1776 designates the river as *Rio Sulfureo de las Piramides,* and Jedediah Strong Smith named it *Adams River* in 1826, for John Quincy Adams, the sixth president of the United States (RWL, p. 145; GGC, p. 155; Wheat II, 128).

VIRGINIA. The name was first used in the state to designate a quartz vein. "On the 22d of February [1859] Fennimore [Old Virginia] located a claim on a large vein lying west of the Comstock, which came to be called the Virginia lead, after the nickname of the claimant" (HHB, Nev., p. 103). **VIRGINIA MINING DISTRICT** (Storey) was the first mining district organized in western Utah Territory. See **COMSTOCK** and **OPHIR.** The **VIRGINIA RANGE** is a mountain range in Lyon, Ormsby (Carson City), and Washoe counties. The **VIRGINIA MOUNTAINS** lie along the west side of Pyramid Lake, between Mullen Pass and Astor Pass. **VIRGINIA PEAK** denotes a mountain peak in the Pah Rah Range, south of Pah Rah Mountain (USGB 5903; NJ 11–1). **VIRGINIA CITY** (Storey). The town on the north end of the Comstock Lode and on the east slope of Mount Davidson is said to have been the largest of old historical mining towns of the West. The name commemorates a prospector who came to Carson Valley in the spring of 1851, working as a teamster for John Reese. "Old Virginia" Fennimore (Fenimore, Finney) joined the miners in Gold Canyon and stayed in the territory until his death (MA, p. 31). See **OPHIR.** William Wright [Dan De Quille], who wrote the basic source book on the history of the Comstock Lode, gave the following account of the naming, apparently accepted by all later historians of the lode and of Nevada.

At this time the camp was spoken of, in documents placed upon the records as "Pleasant Hill" and as "Mount Pleasant Point;" in August 1859 it was designated as "Ophir," and in September as "Ophir Diggings." In October the place is first mentioned as "Virginia Town," but a month later it was proposed to "change the name of the place from Virginia Town to Wun-u-muc-a, in honor of the chief of the Py-utes." Old Winnemucca, chief of all the Piutes, was not so honored, and in November 1859 the town was first called Virginia City, a name it has ever since retained. Comstock says the way the place came to take the name of Virginia City was this: " 'Old Virginia' was out one night with a lot of the 'boys' on a drunk, when he fell down and broke his whisky bottle. On rising he said—'I baptize this ground Virginia.' " (DDQ, p. 32)

VIRGINIA CITY post office was established December 3, 1859 (FTM, p. 30). The name appears on Captain Simpson's 1859 map (Wheat IV, 137).

VISTA (Washoe). Formerly a flag station on the SP RR four miles east of Sparks, at the entrance of Truckee Canyon through the Virginia Range; named for its pleasant prospect (NHS, 1926, p. 345; 1881 Map; T1TR).

VOIGHT (Elko). The post office (named for the Henry Voight ranch) was established October 1, 1892, and discontinued September 20, 1907, when Lamoille became the mail address for its patrons (FTM, p. 30; EP, p. 85).

VYA (Washoe). A settlement north of Forty Nine Canyon, near the junction of State Routes 8A and 34, in Long Valley in the northwestern portion of the county and near the California boundary; named for Vya Wimer, the first white baby born in the valley (OPN, p. 71; GHM, WA 3).

WABUSKA (Lyon). A town of central Lyon County on U.S. Alternate 95 about twelve miles north of Yerington, on a branch line of the SP RR from Hazen to Mina, formerly served by the C and C RR and the NCB RR (NCB Map; SPD, p. 954; VPG). **WABUSKA** post office was established September 18, 1874 (FTM, p. 30). The name is said to be from Washo and to mean "white grass," or "vegetation" (OPN, p. 48; 1881 Map; NJ 11–1).

WADSWORTH (Washoe). The site at the Big Bend of the Truckee River was a seasonal village of the Paiutes when Frémont camped there on January 16, 1844 (JCF, Report, p. 219). In 1854, William Gregory set up a trading post and, later, as a division point for teamsters, the place was called *Drytown*. Being on a trail used by emigrants, the point on the river was known also as *Lower Emigrant Crossing* (MA, p. 645; HPS, 1/29/56). The CP RR reached the area in 1868, and railroad officials established a station, laid out a town, and named it **WADS–WORTH** in honor of an army officer, James Samuel Wadsworth, who was killed in the Battle of the Wilderness in May, 1864 (SPD,

p. 1034; 1864 Map; 1881 Map). Wadsworth was a division point on the SP RR, until 1905 when the shops were moved to Sparks (T1TR; NJ 11–1). **WADSWORTH** post office was established August 20, 1868 (FTM, p. 30).

WAGUHYE PEAK (Nye). A name of unstable orthography for an eminence in the northern end of the Grapevine Mountains, in the southwestern portion of Nye County (HWY Map; VPG). Variants include *Wahguyhe*, used by Rand McNally, and *Wayughe*, used by the Army Map Service (NJ 11–11). According to George R. Stewart, the name is probably Southern Paiute, "summit" (GRS, Amer., p. 517).

WAHMONIE (Nye). The **WAHMONIE MINING DISTRICT** on Shoshone Mountain, thirty miles east of Beatty and about ten miles west of Yucca Pass, was organized in 1928 when two prospectors, McRae and Lefler, rediscovered silver in the old Hornsilver Mine. The boom camp which sprang up about a mile south of the mine was served by a post office so named from April 2, 1928, to April 30, 1929. **WAHMONIE FLAT** lies immediately east of the old mining camp site, about one mile south of Pluto Valley and about twelve miles northwest of Mercury (NM; VPG, p. 145; FTM, p. 30; WA; USGB 6201). See **HORNSILVER.**

WALKER. The **WALKER RIVER** is formed by the uniting of the **EAST WALKER RIVER** and the **WEST WALKER RIVER** in Lyon County and flows into the north end of **WALKER LAKE,** in northwest Mineral County. The **WALKER RIVER RANGE** is a local name for the *Wassuk Range* west of Walker Lake. Early settlements were denoted **WALKER RIVER VALLEY,** in Lyon County (MA, p. 75) and **WALKER RIVER,** in Esmeralda and Douglas counties (1881 Map; HHB, Nev., pp. 255, 261). The latter settlement was served by **WALKER RIVER** post office from September 30, 1872, to January 8, 1883, when its operations were moved to Wellington (FTM, p. 30). **WALKER RIVER INDIAN RESERVATION,** established in 1874, is in Mineral, Churchill, and Lyon counties (NJ 11–4). **WALKER RIVER MINING DISTRICT,** also called *Cat Creek,* was organized on the east slope of the Wassuk (Walker River) Range, about five miles north of Hawthorne and west of Walker Lake in 1866 (VPG, p. 120; Nev. Terr. Map; OPN, p. 52). Frémont named the lake for a man "celebrated as one of the best and bravest leaders who have ever been in the country" (JCF, Report, p. 155). Joseph Reddeford Walker was a member of Bonneville's expedition to the Rocky Mountains in 1832, led a party of trappers to California in 1833, and guided Frémont's third expedition to California in 1845–46. The river and lake were officially designated *Walker* (not Walker's) by the United States Geographic Board in its *Fifth Report.*

WALLEY(S) HOT SPRINGS (Douglas). An early station and health resort three miles from Genoa on the Carson Branch of the Emigrant Trail; named for David and Harriet Walley who developed the spa in 1862 (Dangberg, CV, p. 39; SHM 120; GHM, DO 1).

WALTERS (Lander). Formerly a station on the NC RR, fifty-six miles southeast of Battle Mountain, between Reese River Canyon and Ravenswood stations; named for William Walters, a rancher who owned adjoining land (1881 Map; DM).

WANN (Clark). F. A. Wann, Traffic Manager of the former SPLA and SL RR, is commemorated by **WANN SIDING,** five miles north of Las Vegas on the UP RR, formerly called *Stewart* (Freese, Map 1; WA).

WA–PAI–SHONE (Carson City). The trading post at Stewart has a coined name signifying the three tribes, Washoe, Paiute, and Shoshone, whose craft articles are sold here (OPN, p. 6).

WARD (White Pine). William Ballinger and John Henry, two men in the freighting business, made a discovery in 1872 while hunting "sleeper" bulls near Willow Creek on the east slope of the Egan Range, about ten miles south of Ely. The mining camp that grew up as a result was named for B. F. Ward, one of the locators of the townsite. Nearly all built in 1875, Ward was the most populous camp in the county for a time, largely due to the output of the Paymaster Mine (NHS, 1924, pp. 345–46, 349; 1881 Map; SM, 1875, pp. 167–70). **WARD** post office was active from January 2, 1877, to September 7, 1887 (FTM, p. 30). Shift names are **WARD MOUNTAIN, WARD CHARCOAL OVENS STATE PARK,** south of the mountain, and **WARD MINING DISTRICT** (NJ 11–3; GHM, WP 1; VPG, p. 186).

WARM CREEK (Elko). **WARM CREEK,** a zinc-lead district on the southeast side of **WARM CREEK RIDGE,** east of Clover Valley and twenty-five miles southeast of Halleck Station, is named for **WARM CREEK,** a stream which heads in two warm springs and splits into two unnamed drains (USGB 7004; VPG, p. 49; GHM, EL 5).

WARM SPRINGS. Features named for warm springs in the region are a valley, east of **WARM SPRINGS MOUNTAIN,** south of Winnemucca Valley and west of the Virginia Mountains, between Sparks and Pyramid Lake in Washoe County; a settlement on U.S. 6, southwest of Hot Creek in Nye County, served by a post office so named from January 19, 1924, to June 29, 1929; and a community near Bailey in Lander County. **WARM SPRINGS SETTLEMENT** (White Pine) was served by nearby Cold Creek post office in the early days (FTM, p. 30; TF, p. 23; 1881 Map; NJ 11–1; NJ 11–5; NJ 11–3). **WARM SPRINGS** (Humboldt) is the name for a mining district, also called *Ashdown,* on the west slope of the Pine Forest Range, about twelve miles south of Denio (VPG, p. 78). **WARM SPRINGS** (Carson City). Springs at the prison, east of Carson City, and springs north of the town, also called *Carson Springs* (Car. C. Quad.; NJ 11–1). Near the former, once known as *Currys Hot Springs,* large prehistoric sloth tracks, along with bird, horse and other animal tracks, were uncovered (M&S, p. 279). Southern Nevada features include **WARM SPRINGS,** earlier called *Muddy Spring,* northwest of Moapa in Clark County, and the enigmatically named **WARM OWL SPRINGS,** about a mile north of Panaca in Lincoln County (WA).

WARREN ABLE SPRINGS (Nye). The springs north of Tonopah were named for Warren Able who utilized them as a watering place for stock, including camels once used to carry ore from the Liberty mines. *Warren Averill* is a mistake name for the springs (MM). Jim Butler later changed the name to *Tonopah Springs* (1910 Map). See **TONOPAH.**

WASHAKIE (Pershing). A mining district and former mining camp so named were established in the summer of 1907, near Clear Creek and north of Grand Trunk Canyon on the west slope of the Sonoma Range, about twenty-five miles south from Winnemucca, as noted by the *Reno Evening Gazette* of December 11, 1907 (VPG, p. 167; DM). The name ultimately commemorates a noted Shoshone chief of Wyoming and means "shoots [the buffalo] running" (FWH, p. 919). Washakie was chief of the Wind River Shoshone Indians from the 1840s until 1900 (Fowler, pp. 268, 288).

WASHINGTON. A mountain north of Lincoln Peak in the Snake Range, White Pine County, named for George Washington; a mining district in the Pine Grove Hills (Lyon) in the area of Wichman, described as being between the east and west forks of the Walker River, in the *Gold Hill News* of April 29, 1867; a mining district discovered in 1863 on the west slope of the Toiyabe Range, about twenty-five miles south-south-west of Austin, in Nye County (VPG, pp. 106, 145; NM). A post office so named served the Nye County mining camp from July 29, 1870, to August 27, 1872 (Census, 1870; 1881 Map; FTM, p. 30). The Lyon County district had a short-lived post office, active from April 7, 1879, to July 12, 1880 (HHB, Nev., p. 261; FTM, p. 30). **WASHINGTON HILL** (Storey) is a rhyolite peak in the Virginia Range, eleven miles southeast of Reno (VPG; NJ 11–1). The old settlement so denoted was north of Lousetown and served by Virginia City post office (1881 Map; TF, p. 23).

WASHOE. WASHOE COUNTY was created November 25, 1861. On January 18, 1883, Roop County, formerly a part of Lake County, was added to Washoe. See **LAKE** and **ROOP.** A portion of Lake Tahoe is in the extreme southwest part of the county. **WASHOE VALLEY** lies between the Virginia Range and the Carson Range of the Sierra Nevada. **WASHOE** post office, in Washoe Valley, first established November 13, 1861, operated with only minor interruptions of service until December 15, 1920. From July 3, 1862, until December 13, 1894, it was named **WASHOE CITY.** From the necessity of cheap fuel and water with which to work Comstock ore, **WASHOE CITY,** at the foot of **WASHOE HILL** near **LITTLE WASHOE LAKE,** sprang into existence in 1860. In 1861, the Atchison Mill was built by J. H., S. M., and S. S. Atchison, and soon thereafter the New York, Buckeye, and Minnesota mills. Washoe City was the first county seat of Washoe County and is said to have had the first stock exchange in the West, established a few years before the San Francisco exchange came into existence. **BIG WASHOE LAKE** is in the south end of Washoe Valley (MA, p. 625; C&C, pp. 588, 593; Nev. Terr. Map; FTM, p. 31; NJ 11–1). The graphic variant *Washoo* appears on maps of the 1850s (Wheat IV, 60, 137). The ethnic name is that of the small Hokan-speaking tribe that inhabited the region, the Washo from *Washiu,* "person" (FWH, p. 920; RGE, p. 3).

WASHOUT (Lyon). The station on the old C and C RR, twenty-eight miles from Mound House, was so named because each year melting snows washed out both wagon roads and railroad tracks near the station (NHS, 1913, p. 217).

WASSUK. A name of undetermined origin (Northern Paiute?) for a mountain range west of Walker Lake, extending the length of Mineral County and into Lyon County (NJ 11–4). The northern part of the range is known as the *Walker River Range.* See **WALKER.**

WATER. A name for well-watered canyons in Douglas, Humboldt, Lincoln, Nye, and Pershing counties. Five canyons in White Pine County and four canyons in Lander County are so named (Dir. 1971). **WATERHOLE CANYON** (Washoe) is west of Pyramid Canyon and north of Sutcliffe; **WATER TANK SPRING** (Mineral) is northwest of Bald Mountain in the Wassuk Range (GHM, WA 1; MI 1). **WATERLOG SUMMIT** (Elko). A pass at the head of a long canyon,

which heads northwest of Gold Creek Ranger Station and descends with Meadow Creek to the Bruneau River (Nev. Guide, p. 169; GHM, EL 3).

WATER PIPE. A canyon and a creek, tributary to the South Fork Owyhee River; named for a pipe which carries water from the creek to Tuscarora, in Elko County (EP, p. 86).

WATERLOO (Douglas). A settlement founded in 1892 at the crossing of Mottsville Lane and State Route 88; named by a German-born resident, Heinrich Behrmann (NHS, 1913, p. 203; Dangberg, CV, p. 114). **WATERLOO** post office was active from September 7, 1907, to May 15, 1911 (FTM, p. 31).

WATERPOCKET WASH (Clark). A wash draining into Moapa Valley from the west, cutting through Overton Ridge, south of South Fork Overton Wash; named for "pockets" or holes in sand rock that catch and hold rain and flood water (WA). The name is an alternate for *Kaolin Wash* (NJ 11–12).

WEAVER CREEK (White Pine). A stream heading in the Snake Range and flowing into Snake Valley, northwest of Strawberry Creek (NJ 11–3); a mining district named for the creek and also called *Osceola* (VPG, p. 181).

WEBSTER (Washoe). The early town laid out in the vicinity of Peavine Mountain was named for Daniel Webster, American lawyer and statesman (NHS, 1911, p. 86).

WEBSTERS HOTEL (Douglas). The early station, half way between Genoa and Carson City, was built by Ben Webster, for whom it was named (NHS, 1913, p. 197).

WEDEKIND (Washoe). A locality and former mining camp, two miles north of Sparks; named for George H. Wedekind, a native of Germany, who discovered gold ore there. "One day while eating his lunch he casually kicked over a small rock which appeared a bit unlike others which lay round about. Upon a closer examination he was convinced that it contained ore" (NHS, 1926, p. 344). According to Wedekind, who was a piano tuner in Reno, he discovered the Reno Star Mine, later called *Wedekind,* in 1896. The following year, finding that someone had destroyed the markers, he replaced them, recorded the claim, and built a small cabin at the site. Rich ore was discovered in 1898; production began in 1899. **WEDEKIND** post office was established July 9, 1902, and discontinued March 15, 1905 (SPD, p. 1276; DM; FTM, p. 31).

WEED HEIGHTS (Lyon). An industrial town across the Walker River from Yerington and about ninety miles southeast of Reno, built by the Anaconda Copper Company in 1952; a post office established March 16, 1953; named for Clyde E. Weed, vice president in charge of all Anaconda operations (HPS, 1/24/54; FTM, p. 31).

WEEKS. The name for a non-agency station (Lyon County) on the Mina Branch of the SP RR, south of Appian Station and east of old Fort Churchill in Churchill Valley (NJ 11–1). **WEEKS** (Elko). A creek flowing from east of Hole in the Mountain in the East Humboldt Range to Clover Valley and **WEEKS RANCH** on the creek; named for S. Weeks, an early settler (EP, p. 86). *Leach* is a variant name for the creek (GHM, EL 5).

WEEPAH (Esmeralda). The mining camp and district on the southeast slope of Lone Mountain, about twenty-six miles southwest of Tonopah, was the scene of a boom in 1927. It is said that newsreel cameramen photographed Weepah, where Tonopah dancehall girls staked claims by moonlight (NM; VPG, p. 57). The post office named for the camp was active from April 8, 1927, to July 2, 1929 (FTM, p. 31). The Numic (Shoshonean) name derives from Southern Paiute *we*, "knife," + *pa*, "water" (Fowler, p. 277).

WEILANDS (Elko). The name of an early stage stop at the site of later *Dinner Station* (q.v.), commemorative of its builder a Mr. Weiland. When the station burned, it was replaced by a stone structure (EP, p. 86).

WEISER (Clark). A ridge in the Muddy Mountains trending northeastward toward the **WEISER RANCH,** between the Narrows of the Muddy River and Glendale, and **WEISER GAP,** an alternate name for the Narrows; named for Mr. Weiser, the father of Helen J. Stewart (WA). See **LAS VEGAS.**

WELLINGTON (Lyon). The town was established in territorial days, first as a stage station owned by Jack Wright and Len Hamilton. The name honors Daniel Wellington who bought the station and established a stage line to Aurora in 1863. *Wellingtons Station* had 126 inhabitants, according to the Federal Census of 1870 (C&C, p. 589; Nev. Terr. Map; NHS, 1913, p. 227). **WELLINGTON** post office, formerly named *Mammoth Ledge,* was established March 17, 1865 (FTM, p. 31). A mining district so named, also known as *Silver Glance,* is thirty miles south-southeast from Minden (VPG, p. 35).

WELLS (Elko). A town at the junction of U.S. 95 and U.S. 40 served by the WP RR and the SP RR, and the southern terminal of the Idaho Falls-Wells Branch of the UP RR, on the East Fork Humboldt River (NK 11–9). The station of the CP RR was named *Humboldt Wells,* for springs scattered over a meadow northwest of the station. Emigrants over the Fort Hall-Humboldt River Trail camped at the springs which they called *wells.* According to a later observer "when standing on the bank of one of these curious springs, you look on a still

surface of water, perhaps six or seven feet across, and nearly round. No current disturbs it; it resembles a well more than a natural spring" (GAC, p. 129). **WELLS** post office was established July 17, 1869 (FTM, p. 31).

WESO (Humboldt). A coined name for a station because of its location on both the SP RR and the WP RR, east of Winnemucca (NK 11–8).

WEST. The compass-point name is given to show the position of one feature relative to another. **WEST DIVIDE** is an alternate name for Weepah Mining District, in Esmeralda County. **WEST GATE** (Churchill). Three "gates" along U.S. 50, east of the Clan Alpine Range, are merely narrow defiles in the hills, extending for several hundred yards at each pass. They were named by Simpson in 1859. "Immediately after passing through Middle Gate, strike southwestwardly over a pulverulent prairie to a third gate, which we reach in 3½ miles, and which I call the West Gate. It is also a gap in a low range of mountains running north and south" (JHS, p. 83). **WEST GATE STATION** on the route of the Pony Express was midway between Cold Springs and Sand Springs stations (Nev., I, 1961, p. 8). A mining district so named is at the pass on the east slope of the Clan Alpine Range (VPG, p. 21). The **WEST HUMBOLDT RANGE,** in Pershing and Churchill counties, is a mountain range extending generally southwestward from near Mill City in Pershing County to opposite the Carson Sink in Churchill County. In the early 1900s, Professor Louderback of the University of California applied the name *Lake Range* to the southern portion of the mountain range, reserving the name West Humboldt Range for the northern part only; however, the practice has been to call the two mountain masses the West Humboldt Range (VPG). *West Humboldt Range* appears on Captain James H. Simpson's 1859 map of his explorations across the Great Basin (Wheat IV, 137). **WEST LAKE** (Washoe). One of a group of three lakes in northwestern Washoe County; named for its position west of the other two (NJ 11–7). **WEST POINT** (Clark) was the name for a settlement of the 1860s near the site of present Moapa and about fifteen miles west of former Saint Joseph (JGS, I, p. 593; Wheeler 1871 Map; WA). **WEST RANGE** (Lincoln) denotes a mountain range west of the Bristol Range (WA). **WEST RENO,** a station on the SP RR, was established August 4, 1948 (NJ 11–1; DM). **WEST END,** a borate district in Callville Wash, twenty-six miles east of Las Vegas, apparently took its name from West End Chemical Company (WA; VPG, p. 32). **WEST WALKER.** See **WALKER.**

WHEELER PEAK (White Pine). A mountain peak west of Lehman Caves National Monument in the Snake Range; named for Captain George M. Wheeler of the United States Army Engineers and of the Corps which made surveys west of the 100th meridian, 1875–89 (NJ 11–6; OPN, p. 76).

WHIPPLE CAVE (Lincoln). A cave near Lund whose chief attraction is a room one hundred feet in width and height and five hundred feet long, in which a stalagmite called the "Great Column" extends from the floor to the over-arching roof. John L. Whipple, the discoverer and developer of this natural phenomenon, is commemorated (JGS, III, p. 524; Nev. Guide, p. 243; GHM, LN 1).

WHIRLWIND VALLEY. A valley extending westward from Beowawe in Lander County into Eureka County, north of the malpais; named for whirlwinds (NK 11–11). The desert dust devils were well described by Dan De Quille, who viewed them in the western portion of Nevada.

> In the morning and during the forenoon there is no dust seen to rise on this desert, all is clear and bright as far as the eye can see; but about one o'clock begins to be seen tall slender columns of dust, rising often perpendicularly to the height of a thousand feet, till reaching a current in the upper air when the top of the column is bent over or flattened and streams away to the eastward. In the commencement there is often but a single pillar, but soon another and another arises and like stately giants they chase each other across the plain, till soon all mingle into one confused, flying mass, and so continues till sundown or after. (REL, p. 86)

WHISKY. WHISKY FLAT (Mineral), south of Hawthorne and north of the Excelsior Mountains, may have been named for **WHISKY SPRINGS** at its eastern edge, an early stage, mail, and telegraph stop for travelers on the Bodie-Candelaria road (NJ 11–4). **WHISKY FLAT MINING DISTRICT** is at the south end of Whisky Flat on the north slope of the Excelsior Mountains, twenty miles south of Hawthorne (VPG, p. 120). A local legend relates that Indians stole whisky from Knapp's store and frolicked on the flat, hence the name (MM). **WHISKEY SPRING** (Lincoln). A spring in **WHISKEY SPRING CANYON**, which drains into the Meadow Valley Wash from the east, opposite the Elliott Ranch, about a mile south of Stine. The remains of a still are visible near the spring (WA).

WHISPER FERRY (Clark). The ferry so named was a suspension type, which hung from an overhead cable, at Eldorado Canyon, now under Lake Mohave, and was also called *Eldorado Ferry* (WA).

WHITE. White is the adjective of color most frequently used in place-naming in Nevada. Land features named descriptively for an over-all white appearance may be composed of or contain any of the following: quartz and feldspar (of which white sand is commonly composed), quartz veins, pegmatite veins, white quartzite, limestone, certain clays and tuffs, alkali and salt, or alkali efflorescences. In addition, many otherwise dark rocks, after mineralization, may be weathered and leached to almost, or entirely, white. Hydrographic features containing certain minerals which cause water to appear white are usually named White or Silver (q.v.).

WHITE BASIN (Clark). A basin east of Muddy Peak and north of Bitter Ridge, the site of **WHITE BASIN MINING DISTRICT**; named for borax deposits (VPG, p. 32; NJ 11–12). **WHITE BUTTE** (Clark) denotes a butte north of the Valley of Fire (WA). **WHITE CAPS** (Nye). A gold mine, a notable producer near Manhattan. Rich ore discovered in the lower levels of the mine caused a boom in 1915 (Nev. Guide, p. 257). **WHITE CLOUD** (Churchill). **WHITE CLOUD CITY**, in the Desert Mountains, was named for **WHITE CLOUD CANYON** in the northwest part of the county. A mining district so named (1881 Map) and also known as *Coppereid* is on the west slope of the Stillwater Range. Iron mines were discovered in the district in 1898 (NHS, 1913, p. 176; VPG, p. 20; DM). **WHITE DRY LAKE**. See **DRY**. **WHITE EAGLE** (Clark). The **WHITE EAGLE MINE** is a gypsum mine northeast of Whitney (NJ 11–12). **WHITE ELEPHANT** (Elko). The mountain peak northeast of Jarbidge was named for its shape and color (OPN, p. 30). **WHITE HORSE** (Elko). A war chief of the Gosiutes, White Horse, who on March 22, 1863, burned Eight-Mile Station and started the Overland War in Nevada, is commemorated by a name group in the Goshute Mountains. **WHITE HORSE PASS** is on U.S. Alternate 50, north of **WHITE HORSE FLAT**. The copper-lead district so denoted is forty-five miles east of Currie in the Goshute Mountains. **WHITE HORSE MOUNTAIN** is south of Sugar Loaf Peak in the range (VPG, p. 49; NK 11–12; SPD, p. 156). **WHITE HORSE** (Washoe) is the alternate name for Olinghouse Mining District, nine miles west of Wadsworth in the Pah Rah Range (VPG, p. 172). **WHITE MOUNTAINS** (Esmeralda) denotes a range of the Sierra Nevada extending northward from California into the northwest corner of Esmeralda County (NJ 11–7) and a mercury-salines district, named for the mountain range, but also known as *Fish Lake Valley* (VPG, p. 53). **WHITE PEAKS** (Elko). A mountain east of Granite Peak in the Granite Range, north of Knoll Creek (NK 11–9).

WHITE PINE. Silver, lead, and copper deposits were discovered in 1865, about 120 miles east of Austin on a high mountain range in old Lander County. The mining district was organized and named **WHITE PINE** because of the heavy stand of pine trees in the range, thought to be white pine (M&S, p. 158; OPN, p. 76; RRE). When the Hidden Treasure Mine was discovered near the summit of a 9,000-foot mountain, an estimated 15,000 people rushed to the district. **WHITE PINE CITY** was established on the south side of Treasure Hill. **WHITE PINE COUNTY,** named for the district, was created out of Lander County, by an act passed March 2, 1869, and Hamilton was named county seat. Ely was made the county seat on August 1, 1887. The **WHITE PINE RANGE** extends from the southwest end of the Butte Mountains in White Pine County, into Nye County west of the Horse Range. **WHITE PINE PEAK** is at the south end of the mountain range, in Nye County (NJ 11–3; NJ 11–6).

WHITE PLAINS (Churchill). The settlement and post office (June 4, 1879–July 15, 1909) in the northwest part of the county, forty miles north of Fallon, was also a side track station on the CP RR (FTM, p. 31; 1881 Map; Car. Sink 1908; HHB, Nev., p. 262). "As indicated by the name the plains immediately around the station are white with alkali, solid beds of which slope away to the sinks of Carson and Humboldt lakes. . . . No vegetation meets the eye when gazing on the vast expanse of dirty white alkali" (GAC, p. 156). **WHITE PLAINS FLAT MINING DISTRICT,** the site of the Desert Crystal Salt Company in the vicinity of Huxley, was named for the white appearance of the valley floor (VPG, p. 21). **WHITE RIDGE** (Nye) is on the eastern side of the Kawich Range and about one mile west of Cedar Wells (USGB 6303). The **WHITE RIVER** rises in the Egan Range, southwest of Ely, in White Pine County, and flows through **WHITE RIVER VALLEY** in Nye County, then southeastward to its sink above Hiko, in Lincoln County (NJ 11–3; NJ 11–6; NJ 11–9). In times long past, when Nevada was blessed with greater precipitation, White River flowed from its source to the Colorado River, as indicated by the fish which still survive in springs along the valley (VPG). **WHITE RIVER RANGE** was a local name for the White Pine Mountains, which were known also in the early days as the *Sawmill Mountains,* because from their slopes came most of the lumber which built Shermantown, Hamilton, and Eberhardt (NHS, 1924, p. 389). **WHITE RIVER** also denoted an early settlement and post office (June 6, 1889–May 31, 1905) in Nye County, named for **WHITE RIVER VAL-**

LEY, one of the first settled and most fertile valleys in the state (FTM, p. 31; OR, 1899; Census, 1870). The White River name group honors F. A. White, a member of the Blasdel Party in 1866 (OPN, p. 58). **WHITE ROCK.** The **WHITE ROCK MOUNTAINS** of northeast Lincoln County are along the Utah border, separated from the Wilson Creek Range by Camp Valley Creek and Spring Valley Wash. The principal peak in the range is so named (NJ 11–6). In Elko County, a former settlement named **WHITE ROCK,** or *White Rock City,* served the Bull Run Mining District and was near **WHITE ROCK CREEK** which rises on the west slope of the Bull Run Mountains and flows northwestward to Silver Creek (NK 11–8; Wheeler, 1872, p. 34). A post office named for the camp was established June 21, 1871. On December 31, 1925, its operations were transferred to Tuscarora (FTM, p. 31). **WHITE ROCK** (Clark) denotes a spring in the Red Rocks area (Blue D. Quad.). **WHITE ROCK CANYON** (Eureka) heads at **WHITE ROCK SPRING** in the Monitor Range and trends eastward to Copenhagen Canyon (NJ 11–2; SG Map 6). **WHITE ROCK HOUSE** (Churchill), an early station and watering place about six miles east of East Gate, was so named because the house had been cut out of soft, white rock, volcanic tuff (HHB, Nev., p. 262; 1881 Map; NHS, 1913, p. 176; VPG). **WHITE ROCKS CANYON** (Nye), fifteen miles southwest of Morey Peak, was named by the United States Board on Geographic Names in 1969 "for the white rocks in the upper reaches of the canyon" (USGB 6903). **WHITE SADDLE PASS** (Nye) is about six miles north of Belted Peak in the Belted Range and sixty-three miles east of Goldfield (USGB 6303). **WHITE SAGE CANYON** which heads on the west slope of the Monitor Range, in Eureka County, and trends southward into Nye County, is named for sagebrush in the canyon (NJ 11–2).

WHITES. An early settlement in Eureka County known as **WHITES RANCH** was served by *White* post office from July 31, 1890, to November 30, 1899 (Census, 1900; FTM, p. 31). **WHITES CANYON** (Washoe) drains eastward from the Carson Range into Steamboat Valley, south of Thomas Creek (NJ 11–1).

WHITNEY (Clark). The town, renamed *East Las Vegas* in October, 1958, is southeast of Las Vegas. The townsite was originally part of the Stowell E. Whitney ranch, which he subdivided about 1931. **WHITNEY** post office, established March 28, 1932, and **WHITNEY MESA,** southwest of Whitney, as well as the town name, commemorate Mr. Whitney (NJ 11–12; WA; OPN, p. 18). See **TUCK RANCH.**

WHITTON SPRINGS. See **CHASE SPRING.**

WICHMAN (Lyon). A settlement on State Route 2, at the East Walker River, east of the Pine Grove Hills; a former post office, active from December 6, 1911, to September 15, 1941, when Yerington became the mail address for its patrons (NJ 11–4; FTM, p. 31); a canyon west of the settlement.

WICKIUP CREEK (Elko). A tributary of the Bruneau River west of Jarbidge; named for **WICKIUP CAMP.** The camp had a rough shelter to accommodate range riders (GHM, EL 3; EP, p. 87).

WILD BURRO WASH (Clark). The wash south of Bonelli Peak in southeast Clark County presumably is named for the desert burro (WA).

WILDCAT. Features named for the wildcat are a canyon heading on the north side of **WILDCAT PEAK** in the Toquima Range and extending into Big Smoky Valley, north of Northumberland Canyon; a peak southeast of Beatty in the Bare Mountains, all in Nye County (GHM, NY 3, 8). **WILDCAT CREEK** denotes a creek rising in the Humboldt National Forest, south of Sun Creek in Elko County; a tributary of Washburn Creek, southwest of Cordero in Humboldt County. **WILDCAT SPRING** (Washoe) is northeast of Spanish Springs Peak (GHM, EL 3; HU 4; WA 1). **WILDCAT** was also the name of an early stage station in Churchill County (NHS, 1913, p. 181). See **CAT.**

WILD HORSE. Large herds of wild horses formerly roamed the northern and central portions of the state, particularly the well-watered areas. **WILD HORSE** (Elko). A name group occurs southeast of the Duck Valley Indian Reservation in the Humboldt National Forest consisting of **WILD HORSE CREEK,** tributary to the Owyhee River; **WILD HORSE RESERVOIR,** southeast of **WILD HORSE CROSSING;** and **WILD HORSE MOUNTAIN** in the south end of the **WILD HORSE RANGE.** An early settlement so named is on State Route 43 above North Fork and was served by a post office established July 3, 1945, and discontinued February 28, 1948, when its services were transferred to Mountain City (NI 11–3; GHM, EL 3; FTM, p. 31). **WILD HORSE** (Mineral). A canyon heading in the Gillis Range and extending to Nolan Station, east of Walker Lake, where a herd of four-hundred to five-hundred horses was reported in May, 1908 (NJ 11–4; DM); a canyon and a spring in the Gabbs Vally Range near Red Rock Canyon. **WILD HORSE BASIN** denotes a basin in the Desert Mountains, in Lyon County, and a valley north of Antler Peak in Lander County (GHM, LA 2; DM). **WILD HORSE CANYON** (Washoe) heads in the Lake Range and extends into the Smoke Creek Desert, south of Reynard (GHM, WA

2). **WILD HORSE CREEK** (Nye) is a creek rising near the middle summit of Mount Jefferson, and tributary to Jefferson Creek (SG Map 6). **WILD HORSE MINING DISTRICT** is the name for a mercury district thirty-five miles northwest of Austin, in Lander County; a district twelve miles southeast of Lovelock on the east side of the Humboldt Range, in Pershing County; and a former district about twelve miles south of Hazen, in Lyon County, as noted in the *White Pine News* of February 13, 1908 (VPG, pp. 91, 167; DM; NJ 11–1).

WILKINS (Elko). A town, a station on the UP RR between Herrell and Shores sidings, at Thousand Spring Creek; a post office established July 1, 1948 (NK 11–9; FTM, p. 31); named for Russel Wilkins, a rancher (EP, p. 87).

WILLARD (Pershing). A mining district, also called *Loring,* located in the West Humboldt Range at the west end of Coal Canyon, about ten miles northeast of Lovelock; a former mining camp which sprang up following a gold strike on the Honey Bee Claim in April, 1915 (VPG, p. 167; DM).

WILLIAMS. A ridge in Nye County on the east side of Hot Creek Valley about one mile north of Halligan Mesa; "named for the Williams family, first settlers of Hot Creek Valley" (USGB 7101). Other geographical features bearing this surname are a creek, tributary to Marys River and south of Marys River Basin, in the Humboldt National Forest, Elko County; a creek rising on the east slope of the Cherry Creek Mountains, north and west of Goshute Lake in Elko County; and a canyon extending from the west slope of the Snake Range, north of Mount Washington, into Baking Powder Flat in White Pine County (SG Map 11; ECN Map; NJ 11–6). **WILLIAMS SALT MARSH** is an alternate name for the Diamond Marsh district, thirty miles north of Eureka in Eureka County (VPG, p. 64).

WILLIAMSBURG (Pershing). A former mining camp, established in the early 1860s, about eighteen miles northeast of Lovelock in the Sacramento Mining District, and later named *Lime* (NM).

WILLIAMS STATION (Lyon). The station on the Emigrant Trail, nine miles up the river from Eight-Mile Station and about ten miles northeast of where old Fort Churchill later was constructed, was named for three brothers, James O., Oscar, and David Williams. An Indian massacre here in May, 1860, led to the Pyramid Lake Indian War, provoked by the Bannocks, according to Dan De Quille, but probably nonetheless imminent.

In the absence of Williams, proprietor of the station where the massacre, as it was called, occurred, two or three men left in charge had seized upon two young Piute women and had treated them in the most outrageous manner, keeping them shut up in an outside cellar or cave for a day or two. . . . It so happened that the women who had been outraged were of the branch of the Piute tribe living at Walker Lake, who had married men of the Bannock tribe. . . . When the chief of the Bannocks had heard the man's [Bannock husband's] story, he at once gave him thirty of his best men, and told him to go and avenge the wrong that had been done him. He went and the result is known. (DDQ, pp. 81, 82)

Dan De Quille camped at the site, later named Honey Lake Smiths (q.v.), during his prospecting trip of 1861.

WILLOW. The name of most frequent occurrence in Nevada, used principally for creeks and springs for willow trees growing there. **WILLOW CREEK** denotes thirty-one creeks in ten of Nevada's seventeen counties; seven ranches in Eureka, Humboldt, Lander, Nye, and Pershing counties; a campground in Clark County; and a reservoir in southwest Elko County. In Humboldt County, **WILLOW CREEK** denotes an early settlement and former post office (May 8, 1879–April 19, 1902), serving a mining district so named and also called *Rebel Creek*. The district was discovered in November, 1883, on the west slope of the Santa Rosa Range, fifty-four miles north of Winnemucca (VPG, p. 75; FTM, p. 31; 1881 Map). **WILLOW SPRING(S)** is the name for twenty-three springs in nine counties. **WILLOW PATCH SPRING** is a spring south of Black Horse in the Snake Range, White Pine County (Dir. 1971). See **INDIAN SPRING(S).**

WILLOW POINT (Humboldt). An early settlement in Paradise Valley about twenty miles northeast of Winnemucca, served by a post office which, except for two intervals, was active from June 2, 1865, to April 30, 1910. A copper-silver district so named is on the west side of the Hot Springs Range. A military camp was established at **WILLOW POINT** on the Little Humboldt River, by Major Michael O'Brien, Sixth Infantry, California Volunteers, who took command of the troops stationed at Quinn River Camp No. 33, after Colonel Charles McDermit was killed by Indians on August 7, 1865. The troops at Willow Point withdrew to Camp Dun Glen in October, 1865 (Ruhlen; VPG, p. 79; 1881 Map; FTM, p. 31).

WILLOWTOWN (Churchill). An early settlement four miles west of old Ragtown; named for willow trees growing in the valley of the Carson River (NHS, 1913, p. 176).

WILSON. A locality and station on the former NCB RR between Nordyke and Hudson, a mountain, and a scenic canyon cut by the West Walker River, through which ran the railroad and later a highway, in Lyon County; named for David Wilson, whose wife Abigail was the first white woman to settle in Mason Valley. **WILSON MINING DISTRICT** was named for "Uncle Billy" Wilson, the brother of David Wilson who came to Virginia City in 1859 and to Mason Valley in 1863, where he took up a ranch. He discovered the district, also called *Pine Grove,* on the east slope of the Pine Grove Hills, twenty-three miles south of Yerington in July of 1865 (Well. Sheet; DM; OPN, p. 48; JGS, II, p. 506; SPD, p. 952; VPG, p. 103). **WILSON** (Nye) was the name for an early post office (July 18, 1898–August 31, 1899), which commemorated Isaac J. Wilson, postmaster (FTM, p. 31; OR, 1899). A silver-gold district, thirty-eight miles east-southeast of Goldfield, in Nye County is named **WILSONS** (VPG, p. 146). **WILSON CREEK RANGE** (Lincoln) is in the northeast part of the county, with **MOUNT WILSON** near the center of the mountain range and **WILSON CREEK** flowing from the northwest slope of the mountains into Lake Valley (NJ 11–6). The features honor Charles Wilson, an early county commissioner (OPN, p. 46). *Cedar Mountain Range* was an earlier name for the range (WA). **WILSONS CREEK** was the name of the small settlement listed in the Federal Census of 1900. **WILSON** (Elko). A creek flowing from the Bull Run Mountains to **WILSON RESERVOIR** west of Edgemont; named for Jimmy Wilson, an early settler (EP, p. 89; GHM, EL 2).

WINDYPAH (Esmeralda). A hybrid name consisting of "windy" + the Southern Paiute generic *pah,* "water," for a mining district, also called *Pigeon Spring,* in the Palmetto Mountains (VPG, p. 58).

WINDY WASH (Nye). The watercourse so named extends from the west side of Yucca Mountain to Crater Flat, about thirteen miles southeast of Beatty (DL 58).

WINES (Elko). Ira D. Wines, a rancher in the early days, is commemorated by **WINES CREEK** which rises in the Ruby Mountains east of **WINES PEAK** and flows into Ruby Valley (EP, p. 89; NJ 11–12).

WINFIELD SCOTT, CAMP (Humboldt). The camp, in the northwest corner of Paradise Valley and about two miles north of the town so named, was established by Captain Murray Davis, of Company A, Eighth U.S. Cavalry, on December 12, 1866, for the protection of travelers and settlers in Paradise Valley. Since 1864, hostile Indians in the valley had been stealing stock, murdering prospectors and settlers, and committing other depredations. The camp, abandoned February 19, 1871, was named for a distinguished U.S. Army officer, General Winfield Scott (Ruhlen).

WINNEMUCCA. The Humboldt County name group may stem from **WINNEMUCCA**

MINE, in the **WINNEMUCCA MINING DISTRICT** (discovered in 1863), from **WINNEMUCCA MOUNTAIN,** called *Old Winnemucca Mountain* in 1863, or from **WINNEMUCCA SPRING,** mentioned by Bancroft (HHB, Nev., p. 264; SM, 1867, pp. 48–49, 55). **WINNEMUCCA** post office was established February 1, 1866 (FTM, p. 31). Until the establishment of the post office in 1866, the town of **WINNEMUCCA** on the Humboldt River was known as *French Ford* or *French Bridge,* for a bridge built at the noted crossing place by the Lay brothers and a Frenchman, Frank Band, in 1850 (SPD, p. 912; HHB, Nev., pp. 263–64, 268, n. 18). According to James Scrugham, the place was called *Centerville* for a time because it was a center for northbound travelers (JGS, I, p. 257). When the CP RR reached the settlement in 1868, the station was named Winnemucca by "C. B. O. Bannon, nephew of the Secretary of the Interior under Lincoln, who wished to perpetuate the name of the famous Indian chief" (MA, pp. 459–60; HHB, Nev., p. 268, n. 18; SPD, p. 912) and adopted the name of the post office, mining district, and mountain. The combined name *Winnemucca of French Ford* is said to have been current for a short time (B&H, p. 121; ELS, Pacific, pp. 254–55). Winnemucca became the county seat of Humboldt County in 1872 (MA, pp. 459–60).

Of the three Winnemuccas who helped to make Nevada history, Na-ana (Chiquito, or Little Winnemucca), Numaga (Young Winnemucca), and Poito (Old Winnemucca), undoubtedly the last is commemorated, as the mountain name would indicate. In the *History of the Big Bonanza* (pp. 196, 203), Dan De Quille described Old Winnemucca as a man of about seventy years who wore a stick four inches long in his nose. An inveterate gambler among his own people, Old Winnemucca was a "good-natured, kind-hearted old man, but not a man remarkable for either wisdom or cunning." The name has been variously interpreted to mean "place by the river," "bread giver," "the giver," "the charitable man," and "one moccasin" (NHS, 1922, p. 16; SPD, p. 912; FES, p. 191; HHB, Nev., p. 222, n. 28; DDQ, p. 203). Chief Harry Winnemucca of the present-day Pyramid Lake Indian Reservation accepts the following explanation which was passed down to him by word of mouth. "By legend, my great great grandfather, Old Winnemucca, long ago lost one moccasin in the area of the Forty Mile Desert [south and east of the Truckee River] when the cavalry was coming, and he had to flee. 'One' is used by white people. 'Shoe' in Paiute is 'mau-cau.' 'One-a-mau-cau,' his and my name came to be" (RH, p. 111). *Mo-ko,* "moccasins" is contained in John Wesley Powell's Paviotso vocabulary

given by Naches in 1873 (Fowler, p. 211). Captain James H. Simpson reported in 1859 that the chief of the Paiutes was *Wan-muc-ca* (The Giver) and spelled the name of Numaga, the younger, *Won-amuc-a* (JHS, pp. 37, 94). According to Frederick Hodge, Winnemucca meant "The Giver" (FWH, p. 962). *Poito* was reported by Stephen Powers to be from *Pu-i-dok,* "deep eyes" (Fowler, p. 230). The present chief, Harry Winnemucca, provided the following explanation of the name. "Old Winnemucca, to show his rank within all the Paiute tribes, wore a stick of wood or bone through his pierced nose. Therefore, he was called 'Poito' the Paiute word for 'hole through nose' " (RH, p. 111). Lack of conclusive evidence precludes a positive statement of the meaning of *Winnemucca,* but Poito was the first to bear the name.

WINNEMUCCA LAKE and **WINNEMUCCA WILDLIFE REFUGE** are in western Pershing County and eastern Washoe County (NK 11–10). The dry lake, east of the Lake Range and west of the Nightingale Mountains, is a remnant of ancient Lake Lahontan. The name of the lake appears on an 1860 map of the Washoe Mining Region, by R. M. Evans (Wheat V (I), 16). **WINNEMUCCA LAKE CAVES** (Pershing) is a group name for nine caves along the northeastern shore of the lake. The caves were explored by the Nevada State Museum in the early 1950s and individually named *Chimney, Cowbone, Crypt, Fishbone, Guano, Horse, Owl, Stick,* and *Thinolite* (M&M, p. 178). **WINNEMUCCA VALLEY** (Washoe) extends northwestward from Warm Springs Valley, bounded by the Virginia Mountains on the east and by the Dogskin Mountains on the west (NJ 11–1). **LITTLE WINNEMUCCA,** a settlement of old Roop County, was named to commemorate Na-ana (Chiquito, or Little Winnemucca), who proved himself a formidable foe in the first battle of the Pyramid Lake Indian War of 1860 (SPD, pp. 52–61).

WINNEMUC HILL (Clark). Old timers in Nevada were apt to say that a person ill with chills and fever had "the winnemucs," although the origin of the expression and its connection with Chief Winnemucca are unknown. During the construction of a road in Clark County, an Indian boy was seized by chills and fever. The workers named a steep dugway, at the mouth of Toquop Wash, **WINNEMUC HILL** (WA).

WINTER CREEK (Elko). The stream so named flows into the East Fork Humboldt River six miles west-southwest of Deeth and commemorates "Frank Winter, a longtime resident of the area" (USGB 7002). A variant name is *Waiter* Creek (NK 11–9).

WONDER (Churchill). A mining district and

the site of an abandoned settlement on the west slope of the Clan Alpine Mountains, seventeen miles northeast of Frenchman and about thirty-nine miles east of Fallon; named for the **NEVADA WONDER MINE**, discovered either by J. L. Stroud, or by a man named Horgan, on April 7, 1906. **WONDER MOUNTAIN** is about one mile north of the old mining camp for which it is named (VPG, p. 21; DM; USGB 5904; M&S, pp. 121, 150; NJ 11–1). **WONDER** post office was active from September 17, 1906, to August 14, 1920, when Fallon became the mail address for its patrons (FTM, p. 32).

WOOD (Elko). A short-lived post office, established April 18, 1900, and discontinued December 15, 1902, when its operations were transferred to Clover (FTM, p. 32).

WOODRUFF. WOODRUFF CREEK is tributary to the Humboldt River southwest of Carlin, in Elko County, and was named by Simpson for Captain I. C. Woodruff, Corps Topographical Engineers (JHS, p. 79). A post office of Esmeralda County, active from July 5, 1882, to July 21, 1885, was named for the postmaster, A. Woodruff (FTM, p. 32; OR, 1883, 1885).

WOOD YARD (Esmeralda). The station, established in 1913 ten miles north of Blair on the SP RR, was named for the wood fuel hauled down from the mountains, for transport on the railroad from this point (DM).

WOOLSEY (Pershing). A non-agency station on a spur line of the SP RR, southwest of Oreana and nine miles northeast of Lovelock, on U.S. 40 (T75; NK 11–10).

WORTHINGTON (Lincoln). The **WORTHINGTON MOUNTAINS** extend northward from the Timpahute Range, bounded on the west by Sand Spring Valley and on the east by Garden Valley. **WORTHINGTON PEAK** in the north end of the mountains is the site of the **WORTHINGTON MINING DISTRICT**, located in 1865 by two prospectors named Didlake and Aikens. The principal mines of this district, reorganized as *Freiberg* (Freyberg, Fryberg) in 1869, are the Ellen, Shoupe, Trident, Boulder, and Neptune (WA; SM, 1867, p. 66; VPG, p. 94; NJ 11–9). The name is honorific of Henry G. Worthington, Nevada's first Congressman, elected in 1864 (SPD, p. 194).

YANDAI CREEK. See **REED CREEK**.
YANKEE BLADE (Lander). A mining district, also called *Reese River, Amador,* and *Austin,* and a former mining camp about four miles north of Austin, which grew up because of silver discoveries in 1863 (VPG, p. 88; Wheeler 1871 Map). The *Reese River*

Reveille, Austin's famous newspaper, "likened Yankee Blade's activity to a Missouri sawmill, in which the saw went up one day and came down the next, and laid off on Sundays" (NM, p. 271). The camp was named for a New England newspaper so denoted (MM).

YELLAND (White Pine). The early settlement, just south of McCoy in Spring Valley, was named for John ("Josh") Yelland of Cornwall, England, who came to eastern Nevada in 1881 and established the Yelland ranch (JGS, I, pp. 280–81; NHS, 1924, p. 307; GHM, WP 1). **YELLAND** post office was active from November 17, 1924, to January 15, 1927 (FTM, p. 32).

YELLOW. Mountains named for predominantly yellow rock coloration include **YELLOW HILL**, a peak in the Ely Springs Range in Lincoln County, and **YELLOW PEAK**, east of Mud Lake in northern Washoe County (WA; GHM, WA 3). **YELLOW ROCK** (Elko) is the name for a peak southeast of Owyhee in the Western Shoshone (Duck Valley) Indian Reservation (GHM, EL 3).

YELLOW CLEFT (Nye). A canyon heading about one mile east of the peak of Black Mountain and extending to Labyrinth Canyon, about twenty-three miles north-northeast of Beatty; named for the yellow tinged rock walls and floor of the precipitous canyon (USGB 6302; DL 56).

YELLOW JACKET (Storey). The Comstock claim was taken up on May 1, 1859, and recorded the following June 27 (GH–A). The ground is between the Kentuck and the Consolidated Imperial and includes 957 feet, controlled presently by the Sutro Tunnel Coalition, Inc. (IH; AAL). "This claim was called the Yellow-Jacket because of the fact of the locators' finding a nest of yellow-jackets in the surface rock while they were digging about for the purpose of prospecting the vein" (DDQ, p. 36). The location notice for the Yellow Jacket was signed by Camp, Rogers, and John Bishop, "Big French John," who named the town of Gold Hill (q.v.). The anecdote concerning an accidental encounter with insects seems to be traditional. Mosquito, a Colorado mining camp, was reportedly so named because of the first settlers having found a mosquito in the record book of the still nameless settlement (GTC, p. 28). Miners seem to have been fond of the "jacket" name described as yellow, blue, and red. Kern, El Dorado, and Sierra counties, California, each had a Yellow Jacket mine; Tuolumne County had two (CMA, pp. 180, 318, 359; OPJ, p. 81). A mine and a mountain range named Yellow Jacket are in Idaho. Blue Jacket mines were in Lander County, Nevada, and in Amador and San Bernardino counties, California (RWR, p. 135; JRB, Res.,

p. 74; CSMB, p. 500). San Bernardino County, in addition, had a Red Jacket mine (CSMB, p. 498).

YELLOW PINE (Clark). An early and alternate name for the Goodsprings Mining District (q.v.), whose principal producers were the Potosi and YELLOW PINE mines (VPG, p. 26; Wheeler 1871 Map; WA). "The Yellow Pine district as organized, however, is of great extent, and is said to show a multiplicity of locations and ores. There is an immense body of heavy pine timber distributed over a great share of the higher elevations of the Spring Mountain Range" (Wheeler, 1872, p. 53).

YELLOW ROCK (Washoe). A canyon of this name joins High Rock Canyon from the west. The name is derived from the striking, yellow-colored rocks in the canyon walls (VPG; NK 11-7). See YELLOW.

YERINGTON (Lyon). A town and post office established February 6, 1894, in the east-central portion of Lyon County on U.S. 95A, the county seat, formerly served by the C and C RR and the NCB RR (FTM, p. 32; NCB Map; NJ 11-1). At the time of settlement the town was known as *Poison* or *Pizen Switch,* for a saloon owned by a Mr. Downey, who made his own liquor which the men called "pizen." The name "switch" was derived from a small saloon made of willows and called *Willow Switch.* According to the legend, the "boys" would race their horses from one place to the other and frequently use the expression "Let's switch off and get some pizen." Another version relates that the expression was used by "buckeroos" when they reached the crossroads (SPD, pp. 953-54; OPN, p. 48; NHS, 1913, pp. 215-16). The place was called *Greenfield* next for its location in the green fields of Mason Valley. The station on the former C and C RR was named Yerington, in honor of Henry Marvin Yerington, a native of Calborne, Canada, and the superintendent of the former V and T RR and builder of the former LTNG RR, in partnership with Duane L. Bliss. YERINGTON MINING DISTRICT, also called *Ludwig* and *Mason,* is four miles southwest of the town in the central portion of the Singatse Range (VPG, p. 107). The district earlier was called the *Crazy Louse.* At one time all of the district was owned by Mark Twain, who did not realize its values. Lyon County records note the sale of the property to him. It is the site of a large copper-producing mine at the present time (CBG, Gold, p. 205; VPG).

YOACHAM (Lincoln). The post office, active from July 19, 1893, to October 31, 1902, when Caliente became the mail address for its patrons, was named for Susie Yoacham, postmaster (FTM, p. 32; OR, 1899), and was at the Archie Yoacham ranch (WA).

YOMBA (Nye). The YOMBA INDIAN RESERVATION is in Reese River Valley in the northern portion of the county, between the Shoshone Mountains and the Toiyabe Range (NJ 11-2).

YOUNTS RANCH (Clark). The old ranch south of Manse in Pahrump Valley presumably commemorated the Joseph Yount family, who settled the Manse Ranch (q.v.) in 1875 (Vegas Quad.).

YP (Elko). The YP DESERT is a flat in the extreme northwest corner of Elko County where "the Garat Ranch used to run cattle. It was named for the cattle brand of the Garats" (EP, p. 90). The YP RANCH is southeast of the flat and west of White Rock (GHM, EL 2).

YUCCA (Nye). A mountain group named YUCCA MOUNTAIN is bounded on the north by Beatty Wash, on the east by Forty-mile Canyon, and on the west by Crater Flat, about twenty miles west-southwest of YUCCA FLAT, in the Nevada Test Site. The mountains were named *Yucca* (not Joshua) by decision of the United States Geographic Board in its *Fifth Report.* YUCCA WASH is a watercourse on Yucca Mountain, heading just south of Pinyon Pass and extending to Fortymile Canyon, southwest of the Calico Hills and about twenty miles west-southwest of Yucca Flat. YUCCA LAKE, on the flat, is northwest of Massachusetts Mountain (NJ 11-12; NJ 11-8; DL 58). The name is descriptive of the *Yucca brevifolia* in the area.

ZELDA (Churchill). A former post office, established September 23, 1891, and discontinued November 3, 1902, when its name was changed to *Massie;* a side track station on the old line of the CP RR, southwest of White Plains (FTM, p. 32; NHS, 1913, p. 184).

ZEPHYR (Douglas). ZEPHYR COVE, a summer resort and post office, established July 11, 1930, on the east shore of Lake Tahoe near ZEPHYR POINT, may have been named for gentle breezes playing about its natural features, unless humorous reference was made to the "Washoe Zephyr," a native term for a furious westerly gale in Nevada (NJ 11-1; FTM, p. 32). This "peculiarly Scriptural wind" is no less vigorous now than it was when Mark Twain, on the day of his arrival at Carson City, felt one set in, observing characteristically that "a soaring dust-drift about the size of the United States set up edgewise came with it, and the capital of Nevada Territory disappeared from view" (SLC, I, pp. 146, 147).

RAILROAD
ABBREVIATIONS

AC RR	Austin City Railroad
AT and SF RR	Atchison, Topeka, and Santa Fe Railroad
B and S RR	Barnwell and Searchlight Railroad
BG RR	Bullfrog-Goldfield Railroad
BM and L RR	Battle Mountain and Lewis Railroad
C and C RR	Carson and Colorado Railroad
CP RR	Central Pacific Railroad
E and P RR	Eureka and Palisade Railroad
EM RR	Eureka Mill Railroad
LTNG RR	Lake Tahoe Narrow Gauge Railroad
LV and T RR	Las Vegas and Tonopah Railroad
N and C RR	Nevada and California Railroad
NC RR	Nevada Central Railroad
NCB RR	Nevada Copper Belt Railroad
NCO RR	Nevada-California-Oregon Railroad
NN RR	Nevada Northern Railroad
OSL RR	Oregon Short Line Railroad
P and B RR	Pioche and Bullionville Railroad
PC RR	Prince Consolidated Railroad
RH RR	Ruby Hill Railroad
SC RR	Six Companies Railroad
SP RR	Southern Pacific Railroad
SPK RR	Silver Peak Railroad
SPLA and SL RR	San Pedro, Los Angeles, and Salt Lake Railroad
ST RR	Sutro Tunnel Railroad
T and G RR	Tonopah and Goldfield Railroad
T and T RR	Tonopah and Tidewater Railroad
UP RR	Union Pacific Railroad
V and T RR	Virginia and Truckee Railroad
WP RR	Western Pacific Railroad

ALPHABETICAL
KEY TO SOURCES

AAL	Affidavit	C&CR	"Carson & Colorado"
AAR	Association	C 4	Southern Pacific
ABH	Hulbert		
AC	Child	Dangberg, CV	Dangberg
AD	Delano	DB	Basso
AEH	Hutcheson	DDQ	Wright
AJ	Jenson	DE	Emrich
AJM	Maestretti	Deeds	Deeds
AN	Nevins	Dir.	Directories
AR	Assessment	DL	U.S. Geographic
AS	"Archeological"	DM	Myrick
A&LH	Heilprin	DMP	Potter
		DRL	Lane
Barnes	Barnes		
BFB	Bonney	EBB	Buckbee
BFS	Sawyer, B. F.	EC	Cronkhite
Black Gold	"Black Gold"	ED	Dick
BLK	King, B. L.	EEA	Newberry Library
Brand	Nevada State	EED	Dye
BS	Storm	EH	Hungerford
BT	Taylor	EL	Lord
Bullfrog	"Bullfrog"	ELK	King, E. L.
BW	Woon	ELS	Sabin
B&C	Beebe and Clegg	EM	Manter
B&H	Botkin	EMM	Mack
		EP	Patterson
Cal. Guide	California	EPA	Alexander
CBG	Glasscock	ERH	Hall
CC	Carson, Christopher	ES	Sapir
Census	U.S. Bureau	EWB	Billeb
CES	Carpenter	E&P	Elliott & Poulton
CFV	Voegelin		
CH	Haymond	FBG	Goddard
CHL	Labbe	FCL	Lincoln
CHS	Shinn	FES	Shearer
CIW	Wheat	FG .	Greulich
CJ	Jones	FHH	Hart
CK	King, C.	FHL	Leavitt
CL	Laird, C.	FLK	Kramer
CLS	Skinner	FLR	Ransome
CMA	California Miners'	FNF	Fletcher
CO	Oman	Fowler	Fowler
COP	Paullin	FP	Parkman
Coues	Coues	FPWR	Richthofen
CSMB	California State	FSD	Dellenbaugh
C&C	Chase	FTM	Frickstad

FWCG	Gerstäcker
FWH	Hodge
GAC	Crofutt
GCC	Christensen
GCQ	Quiett
GD	Dangberg
GDL	Lyman
GES	Shankle
GFB	Becker
GG	Griffen
GGC	Cline
GH	Gold Hill
GHK	Kneiss
GHS	Smith, G. H.
GMD	Dodge
GRB	Brown, G. R.
GRS	Stewart, G. R.
GS	Stokes
GTC	*Ghost Towns*
GTM	Marye
Gudde	Gudde
GWK	Keller
HAR	Rundell
HCD	Dale
HD	Denton
HDG	De Groot
HG	Gannett
HH	Hoffman
HHB	Bancroft
HHR	Roberts
HK	Kenny
HKW	White, H. K.
HL	Laird, H.
HLM	Mencken
HMC	Chittenden
HMG	Gorham
HNS	Smith, H. N.
HPS	Historical
HRD	Driggs
HRM	Mighels
HSC	Carlson
HWB	Bentley
H&E	Hague
ICC	Indian Claims
ICR	Russell
IH	"Individual Histories"
JA	Atwater
JAC	Church
JAP	Price
JB	Bigelow
JBF	Frémont, J. B.
JC	Codman
JCF	Frémont, J. C.
JDF	Forbes
JGF	Folkes
JGS	Scrugham
JHC	Curle
JHJ	Jackson, J. H.
JHS	Simpson

JJP	Powell
JLF	French
JLK	King, J. L.
JLM	Marshall
JM	McElrath
JML	Linsdale
JRB	Browne
JRS	Swanton
JS	Smith, J.
JTA	Adams, J. T.
JWC	Calhoun
JWH	Hulse
Kilmartin	Kilmartin
Kroeber	Kroeber
KU	Upland
KWC	Clarke
LAM	McArthur
LB	Beebe
LES	Seltzer
LF	Florin
LHC	Creer
Lillard	Lillard
LKM	McNary
LPB	Brockett
LRB	Berg
LRH	Hafen
LS	Sawyer, L.
LVL	Loomis
MA	Angel
MM	Myles
MMQ	Quaife
Moody	Moody
Morgan	Morgan
MSS	Sullivan
MSW	Wolle
M&F	McVaugh
M&M	Mordy
M&S	Mack & Sawyer
M&SP	Mining
NA	Anderson
Nev.	Nevada Highways
Nev. Guide	Nevada
NHS	Nevada Historical
NHS, Quarterly	Nevada Historical
NM	Murbarger
NP	*Nevada's Parks*
NS	Sanchez
NSS	U.S. Post Office
OCC	Coy
OCS	Stewart, O. C.
OFM	McKeon
OG	*Official Guide*
OJH	Hollister
OL	Lewis, O.
OPJ	Jenkins, O. P.
OPN	*Origin*
OR	Official Register
OW	Weston

Paul	Paul	Steward	Steward
Pearce	Pearce	SW	Wood
PRRS	U.S. Congress	SWH	Hopkins
PSF	Fritz	SWP	Paher
PT	Trego, P.	SWS	Scott
PTH	Hanna	S&H	Schilling
		S&S	Savage
RBM	Marcy		
RBS	Sealock	TAR	Rickard
RC	Chatham	TBHS	Stenhouse
RDH	Hunt, R. D.	TDB	Bonner
REC	Cowan	TF	Fox
REL	Wright	TGG	Grieder
RER	Riegel	TMP	Pearce
RFA	Adams, R. F.	TP	U.S. State
RFB	Burton	TPB	Brown, T. P.
RGL	Lewis, R. G.	TS	Sutro
RH	Hermann	TW	Wren
RL	Laxalt	T1SL	Southern Pacific
RPC	Conkling	T1TR	Southern Pacific
RR, 1888	U.S. Interstate	T54	Western Pacific
RRE	Elliott	T75	Southern Pacific
RS	Shutler	T187	Southern Pacific
RSH	Henry		
RT	Trego, R.	USGB	U.S. Geographic
Ruhlen	Ruhlen	USPO	U.S. Post Office
RWL	Leigh		
RWP	Prince	VF	Fisher
RWR	Raymond	VH	Harland
		VMR	Virginia
SB	Bowles	VPG	Gianella
SD	Daggett		
SFH	Hunt, S. F.	WA	Averett
SHH	Holbrook	Washoe	Woon
SHM	State Historical	WBM	Malloy
SKF	Farrington	WCM	Miller
SLC	Clemens	WD	Drury
SLL	Lee, S. L.	Wheeler	Wheeler
SM, 1867	Stretch	WHJ	Jacobsen
SM, 1869	White, A. F.	WI	Irving
SM, 1871	White, A. F.	WLP	Park
SM, 1873	Whitehill	WMT	Thayer
SM, 1875	Whitehill	WSJ	Jenkins, W. S.
SM, 1877	Whitehill	WSS	Shepperson
SP	Paine	WTJ	Jackson, W. T.
SPB	Southern Pacific	WTL	Lee, W. T.
SPD	Davis		
SP, Hist.	Southern Pacific	ZL	Leonard
SP, Rules	Southern Pacific		

MAP KEY

Wheat, Carl Irving. Mapping the Transmississippi West, 1540–
1861. 5 vols. San Francisco: Institute of Historical Cartog-
raphy, 1957–1963.   (Wheat)

Map of an Exploring Expedition to the Rocky Mountains in
the Year 1842 and to Oregon & North California in the
Years 1843–44. By Brevet Capt. J. Frémont of the Corps of
Topographical Engineers under the Orders of Col. J. J.
Abert, Chief of the Topographical Bureau. Lith. by E.
Weber & Co., Baltimore, Md.   (Frémont Map)

Explorations and Surveys for Railroad Routes from the Mis-
sissippi River to the Pacific Ocean. Profiles of the Main
Routes Surveyed. Compiled in 1855, by Lieutenants C. K.
Warren & H. L. Abbott, Corps Top. Engineers, Capt. A. A.
Humphreys, Corps Top. Engineers, in charge.

From Great Salt Lake to the Humboldt Mountains, by
Capt. E. G. Beckwith, 1855. Map No. 2.   (PRR–2 Map)

From the Humboldt Mountains to the Mud Lakes, by Capt.
E. G. Beckwith, 1855. Map No. 3.   (PRR–3 Map)

From the Valley of the Mud Lakes to the Pacific Ocean, by
Capt. E. G. Beckwith, 1855. Map. No. 4.   (PRR–4 Map)

Profiles of Wagon Routes in the Territory of Utah, by Capt.
J. H. Simpson, Top'l. Engr. U.S.A., 1858–59, assisted by
Mr. Henry Engelmann. Facsimile Reproduction by The
Graphic Co., 39 & 41 Park Place, N.Y. Drawn by J. P.
Mechlin. Reproduced in JHS.   (JHS Map)

Trails Across Nevada. Reproduced in NHS, 1924, p. 40.   (Trails Map)

Map of Carson Valley. Reproduced in NHS, 1922, p. 13.   (CV Map)

Pony Express Route April 3, 1860–October 24, 1861, by
W. H. Jackson. Issued by the American Pioneer Trails Association.   (Jackson Map)

Bancroft's Map of The Washoe Silver Region of Nevada Territory, 1862.   (Bancroft Map)

Map of Nevada Territory 1863, County Boundaries and Mining Districts, by Henry De Groot. (De Groot Map)

Nevada Territory Map. Reproduced in C&C, p. 587. (Nev. Terr. Map)

Map of Virginia City, Nev. Townsite and Mining Claims, by Evalin Curran. (Curran Map)

Map of the Reese River Mines, Located in the Vicinity of the Town of Austin, Lander County, N. T., 1863. Reproduced in NHS, 1913, p. 145. (1863 Map)

The New State of Nevada: The Thirty-sixth Star in the Union —Its Latitude and Longitude, 1864. Reproduced in NHS, 1917, p. 36. (1864 Map)

Nevada 1866, Wagon Roads 1871—Proposed and Completed. Reproduced in M&S, p. 106. (1866 Map)

County Map of Nevada 1867. Drawn and Engraved by W. H. Gamble, Philadelphia. Reproduced in TF, pp. 12–13. (1867 Map)

Map of the White Pine Range and White Pine Mining District. Compiled by A. Cadwalader, published by H. H. Bancroft & Co., San Francisco, 1869. Reproduced in NHS, 1924, pp. 272, 280. (Cad. Map)

Map of East Central Nevada. Reproduced in NHS, 1924, p. 289. (ECN Map)

Explorations and Surveys South of Central Pacific R. R. Preliminary Topographical Map. Prepared under the immediate direction of 1st Lieut. Geo. M. Wheeler, Corps of Engineers. Louis Nell, Chief Topographer and Draughtsman, 1871. (Wheeler 1871 Map)

Las Vegas and Vicinity 1878. Reproduced in NHS, 1926, p. 151. (LV Map)

Sketch Indicating the Advancement of the Surveys of the Public Lands and the Military Topographical and Geographical Surveys West of the Mississippi. Prepared under the Direction of 1st Lieut. Geo. M. Wheeler, Corps of Engineers, U.S. Army, 1879. (Wheeler 1879 Map)

The Comstock Lode—Showing Location of Important Mines and Deep Shafts in 1880. From the Atlas accompanying GFB. (Becker Map)

Map of Nevada 1881. Fold-in Map in TF. (1881 Map)

Map of Glendale and Vicinity, 1893. Reproduced in NHS, 1926, p. 290. (1893 Map)

Map Showing Prinicpal Mining Camps in Nevada and How Reached by Railroad. Reproduced in *Los Angeles Mining Review*, XXVI (March, 1909), p. 30. (1909 Map)

Nevada California Oregon Railway. From the N–C–O Annual
Report for 1910. Reproduced in *The Western Railroader,*
XVIII (June, 1955), p. 2.   (N–C–O Map)

Population and Railroads 1910 (Proposed and Completed).
Reproduced in M&S, p. 127.   (1910 Map)

Map of the Virginia and Truckee Railway. Reproduced in
GHK, V&T, p. 32.   (V&T Map)

Nevada Copper Belt Railroad 1919. Reproduced in *The Western Railroader,* XVIII (December, 1954), p. 2.   (NCB Map)

Map of the State of Nevada Existing Park and Recreational
Areas. Reproduced in NP, p. 56.   (Park Map)

State of Nevada 1940. Fold-in Map in Nev. Guide.   (Guide Map)

Landforms of California and Nevada. Second Revised Edition
1951, by Erwin Raisz. Published by Ginn and Co., Boston,
Mass.   (Landforms)

Map of the Salt Lake Division. January 9, 1955. Printed on
the cover of T75.   (T75 Map)

Map of the Sacramento Division. January 9, 1955. Printed on
the cover of T187.   (T187 Map)

Road Map of Nevada. Prepared for Standard Oil Company of
California. Copyright 1956 by The H. M. Gousha Company,
Chicago-San Jose.   (1956 Map)

Sportsmen's Guide Maps. Published by Ed. W. Pulver & Son,
Seattle, Washington.   (SG Map)

Tahoe Fishing Hunting Recreation Map. Evergreen Publishing
Company, Sacramento, California.   (Tahoe Map)

Nevada County Maps. Compiled from state-wide highway
planning survey and private data. Published by Harry
Freese, Oakland, Calif. Distributed by Thomas Bros. (Freese)

General Land Office Map of the State of Nevada. Compiled
from the official records of the General Land Office and
other sources, 1941.   (Gen. Land Off. Map)

United States Department of the Interior Geological Survey.
Quadrangles and Sheets. 1889–1969.   (Quad.) (Sheet)

United States Army Map Service, Corps of Engineers. 1947–
1962.   (NI, NJ, NK)

General Highway Maps. Prepared by Nevada State Highway
Department, Planning Survey Division, in cooperation with
U.S. Department of Commerce, Bureau of Public Roads.
1959–1971.   (GHM)

Official Highway Maps of Nevada. Nevada State Highway
Department, Carson City, Nevada. Prepared by Rand
McNally & Co., Chicago. 1958–1973.   (HWY Map)

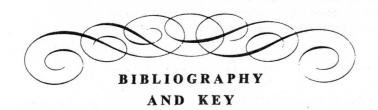

BIBLIOGRAPHY
AND KEY

Adams, James Truslow (ed.). *Atlas of American History*. New York: Charles Scribner's Sons, 1943. (JTA)

Adams, Ramon F. *Western Words: A Dictionary of the Range, Cow Camp and Trail*. Norman, Okla.: University of Oklahoma Press, 1944. (RFA)

Affidavit of Annual Labor, Book V, P of A, Storey County Records 1954. Exhibited by Edna J. James, Storey County Recorder and Auditor, Courthouse, Virginia City, Nevada. (AAL)

Alexander, E. P. *Iron Horses: American Locomotives 1829–1900*. New York: W. W. Norton and Co., Inc., 1941. (EPA)

Anderson, Nels. *Desert Saints*. Chicago: University of Chicago Press, 1942. (NA)

Angel, Myron (ed.). *History of Nevada*. Oakland: Thompson and West, 1881 (MA)

"Archeological Sites in Washoe, White Pine and Nye Counties." Unpublished MS, at the Nevada State Museum, Carson City, Nevada, furnished by Mrs. Ralph W. Smith, 1665 McKinley Drive, Reno, Nevada. (AS)

Assessment Roll of Storey County, Nevada, 1954. Exhibited by Eric A. Jacobsen, Storey County Assessor and Sheriff, and by William E. Murry, Deputy Sheriff of Storey County, Courthouse, Virginia City, Nevada. (AR)

Association of American Railroads. Railroad Committee for the Study of Transportation. *Transportation in America*. Washington, 1947. (AAR, 1947)

.... *American Railroads, Their Growth and Development*. Washington, 1951. (AAR, 1951)

Atwater, Jane. " 'Best Kept' Ghost Town." *Nevada State Journal*, August 7, 1955, p. 8. (JA)

Averett, Walter R. "Directory of Southern Nevada Place-Names." Fifth draft MS of first revision (March 15, 1960), from the private files of Mr. Averett, used with his permission. (WA)

.... *Directory of Southern Nevada Place-Names.* Las
Vegas: By the author, 1962. (WA, 1962)

Bancroft, Hubert Howe. *History of California 1848–1859.* Vol.
VI. San Francisco: The History Co., 1890. (HHB, Cal.)

.... *History of Nevada, Colorado, and Wyoming.* San
Francisco: The History Co., 1890. (HHB, Nev.)

.... *History of Utah.* San Francisco: The History Co.,
1889. (HHB, Utah)

Barnes, Will C. *Arizona Place Names.* Revised and enlarged by
Byrd H. Granger. Tucson: University of Arizona Press,
1960. (Barnes)

Basso, David. *Ghosts of Humboldt Region.* Sparks, Nev.:
Western Printing & Publishing Co., 1970. (DB)

Becker, George F. *Geology of the Comstock Lode and the
Washoe District with Atlas.* Washington: U.S. Government
Printing Office, 1882. (GFB)

Beebe, Lucius. *Mixed Train Daily.* New York: E. P. Dutton
and Co., 1947. (JRB, Res.)

.... *Trains in Transition.* New York: D. Appleton-Century
Co., Inc., 1941. (LB, Trains)

Beebe, Lucius and Clegg, Charles. *Legends of the Comstock
Lode.* Stanford, Calif.: Stanford University Press, 1950. (B&C, Legends)

.... *U.S. West: The Saga of Wells Fargo.* New York: E. P.
Dutton and Co., 1949. (B&C, US West)

.... *Virginia and Truckee.* Stanford, Calif.: Stanford University Press, 1949. (B&C, V&T)

Bentley, Harold W. *Dictionary of Spanish Terms in English.*
New York: Columbia University Press, 1932. (HWB)

Berg, Lucile Rae. "A History of the Tonopah Area and Adjacent Region of Central Nevada, 1827–1941." Unpublished
Master's thesis, University of Nevada, 1942. (LRB)

Bigelow, John. *Memoir of the Life and Public Services of John
Charles Frémont.* New York: Derby and Jackson, 1856. (JB)

Billeb, Emil W. *Mining Camp Days.* Berkeley, Calif.: Howell-
North Books, 1968. (EWB)

"Black Gold Comes to Nevada." *Nevada Highways and Parks*
XIV (September–December, 1954): 12–19. (Black Gold)

Bonner, T. D. *Life and Adventures of James P. Beckwourth.*
New York: Harper and Brothers, 1856. (TDB)

Bonney, Benjamin Franklin. *Personal Narrative.* Eugene,
Oreg.: Koke-Tiffany Co., 1923. (BFB)

Botkin, B. A. and Harlow, Alvin F. (eds.). *A Treasury of Railroad Folklore.* New York: Crown Publishers, Inc., 1953. (B&H)

Bowles, Samuel. *Our New West.* Hartford: Hartford Publishing
Company, 1869. (SB)

Brockett, Linus Pierpont. *Our Western Empire or the New
West Beyond the Mississippi.* Columbus: W. Garretson and
Co., 1882. (LPB)

Brown, George Rothwell (ed.). *Reminiscences of Senator William M. Stewart of Nevada.* New York: Neale Publishing Co., 1908. (GRB)

Brown, Thomas P. *Colorful California Names.* San Francisco: American Trust Co., 1952. (TPB)

.... "Elko, Nevada." *Western Folklore* IX (October, 1950): 378–79. (TPB, Elko)

Browne, J. Ross. *A Peep at Washoe* and *Washoe Revisited.* Balboa Island, Calif.: Paisano Press, 1959. (JRB)

.... *Crusoe's Island: A Ramble in the Footsteps of Alexander Selkirk with Sketches of Adventure in California and Washoe.* New York: Harper and Brothers, 1864. (JRB, Crusoe)

.... *Resources of the Pacific Slope.* New York: D. Appleton and Co., 1869. (JRB, Res.)

Buckbee, Edna Bryan. *Saga of Old Tuolumne.* New York: The Press of the Pioneers, Inc., 1935. (EBB)

"Bullfrog Area." *Nevada State Journal,* January 15, 1956, p. 7. (Bullfrog)

Burton, R. F. *The City of the Saints and Across the Rocky Mountains to California.* New York: Harper and Brothers, 1862. (RFB)

Calhoun, J. W. The Nevada State Museum Director, Carson City. Personal letter, February 10, 1964. (JWC)

California: *A Guide to the Golden State.* Federal Writers' Project, W. P. A. New York, 1939. (Cal. Guide)

California Miners' Association. *California Mines and Minerals.* San Francisco, 1899. (CMA)

California State Mining Bureau. *Eighth Annual Report of the State Mineralogist.* Sacramento, 1888. (CSMB)

Carlson, Helen Swisher. "Comstock Mine Names." *Reno Evening Gazette,* May 9, 1955–May 24, 1955 (daily). (HSC, Com.)

.... "Influence of Nineteenth-century Nevada Railroads on Names along the Line." *Western Folklore* XV (April, 1956): 113–121. (HSC, RR)

.... "Mine Names on the Nevada Comstock Lode." *Western Folklore* XV (January, 1956): 49–57. (HSC, Mine)

.... "Names and Places: Nevada." *Western Folklore* XIV (January, 1955): 44–49. (HSC, Nev.)

.... "Nevada Place Names: Origin and Meaning." Unpublished Ph.D. dissertation, University of New Mexico, 1959. (HSC, NPN)

Carpenter, Jay A., Elliott, Russell Richard, and Sawyer, Byrd Fanita Wall. "The History of Fifty Years of Mining at Tonopah, 1900–1950." University of Nevada *Bulletin,* January, 1953. (CES)

Carson, Christopher. *Kit Carson's Own Story of His Life.* Edited by Blanche C. Grant. Taos, New Mex., 1926. (CC)

"Carson & Colorado Railroad." *The Western Railroader* XI (April, 1942): 3–4. (C&CR)

Chase, Carroll and Caheen, Richard McP. "The First Hundred Years of U.S. Territorial Postmarks, 1787–1887. Nevada Territory." *American Philatelist* LVI (June, 1943): 586–94. (C&C)

Chatham, Ronald Lewis. "Nevada Town Names." Unpublished Master's thesis, Sacramento State College, 1956. (RC)

Child, Andrew. *Overland Route to California.* Los Angeles: N. A. Kovach, 1946. (AC)

Chittenden, Hiram Martin. *The American Fur Trade of the Far West.* 2 vols. New York: R. R. Wilson, Inc., 1936. (HMC)

Christensen, Glen C. "The Chukar Partridge in Nevada." *Biological Bulletin, No. 1.* Carson City: State Printing Office, 1954. (GCC)

Church, John A. *The Comstock Lode: Its Formation and History.* New York: J. Wiley and Sons, 1879. (JAC)

Clarke, K. W. "More on Beowawe, A Nevada Place Name." *Western Folklore* XX (April, 1961): 112. (KWC)

Clemens, Samuel Longhorne (Mark Twain). *Roughing It.* 2 vols. New York: Harper and Brothers, 1913. (SLC)

Cline, Gloria Griffen. *Exploring the Great Basin.* Norman, Okla.: University of Oklahoma Press, 1963. (GGC)

Codman, John. *The Round Trip: By Way of Panama Through California, Oregon, Nevada, Utah, Idaho, and Colorado.* New York: G. P. Putnam's Sons, 1879. (JC)

Conkling, Roscoe Platt and Margaret B. *The Butterfield Overland Mail, 1857–1869.* Glendale, Calif.: The Arthur H. Clark Co., 1947. (RPC)

Coues, Elliott (ed.). *On the Trail of a Spanish Pioneer: Diary and Itinerary of Francisco Garces, 1775–1776.* 2 vols. New York: F. P. Harper, 1900. (Coues)

Cowan, Robert Ernest. *A Bibliography of the History of California and the Pacific Coast 1510–1906.* Columbus: Long's College Book Co., 1952. (REC)

Coy, Owen Cochran. *Gold Days.* Los Angeles: Powell Publishing Co., 1929. (OCC)

Creer, Leland Hargrave. *Utah and the Nation.* Seattle: University of Washington, 1929. (LHC)

Crofutt, George A. *Crofutt's Trans-Continental Tourist's Guide.* New York: George A. Crofutt, 1873. (GAC)

Cronkhite, Eric. Administrator, Nevada State Park System, Carson City, Nevada. Personal communication, July, 1973. (EC)

Curle, J. H. *The Gold Mines of the World.* London: G. Routledge and Sons, Ltd., 1905. (JHC)

Daggett, Stuart. *Chapters on the History of the Southern Pacific.* New York: The Ronald Press Co., 1922. (SD)

Dale, Harrison Clifford (ed.). *The Ashley-Smith Explorations and the Discovery of a Central Route to the Pacific 1822–1829.* Glendale, Calif.: The Arthur H. Clark Co., 1941. (HCD)

Dangberg, Grace. *Carson Valley: Historical Sketches of Nevada's First Settlement.* Carson City: The Carson Valley Historical Society, 1972. (Dangberg, CV)

.... "Washo Texts." University of California *Publications in American Archaeology and Ethnology* XXII (March, 1927): 391–443. (GD)

Davis, Sam P. *The History of Nevada.* 2 vols. Los Angeles: Elms Publishing Co., 1913. (SPD)

Deeds, Checks, and Stock Certificates. In the files of the Nevada State Museum, Carson City, Nevada. (Deeds)

De Groot, Henry. "Comstock Papers." *Mining and Scientific Press,* July–December, 1876. (HDG, CP)

.... "Early Times." *Territorial Enterprise,* June 20, 1875. (HDG, ET)

.... *Sketches of the Washoe Silver Mines.* San Francisco: H. Keller and Co., 1860. (HDG, Washoe)

Delano, Alonzo. *Across the Plains and Among the Diggings.* New York: Wilson-Erickson, Inc., 1936. (AD)

Dellenbaugh, Frederick S. *Frémont and '49.* New York: G. P. Putnam's Sons, 1914. (FSD)

Denton, Hazel. "Tempiute." *Nevada State Journal,* December 6, 1953, p. 6. (HD)

Dick, Everett. *Vanguards of the Frontier.* New York: D. Appleton-Century Company, Inc., 1941. (ED)

Directories.

Kelly, J. Wells. *First Directory of Nevada Territory.* San Francisco: Valentine and Co., 1862. (Dir. 1862)

.... *Second Directory of Nevada Territory.* n.p., 1863. (Dir. 1863)

Virginia, Gold Hill, Silver and American City Directory 1864–65. San Francisco: Valentine and Co., 1865. (Dir. 1865)

Storey, Ormsby, Washoe and Lyon Counties Directory 1871–72. n.p., 1871. (Dir. 1871)

Uhlhorn, John F. *Virginia and Truckee Railroad Directory 1873–74.* San Francisco: Valentine and Co., 1873. (Dir. 1873)

A General Business and Mining Directory of Storey, Lyon, Ormsby and Washoe Counties, Nev. np., n.d. [1875] (Dir. 1875)

Business Directory of San Francisco and Principal Towns of California and Nevada. San Francisco: Valentine and Co., 1877. (Dir. 1877)

Nevada State Gazeteer and Business Directory 1907–1908. Salt Lake City: R. L. Polk and Co., 1910. (Dir. 1910)

Directory of Geographic Names. Prepared by State of Nevada, Department of Highways, Planning Survey Division, Cartographic Section. In cooperation with U.S. Department of Transportation, Federal Highway Administration, 1971. (Dir. 1971)

Dodge, Major-General Grenville M. *How We Built the Union Pacific Railway.* Washington: U.S. Government Printing Office, 1910. (GMD)

Driggs, Howard R. *Westward America.* New York: Follett
Publishing Co., 1942. (HRD)

Drury, Wells. *An Editor on the Comstock Lode.* New York:
Farrar and Rinehart, Inc., 1936. (WD)

Dye, Eva Emery. *McLoughlin and Old Oregon.* Chicago: Binfords and Mort, 1901. (EED)

Elliott, Russell Richard. *History of Nevada.* Lincoln: University of Nebraska Press, 1973. (RRE, Hist.)

.... *Nevada's Twentieth-Century Mining Boom: Tonopah
Goldfield Ely.* Reno: University of Nevada Press, 1966. (RRE, p.)

.... University of Nevada, Reno, Nevada. Personal correspondence, 1963–1964. (RRE)

Elliott, Russell Richard and Poulton, Helen J. "Writings on
Nevada: A Selected Bibliography," *Nevada Studies in His-
tory and Political Science,* No. 5 (1963). Carson City:
University of Nevada Press, 1963. (E&P)

Emrich, Duncan. *Comstock Bonanza.* New York: Vanguard
Press, 1944. (DE)

Farrington, Selwyn Kip. *Railroads at War.* New York: Coward-
McCann, Inc., 1944. (SKF)

Fisher, Vardis. *City of Illusion.* Caldwell, Idaho: Caxton Printers, Ltd., 1941. (VF)

Fletcher, Fred Nathaniel. *Early Nevada.* Reno: Carlisle and
Company, 1929. (FNF)

Florin, Lambert. *Nevada Ghost Towns.* Seattle: Superior Publishing Co., 1971. (LF)

Folkes, John Gregg. "Nevada's Newspapers: A Bibliography.
A Compilation of Nevada History, 1854–1964." *Nevada
Studies in History and Political Science,* No. 6 (1964).
Reno: University of Nevada Press, 1964. (JGF)

Forbes, Jack D. (ed.). *Nevada Indians Speak.* Reno: University of Nevada Press, 1967. (JDF)

Fowler, Don D. and Catherine S. (eds.). *Anthropology of the
Numa: John Wesley Powell's Manuscripts on the Numic
Peoples of Western North America 1868–1880.* City of
Washington: Smithsonian Institution Press, 1971. (Fowler)

Fox, Theron. *Nevada Treasure Hunters Ghost Town Guide.*
San Jose, Calif.: By the author, 1296 Yosemite Ave., San
Jose, n.d. (TF)

Frémont, Jessie Benton. *Far-West Sketches.* Boston: D. Loth-
rop Co., 1890. (JBF)

Frémont, John Charles. *Memoirs of My Life.* New York: Bel-
ford, Clarke and Co., 1887. (JCF, Memoirs)

.... *Report of the Exploring Expedition to the Rocky
Mountains in the Year 1842 and to Oregon and North California in the Years 1843–'44.* Washington: Blair and Rives,
1845. (JCF, Report)

French, Joseph Lewis (ed.). *Pioneer West*. Boston: Little,
Brown and Co., 1923.   (JLF)

Frickstad, Walter N. and Thrall, Edward W., with the collabo-
ration of Ernest G. Meyers. *A Century of Nevada Post
Offices 1852–1957*. Oakland, Calif.: Philatelic Research
Society, 1958.   (FTM)

Fritz, Percy Stanley. *Colorado: The Centennial State*. New
York: Prentice-Hall, Inc., 1941.   (PSF)

Gannett, Henry. *American Names*. Washington: Public Affairs
Press, 1947.   (HG)

Gerstäcker, Friedrich Wilhelm Christian. *California Gold
Mines*. Oakland, Calif.: Biobooks, 1946.   (FWCG)

Ghost Towns of Colorado. American Guide Series. Federal
Writers' Project, W. P. A. New York, 1947.   (GTC)

Gianella, Vincent P. "Bibliography of Geologic Literature of
Nevada." University of Nevada *Bulletin*, December, 1945.   (VPG, p.)

.... "Geology of the Silver City District and the Southern
Portion of the Comstock Lode, Nevada." University of
Nevada *Bulletin*, December, 1936.   (VPG, CL)

.... Professor Emeritus and Consulting Geologist, University of Nevada, Reno, Nevada. Personal correspondence,
1961–1964.   (VPG)

Glasscock, Carl Burgess. *The Big Bonanza*. Indianapolis:
Bobbs-Merrill Co., 1931.   (CBG, Bonanza)

.... *Gold in Them Hills*. Indianapolis: Bobbs-Merrill Co.,
1932.   (CBG, Gold)

Goddard, Frederick B. *Where to Emigrate and Why: Homes
and Fortunes in the Boundless West and the Sunny South*.
New York: F. B. Goddard, 1869.   (FBG)

Gold Hill Mining Records, Books A–E. Located at the Storey
County Courthouse, Virginia City, Nev.   (GH)

Gorham, Harry M. *My Memories of the Comstock*. Los Angeles: Sutton-house Publishers, 1939.   (HMG)

Greulich, Fred. "Silver Peak." *Nevada State Journal*, January
29, 1956, p. 7.   (FG, Silver)

.... "Uranium." *Nevada State Journal*, January 15, 1956,
p. 2.   (FG, Uran.)

Grieder, T. G., Jr. "Beowawe: A Nevada Place Name." *Western Folklore* XIX (January, 1960): 53–54.   (TGG)

Griffen, Gloria. "Early Exploration, Routes, and Trails in
Nevada." Unpublished Master's thesis, University of Nevada,
1951.   (GG)

Gudde, Erwin G. *California Place Names*. 2d ed. revised.
Berkeley: University of California Press, 1960.   (Gudde)

Hafen, LeRoy R. and Ann W. (eds.). *The Far West and the
Rockies Historical Series 1820–1875*. 15 vols. Glendale,
Calif.: 1952–1961.   (LRH)

Hague, Arnold and Emmons, S. F. *Descriptive Geology: Report of the Geological Exploration of the Fortieth Parallel.* Washington: U.S. Government Printing Office, 1877. (H&E)

Hall, E. Raymond. *Mammals of Nevada.* Berkeley: University of California Press, 1946. (ERH)

Hanna, Phil Townsend. *The Dictionary of California Land Names.* Los Angeles: Automobile Club of Southern California, 1946. (PTH)

Harland, Victor. "Alpine County—Its Mines and Resources Past, Present and Future." *Mining and Scientific Press,* August 5, 1876. (VH)

Hart, Fred H. *The Sazerac Lying Club.* San Francisco: H. Keller and Co., 1878. (FHH)

Haymond, Creed. *The Government and the Pacific Railroads.* Reported by James L. Andem, Stenographer of the Committee. Oral argument made before the Select Committee of the U.S. Senate. Senator Frye, Chairman, Senators Dawes, Hiscock, Davis, Morgan, Butler, and Hearst. March 17th and 26th and April 7th, 1888. San Francisco: H. S. Crocker and Co., 1888. (CH)

Heilprin, Angelo and Louis (eds.). *Lippincott's New Gazeteer: A Complete Pronouncing Gazeteer or Geographical Dictionary of the World.* Philadelphia: J. B. Lippincott Co., 1916. (A&LH)

Henry, Robert Selph. *This Fascinating Railroad Business.* Indianapolis: Bobbs-Merrill Co., Inc., 1942. (RSH)

Hermann, Ruth. *The Paiutes of Pyramid Lake.* San Jose, Calif.: Harlan-Young Press, 1972. (RH)

Historical-Pictorial Supplement, *Nevada State Journal,* January 24, 1954; January 29, 1956. (HPS)

Hodge, Frederick Webb (ed.). *Handbook of American Indians North of Mexico.* 2 vols. Washington: U.S. Government Printing Office, 1910. (FWH)

Hoffman, Hermann. "California–Nevada and Mexico: Wanderungen eines Polytechniker, 1863–1868." MS at Nevada State Museum, Carson City, Nevada. (HH)

Holbrook, Stewart H. *The Story of American Railroads.* New York: Crown Publishers, Inc., 1947. (SHH)

Hollister, Ovando J. *The Mines of Colorado.* Springfield, Massachusetts: S. Bowles and Company, 1867. (OJH)

Hopkins, Sarah Winnemucca. *Life among the Piutes: Their Wrongs and Claims.* Edited by Mrs. Horace Mann. New York: G. P. Putnam's Sons, 1883. (SWH)

Hulbert, Archer Butler. *Forty-Niners: The Chronicle of the California Trail.* Boston: Little, Brown and Co., 1931. (ABH)

Hulse, James W. *The Nevada Adventure: A History.* Reno: University of Nevada Press, 1969. (JWH, Nev.)

.... Professor of History, University of Nevada, Reno,
Nevada. Personal communications, August, 1959, and June,
1973. (JWH)

Hungerford, Edward. *Wells Fargo: Advancing the American
Frontier.* New York: E. P. Dutton and Co., 1949. (EH)

Hunt, Rockwell D. *John Bidwell, Prince of California Pioneers.*
Caldwell, Idaho: Caxton Printers, Ltd., 1942. (RDH)

Hunt, S. Frank. *Mining Geology Outlined.* Reno: By the
author, 1936. (SFH)

Hutcheson, Austin E. "Before the Comstock 1857–1858:
Memoirs of William Hickman Dolman." *New Mexico Historical Review,* July, 1947, pp. 31–42. (AEH, Comstock)

.... Professor of History, University of Nevada, Reno,
Nevada. Personal correspondence, 1961–1962. (AEH)

Indian Claims Commission Case. Shoshone Tribe of Indians of
the Wind River Reservation, Wyoming, *et al.,* Petitioners, v.
The United States of America, Defendant. *Docket No. 326.*
Shoshone Nation or Tribe of Indians, on the relation of and
represented by Edward Queep Boyer, *et al.,* Petitioner, v.
The United States of America, Defendant. *Docket No. 367.*
From the personal files of Justice Milton B. Badt of the
Nevada Supreme Court.

    "Petitioners' Proposed Findings of Fact and Brief (Vol-
ume I – Findings)." Filed February 16, 1961. (ICC, I)

    "Petitioners' Proposed Findings of Fact and Brief (Vol-
ume II – Brief)." Filed February 16, 1961. (ICC, II)

    "Defendant's Requested Findings of Fact, Defendant's
Objections to Petitioners' Proposed Findings of Fact, and
Defendant's Brief." Filed July 28, 1961. (ICC, III)

    "Petitioners' Objections to Defendant's Requested Find-
ings of Fact, Petitioners' Comments on Defendant's Objections to Petitioners' Proposed Findings of Fact and
Petitioners' Reply Brief." Filed September 19, 1961. (ICC, IV)

"Individual Histories of the Mines of the Comstock." Unpublished MS compiled by the Nevada State Bureau of Mines
and the Federal Writers' Project, W.P.A., 1941. MS at the
Mackay School of Mines, University of Nevada, Reno,
Nevada. (IH)

Irving, Washington. *The Adventures of Captain Bonneville,
U.S.A., in the Rocky Mountains and the Far West.* New
York: Binfords and Mort, 1954. (WI)

Jackson, Joseph Henry. *Anybody's Gold: The Story of California's Mining Towns.* New York: D. Appleton-Century
Co., Inc., 1941. (JHJ, Min.)

.... *Gold Rush Album.* New York: Charles Scribner's
Sons, 1949. (JHJ, Album)

Jackson, W. Turrentine. *Wagon Roads West: A Study of Fed-, eral Road Surveys and Construction in the Trans-Mississippi West 1846–1869.* Berkeley: University of California Press, 1952. (WTJ)

Jacobsen, William H., Jr. "Washo Linguistic Studies." In d'Azevedo, Warren L. et al. *The Current Status of Anthropological Research in the Great Basin: 1964.* Social Sciences and Humanities Publications, No. 1, Reno: Desert Research Institute, 1966. (WHJ)

Jenkins, Olaf P. *Guidebook along Highway 49.* San Francisco: California Division of Mines, 1948. (OPJ)

Jenkins, William Sumner (ed.). *Records of the States of the United States of America, Nev. D2, Reel 1A.* Prepared by the Library of Congress in Association with the University of North Carolina. Microfilmed by the Library of Congress Photoduplication Service, 1949.

Unit 1, 1851–1864. *First Records of Carson Valley Utah Ter. 1851.* (WSJ–1)

Unit 2. *Records of the Probate Court of Carson County, U. T.* Hon. O. Hyde, Judge, Oct. 3, 1855 to July 5, 1856. Stephen A. Kinsey, Clerk, 1856–1857. (WSJ–2)

Unit 3. *County Book of Carson County Court Oct. 2d, 1855 to July 30, 1861.* (WSJ–3)

Unit 4. *Probate Records of Carson County Utah Territory Wills and Estates of Deceased Persons.* Orson Hyde, Probate Judge, Stephen A. Kinsey, Clk. 1855. (WSJ–4)

Jenson, Andrew. "Origin of Western Geographic Names Associated with the History of 'Mormon' People." *The Utah Geneal. and Hist. Mag.,* x–xiii (1919–1922). (AJ)

Jones, Casey. "Steptoe." *Nevada State Journal,* February 27, 1955, p. 7. (CJ)

Keller, G. W. "Vernon of 1907." *Nevada State Journal,* January 15, 1956, p. 8; January 22, 1956, p. 6; January 29, 1956, p. 6. (GWK)

Kenny, Hamill. *The Origin and Meaning of the Indian Place Names of Maryland.* Baltimore: Waverly Press, 1961. (HK)

Kilmartin, J. O. Executive Secretary, Domestic Geographic Names, United States Department of the Interior, Board on Geographic Names, Washington, D.C. Personal correspondence, 1962–1964. (Kilmartin)

King, Buster L. "The History of Lander County." Unpublished Master's thesis, University of Nevada, 1954. (BLK)

King, Clarence. *Systematic Geology: Fortieth Parallel Survey.* Washington: U.S. Government Printing Office, 1878. (CK)

King, Ernest La Marr. *Main Line: Fifty Years of Railroading with the Southern Pacific.* Garden City, New York: Doubleday and Co., 1948. (ELK)

King, Jos. L. *History of the San Francisco Stock and Exchange Board*. San Francisco: J. L. King, 1910. (JLK)

Kneiss, Gilbert H. *Bonanza Railroads*. Stanford, Calif.: Stanford University Press, 1947. (GHK, Bonanza)

.... *The Virginia and Truckee Railroad*. Boston: The Railway and Locomotive Historical Society, Inc., 1938. (GHK, V&T)

Kramer, Fritz L. "Idaho Town Names." *Twenty-third Biennial Report of the Idaho State Historical Department 1951–1952*, pp. 14–144. (FLK)

Kroeber, A. L. *Handbook of the Indians of California*. Washington: U.S. Government Printing Office, 1925. (Kroeber, Handbook)

.... "Shoshonean Dialects of California." University of California *Publications in American Archaeology and Ethnology*, Vol. IV, No. 3, Berkeley, University of California Press, 1906. (Kroeber, Shoshonean)

.... "The Washo Language of East Central California and Nevada," University of California *Publications in American Archaeology and Ethnology*, Vol. IV, No. 5, Berkeley, University of California Press, 1919. (Kroeber, Washo)

Labbe, Charles (H.). *Rocky Trails of the Past*. Las Vegas: By the author, 1960. (CHL)

Laird, Charlton. *Language in America*. New York and Cleveland: The World Publishing Company, 1970. (CL, Lang.)

.... *The Miracle of Language*. New York: The World Publishing Co., 1953. (CL)

Laird, Helene and Charlton. *The Tree of Language*. New York: The World Publishing Co., 1957. (HL)

Lane, D. R. "Nevada." *Motorland* LXVII (January–February, 1956): 1–16. (DRL)

Laxalt, Robert. *States of the Nation: Nevada*. New York: Coward, McCann, Inc., 1970. (RL)

Leavitt, Francis H. "Influence of the Mormons in the Settlement of Clark County." Unpublished Master's thesis, University of Nevada, 1934. (FHL)

Lee, Simeon Lemuel. Collection containing 3,198 entries—arrowheads, Indian curios, and specimens with sites. Located at the Nevada State Museum, Carson City, Nevada. (SLL)

Lee, Willis T. and others. *Guidebook of the Western United States, Part B: The Overland Route*. Washington: U.S. Government Printing Office, 1915. (WTL)

Leigh, Rufus Wood. "Naming of the Green, Sevier, and Virgin Rivers." *Utah Historical Quarterly* XXIX (April, 1961): 137–147. (RWL)

Leonard, Zenas. *Adventures of Zenas Leonard, Fur Trader and Trapper, 1831–1836*. Edited by W. F. Wagner. Cleveland: Burrows Brothers Co., 1904. (ZL)

Lewis, Oscar. *Sagebrush Casinos*. Garden City, New York: Doubleday and Co., Inc., 1953. (OL, Casinos)

.... *Silver Kings.* New York: Alfred A. Knopf, Inc., 1947.　(OL, Silver)

.... *The Town that Died Laughing.* Boston: Little, Brown
and Co., 1955.　(OL, Town)

Lewis, Robert G. *The Handbook of American Railroads.* New
York: Simmons-Boardman Publishing Co., 1956.　(RGL)

Lillard, Richard G. *Desert Challenge: An Interpretation of
Nevada.* New York: Alfred A. Knopf, Inc., 1942.　(Lillard)

Lincoln, Francis Church. *Mining Districts and Mineral
Resources of Nevada.* Reno: Newsletter Publishing Co.,
1923.　(FCL)

Linsdale, Jean M. *The Birds of Nevada.* Berkeley: Cooper
Ornithological Club, 1936.　(JML)

Loomis, Leander V. *Journal of the Birmingham Emigrating
Company: The Record of a Trip from Birmingham, Iowa, to
Sacramento, California, in 1850.* Salt Lake City: Legal
Printing Company, 1928.　(LVL)

Lord, Eliot. *Comstock Mining and Miners.* Washington: U.S.
Government Printing Office, 1883.　(EL)

Lyman, George D. *Ralston's Ring: California Plunders the
Comstock.* New York: Charles Scribner's Sons, 1937.　(GDL, Ralston)

.... *The Saga of the Comstock Lode.* New York: Charles
Scribner's Sons, 1946.　(GDL, Saga)

McArthur, Lewis A. *Oregon Geographic Names.* Portland,
Oregon: Binfords and Mort, 1952.　(LAM)

McElrath, Jean. "Fort Ruby." *Nevada State Journal,* December 11, 1955, p. 9.　(JM)

Mack, Effie Mona. *Mark Twain in Nevada.* New York:
Charles Scribner's Sons, 1947.　(EMM, Twain)

.... *Nevada: A History of the State from the Earliest
Times Through the Civil War.* Glendale, California: Arthur
H. Clark Co., 1936.　(EMM, Nev.)

Mack, Effie Mona and Sawyer, Byrd Wall. *Our State: Nevada.*
Caldwell, Idaho: Caxton Printers, Ltd., 1940.　(M&S)

McKeon, Owen F. " 'Ten Cents Per Mile' Life on the Lake
Tahoe Narrow Gauge." *The Western Railroader* V (April,
1942): 3–7.　(OFM)

McNary, Laura Kelly. *California Spanish and Indian Place
Names.* Los Angeles: Wetzel Publishing Co., Inc., 1931.　(LKM)

McVaugh, Rogers and Fosberg, F. R. *Index to the Geographical Names of Nevada.* Contributions Toward a Flora of
Nevada No. 29. Washington: National Arboretum, 1941.　(M&F)

Maestretti, A. J., Hicks, Charles Rogers, and Smith, Claude C.
"The Constitution of the State of Nevada: Its Formation and
Interpretation." University of Nevada *Bulletin,* December,
1951.　(AJM)

Malloy, William Boyle. "Carson Valley 1852–60." Unpublished Master's thesis, University of California, 1931. Microfilm copy at the main University of Nevada library, Reno, Nevada. (WBM)

Manter, Ethel. *Rocket of the Comstock.* Caldwell, Idaho: Caxton Printers, Ltd., 1950. (EM)

Marcy, Randolph B. (ed.). *The Prairie Traveler: A Hand-Book for Overland Expeditions.* New York: Harper and Brothers, 1859. (RBM)

Marshall, James L. *Santa Fe: The Railroad that Built an Empire.* New York: Random House, Inc., 1945. (JLM)

Marye, George Thomas, Jr. *From '49 to '83 in California and Nevada: Chapters from the Life of George Thomas Marye a Pioneer of '49.* San Francisco: A. M. Robertson Co., 1923. (GTM)

Mencken, H. L. *The American Language, Supplement II.* New York: Alfred A. Knopf, Inc., 1948. (HLM)

Mighels, Henry R. *Sage Brush Leaves.* San Francisco: E. Bosqui and Co., 1879. (HRM)

Miller, William Charles. "Bonanza and Borasca Theatres on the Comstock (1860–1875)." Unpublished Ph.D. dissertation, University of Southern California, 1947. Microfilm copy at the main University of Nevada library, Reno, Nevada. (WCM)

Mining and Scientific Press, July 3–December 25, 1869; January 3–June 27, 1874; July 4–December 26, 1874; January 3–June 26, 1880; July 3–December 25, 1880. (M&SP)

Moody, John. *The Railroad Builders.* The Chronicles of America Series. New Haven: Yale University Press, 1919. (Moody)

Mordy, Brooke D. and McCaughey, Donald L. *Nevada Historical Sites.* A Study by the Western Studies Center, Desert Research Institute, University of Nevada System, under contract to the State of Nevada, Department of Conservation and Natural Resources, 1968. (M&M)

Morgan, Dale. *The Humboldt, Highroad of the West.* New York: Rinehart and Co., Inc., 1943. (Morgan)

Murbarger, Nell. *Ghosts of the Glory Trail.* Palm Desert, California: Desert Magazine Press, 1956. (NM)

Myles, Myrtle T. Nevada Historical Society, Reno, Nevada. Personal correspondence, 1961–1963. (MM)

Myrick, David (F.). "Nevada-California-Oregon Railway." *The Western Railroader* XVIII (June, 1955): 3–20. (DM–NCO)

.... *Railroads of Nevada and Eastern California.* 2 vols. Berkeley, Calif.: Howell-North Books, 1962–1963. (DM, RR)

.... Personal correspondence, September, 1961–April, 1962. (DM)

Nevada: A Guide to the Silver State. Federal Writers' Project, W. P. A. Portland, 1940. (Nev. Guide)

Nevada Highways and Parks. Department of Highways, Carson City, Nevada, 1954–1960.   (Nev.)

Nevada Historical Society.

> *First Biennial Report Nevada Historical Society 1907–1908.* Carson City: State Printing Office, 1908.   (NHS, 1908)

> *Second Biennial Report Nevada Historical Society 1909–1910.* Carson City: State Printing Office, 1911.   (NHS, 1911)

> *Third Biennial Report Nevada Historical Society 1911–1912.* Carson City: State Printing Office, 1913.   (NHS, 1913)

> *Nevada Historical Society Papers 1913–1916.* Carson City: State Printing Office, 1916.   (NHS, 1916)

> *The Celebration of Nevada's Semicentennial of Statehood.* Carson City: State Printing Office, 1917.   (NHS, 1917)

> *Nevada Historical Society Papers 1917–1920.* Carson City: State Printing Office, 1920.   (NHS, 1920)

> *Nevada Historical Society Papers 1921–1922.* Carson City: State Printing Office, 1922.   (NHS, 1922)

> *Nevada Historical Society Papers 1923–1924.* Carson City: State Printing Office, 1924.   (NHS, 1924)

> *Nevada Historical Society Papers 1925–1926.* Carson City: State Printing Office, 1926.   (NHS, 1926)

> *Nevada Historical Society Quarterly,* Vol. I–XVI (1957–1973)   (NHS, Quarterly)

> State Historical Markers, Nos. 26–197. Prepared in cooperation with the Nevada State Park System. Texts furnished by John Townley, Director, Nevada Historical Society, Reno.   (SHM)

Nevada's Parks. Carson City: State Printing Office, 1938. Prepared by the Nevada State Planning Board, Robert A. Allen, Chairman, in cooperation with the National Park Service.   (NP)

Nevada State Board of Stock Commissioners. *The Nevada Brand Book.* Reno: Brand Book Co., 1924.   (Brand)

Nevins, Allan. *Frémont: The West's Greatest Adventurer.* 2 vols. New York: Harper and Brothers, 1928.   (AN)

Newberry Library, Chicago. Edward E. Ayer Collection. *A Bibliographical Check List of North and Middle American Indian Linguistics in the Collection.* 2 vols. Chicago, 1941.   (EEA)

Official Guide of the Railways. New York: National Railway Publication Co., 1952.   (OG)

Official Register.

> *Register of Officers and Agents, Civil, Military, and Naval, in the Service of the United States on the Thirtieth of September, 1877.* Washington: U.S. Government Printing Office, 1878, pp. 639–640.   (OR, 1878)

> *Official Register of the United States Containing a List of Officers and Employes in the Civil, Military, and Naval*

Service on the Thirtieth of June, 1879. Vol. II. Washington: U.S. Government Printing Office, 1879, pp. 267–268. (OR, 1879)

Official Register of the United States Containing a List of Officers and Employes in the Civil, Military, and Naval Service on the First of July, 1881. Vol. II. Washington: U.S. Government Printing Office, 1881, p. 487. (OR, 1881)

Official Register of the United States Containing a List of Officers and Employes in the Civil, Military, and Naval Service on the First of July, 1883. Vol. II. Washington: U.S. Government Printing Office, 1884, pp. 513–514. (OR, 1884)

Official Register of the United States Containing a List of Officers and Employes in the Civil, Military, and Naval Service on the First of July, 1885. Vol. II. Washington: U.S. Government Printing Office, 1885, pp. 549–550. (OR, 1885)

Official Register of the United States Containing a List of Officers and Employes in the Civil, Military, and Naval Service on the First of July, 1899. Vol. II. Washington: U.S. Government Printing Office, 1899, pp. 221–222. (OR, 1899)

Oman, Charles. *A History of England.* London: Edward Arnold, 1895. (CO)

Origin of Place Names: Nevada. Federal Writers' Project, W. P. A. Reno, 1941. (OPN)

Paher, Stanley W. *Nevada Ghost Towns & Mining Camps.* Berkeley, Calif.: Howell-North Books, 1970. (SWP)

Paine, Swift. *Eilley Orrum: Queen of the Comstock.* Palo Alto: Pacific Books, 1949. (SP)

Park, William Lee. *Pioneer Pathways to the Pacific.* Clare, Michigan: Clara Aire, 1935. (WLP)

Parkman, Francis. *The Oregon Trail.* New York: Random House, Inc., 1949. (FP)

Patterson, Edna. With Foreword by Velma Stevens Truett. *Who Named It? History of Elko County Place Names.* Elko, Nev.: Warren L. and Mary J. Monroe, in cooperation with *The Elko Independent,* 1964. (EP)

Paul, Rodman W. *California Gold.* Cambridge: Harvard University Press, 1947. (Paul)

Paullin, Charles O. *Atlas of the Historical Geography of the United States.* Published jointly by Carnegie Institution of Washington and the American Geographical Society of New York. Baltimore, 1932. (COP)

Pearce, Thomas Matthews (ed.). *New Mexico Place Names: A Geographical Dictionary.* Albuquerque: The University of New Mexico Press, 1965. (Pearce)

.... "Spanish Place Name Patterns in the Southwest." *Names,* III (December, 1955): 201–209. (TMP, Patterns)

Potter, David Morris. *Trail to California: The Overland Journal of Vincent Geiger and Wakeman Bryarly.* New Haven, Conn.: Yale University Press, 1945. (DMP)

Powell, John J. *Nevada: The Land of Silver.* San Francisco: Bacon and Company, 1876. (JJP)

Price, John Andrew. "Washo Economy." *Nevada State Museum Anthropological Papers,* No. 6. Carson City: State Printing Office, 1962. (JAP)

Prince, Robert W. "Bibliography of Geologic Maps of Nevada Areas." University of Nevada *Bulletin,* December, 1945. (RWP)

Quaife, Milo Milton. *Narrative of the Adventures of Zenas Leonard.* Chicago: The Lakeside Press, R. R. Donnelley & Sons, 1934. (MMQ)

Quiett, Glenn Chesney. *Pay Dirt: A Panorama of American Gold-Rushes.* New York: D. Appleton-Century Co., Inc., 1936. (GCQ)

Ransome, Frederick Leslie. *Preliminary Account of Goldfield, Bullfrog, and Other Mining Districts in Southern Nevada.* Washington: U.S. Government Printing Office, 1907. (FLR)

Raymond, Rossiter W. *Statistics of Mines and Mining in the States and Territories West of the Rocky Mountains.* Washington: U.S. Government Printing Office, 1870. (RWR)

Richthofen, Ferdinand Paul Wilhelm. *The Comstock Lode.* San Francisco: Sutro Tunnel Co., 1866. (FPWR)

Rickard, T. A. *A History of American Mining.* New York: McGraw-Hill Book Co., 1932. (TAR)

Riegel, Robert Edgar. *The Story of the Western Railroads.* New York: The Macmillan Co., 1926. (RER)

Roberts, Harriett Hale. Letter dated June 1, 1955, written by the granddaughter of Calvin Hale. (HHR)

Ruhlen, George. "Early Nevada Forts, Posts and Camps." Revised MS, dated November 22, 1958. From the private files of Colonel Ruhlen, 3440 Park Blvd., San Diego, California, and used with his permission. (Ruhlen)

Rundell, Hugh A. *Washington Names: A Pronunciation Guide.* 2d ed. Pullman, Washington, n.d. Issued jointly by Radio Station KWSC and the Extension Service, Institute of Agricultural Sciences, Washington State University. (HAR)

Russell, Israel Cook. *Geological History of Lake Lahontan: A Quaternary Lake of Northwestern Nevada.* Washington: U.S. Government Printing Office, 1885. (ICR, Geol.)

.... *Present and Extinct Lakes of Nevada.* New York: American Book Co., 1895. (ICR, Lakes)

Sabin, Edwin L. *Building the Pacific Railway.* Philadelphia: J. B. Lippincott Co., 1919. (ELS, Pacific)

.... *Kit Carson Days.* Chicago: A. C. McClurg and Co., 1914. (ELS, Carson)

Sanchez, Nellie Van De Grift. *Spanish and Indian Place Names of California.* San Francisco: A. M. Robertson, 1914. (NS)

Sapir, Edward. *Selected Writings of Edward Sapir.* Edited by David G. Mandelbaum. Berkeley and Los Angeles: University of California Press, 1958. (ES)

Savage and Son, Inc. (advertisement). *Reno Evening Gazette,* September 25, 1954, United States Mining Bureau Supplement. (S&S)

Sawyer, Byrd F. "The Gold and Silver Rushes of Nevada 1900–1910." Unpublished Master's thesis, University of California, 1931. (BFS)

Sawyer, Lorenzo. *Way Sketches Containing Incidents of Travel Across the Plains from St. Joseph to California in 1850.* New York: E. Eberstadt, 1926. (LS)

Schilling, John and Hyde, Philip. "The Mountains of Nevada: The Volcanic Ranges." *Nevada Highways and Parks,* 31 (Fall, 1971): 34–45, 58. (S&H, III)

.... "The Mountains of Nevada: The Limestone Ranges." *Nevada Highways and Parks,* 32 (Summer, 1972): 16–27, 44. (S&H, V)

.... "The Mountains of Nevada: The Rubys and the Eldorados." *Nevada Highways and Parks,* 32 (Fall, 1972): 16–24, 44. (S&H, VI)

Scott, Sir Walter. *Rob Roy.* Boston: Houghton Mifflin Company, 1956. First published 1817. (SWS)

Scrugham, James G. (ed.). *Nevada: A Narrative of the Conquest of a Frontier Land.* 3 vols. New York: The American Historical Society, Inc., 1935. (JGS)

Sealock, Richard B. and Seely, Pauline A. *Bibliography of Place Name Literature: United States, Canada, Alaska and Newfoundland.* Chicago: American Library Association, 1948. (RBS)

Seltzer, Leon E. (ed.). *The Columbia Lippincott Gazeteer of the World.* New York: Columbia University, by arrangement with J. B. Lippincott Co., 1952. (LES)

Shankle, George Earlie. *State Names, Flags, Seals, Songs, Birds, Flowers and Other Symbols.* New York: H. W. Wilson Co., 1934. (GES)

Shearer, Frederick E. (ed.). *The Pacific Tourist: Williams' Illustrated Guide to Pacific R. R., California, and Pleasure Resorts Across the Continent.* New York: Adams and Bishop, 1879. (FES)

Shepperson, Wilbur S. *Retreat to Nevada: A Socialist Colony of World War I.* Reno: University of Nevada Press, 1966. (WSS)

Shinn, Charles H. *Mining Camps.* New York: Charles Scribner's Sons, 1885. (CHS, Camps)

.... *Story of the Mine.* New York: D. Appleton and Co., 1914. (CHS, Mine)

Shutler, Richard, Jr. "Lost City: Pueblo Grande de Nevada."
Nevada State Museum Anthropological Papers, No. 5
(1962). Carson City: State Printing Office, 1962. (RS)

Simpson, J. H. *Report of Explorations across the Great Basin
of the Territory of Utah for a Direct Wagon-Route from
Camp Floyd to Genoa, in Carson Valley, in 1859.* Washington: U.S. Government Printing Office, 1876. (JHS)

Skinner, Constance Lindsay. *Beaver, Kings, and Cabins.* New
York: The Macmillan Co., 1933. (CLS)

Skinner, Edmond Norton and Plate, H. Robinson. *Mining
Costs of the World.* New York: McGraw-Hill Book Co.,
1915. (ENS)

Smith, Grant H. "History of the Comstock Lode 1850–1920."
University of Nevada *Bulletin*, July, 1943. (GHS)

Smith, Henry Nash (ed.). *Mark Twain of the Enterprise:
Newspaper Articles and Other Documents 1862–1864.*
Berkeley and Los Angeles: University of California Press,
1957. (HNS)

Smith, Joseph. *History of the Church of Jesus Christ of Latter-
Day Saints.* 7 vols. Salt Lake City: The Deseret Book Company, 1951. Second Revised Edition. (JS)

Southern Pacific Company.
    Circular 4: List of Officers, Agencies, Stations, etc. San
    Francisco: Southern Pacific Company Accounting Office,
    July 1, 1954. Exhibited by Hugh P. Davis, Agent, Sparks,
    Nevada. (C4)
    Salt Lake Division Time Table No. 1 (1892) (T1SL)
    Salt Lake Division Timetable 75. (T75)
    Sacramento Division Timetable 187. (T187)
    Truckee Division Time Table No. 1 (1892) (T1TR)
    Historical Outline. San Francisco: Bureau of News,
    Development Department, March, 1933. (SP, Hist.)
    Rules and Regulations of the Transportation Department,
    December 1, 1951. (SP, Rules)
    Southern Pacific Bulletin Pacific Lines, March, 1955. (SPB)

Stenhouse, T. B. H. *The Rocky Mountain Saints: A Full and
Complete History of the Mormons.* New York: D. Appleton
and Co., 1873. (TBHS)

Steward, Julian Haynes. "Basin Plateau Aboriginal Sociopoliti-
cal Groups." Bureau of American Ethnology *Bulletin*, No.
120, Washington, D.C.: Smithsonian Institution, 1938. (Steward)

Stewart, George R. *American Place-names: A Concise and
Selective Dictionary for the Continental United States of
America.* New York: Oxford University Press, 1970. (GRS, Amer.)

.... "A Classification of Place Names." *Names*, II (March,
1954): 1–13. (GRS, Class.)

.... "Elko, Nevada." *Western Folklore* IX (April, 1950):
156. (GRS, Elko)

.... *Names on the Land*. New York: Random House, Inc., 1945. (GRS, Names)

.... *U.S. 40: Cross Section of the United States of America*. Boston: Houghton Mifflin Co., 1953. (GRS, US40)

Stewart, Omer Call. *Northern Paiute*. Berkeley: University of California Press, 1941. (OCS)

Stokes, George. "The Men in the Mines." *Mining and Scientific Press,* October 28, 1876. (GS)

Storm, Barry. *Thunder Gods Gold*. Tortilla Flat, Arizona: Southwest Publishing Co., 1946. (BS)

Stretch, R. H. *Annual Report of the State Mineralogist of the State of Nevada for 1866*. Carson City: State Printing Office, 1867. (SM, 1867)

Sullivan, Maurice S. *Jedediah Smith*. New York: Press of the Pioneers, 1936. (MSS)

Sutro, Theodore. *The Sutro Tunnel Company and The Sutro Tunnel*. New York: J. J. Little and Co., 1887. (TS)

Swanton, John R. *Indian Tribes of North America*. Washington: U.S. Government Printing Office, 1952. (JRS)

Taylor, Bayard. *Cyclopaedia of Modern Travel: A Record of Adventure, Exploration and Discovery for the Past Sixty Years*. New York: Moore, Wilstack, Keys and Co., 1860. (BT)

.... *Eldorado, or, Adventures in the Path of Empire*. New York: G. P. Putnam's Sons, 1856. (BT, Eldorado)

Thayer, William Makepeace. *Marvels of the New West*. Norwich, Connecticut: The Henry Bill Publishing Co., 1887. (WMT)

Trego, Peggy. "White Pine Fever." *Nevada State Journal,* October 16, 1955, p. 10. (PT)

Trego, Robert. "Black Rock Desert Roads." *Nevada State Journal,* October 23, 1955, pp. 10–11. (RT)

Upland, Keith. "New Discoveries." *Nevada State Journal,* September 26, 1954, p. 7. (KU)

U.S. Bureau of the Census.

Sixth Census or Enumeration of the Inhabitants of the United States in 1840. (Census, 1840)

Seventh Census of the United States: 1850. (Census, 1850)

Population of the United States in 1860: Eighth Census. (Census, 1860)

The Statistics of the Population of the United States: Ninth Census, Vol. I. (Census, 1870)

Statistics of the Population of the United States at the Tenth Census: 1880. (Census, 1880)

Report on Population of the United States at the Eleventh Census: 1890. (Census, 1890)

Twelfth Census of the United States Taken in the Year 1900. Population, Part I. (Census, 1900

U.S. Census of Population: 1950. Vol. II. *Characteristics of the Population,* Part 28, Nevada. (Census, 1950)

U.S. Census of Population: 1960. Vol. II. *Characteristics of the Population: Nevada.* (Census, 1960)

Census of Population: 1970. General Population Characteristics: Final Report PC (1)–B30 Nevada. (Census, 1970)

U.S. Congress. *Reports of Explorations and Surveys, to Ascertain the Most Practicable and Economical Route for a Railroad from the Mississippi River to the Pacific Ocean.* 36th Cong., 2d Sess., 1861. 13 vols. (PRRS)

U.S. Geographic Board.

First Report of the United States Board on Geographic Names, 1890–1891. (USGB–1)

Second Report of the United States Board on Geographic Names, 1890–1899. (USGB–2)

Fifth Report of the United States Geographic Board, 1890–1920. (USGB–5)

Sixth Report of the United States Geographic Board, 1890–1932. (USGB–6)

Decision List No. 5901 (April, 1957–December, 1958) (USGB 5901)

Decision List No. 5902 (January, 1959–April, 1959) (USGB 5902)

Decision List No. 5903 (May, June, July, August, 1959) (USGB 5903)

Decision List No. 5904 (September, 1959–December, 1959) (USGB 5904)

Decision List No. 6001 (January–April, 1960) (USGB 6001)

Decision List No. 6002 (May–August, 1960) (USGB 6002)

Decision List No. 6003 (September–December, 1960) (USGB 6003)

Decision List No. 6102 (May–August, 1961) (USGB 6102)

Decision List No. 6103 (September–December, 1961) (USGB 6103)

Decision List No. 6201 (January–April, 1962) (USGB 6201)

Decision List No. 6202 (May–August, 1962) (USGB 6202)

Decision List No. 6203 (September–December, 1962) (USGB 6203)

Decision List No. 6301 (January–April, 1963) (USGB 6301)

Decision List No. 6302 (May–August, 1963) (USGB 6302)

Decision List No. 6303 (September–December, 1963) (USGB 6303)

Decision List No. 6403 (September–December, 1964) (USGB 6403)

Decision List No. 6601 (January–March, 1966) (USGB 6601)

Decision List No. 6603 (July–September, 1966) (USGB 6603)

Decision List No. 6604 (October–December, 1966) (USGB 6604)

Decision List No. 6703 (July–September, 1967) (USGB 6703)

Decision List No. 6704 (October–December, 1967) (USGB 6704)

Decision List Nos. 6801 (January–March, 1968) (USGB 6801)

Decision List No. 6803 (July–September, 1968) (USGB 6803)

Decision List No. 6901 (January–March, 1969) (USGB 6901)

Decision List No. 6902 (April–June, 1969) (USGB 6902)

Decision List No. 6903 (July–September, 1969) (USGB 6903)

Decision List No. 7001 (January–March, 1970) (USGB 7001)

Decision List No. 7002 (April–June, 1970) (USGB 7002)

Decision List No. 7003 (July–September, 1970) (USGB 7003)

Decision List No. 7004 (October–December, 1970) (USGB 7004)

Decision List No. 7101 (January–March, 1971)	(USGB 7101)
Decision List No. 7103 (July–September, 1971)	(USGB 7103)
Decision List No. 7104 (October–December, 1971)	(USGB 7104)
Decision List No. 7202 (April–June, 1972)	(USGB 7202)
Decision List No. 7203 (July–September, 1972)	(USGB 7203)
Docket List No. 29 (April 13, 1961)	(DL 29)
Docket List No. 50 (January 10, 1963)	(DL 50)
Docket List No. 51 (February 12, 1963)	(DL 51)
Docket List No. 52 (March 12, 1963)	(DL 52)
Docket List No. 53 (April 9, 1963)	(DL 53)
Docket List No. 54 (May 14, 1963)	(DL 54)
Docket List No. 56 (July 9, 1963)	(DL 56)
Docket List No. 57 (August 13, 1963)	(DL 57)
Docket List No. 58 (September 10, 1963)	(DL 58)
Docket List No. 60 (November 12, 1963)	(DL 60)
Docket List No. 61 (December 10, 1963)	(DL 61)
Docket List No. 62 (January 14, 1964)	(DL 62)
Docket List No. 64 (March 10, 1964)	(DL 64)

U.S. Interstate Commerce Commission, Bureau of Transport Economics and Statistics. *Annual Report on the Statistics of Railways in the United States, 1887–88.* (RR, 1888)

U.S. Post Office.
Postal Bulletin, LXXV (1954); LXXVI (1955). (USPO)
"Nevada State Sheet," *Directory of Post Offices* TL6, 1–1–57. (NSS, 1957)
Post Office Publication No. 26 (July, 1962), pp. 241–42. (NSS, 1962)
Post Office Publication No. 26 (July, 1963), p. 149. (NSS, 1963)
National ZIP Code Directory 1973. (NSS, 1973)

U.S. State Department. *Territorial Papers, Nevada Series, May 13, 1861–October 31, 1864.* File Microcopies of Records in the National Archives: No. 13, Roll 1. (TP)

Virginia Mining Records. Books A–G. Located at the Storey County Courthouse, Virginia City, Nevada. (VMR)

Voegelin, C. F. and F. M., and Hale, Kenneth L. "Typological and Comparative Grammar of Uto-Aztecan: I (Phonology)." Indiana University *Publications in Anthropology and Linguistics;* Memoir 17 of the *International Journal of American Linguistics,* Vol. XXVIII, No. 1, Baltimore, 1962. (CFV)

Western Pacific Railroad Company. *Eastern Division Timetable 54.* (T54)

Weston, Otheto. *Mother Lode Album.* Stanford, Calif.: Stanford University Press, 1948. (OW)

Wheat, Carl I. *Books of the California Gold Rush.* San Francisco: The Grabhorn Press, 1949. (CIW, Books)

.... *The Maps of the California Gold Region 1848–1857.* San Francisco: The Grabhorn Press, 1942. (CIW, Maps)

Wheeler, Geo. M. *Preliminary Report Concerning Explorations and Surveys Principally in Nevada and Arizona.* Washington: U.S. Government Printing Office, 1872.   (Wheeler, 1872)

.... *United States Geographical Surveys West of the 100th Meridian.* Washington: U.S. Government Printing Office, 1879.   (Wheeler, 1879)

White, A. F. *Report of the State Mineralogist of Nevada for the Years 1867–1868.* Carson City: State Printing Office, 1869.   (SM, 1869)

.... *Report of the Mineralogist of the State of Nevada for the Years 1869 and 1870.* Carson City: State Printing Office, 1871.   (SM, 1871)

White, Henry Kirke. *History of the Union Pacific Railway.* Chicago: University of Chicago Press, 1895.   (HKW)

Whitehill, H. R. *Biennial Report of the State Mineralogist of the State of Nevada, for the Years 1871 and 1872.* Carson City: State Printing Office, 1873.   (SM, 1873)

.... *Biennial Report of the State Mineralogist of the State of Nevada, for the Years 1873 and 1874.* Carson City: State Printing Office, 1875.   (SM, 1875)

.... *Biennial Report of the State Mineralogist of the State of Nevada, for the Years 1875 and 1876.* Carson City: State Printing Office, 1877.   (SM, 1877)

Wolle, Muriel Sibell. *The Bonanza Trail.* Bloomington, Indiana: Indiana University Press, 1953.   (MSW)

Wood, Stanley. *Over the Range to the Golden State.* Chicago: R. R. Donnelley and Sons, 1889.   (SW)

Woon, Basil. "Franktown." *Nevada State Journal,* November 11, 1955, p. 8; December 18, 1955, p. 10; January 22, 1956, p. 8.   (BW)

.... "Northern Washoe." *Nevada State Journal,* June 5, 1955, p. 25.   (Washoe)

Wren, Thomas (ed.). *A History of the State of Nevada.* New York: The Lewis Publishing Co., 1904.   (TW)

Wright, William (Dan De Quille). *The Big Bonanza.* New York: Alfred A. Knopf, Inc., 1953. First published as *History of the Big Bonanza.* San Francisco: A. L. Bancroft and Co., 1877.   (DDQ)

.... *Washoe Rambles.* Introduction by Richard E. Lingenfelter. Los Angeles: Dawson's Book Shop, 1963. First published between July 28 and December 1, 1861, in the *Golden Era* and in the *California Magazine and Mountaineer.*   (REL)